The Blackwell Dictionary of Sociology

The Blackwell Dictionary of Sociology

A User's Guide to Sociological Language

Second edition

Allan G. Johnson

 BLACKWELL
Publishers

First published 1995
Reprinted 1996 (twice), 1997 (twice), 1999

Second edition published 2000

2 4 6 8 10 9 7 5 3 1

Blackwell Publishers Inc.
350 Main Street
Malden, Massachusetts 02148
USA

Blackwell Publishers Ltd
108 Cowley Road
Oxford OX4 1JF
UK

Library of Congress Cataloging-in-Publication Data

Johnson, Allan G.
  The Blackwell dictionary of sociology: a user's guide to sociological language/Allan G. Johnson.—2nd ed.
    p. cm.
  Includes bibliographical references and index.
  ISBN 0-631-21680-4 (hb: alk. paper)—ISBN 0-631-21681-2 (pb: alk. paper)
    1. Sociology—Dictionaries. I. Title: Dictionary of sociology. II. Title.
HM425 J64 2000
301'.03—dc21   99-049053

British Library Cataloguing in Publication Data

A CIP catalogue record for this book is available from the British Library.

Typeset in 9.5/11 Plantin
by Newgen Imaging Systems (p) Ltd, Chennai, India.
Printed in Great Britain by TJ International, Padstow, Cornwall

This book is printed on acid-free paper.

Contents

For Peter Dougherty

About this Book

Every discipline has its own vocabulary, the words it uses to label and draw attention to what it takes to be worth understanding. In biology, for example, *life*, *cell*, and *organism* are essential for knowing what biology is about, just as *sharp*, *flat*, and *tempo* are essential in music, and *culture*, *interaction*, and *structure* are essential in sociology.

For beginning students, vocabulary often appears as just a daunting collection of definitions to be memorized for the next quiz. What students often miss is that such words are far more than mental hurdles to clear, far more than jargon invented by professionals to distinguish themselves. Taken as a whole, the language of a discipline is a map that identifies a territory of study and provides points of view from which to look at it. Learning a new discipline is like traveling to a foreign land, and technical language is a guide to significant sights to look for and how to pay attention to them.

As such, language plays a key role in drawing attention to different aspects of reality, and in the process it shapes the reality that you perceive and experience. The first time you walk through a field of wildflowers, for example, you may see only a soft sea of colors blending into an undifferentiated whole. But what happens if you take along someone who knows one flower from another, who bends you down to see the details of each? Strolling through country fields will never be the same again. Now you will know the distinct individuality of each variety of flower and how they come together to make this thing you experience as a field. You will find yourself saying, "I never *saw* that flower before," when in fact, of course, you saw it a thousand times; what you never did before was to *notice* it.

Noticing is a great deal of what technical language is about. When we learn the word for a concept – such as *system* – we can then think about that concept in relation to other concepts – such as *family* – and thereby understand both in a different way than before. In many ways, this is what thinking is about: noticing and making connections. Whether word labels refer to colors, types of flowers, types of political systems, or theories of social change, they are essential for noticing, connecting, thinking, and understanding.

The language of sociology is what sociologists use to study social life in all its diversity and complexity – to see how this system works differently from that or how one pattern of small group interaction differs from another. It is this language that takes us beyond merely seeing what is all around us, to *noticing*, to paying attention in ways that enable us to understand social life in a more systematic way. The word "culture," for example, points to a collection of things, symbols, ideas, and practices that shape life in a social system such as a society. Culture includes the languages people speak, the foods they prefer, the rules they live by, and the values that shape their choices. Once "culture" becomes part of our active vocabulary, we are more likely to notice the distinction between an individual's personality and the culture in which they participate. We can become more aware that there is something larger than ourselves that we and other people participate in, an "it" to be understood in its own right. From here we can realize that we cannot understand the behavior of individuals without paying attention to the culture of the society in which they live. Instead of merely seeing destructive individual personalities as the cause of social problems, for example, we also notice the many ways in which a society can reward or otherwise promote destructive behavior. In short, we start to notice that everything individuals experience or do always takes place in and is shaped by a cultural context.

Inventing words to label social reality is not a straightforward kind of work and is itself full of controversy. Sociologists may disagree on how to define a particular concept such as "family" or "culture" or "power" in part because each stands for something so complex and varied in form that it is difficult to come up with a single neat definition. This means that the same word may be used in several different ways. Any reader of this book should therefore be aware that although for reasons of space I may not go into such complications in great detail, they often do exist.

There is also disagreement over the process of naming itself. Some argue that the social world does not exist in a fixed, concrete way waiting for us to name it. Instead, naming is a creative act in which we construct what we then experience as "real." The French philosopher Michel Foucault, for example, maintained that there is no such thing as "sexuality" existing as a fixed "thing" for us to discover. Foucault believed instead in the existence of a variety of sexualities that have been (and continue to be) socially constructed through cultural ideas about sexuality. The word "homosexual," for example, has only during the last century or so been used as a noun to identify a type of person, rather than as an adjective to describe a kind of behavior. Once we start labeling people rather than behavior, it fundamentally alters how we experience the "reality" of both them and what they do.

This book is a dictionary of sociological language, but saying that really does not convey what this book is about or how you might use it. There are many terms that refer in some way to social life, but which are not included here because they are not part of the language that sociologists use to describe and analyze social life. The Ku Klux Klan, for example, is an organization that has had an important impact on race relations in the United States, but that alone does not make it part of sociological language. You will find *social movement* in this dictionary, however, because this is a concept that sociologists use to make sense of organizations such as the Klan.

You also will not find here every concept and term invented by sociologists to describe social life and how it works. That kind of dictionary could never fit handily between two covers (and even if it did, it would be much too large to carry about and read from in a spare moment, as I hope you will do with this book). The accumulated store of sociological terms is not only enormous but growing at such a rate that any attempt to cover it all would be out of date before it ever appeared in print. Social life includes an extraordinary range of social phenomena, from why married couples divorce to the workings of the world economic system. This means that any systematic attempt to understand social life inevitably involves the invention of an ever-growing collection of concepts and language that refers to them. In light of this, I have not tried to cover the length and breadth of this diverse discipline or to keep up with all the latest additions to it. I have tried to represent the classical conceptual core of the discipline along with a representative sampling of diverse areas within sociology and a few fundamentally important concepts from related disciplines such as philosophy. I have also provided brief biographical sketches of major figures – both historic and, to a lesser degree, contemporary – in the development and practice of sociology.

Neither is this an encyclopedia providing in-depth discussions of each concept's various shades of meaning. Any student of social life will encounter those complexities soon enough and in contexts that allow for the kind of full discussion that does them justice. A single-volume, portable dictionary must work within a limited length to strike a balance between depth on the one hand and accessibility on the other. In general, the deeper it goes, the more it must assume its readers already know about sociology and related disciplines such as philosophy. This is a particularly weak assumption with beginning undergraduates and even with graduate students who may lack training in sociology. As a teacher and writer, I place a premium on being understood: I would rather attempt less and be understood than attempt too much in the name of sophistication and leave the average intelligent reader feeling lost.

If, then, this is neither exhaustive dictionary nor expansive encyclopedia, what is it? The answer lies in my reasons for writing this book in the first place. I have been asked more than once why I chose to write a dictionary of sociology since most dictionaries are compilations of entries written by scores of authors. The writer in me replies that I was attracted to the idea of writing a dictionary with a single author's voice that would give it a greater sense of continuity and wholeness. The sociologist and teacher replies that this is interesting and important work, in part because

I have had to learn a great deal in order to do it, but also because it provides yet another way to promote clear understandings of what sociological thinking is about.

Like all sociologists, I am committed to the goal of systematically understanding social life. Like many of my colleagues, I also believe in the importance of making what we know more accessible to students and other curious readers. Although the world suffers from a multitude of social problems, outside of academia there is little understanding of sociology or how to use it. This means that making clear the conceptual underpinnings of what sociologists do is itself serious sociological work. It requires formal training in sociology and a commitment to clear writing and effective teaching, all which have shaped my professional life. Hence, this book.

In an important sense, this is a dictionary like any other, meant to be consulted from time to time as the need arises to make sense of unfamiliar terms encountered elsewhere. But in a larger sense this is a book in its own right with the simple purpose of conveying a sense of what it means to look at the world in a sociological way. As such, it can be read by itself, although in not quite the same way as most books. You might begin with core concepts such as sociology, social system, culture, social structure, and interaction – the basics of what sociologists pay attention to – and then go on to theoretical perspectives, the major ways to pay attention within sociology.

From here, there are any number of ways to proceed. You can, for example, simply start at the beginning and read your way through, with side excursions suggested in the lists of concepts cross-referenced at the end of each entry. Or, you can identify areas of particular interest such as social stratification or knowledge or the family and go from there. As you read, you will find yourself doing far more than acquiring a list of terms and definitions. You will be building a sense of an entire way of noticing and thinking about both the world and your place in it.

Regardless of how you use this book, you will not find here the last word about anything. What I hope you will find is a clear, engaging, and useful resource, a guidebook to ease the way toward a deeper understanding of social life and of the only discipline dedicated to making sense of it in all its diverse and wondrous complexity.

A Note on How the Book Is Organized

To accomplish the goals I set for myself in writing the dictionary, I made some key decisions that will affect how you use it.

In several cases, I group together terms that might otherwise be covered separately under their own entries. I have done this because I find it much easier to understand some concepts if I also know something about concepts that are closely associated with them. To see what postmodernism is about, for example, it helps to consider how it is related to the concept of modernism. As a result, there is a single entry for "postmodernism and modernism" rather than separate entries for each.

There are many sociological terms that are often preceded by the word "social," as in "social problem," "social class," or "social structure." If you look for such a term under "social" and don't find it, try again using the word that follows. "Social attribution," for example, is listed under "attribution, social."

Finally, I do not include entries for the huge number of social phenomena that sociological concepts are used to think about, such as the "sociology of emotion" or the "sociology of sport." I avoid this because I do not see these as examples of sociological language *per se* but rather as fields of inquiry organized around the *application* of sociological concepts and ideas. The sociology of art, the body, crime and deviance, development, education, the family, gender, health and illness, housing, industry, knowledge, law, leisure, the mass media, medicine, race, religion, science, sexuality, social class, war, and work are all fascinating subjects. In many cases I include entries for the phenomenon itself – as for gender, knowledge, law, race, and science. Having provided that, however, it would then go beyond the scope of this book to discuss how to use the tools of sociology to understand that subject. Hence you will find a discussion of what sociologists mean when they use the words "sociology" and "family," for example, but no entry for "sociology *of* the family."

Also note that the book has an index that lists not only concepts, but substantive examples used to explain them.

Acknowledgments

As the dictionary goes to press, I am mindful of the many people who played important parts in making this happen. I thank my editor at Blackwell Publishers – Susan Rabinowitz for her support and encouragement. I thank Rhonda Pearce for an elegant design, Jean van Altena for smooth copy-editing, and Simon Eckley, Rhonda Pearce, and Mary Dortch for skillful management of the complex process of guiding the book into print. I am also grateful to Mary Jo Deegan for making me more aware of women's contributions to sociological work.

My deepest thanks go to Peter Dougherty. As the one who first suggested that I write this book, he once again showed his editorial vision of what writers can do. He predicted this would be hard work and great fun, and he was right on both counts.

Finally, my thanks go to numerous sociologists in the United States, Britain, Australia, and New Zealand whose critical reviews of various drafts of the manuscript provided invaluable insights and suggestions.

ALLAN G. JOHNSON

Dictionary Entries

A–Z

Names in small capitals have their own entries in the section entitled "Biographical Sketches"; all other words in small capitals denote an entry in the current section.

A

aberrant deviance As described by Robert K. MERTON in his theory of DEVIANCE, aberrant deviance is an act that violates a law or other norm secretly and primarily for personal gain. It can take two forms. *Innovative deviance* uses deviant means to accomplish culturally supported goals (for example, stealing in order to achieve financial success). *Retreatism* is the withdrawal from social life and rejection of society's norms and values. Those who join drug subcultures, for example, reject not only the rules of social life, but what are generally regarded as the most important values.

See also NONCONFORMIST DEVIANCE; OPPORTUNITY STRUCTURE.

Reading

Merton, Robert K. 1968. *Social theory and social structure,* rev. and exp. ed. New York: Free Press.

absolute deprivation *See* DEPRIVATION.

abstracted empiricism According to C. Wright Mills, abstracted empiricism is the practice of gathering sociological data for their own sake without developing a theoretical framework that would give those data meaning and value. Mills was concerned that sociology – especially with the advent of high-speed computers – would become a field awash in information but lacking ideas. Mills was equally critical of what he referred to as *grand theory* – that is a theory uninformed by data gathered in the real world, that is so abstract that it has little significance to anyone but theoreticians.

See also EMPIRICAL; THEORY.

Reading

Mills, C. Wright. 1959. *The sociological imagination.* New York: Oxford University Press.

accommodation, cultural *See* CULTURAL CONTACT.

account In social interaction, an account is what people offer to others when called upon to explain their appearance or behavior – such as being late for an appointment. They range from the relatively insignificant ways we make excuses to friends ("I didn't mean it; I wasn't myself") to formal defenses against accusations of serious crime ("It was self-defense; I had no choice"). Also called *vocabularies of motive*, accounts are sociologically important because they are part of what we use to create impressions of ourselves in the eyes of others. In this way, we influence their perceptions, expectations, attitudes, and behavior in relation to us. The concept has been applied most often in the study of deviance, especially when people use accounts to avoid responsibility and punishment for their actions.

See also ATTRIBUTION, SOCIAL; DELINQUENT DRIFT; DEVIANCE; INTERACTIONIST PERSPECTIVE; NEUTRALIZATION.

Reading
Mills, C. Wright. 1940. "Situated actions and vocabularies of motive." *American Sociological Review* 5: 904–93.

acculturation *See* CULTURAL CONTACT.

achieved status An achieved status (also known as *acquired status*) is a position in a social system that is occupied after birth. Examples include marital status, educational attainment, occupation, and, in some cases, religious affiliation.
See also ASCRIBED STATUS; ROLE; STATUS.

Reading
Linton, Ralph. 1936. *The study of man: An introduction.* New York: Appleton.
Merton, Robert K. 1968. *Social theory and social structure*, rev. and exp. New York: Free Press.

achievement *See* PATTERN VARIABLES.

acquired status *See* ACHIEVED STATUS.

action *See* INTERACTION.

action and behavior A behavior is anything that we do, from scratching our nose or yawning to saying something or driving a car. Action is a type of behavior that takes into account social expectations or how we think other people will interpret and respond to what we do. If we yawn to show someone that we're bored with them, for example, or if we cover our mouths when we yawn so as not to offend people, we are engaging in

action, because the choice of behavior depends in some way on what we think others will think of it. As such, action does not depend on the actual presence of other people, as our behavior while alone can also be affected by what we think other people would make of it if they knew about it.
See also INTERACTION.

action research *See* APPLIED SOCIOLOGY.

action theory *See* INTERACTION.

adaptation Adaptation refers to changes that occur in order to maintain various aspects of a SOCIAL SYSTEM'S culture or structure or, in extreme cases, to aid survival in any form at all. Every social system must adapt in relation to other systems and the natural environment. For example, families must adapt to economies, schools, and the state; and societies must adapt to other societies and the resources and limitations that go with physical environments. Because of this, social systems must deal with changes in other systems and the physical environment.

As the shape of economic life in Europe and the United States shifted from agriculture to urban industry during the nineteenth century, for example, the shape of family production was shifting as well. Increasingly, families stopped producing goods and instead sent family members into the factories to earn cash wages. This profoundly changed the DIVISION OF LABOR and distribution of power in families. It did this by separating mothers (who were left with child care and other domestic work) from the production of goods, which thereby made them dependent upon male wage earners. On a larger scale today, industrial societies are adapting to external changes in order to maintain social systems and their core values. For example, rising levels of air and water pollution due to industrial production and private consumption (of automobiles, for example) have caused governments to increasingly intervene with regulations and restrictions on what were previously considered to be private concerns. Businesses are thus told how to go about making profits, or individuals and families are told what goods they may purchase or how they may use them.

The concept of adaptation plays an important role in Talcott PARSONS's FUNCTIONALIST PERSPECTIVE on society, which views adaptation as one of four basic tasks that every social system must accomplish. It also figures prominently in some theories of SOCIAL CHANGE, most notably evolutionary theories.

See also CULTURAL MATERIALISM; SOCIAL EVOLUTION; FUNCTIONALIST PERSPECTIVE.

Reading

Malinowski, Bronislaw. 1964. *A scientific theory of culture and other essays*. London: Oxford University Press.

Parsons, Talcott, Robert F. Bales, and Edward A. Shils. 1953. *Working papers in the theory of action*. Glencoe, IL: Free Press.

Parsons, Talcott, and Neil J. Smelser. 1956. *Economy and society*. New York: Free Press.

Spencer, Herbert. 1898. *The Principles of sociology*. New York: D. Appleton.

adolescence Adolescence is a stage in the LIFE COURSE that separates childhood from adulthood. It is a relatively recent phenomenon dating to the late nineteenth century and found primarily in industrial societies. In nonindustrial societies, children become economically productive at a relatively early age, and puberty is often the occasion for assuming full adult status. In industrial societies, however, the preadult period is prolonged well after puberty and often into the early twenties. This allows young people to prepare for the relatively sophisticated demands of industrial occupations and keeps them from competing with adults for jobs. Rather than seeing adolescence as inherent in the aging process, sociologists view it as a product of social organization.

See also AGE CATEGORY; AGING.

Reading

Elkind, David. 1984. *All grown up and no place to go: Teenagers in crisis*. Reading, MA: Addison-Wesley.

Hall, G. Stanley. 1904. *Adolescence: Its psychology and its relations to physiology, anthropology, sociology, sex, crime, religion, and education*. New York: Appleton.

Mead, Margaret. [1928] 1961. *Coming of age in Samoa: A psychological study of primitive youth for western civilization*. New York: Morrow.

advanced capitalism *See* CAPITALISM.

affective involvement/affective neutrality *See* PATTERN VARIABLES.

affinal relationship *See* KINSHIP.

affirmative action *See* PREJUDICE AND DISCRIMINATION.

affluent worker *See* EMBOURGEOISEMENT.

age category An age category is a culturally defined span of years – such as childhood or middle age – that is regarded as a social position affecting how people are perceived and treated and what is expected of them. Societies differ a great deal in how many such categories they include in their cultures – from just three among the Nupe of Nigeria, for example, to almost 30 in the Nandi culture of Kenya.

Age categories are often referred to as *age grades* or *age groups*. Although the former is an acceptable term, the latter is inappropriate because a group is a collection of people who interact in regular patterned ways and think of themselves as belonging to a group. This is not true of age categories in all but the smallest tribal societies.

See also AGEISM; AGING; COHORT; SOCIAL CATEGORY.

age grade *See* AGE CATEGORY.

age group *See* AGE CATEGORY.

ageism Ageism is prejudice based on differences in age. Unlike most other forms of prejudice, ageism affects everyone at one time or another since everyone spends time in both subordinate (such as childhood) and dominant (such as middle-age) age categories.

See also AGING; GERONTOLOGY; PREJUDICE AND DISCRIMINATION.

agency and structure Agency and structure are fundamental issues in the study of social life. They revolve around the relationship between individuals and the SOCIAL SYSTEMS in which they participate. In particular, there is disagreement over how much individuals exhibit the capacity for agency by acting independently of

the constraints imposed by social systems. Interactionists such as Georg SIMMEL and Herbert BLUMER, for example, argue that social systems are little more than abstractions that do not actually exist except through what people decide to do in their interactions with one another. "Society," Simmel wrote, "is merely the name for a number of individuals connected by interaction" ([1902] 1950, p. 10). From this perspective, human agency is all important, and what sociologists refer to as social systems are merely the result of it.

In contrast, interactionists such as Manford Kuhn argue that social life is organized primarily around networks of statuses and roles. These are external to individuals and profoundly constrain, if not determine, what people think, feel, and do. Members of a football team, for example, may improvise as they participate in a game, but they also feel constrained by the socially defined situation of the game, which they tend to see as something that exists independently of them (indeed, prior to them) and which exerts a great deal of authority over how they choose to behave. From this perspective, the game produces the patterns of behavior, rather than the other way around.

There is good reason to argue for a middle ground that blends elements of both positions. We certainly feel constrained by the social situations in which we participate. It is also true, however, that those situations do not exist in a concrete way until we actually do something, and although there are recognizable patterns of behavior that distinguish one social situation from others, there is also a great deal of what goes on that cannot be predicted from a knowledge of the social situation alone. In his theory of *structuration*, Anthony GIDDENS argues that it is a mistake to pose social systems and individual agency as separate from each other because neither exists except in relation to the other. There is no such thing as a football player, for example, without the game of football with its rules and structured relationships between players. But it is also true that it is individuals who literally create the reality of a football game every time they set out to play it. When individuals play the game, they draw upon shared understandings of the rules associated with the game and use these in order to construct the game as a concrete reality. In this sense, there is what Giddens calls a *duality of structure*, which is to say, the structure of a system provides individual actors with what they need in order to produce that very structure as a result.

See also ATOMISM AND HOLISM; INTERACTIONIST PERSPECTIVE; METHODOLOGICAL INDIVIDUALISM.

Reading

Blumer, Herbert. 1969. *Symbolic interactionism: Perspective and method*. Englewood Cliffs, NJ: Prentice-Hall.

Giddens, Anthony. 1979. *Central problems in social theory*. London: Macmillan.

Kuhn, Manford H. 1964. "Major trends in symbolic interaction theory in the past twenty-five years." *Sociological Quarterly* 5 (winter): 61–84.

Simmel, G. [1902] 1950. *The sociology of Georg Simmel*. Edited and translated by K. H. Wolf. New York: Free Press.

Age of Enlightenment *See* ENLIGHTENMENT, AGE OF.

Age of Reason *See* ENLIGHTENMENT, AGE OF.

age pyramid *See* AGE STRUCTURE.

age set *See* COHORT.

age structure The age structure of a POPULATION is the distribution of people among various ages. In the simplest sense, it takes the form of a percentage distribution showing relative numbers of people of each age, often grouped into five- or ten-year categories. In graphic form, age structure is portrayed as an *age pyramid* whose relatively broad base indicates the number of children and whose narrowing peak reflects the increasing likelihood of death as people age. A population whose age structure has a very broad base and a sharp narrow peak is said to be "young," while a structure whose base is not much wider than the rest of the pyramid is "old." Most nonindustrial countries, for example, have very young age structures with typically 40–50 percent of their populations below the age of 15 and less than 5 percent over the age of 65. In most industrial countries, the percentage below age 15 is under 20 percent and over 65 ranges from a high of 18 percent in Sweden to a low of 13 percent in the United States and Canada.

Although age structure reflects the long-term effects of both birth and death rates, it is birth rates that affect it the most. Paradoxically, it has been declines in birth rates, not death rates, that have played the greatest part in the aging of populations in Europe and North America. This is because each new birth produces not only an additional person but an additional potential parent who can then add still more children to the population. And while death rates have also declined dramatically over

7

the past two centuries, the greatest effect of this on age structures has been felt among the very young, not the old. The great advances in life expectancy, for example, occurred far more through a drop in infant mortality than the prolongation of life among those who manage to reach old age. Each infant who survives the perilous first year of life can go on to contribute many additional years to the average age for a population. By comparison, a 70-year-old whose life is extended by a few years by medical care contributes a far smaller number of additional years to the overall average.

Age structure is sociologically important because much of social life is organized to some degree around age. The more children there are in a population, for example, the greater is the burden on the adult population to produce not only for themselves but also for a large economically dependent population that must be clothed, fed, and educated. Young adult males have shown themselves in at least some industrialized countries to be unusually likely to engage in criminal behavior. This means that a younger population will be more likely to produce higher crime rates than will an older population (at least for those crimes most likely to be committed by the young). On the other hand, the older a population is, the more resources it will have to devote to expenses such as long-term medical care and retirement and the fewer resources it will need for elementary schooling.

See also DEPENDENCY RATIO; STRUCTURAL LAG.

Reading

Coale, Ansley J. 1964. "How a population ages or grows younger." In *Population: The vital revolution*, edited by Ronald Freedman. New York: Anchor Books.

Shryock, Henry S., and Jacob Siegel and Associates. 1976. *The methods and materials of demography*. New York: Academic Press.

aggregate Aggregate has two meanings in sociology. In the first sense, an aggregate is a sum of individual characteristics, experiences, or behaviors that is used to reflect a collective phenomenon for an entire population. If we add together all of the individual acts of suicide that take place in a year, for example, the result is an aggregation that tells us something about the society in which the suicides occurred. An aggregation may be presented in the form of a rate – such as 6.7 suicides per 100,000 people in England and Wales compared with 11.8 in the United States and 13.0 in Norway. Similarly, the percentage of children who live with both parents, average age at which people marry, or the gross national product are all aggregations.

In a second sense, an aggregate is a collection of people that can be thought of as a whole simply because they happen to be in the same place at the same time. Pedestrians walking along a street, for example, are an aggregate. What distinguishes aggregates from other collections of people (such as GROUPS and SOCIAL CATEGORIES) is that all that is needed for an aggregate to exist is physical proximity regardless of what brings people together. Aggregates typically lack a sense of organization; their members generally do not feel a sense of belonging, and do not interact very much. Although the members of a crowd may share social characteristics such as nationality, race, or religion, it is not these that make them an aggregate.

In a more technical sense, an aggregate is a collection of people who share the same SITUATIONAL STATUS at the same time and place. Aggregates are sociologically important precisely because they tend to be disorganized and lack social cohesion and are, therefore, a prime source of COLLECTIVE BEHAVIOR such as riots and mob action. Explaining such phenomena is, of course, particularly difficult since they are not very predictable and are therefore difficult to observe.

See also COLLECTIVITY; GROUP; LEVEL OF ANALYSIS; SOCIAL CATEGORY; STATUS.

aging Chronological aging is the universal biological process and experience that affects everyone over time. Social aging is a far more complex process that involves the passage from one social position to another. This brings new rights and responsibilities and a changing social identity. All societies divide the life course into a series of age categories, each of which is associated with various cultural ideas about who people are, what they can do, and what is expected of them in relation to other people.

The concept of aging can also be applied to entire populations. For example, the populations of Europe and North America have been aging for a long time as death rates and, particularly, birth rates have fallen. This has resulted in decreasing proportions of young people and increasing proportions of the elderly. In the United Kingdom, for example, 16 percent of the population is 65 or

older, compared with only 5 percent in India. In the United States, centenarians now constitute the fastest growing of all age categories.

See also AGE CATEGORY; AGE STRUCTURE; DISENGAGEMENT THEORY; GERONTOLOGY; LIFE COURSE.

Reading

Eisenstadt, Shmuel N. 1956. *From generation to generation*. Glencoe, IL: Free Press.
Foner, N. 1984. *Ages in conflict: A cross-cultural perspective on inequalities between young and old*. New York: Columbia University Press.
Riley, Matilda White. 1987. "On the significance of age in sociology." *American Sociological Review* 52(1): 1–14.

agrarian society An agrarian society focuses its MODE OF PRODUCTION primarily on agriculture and the cultivation of large fields. This distinguishes it from the HUNTER-GATHERER SOCIETY, which produces none of its own food, and the HORTICULTURAL SOCIETY, which produces food in small gardens rather than fields. Based on the invention of the plow around 3000 B.C., the "agrarian revolution" brought enormous increases in food production. With it came an increasingly complex DIVISION OF LABOR as more and more people were freed from the work of producing food. As a result, the accumulation of great wealth and extremes of social inequality, including slavery, became a major aspect of social life. In general, the degree of social inequality found in agrarian societies appears to be greater than that found in other types of production systems. Some sociologists have argued to the contrary, however, on the grounds that difficulties of measuring the degree of inequality make it all but impossible to make such comparisons.

The ability to produce surpluses and to support a complex division of labor made possible an enormous expansion of knowledge, technology, population, trade, and the size and permanence of communities, including the first true cities. With these changes came major social institutions such as organized religion, the state, universities, and the military.

See also FEUDALISM; INDUSTRIAL SOCIETY; MODE OF PRODUCTION; POSTINDUSTRIAL SOCIETY.

Reading

Childe, V. Gordon. 1964. *What happened in history*. Baltimore: Penguin.

alienation As developed by Karl MARX and others, alienation is a concept referring both to a psychological condition found in individuals and, more importantly, to a social condition that underlies and promotes it. For example, "alienated labor" refers not so much to the psychological condition of workers who feel alienated as it does to economic systems such as CAPITALISM that are organized in ways that estrange workers from their work. In other words, it is the labor rather than the laborer that is alienated, and it is alienated labor that makes people feel alienated.

Marx argued that alienation results from the private ownership of capital and the employment of workers for wages, an arrangement that gives workers little control over what they do. Alienation occurs first in the broken relationship between workers and work. In its fullest sense, producing something involves a complex process that begins with ideas about what to do and how to do it. From this flows a unity of mind and body as the idea is given form in the process of making it. Under capitalism, however, this process is broken, for those who make the goods have no part in deciding what to produce or how to produce it.

Alienation also occurs in the broken relation between workers and the product of their labor since they have no control over what is done with it. Since the sense of self is to some degree grounded in the integrity of a person's work, Marx argues that capitalist production also breaks this connection. This results in the tendency of workers to distance themselves from their work and experience it as a chore (if not an ordeal) to be endured until the closing whistle or the arrival of the weekend. Finally, Marx argues that alienation from the self is connected to alienation from other people.

People who participate in alienated systems tend to feel like cogs in a machine. They are isolated and disconnected from others, themselves, and meaningful work in which they can experience themselves as whole, integrated human beings whose lives have purpose. Since Marx believed that the core of what it means to be human is meaningful work through which people shape and transform their environments, he saw capitalism as a way of organizing social life that dehumanizes by undermining the essence of the species itself. In alienated systems, people no longer work because they experience satisfaction or a sense of connection to the life process, but to earn money which they need in order to meet their needs. Alienated work, then, becomes a routine, mechanical activity directed by others and serving merely as a means to an end. Workers and their work become little more than commodities to be bought and sold in labor markets.

Reading
Blauner, Robert. 1964. *Alienation and freedom*. Chicago: University of Chicago Press.
Marcuse, H. 1964. *One-dimensional man*. London: Sphere.
Marx, Karl. [1927] 1964. *Economic and philosophical manuscripts of 1884*. New York: International Publishers.
Ollman, B. 1971. *Alienation: Marx's critique of man in capitalist society*. Cambridge: Cambridge University Press.

aligning and realigning action An aligning action is any behavior that indicates to others the acceptance of a particular DEFINITION OF THE SITUATION. When the house lights dim in a theater, for example, members of the audience typically stop talking among themselves and turn their attention to the stage. This indicates their acceptance and support for the situation and the expectations that go with it. Erving GOFFMAN, from his DRAMATURGICAL PERSPECTIVE, sees people in social interaction using various techniques to create a definition of the situation from which they can identify expectations that apply to themselves and others.

A realigning action is an attempt to change the definition of the situation. If a member of a theater audience jumps up during the performance and begins an angry speech about the play's political implications, a possibly new definition of the situation is introduced. Depending on whether other audience members perform appropriate aligning actions, it may or may not become the new accepted definition. In a similar way, an employer who makes sexual advances to an employee is trying to change the definition of the situation from one of work to one of sexual intimacy, an attempt that may or may not be met with an aligning action.

See also DEFINITION OF THE SITUATION; DRAMATURGICAL PERSPECTIVE.

Reading
Goffman, Erving. 1959. *The presentation of self in everyday life*. New York: Doubleday.

alternative culture *See* COUNTER-CULTURE.

altruism Altruism is a tendency to see the needs of others as more important than one's own and to therefore be willing to sacrifice for others. Sociologically, the concept appears in several different contexts. Émile Durkheim saw altruism as a basis for patterns of suicide in some societies in which people might identify so strongly with a group or community that they would readily sacrifice themselves to protect its interests or to uphold its traditions.

More recently, altruism has come up in the debate over SOCIOBIOLOGY and its relevance to social life. In arguing that social life has a biological basis, for example, some sociobiologists asserted the existence of an "altruistic gene" that explains the tendency toward altruism found in individual members of communities. Supporters of that view have since distanced themselves from it and acknowledged the overriding importance of social factors in the explanation of social phenomena such as altruism.

The concept of altruism is also found in sociological studies of how people decide how to relate to others through COMPETITION AND COOPERATION, EXPLOITATION, exchange, or sharing. This has been particularly important in the development of EXCHANGE THEORY.

See also EXCHANGE THEORY; GIFT RELATIONSHIP; SOCIAL FACT; SOCIO-BIOLOGY.

Reading

Dovidio, John F. 1984. "Helping behavior and altruism: An empirical and conceptual overview." In *Advances in experimental social psychology*, vol. 17, edited by L. Berkowitz. New York: Academic Press.

Durkheim, Émile. [1897] 1951. *Suicide.* New York: Free Press.

Pilavian, Jane A., and Hongwn, Charng. 1990. "Altruism: A review of recent theory and research." *Annual Review of Sociology.*

amalgamation *See* CULTURAL CONTACT.

analysis of variance Analysis of variance (also known as ANOVA) is one of many statistical techniques used to determine how one variable relates to another. Although most often used in psychology to compare EXPERIMENTAL GROUPS with a CONTROL GROUP, it is sometimes used in sociology as well.

For example, suppose we want to see how group structure affects group performance in a problem-solving task. We vary the structure of small groups so that some have leaders while others are run democratically. Suppose also that we find that the average time it takes groups with leaders to solve a problem is longer than the time taken by groups without leaders. The question that analysis of variance is designed to answer is this: does the fact that the averages differ in our experiment allow us to conclude that leadership makes a difference beyond our experiment in the population of groups in general?

To answer this question, we compare two things. First, we look at groups that are alike – all groups with leaders, for example, or all that are democratic – and measure how much variation there is among them in problem-solving time. Second, we compare groups that are unalike – groups with leaders compared with democratic groups – and see how much variation there is among them. If group structure makes a difference, then groups with different structures should vary more in problem-solving time than groups with the same structure. Analysis of variance compares these two kinds of variation (hence the name, analysis of variance) and if the former is substantially larger than the latter, we conclude that the differences observed in the experiment reflect differences in the population at large.

See also HYPOTHESIS AND HYPOTHESIS TESTING; VARIANCE.

anarchism Although anarchism and anarchy are popularly associated with various sorts of chaos, they have a narrower meaning: the absence of coercive authority used to maintain social order, especially when that authority is held by the STATE. Anarchists are thus not opposed to an orderly way of life but to the undue use of coercion and force to maintain it. Some anarchists argue that the state infringes on the rights of individuals to live as they please. Communist and socialist anarchists argue that the state serves primarily to support the interests of capitalist domination and exploitation. If the private ownership of capital and wage labor could be eliminated, people would tend naturally toward collective, cooperative social arrangements in which order could be maintained without coercion from a centralized authority. Disagreement between Marxists and anarchists arises over the question of whether it would be necessary to maintain a coercive state in the transitional period between the fall of CAPITALISM and the emergence of true COMMUNISM.

As a social movement, the various strands of anarchism were most active during the nineteenth and early twentieth centuries, especially in response to the rise of industrial capitalism in Europe and the United States.

See also COMMUNAL ECONOMY; COMMUNISM; STATE.

Reading

Carter, A. 1971. *The political theory of anarchism*. London: Routledge and Kegan Paul.

Miller, D. 1984. *Anarchism*. London: Dent.

Woodcock, D. 1963. *Anarchism*. Harmondsworth, England: Penguin.

ancestor worship Ancestor worship is a religious practice exemplified by Japanese Shintoism. It is organized around the cultural belief that the spirits of ancestors have the power to influence the lives of their descendants. Practices range from measures intended to avoid offending the spirits of the dead to calling upon them to bring about desired results such as greater fertility.

androcentrism *See* PATRIARCHY.

androcracy *See* PATRIARCHY.

androgyny *See* SEX AND GENDER.

animism Animism is a form of religion based on the belief that spirits inhabit both living and nonliving objects such as trees, rocks, clouds, winds, or animals. Africa's Mbuti, for example, see the forest as the sacred source of death and life. Animist religions often include *shamans*, charismatic figures who are believed to be able to communicate with and influence spirits. Shamans achieve their special status in a variety of ways, including ecstatic religious experiences such as inspirational dreams or visions, or possessing personal characteristics that are culturally defined as having religious significance, such as certain deformities.

See also ANCESTOR WORSHIP.

Annales School The Annales School is the name given to an approach to history initiated in 1929 by a group of French historians who tried to link history and sociology. History is often written as a chronology of events and the people who figure prominently in them. The Annales School combined this with a broad emphasis on social systems, their cultural, structural, population, and ecological aspects, and the role these play in major historical trends in the changing shape of social life. Rather than focus on political leaders and events, for example, the Annales School was more concerned with such major forces as the decline of FEUDALISM, industrialization, and the growth of imperialism and global CAPITALISM. This approach gave the Annales School an especially close link with Marxist thinking.

Lucien Febvre and Marc Bloch were major figures in this school, most notably in their founding of the journal *Annales d'Histoire Economique et Sociale* in 1929. Bloch's study of feudal society is a classic work in this tradition. Most notable among recent writings are Fernand BRAUDEL's multivolume global history and Immanuel WALLERSTEIN's studies of the world economic system.

See also HISTORICAL SOCIOLOGY; WORLD SYSTEM.

Reading

Bloch, Marc. 1961. *Feudal society.* London: Routledge and Kegan Paul.

Braudel, Fernand. 1981. *The structures of everyday life: Civilization and capitalism, 15th–18th century.* vol. 1. New York: Harper and Row.

——. 1983. *The wheels of commerce: Civilization and capitalism, 15th–18th century,* vol. 2. New York: Harper and Row.

——. 1984. *The perspective of the world: Civilization and capitalism, 15th–18th century.* vol. 3. New York: Harper and Row.

Wallerstein, Immanuel. 1976. *The modern world system.* New York: Academic Press.

——. 1980. *The modern world system II. Mercantilism and the consolidation of the European world economy, 1600–1750.* New York: Academic Press.

——. 1989. *The modern world system III: The second era of great expansion of the capitalist world-economy, 1730–1840.* New York: Academic Press.

anomaly *See* SCIENTIFIC REVOLUTION.

anomie Anomie is a social condition in which there is lack of cohesion and order, especially in relation to norms and values. If norms are defined ambiguously, for example, or are enforced in a haphazard or arbitrary way; if a disaster such as war disrupts the usual pattern of social life and creates a situation in which it is unclear just what norms apply; or if a system is organized in a way that promotes individual isolation and autonomy to the extent that people identify more with their own interests than with those of the group or community as a whole – then anomie or "normlessness" can result.

Émile DURKHEIM developed the concept of anomie as part of his explanation of patterns of suicide in nineteenth-century Europe. He argued that suicide rates were higher among Protestants than Catholics because Protestant culture placed a higher value on individual autonomy and self-sufficiency. This made Protestants less likely to develop the kinds of close communal ties that might sustain them during times of emotional distress. This in turn made them more susceptible to suicide.

The concept of anomie has also been applied to the study of DEVIANCE. During natural disasters and wars, for example, it is not uncommon for people to break laws – as by stealing – they would never consider breaking during "normal" times. This results from a loss of social cohesion and normative clarity in the community or society as a whole.

Although anomie is often used to describe a person's psychological condition, sociologically it describes a condition in social systems as a whole. What Durkheim described as anomic suicide was a pattern of behavior that resulted from anomic social conditions – in other words, cultural and structural characteristics of social systems that resulted in low cohesion and a resulting weak sense of attachment of members to their communities.

See also ALIENATION; OPPORTUNITY STRUCTURE.

Reading

Durkheim, Émile. [1897] 1951. *Suicide.* New York: Free Press.

Merton, Robert K. 1938. "Social structure and anomie." *American Sociological Review* 3: 672–82.

Merton, Robert K. 1968. *Social theory and social structure*, rev. and exp. ed. New York: Free Press.

ANOVA *See* ANALYSIS OF VARIANCE.

antecedent variable In the analysis of causal relations among VARIABLES, an antecedent variable is identified as a cause of a variable that is itself regarded as an INDEPENDENT VARIABLE that affects a third variable. Occupation, for example, is an independent variable that causes variation in income. The more education people have, however, the better their jobs tend to be. Thus, in this case, education is called an antecedent variable because it affects an independent variable, occupation.

Note that the use of such labels depends on how the problem is defined initially. Suppose, for example, that we are looking at the relationship between education and income: the more schooling individuals have, the more money they are likely to earn. In this case, education is an independent variable that causes the dependent variable, income. If we then identify variables that cause differences in education – such as the social class background of a person's parents – then social class is called an antecedent variable because in this case it causes variation in an independent variable, education.

See also CONTROL VARIABLE; VARIABLE.

Reading
Rosenberg, Morris. 1968. *The logic of survey analysis*. New York: Basic Books.

anticipated consequence *See* FUNCTIONALIST PERSPECTIVE.

anticipatory socialization SOCIALIZATION is anticipatory when it concerns a role that the person being socialized will perform at some time in the future. For example, when small children dress up in their parents' clothing and play "house," they are practicing basic aspects of adult roles that will be beyond their reach for many years. Students in professional schools go through a similar process as they adopt mannerisms, styles of dress, values, and attitudes characteristic of those in professions for which they are still in training.

See also REFERENCE GROUP; SOCIALIZATION.

Reading
Merton, Robert K., and Alice S. Rossi. 1968. "Contributions to the theory of reference group behavior." In *Social theory and social structure*, rev. and exp., edited by Robert K. Merton, 279–334. New York: Free Press.

apartheid Apartheid was a centuries-old system of rigid racial separation and oppression in South Africa that ended officially with the first multiracial national elections in 1994. Although blacks formed the overwhelming majority of the population, they were denied political and civil rights, segregated from whites in virtually every aspect of social life, and exploited economically. Along with India and the United States, South Africa has provided one of a handful of historical examples of true CASTE systems.

Reading
Frederickson, G. M. 1981. *White supremacy: A comparative study in American and South African history*. New York: Oxford University Press.

appearance and reality Appearance and reality represent the distinction between how social life appears

15

to us and the underlying reality of which we tend to be unaware. It is a topic that Karl MARX, in his analysis of life under CAPITALISM, was particularly interested in. In capitalist societies, for example, people appear to be free to work where they please in a free labor market. Since no one is forced to work for any one employer, economic DEMOCRACY seems to be the rule. Beneath this appearance, however, is the reality that the vast majority of people own no MEANS OF PRODUCTION – no tools or machines they can use to earn a living by producing goods – and must sell their time to someone in exchange for wages. This gives those who own the means of production a great deal of collective power – for example, to dictate conditions of work and rates of pay – because employers know that under capitalism workers have few alternatives to wage labor.

From Marx's perspective, then, beneath the appearance of a free labor market is the reality of a relatively constrained system in which capitalist employers have a great deal of collective economic power in relation to working people. In order to understand the lives of workers, argues Marx, or their relationship with capitalists, we must pay attention to the underlying reality, not superficial appearances.

See also CLASS CONSCIOUSNESS AND FALSE CONSCIOUSNESS; IDEOLOGY.

Reading

Abercrombie, Nicholas. 1980. *Class, structure, and knowledge.* Oxford: Blackwell Publishers.

Marx, Karl. [1867] 1975. *Capital,* vol. 1. New York: International.

applied sociology Applied sociology uses sociological concepts, principles, and insight to deal with practical real-world decisions and problems. Major areas of applied sociological work include gathering data on social indicators – from patterns of consumption of various goods and services to the incidence of disease and injury – to better inform decisions ranging from public health policy to corporate marketing strategies; *evaluation research* to assess the success of programs, from drug rehabilitation to educational reform; and action research designed to change social systems in order to achieve certain goals, from improving student achievement in schools to lowering recidivism rates among criminals.

See also OBJECTIVITY.

Reading

Lazarsfeld, Paul F., and J. G. Reitz. 1975. *An introduction to applied sociology.* New York: Elsevier.

Olsen, M. E., and M. Mickim, 1981. *Handbook of applied sociology.* New York: Praeger.

aristocracy *See* UPPER CLASS.

asceticism Based on the belief that the spiritual and physical aspects of human life are separate and distinct, asceticism is a doctrine that promotes the development of the spirit through the denial of the body – especially its needs and pleasures – and involvement in the mundane aspects of worldly life. Although associated with many religious traditions, its sociological importance traces primarily to Max WEBER'S work on the influence of the PROTESTANT ETHIC on the emergence of CAPITALISM as an economic SYSTEM.

Reading

Weber, Max. [1904] 1958. *The Protestant ethic and the spirit of capitalism.* New York: Scribner's.

ascribed status An ascribed status is a social position that is assigned at (if not before) birth and is, therefore, usually permanent. Ascribed statuses include characteristics such as race, gender, country of origin, and various family of origin characteristics such as religion (in some cases) and ethnicity.

Because ascribed statuses are almost impossible to change (barring sex-change operations, racial "passing" or misrepresentation), they are often at the heart of systems of SOCIAL OPPRESSION, especially in CASTE SYSTEMS. By comparison, CLASS systems are organized more around ACHIEVED STATUSES such as educational attainment and occupation, although ascribed statuses play an important part in limiting the acquired statuses a person can hope to occupy.
See also STATUS.

ascription/achievement *See* PATTERN VARIABLES.

assimilation *See* CULTURAL CONTACT.

asymmetry, statistical *See* SYMMETRY.

atomism and holism Atomism and holism are concepts representing two radically different views of the nature of social life. The atomist perspective is individualistic and psychological. It argues that a SOCIAL SYSTEM is no more than a collection of individuals. If we can understand individuals, then we know all that we need to know about the social systems in which they participate. In short, the whole is the sum of its parts and nothing more. In contrast, holism lies at the heart of sociological thinking. Holism identifies the whole of social

systems as more than the individuals who participate in them. A war, for example, cannot be understood as a simple sum of individuals' aggressive, warlike impulses or behaviors.

Émile Durkheim's pioneering work in sociology during the nineteenth century was in many ways a reaction against the prevailing atomist perspective of his day. It is a debate that continues today within and beyond sociology. On one side are those who argue that social systems consist of networks of statuses and roles that shape and constrain a person's appearance, experience, and behavior. On the other side are a number of interactionists who argue that social systems are mere abstractions that do not exist apart from individuals interacting with one another.

As is often true in such debates, the polarities may represent not a contradiction but a paradox that reflects the complexity of the underlying reality of social life. Social systems cannot exist without individuals who participate in them to some degree; and yet individuals as we know them exist only in relation to one social system or another.
See also AGENCY AND STRUCTURE; INTERACTIONIST PERSPECTIVE; METHODOLOGICAL INDIVIDUALISM.

Reading
Blumer, Herbert. 1969. *Symbolic interactionism: Perspective and method.* Englewood Cliffs, NJ: Prentice-Hall.
Homans, George. 1950. *The human group.* New York: Harcourt Brace.
Kuhn, Manford H. 1964. "Major trends in symbolic interaction theory in the past twenty-five years." *Sociological Quarterly* 5 (winter): 61–84.

attitude An attitude is a concept having two meanings in sociology. The first is often used as a substitute for the concepts of BELIEFS and VALUES. Statements such as "The government spends too little on health care," "Obscene art should be banned," and "There should be tighter controls on immigration" can be accurately described as beliefs, values, or some combination of the two. They are all grounded in beliefs about reality (the relationship between government expenditures and the quality and availability of health care; the idea of obscenity; the actual extent and consequences of immigration, and so on). They also involve value judgments (more health care is desirable, as is government support for it; obscenity is bad; too much immigration is undesirable).

The second meaning of attitude goes beyond beliefs and values to identify a distinct aspect of how we orient ourselves to the world – emotion. In this sense of the word (which is also sometimes referred to as *sentiment*), an attitude is a cultural orientation to something that predisposes us not only to think about it in particular ways but to have positive or negative feelings about it as well. Racism, for example, is more than a matter of beliefs and values, for it also involves emotions such as contempt, hatred, disgust, condescension, and shame. Similarly, what makes patriotism such a powerful cultural force is not simply people's beliefs and values about their country but also deeply held feelings of pride, affection, and attachment that go with them.

Attitudes include a variety of emotions that exist only in a social context. Pride, shame, guilt, disgust, sympathy, love, gratitude, mortification, contempt, awe, reverence, pity – all have a particular relationship with cultural ideas and human beings. Pride, for example, is a positive regard of self that derives not simply from how we evaluate ourselves in relation to some system of values but, most importantly, from how we anticipate others will evaluate us. Similarly, outrage is an emotional state consisting of more than the emotions of anger or rage, for it includes the added factor that something has violated deeply held cultural values and expectations about what is supposed to happen or supposed to be. Since values and expectations are abstract elements of culture, outrage can exist only in relation to a cultural context. For this reason, although infants can feel rage, they cannot feel outrage because, without language, they are incapable of attaching abstract meaning and value to their feelings.

As a concept, attitude is important because it incorporates into sociological thinking an otherwise neglected aspect of social life, the role of emotion and the power of social systems to shape, regulate, and evoke it, producing both social cohesion and conflict. *See also* CULTURE.

Reading

Allport, G. W. 1935. "Attitudes." In *A handbook of social psychology*, edited by C. Murchison. Worcester, MA: Clark University Press.

Hill, R. J. 1981. "Attitudes and behavior." In *Social psychology: Sociological perspectives*, edited by M. Rosenberg and R. H. Turner.

Keicolt, K. J. 1988. "Recent developments in attitudes and social structure." *Annual Review of Sociology* 14: 381–403.

attitude scale An attitude scale is a way of measuring how people view something, whether it be a group of people, a social issue, or a life experience such as dying. Typically, researchers construct a scale by asking respondents a number of questions that are all related to the issue at hand. They ask respondents to agree or disagree with statements such as, "Women and men should be treated equally under the law," or "Women should not have the right to use abortion as a form of birth control." A scale is formed by combining responses to all of the questions into a single numerical score known as an index. This is used to rank respondents in terms of their position on that issue. Support for women's rights, for example, might be measured by questions touching on many different dimensions of the issue, from abortion to employment to church leadership to sexual violence to family relationships. High scores on such a scale might indicate strong support for women's rights, while low scores might indicate strong opposition.

There are different techniques and procedures for deciding which items to include in a scale. Some rely on panels of judges, while others use statistical techniques to determine which items are most closely related to one another and the issue being studied. The most common types are the *Likert,* *Guttman,* and *Thurstone* scales, named for their originators.

See also CLUSTER ANALYSIS; FACTOR ANALYSIS; MEASUREMENT; SOCIAL DISTANCE.

Reading

Dawes, Robyn M., and Tom L. Smith. 1985. "Attitude and opinion measurement." In *Handbook of social psychology*, 3rd ed., edited by G. Lindzey and E. Aronsan. New York: Random House.

Sudman, Seymour, and Norman R. Bradburn. 1983. *Asking questions: A practical guide to questionnaire design.* San Francisco: Jossey-Bass.

attribution, social Social attribution is a process through which people try to explain how other people behave and appear, especially in terms of their motivation. The belief that poor people are poor primarily because they are unwilling to work hard, or that the wealthy are wealthy because they are talented and hard-working are examples of social attributions. Examples of self-attributions might be explaining our own success as the result of talent and hard work or luck.

Such attributions are social not only in the sense of taking place between people. More importantly, they draw on people's social characteristics to form a basis for the attribution. Whether accomplishments are attributed to talent or luck, for example, depends to some degree on whether the person in question is perceived to be a man or a woman. Women are most likely to be seen as getting ahead through luck rather than talent, perhaps as a reflection of their devalued status in male-dominated societies. In explaining others, we draw upon an enormous range of ideas and perceptions of people's characteristics, from class, race, gender, and age to how tall or short, fat or thin, beautiful or ugly people may appear to be as interpreted by a particular culture.

See also FRONT.

Reading

Bierhoff, H.-W. 1989. *Person perception and attribution.* New York: Springer-Verlag.

Weary, G., M. A. Stanley, and J. H. Harvey. 1989. *Attribution*. New York: Springer-Verlag.

audience segregation *See* ROLE CONFLICT.

authoritarianism Authoritarianism is an approach to politics in which government is used to control the lives of the people rather than being subject to democratic control by citizens. Since true DEMOCRACY is quite rare, most governments are to some degree authoritarian and, therefore, problematic for those they govern.

The most extreme form of authoritarianism is *totalitarianism*, a political system designed to achieve complete control over people's inner and outer lives. This is, however, an extremely difficult if not impossible goal which has rarely been achieved for very long except in notable works of fiction such as George Orwell's nightmarish novel, *1984*. Even the most authoritarian societies such as Nazi Germany and the Soviet Union under Stalin failed at controlling most aspects of people's private lives or stifling dissent and subversion.

See also AUTOCRACY; DEMOCRACY, POLITICAL AND ECONOMIC; FASCISM; OLIGARCHY; POWER STRUCTURE; TOTAL INSTITUTION.

Reading
Friedrich, C. J., and Z. Brzezinski. 1965. *Totalitarian dictatorship and autocracy*. Cambridge: Harvard University Press.
Howe, Irving, ed. 1983. *1984 revisited: Totalitarianism in our century*. New York: Harper and Row.

authoritarian personality An authoritarian personality is characterized by rigid conformity, intolerance, wide-ranging prejudice, adulation for the strong and those in positions of authority, and contempt for the weak. Following the 1939–45 war, Theodor ADORNO and his colleagues conducted a classic study in which they tried to identify psychological profiles of people predisposed to PREJUDICE and intolerance and who tend to welcome authoritarian rule such as the fascism that had just devastated Europe. They devised a measurement scale – the *f-scale* – for gauging the degree to which people fit the authoritarian personality model and applied it to various areas of social life, from attitudes towards minorities to support for democratic institutions. With the Holocaust in Europe still recent history, the research focused explicitly on anti-Semitism, but found that prejudice tends to be a generalized rather than a specific view. In other words, people who are prejudiced against one group tend to be prejudiced against many groups, with a hatred of Jews being associated with a hatred of other groups such as Catholics.

Although controversial and the object of considerable criticism, Adorno's work is sociologically important because it seeks a connection between personality and how social systems are organized, in what it says both about how social conditions foster authoritarian personalities and about how AUTHORITARIANISM affects social life.

See also ATTITUDE SCALE; MEASUREMENT.

Reading
Adorno, T. W., E. Frenkel-Brunswik, D. J. Levinson, and R. N. Sandford. 1950. *The authoritarian personality*. New York: Harper and Row.

authority Authority is a concept whose development is most often associated with the German sociologist Max WEBER who saw it as a particular form of POWER. Authority is defined and supported by the norms of a social system and generally accepted as legitimate by those who participate in it. As such, most forms of authority are attached not to individuals but to a social position – STATUS – they occupy in social systems. We tend to obey the orders of police officers, for example, not because of who they are as individuals, about which we most likely know next to nothing. We obey because we accept their right to have power over us in certain situations, and we assume others will support that right should we choose to challenge it. In a similar way, police officers do not act with confidence so much because they possess personal self-confidence but because they share in the cultural belief that the authority of police officers is legitimate. It is for this reason that all that is needed to invoke the authority of a police officer is a convincing impression that the person in question is in fact a police officer, as indicated by the showing of badges or the wearing of appropriate uniforms.

A less formal example of authority is the tendency to refrain from intervening in an adult's punishment of a child on the street if we can find any reason to assume that the adult is the child's parent. In this case we are reluctant to interfere in what we see as a socially sanctioned authority relationship.

Individuals exercise authority only so long as they are seen to occupy the positions to which authority is attached, and the scope of their authority depends on the nature of both the position and the system. Whether a head of state is powerful,

for example, depends less on the individual's characteristics than on the authority vested by the social system in that position. British monarchs lost most of their authority not because they became weaker as individuals but because the structure of the British state was changed to allow them less authority. The transformation was more political and systemic than psychological and personal.

Sociologically, authority is the most important form that power takes in social life, because unlike *personal power*, which is based on such factors as physical strength or personality, authority is produced and controlled by social systems. As such, it tends to be far more stable and enduring than other forms of power because those over whom it is exercised have as much interest in perpetuating the authority as they do in perpetuating the social system itself. To seek to overthrow the authority vested in the state as an institution, for example, is tantamount to overthrowing the state itself (not to be confused with removing a particular individual from a position of authority, as by some mechanism such as impeachment). This threatens the interest not only of office holders but of all those who may suffer the effects of social disruption. In this sense, those who are subordinate to authority often play an active part in supporting their own subordination by accepting its social legitimacy. No authoritarian state can endure for long without substantial support from the population that affirms the legitimacy it must have in order to govern.

The social legitimacy of authority depends on its being used according to the norms that define its scope and the social mechanisms through which it is applied. Unlike schoolyard bullies whose power is based on coercion rather than a shared sense of legitimacy, people in positions of authority can retain it only by maintaining the impression that authority is not being abused. Abuse of authority, however, is often difficult to establish, since part of the legitimacy of authority includes a certain amount of deference to those who wield it. As such, authority is a form of power that is particularly subject to abuse, because it rests on the shared social assumption that those in authority act with the full weight of an entire social system behind them. This means that those who might suffer from abuses of authority may be reluctant to identify it as abuse, much less to challenge the abuser, for to do so can provoke reprisals not only from the individual involved but from the social system itself. The reluctance to question or challenge authority is in fact built into the structure of authority itself and helps account for the fact that authority enables individuals to exercise far more power than their individual abilities and characteristics would otherwise allow. It is for this reason that the abuse of children is so difficult to prevent or even detect, because it is based on the socially supported authority of adults over children.

Weber identified three types of authority that rest on different social bases: legal-rational authority, traditional authority, and charismatic authority. *Legal-rational authority* is based on formally enacted norms that are codified usually, but not always, in written form. A person who exercises legal-rational authority does so because the codes grant that authority to whoever occupies that particular position. This is the form of authority found in workplaces, government, schools, and most major social institutions.

Traditional authority is based on an uncodified collective sense that it is proper and longstanding and should therefore be accepted as legitimate. This is the kind of authority exercised by adults in relation to children, although parental authority also has legal-rational aspects in many societies. Tradition may also be a basis for the authority of husbands over wives in patriarchal societies or of religious leaders over members of a religious community.

Charismatic authority is based on the social attribution of extraordinary personal characteristics or abilities to a person. Note that the authority is based not on the characteristics themselves but on the attribution of those characteristics by those who acknowledge the authority as legitimate. The distinction is crucial, because it underlines the fact that charismatic authority is socially bestowed and may be withdrawn when the leader is no longer regarded as extraordinary. Like traditional authority, charismatic authority is not codified, but unlike both traditional and legal-rational authority, charismatic authority is attached to a person and not the social status occupied by the person. Iran's late Ayatollah Khomeini, for example, had great charismatic authority not simply because he occupied the highest leadership position in the Muslim church but because of the personal qualities he was believed to have brought to that position. Sociologically, it is misleading to refer to someone as "charismatic," because this fosters the impression that such authority derives from and is controlled by the person who exercises it. On the contrary, from a sociological perspective charisma is completely in the eyes of the beholders, and it is on their shared collective attributions that charismatic authority depends.

To Weber's three major types of authority some contemporary sociologists would add a fourth, authority based on expertise (also known as *professional authority*). As societies become dependent on sophisticated technology, for example, and as divisions of labor become more complex, those who can give the impression of possessing specialized knowledge are likely to achieve some authority as a result. The authority of physicians, for example, is to some degree traditional and, increasingly, legal-rational as legislative bodies make deeper inroads into the regulation of medical decisions ranging from abortion to the withdrawal of life support. In addition to this, however, as the practice of medicine becomes increasingly complex and beyond the comprehension of many patients, the perception of expertise becomes a basis for authority in its own right. Similar observations can be made about law, science, and academic scholarship in many fields.

The four types of authority are IDEAL TYPES and as such are usually not found in their pure form in any given situation. In practice, most authority is a blend of two or more types.
See also LEADERSHIP; LEGITIMATION; POWER; TECHNOCRACY.

Reading
Haskell, T. FL., ed. 1984. *The authority of experts.* Bloomington: Indiana University Press.
Weber, Max. 1946. *From Max Weber: Essays in sociology*, edited and translated by Hans Gerth and C. Wright Mills. New York: Oxford University Press.
Willner, A. R. 1984. *The spellbinders: Charismatic political leadership.* New Haven: Yale University Press.

autocracy An autocracy is a state ruled by a single leader, such as a dictator. In agrarian societies, autocratic leadership historically took the form of royal families who ruled by traditional right. In the twentieth century, autocratic rule was based more on charismatic leadership and control over the political and military apparatus of the state, as was the case in Nazi Germany under Hitler, the Soviet Union under Stalin, Nicaragua under Somoza, and Iraq under Saddam Hussein.

Because it tends to rely heavily on the ability to coerce a population into submission, autocracy tends to be a relatively unstable form of government that is especially vulnerable to COUPS D'ÉTAT and REVOLUTION.
See also AUTHORITARIANISM; COUP D'ÉTAT; DEMOCRACY; FASCISM; OLIGARCHY; POWER STRUCTURE; REVOLUTION; STATE.

Reading
Perlmutter, H. V. 1977. *The military and politics in modern times.* New Haven: Yale University Press.

automation Automation is the practice of using machines to replace workers. From an ecological perspective, it greatly increases the human ability to alter the environment, to extract raw materials, and to produce goods in abundant quantities. From a labor relations and social class perspective, it is a major way for the capitalist class to increase profit at the expense of workers (because it causes a net loss of jobs) and controls the working class by invoking the fear of being replaced by machines.

See also ALIENATION; DE-SKILLING; SCIENTIFIC MANAGEMENT.

Reading

Marsh, Peter. 1982. *The robot age.* London: Sphere.

Shaiken, H. 1986. *Work transformed: Automation and labor in the computer age.* Lexington, MA: Lexington Books.

Zuboff, Shoshana. 1988. *In the age of the smart machine.* New York: Basic Books.

B

baby boom   Baby boom is the term referring to a period following the 1939–45 world war when birth rates increased rapidly in North America, Australia, New Zealand, and parts of Western Europe. The boom ended in the early 1960s and was followed in the 1970s by a drop in fertility. The baby boom was due primarily to the sudden "catching-up" of fertility that was delayed by men being away during the war, but also to a modest increase in completed family size.
See also FECUNDITY.

back region   *See* BACKSTAGE AND FRONTSTAGE.

backstage and frontstage   In Erving GOFFMAN'S DRAMATURGICAL PERSPECTIVE on social INTERACTION, frontstage and backstage (also known as *front region* and *back region*) are concepts used to describe the relationship between the ROLES actors play at a given moment and the various audiences these roles involve. When we perform a role in relation to an audience, that role is on frontstage, and our performance is open to judgment by those who observe it. When students go to class, for example, they are on frontstage, and the professor can judge them on how well prepared they are or how well they participate.

The backstage region is a place where actors can discuss, polish, or refine their performances without revealing themselves to their audience. It also allows them to express aspects of themselves that their audience would find unacceptable (such as students saying they don't like the course or, worse, their professor, or that they cheated on the last exam).

Reading

Goffman, Erving. 1959. *The presentation of self in everyday life*. New York: Doubleday.

bar graph   *See* GRAPHICS.

base and superstructure   Base and superstructure are two central concepts in Karl MARX'S view of how societies are organized around material production. The base is the MODE OF PRODUCTION, the basic way a society organizes the production of goods. So critical is the productive system in Marx's view of social life that those who dominate the economic system are also seen as dominating other aspects of social life in their own image and interests. The most important of these areas of dominance are a society's superstructure, the state and institutions such as schools, religious organizations, and the mass media that play a vital role in creating consciousness. This is done through beliefs, values, norms, and attitudes that together provide the raw material for constructing and interpreting social reality.

As with a building, the superstructure rests upon the base and must reflect its shape. The nature of the state, for example, and general ways of thinking will differ in feudal and industrial capitalist societies. This is because the relations of production differ and are dominated in different ways by classes of people with their own sets of interests. The dominant groups in feudal societies depended in part upon the strength of tradition and religious belief to support and justify their power and privilege. In contrast, the dominance of industrial capitalists is based more on legal-rational AUTHORITY, control over state institutions, and, above all, owning the MEANS OF PRODUCTION. As such, the STATE is far more developed and complex in industrial capitalist societies and general ways of thinking are far more organized around rationality, legality, and contractual relations.

Marx argued that it is impossible to understand superstructural aspects of societies without taking the base into account. This does not imply that the base causes or determines the superstructure in a direct, linear way. The superstructure is shaped by noneconomic forces, and it also affects the base. In short, the relationship between base and superstructure is both complex and reciprocal.

See also HEGEMONY; IDEOLOGY; KNOWLEDGE; MODE OF PRODUCTION; STATE.

Reading

Hall, Stuart. 1977. "Rethinking the 'base and superstructure' metaphor." In *Papers on class, hegemony, and party*, edited by J. Bloomfield. London: Lawrence and Wishart.

Marx, Karl. [1859] 1970. *A contribution to the critique of political economy*. New York: International Publishers.

Marx, Karl, and Friedrich Engels. [1846] 1976. "The German ideology." In *Collected works of Marx and Engels*, vol. 5. New York: International.

behavior *See* ACTION AND BEHAVIOR.

behaviorism Behaviorism is a psychological perspective that focuses only on observable behavior and assumes that behavioral patterns result solely from conditioning through the use of reward and punishment. Although it has rarely been used by sociologists (with the notable exception of U.S. sociologist George HOMANS), it is sociologically significant because it conflicts with basic sociological assumptions about human behavior. On the macro level, behaviorism ignores the existence and influence of SOCIAL SYSTEMS and their cultural and structural aspects. On the micro level, it denies the importance of meaning in human ACTION and INTERACTION. It thereby ignores the sociological distinction between simple behavior on the one hand and meaningful ACTION that requires some interpretation on the other. As such, there is disagreement on whether behaviorism can give an adequate account of social life and human behavior in general, including the SOCIALIZATION process through which individuals become social beings capable of participating in social life and social systems.

See also INTERACTION; SOCIALIZATION.

Reading

Skinner, B. F. 1938. *The behavior of organisms*. New York: Appleton-Century-Crofts.

Zuriff, G. E. 1985. *Behaviorism: A conceptual reconstruction*. New York: Columbia University Press.

belief In cultural systems, a belief is any statement or part of a statement that purports to describe some aspect of collective reality. Whether a statement corresponds to what is generally accepted in a SOCIAL SYSTEM as "truth" or "fact" has no bearing on whether it qualifies as a belief. In this sense, all culturally based descriptions of reality are beliefs, including such statements as "God exists," "$E = mc^2$," "Merchants will accept money in exchange for goods," "A person whose brain has no electrical activity is dead," "The sun orbits the earth," "There's no fool like an old fool," "In music, the note one whole step above C is D."

Cultural beliefs are important because it is from them that we construct what we take to be the reality of everyday life as well as not-so-everyday matters such as spirituality and cosmology. This is particularly true of the beliefs that are attached to various positions in social systems. These are assumptions that we use as a substitute for direct personal knowledge of people we interact with and depend on every day. We assume that bank tellers in fact place our deposits in the bank rather than absconding with them for an early retirement; we assume that people who identify themselves as doctors and display all the appropriate appearances know what they are doing; we assume that most people will drive on the correct side of the road. We make these assumptions because they are presented to us as part of our cultural belief system. Even when individuals violate those assumptions – as they invariably do sometimes – we generally don't abandon them unless the exceptions become so numerous that the cultural belief cannot hold (as

when people lost confidence in banks during the Great Depression).

The power of beliefs is most evident in our general lack of awareness of them as such. Some scientists, for example, bridle at the idea that their work is grounded in belief, which they prefer to distinguish from "fact." They, like most of us, take certain aspects of reality as certain and beyond question. They see reality as simply the way things are rather than the way it has been constructed from the raw materials provided by a particular cultural belief system. From a sociological perspective, however, all knowledge is socially constructed and beliefs of all sorts lie at the heart of that construction.

See also CULTURE; PHENOMENOLOGY; POSTMODERNISM; SELF-FULFILLING PROPHECY.

beta weight *See* PATH ANALYSIS; STANDARDIZATION.

bias *See* ERROR.

biased estimate *See* ESTIMATES.

bilateral descent *See* KINSHIP.

bilocal residence *See* MARRIAGE RULES.

bimodal distribution *See* MODE.

biological analogy *See* ORGANIC ANALOGY.

biological determinism *See* DETERMINISM AND REDUCTIONISM.

birth order Birth order is the ranking of children within a family as determined by when each child was born. Research suggests that birth order may affect development in a variety of ways, from personality to occupational achievement. First-born children, for example, may be more likely to seek the company of others when under stress, to conform to social pressure, and to seek positions of power. Prominent leaders are unusually likely to be first-born or only children.

Reading

Ernst, C., and J. Angst. 1983. *Birth order: Its influence on personality.* New York: Springer-Verlag.

birth rate The birth rate is the demographic measure of the rate at which children are born. The most well known is the *crude birth rate*, which is the number of births that occur each year per 1,000 people in the midyear population. This rate is called "crude" because it does not take into account the possible effects of age structure. If a population has an unusually large (or small) number of women in the prime childbearing ages, then its crude birth rate will tend to be relatively high (or low) regardless of the actual number of children each woman has. For this reason, age-adjusted birth rates are preferred for making comparisons, either over time or between populations. One measure that helps to adjust for age is the *general fertility rate*, which is the number of births in a year per 1,000 women aged 15 to 44 years. Age-specific rates, such as the birth rate for 20- to 24-year-olds only, can also be calculated.

In addition to these birth rates, demographers use three hypothetical rates to get some idea of the future consequences of current patterns of reproductive behavior in a population. The *gross reproduction rate* (GRR) is the average number of daughters that would be born to a hypothetical COHORT of women if current birth rates for women of various ages were to remain the same throughout their lifetime. In other words, it is the number of daughters they would have if they went through their twenties having babies at the current rate for women in their twenties, through their thirties having babies at the rate for women in their thirties, and so on. The *net reproduction rate* is the same as the gross reproduction rate except that it uses current mortality rates for women of various ages to take into account the fact that some women will die before they finish their childbearing years and will thus contribute fewer daughters to the population. Finally, the *total fertility rate* is the same as the gross reproduction rate except that it applies to all children, not just daughters.

Sociologists are interested in birth rates primarily as they affect population growth and size and AGE STRUCTURE (high birth rates tend to produce young populations). A host of social consequences are affected by these, especially economic prosperity and development. For this reason birth patterns are important not only on the level of societies but also for different categories of people who differ by SOCIAL CLASS, RELIGION, ETHNICITY, RACE, income, EDUCATION, urban-rural residence, and occupation. Birth rates are a social phenomenon to be explained in terms of the cultural and structural aspects of life in the populations they describe.

See also AGE STRUCTURE; DEATH RATE; FECUNDITY AND FERTILITY; RATE OF NATURAL INCREASE.

Reading

Shryock, Henry S., and Jacob Siegel and Associates. 1976. *The methods and materials of demography.* New York: Academic Press.

blended family *See* FAMILY.

blue-collar worker and white-collar worker In general, a blue-collar worker is a person whose work is primarily *manual,* such as a construction or factory worker. A white-collar worker is a person whose work is primarily *nonmanual,* such as an office worker. The latter usually refers to lower-level workers such as secretaries and clerks rather than higher-level occupations such as executive, lawyer, and professor.

Although the class distinction between blue-collar manual and white-collar nonmanual workers has been important in studies of stratification and mobility, its usefulness appears to be on the decline. The distinction between the two categories is muddy in many cases – a great deal of the work performed by lower-level office workers, for example, involves considerable use of the hands and less mental acuity than a number of skilled blue-collar occupations. In addition, although white-collar work is generally regarded as having higher prestige than blue-collar, many such occupations are in other important respects lower in class standing. Most clerical jobs, for example, have lower levels of power, income, and autonomy than many higher-level blue-collar jobs (such as skilled trades).

See also SOCIAL CLASS; SOCIAL MOBILITY; STRATIFICATION AND IN-EQUALITY.

Reading
Powers, M. G., ed. 1982. *Measures of socioeconomic status.* Boulder, CO: Westview Press.

body, sociology of the *See* FOUCAULT.

Bogardus scale *See* SOCIAL DISTANCE.

boundary A boundary is a point or limit that distinguishes one social system or group from another and identifies and regulates who may participate in it. Military units, for example, are distinguished from one another by uniforms and insignia; communities often use road signs to mark their boundaries; and people may occupy the status of university student only after satisfying the criteria for admission.

Structural boundaries vary in their clarity and openness. While the uniforms worn by athletic teams clearly distinguish members from nonmembers, for example, it is very difficult to identify who occupies the social position of lawyer in a theater crowd. In a courtroom, however, the physical position of lawyers in relation to other participants as well as their behavior clarify their position as well as the boundary separating them from others.

The more open boundaries are, the easier it is for someone to cross them and participate in a social system. Family boundaries, for example, tend to be quite difficult to cross, as are the boundaries for most professions and citizenship in most countries. By comparison, the boundaries of public buses are quite open, requiring only a ticket, and the boundaries of public places such as sidewalks and municipal buildings are more open still – this is what makes them "public."

Boundaries are sociologically significant in many ways, from how the degree of intimacy is regulated in

29

social relationships to nativist hostility toward foreigners to how dominant classes and races maintain their privilege by excluding members of subordinate groups from neighborhoods, occupations, and institutional positions of influence and authority.

See also SOCIAL STRUCTURE; SOCIAL SYSTEM.

bounded rationality Bounded rationality is a decision-making model used by sociologists to explain how decisions are made. When economists explain how decisions are made in business organizations, they typically assume that the process includes rational consideration of all relevant information. From their sociological work on organizations, however, March and Simon argue that the degree to which decision-making can be rational is limited – or bounded – by the fact that decision makers never have access to all the information they need about their alternatives or the consequences of any given decision. In addition, people are inherently limited in their ability to process large amounts of information in a purely rational way. The result is a decision-making model of rationality bounded by such limitations.

Reading
March, J. G., and H. A. Simon. 1958. *Organizations.* New York: Wiley.
Simon, H. A. 1957. *Administrative behavior.* New York: Macmillan.

bourgeoisie *See* SOCIAL CLASS.

brain drain A brain drain is a situation that occurs when talented and highly skilled people migrate from one place to another, especially in search of advanced education and employment. It often occurs when young people migrate from Third World countries to Europe or the United States for university education and then remain upon graduation rather than returning home. The result is a serious loss of human resources for nonindustrial societies. The emigration of skilled and talented people has also been a problem for some advanced industrial societies, including Great Britain.

See also MIGRATION; WORLD SYSTEM.

Reading
Bechhofer, F., ed. 1969. *Population growth and the brain drain.* Edinburgh: Edinburgh University Press.

bureaucracy *See* FORMAL ORGANIZATION.

C

capital   In everyday usage, capital is anything that can be used to generate income or produce wealth, including money lent out at interest, tools and machinery used to make products, and a worker's time sold in exchange for wages. This broad meaning is, however, not very useful for analytical purposes, in part because it includes so much that we can never be sure what it refers to in a particular instance. Most important, if capital is used to refer to anything that generates wealth or income, it is very unclear what should be made of capitalism as an economic system, since wealth and income are produced in almost every economic system whether capitalist or not.

An alternative definition comes from a Marxist perspective that uses the concept of capital to describe not how something is used to produce wealth, but the kind of economic system in which it is used. In particular, capital is some *means of production* – such as machines and tools – used by workers who do not themselves own or control it but who produce wealth with it in exchange for wages. When a machine is owned and operated by the same people, it is a means of production, but not capital, because the social relationships through which it is used, owned, and controlled are one and the same. If those who own the machine hire workers who use it to produce goods in exchange for wages, then the machine becomes capital through the creation of a new set of social relationships.

This way of looking at capital defines it as a fundamentally social phenomenon that both derives from and reflects the social relationships through which economic activity takes place.

See also CAPITALISM; LABOR AND LABOR POWER.

Reading

Marx, Karl. [1867] 1975. *Capital: A critique of political economy*. New York: International Publishers.

capitalism   Capitalism is an economic system that emerged in Europe during the sixteenth and seventeenth centuries. From the perspective developed by Karl MARX, capitalism is organized around the concept of CAPITAL, the ownership and control of the means of production by those who employ workers to produce goods and services in exchange for wages. The key to capitalism as a social system is a set of three relationships among (1) workers, (2) the means of production (factories, machines, tools), and (3) those who own or control means of production. Members of the capitalist class own or control the means of production but do not actually use them to produce wealth; members of the working class neither own nor control the means of production but use them to produce; and the capitalist class employs the working class by buying LABOR POWER (time) in exchange for wages.

The more common definition of capitalism – simply the private ownership of the means of production – overlooks the fact that people have been making goods with privately owned tools for thousands of years, long before the emergence of capitalism. Under capitalism, therefore, the ownership of the means of production is not simply private; it is also exclusionary and forms the basis for SOCIAL CLASS and exploitation in the interests of profit and the accumulation of still more means of production. As such, the common identification of capitalism with "free enterprise" is somewhat misleading since the trio of relations between the means of production, workers, and capitalists is not a necessary condition for free enterprise and in many ways may hinder it. Since competition threatens the success of every capitalist enterprise (however it may contribute to the system as a whole), corporations generally deal with competition by trying to increase their control over labor, production, and markets, with the result that the economy is increasingly dominated by a relatively few large organizations. In this sense, the actual exercise of freedom in free market capitalism becomes possible only at larger and larger levels of social organization. As the myriad of small competing enterprises is replaced by huge CONGLOMERATES (many of them TRANSNATIONAL), so, too, is the freedom of "free enterprise" exercised by a steadily diminishing number of economic players.

The idea of a free market is probably most appropriately associated with what might be called "early capitalism." This was the period before the INDUSTRIAL REVOLUTION when capitalism took the form of profit-seeking through the buying and selling of goods. The forerunners of modern capitalism did not own or control means of production but, as merchants, profited by taking advantage of market conditions such as buying goods and transporting them for sale in a market in which they were unavailable. Merchants contributed to the emergence of capitalism by developing the idea of profit, of using goods as vehicles for turning money into more money. Only later did capitalism emerge as a system whose primary basis for power and profit was control over the production process itself. In the advanced form it has assumed in modern capitalist industrialist societies, it has moved away from competitive capitalism involving a diverse collection of relatively small firms toward what Marx called *monopoly* (or *advanced*) *capitalism*. In this form, corporations merge and form ever larger global centers of economic power that have the potential to rival nation-states in their influence over resources and production, and through these, over the terms on which social life is lived in the broadest sense. As the strains and contradictions within the system grow more severe, governments intervene to control markets, finance, labor, and other capitalist interests with increasing frequency and severity. Marx saw this as the final stage leading to socialist revolution.

See also COMMODITY; CONTRADICTION; LABOR AND LABOR POWER; LABOR MARKET; MARKET; MODE OF PRODUCTION; MONOPOLY; OLIGOPOLY; PROFIT; STATE SOCIALISM; VALUE, ECONOMIC.

Reading

Edwards, Richard C., Michael Reich, and Thomas E. Weisskopf, eds. 1986. *The capitalist system*, 3rd ed. Englewood Cliffs, NJ: Prentice-Hall.

Mandel, Ernest. 1971. *Marxist economic theory*, 2 vols. New York: Monthly Review Press.

——. 1975. *Late capitalism*. London: New Left Books.

Marx, Karl. [1867] 1975. *Capital: A critique of political economy*. New York: International Publishers.

Smith, Adam. [1776] 1982. *The wealth of nations*. New York: Penguin.

career *See* WORK.

case In research, a case is any unit selected for observation. In an opinion SURVEY, for example, each respondent is a case, while in a study of the world economy, a case might be a corporation, a community, or an entire nation. In statistical tabulations, the number of cases is usually represented by the letter n, as in "$n = 1,500.$" A lower-case n denotes a sample size and an uppercase N denotes population size.
See also POPULATION; SAMPLE.

case study A case study is a research method relying on a single case rather than a population CENSUS or a representative SAMPLE.

In spite of the fact that the case study makes it virtually impossible to make generalizations about the population, it has its uses. When researchers focus on a single case, for example, they can make detailed observations over a long period of time, something that cannot be done with large samples without a very high price tag. Case studies are also useful in the early stages of research when the goal is to explore ideas, to test and perfect measurement instruments and observational skills, and to prepare for a larger, more broadly based study.

Sometimes a case study is all that is possible. For example, our interest might be in the dynamics of national elections, but since they occur only at intervals of several years, our only option is to conduct a case study of a particular election, knowing that the results cannot be generalized to all elections. Or, we might want to study a phenomenon that is unlikely to repeat itself in a predictable way, such as the social consequences of a war or of a natural disaster such as a flood, earthquake, or drought.

Because case studies allow an intense focus on social behavior, they are the preferred research design for those who use an INTERACTIONIST PERSPECTIVE and rely on PARTICIPANT OBSERVATION as a research method. Two classic studies are Erving GOFFMAN'S study of asylums and William Foote Whyte's study of urban gangs. Case studies are also used on a much larger scale, however, as in comparative studies of British, U.S., and Japanese business practices, the causes of political revolution, or the impact of technology on the workplace.

Although case studies cannot be used to make reliable statements about populations, they can provide important insights that can be used to design larger, more representative studies. Also, as case studies in a particular area of social life are accumulated, the result can often be used as a substitute for larger single studies based on representative samples.
See also CENSUS; INTERACTIONIST PERSPECTIVE; PARTICIPANT OBSERVATION; SAMPLE.

Reading

Feagin, J. R., A. M. Orum, and G. Sjoberg. 1991. *A case for the case study*. Chapel

Hill: University of North Carolina Press.

cash nexus A nexus is a means of connection or a tie that binds two things together. The term "cash nexus" was coined by Karl MARX and Friedrich ENGELS to describe the depersonalized connection that exists between employers and workers under CAPITALISM. The exchange of cash wages in return for LABOR POWER from workers is often the main source of attachment between workers and employers, with each trying to maximize their return at the expense of the other.

Reading
Marx, Karl, and Friedrich Engels. [1848] 1932. *Manifesto of the communist party.* New York: International Publishers.

caste A caste is a rigid category into which people are born with no possibility of change. In some systems of STRATIFICATION AND INEQUALITY, the distribution of rewards and resources is organized around castes. In India, the caste system historically has consisted of four basic categories – Brahmin, Kshatriya, Vaisya, and Sudra – each with its own specific and rigid location in the stratification system. In addition to these, an "outcaste" of "untouchables" is beneath the lowest caste. The crossing of caste boundaries is rigidly prohibited through controls over occupational distribution and residence, and especially through control over the choice of marriage partners. Within the four major castes, there are numerous subcastes among which a certain amount of mobility is possible.

According to the Indian caste system, which is codified in the Hindu religion, people may move from one caste to another across several lifetimes through the process of reincarnation. Such movements depend upon successful performance in the present caste position, which means that the system provides a powerful incentive for enforcing acceptance of the caste system itself and its inequalities.

Although the concept of caste is associated almost exclusively with India, elements of caste can be found in a few other societies, such as Japan during the seventeenth and eighteenth centuries and more recently in the United States and South Africa. Although the caste system was officially banned in India in 1949, its influence remains in rural areas.

See also SOCIAL CLASS; SOCIAL MOBILITY.

Reading
Frederickson, G. M. 1981. *White supremacy: A comparative study in American and South African history.* New York: Oxford University Press.
Gould, Harold A. 1987. *The Hindu caste system: The sacralization of a social order.* Delhi: Chanakya.

categorical variable *See* SCALE OF MEASUREMENT.

category *See* SOCIAL CATEGORY.

causal explanation and causal model A causal explanation is a statement that one phenomenon is the result of one or more other phenomena that precede it in time. Any full explanation of social inequality, for example, would likely include the idea that occupation has a causal effect on income levels. A causal model takes this a step further by describing causal relationships involving several variables acting together. A model used to explain differences in income, for example, might include not only occupation but additional factors such as educational attainment, race, gender, and age, and family background characteristics such as mother's and father's occupations, educational attainment, and income. The model might specify how each of these affects income in direct or indirect ways. Occupation, for example, has a direct effect on income, with managers being paid more than secretaries. However, educational attainment of parents is more likely to have an indirect effect on income, perhaps through its effects on the educational aspirations of their children.

In research, causal explanations and models are tested through a variety of statistical techniques, including PATH ANALYSIS and LOG-LINEAR ANALYSIS. They are somewhat inconclusive because they rely on various assumptions that often cannot be confirmed. They are nonetheless useful for clarifying how we think about a particular problem, for they force us to specify how variables are related to one another.

The whole issue of causal explanation is also problematic in the social sciences because it is difficult to identify cause-and-effect relationships without conducting EXPERIMENTS, which is usually not possible in sociological work. For example, we can verify that the more highly educated people are, the higher their income tends to be, but this does not mean that educational attainment per se is a causal factor. Although sociologists can rarely prove that a causal relationship exists with the variables they study, they can get close enough to contribute important insights into how social life works. *See also* MODEL; MULTIVARIATE ANALYSIS.

Reading

Blalock, Hubert M. 1964. *Causal inferences in nonexperimental research.* Chapel Hill: University of North Carolina Press.
——, ed. 1985. *Causal models in experimental and panel designs.* Chicago: Aldine.
Blalock, Hubert M., and Anne B. Blalock, eds. 1968. *Methodology in social research.* New York: McGraw-Hill.

cell *See* CROSS-TABULATION.

census A census is a gathering of information from all members of a population rather than from a SAMPLE. In Britain and the United States, for example, a census is conducted every ten years. Although the census is most often associated with data-gathering at the national level, as a concept it applies to any population regardless of its size.

Because a census targets an entire population, it is tempting to assume that its information will be more accurate than that gathered from a sample. This is not necessarily the case, however, for a sample survey can concentrate more heavily on getting answers from every respondent while a census must necessarily accept a higher level of nonresponse. It is for this reason that large sample surveys are often used to assess the accuracy of a census.

See also CASE STUDY; POPULATION; POSTENUMERATION SURVEY; SAMPLE.

Reading

Anderson, M. J. 1988. *The American census: A social history.* New Haven: Yale University Press.

center and periphery The concepts of center and periphery are useful for describing both spatial and social relationships and the connection between the two. In the study of urban areas, for example, the difference between the center and the periphery is often also a difference in how land is used and in the social composition of neighborhoods and COMMUNITIES.

The concepts find their most powerful use as metaphors to describe systems of SOCIAL INEQUALITY. Within SOCIETIES, for example, those privileged by SOCIAL CLASS, RACE, or GENDER are located at the "center" of social life, while subordinate and disadvantaged groups find themselves at the periphery and treated as a marginalized "other." On a larger scale, the WORLD SYSTEM can be described as a system of dominant and subordinate societies, with the elite located at the core and nonindustrial societies in the periphery of power, wealth, and influence.

center nation *See* WORLD SYSTEM.

central limit theorem *See* SAMPLING DISTRIBUTION.

change *See* SOCIAL CHANGE.

charismatic authority *See* AUTHORITY.

Chebyshev's theorem *See* VARIANCE.

Chicago School The Chicago School is the name given to an approach to sociological work associated with the department of sociology at the University of Chicago, formed in 1892 as the first in the United States. It is referred to as a "school" because of its distinctive focus on urban problems, its early use of ecological and ethnographic methods, and its development of basic ideas that grew into what is now the INTERACTIONIST PERSPECTIVE.

The Chicago School is most closely associated with its founder Albion Small (1854–1926) and his colleagues Ernest W. BURGESS, George Herbert MEAD, Roderick McKenzie, Robert Ezra PARK, William I. THOMAS, Louis WIRTH, and Florian ZNANIECKI. Mead and Thomas focused primarily on social interaction, especially as it affects the development of personal identity and the SELF. It is the work of the rest, however – those who focused on the problems of rapid urban growth – that is most often referred to as the Chicago School.

Turn-of-the-century America was a place of rapid change, massive immigration, industrialization, and urbanization, and the members of the Chicago School immersed themselves in the city as if it were a giant laboratory. Their studies ranged from patterns of urban settlement and racism and poverty to the stunning variety of ethnic lifestyles coexisting in the same community. For example, they introduced a theory of urban growth based on the idea that COMPETITION for land results in distinctive patterns of land use and neighborhood composition. They observed the rich diversity of people's lives, from the skid row district to ethnic neighborhoods to the wealthy "Gold Coast" along Lake Michigan. The Chicago School, in short, was distinctive both for its substantive body of sociological work and for its dynamic attitude toward field research and commitment to first-hand understanding of fundamental aspects of social life.
See also ETHNOGRAPHY AND ETHOLOGY; INTERACTIONIST PERSPECTIVE; URBAN ECOLOGY; URBANIZATION AND URBANISM.

Reading

Blumer, Herbert. 1984. *The Chicago School of sociology: Institutionalization, diversity, and the rise of sociological research.* Chicago: University of Chicago Press.

Park, Robert E., Ernest Burgess, and Roderick D. McKenzie, eds. 1925. *The city.* Chicago: University of Chicago Press.

Zorbaugh, Harvey W. 1929. *The gold coast and the slum: A sociological study of Chicago's near north side.* Chicago: University of Chicago Press.

chi-square Chi-square is one of several statistical techniques used to test whether a set of SAMPLE results is simply a chance occurrence or, instead, reflects something real going on in the population. Which statistic is used depends on the mathematical form the results take. Chi-square is used most often to analyze relations between VARIABLES presented in the form of CROSS-TABULATIONS. The test is conducted by constructing a TABLE that shows how the CASES would be distributed among the cells if the two variables were independent of each other.

The computation of chi-square is based on the idea of taking the difference between each pair of corresponding cells as a way to measure how far apart the sample table is from what the same table would look like if the variables were independent of each other. The resulting numerical value of chi-square is then located in a chi-square distribution table that indicates the probability of finding such results simply by chance. If that probability is sufficiently small, this supports the conclusion that the observed sample relationship is more than a matter of chance and reflects a real relationship in the population.

Chi-square is also used in *goodness-of-fit tests* in which one distribution is compared with another to see, once again, if any observed difference is due merely to chance. If we want to test whether a sample is biased by income, for example, we might compare the sample's income distribution with a known population income distribution (gathered as part of a census, for example) and use chi-square to determine whether differences between the two distributions can be attributed to chance or to bias in the sample design.

See also HYPOTHESIS AND HYPOTHESIS TESTING; STATISTICAL INDEPENDENCE AND STATISTICAL DEPENDENCE.

Reading

Bohrnstedt, George W., and David Knoke. 1994. *Statistics for social data analysis,* 3rd ed. Itasca, IL: F. E. Peacock.

church In the sociology of religion, a church is a type of religious organization distinguished by its structural characteristics. Membership is usually ascribed at birth and includes people from a broad range of SOCIAL CLASS backgrounds. The POWER STRUCTURE is bureaucratic and trained leaders have clearly defined authority. Rituals tend to be abstract with little emotional feeling expressed during services. In relation to other major institutions such as the STATE, churches tend to be supportive of the status quo and dominant social categories and groups.

Examples of churches include the Church of England, the Catholic Church outside of Italy, the Greek Orthodox Church, and the Methodist, Episcopalian, and Lutheran churches in the United States.

See also CULT; DENOMINATION; ECCLESIA; RELIGION; SECT.

Reading
Becker, Howard. 1950. *Systematic sociology.* New York: Wiley.
Troeltsch, Ernst. [1912] 1956. *The social teachings of the Christian churches.* London: Allen and Unwin.
Weber, Max. [1922] 1963. *The sociology of religion.* Boston: Beacon.

circulation mobility *See* SOCIAL MOBILITY.

circulation of elites *See* ELITE.

citizen and citizenship As developed by Thomas H. MARSHALL, citizenship is a social position that carries with it three distinct kinds of rights, especially in relation to the STATE: (1) *civic rights* include the right to free speech, to be informed about what is going on, to assemble, organize, and move about without undue restriction, and to be treated equally under the law; (2) *political rights* include the right to vote and run for office in free elections; and (3) *socioeconomic rights* include the right to welfare and social security, to unionize and carry on collective bargaining with employers, and even to have a job in the first place.

A key sociological issue about citizenship is how various groups are included or excluded from it – as in denying women the vote in Britain and the United States until well into the twentieth century, or in denying unionization of workers for much of the early history of capitalism – and how these affect social inequality. Marshall argued, for example, that granting full citizenship to workers has actually disempowered them to some degree. As long as workers feel excluded from the system, they are more likely to organize in opposition to it. As they come to feel more included, they also tend to accept the legitimacy of the very system under which they are exploited as workers and are therefore less likely to rebel against it. Note, for example, that rights of citizenship in capitalist societies do not include equal control over the means of production.

Reading
Barbalet, Jack. 1988. *Citizenship.* Minneapolis: University of Minnesota Press.
Bendix, Reinhard. 1977. *Nation-building and citizenship.* Berkeley: University of California Press.
Marshall, Thomas H. 1950. *Citizenship, social class, and other essays.* Cambridge, England: Cambridge University Press.

city *See* COMMUNITY; URBANIZATION AND URBANISM.

civic rights *See* CITIZEN AND CITIZENSHIP.

civil attention and civil inattention Civil attention and inattention are concepts developed by Erving GOFFMAN in his dramaturgical approach to social interaction and the techniques people use to maintain particular kinds of social impressions. Civil attention is used by individuals to create the impression of being involved in a role when in fact they are not. Students in classrooms, for example, use a variety of techniques to maintain the impression that they are paying attention when they are in fact involved in other activities such as writing letters or daydreaming. Such techniques include pretending to take notes, nodding their heads in agreement at appropriate moments, or laughing at the professor's jokes when others laugh.

In contrast; civil inattention is used to create the impression that a person is unaware of what is going on so that others can maintain the sense that what they say and do is taking place in private. In a doctor's waiting room, for example, the people next to us may be talking about intimate details of their health. As strangers located near enough to overhear, we are not supposed to be privy to their information. In response to this expectation, we refrain from looking at them or otherwise acknowledging our own ability to overhear. Instead, we pretend to have our attention elsewhere. That we can in fact hear everything assumes less social importance than our ability to create the appearance of just the opposite.

See also DRAMATURGICAL PERSPECTIVE; INTERACTIONIST PERSPECTIVE.

Reading
Goffman, Erving. 1963. *Behavior in public places.* New York: Free Press.
——. 1971. *Relations in public: Microstudies of the public order.* London: Allen Lane.

civilization A civilization is a society whose relative freedom from the struggle for mere survival enables it to become more complex in its CULTURE and structure. The hallmarks of civilization include fixed COMMUNITIES; political organization in the form of STATES; a complex DIVISION OF LABOR; trade and commerce within market economies; formal religious institutions; and highly developed art, literature, music, and other forms of expression.

Civilization is most often distinguished from HUNTER-GATHERER and HORTICULTURAL SOCIETIES, which are often referred to as PRIMITIVE by those who count themselves among the civilized. This distinction has often included presumptions of the latter's moral superiority, which history and cross-cultural studies show to be

largely groundless. Indeed, some argue that the development of Western civilization – complete with organized mass welfare, extensive environmental pollution, ALIENATION, economic EXPLOITATION, and SOCIAL OPPRESSION – indicates a moral decline.

Reading
Elias, Norbert. 1939. *The civilizing process: The history of manners.* Oxford: Blackwell Publishers.
——. 1939. *The civilizing process: State formation and civilization.* Oxford: Blackwell Publishers.

civil law *See* LAW.

civil religion Civil religion is a set of secular SYMBOLS and RITUALS that provide some of the sense of belonging, social solidarity, and awe usually associated with religion and the SACRED. As the visibility and public power of institutionalized religion in social life has diminished in industrial societies, some sociologists argue that new frameworks have emerged to take over some of the social functions once performed by it. In some societies, for example, the NATION-STATE serves this function as past leaders, pivotal historical events, and public rituals such as coronations are elevated to mythic if not holy status. Symbols of the state such as flags, memorials, and national anthems are regarded with the kind of deep reverence usually directed toward religious figures and artifacts. Until recently, the importance of Lenin's tomb in Moscow was a clear reflection of the power of civil religion. In similar ways, in the United States, heroic figures such as George Washington and Abraham Lincoln have assumed a mythic significance with the power to generate a measure of social COHESION even in a society that is full of ethnic and racial diversity.

See also RELIGION; SECULARIZATION.

Reading

Bellah, Robert N. 1973. *The broken covenant.* New York: Seabury Press.

——, and Hammond, Philip E. 1980. *Varieties of civil religion.* New York: Harper and Row.

Durkheim, Émile. [1912] 1965. *The elementary forms of religious life.* New York: Free Press.

civil society According to Karl MARX, civil society is a fragmented capitalist world organized around INDIVIDUALISM and materialistic COMPETITION of all against all. The modern STATE became necessary to regulate and contain the resulting conflict and misery. Influenced by the work of philosopher Georg Hegel, Marx used the term civil society to distinguish life under CAPITALISM from the medieval world in which social relations were shaped primarily by family ties and the political bonds of FEUDALISM and the craft GUILD.

More recently, Antonio GRAMSCI has argued that the core of civil society is not only the individual and individualism but also private organizations such as corporations. Gramsci also argued that the state and civil society overlap and merge with each other to such a degree that it is hard to tell where one leaves off and the other begins. From this perspective, it is important to understand the mutually reinforcing relationship between the two.

Reading

Marx, Karl. [1843] 1967. "Critiques of Hegel's philosophy of rights." In *Writings of the young Marx on philosophy and society,* edited and translated by L. D. Easton and K. Guddat. New York: Doubleday.

——. [1927] 1964. *Economic and philosophical manuscripts of 1884.* New York: International Publishers.

——, and Friedrich Engels. [1846] 1976. "The German ideology." In *Collected works of Marx and Engels,* vol. 5. New York: International.

Mouffe, C. ed. 1979. *Gramsci and Marxist theory.* London: Routledge and Kegan Paul.

clan In the study of KINSHIP, a clan is a collection of people who see themselves as descendants of a common ancestor and thereby think of themselves as a group with a shared identity. Clan membership is unilineal: it may be traced through the mother or through the father, but never both.

See also KINSHIP.

Reading

Neville, Gwen. 1979. "Community form and ceremonial life in three regions of Scotland." *American Ethnologist* 6: 93–100.

Rivers, William H. R. 1914. *Kinship and social organization.* London: Constable.

class *See* SOCIAL CLASS.

class conflict and class struggle According to Karl MARX, class conflict and struggle are the inevitable dissension that occurs because of the economic organization of most societies. It happens between peasants and nobility under FEUDALISM, for example, and between workers and employers under CAPITALISM. In his theories of history, Marx argued that such struggles were the engine that drove and shaped SOCIAL CHANGE. It was, for example, the struggle between the landowning aristocracy and the emerging capitalist entrepreneurs that led to the decline of feudalism and the rise of capitalism.

From a Marxist perspective, class conflict and struggle are inevitable in capitalist societies because the interests of workers and capitalists are fundamentally at odds with each other. Capitalists accumulate wealth by exploiting the workers who produce it; and workers maintain or advance their own well-being only by resisting capitalist exploitation. The results of class conflict are reflected in virtually every aspect of social life, from unionizing efforts and strikes to political campaigns to immigration policies to the content of art, literature, and POPULAR CULTURE.

See also CAPITALISM; CONFLICT PERSPECTIVE; MATERIALISM; SOCIAL CLASS.

Reading

Braverman, Harry. 1974. *Labor and monopoly capital.* New York: Monthly Review Press.

Friedman, A. L. 1977. *Industry and labor.* London: Macmillan.

Marx, Karl, and Friedrich Engels. [1848] 1932. *Manifesto of the communist party.* New York: International Publishers.

class consciousness and false consciousness Karl Marx defined class consciousness as a social condition in which members of a SOCIAL CLASS – the working class in particular – are actively aware of themselves as a class. False consciousness is a lack of such awareness, resulting in distorted perceptions of the reality of class and its consequences. More recently, Michael MANN extended Marx's concept to include not only the awareness of class membership, but also awareness of the adversarial relationship between capitalists and workers, the broad range of ways that class systems affect people's lives, and alternatives to class oppression.

Marx defined classes in terms of the positions of individuals in relation to the process of economic production. The capitalist class owns or controls the means of production (factories, machines, tools); workers use the means of production to produce wealth, in exchange for which they are paid wages by their employers. Capitalist profit depends on paying wages that represent less than the value of what workers produce. Hence, the structure of class relations is inherently exploitative and antagonistic since one class can benefit only at the expense of the other.

Class, then, can be described from a Marxist perspective in objective terms. Marx, however, saw classes not only as collections of people with similar characteristics but as participants in a great and continuing struggle that produced SOCIAL CHANGE. To participate in the process of history, classes have to be aware or conscious of themselves as classes, to become classes not only "in themselves" but also "for themselves" by realizing the true causes and extent of their oppression as workers. Marx believed that the exploitative nature of capitalism, coupled with the growing collective misery of the working class, would make class consciousness, and hence revolutionary change, inevitable.

Historically, class consciousness has been the exception rather than the rule, for powerful social forces work against it. Dominant classes tend to control major social institutions, including the STATE and its coercive authority. They also exert great influence over cultural VALUES, BELIEFS, and NORMS. Thus, although the concentration of great wealth depends far more on inheritance than hard work, the prevailing ethic nonetheless emphasizes the importance of hard work in getting ahead. In this way, the unequal distribution of wealth is preserved and the lower classes are left primarily to blame themselves for their own deprivation, presumably on the grounds that they lack sufficient talent and motivation to succeed.

On a more general level, consciousness of the true nature of social life usually results only from considerable effort and training. Most SOCIAL SYSTEMS – from marriages and families to the world economy – do not include in their CULTURE a sustained critical awareness of themselves as social systems. In class systems, however, the dominant class has a vested interest in the existence of false consciousness in the subordinate classes and can use its authority and resources to promote and sustain it.

See also CAPITALISM; CLASS IMAGERY; CLASS INTEREST; IDEOLOGY; MODE OF PRODUCTION; SOCIAL CLASS; SOCIAL CONTROL.

Reading
Mann, M. 1973. *Consciousness and action in the western working class*. London: Macmillan.
Marx, Karl. [1869] 1978. *The eighteenth brumaire of Louis Bonaparte*. Peking: Foreign Languages Press.

class dealignment *See* VOTING BEHAVIOR.

class imagery Class imagery is the name given to people's perceptions of different SOCIAL CLASSES and the relations among them. Although it could apply to the views held by any class, from upper to lower, capitalist to working, sociological work focuses primarily on how working-class people view the class system. The working class tends to use three

models to make sense of the class system: (1) the power model, (2) the prestige model, and (3) the money model. The power model identifies two basic classes, the working class and the upper class, which controls wealth and exerts great power over everyone below it. The prestige model defines the classes less distinctly as separate categories, and people are ranked in terms of the prestige associated with characteristics such as occupation and education along a continuum running from high to low. The world is seen not so much as an "us" and "them" locked in perpetual conflict but as a competition of all against all for standing and advantage. The money model focuses less on prestige and class conflict and more on the different ways people have access to money and the lifestyles they have as a result. From this perspective, some have more, some have less, and regardless of how much they have, they can make decisions about how to spend it that will affect their class standing.

See also CLASS CONSCIOUSNESS AND FALSE CONSCIOUSNESS.

Reading
Bott, E. 1957. *Family and social network*. London: Tavistock.
Bulmer, Martin, ed. 1975. *Working-class images of society*. London: Routledge and Kegan Paul.
Goldthorpe, J. H., D. Lockwood, F. Bechhofer, and J. Platt. 1969. *The affluent worker in the class structure*. Cambridge, England: Cambridge University Press.
Lockwood, David. 1966. "Sources of variation in working class images of society." *Sociological Review* 14: 249–67.

class interest As argued by Karl MARX, class interest is formed by the structure of relations that bind capitalists, the means of production, and workers to one another, creating different priorities for each class. Under CAPITALISM, for example, capitalists own and control the means of production; workers use the means of production to produce goods in exchange for wages. Capitalists depend in part for their wealth on being able to pay workers wages that amount to less than the value of the goods workers produce so that capitalists can keep the difference (as a form of profit) for themselves. Workers, on the other hand, prosper to the extent that they are able to keep for themselves as large a portion as possible of the value of what they produce.

From a Marxist perspective, capitalists have an interest in successfully exploiting workers without so oppressing them that they either rebel or can no longer work. Workers have an interest in increasing wages and other forms of compensation as well as their control over the production process. When these interests are mutually contradictory – as Marx believed class interests inherently are – SOCIAL CONFLICT is the result.

One of the problems with the concept of class interest is deciding whether something constitutes a class interest even if members of a class are unaware of it. Marx, for example, argued that a true social class does not even exist unless its members are aware of themselves as a class. Similarly, it can be argued that class interests become real only through a class that is conscious of itself and do not otherwise exist in any objective sense. Or, it can be argued that class interests are determined objectively – that automation resulting in lost jobs, for example, is against the interests of

the working class whether or not a self-conscious working class exists.
See also CLASS CONSCIOUSNESS AND FALSE CONSCIOUSNESS; CONTRADICTION; MATERIALISM; SOCIAL CLASS.

Reading
Marx, Karl. [1847] 1956. *The poverty of philosophy.* Moscow: Progress Publishers.
——. [1869] 1978. *The eighteenth brumaire of Louis Bonaparte.* Peking: Foreign Languages Press.

class struggle *See* CLASS CONFLICT AND CLASS STRUGGLE.

classical social movement theory
In general, classical social movement theory argues that social movements arise primarily as a collective way for individuals to relieve various forms of emotional strain and distress. Although nominally sociological, the theory is in fact based mostly on psychological processes and mechanisms.

Classical theory is typified by FRUSTRATION-AGGRESSION THEORY, MASS SOCIETY THEORY, AND STRUCTURAL STRAIN THEORY. The classical approach has been widely criticized and has lost much of its influence in contemporary sociology, although variations of it are still common in mass media treatments of social movements and collective behavior.
See also COLLECTIVE BEHAVIOR; FRUSTRATION-AGGRESSION THEORY; MASS SOCIETY; POLITICAL PROCESS THEORY; RESOURCE MOBILIZATION THEORY; STRUCTURAL STRAIN THEORY.

Reading
McAdam, Doug. 1982. *Political process and the development of black insurgency 1930–1970.* Chicago: University of Chicago Press.
Oberschall, A. 1973. *Social conflict and social movements.* Englewood Cliffs, NJ: Prentice-Hall.

Tilly, Charles. 1978. *From mobilization to revolution*. Reading, MA: Addison-Wesley.

clinical sociology Clinical sociology is the practice of applying sociological understandings of how social life works to individual cases of mental or physical illness. It rests on the assumption that individual states of being – including health and illness – are affected by people's participation in SOCIAL SYSTEMS, especially as these produce SOCIAL PROBLEMS such as POVERTY, PREJUDICE AND DISCRIMINATION, ALIENATION, and ANOMIE.

Reading

Bruhn, John G., and Howard M. Rebach. 1996. *Clinical sociology*. New York: Plenum.
Wirth, Louis. 1931. "Clinical sociology." *American Journal of Sociology* 37: 49–66.

cluster analysis Cluster analysis is a statistical technique that is used to identify how various units, such as people, organizations, or societies, can be grouped or "clustered" together because of characteristics they have in common. If we look at societies, for example, we would see that wealthy societies also tend to have complex DIVISIONS OF LABOR, strong militaries, highly developed technology, a diversified industrial base, relatively stable democratic political institutions, and educated populations. On this basis, we might then identify societies such as Britain, Japan, France, the United States, Germany, and Italy as belonging to the same "cluster." By contrast, societies such as China, Uganda, and Nicaragua tend to cluster around a quite different set of characteristics, including low levels of wealth, simpler divisions of labor, a reliance on producing raw materials and agricultural products, relatively unstable and undemocratic political institutions, and low technological development.

As a statistical procedure, cluster analysis includes a collection of techniques used to identify clusters in a set of data. In the most general sense, it is a way to identify types, whether types of societies, people, or organizations.

See also FACTOR ANALYSIS.

Reading

Everitt, Brian S. 1993. *Cluster analysis*, 2nd ed. London: Heinemann.
Sokal, Robert R., and Peter H. A. Sneath. 1963. *Principles of numerical taxonomy*. San Francisco: Freeman.

cluster sample *See* COMPLEX SAMPLE.

coalition A coalition is two or more people, groups, or other units in a SOCIAL SYSTEM who combine in order to have greater POWER or influence. Georg SIMMEL, for example, noted that one of the key differences between a dyad (two people) and a triad (three people) is that with the third person it becomes possible for two to form a coalition against one. As a result, three people living together will tend to have very different power dynamics than will two.

A few sociologists have worked on the problem of predicting when coalitions will appear in social systems and who will be the most likely partners. Caplow, for example, argues that people form coalitions in order to maximize their power over others as well as their own autonomy. Gamson argues that in addition to power, people also form coalitions in order to maximize rewards. Weaker members of a system, for example, might combine against the stronger in the hope of gaining rewards that might be denied to them if they allied with stronger members.

Coalitions are important in political sociology because through them relatively powerless groups can combine to exert considerable influence. *See also* DYAD; POWER STRUCTURE.

Reading
Caplow, Theodore. 1968. *Two against one; Coalitions in triads.* Englewood Cliffs, NJ: Prentice-Hall.
Gamson, William A. 1968. "A theory of coalition formation." *American Sociological Review* 22: 373–79.

code *See* CODING; SPEECH CODES.

coding Coding is the process of assigning numbers or categories to DATA or information. For example, it is much easier to use computers to process, summarize, and display quantitative information if each observation is expressed as a number. We might ask survey respondents which social class category best describes them – lower, working, middle, upper-middle, or upper. When these responses are processed later, each category will be given a numerical equivalent called a *code* – such as lower class = 1, working class = 2, and so on.

Coding can also be used to assign observations to different categories. To study GROUP DYNAMICS, we might videotape a meeting and later try to identify the different types of behavior, gestures, and utterances we observe. How do we decide if a suggestion made by a group member is an attempt to help the group along or a sarcastic attack on the group? Assigning that observation to one category or another and then assigning it

an identifying number is part of the coding process.
See also MEASUREMENT.

Reading
Singleton, Royce A., Bruce C. Straits, and Margaret M. Straits. 1998. *Approaches to social research*, 3rd ed. Oxford and New York: Oxford University Press.

coefficient of alienation In CORRELATION, REGRESSION, and, especially, PATH ANALYSIS, the coefficient of alienation is a STATISTIC that varies in value from 0.00 to 1.00. It is used to indicate the degree to which one or more independent VARIABLES fail to explain variation in a dependent variable. Mathematically, the coefficient is the square root of the proportion of the VARIANCE that is unexplained. If, for example, an analysis shows that the proportion of the variation in personal income that is explained by background variables such as education is 0.40, then 0.60 is the proportion left unexplained, since proportions must add to 1.00. The coefficient of alienation is the square root of this, or 0.77. In a path diagram, this quantity is typically shown connected by an arrow to the dependent variable at the far right-hand side of the model. (For an illustration, see the figure that appears in the entry on PATH ANALYSIS.) The closer it is to 1.00, the poorer is the model as an explanation of the dependent variable. In this sense, the coefficient of alienation is the opposite of a correlation.
See also CORRELATION; COVARIANCE; PATH ANALYSIS; REGRESSION ANALYSIS.

coefficient of determination In CORRELATION, REGRESSION, and PATH ANALYSIS, the coefficient of determination is a statistic that varies in value from 0.00 to 1.00. It indicates the proportion of variation in the dependent variable that is explained statistically by one or more independent variables. It is equivalent to the square of the correlation coefficient. It is represented by the symbol r^2 in simple regression and by R^2 in multiple regression.

See also CORRELATION.

Reading

Bohrnstedt, George W., and David Knoke. 1994. *Statistics for social data analysis*, 3rd ed. Itasca, IL: F. E. Peacock.

coercive power   *See* POWER.

cohesion   Cohesion is the degree to which those who participate in a SOCIAL SYSTEM identify with it and feel bound to support it, especially its NORMS, VALUES, BELIEFS, and structure. The problem of understanding the sources of cohesion has been important in sociology, especially since the work of the nineteenth-century French sociologist Émile DURKHEIM. Durkheim argued that the degree of cohesion depends on how social systems are organized. In this he disagreed with UTILITARIANISM, which viewed cohesion as a result of ongoing decisions of rational individuals to participate in societies because it is in their self-interest to do so.

Durkheim identified two basic sources of cohesion: *mechanical solidarity* and *organic solidarity*. Mechanical solidarity is cohesion based on a shared CULTURE and way of life, a consensus over values, norms, and beliefs resulting from SOCIALIZATION and common experience. Although mechanical solidarity operates to some degree in every social system, it is most closely associated with tribal

societies, where the distinction between individuals and societies is minimal.

In contrast, organic solidarity is based on a complex DIVISION OF LABOR in which people depend on one another because specialization has made it difficult for them to survive on their own. In most industrial societies, for example, people work to earn money to purchase the necessities of life in the market. They do not know how to grow food, build houses, weave cloth, or sew. This means that the only way to meet such needs is through a complex network of interdependency that joins people who in other respects may be quite different and have little in common with one another. In a sense, organic solidarity results not from likeness, but from differences.

More recent versions of Durkheim's approach to social cohesion, especially that developed by Talcott PARSONS, rest on the idea that modern, complex societies are held together by a general *consensus* on values. This collective agreement is cultivated by socializing institutions such as the FAMILY, schools, and the mass media. Although this is to some degree true in every complex society, it needs to be qualified in several ways. First, an apparent consensus on values can mask considerable variation among the subgroups of a population. Second, insofar as dominant groups in a society can control major institutions such as schools and the mass media, they can define and promote universal values that reflect their own interests rather than those of society as a whole. In capitalist societies, for example, most wealth is owned by elites, which means that values that elevate private property rights over other considerations (such as humane living conditions, full employment, or a clean environment) serve elite interests.

In this sense, consensus need not mean that what is agreed to is in fact in the best interests of society as a whole or most of its people. Rather, consensus can reflect the power of some groups to shape things in their own interests. This view is most closely associated with the CONFLICT PERSPECTIVE and the work of Karl MARX and Max WEBER, who argued that cohesion and order are to some degree created and maintained by coercion and domination, most notably through institutions such as the STATE. For example, societies in which there are oppressed minorities may continue to exhibit social cohesion not because of a true value consensus but because minorities fear that if they dare to demand social justice, still greater violence and persecution may result.

See also CONFLICT PERSPECTIVE; CULTURE; FUNCTIONAL PERSPECTIVE; GEMEINSCHAFT AND GESELLSCHAFT; GROUPTHINK; HEGEMONY; POWER; SOCIAL CONTRACT; SOCIAL CONTROL; SOCIAL ORDER; UTILITARIANISM.

Reading

Durkheim, Émile. [1893] 1933. *The division of labor in society*. New York: Free Press.

Parsons, Talcott. 1951. *The social system*. Glencoe, IL: Free Press.

Tönnies, Ferdinand. [1887] 1963. *Community and society*. New York: Harper.

cohort A cohort is a collection of all people who share a particular experience, especially through being born during the same period. Birth cohorts often are defined in terms of five- to ten-year periods, such as those born between 1980–85 or 1940–50.

In some tribal societies, cohorts are formalized and given names that distinguish them from other cohorts. Sociologically, these are known as *age sets*.

The cohort is an important sociological concept, especially in the study of social change. Because each new cohort experiences society in its own way under unique historical conditions, it inevitably contributes to social change by reinterpreting cultural VALUES, BELIEFS, and ATTITUDES and adjusting to structural constraints. A cohort that grows up during times of economic depression, for example, may be expected to develop quite different values about hard work and the importance of frugality and saving than will a cohort growing up during times of economic expansion and prosperity. In similar ways, cohorts who spend their young adult years exposed to a disastrous war such as the U.S. involvement in Vietnam or the former Soviet Union's involvement in Afghanistan can be expected to develop more antiwar attitudes and values than a cohort exposed to what is generally regarded as a "good" war, such as World War II.

Such cohort differences are referred to as *cohort effects*. They are distinguished from *longitudinal effects*, which occur due to aging within a cohort. As women get older, for example, the number of children they have tends to increase simply because they are exposed to a greater number of opportunities to get pregnant – a longitudinal effect. Depending on changing social circumstances, however, the average number of children for each cohort may vary. This was evidenced by the baby boom that followed World War II in Europe and North America which was followed by the decline in fertility starting in the late 1960s.

See also LONGITUDINAL STUDY.

Reading

Riley, Matilda White. 1987. "On the significance of age in sociology." *American Sociological Review* 52(1): 1–14.

Ryder, Norman B. 1965. "The cohort as a concept in the study of social change." *American Sociological Review* 30: 843–61.

cohort effect *See* COHORT.

collective bargaining Collective bargaining is a process for determining wages and other conditions of employment under CAPITALISM. Its "collective" aspect refers to workers and/or employers bargaining not as individuals, but through groups that represent them.

On the one hand, collective bargaining can be seen as a source of POWER for workers who can combine with one another against employers' control of the MEANS OF PRODUCTION. On the other hand, Marxists in particular often see collective bargaining as a tool that ultimately increases employer control over workers by minimizing the possibility of conflict and by regulating workers' demands and containing them within acceptable limits.

collective behavior Collective behavior is a type of social behavior that occurs in crowds and masses. A *crowd* is any temporary collection of people who happen to be in the same place at the same time so that they can affect one another. A theater audience is a crowd as are the people who gather on a street corner to watch a fire. A *mass* differs from a crowd in that although the people share and react to a similar event,

they are not in one another's physical presence. When news of a natural disaster or a political assassination spreads, for example, or when people celebrate a national holiday, they are participating in a common pattern of behavior in relation to a shared event even though they are not in contact with one another. They are participants in mass behavior.

Collective behavior can be organized in a variety of ways, from riots, mobs, panics, and mass hysteria to fads, fashions, rumor, and public opinion. Some sociologists also categorize SOCIAL MOVEMENTS as a form of collective behavior although many social movements have levels of organization that go well beyond what is found in most crowds and masses and are better understood as GROUPS or FORMAL ORGANIZATIONS.

The study of collective behavior has been a significant area in which sociology has largely replaced psychology as a point of view. In the nineteenth century, Gustave Le Bon proposed *mob psychology* as a theory of behavior in crowds. In particular, Le Bon argued that people tend to surrender their individuality, will, and powers of moral judgment in crowds and give in to the hypnotic powers of leaders who shape crowd behavior as they like. Sociologists have shown since that behavior in crowds is far more mindful, rational, and socially organized than Le Bon believed, that it can in fact be understood in the same terms as other forms of social INTERACTION.

See also PUBLIC OPINION; SOCIAL MOVEMENT.

Reading

Le Bon, Gustave. [1895] 1960. *The crowd: A study of the popular mind.* New York: Viking.

Smelser, Neil J. 1962. *Theory* of *collective behavior*. New York: Free Press.

Turner, Ralph H., and Lewis Killian. 1987. *Collective behavior*, 3rd ed. Englewood Cliffs, NJ: Prentice-Hall.

collective conscience *See* CONSCIENCE COLLECTIVE.

collective consumption Collective consumption is a concept that refers to the many goods and services that, in cities, tend to be produced and consumed on a collective level. These include public schools and libraries; roads, bridges and public transportation; health care, waste disposal, public housing, welfare, fire and police protection, and parks and recreational facilities. Manuel Castells uses this term in his work on urban communities, especially as these develop and operate in relation to industrial CAPITALISM. In many ways, capitalist firms depend on such goods and services – such as an educated work force and transportation facilities – in order to function; however, they are reluctant to pay for them because they generate no profit. As a result, city, state, and national governments are the major providers, but struggle with a chronic lack of sufficient funds. This, argues Castells, causes recurring crises, SOCIAL MOVEMENTS, and other forms of political struggle around the provision of services and control over STATE institutions responsible for them.

Reading
Castells, Manuel. 1977. *The urban question: A Marxist approach*. Translated by A. Sheridan. Cambridge, MA: MIT Press.

Saunders, Peter. 1981. *Social theory and the urban question*. London: Hutchinson.

collective representation A collective representation is a SYMBOL or an idea that people internalize as individuals but also experience as something external to themselves. As an individual, for example, I may believe in God or truth, but the *ideas* of God and truth don't originate with me or with any particular collection of individuals I might identify. They are, instead, part of a CULTURE that, like all SOCIAL FACTS, cannot be reduced to a simple sum of the people who share in and make use of it.

The concept of collective representation was introduced by Émile DURKHEIM as a way to understand the power of religious symbols and ideas in social life. Its significance goes far beyond RELIGION, however, because Durkheim laid the groundwork for what became the sociological perspective as an alternative to individualistic thinking.

Reading
Durkheim, Émile. [1912] 1965. *The elementary forms of religious life*. New York: Free Press.

collectivity A collectivity consists of people who think of themselves as belonging to an identifiable social unit such as a political party. Unlike a GROUP, a collectivity lacks regular patterns of INTERACTION among members. Political parties have leadership structures that involve considerable interaction and therefore have group qualities; but the vast majority of members belong only in the sense of registering as such and voting accordingly with little if any regular interaction with other party members. Thus, while governing committees qualify as groups, parties as a whole are more accurately described as collectivities.

Collectivities can take many different forms, including racial, ethnic, national, political, religious, and community identifications (New Yorkers, for example, Oxford graduates, or Protestants) and associations that people join for a variety of reasons, ranging from a simple donation of money to the agreement to subscribe to professional rules of conduct.

See also AGGREGATE; GROUP; SOCIAL CATEGORY.

Reading

Merton, Robert K. 1968. *Social theory and social structure*, rev. and exp. ed. New York: Free Press.

colonialism and imperialism Colonialism is an international system of economic exploitation through which more powerful nations dominate weaker ones. In the typical case, the colonizer controls the colony through a combination of military coercion, dominance of major internal institutions such as the STATE, and, through these, control of MARKETS and production. The colony's role is to provide raw materials so that the colonial power can manufacture goods cheaply and, therefore, profitably. These goods are then sold on world markets, which include the colony. The colonial relationship is usually exclusive, which is to say, the colony may not sell its raw materials to anyone else and must buy finished goods only from its colonizer. This ensures both cheap raw materials and a captive market for the colonial power, a lucrative basis for economic exploitation.

Colonialism played an important role in hastening the development of CAPITALISM in Europe by providing wealth for investment and markets for surplus production. As such, it can be seen as a manifestation of the more general phenomenon of *imperialism*, the practice of one nation dominating another, typically through military force but increasingly through economic dependency. What distinguishes colonialism is its emphasis on economic profit rather than political domination for its own sake, as was the case in the early empires of Rome, Alexander the Great, and Babylonia. Although the colonial system has disappeared through a process of *decolonization* and former colonies are now self-governing, patterns of economic and political dominance and dependency persist through what some refer to as *neocolonialism* or, in Marxism, *neoimperialism*.

The term *internal colonialism* has been used to draw attention to the fact that exploitative relationships can exist within societies as well as between them. This can happen in a number of ways. Industrial regions, for example, may dominate and exploit agricultural regions for food and raw materials; dominant ethnic or racial groups may exploit subordinate groups. First used by Marxists such as Vladimir Lenin and Antonio Gramsci to describe how capitalist exploitation works on a regional level, the concept of internal colonialism has been used in a variety of settings. It has been applied to Latin America, particularly between urban populations with largely European backgrounds and indigenous native populations; to race relations in the United States; and to economic and political inequality in Canada and Europe. In general, it challenges the idea that capitalist industrialization leads to integrated societies governed by principles of equality.

See also CAPITALISM; DEPENDENCY THEORY; THIRD WORLD; WORLD SYSTEM.

Reading
Barratt Brown, M. 1974. *The economics of imperialism*. Harmondsworth, England: Penguin Books.
Hechter, M. 1975. *Internal colonialism*. London: Routledge and Kegan Paul.
Hobson, John A. 1938. *Imperialism*. London: Allen and Unwin.
Mommsen, W. J. 1980. *Theories of imperialism*. London: Weidenfeld and Nicolson.

commodity A commodity is any good or service produced in order to sell or otherwise exchange it for something else in a MARKET system. If you grow tomatoes for your own consumption, the tomatoes are not a commodity; but if you grow them to sell or to barter for goods or services such as clothing or dental work, then the tomatoes you grow are a commodity.

From this perspective, nothing is inherently a commodity; a commodity exists only through its position in relation to markets and the process of EXCHANGE. One of the most important changes brought about by the emergence of industrial CAPITALISM, for example, was that labor became a commodity that people sold in markets in exchange for wages. This extends even to those services once rendered as part of family life, such as child care. At the turn of the twenty-first century, child-care services are emerging as commodities in many industrial societies. Increasing numbers of families depend on the earnings of both parents and turn to commercial child-care services to fill some of the gap in child care, at least among the classes that can afford them.

The transformation of goods and services into commodities is important because it brings with it an increasing dependence on markets to meet basic needs. This, in turn, makes people dependent on the ability to earn cash, usually by selling their work in exchange for wages. In nonindustrial societies, families tend to be relatively self-sufficient in that they produce most of what they consume. As industrialization progresses, however, it takes over the production of almost all goods consumed within the family, from the baking of bread and churning of butter to the weaving of cloth. As a result, a steadily increasing proportion of basic needs can be met only through relations with markets, and families that once lived at stable, albeit modest, standards of living can find themselves suddenly impoverished and without the basic means to make a living.

See also EXCHANGE, ECONOMIC; FETISHISM OF COMMODITIES; LABOR AND LABOR POWER; VALUES, ECONOMIC.

Reading
Rubin, Isaak I. [1928] 1973. *Essays on Marx's theory of value*. Montreal: Black Rose.

commodity fetishism *See* FETISHISM OF COMMODITIES.

commonsense knowledge *See* KNOWLEDGE.

communal economy A communal ECONOMY is a system in which the production and distribution of goods and services are controlled collectively rather than individually. Land, tools, and other productive resources are not held as private property, which means that no individual or subgroup can use economic power to accumulate WEALTH or gain advantage over others. As such, production and the distribution of wealth are based on sharing and cooperation, rather than COMPETITION and domination.

Thus far, most examples of communal economies have been found in HORTICULTURAL or HUNTER-GATHERER societies.

See also COMMUNISM.

Reading

Lenski, Gerhard E., Jean Lenski, and Patrick Nolan. 1998. *Human societies*, 8th ed. New York: McGraw-Hill.

communication structure A communication structure is the pattern of INTERACTION – who communicates with whom, how often, and how long – that exists in every SOCIAL SYSTEM. In families, for example, mothers tend to interact with children more than fathers do, especially when the children are very young, but this pattern may begin to shift somewhat as the children grow older. One of the most serious effects of divorce on family systems is disruption in the communication structure, especially between the newly absent parent and the children.

A distinction should be made between communication structures as they are defined by ROLES and structures that reflect interaction as it actually takes place. In the military, for example, people are expected to limit communication to those no more highly placed than their next highest superior, especially when they have a complaint to make. (To do otherwise is known as "going over your superior's head," which is actively discouraged.) Depending on the circumstances, however, we might observe an actual military unit and find considerable variation from this expectation.

See also SOCIAL STRUCTURE.

Reading

Bavelas, Alex. 1950. "Communication patterns in task-oriented groups." *Journal of the Acoustical Society of America* 22: 725–30.

Leavitt, Harold J. 1951. "Some effects of certain communication patterns on group performance." *Journal of Abnormal and Social Psychology* 46: 38–50.

communism As described by Karl MARX, communism is a MODE OF PRODUCTION in which the means of production, and virtually every other aspect of social life, are controlled by those who participate in them most directly, which is to say, by workers, community members, and the like. People's lives are organized less around greed, competition, and fear than around satisfaction of genuine human needs, cooperation, and sharing. The material basis for communism is the ability to produce an abundance of goods. The social basis includes a general absence of private economic property, SOCIAL CLASS divisions, inequalities of WEALTH and POWER, and oppressive institutions such as the STATE.

Marx envisioned communism as the inevitable result of SOCIALISM, which he believed would result from revolutionary transformations of industrial capitalist societies. After the overthrow of CAPITALISM, the state would rule on behalf of the workers and would ensure that there would be no capitalist counterrevolution. With time, however, the state would lose its reason for being as control over the rhythms of social life would be increasingly concentrated at the local level among those most directly involved. The state, Marx believed, would simply "wither away."

Since there have been no socialist revolutions in advanced industrial capitalist societies, there have also been no communist societies in the Marxist model, although many socialist societies have been mistakenly labeled as such (primarily because while in practice they are socialist, their ideology is communist). The closest that human experience comes to true communism is among tribal societies, especially those engaged primarily in food gathering as a means of subsistence. Whether communism can be achieved in advanced industrial societies remains to be seen.

See also CAPITALISM; HUNTER-GATHERER SOCIETY; SOCIAL CLASS; STATE SOCIALISM; COMPETITION AND COOPERATION.

Reading

Marx, Karl. [1927] 1964. *Economic and philosophical manuscripts of 1884.* New York: International Publishers.

Marx, Karl, and Friedrich Engels. [1848] 1932. *Manifesto of the communist party.* New York: International Publishers.

communism, norm of   *See* SCIENCE, NORMS OF.

community   Community is a term with numerous meanings, both sociological and nonsociological. A community can be a collection of people who share something in common – as in "the artistic community" – without necessarily living in a particular place. It can be a feeling of connection to others, of belonging and identification, as in "community spirit" or "sense of community." It can be a collection of people who do related kinds of work, as in "the health community" or "the academic community." And, in perhaps its most common and concrete sense, it can be a collection of people who share a geographical territory and some measure of

interdependency that provides the reason for living in the same place. There are exceptions to this, such as HUNTER-GATHERER bands that move from place to place in search of food. In general, however, geographically based communities involve living, working, and carrying out the basic activities of life within a territory defined by residents as having geographic identity, most notably reflected in the assigning of place names and the drawing of boundaries.

To some sociologists, such as Ferdinand TÖNNIES, the idea of community includes a fairly strong feeling of belonging and mutual commitment based on a homogeneous CULTURE, shared experience, and close interdependency. Tönnies contrasted this sense of community with other settlement patterns – most notably the city, which in his view does not qualify as a community at all.

Sociologists have developed two dimensions for distinguishing among different types of communities: (1) rural/urban and (2) traditional/modern. A *rural community* is marked primarily by a small, sparsely settled, relatively homogeneous population that engages primarily in agriculture (although there are exceptions to this, especially in small towns and villages within commuting distance of cities in industrial societies). An *urban community* has a large, densely settled, and relatively heterogeneous population. The designation of a community as urban is somewhat arbitrary. The U.S. Census Bureau, for example, draws the line at 2,500 people, although to qualify as an "urbanized area," a city and surrounding territory must contain at least 50,000 people.

The traditional/modern dimension focuses primarily on cultural differences. *Traditional communities* are more homogeneous and resistant to new ideas, and they are less technological and less dependent on mass media; they also place a lower value on literacy and schooling and a higher value on religion. In contrast to this, *modern communities* are culturally heterogeneous, more secular than religious, and dependent on sophisticated technology and complex divisions of labor. They also make use of highly developed mass media and formal education.

Such distinctions are sociologically important because of their effects on community life. For example, the effects of urbanization on social relationships, crime, tolerance, environmental pollution, work, politics, and family life, have long been of sociological interest. In similar ways, modernization has been linked with the FAMILY, promotion of DEMOCRACY and economic development.

See also CHICAGO SCHOOL; GEMEIN-SCHAFT AND GESELLSCHAFT; URBANIZATION AND URBANISM; WORLDVIEW.

Reading

Frankenburg, R. 1966. *Communities in Britain.* Harmondsworth, England: Penguin.

Tönnies, Ferdinand. [1887] 1963. *Community and society.* New York: Harper.

Wirth, Louis. 1938. "Urbanism as a way of life." *American Journal of Sociology* 44: 1–24.

comparable worth Comparable worth is a concept promoting gender equality for jobs having comparable levels of skill and responsibility. Part of the explanation of gender inequality in industrial societies is that women and men tend to work at different occupations with different rates of pay. Research has found, however, that differences in pay are tied not to differences in the skills or responsibilities required by such occupations, but by gender itself. Dispatchers in trucking firms, for example, tend to be men while secretaries tend to be women. The skills and responsibilities associated with each occupation are quite similar, but the dispatchers tend to be paid more than the secretaries.

In working to equalize pay between women and men, especially in the United States, the concept of comparable worth has been used to argue for equal pay not merely for the same work, but for different work calling for comparable levels of skill and responsibility. The intent is to overcome the effects of women's clustering in a relatively small and disadvantaged segment of the LABOR MARKET.

See also PREJUDICE AND DISCRIMINATION.

Reading

Remick, Helen, ed. 1984. *Comparable worth and wage discrimination.* Philadelphia: Temple University Press.

Treiman, Donald J., and Heidi I. Hartmann, eds. 1981. *Women, work, and wages: Equal pay for jobs of equal value.* Washington: National Academy Press.

comparative perspective In sociological research, the comparative (or *cross-cultural*) perspective is based on the idea that a SOCIETY (or other SOCIAL SYSTEM) cannot be fully understood without comparing it with other societies or systems. Developed most extensively by anthropologists, the comparative approach is particularly useful for explaining how social systems change and develop. It is tempting, for example, to conclude that the pattern of change in our own society reflects universal human tendencies, until we compare it with other societies and discover the rich variety of patterns that characterize human social life.

The main limitation of the comparative perspective is that precisely because societies differ in so many ways they may not always be compared meaningfully. Comparing rates of SOCIAL MOBILITY, for example, is difficult because the relative rank of various occupations often differs from one society to another. In another example, the relative social harmony and COHESION of tribal societies are often held up as a lesson for divided, conflict-ridden modern industrial societies. But the fundamental differences between the two kinds of societies are so huge and all-encompassing that it is not clear how to interpret such comparisons.

See also CULTURAL RELATIVISM.

Reading

Kohn, M., ed. 1989. *Cross-national research in sociology.* Beverly Hills, CA: Sage Publications.

Tilly, Charles. 1984. *Big structures, large processes, and huge comparisons.* New York: Russell Sage Foundation.

competition and cooperation
Competition is the struggle that occurs when people try to maximize their own rewards or resources at the expense of others. Cooperation is a coordinated effort to reach mutual goals. Competition is sociologically significant for the positive and negative effects it produces in social life. Early sociological thinkers such as Herbert SPENCER saw competition as a necessary mechanism for achieving social progress, a view that was very much in line with the emergent capitalist system and its belief in competition as the engine that promotes efficiency and low prices. In its approach to urban life, the CHICAGO SCHOOL of sociology stressed the role of competition in urban growth patterns as various ethnic, class, racial, and other groups compete for space.

Max WEBER saw competition as a peaceful form of conflict. Karl MARX also saw its relationship to conflict, but in a less peaceful light. In his critique of CAPITALISM, Marx argued that competition among capitalists, among workers, and between capitalists and workers were major sources of CONTRADICTION and struggle that produced a variety of negative consequences, first among them the exploitation of the working class and a lack of CLASS CONSCIOUSNESS and unity in the face of it.

Whether competition is necessary and unavoidable, and the conditions under which people will choose it over cooperation, are major sociological questions. They cover a wide spectrum from how individuals interact in intimate situations to the structure of the WORLD SYSTEM and relations among nations.

See ZERO-SUM GAME.

Reading

Baran, Paul, and Paul Sweezy. 1964. *Monopoly capitalism.* New York: Monthly Review Press; London: Penguin.

Cowling, K. 1982. *Monopoly capitalism.* London: Macmillan; New York: Halsted.

Marx, Karl. [1867] 1975. *Capital: A critique of political economy.* New York: International Publishers.

Weber, Max. [1921] 1968. *Economy and society.* New York: Bedminster Press.

competitive economy *See* DUAL ECONOMY.

complex organization   *See* FORMAL ORGANIZATION.

complex sample   A complex (or *multistage*) SAMPLE is a subset of a POPULATION selected in more than one step. For example, when sampling from large, complex populations such as an urban area or an entire country, researchers typically select the sample in stages, beginning first with larger units and working from there down to the final units (such as households or people) selected for observation. To sample a nation's secondary school students, researchers might begin by randomly selecting a sample of cities and towns (to ensure geographic representation) and then, within cities and towns, select a sample of secondary schools. Once they have selected the schools, they then select the actual students to be interviewed.

Note that without this kind of procedure it would be very difficult to select a sample of students directly since assembling such a list would be very costly if not impossible. With a multistage design, a list of actual students is required only in the last, and simplest, stage and only for those schools in which students will actually be interviewed.

Cluster sampling is a type of complex sample used to save travel time and expense in conducting surveys without incurring an unacceptable increase in ERROR. For example, a complex sampling design may be used to interview 2,000 residents of London. Researchers might first use a map of the city to select a sample of 2,000 blocks and then interview one randomly chosen resident from each block. This, however, would require interviewers to travel to 2,000 separate places in the city. As an alternative, they might "cluster" interviews by selecting not 2,000 blocks but 400 blocks. On each of these they then interview five randomly chosen residents. Each of these sets of five respondents is called a "cluster" and gives us a total sample size of $400 \times 5 = 2,000$.

Methodological research has shown that clustering is well worth the effort. It substantially cuts survey costs while introducing only a slight amount of bias (tending to produce samples that are more homogeneous than the populations they are used to represent, since people who live on the same block tend to resemble one another more than people living on different blocks). The added error, however, is small and can be estimated statistically and corrected for later on.

See also SAMPLE; STRATIFIED SAMPLE.

Reading

Kalton, G. 1984. *Introduction to survey sampling.* Beverly Hills, CA: Sage Publications.

Kish, Leslie. 1965. *Survey sampling.* New York: Wiley.

component variable   In the statistical analysis of relationships among VARIABLES, a component variable reflects one aspect of a larger phenomenon. SOCIAL CLASS, for example, encompasses a variety of characteristics such as occupational prestige, income, WEALTH, AUTHORITY, consumption patterns, and educational attainment. Each of these may be identified as a component variable of social class.

See also CONTROL VARIABLE; VARIABLE.

Reading

Rosenberg, Morris. 1968. *The logic of survey analysis.* New York: Basic Books.

compound family   *See* FAMILY.

compound status   *See* STATUS.

concentric-zone theory   *See* URBANIZATION AND URBANISM.

conditional relationship   *See* SPECIFICATION.

confidence interval   *See* ESTIMATES.

conflict perspective   The conflict perspective is one of the major theoretical approaches to sociological thinking and analysis. Although it traces its roots to the work of Karl MARX and his critique of CAPITALISM, the conflict perspective has since developed along a number of lines encompassing everything from world politics to interpersonal relations and INTERACTION.

In general, the conflict perspective assumes that social life is shaped by groups and individuals who struggle or compete with one another over various resources and rewards, resulting in particular distributions of WEALTH, POWER, and PRESTIGE in societies and other SOCIAL SYSTEMS. These shape not only the patterns of everyday life and interaction, but also larger patterns such as racial, ethnic, and class inequality, and relations among nations and regions of the world.

Social conflict is based on many different aspects of social life. Marx, for example, argued that most conflict is economic and rests on the unequal ownership and control of property, especially productive property (the MEANS OF PRODUCTION). Max WEBER argued for a broader view encompassing economic relations as well as factors such as race, ethnicity, and religion. Ralf DAHRENDORF argued that conflict centers

primarily on power, on the division between those who control others and those who are controlled, especially in the context of complex organizations such as bureaucracies and corporations.

Whatever the particular focus, the conflict perspective draws attention to important dynamics in which social systems promote and serve as settings for struggle among diverse and competing interests. It also draws attention to the varied consequences of conflict, from SOCIAL OPPRESSION to social COHESION.

See also COHESION; COMPETITION AND COOPERATION; CONTRADICTION.

Reading

Collins, Randall. 1975. *Conflict sociology: Toward an explanatory science.* New York: Academic Press.

Coser, Lewis A. 1964. *The functions of social conflict.* Glencoe, IL: Free Press.

Dahrendorf, Ralf. 1959. *Class and class conflict in industrial society.* Stanford: Stanford University Press.

conformity   Conformity is the practice of obeying a norm. Like DEVIANCE, conformity is a social phenomenon that needs to be understood in terms of the conditions that cause it and the social consequences it produces. Most individuals, for example, find it difficult to resist pressures to conform within small GROUPS, and when taken to extremes, conformity can have disastrous effects on SOCIAL SYSTEMS.

See also DEVIANCE.

Reading

Asch, Solomon E. 1952. *Social psychology.* Englewood Cliffs, NJ: Prentice-Hall.

Roethlisberger, F. J., and W. Dickson. 1939. *Management and the worker.* Cambridge, MA: Harvard University Press.

Scheff, Thomas J. 1988. "Shame and conformity: The deference-emotion system." *American Sociological Review* 53(3): 395–406.

conglomerate A conglomerate is a corporation that owns a number of other corporations that, among them, produce a variety of goods and services. A conglomerate, for example, might own a frozen food company, a luggage manufacturer, a company that makes weapons, an advertising firm, and so on. Conglomerates are sociologically significant because their complex and diversified position in economic MARKETS makes them much more powerful, stable, and competitive than other kinds of firms. As successful corporations use their profits to acquire and merge with other corporations, markets become dominated by conglomerates and the distribution of WEALTH and economic POWER becomes increasingly unequal. This is especially important when conglomerate holdings are international in scope. In some cases their economic resources exceed the gross national product of most nations.
See also TRANSNATIONAL AND MULTINATIONAL CORPORATIONS.

conscience collective (also called *collective conscience*). According to Émile DURKHEIM, the conscience collective is a cultural framework of moral and normative ideas, the belief that the social world exists to some degree apart from and external to the psychological lives of individuals. As individuals, we feel the limitations and constraints imposed by the social world and are affected by them as we make choices about how to appear and behave in relation to others. When an immoral act is committed, for example, it is the conscience collective that is violated. To say that

something is immoral says far more than that it is personally offensive or abhorrent to the person saying it. Rather, such statements appeal to a larger authority that is contained in a moral order associated with entire SOCIAL SYSTEMS. In this sense, the conscience collective is quite different from the individual conscience. It is not a "group mind," but rather a shared framework that individuals experience as external, constraining, and meaningful.
See also COHESION; SOCIAL FACT.
Reading
Durkheim, Émile. [1893] 1933. *The division of labor in society*. New York: Free Press.
——. [1924] 1974. *Sociology and philosophy*. New York: Free Press.

consensus *See* COHESION.

consequence *See* FUNCTIONALIST PERSPECTIVE.

conservatism and liberalism The distinction between conservatism and liberalism is difficult to pin down, in part because the meaning of both words has changed historically. In general, however, there are some basic ideas that set them apart as frameworks for making sense of social life and, in particular, shaping efforts to change it or maintain the status quo.

As a political ideology, conservatism emerged primarily in reaction to the French Revolution. In *Reflections on the Revolution in France* (1855), Edmund Burke argued that the status quo was always preferable to an alternative that existed primarily as theory which, when he wrote, was true of DEMOCRACY as a form of government. Change, if it is to occur, should come about slowly and as a logical extension of the natural order of things, not as a revolutionary shift in direction.

Conservatism is based on a relatively pessimistic view of human nature as basically evil, unreasonable, and violent if left to its own devices. The only way to control this destructive potential is to enforce rigid moral codes through strong traditions, social INSTITUTIONS, and a hierarchical society governed by ELITES whose power rests on both their inherent superiority and private property inherited across the generations. This implies that social inequality is inevitable and, indeed, necessary to maintain society.

Liberalism traces its roots to the European ENLIGHTENMENT and the conflict between free-market capitalist entrepreneurs and the entrenched feudal aristocracy. It is based on a commitment to individual liberty. As CAPITALISM developed in the nineteenth and twentieth centuries, however, liberals saw it becoming a new and oppressive threat to individual liberty and well-being. Under FEUDALISM, the ELITE had been the aristocracy that opposed free-market capitalism. Under advanced capitalism, however, the capitalist class became the elite. Liberalism's answer to this has been increased reliance on the STATE to defend individual rights against the excesses of capitalist expansion and exploitation – for example, by protecting workers and consumers or by shielding key corporations from some of the more damaging consequences of unrestrained competition. In doing so, liberalism perpetuates capitalism by protecting it from its own excesses.

There is much inconsistency in the use of conservative and liberal as labels, especially when they refer merely to attitudes about change. During the Cold War, for example. Americans often associated liberals with communism and conservatives with anticommunism. But during the anticommunist revolutions in the Soviet Union and Eastern Europe during the late 1980s and 1990s, the diehard defenders of the communist status quo were often referred to as conservative and procapitalists were considered liberal.

Reading

Laski, Harold J. [1936] 1962. *The rise of European liberalism*. New York: Barnes and Noble.

Nisbet, Robert. 1986. *Conservatism*. Minneapolis: University of Minnesota Press.

conspicuous consumption In *The Theory of the Leisure Class*, Thorstein VEBLEN defines conspicuous consumption as the practice of buying and displaying material possessions in order to indicate or enhance one's PRESTIGE in the eyes of others. Conspicuous consumption occurs in both grand and subtle forms. At one extreme are ostentatious displays through which the very wealthy (whom Veblen dubbed the *leisure class*) indicate their superior standing by showing they have so much that they can afford to waste on a huge scale (similar to the practice of POTLATCH among Northwest Native Americans). The great WEALTH of U.S. industrialists such as the Rockefellers and Vanderbilts at the turn of the twentieth century, for example, was often displayed at outlandish parties in which vast quantities of food were served on solid gold dishes by a host of servants – all of which served the primary function of showing how highly placed they were.

On a more ordinary scale, people from various SOCIAL CLASS backgrounds use conspicuous consumption to draw attention to themselves and enhance their position. From designer labels on clothing to owning a particular car (or any car at all); from "being seen" in particular restaurants to living in upscale or fashionable neighborhoods; from eating by candlelight to playing classical music for one's guests to taking long and expensive vacations, consumption often has consequences that have nothing to do with the uses for which a particular item was made or service was rendered. In short, wherever societies include systems of prestige ranking, the goods and services that people consume will play a part.

Conspicuous consumption is important to sociological thinking because it draws attention to the problem of how to identify the subtle, often UNANTICIPATED CONSEQUENCES of various aspects of social life. Much of what we regard as personal behaviour, taste, and preference have social consequences whose significance and power are often beyond our awareness.

See also PRESTIGE; SOCIAL CLASS.

Reading
Veblen, Thorstein. 1934. *The theory of the leisure class*. New York: Modern Library.

constant *See* VARIABLE.

consumption cleavage A basic assumption of the CONFLICT PERSPECTIVE is that SOCIAL INEQUALITY produces divisions in societies along SOCIAL CLASS lines. The concept of consumption cleavage points to another source of division – different patterns of consumption of goods and services, especially in major areas of

social life such as housing and medical care. Thorstein VEBLEN, for example, argued that people often buy things as a way to indicate to others that they occupy a superior or unique status in life, a practice he called CONSPICUOUS CONSUMPTION. This produces a consumption cleavage to the extent that it shapes people's identities, divides one group from another, and shapes their LIFE CHANCES or behavior (such as voting).

Similar differences might occur between urban and suburban housing, or between people who buy housing on the private market through their own resources and those who must depend on government assistance (also known as *housing classes*). A key issue is whether consumption cleavages operate independently of social class.

Reading
Saunders, Peter. 1986. *Social theory and the urban question*. New York: Holmes and Meier.
——. 1990. *A nation of home owners*. London: Unwin Hyman.

content analysis Content analysis is a research method that is used to analyze social life by interpreting words and images contained in documents, films, art, music, and other cultural products and media. Content analysis has been used extensively, for example, to examine the place of women in society. Studies of school textbooks find that characters in stories or examples tend to be male, especially when the character is dominant, active, or heroic. In advertising, women tend to be portrayed as subordinate, often through their lower physical positioning in relation to males or the tentative, unassertive nature of their posture or gestures.

Although content analysis can take a relatively objective quantitative form (as in counting the number of female and male characters in a book or the percentage of front-page news stories that focus on women), in general practice it tends to be more subjective than other research methods unless done very carefully. Researchers, for example, must specify what they are looking for and establish clear categories in which to sort their observations.

See also SECONDARY ANALYSIS.

Reading

Holsti, O. R. 1969. *Content analysis for the social sciences and humanities.* Reading, MA: Addison-Wesley.

Weber, R. P. 1990. *Basic content analysis.* Beverly Hills, CA: Sage Publications.

contest mobility *See* SPONSORED MOBILITY AND CONTEST MOBILITY.

continuous variable *See* DISCRETE VARIABLE AND CONTINUOUS VARIABLE.

contract *See* SOCIAL CONTRACT.

contradiction In sociological thinking (especially in the tradition of Karl MARX), a contradiction is any instance in which two or more aspects of a SOCIAL SYSTEM are incompatible or conflict with one another. For example, a SOCIETY whose CULTURE values equality, fairness, and justice, exists in a state of contradiction if it also includes racial and gender PREJUDICE and OPPRESSION. This produces social tension and pressures toward change. In his classic 1940s study of race relations in the United States, for example, Swedish sociologist Gunnar Myrdal correctly predicted that the contradiction between egalitarian ideals and the reality of racism constituted an "American dilemma" that would inevitably lead to change, as it began to do several decades later with the emergence of the civil rights movement.

Marx argued that the most important contradictions involve economic factors. The transition between FEUDALISM and CAPITALISM, for example, resulted from tensions between two contradictory forces. On the one hand was the feudal order based on peasant production, attachments to land, and ties of loyalty, obligation, and domination between nobility and serfs. On the other hand was the emerging system of towns and markets in which people produced for the purpose of buying and selling. Because capitalism thrived on freedom from feudal obligations, the resulting contradiction produced profound social tensions that eventually led to the downfall of feudalism and the aristocracy.

Capitalism also produces contradictions, which occupy a central place in Marxist analysis. One of the most important contradictions is that between the conflicting interests of capitalists (who gain at the expense of workers) and workers (who gain at the expense of capitalists).

See also MATERIALISM.

Reading

Godelier, Maurice. [1966] 1972. "System, structure, and contradiction in capital." In *Rationality and irrationality in economics.* London: New Left; New York: Monthly Review Press.

Lukács, Georg. [1923] 1971. *History and class consciousness.* London: Merlin; Cambridge, MA: MIT Press.

Myrdal, Gunnar. 1945. *An American dilemma.* New York: Harper and Row.

control *See* SOCIAL CONTROL.

control group *See* EXPERIMENT.

control variable In the analysis of relationships between VARIABLES, a control variable is one that is held constant through the use of statistical techniques. The purpose of this is to understand the relationship between an independent and a dependent variable. If we look at the relationship between educational attainment and income, for example, we will find a positive relationship in which higher education tends to be associated with higher income. If we then control for gender, we would look at the same relationship – between education and income – but separately for women and men to see if the DIRECTION OF THE RELATIONSHIP or its STRENGTH is the same for both categories of people. By looking just at women and then just at men we statistically hold the variable gender constant by looking at people who are alike on that characteristic. Gender, then, is a control variable in this case.

Sociologists use a variety of statistical techniques to control for one or more variables. This is generally done to answer four basic kinds of questions: (1) Is an observed relationship between two variables just a statistical accident? (2) If one variable has a causal effect on another, is this effect a direct one or is it indirect with other variables intervening between them? (3) If several variables all have causal effects on a dependent variable, how does the strength of those effects vary? (4) Does a particular relationship between two variables look the same under various conditions?

See also ANTECEDENT VARIABLE; COMPONENT VARIABLE; DISTORTER VARIABLE; INTERVENING VARIABLE; MULTIVARIATE ANALYSIS; SPECIFICATION; SUPPRESSOR VARIABLE.

Reading
Rosenberg, Morris. 1968. *The logic of survey analysis*. New York: Basic Books.

conurbation *See* MEGALOPOLIS.

convergence theory According to convergence theory, as societies become increasingly industrialized, they begin to resemble other industrial societies in important ways. In other words, they "converge" toward similar forms of social organization. Just how much of social life is included in this process varies from one theorist to another. Some, for example, would include political institutions (a tendency toward DEMOCRACY) while others argue that industrialization can exist in a variety of political settings.

Convergence theory is rooted in basic ideas drawn from the FUNCTIONALIST PERSPECTIVE, which assumes that societies have certain requirements that must be met if they are to survive and operate effectively. In line with this approach, convergence theory argues that industrialization brings with it certain needs or requirements that will be solved in similar ways from one industrial society to another. For example, industry requires large pools of labor that can adapt to changing demands for particular skills in particular locations. As a result, industrial societies will tend to be heavily urbanized and their populations will tend to be both socially and geographically mobile. Other aspects of social organization often associated with convergence theory are complex DIVISIONS OF LABOR, the separation of family and work life, highly developed mass media and communication systems, high levels of literacy and formal education, and a disciplined work force.

Convergence theory has numerous limitations. Industrialization, for example, is certainly a powerful influence, but it is only one among many that shape social life. In addition, similarities between societies may be due not so much to industrialization itself as to other factors such as CAPITALISM. The need for a mobile work force, for example, stems more from the demands of capitalist COMPETITION and changing MARKETS than it does from industrialization.

See also INDUSTRIAL SOCIETY AND INDUSTRIALIZATION; MODERNIZATION THEORY.

Reading

Kerr, Clark. [1960] 1962. *Industrialism and industrial man.* Cambridge, MA: Harvard University Press; London: Heinemann.

Scott, J. 1979. *Corporations, classes, and capitalism.* London: Hutchinson.

conversation analysis *See* ETHNO-METHODOLOGY.

cooperation *See* COMPETITION AND COOPERATION.

core economy *See* DUAL ECONOMY.

core society *See* WORLD SYSTEM.

corporate class In industrial capitalist societies, the corporate class is a social division near the top of the class structure, just beneath the upper class. Although it shares many of the characteristics of the upper class, the basis for its position lies less with ownership of the MEANS OF PRODUCTION than with control over them. This places chief executive officers and other upper management in the corporate class as well as, in some cases, government officials whose job it is to serve the interests of CAPITALISM (hence they are sometimes referred to as the *service class*).

There is some disagreement among sociologists about the relative influence of the upper and corporate classes, with some arguing that the rapid increase in the size and power of the corporate class threatens to eclipse the upper class. Others point out that although the corporate class has become increasingly important, its security still depends on serving interests that coincide with those of the upper class.

See also MANAGERIAL REVOLUTION; SOCIAL CLASS; UPPER CLASS.

Reading

Abercrombie, Nicholas, and John Urry. 1983. *Capital, labour, and the middle classes.* London: Allen and Unwin.

Renner, Karl. [1953] 1978. "The service class." In *Austro-Marxism,* edited by Tom Bottomore and P. Goode. Oxford: Oxford University Press.

Useem, Michael. 1984. *The inner circle: Large corporations and the rise of business political activity in the U.S. and U.K.* New York: Oxford University Press.

corporatism Corporatism is a system of distributing power in a SOCIETY among various organizations such as the STATE, TRADE UNIONS, corporations, and professional associations. The basic idea is that POWER is held by these organizations in coordination with one another and that individuals have power only insofar as their interests are represented by one or more of these. In this sense, corporatism differs from representative DEMOCRACY in which individuals exercise their share of power directly by voting for candidates. It differs even more sharply from direct democracy in which individuals vote in town meetings, for referendum propositions, and the like.

Corporatism first appeared in Spain under Franco and as part of Italian FASCISM. During the 1970s, it also emerged in several European countries including Austria, Britain, and much of Scandinavia. For the most part it has consisted of a working relationship among government, business, and trade unions in which most major social policy decisions reflect a balance of interests among these groups. There is some disagreement about its origins and underlying purpose. In Italy it was used to forge a sense of national unity and minimize internal conflict. Some have argued that in its most recent manifestations, it represents a way for government and business to control labor unions.

See also DEMOCRACY, POLITICAL AND ECONOMIC; STATE.

Reading

Goldthorpe, J. H. 1985. *Order and conflict in contemporary capitalism.* Oxford, England: Oxford University Press.

Panitch, L. 1980. "Recent theorizations of corporatism." *British Journal of Sociology* 31: 159–87.

correlation Correlation is often used as an umbrella term referring to MEASURES OF ASSOCIATION that indicate the strength of relationship between two variables. Usually, however, it is associated more specifically with REGRESSION ANALYSIS. In regression analysis, the dependent VARIABLE, Y, is plotted against the independent variable, X. A line is fitted to the points to provide the most accurate prediction of Y based upon knowledge of X. The correlation coefficient is a statistical quantity that indicates the degree to which the points lie on the line used to predict Y from X. In other words, the stronger the correla-

tion, the more accurately X can be used to predict Y.

The correlation coefficient (also known as the Pearson *product–moment correlation coefficient*) is represented by r. Its numeric value ranges between -1.0 and $+1.0$, with the positive or negative sign indicating the DIRECTION OF RELATIONSHIP and the number itself indicating the STRENGTH OF THE RELATIONSHIP. A value of 1.0 (positive or negative) indicates a perfect relationship, which means that knowing X allows us to predict Y without error. A value of 0.00 indicates no relationship, which means that in trying to predict values of Y we will make as many mistakes knowing X as we will not knowing X. When interpreting correlations, it is always important to keep in mind that correlation and causation are not the same. The ability to predict Y from knowledge of X does not mean that X causes Y, only that they tend to vary together in predictable ways.

Correlation can also be used to examine the relationship between a dependent variable and two or more independent variables simultaneously. For example, we might want to explain variation in income, using variables such as education, occupation, experience, race, and gender. In this case, we would calculate a *multiple correlation coefficient* (R) indicating the degree to which income can be predicted from the information contained in all the independent variables working together.

In statistical analyses involving a set of variables, it is often useful to compute the correlation for each possible pair of variables. These are then displayed in a *correlation matrix* which for each row and column variable shows the correlation value in the cells of the table.

See also MEASURE OF ASSOCIATION; PARTIAL ASSOCIATION; REGRESSION ANALYSIS.

Reading

Bohrnstedt, George W., and David Knoke. 1994. *Statistics for social data analysis*, 3rd ed. Itasca, IL: F. E. Peacock.

correlation matrix *See* CORRELATION.

counterculture A counterculture (or *alternative culture*) is a SUBCULTURE that rejects and opposes significant elements of the dominant CULTURE of which it is a part. During the 1960s, for example, countercultural movements in the United States were highly critical of mainstream values such as materialism, support for the Vietnam War, respect for authority, and conservative lifestyle choices as reflected in clothing, hairstyles, and the avoidance of drugs such as marijuana and LSD. Countercultures can take a variety of forms, from religious CULTS to communes to political movements such as the Green Party in Western Europe.

See also SOCIAL MOVEMENT.

Reading

Roszak, Theodore. 1968. *The making of a counterculture*. Garden City, NY: Doubleday Anchor Books.

counterfactual A counterfactual statement is based on the occurrence of something that in fact did not happen. "If I were in charge of the world, things would be a lot better than they are now" is a counterfactual statement since, clearly, I am not in charge of the world. Counterfactual statements are important in thinking about the causes of social phenomena

because when we argue that *A* caused *B*, we often assume the counterfactual, that if *A* had not happened, then *B* would not have occurred either, which may not be the case at all. Any argument, for example, about the effects of the Russian Revolution on the course of history would also have to consider counterfactual statements about what would have happened if there had been no revolution, a hypothetical case for which it is obviously difficult to make a convincing argument.

See also FALSIFICATIONISM.

coup d'état In changing political systems, a coup d'état is a sudden action through which one leader or government is replaced by another through the use of force. This is typically carried out by factions of the military since in many societies, especially in the Third World, the military has a monopoly over the instruments of force.

Because coups focus more on changing governments than on the nature of the STATE itself as a SOCIAL INSTITUTION, they tend to produce only a small and often temporary level of SOCIAL CHANGE, if any at all.

See also INSTITUTION; REBELLION, POLITICAL; REVOLUTION; STATE.

Reading

Luttwak, E. 1968. *Coup d'état: A practical handbook*. London: Allen Lane.

Malaparte, C. 1948. *Technique of the coup d'état*. Paris: Grasset.

covariance Covariance is a particular kind of VARIANCE. It is a statistical quantity that measures the degree to which two VARIABLES vary together in relation to each other. If there is a positive relationship between *X* and *Y*, for example, then for every case when the value of X is high, the value of Y will also tend to be high; when the value of X is low, the value of Y will tend to be low.

Another way of expressing this is to say that when the value of X is greater than the mean of X, the value of Y will tend to be greater than the mean of Y, and so on. This is particularly important for calculating the covariance. For each observation (such as a person in a survey), we take the score on variable X and subtract from it the mean for X. We then take the score on Y and subtract from it the mean for Y. Finally, we multiply these two differences. We do this for every observation and then add all of these products. The resulting total is the covariance. When the relationship between the variables is positive, the covariance will be positive. When there is no relationship and the variables are independent of each other, the covariance will equal zero.

As is noted in the entry on VARIANCE, one of the main goals of sociological research is to explain differences, to account for the statistical fact that people or other units of observation differ in characteristics such as income or age at death. Since the variance indicates how much variable Y varies altogether, and the covariance indicates the degree to which Y varies with X, then if the covariance is subtracted from the variance, the remainder is the amount of variance in Y that does not vary with X. This is called the *unexplained variance*. The covariance is often referred to as the *explained variance*.

Both explained and unexplained variance are often presented as percentages of the total variance. In other words, if the numerical value for the total variance in Y is 347 and the value for the covariance between X and Y is 83, then we can say that $83/347 = 0.24$, or 24 percent of the variation in Y, is statistically accounted for or "explained" by its relationship with X. By subtraction $(1.00 - 0.24)$, we can say that 76 percent of the variance is "unexplained."

The qualified use of the terms "explained" and "unexplained" is made because these terms refer to a statistical accounting that may have nothing to do with cause and effect. That variable Y varies with variable X – even perfectly – does not mean that X causes Y.

See also COEFFICIENT OF ALIENATION; COEFFICIENT OF DETERMINATION; CORRELATION; SPURIOUSNESS; VARIANCE.

Reading

Bohrnstedt, George W., and David Knoke. 1994. *Statistics for social data analysis*, 3rd ed. Itasca, IL: F. E. Peacock.

credentialism Credentialism refers to the practice of using educational degrees and other credentials to decide who is best qualified to occupy a SOCIAL STATUS, especially an OCCUPATION. Credentialism encourages people to assume that those having the "right" credentials also know what they are doing and are qualified to do the job. One consequence of this is that educational degrees take on a value of their own independent of what they actually represent in terms of learning and competence, a phenomenon sometimes known as *diploma disease*.

Reading

Berg, Ivar. 1970. *Education and jobs: The great training robbery*. Harmondsworth, England: Penguin.

Collins, Randall. 1979. *The credential society*. New York: Academic Press.

Dore, Ronald. 1976. *The diploma disease.* London: Allen and Unwin.

crime and criminology *See* DEVIANCE.

criminal law *See* LAW.

critical theory In its most general sense, critical theory is a sociological theory that aims to dig beneath the surface of social life and uncover the assumptions and masks that keep us from a full and true understanding of how the world works. The countries of Western Europe and North America, for example, are often described as DEMOCRACIES, and their people would typically describe them as such. But a critical analysis of politics under industrial CAPITALISM would reveal the many ways in which political and economic POWER actually are concentrated in the hands of a relative few, contradicting basic democratic principles. A major goal of critical theory is to reveal how surface reality often contradicts the underlying reality. Marxists take this one step further by arguing that critical thought must be combined with critical action (PRAXIS) to bring about change in what we criticize.

Critical theory is most often associated with a group of social scientists at the University of Frankfurt in Germany who referred to themselves as the *Frankfurt School.* Formed in 1922, the group moved to the United States during World War II, and returned to Germany in 1949, where it continued until 1969. The basic thrust of their work was to criticize life under CAPITALISM and prevailing ways of explaining it. Although their approach was grounded in Marxism, they modified some of its basic assumptions and blended it with other approaches that gave the work of the Frankfurt School a distinctive appeal. As such, they were in some ways returning to the work of the young Marx, which was more humanistic and less rigidly deterministic than the Marxism being promoted as part of the Soviet Union's political IDEOLOGY.

Contrary to prevailing versions of Marxism, for example, members of the Frankfurt School argued that economics did not determine the shape of social life. They stressed the importance of CULTURE and developed a critical approach to art, aesthetics, and the mass media. They combined Marxism with Freudian analysis to create an understanding of personality and the individual in relation to capitalist society. Throughout, they were committed to liberating human existence from what they saw as the stifling control of a society increasingly dominated by values of efficiency and control, especially through the use of sophisticated technology. From their perspective, the potential of the ENLIGHTENMENT to liberate humanity had been coopted and perverted into an increasingly oppressive way of life that progressively deprived people of their freedom.

Best known among the numerous people associated with the Frankfurt School are Theodor ADORNO, Erich Fromm, Jürgen HABERMAS, Max Horkheimer, Herbert MARCUSE, and Felix Weil (who founded the school). *See also* APPEARANCE AND REALITY; AUTHORITARIAN PERSONALITY; RATIONALIZATION.

Reading
Habermas, Jürgen. 1971. *Knowledge and human interests.* Boston: Beacon Press.

Held, David. 1980. *Introduction* to *critical theory*. Berkeley: University of California Press.

Marcuse, Herbert. 1964. *One-dimensional man*. Boston: Beacon Press.

cross-cultural   perspective *See* COMPARATIVE PERSPECTIVE.

cross-sectional data Cross-sectional (or *period*) data are information that is gathered at one time to reflect social conditions in the same way that a still photograph captures a visual image. Most of the data gathered by sociologists – especially in the form of SURVEYS – take this form and are therefore of limited use in describing the process through which people or SOCIAL SYSTEMS change or, for that matter, the cause-and-effect process through which one VARIABLE affects another over time. Cross-sectional studies can be used to make inferences about such processes if they are repeated, especially if the same SAMPLE is observed at each point. Even if the samples are different, however, it is still possible to use a series of cross-sectional studies to make inferences about change. A representative sample of 15–19-year-olds, for example, can be compared ten years later with a sample of 25–29-year-olds. Even though the individuals are not the same, the population from which the samples are drawn is the same, with the exception of those who have entered or left through migration or death.

See also COHORT; LONGITUDINAL RESEARCH.

Reading

Blalock, Hubert M. 1964. *Causal inferences in nonexperimental research*. Chapel Hill: University of North Carolina Press.

Singleton, Royce A., Bruce C. Straits, and Margaret M. Straits, 1998. *Approaches* to *social research*, 3rd ed. Oxford and New York: Oxford University Press.

cross-tabulation A cross-tabulation (or "cross-tab" for short) is a display of data that shows how CASES in each category of one VARIABLE are divided among the categories of one or more additional variables. The table below is a two-variable cross-tabulation of SOCIAL CLASS self-identification by RACE in the United States. The first column shows how people who fall in the category "white" are divided among the four social class categories; the second column shows the same thing for blacks. Also note that each row shows how people who fall into different social class categories are divided between the two racial categories.

In a cross-tabulation, a *cell* is a combination of two or more characteristics, one from each variable. The table below has eight cells, one for each of the four combinations of race and social class (such as 139 lower-class whites). The bottom row and the far-right column give the total number of cases with each racial or class characteristic (such as 197 lower-class respondents), and are known as marginal totals or *marginals* for short. The total in the lower right corner gives the

Table 1 Social Class by Race, United States

Social Class	RACE		Total
	Whites	*Blacks*	
Lower	139	58	197
Working	1,566	272	1,838
Middle	1,865	153	2,018
Upper	120	13	133
Total	3,690	496	4,186 = *n*

total number of cases in the cross-tabulation and is usually designated by *n*.

In many cross-tabulations the numbers in each cell are not frequencies as they are in the above table. If we wanted to compare blacks and whites in terms of social class, for example, we would convert each cell into a *percentage* by dividing it by the total number of people in each racial group. Hence, the percentage of whites who place themselves in the lower class is 139/3690 = 3.8 percent. The percentages calculated for all of the cells are shown in the table below.

Table 2 Social Class by Race, United States

Social Class	RACE		Total
	Whites	Blacks	
Lower	3.8%	11.7%	4.7%
Working	42.4	54.9	43.9
Middle	50.5	30.8	48.2
Upper	3.3	2.6	3.2
Total	100.0	100.0	100.0

With percentages, whites and blacks can be compared even though there are more than seven times as many whites as blacks. The results show quite clearly that blacks are far more likely than whites to identify themselves as members of the lower and working classes (11.7% v. 3.8%; 54.9% v. 42.4%) and far less likely to identify themselves as members of middle and upper classes (30.8% v. 50.5%; 2.6% v. 3.3%).

Note that if we had not percentaged the table, the results would have been quite misleading. As the first table shows, there are more whites than blacks in virtually every class category simply because there are so many more whites than blacks in the United States as a whole. Because of this imbalance, the only way to compare the two racial categories is to obtain a percentage within each of them, as we have done above.

See also STANDARDIZATION.

Reading
Rosenberg, Morris. 1968. *The logic of survey analysis.* New York: Basic Books.

Zeisel, Hans. 1985. *Say it with figures,* rev. ed. New York: Harper and Row.

crowd *See* COLLECTIVE BEHAVIOR.

crude birth rate *See* BIRTH RATE.

crude death rate *See* DEATH RATE.

cult A cult is a particular structural type of religious INSTITUTION. Membership is predominantly lower-class and usually gained through conversion, often during an emotional crisis that joining a cult is seen to resolve. Unlike other religious institutions, cults tend to be short-lived, primarily because of their SOCIAL STRUCTURE – an informal, loose organization formed around a single leader's charismatic authority; highly emotional services that lack formalized RITUAL; and a retreatist, hostile orientation to major social institutions. Virtually all major religions began as cults, including Buddhism, Islam, and Christianity.

See also AUTHORITY; CHURCH; DENOMINATION; ECCLESIA; RELIGION; RETREATISM; SECT.

Reading
Becker, Howard. 1950. *Through values to social interpretation.* Durham, NC: Duke University Press.

Merton, J. G., and R. L. Moore. 1982. *The cult experience.* New York: Pilgrim Press.

cultural capital According to French sociologist Pierre BOURDIEU, cultural capital consists of ideas and knowledge people draw upon as they participate in social life. Everything from rules of etiquette to being able to speak and write effectively can be considered cultural capital. Bourdieu was particularly interested in the unequal distribution of cultural capital in stratified societies and how such inequality disadvantages people. This is especially true in schools and occupations, where ignorance of what the dominant classes define as basic knowledge makes it very difficult for those in marginal or subordinate groups to compete successfully. Ethnic immigrants, for example, often do poorly in school because they lack important cultural capital required by their adopted society. Bourdieu referred to this lack as *cultural deprivation*.

See also CULTURE; CULTURAL REPRODUCTION AND SOCIAL REPRODUCTION; STRATIFICATION AND INEQUALITY.

Reading

Bourdieu, Pierre, and Jean-Claude Passeron. 1977. *Society, culture, and education*. Beverly Hills, CA: Sage Publications.

cultural contact Cultural contact is what occurs when two or more CULTURES come in contact with one another through images in the mass media, trade, immigration, or conquest so that they affect one another. With *assimilation* (also known as *acculturation*), a dominant group imposes its culture on subordinate groups so effectively that these become virtually indistinguishable from the dominant culture. A lesser form of assimilation occurs when newcomers to a SOCIETY conform outwardly to VALUES and NORMS as a way to adapt to their situation. It is

easier for immigrants to succeed in their adopted country, for example, if they conform by learning a new language, using a new currency, and obeying norms. By not surrendering their own culture entirely, such groups form the basis for *cultural pluralism* through which diverse cultures coexist and maintain some degree of separate identity. In addition, assimilation is rarely a one-way street and the culture of dominant groups is itself affected. Blacks in Europe and the United States, for example, have lost many of their African cultural traditions; but it is also true that white society is quick to adopt many vestiges of African culture and its derivatives, from jazz and clothing to slang and styles of speech.

Amalgamation occurs when two or more cultures merge into a single new culture that contains elements of both as well as some entirely new elements representing a synthesis of the two. Mexico, for example, is an amalgamation of Spanish and Native American cultures.

See also MULTICULTURALISM; SEGREGATION AND INTEGRATION.

Reading

Blauner, Robert. 1972. "Racism as the negation of culture." In *Racial oppression in America*. New York: Harper and Row.

Castles, Stephen, with Heather Booth and Tina Wallace. 1984. *Here for good: Western Europe's new ethnic minorities*. London: Pluto Press.

Park, Robert E. 1950. *Collected papers of Robert Ezra Park*. New York: Free Press.

cultural deprivation *See* CULTURAL CAPITAL.

cultural determinism *See* DETERMINISM AND REDUCTIONISM.

cultural lag Cultural lag is a term originated by William F. Ogburn to describe what happens in a SOCIAL SYSTEM when the cultural ideas used to regulate social life do not keep pace with other SOCIAL CHANGES. Nuclear weapons, for example, are being developed by an increasing number of nations without an effective international system of NORMS and VALUES to control their use. On a smaller scale, new medical TECHNOLOGY makes it possible to keep people's bodies functioning long after they would otherwise have been considered dead. This, in turn, raises cultural questions about the definition of when life ends, who has the right to withdraw artificial life supports, and how to balance competing values about the absolute length of life and its quality. In all of these cases, the development of new cultural BELIEFS, values, and norms lags behind the dilemmas posed by technological change. Hence the term, cultural lag.

See also STRUCTURAL LAG.

Reading
Ogburn, William F. 1922. *Social change*. New York: Viking.
——. 1964. "Cultural lag as theory." In *On culture and social change*, edited by William F. Ogburn, 86–95. Chicago: University of Chicago Press.

cultural materialism Cultural materialism is a theory that explains aspects of CULTURE, such as religious BELIEFS, as being adaptations to the physical or material conditions of life in a particular society, especially as these relate to geography, climate, and population. Most closely associated with the work of anthropologist Marvin Harris, cultural materialism has been applied to a wide range of social phenomena, from war and male supremacy to cannibalism and the Jewish prohibition on eating pork. Harris argues that the SACRED status of cattle among Hindus is an adaptation to climatic conditions. During India's frequent and prolonged droughts, families might have felt tempted to eat their draft animals as a last resort. In the long run, however, such desperate measures would have been disastrous because farmers would be unable to cultivate the crops needed to survive when the rains returned. Hence, Harris argues, cattle were initially protected for practical reasons having to do with the demands of material existence.

See also ADAPTATION; ECOLOGY; POPULATION.

Reading
Harris, Marvin. 1974. *Cows, pigs, wars, and witches*. New York: Random House.
——. 1977. *Cannibals and kings: The origins of cultures*. New York: Random House.
——. 1979. *Cultural materialism*. New York: Random House.

cultural pluralism *See* CULTURAL CONTACT.

cultural relativism Cultural relativism is a concept that refers to the fact – so amply documented by anthropologists – that what is regarded as true, valued, or expected in one SOCIAL SYSTEM may not be so in another. A *lorry* in Britain is a *truck* in the United States. In Iceland, one of the great delicacies is buried shark that after several months has the consistency of an aged soft Camembert cheese: the true test of its quality is the degree to which the fumes bring tears to the eyes of the person eating it. The deliberate killing of a child

71

is considered murder in most societies, but in Brazil's Tenetehara it is a legitimate practice.

One of the most profound benefits of being aware of cultural relativism is that it undermines the common perception that a particular society's way of going about social life is rooted in a natural order of things, that its moral codes are universal and absolutely correct, or that the tastes and preferences of its people are something more than just one more manifestation of the collective potential of human imagination and ingenuity. This awareness, of course, does not free us from the constraints imposed by our own CULTURE, since each culture defines reality for those who participate in it. Westerners may be aware that in Tibet brothers often share a single wife, but this awareness is unlikely to make them more tolerant of such practices in their own societies. Thus the consequences produced by a culture hold within that culture regardless of how differently things might be done elsewhere.

Another effect of being more aware of cultural relativism is that we tend to be less blind and arrogant in relation to other societies and less rigid and dogmatic in evaluating the idea of changing our own. It can be a humbling experience to realize that what we take for granted as natural, universal, and immutable in fact takes many different forms both historically and cross-culturally.

See also CULTURAL UNIVERSAL; ETHNOCENTRISM.

cultural reproduction and social reproduction

According to French sociologist Pierre BOURDIEU, cultural reproduction is the social process through which CULTURE is reproduced across generations, especially through the socializing influence of major INSTITUTIONS. Bourdieu applied the concept in particular to the ways in which social institutions such as schools are used to pass along cultural ideas that underlie and support the privileged position of the dominant or UPPER CLASS.

Cultural reproduction is part of a larger process of social reproduction through which entire societies and their cultural, structural, and ecological characteristics are reproduced through a process that invariably involves a certain amount of change. From a Marxist perspective, social reproduction is primarily economic in scope, including the RELATIONS OF PRODUCTION, FORCES OF PRODUCTION, and the LABOR POWER of the WORKING CLASS. In a broader sense, however, social reproduction includes much more than this, from the shape of religious institutions to language and varieties of music and other cultural products.

See also CULTURAL CAPITAL; IDEOLOGY; SOCIALIZATION.

Reading

Bourdieu, Pierre, and Jean-Claude Passeron. 1977. *Society, culture, and education.* Beverly Hills, CA: Sage Publications.

Marx, Karl. [1867] 1975. *Capital: A critique of political economy.* New York: International Publishers.

cultural studies

Cultural studies is an area of sociology that focuses on how CULTURE is produced and experienced in a SOCIETY. More specifically, it looks at how culture is shaped by major social INSTITUTIONS such as the STATE and the ECONOMY. How, for example, does CAPITALISM shape cultural products such as literature and film, and how do the social dynamics of class, race, age, gender, and ethnic relations affect how people experience them? How are subordinate groups such as minorities, young people, and the working class able to shape their own POPULAR CULTURE in spite of control of the mass media and other means of cultural production by an ELITE?

As an area of interest within sociology, cultural studies is most closely associated with the Center for Contemporary Cultural Studies at the University of Birmingham, England, which was founded in 1964.

Reading

Hoggart, Richard. [1957] 1967. *The uses of literacy: Aspects of working-class life with special reference to publications and entertainment.* London: Chatto and Windus.

Williams, Raymond. 1961. *The long revolution.* New York: Columbia University Press.

——. 1980. *Problems in materialism and culture.* London: Verso.

cultural universal A cultural universal is an aspect of social life that is found in all known societies. This might include some form of dance, courtship, folklore, incest taboo, magic, sport, and BELIEF about what happens after people die. The actual form that these universals take differs greatly (something of particular interest to anthropologists), a phenomenon known as CULTURAL RELATIVISM.

See also ETHNOCENTRISM.

Reading

Murdock, George P. 1943. "The common denominator of cultures." In *The science of man in the world crisis*, edited by Ralph Linton. New York: Columbia University Press.

——. 1967. *Ethnographic atlas.* Pittsburgh: Pittsburgh University Press.

culture Culture is the accumulated store of SYMBOLS, ideas, and material products associated with a SOCIAL SYSTEM, whether it be an entire SOCIETY or a family. Along with SOCIAL STRUCTURE, POPULATION, and ECOLOGY, it is one of the major elements of every social system and a key concept in defining the sociological perspective.

Culture has both material and nonmaterial aspects. *Material culture* includes everything that is made, fashioned, or transformed as part of collective social life, from the preparation of food to the manufacture of steel and computers to the landscaping that produces English country gardens. *Nonmaterial culture* includes symbols – from words to musical notation – as well as ideas that shape and inform people's lives in relation to one another and the social systems in which they participate. The most important of these ideas are ATTITUDES, BELIEFS, VALUES, and NORMS.

It is important to note that culture does not refer to what people actually do, but to the ideas they share about what they do and the material objects that they use. The act of eating with chopsticks rather than with silverware or one's hands, for example, is not a part of culture. It is something that people do that makes the influence of culture visible. The chopsticks themselves, however, are indeed a part of culture as are the shared expectations that define this as an appropriate if not expected way to eat in certain societies.

The distinction between culture on the one hand and what we do on the other is important because the POWER and AUTHORITY of culture in human life derive primarily from our experience of culture as something external

73

to ourselves that transcends what we actually do. Our appearance or behavior may conform to or deviate from cultural standards, but the appearance or behavior is not itself part of culture and should not be confused with those standards. What makes an idea cultural rather than personal is not simply that it is shared by two or more people. Rather, it must be perceived and experienced as having an authority that transcends the thoughts of individuals. We do not perceive a symbol or idea as cultural because most people share in it, for in fact we have no way of knowing what most people in a society think. Instead, we assume that most people share in a cultural idea because we identify it as cultural.

See also CULTURAL RELATIVISM; SOCIETY; TECHNOLOGY.

culture of poverty

The culture of poverty (also known as the *cycle of deprivation*) is the name given to a theory developed by anthropologist Oscar Lewis in his studies of communities in Puerto Rico and Mexico. Lewis identified what he believed to be an important factor in the perpetuation of poverty. Regardless of what originally caused patterns of inequality and poverty to exist in society, Lewis argued, once established, life in poverty tends to produce cultural ideas that promote behaviors and outlooks that perpetuate poverty. The poor may lose the ambition to improve their lives by adopting the fatalistic belief that hard work and ambition will not make any difference. This CULTURE, in turn, is passed from one generation to the next. In a sense, Lewis argued that as people collectively adapt to impoverished circumstances, they tend to

develop a culture consistent with and therefore supportive of it. This *transmitted deprivation* would help to explain not only patterns of poverty within societies, but the inability of nonindustrial countries to develop economically as well.

Although Lewis was careful to point out that he did not believe the concept applied beyond the societies he was studying when he developed it, this has not prevented its widespread application to the poverty found in industrial societies such as the United States, especially in relation to African-Americans and other members of the expanding urban UNDERCLASS. There has been considerable debate, however, not only over this, but over whether the concept applies in any society, and whether its primary effect is to unjustly blame the victims of poverty for their own circumstances.

Reading

Gans, Herbert. 1969. "Culture and class in the study of poverty." In *On understanding poverty*, edited by Daniel P. Moynihan, 201–28. New York: Basic Books.

Lewis, Oscar. 1959. *Five families: Mexican case studies in the culture of poverty.* New York: Basic Books.

——. 1966. *La Vida: A Puerto Rican family in the culture of poverty.* New York: Random House.

Valentine, Charles. 1968. *Culture and poverty.* Chicago: University of Chicago Press.

curvilinear relationship

See DIRECTION OF RELATIONSHIP; REGRESSION ANALYSIS.

custom

A custom is a cultural idea that describes a regular, patterned way of appearing or behaving that is considered characteristic of life in a

SOCIAL SYSTEM. Shaking hands, bowing, and kissing, for example, are all customary ways of greeting people that distinguish one SOCIETY from another. Similarly, individual families often have different customs, such as distinctive ways of celebrating holidays or marking significant events in family history.

See also CULTURE; FOLKWAYS.

Reading

Murdock, George P. 1967. *Ethnographic atlas*. Pittsburgh: Pittsburgh University Press.

cybernetics Cybernetics is a science that focuses on the use of communication as an instrument of control. The basic idea is that flows of information provide feedback on conditions that affect the behavior of people or animals or the operation of machines. A household thermostat, for example, senses room temperature and provides information that regulates when the furnace turns on and off. Feedback that the room is too cold triggers the furnace, which then warms the room. This, in turn, affects the thermostat, which sends a new message to the furnace, signalling it to turn off. Cybernetics is the study of how such feedback loops work in the interest of control and adaptation to changing conditions.

In sociology, cybernetics is applied primarily to the operation of SOCIAL SYSTEMS such as FORMAL ORGANIZATIONS.

Reading

Parsons, Talcott. 1951. *The social system*. Glencoe, IL: Free Press.

Weiner, Norbert. 1949. *Cybernetics: Control and communication in man and machine*. Cambridge, MA: MIT Press.

cycle of deprivation *See* CULTURE OF POVERTY.

cyclical change *See* SOCIAL EVOLUTION.

cyclical unemployment *See* UNEMPLOYMENT AND UNDEREMPLOYMENT.

D

Darwinism, social *See* SOCIAL DARWINISM.

data In a sociological context, data are facts that social scientists gather, analyze, and interpret. In conversation as well as print, the word *data* is commonly, and erroneously, treated as singular (as in "The data is accurate") rather than plural ("The data are accurate"). A lone bit of information such as a percentage or a respondent's answer to a survey question is a datum; a flock of percentages, however, should always be referred to as data.

Davis–Moore debate The Davis–Moore debate refers to an exchange between Kingsley Davis and Wilbert Moore, on the one hand, and Melvin Tumin, on the other, concerning the FUNCTIONALIST PERSPECTIVE on STRATIFICATION. A functionalist, Davis argued that social inequality results from the needs of SOCIAL SYSTEMS to have the most important jobs performed by the best-qualified people. Since such people tend to be in short supply and must be motivated to undergo the difficult training required for such jobs, they must be rewarded accordingly. The result is social inequality.

Moore criticized the functionalist argument on numerous grounds. Money is not the only – or even the best – motivation for becoming a doctor, for example, and the number of qualified people who want to attend medical school is always much greater than the number of positions available. In addition, many jobs such as garbage collector are poorly paid, yet crucial to the operation of any community (as we discover when workers go on strike); it is unclear why motivation to undergo training must result in a lifetime of privilege; much of the cost of professional training is borne by government and other institutional resources, not by individuals; and the degree of inequality among many positions is far larger than differences in the value of what people actually contribute to SOCIETY.

Reading
Davis, Kingsley, and Wilbert E. Moore. 1945. "Some principles of stratification." *American Sociological Review* 10: 242–9.
Tumin, Melvin M. 1953. "Some principles of stratification: a critical analysis." *American Sociological Review* 18: 378–94.
Davis, Kingsley. 1953. "Reply to Tumin." *American Sociological Review* 18 (Aug.): 394–7.

death rate The death (or *mortality*) rate is most commonly measured by the *crude death rate*, which is the annual number of deaths per 1,000 people in the midyear POPULATION. When used to make comparisons, crude death rates are often misleading because they do not take into account differences in AGE STRUCTURE. A population with a relatively large proportion of the elderly, for example, will generate a relatively large number of deaths regardless of health conditions. For this reason, crude death rates in some nonindustrial, relatively poor societies are similar if not below those of some industrial societies, even though health conditions are worse and death rates are higher at most ages. Mexico, for example, has a large percentage of children in its population and a relatively small percentage of the elderly, an age structure that is conducive to low overall mortality. By comparison, Britain's population is much older and, although on the whole healthier, produces a larger number of deaths relative to the size of its population.

There are two ways to deal with the distorting effects of age structure on the measurement of mortality. The first is the *age-adjusted* (or *standardized*) *rate*, a rate that uses a single standard age structure in order to isolate the effects of mortality alone. The second is *life expectancy*, a hypothetical measure of how long a group of people could expect to live on the average if their risk of dying at each age continued to be as it is now. Although long life expectancy is often associated with living to be old, upward trends in life expectancy have been more profoundly influenced by improvements in INFANT MORTALITY than the prolongation of life among the elderly. Infancy is a relatively risky period of life. If an infant is saved from dying, the result is likely to be an entire lifetime added to the collective average. If an elderly person's life is saved, however, the number of additional years added to the collective average is much smaller – hence the more profound effect on life expectancy caused by improvements in infant mortality.

This applies not only to historical trends but to most differences between societies and population groups.

See also EPIDEMIOLOGY; INFANT MORTALITY RATE; LIFE TABLE; RATE OF NATURAL INCREASE; STANDARDIZATION.

Reading
Shryock, Henry S., and Jacob Siegel and Associates. 1976. *The methods and materials of demography.* New York: Academic Press.

decentered self or decentered subject The basic idea behind the concept of the decentered self is that individual people are not the ultimate source of knowing. In other words, our egos and thinking minds are not at the center of things as autonomous knowers. Instead, we and what we know are relational, which is to say that they exist only in relation to other people and to SOCIAL SYSTEMS and shift in character from one social situation to another. There is no "I" out there in the middle of things, observing the world from its own isolated point of view, and figuring things out on its own.

Reading
Giddens, Anthony. 1987. "Structuralism, poststructuralism and the production of culture." In *Social theory today*, edited by Anthony Giddens and Jonathan Turner. Stanford, CA: Stanford University Press.

decision theory *See* RATIONAL CHOICE THEORY.

decolonization *See* COLONIALISM AND IMPERIALISM.

deconstruction Deconstruction is an approach to understanding meaning by relating words to other words rather than directly to what we think the words represent. As argued by Jacques Derrida and other advocates of a perspective known as

POSTSTRUCTURALISM, the meaning of LANGUAGE is not to be found in some concrete reality or truth but only in relation to language itself, which is socially constructed. The word *masculine*, for example, does not name some concrete truth that can be observed in human beings. Instead, the word's meaning can only be identified through an intellectual process (deconstruction) that links *masculine* with other words such as *feminine* or *androgynous*. Included in deconstruction is the argument that some ideas (such as *masculine*) are culturally privileged in relation to others (such as *feminine*), and help enforce an underlying social hierarchy and SOCIAL OPPRESSION.

Since the meaning of language is fluid and unstable, so too is the reality that we use language to name and explain. Derrida saw in this approach the radical potential to use deconstruction to expose how language is used to promote inequality and oppression. In other fields, however, deconstruction has been used in quite different ways. Some schools of literary criticism, for example, argue that it is impossible to decide what anything means, a stance that others argue could help ensure the perpetuation of the status quo, including inequality and oppression.

See also POSTMODERNISM.

Reading

Derrida, Jacques. 1978. *Writing and difference*. Chicago: University of Chicago Press.

deductive reasoning *See* HYPO-THETICO-DEDUCTIVE METHOD.

de facto and de jure segregation *See* SEGREGATION AND INTEGRATION.

definition of the situation The definition of the situation is what people use to obtain some sense of the STATUSES and ROLES that are involved in a situation so that they can know what is expected of them and what to expect of others. They must know, for example, whether they are in a bank, a Turkish bath, a movie theater, or a market. They must know, in a social sense, just whom they are interacting with and for what purpose.

One of the more interesting problems with this is that defining the situation is not a straightforward matter of identifying objective facts readily apparent to anyone who cares to look at them. Rather, the definition of the situation can be highly subjective and open to negotiation. Indeed, as people participate in social life they may "make up" the definition of the situation as they go along by interpreting various cues. If you are walking down a darkened street and a man approaches you and asks you to light his cigarette, you may define that situation as an impending assault or robbery, and if so you are likely to behave quite differently than if you interpret his intentions as friendly. What ensues may have much less to do with the objective facts of the situation than with the definitions formulated by those involved.

This important relationship between subjective interpretations and definitions on the one hand and the objective outcomes of interaction on the other, gave rise to William I. THOMAS's classic notion that what we define as real is real in its consequences.

See also DRAMATURGICAL PERSPECTIVE; ETHNOMETHODOLOGY.

Reading

McHugh, P. 1968. *Defining the situation*. Indianapolis: Bobbs-Merrill.

Thomas, William I. 1927. "The behavior pattern and the situation." *Publications of the American Sociological Society* (papers and proceedings), 1–13.

——. with Dorothy Swain Thomas. 1928. *The child in America.* New York: Alfred A. Knopf.

degradation ceremony A degradation ceremony is a RITE OF PASSAGE sometimes used to initiate people into TOTAL INSTITUTIONS such as mental hospitals, prisons, and military units. The purpose of degradation ceremonies is to deprive people of their former identities and dignity in order to make them more accepting of external control. In prisons, for example, this might include being stripped, searched (including body cavities), and verbally harassed in ways that label prisoners as inferior and underscore their lack of POWER and autonomy.

Reading

Garfinkel, Harold. 1956. "Conditions of successful degradation ceremonies." *American Journal of Sociology* 61: 420–24.

de-industrialization De-industrialization is the process through which manufacturing declines in a SOCIETY or region as a proportion of total economic activity. This occurs, for example, when the service ECONOMY grows faster than industries that manufacture goods. It also happens when corporations close production facilities under pressure from foreign competition, or shift production to THIRD WORLD countries where wages and taxes are lower and TRADE UNIONS are less powerful.

Reading

Bluestone, Barry, and Bennett Harrison. 1982. *The de-industrialization of America: Plant closings, community abandonment,* *and the dismantling of basic industry.* New York: Basic Books.

delinquency Delinquency is a concept generally referring to criminal and other deviant behavior committed by children and adolescents who are not yet considered adults. In some cases it refers to acts that for adults would be treated as crimes – such as theft – but which when committed by children are regarded less severely. As a result, "youthful offenders" may not be tried in regular courts or imprisoned with adults, and may have their criminal records sealed or even erased upon reaching adult status.

Delinquency also includes behavior that violates the law only when committed by nonadults, such as running away from home, refusing to attend school, chronically disobeying one's parents, or (for girls especially) being sexually active at an early age. These are also sometimes known as status offences, because they are defined primarily in relation to the age status of the offender.

See also ADOLESCENCE; AGE CATEGORY; DELINQUENT DRIFT; DEVIANCE.

Reading

Cloward, Richard A., and Lloyd E. Ohlin. 1960. *Delinquency and opportunity: A theory of delinquent gangs.* New York: Free Press.

Sutton, J. R. 1983. "Social structures, institutions, and the legal status of children." *American Journal of Sociology* 88(5): 915–47.

delinquent drift As developed by sociologists David Matza and Gresham Sykes, delinquent drift is the process through which young people rationalize delinquent behavior and therefore are able to engage in it without thinking they are doing anything wrong.

In general, the "drift" toward delinquency occurs when young people define laws as unfair or having little to do with them and disassociate themselves from the consequences of their behavior. This typically includes perceptions that police and other AUTHORITY figures are corrupt, that no one is really hurt by deviant behavior (as when a school is vandalized), that victims deserve what they get, and that the delinquency is done for a good reason or results from an accident or the behavior of others. In such cases, the link that connects the offender to other people and to SOCIAL SYSTEMS and their NORMS is weakened and explained away with a complex set of RATIONALIZATIONS.

See also ANOMIE; DELINQUENCY.

Reading

Matza, David. 1964. *Delinquency and drift.* New York: Wiley.

Sykes, Gresham, and David Matza. 1957. "Techniques of neutralization." *American Sociological Review* 22: 664–70.

democracy, political and economic As applied to politics, a democracy (from the Greek, meaning "rule of the people") is a SOCIAL SYSTEM in which everyone has an equal share of POWER. Although there are many relatively small and simple social systems (such as a GROUP of friends) that are organized as pure democracies, on the level of ORGANIZATIONS, COMMUNITIES, and entire SOCIETIES, pure democracy is quite rare. In part this is because the definition of "everyone" almost always excludes some portion of the POPULATION – such as women, children, or minorities. In addition, most societies that describe themselves as political democracies are actually representative democracies in which citizens elect officials who actually hold and exercise political AUTHORITY.

Even societies that enjoy relatively high levels of political democracy often do not extend such equality to economics. Every industrial capitalist society, for example, functions politically as a representative democracy, but a small ELITE controls the vast majority of WEALTH, including means of production such as factories. While workers have the freedom to choose not to work for a particular employer, they generally do not have the freedom to work for themselves and avoid the relatively powerless position of wage earner.

Marxists argue that the relationship between political and economic democracy is complex and important for understanding SOCIAL CLASS and SOCIAL OPPRESSION. The existence of political democracy in a SOCIETY, for example, may be used to mask the lack of economic democracy. In addition, political organizations such as the STATE are often used to protect the interests of economic elites.

See also AUTHORITARIANISM; AUTOCRACY; OLIGARCHY; POLITICAL ECONOMY.

Reading

Bottomore, Tom B. 1993. *Political sociology.* Minneapolis: University of Minnesota Press.

Bollen, Kenneth, and Robert W. Jackman. 1985. "Political democracy." *American Sociological Review* 50(4): 438–57.

Held, David. 1987. *Models of democracy.* Cambridge, England: Polity Press.

democratic socialism *See* STATE CAPITALISM.

demographic transition First used by Warren S. Thompson, demographic transition is a term referring to an historical account of trends in births, deaths, and POPULATION growth that occurred in today's industrialized societies, for the most part beginning in the late eighteenth century.

The transition is divided into three stages, the first of which covers almost all of human history. In this stage, birth and death rates were both relatively high with resulting low rates of population growth. The second stage began in Europe late in the eighteenth century with a decline in death rates brought about primarily by advances in public health, sanitation, and stable food supplies that came with the early stages of the INDUSTRIAL REVOLUTION. As death rates dropped, populations grew rapidly. Eventually, however, the same underlying social forces that promoted lower death rates – urbanization, industrialization, the growth of wage labor, and opportunities to take advantage of economic prosperity – also prompted a corresponding decline in birth rates. As a result, rates of population growth declined in the third stage as falling birth rates caught up with the death rates. In some cases – most notably in eastern and central Europe – birth rates have fallen so low that the RATE OF NATURAL INCREASE is actually zero or negative. Some demographers expect similar developments in North America by early in the twenty-first century.

The diffusion of KNOWLEDGE and cheap medical TECHNOLOGY has brought many nonindustrial societies into the second stage of the demographic transition. Without the underlying social forces such as industrialization that promote similar declines in birth rates, however, these societies have thus far been unable to enter the third stage. The result has been very high rates of population growth in countries that are not experiencing corresponding economic growth.

Although sometimes referred to as a theory, the demographic transition is more a model that describes what happened than an explanation that can be tested. In addition, there is historical evidence suggesting that the transition may not have proceeded in a uniform, linear fashion in European countries. If and how it will apply to the world's nonindustrial and industrializing countries remains to be seen.

Reading

Coale, Ansley, and Susan Watkins, eds. *The decline of fertility in Europe.* Princeton: Princeton University Press.

Thompson, Warren S. 1929. "Population." *American Journal of Sociology* 34.

Weinstein, J. A. 1976. *Demographic transition and social change.* Morristown, NJ: General Learning Press.

demography Demography is the systematic study of the growth, size, composition, distribution, and movement of human POPULATIONS. It is traced to a seventeenth-century Englishman, John Graunt, who used church and city records of deaths and christenings to identify social patterns of mortality in the London area. Graunt was not the first to think about population matters, but he was the first to base observations on systematic records. He used his observations to make a variety of estimates – of the size of London's population, for example, which was unknown at the time – and the relative effects of MIGRATION, births, and deaths on population size and growth.

Demography plays an important part not only in the social sciences, and sociology in particular, but in the formulation of government and economic policy. Demographic data are gathered on a regular basis throughout the industrialized world and, to a much lesser degree, in nonindustrial societies as well.

The close connection between demography and sociology is most apparent in the field of *population studies*, which focuses on the relationship between demographic VARIABLES on the one hand and the characteristics of SOCIAL SYSTEMS on the other. This kind of work includes both questions about how social systems affect demographic processes and how demographic processes affect the conditions of social life.

See also BIRTH RATE; DEATH RATE; DEMOGRAPHIC TRANSITION; RATE OF NATURAL INCREASE.

Reading

Namboodiri, K. 1968. "Ecological demography: Its place in sociology." *American Sociological Review* 5(4): 619–33.

Shryock, Henry S., and Jacob Siegel and Associates. 1976. *The methods and materials of demography*. New York: Academic Press.

Wrigley, E. A. 1969. *Population and history*. London: Weidenfeld and Nicolson.

denomination A denomination is a religious organization that is smaller than a CHURCH but larger than a SECT. Membership tends to be ascribed at birth and to include a relatively narrow mix of SOCIAL CLASS backgrounds. The AUTHORITY structure is formal with a trained clergy, but is rarely bureaucratic. As with larger types of religious organizations, the denomination uses a highly abstract form of religious service with little emotional display. In relation to other major INSTITUTIONS such as the state, the denomination neither supports nor opposes the status quo but, rather, coexists with it.

In the United States, the concept of a denomination is most often applied to Protestant religions, such as the Congregationalist, Unitarian Universalist, and Presbyterian denominations. *See also* BUREAUCRACY; CULT; ECCLESIA; RELIGION.

Reading

Becker, Howard. 1950. *Systematic sociology*. New York: Wiley.

Troeltsch, Ernst. [1912] 1956. *The social teachings of the Christian churches*. London: Allen and Unwin.

Weber, Max. [1922] 1963. *The sociology of religion*. Boston: Beacon.

dependence, statistical *See* STATISTICAL INDEPENDENCE AND STATISTICAL DEPENDENCE.

dependency ratio In a POPULATION, the dependency ratio is the number of young and elderly people divided by the total adult population. "Young" usually is defined as under 16 years old and "elderly" is defined as over 64, although other cutoff points are sometimes used. The dependency ratio is a significant statistic for societies in which these age groups do not engage in much economically productive work, for this means that their needs must be met by the rest of the adult population. The larger the dependency ratio is, the greater is the burden on the average adult. High dependency ratios are socially problematic in societies with particularly young populations, such as the high-fertility countries of the THIRD WORLD, or old populations such as those in the low-fertility countries of Europe and, increasingly, North America. *See also* AGE STRUCTURE.

dependency theory Dependency theory is used to explain the failure of nonindustrialized countries to develop economically in spite of investments from industrial countries. In the decades following World War II, it was widely believed in industrial capitalist countries such as Britain and the United States that the key to economic development in the THIRD WORLD was MODERNIZATION, the infusion of TECHNOLOGY, formal education, and "modern VALUES" such as an emphasis on long-range planning and openness to innovation and change.

Dependency theory developed as a critical response to the failure of modernization theory to produce any more than scattered success. The central argument of dependency theory is that the world economic system is highly unequal in its distribution of POWER and resources and places most nations in a dependent position in relation to the industrial powers. This dependency limits development in the Third World largely because it dictates that any infusions of technology and other investment will be done in ways that ensure the continued dominance of the wealthy countries. When TRANSNATIONAL CORPORATIONS build factories in Third World countries, for example, profits are typically removed rather than reinvested in the host country. Agriculture is transformed from subsistence crops that feed local populations to cash export crops (such as fruits, vegetables, coffee, and sugar) that make producer countries highly dependent on wealthier countries that buy their produce. What were once relatively self-sufficient albeit poor economies in which local needs were locally met become dependent economies in which the ability to earn cash in international markets – in which demand and prices can fluctuate wildly – is central to survival.

Dependency theory argues that we cannot understand the course of economic development in the Third World without taking into account the essentially dependent relationship that exists between these countries and the industrial powers' vested interest in maintaining and extending their dominant position in the world economy. Critics argue that dependency theory is overly general and ignores the effects of internal conditions on local economies.

See also STRATIFICATION AND INEQUALITY; WORLD SYSTEM.

Reading
Amin, Samir. 1976. *Unequal development: An essay on the social formation of peripheral capitalism.* New York: Monthly Review Press; Hassocks: Harvester Press.
Frank, Andre G. 1967. *Capitalism and underdevelopment in Latin America.* New York: Monthly Review Press.

dependent variable *See* VARIABLE.

deprivation In general, deprivation refers to a condition in which people lack what they need. The concept is sociologically important because of the social significance of what people are willing to go through in order to improve their lives, from crime to participation in social movements.

Absolute deprivation is a lack of life necessities such as food, water, shelter, and fuel. A state of *relative deprivation*, however, is based on a perceived difference between what people have in comparison with others. Implicit in this is the idea that people are selective in whom they choose to compare themselves to. Those at the bottom of SOCIAL CLASS systems in many INDUSTRIAL SOCIETIES, for example, are objectively better off than many of those more highly placed in class systems of nonindustrial societies. Those in industrial societies take no comfort from this, however, because they do not use such societies as points of comparison. In this sense, relative deprivation exists when individuals see themselves as lacking what they believe they *should* have within the context of the particular SOCIAL SYSTEM they live in and their position in it.

The concept of relative deprivation has been most used in the study of SOCIAL MOVEMENTS and REVOLUTION, where it is argued that relative, not absolute, deprivation is most likely to lead to pressure for change.

Whether absolute or relative, *multiple deprivation* occurs when one form of deprivation (such as low income) tends to overlap with others (such as low access to healthy food, safe neighborhoods, and quality education). *See also* REFERENCE GROUP.

Reading
Brown, M., and N. Madge. 1982. *Despite the welfare state*. London: Heinemann Educational Books.
Davies, James C. 1962. "Toward a theory of revolution." *American Sociological Review* 27: 5–19.
Tilly, Charles. 1978. *From mobilization to revolution*. Reading, MA: Addison-Wesley.

derivations *See* RESIDUES AND DERIVATIONS.

descent *See* KINSHIP.

descriptive statistics *See* STATISTICS.

de-skilling De-skilling is the process of using TECHNOLOGY and the fragmentation of work in order to lower the breadth and depth of skill possessed by workers. In the early stages of industrial CAPITALISM, for example, production workers were generally highly skilled in all areas of the productive process. This, however, gave them considerable leverage and power because it was difficult to replace them. As mass production technology grew, assembly lines were used both to make production more efficient and to fragment the work process so that each worker focused on a narrower range of simplified tasks requiring less training and expertise.

As a result, today's generation of workers are more easily replaced, and meeting worker demands becomes less compelling. De-skilling also appears to be spreading among lower-level white-collar occupations, a trend related to the increased use of computers. The professions are the only occupations that are generally impervious to de-skilling, in part because they still manage to retain control over conditions and methods of work.

There is some disagreement over whether de-skilling is in fact taking place, especially from those who foresee a more highly skilled work force in POSTINDUSTRIAL SOCIETY.

See also ALIENATION; PROLETARIANIZATION; SCIENTIFIC MANAGEMENT.

Reading
Braverman, Harry. 1974. *Labor and monopoly capital*. New York: Monthly Review Press.
Wood, Stephen. 1982. *The degradation of work?* London: Hutchinson.

determinism and reductionism In general, determinism is a way of thinking that assumes everything is caused by something in a predictable way. More specifically, determinism describes any THEORY that explains the world in terms of a few narrowly defined factors to the exclusion of all others (a practice also known as *reductionism*). *Biological determinism,* for example, argues that physiology, genetics, and POPULATION pressures determine how societies are organized. *Social* (or *cultural*) *determinism* goes to the other extreme by attributing social life solely to SOCIAL SYSTEMS which are assumed to be beyond the influence of biological aspects of human existence. Both perspectives imply that individuals have relatively little control or free choice in the face of biological or social factors.

Marxist theory has been criticized as a form of *economic determinism* (also known as *economism*) when it argues that the forces and RELATIONS OF PRODUCTION that define economic systems determine social conditions from religion and literature to government and family life.

From a sociological perspective, deterministic/reductionistic thinking is by its very nature flawed because it fails to appreciate the inherent complexity of social life, which sociology tries to embrace and articulate. Indeed, the emergence of sociology in the nineteenth century was in part grounded in Émile DURKHEIM's critique of the tendency to reduce social phenomena to individual psychology.

See also AGENCY AND STRUCTURE; BASE AND SUPERSTRUCTURE; METHODOLOGICAL INDIVIDUALISM; SOCIOBIOLOGY.

Reading

Durkheim, Émile. [1895] 1938. *The rules of the sociological method.* New York: Free Press.

——. [1924] 1974. *Sociology and philosophy.* New York: The Free Press.

deviance Deviance is any behavior or appearance that violates a NORM. Sociologically, it differs from behavior or appearance that is merely unusual in a statistical sense. For example, it is highly unusual, but not deviant, for someone to be elected prime minister or president of a country. In contrast, using illegal drugs and committing adultery are fairly common behaviors in spite of the fact that they are defined as deviant in many CULTURES.

As Émile DURKHEIM pointed out, from a FUNCTIONALIST PERSPECTIVE deviance is a cultural creation because it is only through the creation of norms that the possibility for people to violate norms exists.

Norms, and hence deviance, are socially important because they help define and regulate the BOUNDARIES of a SOCIAL SYSTEM. Our shared, visible allegiance to a culture's norms defines us as members; but in a similar way those who violate norms heighten awareness of boundaries by violating them. In so doing, they reinforce the sense of COHESION and belonging for those who conform.

From a CONFLICT PERSPECTIVE, the POWER to define norms, and therefore to define deviance, is usually distributed unequally in societies. This means dominant groups can shape norms to serve their own interests, including control over subordinate groups at their expense. Dominant groups in most societies can use legislatures, courts, police, and, in some cases, the military to enforce norms that protect their property and privilege, especially their control over WEALTH and major social INSTITUTIONS.

From an INTERACTIONIST PERSPECTIVE, deviance and conformity are created through people's behavior in relation to one another and through the perception and interpretation of the appearance and behavior of others. All forms of deviance – from criminal behavior to the STIGMA of physical deformity to simply being regarded as "odd" – occur only when people perceive, interpret, and respond to behavior or appearance as deviant.

Criminology is concerned primarily with describing and explaining patterns of deviance that violate criminal laws. The sociology of deviance, however, takes a broader view that includes all of the ways in which people conform to or deviate from the normative expectations found in social systems, and how such behavior produces consequences not only for themselves and other people but for social systems as a whole. In the sociology of deviance, the focus is not only on why individuals violate norms, but on how the characteristics of social systems produce patterns or rates of deviance, such as homicide and suicide rates or the rate of cheating in a university. Rates of deviance are of interest because they describe social systems and categories of people within them.

The accompanying table illustrates several patterns of interest. Countries differ in their suicide rates, but the differences vary with age. Denmark is highest among all men and women, for example, but France has the highest rate among elderly men and Japan has the highest rate among elderly women. Men have uniformly higher rates than women, but men in Australia, Britain, Italy, and the United States have a lower rate than women in Denmark. This difference disappears at older ages, however, because although men's rates increase sharply with advancing age, rates for women tend to decline.

Table 3 Suicide Rates by Gender and Age for Selected Countries, per 100,000

	All men	75 or older	All women	75 or older
Australia	17.0	39.3	5.4	8.2
Britain	11.5	22.5	5.9	9.7
Canada	22.3	26.4	6.4	4.6
Denmark	37.1	69.1	21.2	27.8
France	28.5	97.9	11.1	24.8
Italy	10.1	37.4	4.6	10.2
Japan	27.6	79.1	13.3	56.9
Sweden	27.8	56.7	11.2	13.1
United States	19.2	46.1	5.6	5.3

Source: Statistical abstract of the United States, U.S. Census Bureau 1987.

From a sociological perspective, the explanation for such patterns are to be found in the social conditions in which these different POPULATIONS live.

See also ANOMIE; DEVIANCE AND SOCIAL CONTROL; DIFFERENTIAL ASSOCIATION; LABELING THEORY; OPPORTUNITY STRUCTURE; VICTIMLESS CRIME.

Reading

Becker, Howard S. 1963. *Outsiders: Studies in the sociology of deviance.* Glencoe, IL: Free Press.

Downes, D., and P. Rock. 1982. *Understanding deviance.* Oxford, England: Oxford University Press.

Sutherland, Edwin H., and Donald R. Cressey. 1978. *Criminology*, 16th ed. Philadelphia: Lippincott.

deviance amplification Deviance amplification is a situation that occurs when the social response to deviant behavior – by police and the media, for example – has the effect of increasing deviance rather than curbing it. Suppose, for example, that the U.S. media focus intensely on the problem of urban crime, especially the traffic in illegal drugs. Since blacks are more likely to be arrested for crimes than are whites, it would be relatively easy for the media to fall back on racial stereotypes and identify blacks as the primary perpetrators of crime. This in turn pressures police to focus their efforts on black neighborhoods, to stop and search blacks and their cars on the chance that drugs might be found, to search apartments on the slightest pretext of wrongdoing. Whites become increasingly afraid to be around blacks, spend less time downtown, and contribute to economic and social decline. Blacks feel increasingly isolated, besieged, harassed, and, perhaps, defiant of police and other authorities. The ultimate result may be an amplification of deviant behavior, brought about by social responses intended to curb it.

The concept of deviance amplification has been applied to numerous groups, including drug users and people with AIDS.

See also LABELING THEORY.

Reading
Wilkins, L. T. 1964. *Social deviance: Social policy, action, and research.* London: Tavistock.
——. 1965. "Some sociological factors in drug addiction control." In *Mass society in crisis*, edited by B. Rosenberg, I. Bernard, and F. Howlen. New York: Free Press.

diachronic and synchronic The Swiss linguist Ferdinand de SAUSSURE (1857–1913) used the terms diachronic and synchronic to refer to aspects of LANGUAGE that contribute to change (diachronic) and permanence (synchronic). Historically, the meaning of words is subject to change. The word "bitch," for example, was originally a positive reference to the hunting dogs that accompanied the goddess Artemis-Diana. Today, however, the word is used as an insult directed at women. Diachronics refers to the social and historical dynamics that lead to such changes.

Synchronics are aspects of language that promote permanence. The meaning of a word such as "apple," for example, is not contained simply in the word itself. Instead, it is embedded in relationships between the word and other words (such as "fruit") and rules of usage (such as those governing the placement of nouns) that anchor the word in social space and allow us to use it reliably as we communicate with one another. Such relationships exist as part of CULTURE and draw their authority from it rather than from individuals. These synchronic aspects of language are what give them a sense of permanence and predictability.

See also SEMIOTICS.

Reading
Saussure, Ferdinand de. [1916] 1974. *The course in general linguistics.* London: Fontana.

dialectical materialism *See* MATERIALISM.

dichotomy A dichotomy is a VARIABLE that has only two categories, such as gender and answers (Yes or No) to the question, "Do you believe in God?" Any variable with several categories can be converted into a dichotomy simply by combining categories. Age, for example, could be collapsed into a dichotomy with the two categories of 0–45 and 46 and older.

There are several reasons to collapse a variable with several categories into a dichotomy. Sometimes there are so few observations in some categories that it is impossible to analyze them – such as the extremely small number of 90–100-year-olds to be found in the typical survey. One of the most appealing reasons for doing this is that a dichotomy can be considered to have INTERVAL-SCALE properties since it has only one interval, the one that exists between the two categories. Since many sophisticated statistical techniques can be used with interval-scale variables, this means that lower-scale variables such as gender can be treated as interval-scales and incorporated into more sophisticated analyses than would otherwise be possible.

The danger in this practice is that collapsing variables often masks important information. If we collapse the variable religion into two categories such as "Christian" and "non-Christian," for example, we lump together religious groups that differ in profound ways. If such differences are relevant to the other variables being studied, this can be a serious mistake.

See also DUMMY VARIABLE; SCALE OF MEASUREMENT.

differential association According to Edwin SUTHERLAND, differential association is the process of learning some types of deviant behavior requiring specialized knowledge and skill as well as the inclination to take advantage of opportunities to use them in deviant ways. All of this is learned and promoted primarily within groups such as urban gangs or business GROUPS that condone fraud, tax evasion, or insider trading on the stock market. The overall rate of deviance in a society or variations in rates among class, racial, and other groupings therefore depends on the availability of such groups and the SOCIALIZATION they offer.

We also can argue that a more complex SOCIAL SYSTEM is bound to generate more deviance than a simpler system because it cannot ensure a uniform and universal socialization experience for each new generation. The greater the variety of NORMS and VALUES that people grow up (or "associate") with, the less likely will there be a strong sense of COHESION around the values and norms of a given social system.

Sutherland's theory was first developed in the 1930s in response to individualistic theories of deviance that focused only on factors such as heredity and personality. Sutherland argued instead that the rate of crime is a social phenomenon whose explanation must include the characteristics of social systems such as the frequency, duration, and intensity of people's interactions with various kinds of groups. His theory is particularly useful in understanding career criminals.

Reading
Sutherland, Edwin H. 1934. *Principles of criminology.* Chicago: Lippincott.
Sutherland, Edwin H., and Donald R. Cressey. 1978. *Criminology,* 10th ed. Philadelphia: Lippincott.

differentiation Differentiation is a concept having two distinct meanings in sociology, both of which describe the structure of SOCIAL SYSTEMS. In the first sense, differentiation is the tendency of social systems to become increasingly complex as they develop, in particular through specialization. As governments grow, for example, they tend to invent greater and greater numbers of separate departments to handle specialized functions.

In the second sense, differentiation is the general social process of distinguishing among people according to the social STATUSES they occupy. *Horizontal differentiation* refers to distinctions between dissimilar statuses – office workers have different ROLE expectations than combat soldiers, for example. *Vertical differentiation* adds the element of ranking by making distinctions based on the amount of WEALTH, POWER, PRESTIGE, and other valued rewards and resources people receive by virtue of the statuses they occupy. The SOCIAL CLASS system, for example, differentiates among people both horizontally (differences in lifestyle, political behavior, and so on) and vertically (inequalities of wealth, power, and prestige).

See also DIFFERENTIAL ASSOCIATION; DIVISION OF LABOR; STRATIFICATION AND INEQUALITY.

Reading
Durkheim, Émile. [1893] 1933. *The division of labor in society.* New York: Free Press.

diffuseness *See* PATTERN VARIABLES.

diffusion As first described by anthropologist Edward Tylor, diffusion is a social process through which cultural KNOWLEDGE and practices and material products spread from one SOCIAL SYSTEM to another. Printing, for example, was first invented by the Chinese in the sixth century. From China it spread to the rest of the world and revolutionized the ability to store, retrieve, and share knowledge and ideas. As opportunities for interaction across CULTURES have increased, so has the rate of diffusion. Since the development of nuclear weapons TECHNOLOGY, for example, there have been great efforts to prevent its diffusion beyond the core of dominant industrial societies.

See also SOCIAL CHANGE.

Reading
Rogers, Everett M. 1983. *Diffusion of innovations*, 3rd ed. New York: Free Press.
Tylor, Edward. [1871] 1958. *Primitive culture*. New York: Harper.

diploma disease *See* CREDENTIALISM.

direct effect *See* EFFECT, STATISTICAL.

direction of relationship The direction of relationship is the statistical connection between two VARIABLES which can be described in terms of its direction or shape. This is the patterned way in which scores on one variable vary in relation to scores on the other.

A *linear relationship* usually takes the shape of a straight line and can be either *positive* or *negative*. If scores on Y tend to increase as scores on X increase, then the relationship is described as positive (or *direct*). This is the case with the relationship between income (Y) and education (X). If scores on Y tend to decrease as scores on X increase, then the relationship is negative (or *inverse*). This is the case with the relationship between how well children do in school (Y) and the number of siblings they have (X).

A *nonlinear relationship* can be either *curvilinear* or *irregular*. Irregular relationships lack a clear pattern. If we look at how people's support for a particular belief differs as income increases, for example, we might find a jerky pattern of alternating increases and decreases that resembles neither a straight line nor a curve.

Curvilinear relationships have been quite important in sociology. The relationships between SOCIOECONOMIC STATUS and FERTILITY, for example, varies according to country and historical period. In many cases it is linear (either positive or negative) but in a few it has resembled a "U" with the highest levels of fertility among those at the top and bottom of the class system. The U-shape is also found in Émile DURKHEIM's study of suicide where the highest rates of suicide occur where the degree of social COHESION is very low and where it is very high. The suicide rate was lowest in the more moderate ranges of cohesion.

In practice, researchers tend to assume relationships are linear, in part because the statistical techniques for analyzing curvilinear relationships are less well developed and are more complicated and difficult to use and interpret. Nonetheless, curvilinear relationships are among the most fascinating in sociology.

See also STATISTICAL INDEPENDENCE AND STATISTICAL DEPENDENCE; REGRESSION ANALYSIS.

direct relationship See DIRECTION OF RELATIONSHIP.

discourse and discourse formation
Discourse is written and spoken conversation and the thinking that underlies it. According to Michel FOUCAULT, discourse is sociologically important because how we talk and think about the world shapes how we behave and the kind of world we help to create as a result. It is through discourse that we construct what we experience as reality, and as soon as we learn to think and talk about reality in a particular way, we cannot help but shut off our ability to think of it in countless other ways.

Foucault was particularly interested in discourse formation – how ways of thinking and conversation come into being in a SOCIETY and how they affect social life. Two major areas of interest for him were madness and sexuality, both of which he regarded as socially constructed. There is, he argued, no such thing as sexuality or madness except as human beings create ideas about them through conversation and other forms of discourse. Whether we regard madness as divinely inspired or evil or a biologically caused pathology, for example, depends on what the discourse on madness looks like in our society. Similarly, if we equate CAPITALISM with DEMOCRACY or sexuality with male-dominated heterosexuality, we cannot help but shape economic and sexual life in ways that make it difficult to consider the possibility of democratic alternatives to capitalism or sexual lives that are egalitarian, gay, or lesbian.

See also CULTURE; KNOWLEDGE.

Reading
Foucault, Michel. 1971. *Madness and civilization: A history of insanity in the age of reason.* London: Tavistock.
——. [1976] 1979. *The history of sexuality.* London: Tavistock.

discrete variable and continuous variable A VARIABLE is discrete if observations can take only a limited number of values within a given range. The variable "ideal number of children," for example, can have only whole numbers as values since it is impossible to have a fractional number of children. Income is likewise discrete since the number of denominations in which coins and bills occur is limited. A variable is continuous if within a given range it can take on an infinite number of possible values. Age, for example, can be measured in virtually any unit from decades to milliseconds and beyond.

Reading

Bohrnstedt, George W., and David Knoke. 1994. *Statistics for social data analysis,* 3rd ed. Itasca, IL: F. E. Peacock.

discrimination *See* PREJUDICE AND DISCRIMINATION.

disengagement theory According to disengagement theory, in every SOCIETY the elderly undergo a process of adjustment in which they leave important public roles and narrow their social world to family and friends. The process benefits societies by avoiding the potential disruption of its key members dying suddenly. It also benefits individuals by enabling them to die without the stress and strain of fuller participation in social life.

Disengagement theory was part of a heated debate that led to considerable progress in sociological thinking about aging and the elderly. Critics observed, for example, that many elderly people do not disengage from important roles; that disengagement is unknown in numerous societies; and that continued engagement throughout the life course is often associated with higher levels of personal well-being. Instead of a FUNCTIONALIST EXPLANATION of disengagement, critics argued that disengagement is more likely to result from PREJUDICE against the elderly and COMPETITION from those in younger AGE CATEGORIES.

See also AGEISM; STRUCTURAL LAG.

Reading

Cumming, Elaine, and William Henry. 1961. *Growing old: The process of disengagement.* New York: Basic Books.

Hochschild, Arlie E. 1975. "Disengagement theory: A critique and proposal." *American Sociological Review* 40: 553–59.

Binstock, Robert H., and Linda K. George. 1996. *Handbook of aging and the social sciences,* 4th ed. San Diego: Academic Press.

disinterestedness, norm of *See* SCIENCE, NORMS OF.

dissimilarity, index of The index of dissimilarity is a statistic used to measure the overall difference between two percentage DISTRIBUTIONS. The index is expressed as a percentage ranging from 0 to 100 that indicates the percentage of CASES in one distribution that would have to be redistributed in order for it to exactly match the other distribution. It has been used as a measure of racial SEGREGATION, with findings showing that roughly 80 to 90 percent of the people in the United States would have to change residence in order for the POPULATION to be racially integrated. It has also been used to measure occupational segregation, especially by gender.

The index is computed by placing the two percentage distributions next to each other and then taking the difference between each corresponding pair of values. Some of the differences will be positive and some will be negative. The sum of the positive or negative differences can be used for the index; either will yield the same numerical value (the negative signs are ignored since the index is always positive). The index can be used in combination with a GOODNESS-OF-FIT test. *See also* CHI-SQUARE.

Reading

Taeuber, Karl E. 1965. "Residential segregation." *Scientific American* 213(2): 42–50.

distance *See* SOCIAL DISTANCE.

distorter variable In the statistical analysis of relationships among variables, a distorter VARIABLE is one which, when controlled, causes the relationship between the independent and dependent variables to change direction, from positive to negative or from negative to positive. In his classic study of suicide, for example, Émile DURKHEIM initially found a positive relationship between being married and committing suicide. This two-variable relationship, however, does not take into account the effects of a third variable – age – which has important relations to both marital status and the tendency to commit suicide. In particular, married people tend to be older than single people and older people are generally more likely to commit suicide.

In looking at people of similar age, Durkheim found that the relationship between marital status and suicide changed direction. It was single people who were more likely to kill themselves. In this case, age is called a distorter variable.

See also CONTROL VARIABLE; DIRECTION OF RELATIONSHIP; VARIABLE.

Reading
Rosenberg, Morris. 1968. *The logic of survey analysis*. New York: Basic Books.

distribution Distribution is a concept having two primary definitions in sociology. In a statistical sense, a distribution is a set of scores such as people's ages and the relative number of times each score occurs. In the United States, for example, the distribution of how adults identify their SOCIAL CLASS position has shifted markedly downward in the second half of the twentieth century. In 1964, 61 percent placed themselves in the middle class and 35 percent in the working class, with the remaining 4 percent split between the upper and lower classes. By comparison, the distribution in 1993 showed only 45 percent putting themselves in the middle class, 45 percent in the working class, 7 percent in the lower class, and 3 percent in the upper class.

In the study of SOCIAL INEQUALITY, distribution is the process of dividing up social rewards and resources and the result of that process. Class systems and other forms of systematic inequality are not static; rather they are ongoing systems of production and distribution that affect not only people's lives but the shape of entire SOCIAL SYSTEMS.

Distributions also figure prominently in statistical analysis through the use of, for example, the NORMAL CURVE DISTRIBUTION and the distribution of CHI-SQUARE.

See also AGE STRUCTURE; CHI-SQUARE; DIFFERENTIATION; DISSIMILARITY, INDEX OF; FREQUENCY DISTRIBUTION; GRAPHICS; SAMPLING DISTRIBUTION STATISTICS; SOCIAL STRUCTURE.

division of labor The division of labor is the range of tasks within a SOCIAL SYSTEM. This can vary from everyone doing the same thing to each person having a specialized ROLE. It has long been an important sociological concept because it is through the division of labor that social life actually takes place and individuals are connected to it.

The concept is used primarily in relation to the study of economic production. In HUNTER-GATHERER SOCIETIES, for example, divisions of labor are relatively simple since the sheer number of tasks to be performed is not very great. By comparison,

INDUSTRIAL SOCIETIES have extremely complex divisions of labor, largely because the ability to produce a vast surplus of food allows most people to pursue a variety of tasks having little to do with survival needs. As first argued by Émile DURKHEIM, such differences in the division of labor profoundly affect what holds societies together. With simple divisions of labor, social COHESION is based primarily on people's similarities to one another and the sharing of a common way of life. With complex divisions of labor, however, cohesion is based on the interdependency that results from specialization. In an ironic sense, what holds us together is our differences.

The division of labor also figures prominently in the study of SOCIAL INEQUALITY. From a Marxist perspective, CAPITALISM uses a complex division of labor to control workers more effectively. Work is divided into a large number of narrowly specialized tasks for which the amount of training and skill is minimal. This enables employers to monitor and control the production process and to replace workers easily, which deprives workers of power in relation to employers. The division of labor is also important in the study of gender, racial, and other forms of social inequality since the kinds of roles people perform greatly affect their share of WEALTH, POWER, and PRESTIGE.

See also GEMEINSCHAFT AND GESELL-SCHAFT; INTERNATIONAL DIVISION OF LABOR; LABOR MARKET; OCCUPATIONAL STRUCTURE; ROLE STRUCTURE.

Reading

Braverman, Harry. 1974. *Labor and monopoly capital.* New York: Monthly Review Press.

Durkheim, Émile. [1893] 1933. *The division of labor in society.* New York: Free Press.

divorce   *See* MARRIAGE AND DIVORCE.

divorced family   *See* FAMILY.

domestic labor   Domestic (from the Latin word for "house") labor is work done primarily to maintain households and the people who live in them. It includes providing food and other necessities, cleaning, mending clothes, caring for children, the sick, and the elderly, shopping for goods and services, and disposing of waste and other discards. From a Marxist perspective, domestic labor is done to produce use value, which means that goods and services produced in households are intended for immediate consumption, not for sale or exchange beyond the household.

In INDUSTRIAL SOCIETIES domestic labor is generally unpaid, undervalued, and relegated to women either in the role of housewife or as paid domestic workers. From both Marxist and feminist perspectives, the gendering of domestic work is a primary way in which male dominance and privilege are realized and enforced. Men's freedom from domestic work, for example, enables them to establish themselves in the cash-based economy, whereas holding women responsible for domestic labor interferes with establishing a financial base independent of their husbands. This in turn promotes wives' vulnerability and dependency in relation to husbands.

Although it is now common to refer to the private world of domestic labor and the public world of political and economic affairs as "separate spheres," this view has been criticized as misleading and inaccurate. To see domestic labor as economically unproductive ignores the fact that it involves the production of real goods and services, from health care to meal preparation, which are also to be found in markets. The separate spheres view also ignores the vital role domestic labor plays in making economic activity possible, by socializing new workers, for example, and by caring for the needs of adult workers.

See also FEMINISM; PRIVATE SPHERE AND PUBLIC SPHERE; VALUE, ECONOMIC.

Reading

Engels, Friedrich. [1891] 1972. *The origin of the family, private property, and the state.* New York: Pathfinder Press.

Hartmann, Heidi I. 1981. "The family as the locus of gender, class, and political struggle: The example of housework." *Signs: Journal of Women in Culture and Society* 6 (spring): 366–94.

Oakley, Ann. 1974. *Woman's work: The housewife, past and present.* New York: Pantheon.

dominant ideology thesis An outgrowth of Marxist thinking, the dominant ideology thesis argues that subordinate classes and minority groups tend to accept their disadvantaged condition because the CULTURE in which they live is largely controlled by dominant groups. Culture is important because it contains the basic ideas that we draw upon in constructing our sense of what is real, important, and expected. The cultures of many class societies, for example, include the belief that hard work and talent are the most important determinants of financial success, and that hard work should be valued for its own sake regardless of how demeaning it may be. The dominant ideology thesis argues that such BELIEFS are widely promoted by educational INSTITUTIONS and the mass media,

all of which are heavily influenced by the UPPER CLASS whose privilege they support. Most members of the upper class, for example, began their lives in privileged circumstances and inherited their WEALTH. This suggests that the deprived circumstances of those below them result not from a lack of talent or unwillingness to work hard but from the fact that a tiny minority of the population controls most of the wealth. The belief in the efficacy and value of hard work benefits dominant classes by obscuring these fundamental points and promoting the idea that SOCIAL INEQUALITY is legitimate.

This thesis is controversial. There is disagreement, for example, over how powerful the upper classes are when it comes to controlling culture, and the degree to which members of subordinate classes can and do develop their own ideas about how the world works that are quite at odds with versions favorable to the upper classes.

See also CLASS CONSCIOUSNESS AND FALSE CONSCIOUSNESS; HEGEMONY; IDEOLOGY; UPPER CLASS.

Reading

Abercrombie, Nicholas, Stephen Hill, and Bryan S. Turner. 1980. *The dominant ideology thesis.* London: Allen and Unwin.

double hermeneutic *See* HERMENEUTICS.

doubling time In DEMOGRAPHY, doubling time is the number of years it will take a POPULATION to double in size at a given rate of annual growth. A population with a 2 percent annual growth rate, for example, will double in just under 35 years and quadruple in just under 70 years. Doubling time is calculated by dividing 69.3 by the growth rate expressed as a percentage. (The constant 69.3 is derived from the formula for exponential growth; it is the natural logarithm of 2 multiplied by 100.) Doubling time is a useful statistic because it dramatizes the enormous potential consequences of what otherwise appear to be low rates of population growth.

See also RATE OF NATURAL INCREASE.

dramaturgical perspective Developed primarily by the symbolic INTERACTIONIST Erving GOFFMAN, the dramaturgical perspective is a method that uses a theatrical metaphor of stage, actors, and audience to observe and analyze the intricacies of social INTERACTION. Everyone is at once actor in relation to others as audience and audience in relation to others as actors. Expectations that apply in each situation constitute a *social script* that actors use to guide or even dictate their performance.

From the dramaturgical perspective, the SELF is made up of the various parts that people play, and a key goal of social actors is to present their various selves in ways that create and sustain particular impressions, especially favorable ones (known as *impression management*). This includes protecting the integrity of performances. Since actors and audiences are mutually dependent on one another, it is in everyone's interest to support and protect the performances of all those involved. This is an effort that brings into play various techniques and devices. When we show signs of embarrassment, for example, it serves to remind others that although we may have failed in some aspect of our performance, we are committed to the ROLE and will try to do better in the future.

One of the more interesting questions raised by the dramaturgical perspective is whether the playing of roles implies a lack of authenticity and honesty in social actors. Goffman's position is that there is nothing inherently unreal about the scripts and parts we play, that they in fact reflect real aspects of our complex selves. Roles are real and authentic parts of who we are, not false masks that cover up some deeper self.

See also ALIGNING AND REALIGNING ACTION; BACKSTAGE AND FRONTSTAGE; FRONT; INTERACTIONIST PERSPECTIVE; STIGMA.

Reading
Brisset, D., and C. Edgley, eds. 1990. *Life as theater: A dramaturgical sourcebook.* New York: Aldine de Gruyter.
Goffman, Erving. 1959. *The presentation of self in everyday life.* New York: Doubleday.
Hare, A. P. 1985. *Social interaction as drama.* Beverly Hills, CA: Sage Publications.

dual consciousness Dual consciousness exists when people hold one set of BELIEFS based on the mainstream CULTURE and a contradictory set of beliefs based on their actual experience. American workers, for example, are often harshly critical of COMMUNISM and anything associated with Marxist critiques of it. At the same time, they may also criticize the excesses of CAPITALISM, the POWER that capitalists have over workers and production, and the hardship and economic EXPLOITATION that result from it. In similar ways, workers may see strikes as badly motivated and largely caused by "trouble makers," and yet participate in strikes when they see their own interests threatened.

See also CLASS CONSCIOUSNESS AND FALSE CONSCIOUSNESS; DOMINANT IDEOLOGY THESIS.

dual economy A dual economy is the system that emerged as industrial CAPITALISM moved away from its formative stage, which consisted primarily of a large number of relatively small firms that competed intensely with one another. As capitalism developed toward more oligopolistic and monopolistic forms, the result has been two economies – monopolistic and competitive – each with distinct types of firms, market mechanisms, and labor markets.

The *monopolistic* (or *core*) economy consists of large, powerful firms whose products or services are in such reliable demand that their position in the market is relatively stable over the long run. Steel, automobiles, chemicals, oil, and pharmaceuticals are all examples of core industries. In contrast, the *competitive* (or *peripheral*) economy consists of firms of varying size whose market position tends to be highly competitive and therefore unstable. Examples include retail sales, airlines, and small suppliers for large core corporations.

The dual economy is sociologically significant in several ways. As capitalism develops, for example, it tends toward domination by the core over the periphery and, with this, an increasing concentration of economic and political POWER. In addition, the advantages enjoyed by workers in the core tend to alienate them from workers in the periphery with the effect of undermining the potential for organizing labor around common interests. Core workers, for example, tend to be better paid, are more likely to be unionized, and enjoy greater job security than do workers in similar occupations in the periphery. As such, they are less likely to identify with the labor problems of other workers.

See also CAPITALISM; LABOR MARKET; MONOPOLY; OLIGOPOLY; STATUS ATTAINMENT AND NEW STRUCTURALISM.

Reading

Averitt, Robert T. 1968. *The dual economy: The dynamics of American industry structure.* New York: Norton.

O'Connor, James. 1973. *The fiscal crisis of the state.* New York: St. Martin's Press.

dual labor market *See* LABOR MARKET.

dummy variable A dummy variable is a VARIABLE with two categories: one for observations that have a particular characteristic and one for those that do not. Dummy variables are usually constructed from the categories of a larger variable, such as marital status. The category "married," for example, becomes a dummy variable with two categories "married" and "not married"; the category "single" becomes a dummy variable with the two categories of "single" and "not single"; and so on. Thus a variable with five categories is transformed into five separate dummy variables. Usually a case is scored "1" if it has that characteristic and scored "0" if it does not. This means that each CASE in a study will score 1 on one dummy variable and 0 on all the rest (a person who is married cannot also be single).

Dummy variables are used when researchers have nominal- or ordinal-scale variables but want to use statistical techniques designed for higher scales, such as multiple REGRESSION ANALYSIS. Since a variable with only two categories has only one interval (between its two scores), it can be treated as an interval scale.

See also DICHOTOMY; SCALE OF MEASUREMENT; REGRESSION ANALYSIS VARIABLE.

Reading

Bohrnstedt, George W., and David Knoke. 1994. *Statistics for social data analysis,* 3rd ed. Itasca, IL: F. E. Peacock.
Suits, Daniel. 1957. "The use of dummy variables in regression equations." *Journal of the American Statistical Association* 52: 548–51.

dyad A dyad is a social relationship involving two participants. The importance of numbers in social INTERACTION is often associated with the German sociologist Georg SIMMEL who noted, for example, that when a dyad becomes a *triad* (with three participants) the possibility of a COALITION emerges and with it, an increased potential for an imbalance of POWER.

Reading

Simmel, Georg. [1908] 1965. "The poor." *Social Problems* 13: 118–40.

dysfunctional consequence *See* FUNCTIONALIST PERSPECTIVE.

E

ecclesia An ecclesia is a type of religious organization whose cultural and structural characteristics set it apart from other forms such as the CHURCH, DENOMINATION, or SECT. The ecclesia is the largest, most formalized, and most powerful of all religious organizations.

Membership is usually ascribed at birth and is nearly universal in the SOCIETY in which it exists. Its POWER STRUCTURE is highly formalized and bureaucratic, and it relies on a trained clergy. RITUAL is highly abstract and includes relatively little display of emotion. In relation to other forms of religious organization, it is highly identified with dominant INSTITUTIONS such as the STATE and ECONOMY; indeed, in some societies the ecclesia is the prevailing political and religious institution.

Examples of ecclesia include the Catholic Church in Italy and Islam in Iran.
See also CULT; RELIGION.

ecological fallacy *See* LEVEL OF ANALYSIS.

ecology Ecology is the study of the relationships through which POPULATIONS of various species affect and are affected by their physical environments. From an ecological perspective, life is organized into *ecosystems*, which consist of all forms of life that live in relation to one another and a particular physical ENVIRONMENT. How that environment is defined depends entirely on the interests of whoever does the defining. It might be as small as a drop of pond water, for example, or as large as a city or country, or the entire universe. In human ecology, ecosystems are always defined in relation to human populations.

Within ecosystems, various populations occupy functional positions known as *niches*. These describe how populations affect and are affected by other participants in the system as well as the system as a whole. Most nonhuman niches are relatively simple. Plants absorb certain nutrients, for example, and give off oxygen. When they die and decompose, they provide nutrients for other living things. Such niches are relatively slow to change since they are for the most part embodied in genetic codes. Human niches, by contrast, are extremely complex because human populations affect ecosystems in so many different and interdependent ways. In addition, CULTURE makes it possible to alter human niches with great speed, especially through the use of new TECHNOLOGY.

In sociology, the ecological perspective is used in a variety of ways. On the smallest level, interactionists may take into account the effects of physical arrangements on patterns of INTERACTION. A classroom arranged in a circle, for example, will promote more discussion than one arranged with rows of chairs all facing front. On a larger level of analysis, ecological sociology is concerned with the effects of physical factors such as climate and topography on the development of SOCIAL SYSTEMS as well as the effects of social systems on the physical environment. INDUSTRIALIZATION and URBANIZATION, for example, are two major social developments that continue to produce environmental consequences that, in turn, affect human societies in complex and often unforeseen ways.

Some sociologists argue that the ecological perspective has the potential to organize much of the basic concerns of sociology. Hints of this can be found in Duncan and Schnore's framework, which is represented by the acronym *POET* (population, organization, environment, and technology). Substantial portions, although certainly not most, of what sociologists study can be framed in terms of these four classes of VARIABLES. Other ecologically minded sociologists have argued that the basic model of ecosystem analysis – that species make use of various inputs from the environment to produce various results – can be applied usefully to social systems as well.

Although the ecological perspective is still not widely used in sociological thinking, its place in the discipline is secured by the simple fact that every social system involves some population of people who participate in it as well as in physical arrangements and environments.

See also CHICAGO SCHOOL; HOMEOSTASIS; MICROECOLOGY; SUCCESSION, ECOLOGICAL; URBAN ECOLOGY.

Reading
Duncan, Otis Dudley. 1961. "From social system to ecosystem." *Sociological Inquiry* 31: 140–49.
——, and L. F. Schnore. 1959. "Cultural, behavioral, and ecological perspectives in the study of social organization." *American Journal of Sociology* 65.
Hawley, Amos H. 1986. *Human ecology: A theoretical essay.* Chicago: University of Chicago Press.
Namboodiri, K. 1988. "Ecological demography: Its place in sociology." *American Sociological Review* 5(4): 619–33.

economic determinism *See* DETERMINISM AND REDUCTIONISM.

economism *See* DETERMINISM AND REDUCTIONISM.

economy An economy is a set of institutional arrangements through which goods and services are produced and distributed in a society. From the time of Karl MARX, Max WEBER, and Émile DURKHEIM, sociologists have had a long and complex interest in economic INSTITUTIONS, especially as these relate to non-economic aspects of social life such as the STATE, EDUCATION, and the FAMILY.

Historically, economies vary along several dimensions, including their complexity, the sophistication of their TECHNOLOGY, their underlying values (COOPERATION and sharing versus EXPLOITATION and COMPETITION, for example), reliance on MARKETS, and, especially in the Marxist tradition, the structure of control over the MEANS OF PRODUCTION and the relation of this to CLASS CONFLICT.

See also DETERMINISM AND REDUCTIONISM; DIVISION OF LABOR; MODE

OF PRODUCTION; POLITICAL ECONOMY; SOCIAL CLASS.

Reading

Durkheim, Émile. [1893] 1933. *The division of labor in society.* New York: Free Press.

Moore, Wilbert. 1955. *Economy and society.* New York: Doubleday.

Swedberg, Richard. 1990. *Economics and sociology.* Princeton: Princeton University Press.

Weber, Max. [1904] 1958. *The Protestant ethic and the spirit of capitalism.* New York: Scribner's.

——. [1921] 1968. *Economy and society.* New York: Bedminster Press.

ecosystem *See* ECOLOGY.

education In every SOCIAL SYSTEM, SOCIALIZATION ensures that new members know how to participate. In simpler systems, such training can be accomplished informally, but in more complex systems such as INDUSTRIAL SOCIETIES the amount of knowledge required is so great and diverse that formal, systematic training is necessary. In sociological usage, the concept of education refers to such training in order to distinguish it from less formal modes of socialization. Schools are the social INSTITUTIONS in which education takes place.

Reading

Chapman, Karen. 1986. *The sociology of schools.* London: Tavistock.

Mulkey, Lynn M. 1993. *Sociology of education.* Fort Worth, TX: Harcourt Brace Jovanovich.

effect, statistical A statistical effect is a difference in the value of one VARIABLE that is associated with a difference related to one or more other variables. People with more years of schooling (a difference in education), for example, tend to have higher incomes (a difference in income); and countries with higher levels of poverty tend to have higher infant mortality rates.

There are two general types of statistical effect: *direct* and *indirect* (see figure). A direct effect does not involve the influence of an additional variable that comes between the two variables. Having upper-class parents, for example, may have a direct effect on the chance of getting a good job (through influence with potential employers). An indirect effect, however, works through other variables. Having upper-class parents may affect aspirations, the development of skills and talents, and access to higher education, all of which may themselves have direct effects on occupational

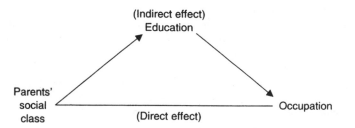

Figure 1 *Diagram showing direct and indirect (through education) effects of parents' social class on children's occupation*

achievement. In this sense, parental class background may have both direct and indirect effects on occupation.

Statistical effects may or may not indicate a CAUSAL relationship between variables. In some cases, the relationship is SPURIOUS rather than causal.

See also DIRECTION OF RELATIONSHIP; INTERVENING VARIABLE; PATH ANALYSIS.

Reading
Rosenberg, Morris. 1968. *The logic of survey analysis.* New York: Basic Books.

efficiency, sampling Sampling efficiency is the amount of accuracy a SAMPLE design provides in relation to sample size. For example, if two sample designs can both be used to estimate a population MEAN with the same degree of accuracy, the smaller of the two samples is the more efficient. Given the great expense of sample surveys in sociological research, efficiency is highly valued and has led to the development of numerous techniques for improving it.

See also STRATIFIED SAMPLE.

Reading
Kalton, G. 1984. *Introduction to survey sampling.* Beverly Hills, CA: Sage Publications.
Kish, Leslie. 1965. *Survey sampling.* New York: Wiley.

egoism Egoism is the tendency of individuals to focus intensely on themselves in isolation from other people and SOCIAL SYSTEMS such as GROUPS, COMMUNITIES, and SOCIETIES. In sociology it is most closely associated with the theory of suicide developed by Émile DURKHEIM, who argued that egoistic suicide results from low social COHESION in groups that stress INDIVIDUALISM, such as

Protestants in comparison with Catholics or Jews. Durkheim's theory has been much criticized, primarily on the grounds that official records of suicide are biased in ways that tend to support the theory. Jack Douglas, for example, argues that groups with high cohesion are more successful at concealing suicides among their members, giving the appearance of a low suicide rate.

Reading
Douglas, Jack. 1967. *The social meanings of suicide.* Princeton: Princeton University Press.
Durkheim, Émile. [1897] 1951. *Suicide.* New York: Free Press.

elaborated speech code *See* SPEECH CODES.

elite An elite is any GROUP or SOCIAL CATEGORY of people in a SOCIAL SYSTEM that occupies a position of privilege or dominance. Examples include the upper class, the top ranks of military hierarchies, senior tenured professors in some universities, chief executive officers of corporations, leaders of organized religion, top party officials in a political OLIGARCHY, or technical experts in social systems that depend on specialized KNOWLEDGE.

The study of elites includes research into how they recruit members, how much an elite can unite around common goals and a clear sense of itself, and how different elites coordinate efforts to advance common interests. In the political systems of representative democracies, for example, POWER is often distributed among a variety of elites who compete with one another over specific issues. They tend to unite, however, over fundamental issues such as the question of whether

101

nonelites should be allowed to enter the competition. Sociologist C. Wright MILLS argued that there exists a power elite among the top echelons of military, economic, and political INSTITUTIONS who move freely from one position of AUTHORITY to another and enjoy other common associations and background characteristics such as schooling and family ties.

This theory is related to Italian sociologist Vilfredo PARETO's concept of CIRCULATION OF ELITES, which refers to the tendency for societies to be ruled by elites regardless of how democratic their political institutions might appear to be. In Britain, for example, top government officials tend to be graduates of a few elite schools. In the United States, members of presidential cabinets tend to be drawn from the upper classes regardless of which political party is in power. While an election may bring with it the appearance of change, the interests of privileged groups are rarely if ever truly threatened by either party. *See also* OLIGARCHY; POWER STRUCTURE; RESIDUES AND DERIVATIONS; UPPER CLASS.

Reading
Mills, C. Wright. 1956. *The power elite.* New York: Oxford University Press.
Pareto, Vilfredo. [1916] 1935. *The mind and society.* London: Cape; New York: Harcourt Brace.

elite pluralism *See* POWER STRUCTURE.

embourgeoisement Embourgeoisement is the process through which the working class becomes more like the MIDDLE CLASS by achieving relatively comfortable levels of financial security and material well-being, especially through the influence of unions. In his analysis of CAPITALISM,

Karl MARX believed that workers would eventually become so deeply oppressed by low wages and other forms of exploitation under capitalism that they would bring about a revolution leading to SOCIALISM. One reason this has not come about is that significant segments of the working class have experienced embourgeoisement. As a result, the working class has been split between a relatively small elite of affluent workers and the vast majority who live closer to the class realities under capitalism that Marx described. This split affects political and other VALUES as well as consumption patterns, which weaken feelings of solidarity among workers and with it the potential for revolutionary thought and action.

There is evidence of embourgeoisement in the United States and some other industrial societies during the decades following World War II. Some have argued that since that time, economic declines – particularly those affecting manufacturing and highly skilled workers – have ended if not reversed that process.
See also CAPITALISM; CLASS CONSCIOUSNESS AND FALSE CONSCIOUSNESS; LIFESTYLE; PROLETARIANIZATION; SOCIAL CLASS.

Reading
Goldthorpe, John H., David Lockwood, F. Bechhofer, and J. Platt. 1969. *The affluent worker in the class structure.* Cambridge, England: Cambridge University Press.

emergent norm theory Emergent norm THEORY is a concept used to explain TOLLECTIVE BEHAVIOR, such as what patterns develop in crowds of strangers. Turner and Killian argue that the NORMS that ultimately govern a situation may not be initially apparent to the participants. Instead, norms may emerge through a process of social INTERACTION in which people look to one another for cues and signs indicating various possibilities of what they might expect. Some of this is based on earlier experience in similar situations, but to some degree the outcome cannot be predicted on that basis alone. Because people tend to feel uncomfortable in situations that lack clear norms, some will tend to seize upon whatever "emerges" first. As Turner and Killian point out, however, this is far from a universal response. Careful observation of crowds reveals a variety of different norms operating at the same time, resulting in various patterns of behavior only some of which conform to emergent norms. In a riot, for example, some may join in the violence, some may play a more passive role, and still others may remain little more than bystanders.

Reading
Turner, Ralph H., and Lewis M. Killian. 1987. *Collective behavior*, 3rd ed. Englewood Cliffs, NJ: Prentice-Hall.

emergent properties Emergent properties is a concept first developed by Émile DURKHEIM as part of the FUNCTIONALIST PERSPECTIVE, which was expanded by Talcott PARSONS. Parsons argued that the properties of SOCIAL SYSTEMS emerge (hence, "emergent properties") from social INTERACTION but cannot be understood simply by studying the individuals who take part in that interaction. In addition, individual experience and behavior can be understood fully only in relation to those properties. This reflects a major assumption in sociology that social life amounts to more than the motivations and characteristics of individual people, for these are shaped by a social context that we can understand in its own right. The whole, in short, is more than the sum of its parts.

See also ATOMISM AND HOLISM; DETERMINISM AND REDUCTIONISM.

Reading
Durkheim, Émile. [1895] 1938. *The rules of the sociological method*. New York: Free Press.
Parsons, Talcott. 1937. *The structure of social action*. New York: McGraw-Hill.

emigration *See* MIGRATION.

empathy *See* MIND.

empire *See* WORLD SYSTEM.

empirical An empirical statement describes observations or research based on actual observations. It is thus distinguished from something based only on theoretical or other abstract thinking processes. "Most well-educated people vote in national elections" is an empirical statement based on actual observations of voting behavior. The question of what we mean by a "well-educated person" is not, however, an empirical question. Instead, the answer is arrived at through abstract reasoning.

Empiricism is a philosophical approach based on the idea that the only valid form of KNOWLEDGE is that which is gathered through the use of the senses. According to this perspective, if something cannot be observed, then it is of no use in trying to explain natural or other phenomena.

See also ABSTRACTED EMPIRICISM; POSITIVISM; REALISM; THEORY.

empirical generalization *See* THEORY.

empiricism   *See* EMPIRICAL.

encounter   In the study of social INTERACTION, an encounter is a face-to-face meeting in which two or more people interact. As such, it is the primary unit and focus of analysis.
See also INTERACTIONIST PERSPECTIVE.
Reading
Goffman, Erving. 1961. *Encounters*. Indianapolis: Bobbs-Merrill.
——. 1967. *Interaction ritual*. New York: Anchor Books.
——. 1971. *Relations in public: Micro-studies of the public order*. New York: Basic Books.

end-of-ideology theory   End-of-ideology theory was first presented in the 1950s by Daniel BELL, Seymour Martin LIPSET, and others who suggested that the political and economic climate of industrial capitalist societies was changing in ways that would put an end to conflict between workers and capitalists. Bell believed, for example, that as INDUSTRIAL SOCIETIES focused more on providing services than on producing goods, styles of management would change as well. Communication skills and relations among people, for example, are more important in service occupations than in industry, where the relation between worker and machine is of paramount importance. As workplaces shift more toward human relations, Bell argued, they will be governed more by negotiation and consensus than by POWER plays and authoritarian attempts to control workers. This will be reflected in the larger political process of society as a whole as workers increasingly participate in party politics and elections, replacing the more confrontational and aggressive methods of the past.

The expansion of welfare systems also plays a part in Bell's argument, with the availability of public assistance in times of economic need taking much of the sting out of management–worker relations and removing a major basis for CLASS CONFLICT.

Although there may have been truth to this thesis in the 1950s, there is little support for it in the decades since. Labor–management conflict, the exploitation of service workers, and civil unrest over racial inequality, immigrant workers, and numerous civil and other wars all suggest that polarization around conservative, liberal, and radical ideologies is far from over. The intensity of the debate does seem to have faded somewhat, however, especially following the collapse of the Soviet Union.
See also POSTINDUSTRIAL SOCIETY.
Reading
Bell, Daniel. 1960. *The end of ideology*. New York: Collins.
Waxman, C. I., ed. 1986. *The end of ideology debate*. New York: Funk and Wagnalls.

endogamy   *See* MARRIAGE RULES.

Enlightenment, Age of   The Age of Enlightenment (or *Age of Reason*) was a period of European history that extended throughout the eighteenth century to the French Revolution. It revolved around the emergence of a way of thinking about the natural world and the relation of human beings and societies to it. This rested on the assumption that understanding based on reason and experience in the form of SCIENCE was superior to that based on religious faith, and made it possible for human beings to both explain and control natural phenomena. The seat of knowledge and truth shifted from God and religious authority to the individual mind, which was now seen as free to think and express itself. This became the basis for INDIVIDUALISM and UTILITARIANISM.

Reason also promised to provide a basis for a science of society that would make it possible to shape and control the social environment, especially through the discovery of fixed laws governing human behavior and SOCIAL CHANGE. As such, it was an era of hope for the future grounded in the cultural BELIEF that progress was both possible and controllable and that SOCIAL PROBLEMS such as SOCIAL OPPRESSION might be solved through DEMOCRACY and representative government.

Among the major contributors to the Enlightenment were the Marquis de Condorcet, Denis Diderot, David Hume, Immanuel Kant, the Baron de MONTESQUIEU, Jean-Jacques Rousseau, Adam SMITH, and Voltaire. *See also* HABERMAS; INDUSTRIAL REVOLUTION; MODERNISM; RATIONALISM; SCOTTISH ENLIGHTENMENT; SOCIAL CONTRACT.

enterprise culture Enterprise culture refers to STATE policies designed to promote INDIVIDUALISM, self-reliance, innovation, profit making, COMPETITION, and initiative in economic activities. It is most closely associated with government policies in Great Britain and the United States during the 1980s, and applies especially to the deregulation and PRIVATIZATION of key industries such as public utilities, airlines, and communications companies. There is disagreement over whether these policies increased economic innovation or efficiency.

entrepreneur In economic life, an entrepreneur is someone who innovates, who invents new products or more effective ways to produce and market them. Joseph Schumpeter argued that entrepreneurs are crucial for economic growth. It is for lack of such people that THIRD WORLD countries lag behind in their development. This view contrasts with DEPENDENCY THEORY which attributes global INEQUALITY to the dominance of core INDUSTRIAL SOCIETIES.

Reading
Schumpeter, Joseph. 1934. *Theory of economic development.* Cambridge, MA: Harvard University Press.

environment In general, an environment is any set of things, forces, or conditions in relation to which something exists or takes place. Sociologists typically distinguish between natural physical environments and social environments. The latter includes both material CULTURE (such as buildings and computers) and the abstract cultural and structural characteristics of SOCIAL SYSTEMS that constrain and shape the terms on which social life is lived. Since sociology's major contribution to understanding human behavior focuses on the influence of factors external to individuals, the existence of various kinds of environments is a fundamental assumption that underlies all sociological work.
See also ECOLOGY; SOCIAL STRUCTURE.

epidemiology Epidemiology is a branch of ECOLOGY that studies how disease and illness and other causes of death and disability (such as accidents) are spread and distributed among POPULATIONS. Epidemiology focuses on both the incidence of conditions (the number of new cases occurring each year), their prevalence (the accumulated sum of cases that exist at a given time in a population regardless of when they first appeared), and environmental and other risk factors that explain such patterns.

A key focus is on how conditions are distributed both geographically and according to social characteristics such as age, gender, race, income, occupation, and marital status. For example, when AIDS was first discovered, cases were concentrated among homosexuals, drug users, and recipients of blood transfusions, a pattern that provided critical clues to its geographic origins and the mechanisms through which it was being transmitted from one person to another. Similarly, maps showing the distribution of various forms of cancer raise questions about living conditions, occupational hazards, and environmental characteristics.

When epidemiology is combined with a sociological perspective, it raises questions about the connection between the life of human beings as biological organisms on the one hand and cultural and structural characteristics of SOCIAL SYSTEMS on the other. The fact that cigarette smoking is more prevalent among the lower and working classes, for example, suggests connections between SOCIAL CLASS systems and the distribution of life-enhancing and self-destructive behaviors. There has been some tendency among epidemiologists to resort to individualistic explanations for such patterns – to see cigarette smoking, for example, as nothing more than a personal choice rather than looking to see how social environments affect patterns of choice. There is, however, great potential to go beyond such narrow individualistic frameworks to develop a truly social epidemiology.

See also DEATH RATE.

Reading

Friedman, Gary D. 1994. *A primer of epidemiology.* New York: McGraw-Hill.

Valanis, Barbara. 1992. *Epidemiology in nursing and health care.* Norwalk, CT: Appleton and Lange.

episodic approach *See* SOCIAL EVOLUTION.

epistemology In philosophy, epistemology is the study of knowing, of the basis for knowing and how it is that people come to know what they know. Sometimes the term is applied only to what is known through scientific means, but it is often used more generally to refer to all types of KNOWLEDGE and knowing.

Epistemology is concerned with various issues about knowing, including the relationship between the knower and the object of knowledge; variations among different types of knowledge (scientific, spiritual, and so on); the nature of truth; the possibility of understanding social life using scientific data alone; the possibility of attaining any kind of valid knowledge about anything at all; the most valid methods for acquiring different kinds of knowledge; and the role of reason and the senses in knowing.

Within sociology there is considerable disagreement about the most appropriate epistemology for sociological work – in other words, the most appropriate way to know about social life. Those who embrace the scientific method, for example, generally do not question whether empirical techniques are adequate for understanding the social world and focus instead on deciding which methods to use. A contrary view is that to understand the underlying basis for social life, sociologists must pay as much attention to what they cannot observe directly as to what they can.

See also IDIOGRAPHIC AND NOMOTHETIC; KNOWLEDGE; METHODOLOGY; OBJECTIVITY; ONTOLOGY; POSITIVISM; POSTMODERNISM; REALISM; SCIENCE; VALIDITY.

Reading
Keat, R., and John Urry. 1975. *Social theory as science*. London: Routledge and Kegan Paul.

equality The concept of equality is used in three ways. In the first sense, people may be seen as sharing a common human essence, and, therefore, an equal social standing under the law, as in the U.S. Constitution's declaration that all people are created equal. In a second sense, SOCIAL SYSTEMS vary in equality of opportunity, the degree to which people have the same freedom to seek education, training, and work, and to otherwise develop and apply themselves to the best of their ability. The third sense refers to equality of outcomes or conditions, the degree to which people have access to similar shares of rewards and resources such as food, shelter, health care, and leisure.

The struggle over SOCIAL INEQUALITY by characteristics such as SOCIAL CLASS, RACE, and GENDER often centers on a disagreement over whether the ultimate goal should be equality of opportunity or equality of outcome.

Reading
Tawney, Richard Henry. 1931. *Equality*. New York: Barnes and Noble.

Turner, Bryan S. 1986. *Equality*. London: Tavistock.

equilibrium In his FUNCTIONALIST PERSPECTIVE on social life, Talcott PARSONS argued that each SOCIETY exists in a state of tension between forces for SOCIAL CHANGE and forces that maintain the status quo. It is a process that always tends toward a balance between the two, a state he called "equilibrium." In contrast with the CONFLICT PERSPECTIVE, functionalism sees equilibrium as a natural tendency rather than a social condition achieved through coercion and OPPRESSION of subordinate groups by the powerful.

See also SUCCESSION.

Reading
Parsons, Talcott. 1951. *The social system*. Glencoe, IL: Free Press.

error One of the most important aspects of any research is estimating the amount of error in a set of data. There are two types of error: random error and bias. If the error is *random*, then all possible patterns of error are equally likely. For example, if we ask respondents to report whether they have been victimized by crime during the past year, we can make two kinds of mistakes: to record that they have been victimized when they have not or that they have not been victimized when in fact they have. If our goal, however, is to estimate the percentage of people who have been victimized, then these errors will not alter the result so long as there are equal numbers of each type. If for each person incorrectly listed as a victim, someone is incorrectly listed as a nonvictim, the two errors will cancel each other out in the long run.

With *bias*, however, error tends to be more systematic, with the result that some patterns of error are more likely than others. This in fact happens to be the case with the reporting of crime. People are far more likely to withhold reports of being victimized than they are to falsely claim victimization. This means that if we rely on reports to police as indicators of the actual incidence of crime, the results will underestimate the amount of crime.

Bias and random error can pose problems for researchers both in the MEASUREMENT process and in using SAMPLES to describe POPULATIONS. Of the two forms of error, bias is far more serious because of its potential for distortion. Random error, on the other hand, tends to cancel itself out in the long run and, if proper research methods are used, can be estimated statistically and thereby taken into account.

See also ESTIMATE; INTERVIEW; MEASUREMENT; REGRESSION ANALYSIS; SAMPLING DISTRIBUTION; SAMPLING ERROR; STANDARD ERROR; STATISTICS.

essentialism Essentialism has two meanings in sociological thinking. In a philosophical sense, essentialism refers to the BELIEF that it is possible to discover and articulate the truth behind natural phenomena, a truth that defines their essence (hence the term "essentialism"). In a related and more general sense, essentialism is the belief that it is possible to establish the truth of any scientific THEORY.

In FEMINISM, essentialism is the belief that GENDER inequality is rooted in biological and psychological differences between women and men (such as a greater male tendency toward aggression) that operate independently of SOCIALIZATION and other influences of SOCIAL SYSTEMS.

See also DECONSTRUCTION; POSTMODERNISM.

Reading
Popper, Karl R. 1963. *Conjectures and refutations*. London and New York: Routledge.
Tong, Rosemarie. 1998. *Feminist thought: A more comprehensive introduction*. Boulder, CO: Westview Press.

estate system *See* FEUDALISM.

estimates Estimates are calculations in sociological research that use SAMPLES to determine the characteristics of POPULATIONS. We might, for example, ask a sample of women if they have ever been sexually harassed at work and then use this information to estimate the percentage of women in the entire population who have experienced harassment. Estimates take one of two basic forms: the *point estimate* and the *confidence interval*. A point estimate uses a single number such as a sample MEAN or percentage as an estimate of the population mean or percentage. If 62 percent of the women in the sample reported being harassed, a point estimate for the population would also be 62 percent. The appeal of point estimates is that they are very precise. The disadvantage is that it is highly unlikely that they are accurate given the random error inherent in even the best sample design. In other words, it is very unlikely that the percentage of women in the population who have been harassed is exactly 62.

The confidence interval is formed by a range of scores with a confidence level attached to it in the form of a probability. With a sample of 1,500 respondents, for example, we could construct a 99 percent confidence interval that would estimate the percentage of women in the population who have been harassed as falling somewhere between 62 percent plus or minus 3 percent, or between 59 and 65 percent. While an interval estimate lacks the precision of a point estimate, we can assume with greater confidence that it accurately reflects the population.

Estimates can be characterized as *biased* or *unbiased*. An estimate is unbiased if it can be shown mathematically that over the long run of making many such estimates the average value for all the estimates combined will equal the population value we are trying to estimate. In other words, if we imagine drawing many different samples and calculating for each the percentage of women who have been harassed, the sample percentage will be an unbiased estimate if the average of all these sample percentages in fact equals the population percentage.

An estimate is biased if the average sample value does not equal the population value. If we use sample STAN-DARD DEVIATIONS, for example, in order to estimate the population standard deviation, the estimate will tend to be too small because samples tend to be more homogeneous – to have less variation – than populations, primarily because they are smaller. Sample standard deviations, then, are biased estimators of population standard deviations.
See also ERROR.

ethicalist religion Ethicalist religion is sometimes considered not to be a religion at all because it relies very little, if at all, on belief in supernatural forces, deities, or other features most often associated with the idea of religion. Instead, ethicalist religion is concerned primarily with developing and applying principles that improve the quality of human life both socially and in relation to the rest of the natural world. Buddhism, for example, focuses a great deal on giving up excessive attachments to the material world as a way of alleviating the suffering of earthly existence. Confucianism emphasizes duty to family and community as ways of achieving a sense of harmony and serenity. Taoism sees the universe itself as bound together by ethical principles that, if followed successfully by humans, also result in a sense of harmony.
See also ANIMISM; RELIGION; THEISTIC RELIGION; TOTEMIC RELIGION.

ethnicism *See* PREJUDICE AND DISCRIMINATION.

ethnicity Ethnicity is a concept referring to a shared CULTURE and way of life, especially as reflected in LANGUAGE, FOLKWAYS, religious and other institutional forms, material culture such as clothing and food, and cultural products such as music, literature, and art. The collection of people who share an ethnicity is often called an ethnic group, although technically the use of "GROUP" is inappropriate in sociological usage because a group is a SOCIAL SYSTEM with some degree of regular interaction among its members. An ethnicity, however, typically includes far too many people for regular interaction. Therefore, a more accurate term would be ethnic COLLECTIVITY or ethnic category.

Ethnicity is sociologically important because it is often a major source of social COHESION and social conflict. Nationalism, for example, often has a strong ethnic base as does the oppression of minorities. Ethnicity is also an important basis for the formation of subcultures in complex societies.

See also COLLECTIVITY; CULTURAL CONTACT; ETHNIC MARKER; FOLKWAYS; MINORITY; SOCIAL CATEGORY.

Reading

van den Berghe, Pierre L. 1981. *The ethnic phenomenon.* New York: Praeger.
Lieberson, Stanley, and M. C. Waters. 1988. *From many strands: Ethnic and racial groups in contemporary America.* New York: Russell Sage Foundation.
Peach, P. 1981. *Ethnic segregation in cities.* London: Croom Helm.

ethnic marker An ethnic marker is any identifiable cultural characteristic such as LANGUAGE or distinctive style of dress that identifies members of a particular ETHNICITY. Markers also include rules that govern marriage and other forms of social connection that affect the BOUNDARIES that separate different people of different ethnicities. Markers are important because as they decline in number and effectiveness, so does the ethnic identity associated with them. For example, as children of immigrants learn the language of their adopted country, their language, customs, and styles of dress may change as well, leading to intermarriage and a loss of ethnic identity.

See also MARRIAGE RULES; SELF.

ethnocentrism In its first sense, ethnocentrism is a blindness to cultural differences, a tendency to think and act as if they do not exist. In its second sense, ethnocentrism refers to the negative judgments that people tend to make about other CULTURES.

As anthropology has made abundantly clear, cultures differ greatly from one another, but there is also considerable variation in the degree to which people are aware of or willing to accept this simple fact. Ethnocentrism can be looked at as the sociological counterpart to the psychological phenomenon of egocentrism. The difference is that instead of individuals defining themselves as the center of the universe in relation to which everything else derives its existence and significance, an entire culture is placed in this exalted position. Like egocentrism, ethnocentrism is a prism through which everything is perceived and interpreted in relation to a single cultural framework to the exclusion of all other possibilities. When people who live in INDUSTRIAL SOCIETIES assume that the entire world shares their appetite for consumer goods and Western-style democratic political INSTITUTIONS and that those who prefer otherwise are therefore "primitive"; when the descendants of white European immigrants now living in the United States assume that it was Columbus, and not Native Americans, who "discovered" North America; when outsiders are regarded, by definition, as "barbarians"; or when "classical" music is defined as only that which originated in Europe, we are witnessing the assumptions, blindness, and judgments inherent in ethnocentrism.

In an important sense, ethnocentrism is not a problem; it is an inherent consequence of living under the influence of any particular culture and the social construction of reality that goes with it. Just as every individual is to some degree egocentric, so too will every SOCIAL SYSTEM to some degree promote a view of itself and the world around it in relation to itself and the reality it has constructed. Like its psychological counterpart, ethnocentrism becomes a problem to the extent that it distorts perceptions of other cultures, especially when it is used ideologically as a basis for SOCIAL OPPRESSION.

See also XENOCENTRISM.

Reading

Sumner, William Graham. 1906. *Folkways*. Boston: Ginn.

ethnography and ethnology An ethnography is a descriptive account of social life and CULTURE in a particular SOCIAL SYSTEM based on detailed observations of what people actually do. It is a research method most closely associated with anthropological studies of tribal societies, but it is also used by sociologists, especially in relation to GROUPS, ORGANIZATIONS, and COMMUNITIES that are part of larger and more complex SOCIETIES such as hospitals, ethnic neighborhoods, urban gangs, or religious CULTS.

Ethnography plays an important part in ethnology, a branch of anthropology that studies how cultures develop historically and compare with other cultures.

See also PARTICIPANT OBSERVATION.

Reading

Gurbrium, Jaber F. 1988. *Analyzing field reality*. Newbury Park, CA: Sage Publications.

Hammersley, Martyn, and Paul Atkinson. 1995. *Ethnography: Principles and practice*. New York: Routledge.

ethnology *See* ETHNOGRAPHY AND ETHNOLOGY.

ethnomethodology As originated by Harold GARFINKEL, ethnomethodology (meaning "people's methods") is the study of how people actually use social INTERACTION to maintain an ongoing sense of reality in a situation. A conversation, for example, is a social process that requires certain things in order for participants to identify it as a conversation and to keep it going as such. People look at one another while talking or listening, for example, nod or murmur to acknowledge their ongoing interest in keeping the conversation going, ask and respond to questions, take turns talking, and so on. If these methods are not used successfully, the conversation breaks down to be replaced by a social situation of a different sort. To gather data, ethnomethodologists rely on conversation analysis and a rigorous set of techniques for systematically observing and recording what actually happens when people interact in everyday, natural settings.

See also ACCOUNT; INDEXICALITY; MACROSOCIOLOGY AND MICROSOCIOLOGY.

Reading

Atkinson, J. Maxwell, and John Heritage, eds. 1984. *Structures of social action: Studies in conversation analysis*. Cambridge, England: Cambridge University Press.

Garfinkel, Harold. 1967. *Studies in ethnomethodology*. Englewood Cliffs, NJ: Prentice-Hall.

Hilbert, R. A. 1990. "Ethnomethodology and the micro-macro order." *American Sociological Review* 55(6): 794–808.

Livingston, E. 1987. *Making sense of ethnomethodology*. London: Routledge and Kegan Paul.

ethology Ethology is the study of nonhuman animal behavior. Its relevance to sociology is that observations of nonhuman species are sometimes used as evidence in support of theories about human behavior, especially those that argue that social life is shaped primarily by biological and genetic forces. Primate studies, for example, have often been used to argue that human social patterns such as male dominance, sexual aggressiveness, and other gendered phenomena are innate rather than products of SOCIAL SYSTEMS. With the advent of feminist analysis, however, much of this research is now controversial and is undergoing considerable challenge and reinterpretation.

In some cases, ethological research has pointed toward the learned nature of much of human behavior. Harlow's famous experiments with monkeys found that unless young females are exposed to adult models they never develop the necessary skills and predispositions to be effective mothers to their own young.

See also FEMINISM; SOCIOLOGY.

Reading
Harlow, H. F., and M. K. Harlow. 1969. "Effects of various mother-infant relationships on rhesus monkey behaviors." In *Determinants of infant behavior*, vol. 4, edited by M. Foss. London: Methuen.
Hinde, R. A. 1982. *Ethology*. Glasgow: Fontana.
Lopreato, Joseph. 1984. *Human nature and biocultural evolution*. Boston: Unwin Hyman.

eufunction *See* FUNCTIONALIST PERSPECTIVE.

eugenics Derived from the Greek *eu* ("well") and *genics* ("produce") – or "produce well" – eugenics is the THEORY and practice of using KNOWLEDGE of genetics and heredity to improve the quality of human POPULATIONS. It is based on the assumption that human qualities such as intellectual ability, talent, and personality are largely inherited. In practice, it focuses primarily on controlling reproductive behavior – especially through sterilization of those deemed less "fit" to reproduced. The term was first coined by Francis Galton in the nineteenth century and was linked to SOCIAL DARWINISM and a widespread eugenics movement in the United States and Great Britain. This model, and especially the high value it places on racial "purity," was later adopted enthusiastically in Nazi Germany during the 1930s and implemented in the Holocaust.

Reading
Galton, Francis. [1869] 1978. *Hereditary genius*. New York: St. Martin's Press.

evaluation research *See* APPLIED SOCIOLOGY.

evolutionary theory *See* SOCIAL EVOLUTION.

exchange, economic Economic exchange takes several different forms that are sociologically significant because of their effects on SOCIAL SYSTEMS and social life. The simplest form of economic exchange is to give one COMMODITY and to receive another (commodity-commodity). This occurs when someone who makes clothing makes a trade with someone who grows vegetables, for example, or when a community supports its school teacher or minister by providing locally produced goods and services such as food, lodging, or health care. The main cultural VALUE involved in such exchanges is to procure what cannot be produced in exchange for what can be and, in doing so, to effect a "fair trade" of equal value.

The introduction of money greatly expands and complicates exchange. With commodity-money-commodity exchange, people produce goods or services, exchange them for money, and then use the money in the marketplace to buy goods or services they do not themselves produce. This is still primarily an exchange between producers designed to expand the range of goods and services available to people.

Money also makes possible money-commodity-money exchange in which people use surplus cash to buy goods that they then sell in exchange for money. Since it would make no sense to end up with as much money as they began with, the point of this form of exchange is to generate PROFIT and is the basis for CAPITAL-ISM. Early capitalists were traders who bought goods in one location and then transported them to another where they could fetch a higher price because the goods were not otherwise available there. Or, goods that stored well (such as grain) were bought and then held on the chance that poor weather or other conditions might create a shortage and thereby increase the price in response to lowered supply. Under advanced capitalism, the capitalist actually controls the production of goods and services and makes a profit by buying materials, workers' LABOR POWER, and so on and then selling the resulting goods and services for more than the cost of production. This is accomplished in large part by controlling labor costs.

Since the point of money-commodity-money exchange is to turn money into still more money, the commodities involved in the exchange can take almost any form

as long as they can be bought and then sold at a profit (indeed, money itself is exchanged as a commodity in international currency markets in which traders speculate on the rising and falling value of various currencies in relation to one another). Because of this, the role of advertising through which the desire for commodities is created and stimulated is particularly important since without such persuasion the commodities might not attract buyers on their own merits.
See also ECONOMY.

Reading
Parry, J., and M. Bloch, eds. 1989. *Money and the morality of exchange.* Cambridge, England: Cambridge University Press.
Simmel, Georg. [1900] 1978. *The philosophy of money.* London: Routledge and Kegan Paul.

exchange theory Exchange theory includes two similar but quite distinct approaches to social INTERACTION and relationships. The first, which is primarily American, views people as rationally trying to get what they need by exchanging valued resources with others. The model usually takes the form of two people interacting, as when spouses exchange love with each other, friends exchange favors, or subordinates in bureaucracies give compliance in return for rewards from superiors. This somewhat narrow approach has been criticized for relying so heavily on economic assumptions of rational calculations of self-interest in social relationships, as if social life were conducted like a MARKET. It has also been criticized for not shedding much light on interactions involving more than two people.

A European version of exchange theory focuses not on pairs of actors but on exchange between individuals and GROUPS or other SOCIAL SYSTEMS as a whole. By participating in a system based on mutual loyalty and sharing, individuals may contribute and derive benefits not from interactions with particular people but from their overall participation in the system. Families often operate in this way, as do many preindustrial, premarket tribal societies. The VALUES are quite different from the first version of exchange theory – sharing, loyalty, and mutual cooperation, for example, rather than calculations of self-interest and maximization of individual gain.

See also GIFT RELATIONSHIP; UTILITARIANISM; COMPETITION AND COOPERATION.

Reading

Blau, Peter M. 1986. *Exchange and power in social life*, rev. ed. New York: Wiley.

Cook, K. S., ed. 1987. *Social exchange theory*. Newbury Park, CA: Sage Publications.

Mauss, Marcel. [1925] 1954. *The gift*. New York: Free Press.

exchange value *See* VALUE, ECONOMIC.

exogamy *See* MARRIAGE RULES.

exogenous variable *See* PATH ANALYSIS.

expectation states theory Expectation states theory is an approach to understanding how people evaluate other people's competence in small task GROUPS and the amount of credibility and influence they give to them as a result. The basic idea is that we evaluate people according to two kinds of criteria, or *status characteristics*. The first are specific skills and abilities that are relevant to the task at

hand, such as prior experience or training with a particular type of problem. The second are diffuse status characteristics – such as GENDER, RACE, EDUCATION, AGE, or physical attractiveness – that encourage people to believe that someone will be superior to others even though the characteristics have no direct bearing on the work of the group. In societies where whiteness is valued over color, for example, and where men are valued over women, white males are often assumed to be more competent as a general condition regardless of their actual abilities in a particular area. This is an example of STATUS GENERALIZATION, in which cultural ideas about the STATUSES of "white" and "male" are generalized to influence a situation where they have no direct bearing on the task of the group.

Judgments based upon status characteristics are used to assess competence and to predict future performance, and are known as *performance expectations*. These are important because they affect how people are treated, the kinds of opportunities they are given, how much influence they have, and how they are evaluated for what they do.

Reading

Berger, Joseph. 1988. "Directions in expectation states research." In *Status generalization: New theory and research*, edited by Murray Webster, Jr., and Martha Foschi. Stanford, CA: Stanford University Press.

Berger, Joseph, and Morris Zelditch, Jr., eds. 1985. *Status, rewards, and influence: How expectations organize behavior*. San Francisco: Jossey-Bass.

experiment An experiment is a scientific research method used to establish cause-and-effect relationships between VARIABLES. In its simplest form, the experiment compares two groups of observations under two conditions that are identical in every respect but one. The *experimental group* is exposed to a condition believed to have some kind of causal effect. The *control group* is not exposed to that condition. If the resulting observations differ, then it can be concluded that the difference is caused by the varying conditions.

Let's assume we have two groups of men. The groups are alike in every way except that one group has been exposed to a pornographic film and the other has not. If we observe changes in the first group's attitudes toward women but no changes in the attitudes of the second group, then we may conclude that the change was due to exposure to the experimental condition, the pornographic film.

In practice, the requirement that the two groups are identical in every way except the experimental condition is impossible to verify since there is no way to account for all the ways people might differ from one another. Experimenters respond to this problem by selecting subjects using a RANDOM SAMPLING design or something close to it. They then assume that over the long run, the only systematic difference between the two groups will be the experimental condition with all other differences being no more than random ERROR that is free of bias.

Experiments suitable for sociological questions tend to be costly and impractical. The method is also limited by the relative artificiality of typical laboratory settings. One solution to this is the *field experiment* in nonlaboratory settings. To test for sex discrimination, for example,

experimenters have conducted studies in which they mailed resumés to potential employers and requested evaluation of the candidates. The resumés were all the same except that half identified candidates as men and half identified them as women. The finding that men received consistently higher ratings supports the conclusion that gender is used as a basis for discrimination.

Although the classic experimental design is rarely used in sociology, a variety of statistical analysis techniques can be used to approximate cause-and-effect analyses.

See also CAUSAL EXPLANATION AND CAUSAL MODEL; ERROR; HAWTHORNE EFFECT; HYPOTHESIS AND HYPOTHESIS TESTING; STATISTICS; VARIABLE.

Reading

Blalock, Hubert M. 1964. *Causal inferences in nonexperimental research.* Chapel Hill: University of North Carolina Press.

Singleton, Royce A., Bruce C. Straits, and Margaret M. Straits. 1998. *Approaches to social research*, 3rd ed. Oxford and New York: Oxford University Press.

experimental effect *See* HAWTHORNE EFFECT.

experimental group *See* EXPERIMENT.

explained variance *See* COVARIANCE.

explanation *See* CAUSAL EXPLANATION AND CAUSAL MODEL.

exploitation Exploitation is a central concept in the study of SOCIAL OPPRESSION, especially from a Marxist perspective. It occurs when one GROUP is able to take for itself what is produced by another group. Slavery, for example, is an exploitative system based on the slaveowner's ownership of the slave and, hence, all that the slave produces. To Karl MARX, CAPITALISM is also an exploitative system based not on ownership of the producers, as in slavery, but of machinery and other MEANS OF PRODUCTION.

The concept of exploitation can be extended to include noneconomic forms, such as the sexual exploitation of women by men under PATRIARCHY. Men's AUTHORITY as husbands, employers, and other authorities, for example, gives them a socially legitimate basis from which to coerce sexual compliance from women. In a larger sense, women's bodies and sexuality are exploited by capitalist advertising and mass media entertainment.
See also COLONIALISM AND IMPERIALISM.

expressive role and task role As developed by Robert F. Bales in his studies of GROUP DYNAMICS, the concepts of expressive and task (or *instrumental*) ROLES describe two ways of participating in social relationships. In GROUPS, for example, expressive leaders pay attention to how well everyone gets along, to managing conflict, soothing hurt feelings, encouraging good humor, and taking care of the countless little things that contribute to good feelings about being in a group. In contrast, task leaders pay more attention to achieving whatever goals are important in the group, whether it be making sure dinner is cooked in a family or meeting the terms of a business contract. As Bales and his colleagues discovered, both expressive and task roles

profoundly affect what goes on in groups and how members are affected, and how well a group achieves its goals.
See also COHESION.

Reading
Bales, Robert F. 1950. *Interaction process analysis: A method for the study of small groups.* Reading, MA: Addison-Wesley.

expulsion Expulsion is a POPULATION measure for controlling people by forcing them to leave a particular territory. Many Native American tribes in the United States, for example, were forcibly removed from their ancestral lands so that whites could exploit and profit from resources such as land and gold. Following the U.S. Civil War, there were calls to solve the "race question" by forcibly sending blacks to Africa.

In this century, the genocide perpetrated by Nazi Germany on Jews and other ethnic groups was initially described as no more than an expulsion from Germany and other occupied countries to Eastern Europe. More recently, entire ethnic groups have been expelled from some African societies as a result of economic pressures, civil war, and other disturbances. In several European countries, most notably France, social movements have been calling for the removal of immigrant populations, most of them nonwhite, in order to ease competition for jobs and other resources.
See also GENOCIDE.

extended family *See* FAMILY.

extraneous variable *See* SPURIOUSNESS.

F

fact *See* SOCIAL FACT.

facticity Facticity is the state of experiencing and thinking of the external world as if it had a concrete reality rather than being largely made up as a product of social life. For example, we tend to experience SOCIAL SYSTEMS such as the FAMILY as solid and "thing-like" even though they are largely abstract ideas – cultural creations – about relationships, expectations, VALUES, and so on. We live unaware of the social origins of the reality we experience and its often arbitrary nature as revealed by comparisons with other SOCIETIES. In short, we tend to assume that the world is, in fact, just what it appears to be as identified and interpreted through culturally defined frameworks. *See also* PHENOMENOLOGY AND PHENOMENOLOGICAL SOCIOLOGY.

Reading

Berger, Peter L., and Thomas Luckman. 1967. *The social construction of reality.* Garden City, NY: Doubleday.

factor analysis In STATISTICS, factor analysis is a technique for replacing a large number of VARIABLES with a smaller number of "factors" that reflect what sets of variables have in common with one another. It was developed by Charles Spearman to identify basic factors that underlie various measures of intelligence. He argued that different measures of mental ability are correlated with one another because they reflect two basic factors: (1) a general intelligence level that affects people's ability to deal with all kinds of problems and (2) intelligence that is specific to certain kinds of problems. Through factor analysis, Spearman tried to reduce a large and unwieldy number of intelligence test results to a few underlying factors that account for most of the variation observed in individual ability.

Factor analysis is most often used in an exploratory way to identify what underlies a set of otherwise loosely related variables. For example, measures of people's ATTITUDES toward social issues such as abortion or race may all reflect an underlying view of the world, such as a tendency toward intolerance of diversity or change. *See also* CLUSTER ANALYSIS.

Reading

Gorsuch, Richard L. 1984. *Factor analysis,* 2nd ed. Hillsdale, NJ: Lawrence Erlbaum.

Lawley, D. N., and A. E. Maxwell. 1971. *Factor analysis as a statistical method.* London: Butterworth.

Spearman, Charles. 1947. *Multiple factor analysis.* Chicago: University of Chicago Press.

false consciousness *See* CLASS CONSCIOUSNESS AND FALSE CONSCIOUSNESS.

falsificationism As developed by the philosopher Karl POPPER, falsificationism is a scientific approach based on the BELIEF that it is impossible to actually prove anything. Instead, science advances only by coming up with HYPOTHESES stated in such a way that it is possible to test them (a practice that Popper believed separates science from nonscience). When a hypothesis is tested, it is either disproved or not disproved, but the inability to disprove it does not make it necessarily true. What is accepted as KNOWLEDGE, then, is a THEORY or finding that, so far, no one has been able to disprove.

Although a great deal of scientific work proceeds in this way, there are key propositions that make science possible and yet are not testable, beginning with the belief that everything has a cause that can be discovered through the scientific method. In addition, whether a hypothesis is considered disproved in practice often depends on judgments that go beyond the results of an empirical test.

See also EMPIRICAL; HYPOTHESIS AND HYPOTHESIS TESTING; POSITIVISM.

Reading

Feyerabend, Paul. 1975. *Against method.* London: New Left Books.

Popper, Karl R. [1934] 1959. *The logic of scientific discovery.* London: Hutchinson.

family As a social INSTITUTION, the family is defined by the social functions it is expected to perform: reproducing and socializing the young, regulating sexual behavior, acting as a major focus of productive work, protecting children and providing emotional comfort and support for adults, and serving as a source of ASCRIBED STATUSES, such as ethnicity and race. Although the shape of family institutions varies enormously from one SOCIETY or historical period to another, basic family functions appear to be quite constant and nearly universal.

There is a difference between the family as an institution and the individual families that exist at any given time in a society. As an institution, the family is an abstract blueprint that describes the organization and activities of families. In many societies, for example, the institution of the family describes a safe, protected environment for children, even though the reality of life in individual families often includes abuse and neglect. Failing to see the gap between ideals and reality has important social consequences. In the United States, for example, many government assistance programs are based on a family model in which parents and children live together, the father is the primary breadwinner, and the mother stays at home to care for the children. In reality, however, only a small portion of U.S. families fit this model.

As SOCIAL SYSTEMS, families vary in their structural characteristics which, in turn, produces great variations in family life. The *nuclear family*, for example, consists of parents and their natural or adopted children living in the same household in the absence of other relatives. This model is most often associated with life in INDUSTRIAL SOCIETIES where geographic and economic mobility go hand in hand: the smaller the family unit, the more easily it can respond to economic opportunities in distant places. The nuclear family is also associated with social isolation and lack of contact with relatives and, as a result, a variety of problems such as role overload. In this respect, the nuclear family model is most often contrasted with the *extended family* – parents, their children, and assorted relatives living in the same household – which is widely perceived as the dominant and somewhat idealized form of family life in nonindustrial societies. But research suggests that historically the nuclear family model rather than the extended has been more the case. Also, even in individualistic societies such as the United States, the nuclear family is more extended than is commonly believed. Although physically separate from extended kin, families maintain regular and frequent ties through visits, letter writing, and telephoning.

The dissolution of families through death and divorce results in three additional structures that have important effects on family life. A *compound* (also known as *melded* or *blended*) *family* has a ROLE STRUCTURE in which at least one parent has been previously married and which includes children from one or both of those marriages. This means that the traditional system of blood relations between parents and children is complicated by one or even two sets of step-relationships. This is sociologically interesting because it can create complex structures in very small GROUPS with much opportunity for conflict. Stepparents, for example, often find themselves competing with the absent natural parent for the affection of the children; or they find themselves feeling excluded from the bond between their spouses and their spouse's natural children.

In some countries where divorce is relatively common, so too is the formation of compound families. It is, for example, one of the most rapidly increasing forms of family structure in the United States where roughly half of all marriages are remarriages for at least one spouse and a sixth of all children live with a stepparent.

Another rapidly expanding type of family system in societies with high divorce rates is the *single-parent family*, which is sociologically most significant for its lack of adult role models of both genders, the potential for strain on the resident parent, and the tendency toward poverty, especially in families headed by women.

Compound and single-parent families are often (although not always) also *divorced families* in that at least some of their members have experienced divorce. As a result, there are complex ties to nonresident parents, children, and former spouses. Some sociologists argue that the divorced family should be recognized as a distinct type of family structure whose complex and often conflicting relationships profoundly affect the nature of family life.

See also HOUSEHOLD; INSTITUTION; KINSHIP; MARRIAGE AND DIVORCE.

Reading

Sussman, Marvin B., and Suzanne K. Steinmetz, eds. 1987. *Handbook of marriage and the family*. New York: Plenum Press.

fascism As it appeared in Europe during the first half of the twentieth century, fascism was an IDEOLOGY and a SOCIAL MOVEMENT, and in Italy and Nazi Germany, a form of STATE. As an ideology, fascism opposed INDIVIDUALISM, LIBERALISM, Marxism, and unfettered CAPITALISM conducted purely for private gain. In their stead, fascism argued for the primacy of the GROUP, especially the NATION-STATE, as the core that defined and provided the basis for social and individual life. The state, often dominated by a charismatic leader seen as the embodiment of national identity, sought control over almost every aspect of social life, from the family to economics, religion, and education. To justify and accomplish these ends, fascist states relied heavily on racist and other supremacist ideologies and made extensive use of the military and police and their potential for surveillance, violence, terrorism, and mass elimination of any opposition. *See also* AUTHORITARIANISM; AUTHORITY; NATION, NATION-STATE AND NATIONALISM.

Reading

Kitchen, Martin. 1976. *Fascism*. London: Macmillan.

Woolf, S. J., ed. 1968. *The nature of fascism*. New York: Random House.

fecundity and fertility Demographers define fecundity as the biological potential for reproduction, and define fertility as the number of children people actually have. Although in theory the concepts apply to both men and women, in practice the focus has been primarily on women. This has been criticized by those who argue that BIRTH RATES cannot be understood without paying attention to men's social and biological roles in reproduction.

In understanding levels and trends of birth rates, the distinction between fertility and fecundity is important because each is affected by different social factors and therefore should not be confused. Indeed, one of the primary interests of DEMOGRAPHY lies in understanding the social factors that keep human fertility far below the potential of its fecundity.

Reading

Bulatao, Rodolfo, and Ronald D. Lee. eds. 1983. *Determinants of fertility in developing countries*. New York: Academic Press.

Coale, Ansley, and Susan C. Watkins, eds. 1988. *The decline of fertility in Europe*. Princeton: Princeton University Press.

Knodel, John. 1988. *Demographic behavior in the past*. Cambridge: Cambridge University Press.

femininity *See* SEX AND GENDER.

feminism Feminism can be defined in two major ways. In the narrowest sense it is a complex set of political IDEOLOGIES used by the women's movement to advance the cause of women's equality and to end sexist theory and the practice of SOCIAL OPPRESSION. In a broader and deeper sense, feminism is a variety of interrelated frameworks used to observe, analyze, and interpret the complex ways in which the social reality of GENDER and gender inequality is constructed, enforced, and manifested from the largest institutional settings to the details of people's daily lives. These frameworks generate THEORIES about psychological, spiritual, and social life and their consequences – from music, literature, and religious ritual to patterns of violence to unequal distributions of income, wealth, and power. They also produce distinct research methodologies that are often at odds with established approaches such as the scientific method. Part of the feminist criticism of standard research practices is that they serve the patriarchal status quo by rendering the experience and perspectives of women largely invisible.

Most feminist thinking and research draws upon one or more of three perspectives: (1) liberal, (2) socialist or Marxist, and (3) radical. Like liberal thinking in general, liberal feminism traces its roots to the period of

European history known as the ENLIGHTENMENT. Its central premise is that a just society results from the free choices of educated, aware – or "enlightened" – people. By extension, liberals argue that social problems arise primarily from ignorance and social constraints on freedom of choice.

From a liberal perspective, gender inequality results primarily from SOCIALIZATION that forces people to grow up with distorted and harmful ideas about males and females and from CULTURAL ideas that restrict people's freedom to freely choose how to live their lives. Liberal solutions typically focus on changing ideas and cultural practices, from rewriting school textbooks to reforming legal codes and outlawing discrimination.

Although liberal feminism is the dominant feminist framework in most INDUSTRIAL SOCIETIES today, it has many critics. In particular, liberal feminism lacks any kind of historical analysis that explains the origins of gender inequality or a sociological analysis that relates it to a larger institutional context. Instead, the liberal feminist approach generally accepts as given the major features of patriarchal societies such as CAPITALISM, militarism, adversarial legal systems, competition, and hierarchy. These larger SOCIAL SYSTEMS are not seen as problematic; the problem is women's lack of free access to positions within them. Thus a liberal feminist would fight to allow women to be military commanders or corporate leaders but would generally not regard war or corporate capitalism themselves as problems in need of feminist analysis.

Unlike liberal feminism, Marxist feminism makes a direct causal connection between capitalism and the patriarchal subordination of women. From this perspective, women are an exploited class in the capitalist MODE OF PRODUCTION, both by their husbands within families and by employers in the paid labor market. Within families, women provide a great deal of labor either free or in return for what amounts to subsistence wages (their husbands provide food, shelter, and so on), a system that some writers liken to slavery. In the paid labor market, women provide cheap labor, especially as part-time workers, and can be exploited because they are regarded primarily as wives and mothers and can thus not command decent wages.

The strongest criticism of Marxist feminism is that it ignores the fact that PATRIARCHY predates capitalism by several thousand years and as such cannot be understood as a product of capitalism. It also ignores the fact that male dominance continues in noncapitalist countries such as China and the former Soviet Union. And as socialist feminists argue, a purely Marxist approach pays too little attention to reproduction as an important form of production in societies.

In either case, the role of capitalism in patriarchy is important, for as the dominant mode of production in the world today, capitalism shapes male dominance in ways that need to be explained as part of a broader understanding of gender inequality. Under traditional patriarchy, for example, men dominate women in part by controlling land and the means of production, especially on family farms. Under industrial capitalism, however, most people own neither productive land nor capital, which means that men must find other ways to assert dominance (such as control over jobs and wages and, with them, family income). Male dominance remains, but in an altered form that also has its effects on men.

From a radical feminist perspective, gender inequality is due neither to ignorance and a lack of freedom nor to capitalism; rather it is the result of the collective efforts of men to dominate, control, and exploit women. From this perspective, the central problem of radical feminist analysis is to understand how the subordination of women is accomplished and sustained, the consequences it produces, and how it might be ended. This includes seeing how men's dominance of major social INSTITUTIONS enables them to shape the world in ways that reinforce their collective dominance. Thus, unlike liberal feminism, radical feminism sees capitalism, militarism, hierarchy, and competition as manifestations of core patriarchal VALUES and BELIEFS and vehicles through which men maintain dominance. Violence against women, compulsory heterosexuality, and the organization of the traditional family are all viewed as ways to ensure male dominance through female subordination to and dependence upon men.

One of the main criticisms of radical feminism is that it is sometimes tied in with ESSENTIALIST thinking, according to which patriarchy and women's oppression are rooted in inherent male tendencies toward domination and aggression.

In addition to the major perspectives, feminism continues to develop a rich variety of approaches to understanding gender inequality. POST-MODERN feminism, for example, raises fundamental issues about how we think about gender and gender inequality, beginning with what we mean when we use words like "women" or "men" to describe people's experience. (Often, for example, when the word "women" is used, the actual referent is women of a particular class or race rather than all women.) Psychoanalytic feminism focuses on how gender emerges as part of psycho-social development, and existentialist feminism builds on the early pioneering work of Simone de BEAUVOIR and her analysis of woman as "other." Ecofeminism argues that patriarchal dynamics shape relations not only among humans, but between humans and the rest of the natural world, to the detriment of both.

As with any way of thinking that involves multiple perspectives, feminist analysis is most powerful when it combines elements of all its various frameworks.

See also PATRIARCHY; SEX AND GENDER.

Reading

hooks, bell. 1984. *Feminist theory: From margin to center*. Boston: South End Press.

Lovell, Terry, ed. 1990. *British feminist thought*. Oxford: Blackwell Publishers.

Tong, Rosemarie. 1998. *Feminist thought: A more comprehensive introduction*. Boulder, CO: Westview Press.

feminization and masculinization

Feminization is a process in which some aspect of social life changes toward an increasing focus on women. An occupation, for example, becomes feminized to the extent that the number of women involved in it grows into a majority. Similarly, poverty is becoming feminized in the United States as women (single mothers and their children in particular) comprise an increasingly large segment of the population of impoverished people.

Masculinization is less common because men are less likely to take over occupations dominated by women, since such occupations are usually regarded as having less cultural VALUE in male-dominated patriarchal societies. A notable exception is found in the healing arts, where the central position of midwives and wise-woman healers was overthrown and suppressed by the male-dominated medical profession several centuries ago.
See also PATRIARCHY.

fertility *See* FECUNDITY AND FERTILITY.

fetishism of commodities In his analysis of CAPITALISM, Karl MARX identified the fetishism of commodities as the tendency to treat COMMODITIES as fetishes, objects with magical properties that give them a life of their own. We act, for example, as though goods and services have a natural VALUE in relation to other goods and services in the marketplace; as though money, gold, and other commodities are by their nature "precious"; as if commodities can pursue and attract one another, as when inflation is explained as a case of "too much money chasing too few commodities." The problem with this kind of thinking is that it tends to obscure the underlying social relationships among people that are the actual source of what we attribute to commodities. We would not have to buy and sell in competitive markets, for example, if we organized economic life in a cooperative way based on sharing and common effort.

Reading
Abercrombie, Nicholas. 1980. *Class, structure, and knowledge.* Oxford: Blackwell Publishers.
Geras, Norman. 1971. "Fetishism in Marx's *Capital.*" *New Left Review* 65: 69–85.

feudalism Feudalism is a political and economic system that prevailed primarily in Europe during the Middle Ages. Feudalism also has been found in various forms at other times in other regions of the world. At its heart, feudalism is a core of social relationships organized around agriculture and control over land. In Europe, land was controlled by militarily powerful lords who enlisted the military support of lesser nobles in return for granting them control over a specified territory. This control included the right to appropriate for themselves a portion of what was produced by the peasants who were tied to the land by tradition and the nobility's monopoly over military hardware and expertise. Peasants were dominated by the local nobility, but they nonetheless had some control over the means and process of production and enjoyed traditional rights to use the land. Each portion of land with its resident peasants and ruling nobles constituted a *manor,* which was a relatively autonomous and self-sufficient SOCIAL SYSTEM.

As a system of STRATIFICATION, the feudal system included several distinct social categories, or *estates,* each of which occupied a position in a rigid hierarchical system that strictly regulated mobility from one estate to another. Each estate had its own set of rules governing appearance and behavior within the estate and was subordinate to the laws of higher estates which, in turn, were generally responsible for providing protection for estates below them. Most feudal systems consisted of three estates – nobility, clergy, and commoners – although during the early stages of CAPITALISM toward the end of the feudal period a fourth estate emerged as urban merchants and craftspeople became more distinguishable from peasants on feudal manors. The towns and their capitalist activity eventually developed to such a degree that they led to the disintegration of feudalism.

See also CAPITALISM; STRATIFICATION AND INEQUALITY.

Reading
Bloch, Marc. 1961. *Feudal society*. London: Routledge and Kegan Paul.
Holton, Robert J. 1985. *The transition from feudalism to capitalism*. London: Macmillan.
Weber, Max. [1921] 1968. *Economy and society*. New York: Bedminster Press.

fictive kin   *See* KINSHIP.

field experiment   *See* EXPERIMENT.

figurational sociology   *See* ELIAS.

folk society   As described by anthropologist Robert Redfield, a folk society is a small, isolated, homogeneous COMMUNITY governed primarily by tradition and a shared commitment to the welfare of the community rather than individual advantage or gain at the expense of others. As an IDEAL TYPE, it was often held up in contrast to urban life, but research suggests that the realities of such communities depart significantly from Redfield's somewhat romantic vision.

See also COHESION; COMMUNITY; GEMEINSCHAFT AND GESELLSCHAFT.

Reading
Redfield, Robert. 1947. "The folk society." *American Journal of Sociology* 52: 293–308.

folkways   As described by William Graham SUMNER, the folkways of a SOCIAL SYSTEM are a set of NORMS governing commonly accepted practices, customs, and habits that make up the fabric of everyday life. Table manners, accepting one's place in line rather than cutting in ahead, showing respect when speaking to people, and wearing appropriate clothing to social gatherings are all among the folkways of a SOCIETY. In comparison with other norms, folkways tend to involve relatively unimportant matters of behavior and appearance and carry SANCTIONS that are correspondingly mild. In addition, there are few restrictions on who may legitimately punish a person who violates folkways. These characteristics distinguish folkways from LAWS and MORES.

Reading
Sumner, William Graham. 1906. *Folkways*. Boston: Ginn.

forager   *See*   HUNTER-GATHERER SOCIETY.

forces of production   *See* MODE OF PRODUCTION.

Fordism   *See* SCIENTIFIC MANAGEMENT.

forecasting   *See* PREDICTION AND PROJECTION.

formal organization   A formal (or *complex*) organization is a SOCIAL SYSTEM organized around specific goals and usually consisting of several interrelated groups or subsystems. Formal organizations are governed by clearly stated, rigidly enforced norms. Corporations, the Catholic Church, court systems, university administrations, and military organizations all have properties of formal organizations.

Bureaucracy is the most complex and highly developed type of formal organization. As the concept was developed by Max WEBER, it refers to an organization in which power is distributed in a rigid HIERARCHY with clear lines of AUTHORITY. The DIVISION OF LABOR is complex, which is to say people engage in narrowly specialized tasks and work under rules and expectations that are clearly defined, typically in writing. Written records are kept and managers specialize in overseeing the system. The accomplishment of organizational goals takes precedence over the welfare of individuals, and impersonal rationality is prized as a basis for making decisions in light of those goals.

Weber believed that the bureaucratic model would spread because it was the most efficient way to handle complex tasks and coordinate complex divisions of labor. While this is true to a degree, as subsequent sociologists have argued, the nature of bureaucracy renders it ineffective if not counterproductive in a variety of ways. The same rigidity that gives bureaucracy its sense of predictability and stability, for example, also makes it difficult for such organizations to deal with unpredictable and radically new situations. It also encourages employees to blindly follow the rules even when this may undermine the organization's goals.

Bureaucracy is perhaps one of the most important social innovations to occur over the past several centuries, as an increasing range of social activity is organized bureaucratically. The growth of bureaucracy has resulted in extreme concentrations of power at ever larger levels of social organization, perhaps best exemplified in modern STATES and TRANSNATIONAL CORPORATIONS. As power concentrates in bureaucracies, these become major sites for SOCIAL CONTROL, SOCIAL OPPRESSION, and conflict.

Within formal organizations people often participate in networks of *informal relations* in which expectations are less rigidly defined and less focused on specific goals. Office friendships, for example (and animosities), often play an important part in the conduct of more formal roles.

See also AUTHORITY; IMPERATIVELY COORDINATED ASSOCIATION; PRIMARY RELATIONSHIP AND SECONDARY RELATIONSHIP; RATIONALIZATION.

Reading

Albrow, Martin. 1970. *Bureaucracy.* London: Macmillan.

Kamenka, Eugene. 1989. *Bureaucracy.* Oxford: Blackwell Publishers.

Rheinstein, M., ed. 1954. *Max Weber on law in economy and society.* Cambridge: Harvard University Press.

Weber, Max. [1922] 1958. "Bureaucracy." to *From Max Weber: Essays in sociology,* edited and translated by Hans H. Gerth and C. Wright Mills. New York: Oxford University Press.

formal sanction *See* SANCTION.

frame, sampling A sampling frame is a list or other representation of a population from which researchers select samples. The simplest kind of frame is a list of every member of a POPULATION from which a SAMPLE is to be drawn. In more complex designs, a frame has several different parts or layers ranging from larger units to smaller units. A frame for sampling factory workers, for example, might consist of a list of factories from which a sample of factories is selected; a list of departments within factories from which a sample of departments is drawn; and finally a list of workers within selected departments from which a sample of workers is drawn. *See also* COMPLEX SAMPLE.

Reading

Kalton, Graham. 1984. *Introduction to survey sampling*. Beverly Hills, CA: Sage Publications.

Kish, Leslie. 1965. *Survey sampling*. New York: Wiley.

Singleton, Royce A., Jr, Bruce C. Straits, and Margaret M. Straits. 1998. *Approaches to social research*, 3rd ed. Oxford and New York: Oxford University Press.

Frankfurt School *See* CRITICAL THEORY.

frequency distribution A frequency distribution is a description of a VARIABLE providing a count of the number of CASES that fall into each of the variable's categories. Consider, for example, the following statement: "It is much better for everyone involved if the man is the achiever outside the home and the woman takes care of the home and family." As measured in the 1993 General Social Survey of the United States adult population, this variable had four categories with the frequencies shown in the accompanying table.

Table 4 Frequency Distribution

Strongly agree	64
Agree	318
Disagree	491
Strongly disagree	181
Don't know	23
Total	$1,077 = n$

Source: James A. Davis and Tom W. Smith, *General Social Surveys, 1972–1993: Cumulative Codebook* (Chicago: National Opinion Research Center, 1993).

The table represents the frequency distribution for the variable, with n denoting the total number of cases in the distribution. Frequency distributions are useful for getting a rough idea of results (we can see, for example, that a majority – 672 out of 1,077 – disagree or strongly disagree), but they are usually converted to other forms – such as percentages – in order to answer sociological questions.

See also CROSS-TABULATION; GRAPHICS; VARIABLE.

frequency polygon *See* GRAPHICS.

frictional unemployment *See* UNEMPLOYMENT AND UNDEREMPLOYMENT.

front In Erving GOFFMAN'S DRAMATURGICAL PERSPECTIVE, a front consists of all the elements people use to create an impression of themselves in the eyes of other people who serve as their audience. This includes physical appearance (clothing, make-up, hairstyle, posture), but it also includes such things as manner of speaking (the use of accents and the choice of vocabulary, for example) and the use of various props such as the type of car driven, the kinds of food served at meals, and so on. Together, all of these elements play a role in the way people present themselves to others which, in turn, profoundly affects the expectations and behavior of others in social INTERACTION.

See also CONSPICUOUS CONSUMPTION; DRAMATURGICAL PERSPECTIVE; ROLE; SELF.

Reading

Goffman, Erving. 1959. *The presentation of self in everyday life*. New York: Doubleday.

front region *See* BACKSTAGE AND FRONTSTAGE.

frontstage *See* BACKSTAGE AND FRONTSTAGE.

frustration-aggression theory Most closely associated with the work of John Dollard and his colleagues, frustration-aggression theory argues that SOCIAL MOVEMENTS occur when frustration leads to collective, often aggressive behavior. According to the THEORY and its later variations, frustration has a variety of sources. It may, for example, result from DEPRIVATION caused by poor economic conditions or SOCIAL OPPRESSION. As Ted Gurr argued, deprivation can in turn take two forms. It can be absolute – when people simply do not have enough to survive – or relative – when people have enough to survive but have less than those around them with whom they make comparisons.

James Davies argued that frustration is likely to occur not when conditions are bad, but when they have been improving for some time and then take a turn for the worse. It is, he believed, when people's expectations for a better life are on the rise that they are most prone to aggressive social behavior if those expectations are then frustrated. This is known as the *J-curve theory* because the pattern of rising and then tumbling fortunes looks like an upsidedown "J."

In general, variations on the frustration-aggression theme have little influence on contemporary sociological approaches to social movements. Researchers have been unable to link social movements with observed frustration levels; some evidence indicates that those who participate in social movements are no more frustrated than those who do not; and the organization and maintenance of social movements requires far more than aroused emotional states. In short, frustration-aggression theories have too little to say about the social causes of social movements.

See also CLASSICAL SOCIAL MOVEMENT THEORY; DEPRIVATION.

Reading

Davies, James C. 1962. "Toward a theory of revolution." *American Sociological Review* 27: 5–18.

Dollard, John, Leonard M. Doob, Neal E. Miller, Orval H. Mowrer, and Robert R. Sears. 1939. *Frustration and aggression.* New Haven: Yale University Press.

Gurr, Ted. R. 1970. *Why men rebel.* Princeton: Princeton University Press.

f-scale *See* AUTHORITARIAN PERSONALITY.

functional consequence *See* FUNCTIONALIST PERSPECTIVE.

functional imperative (also called *functional prerequisite*). As identified by various theorists, functional imperatives or prerequisites range from communication and shared ways of thinking, setting goals, and regulating behavior to adapting to and making effective use of the physical environment. From a FUNCTIONALIST PERSPECTIVE, societies survive and function only if certain tasks are accomplished. Without reproduction and SOCIALIZATION, for example, there would be no supply of new members capable of participating in social life and, as a result, SOCIETIES could not continue to exist.

Criticism of the functionalist perspective often focuses on its reliance on the concepts of imperatives and prerequisites. One problem is that the concepts lend themselves too readily to the misleading idea that societies have needs and are somehow able to act to meet those needs in an intentional way – in other words, that societies are like people. A second problem is the tendency to assume that every characteristic of a society must have some "good" reason for existing that is connected to one or more vital needs of society. This distracts attention from other issues, such as the ability of dominant groups to shape societies in ways that advance their own narrow interests rather than the functioning of societies as a whole.

See also CONFLICT PERSPECTIVE; CONVERGENCE THEORY; FUNCTIONALIST PERSPECTIVE.

Reading

Gouldner, Alvin W. 1979. *The coming crisis of Western sociology*. New York: Avon.

Malinowski, Bronislaw. 1944. *A scientific theory of culture*. Chapel Hill: University of North Carolina Press.

Parsons, T. 1937. *The structure of social action*. New York: McGraw-Hill.

——. 1951. *The social system*. Glencoe, IL: Free Press.

Radcliffe-Brown, A. R. 1952. *Structure and function in primitive society*. Glencoe, IL: Free Press.

functionalist perspective In sociology, the functionalist perspective is traced primarily to the pioneering work of nineteenth-century French sociologist Émile DURKHEIM and, in the twentieth century, to the American sociologist Talcott PARSONS and his students. Its anthropological roots extend to the work of Bronislaw MALINOWSKI and A. R. RADCLIFFE-BROWN. The functionalist perspective focuses on SOCIAL SYSTEMS as a whole, how they operate, how they change, and the social consequences they produce. In evaluating or trying to explain any aspect of a social system or its consequences, functionalism asks several basic questions: How is this aspect related to other aspects of the system? What is its place in the overall operation of the social system? What kinds of consequences result from this? How do these consequences contribute to or interfere with the operation of the system and the realization of the cultural VALUES on which the system is based?

In studying family life, for example, a functionalist will think of the FAMILY as a social system organized around particular cultural values, such as the importance of nurturing and socializing the young, of providing love and protection for family members, of regulating sexual behavior, of passing on the accumulated wealth of the family, and, of course, of perpetuating the family as a social system. Like any social system, a family can have a variety of characteristics which, individually and together, produce consequences both for individual members and, most importantly to the functionalist, for the system as a whole.

Differences in family characteristics produce a variety of consequences for the family as a system. Unless the wife has an independent ability to support herself and her children financially, for example, divorce is likely to plunge the family into poverty, assuming that she has custody of the children as is typically the case. From a functionalist perspective, such consequences are evaluated in terms of their effects on the operation and values of the system. Consequences that interfere with the system and its values are called *dysfunctional* while those that contribute are called *functional* (or, formerly, *eu-functional*). As with divorce, aspects of systems often have both functional and dysfunctional consequences. Divorce often has the dysfunctional consequence of interfering with family members' material needs, but it also can have the functional consequence of providing a solution to destructive conditions such as family violence.

Functionalists also distinguish between *manifest consequences* (or *intended consequences*) that are anticipated and *latent consequences* (or *unintended consequences*) that are not. A manifest consequence of the close-knit nuclear family model, for example, is that it may enhance emotional intimacy, interdependency, and support, especially between spouses. A latent consequence is that by isolating the family from KINSHIP support networks, the emotional burdens placed on each spouse are greatly increased and this can lead to tension, conflict, and violence. Isolation has the further effect of making what goes on within the family less visible and, therefore, less subject to SOCIAL CONTROL. This also may make violence and abuse more likely to occur.

Sociological functionalism is closely related to the *structural-functionalist approach* in anthropology, which tries to explain the various social forms found in tribal societies in terms of their contributions to social cohesion. This perspective has been criticized for paying too little attention to social conflict and change and for a tendency to assume that every aspect of social systems must in some way be connected to the "needs" or "requisites" of that system such as social stability and cohesion or

defense against external threats. But this, especially today, reflects a relatively narrow view of functionalism's potential to enhance sociological thinking. The enduring contribution of functionalism – and of Durkheim – is a focus on social systems and how they operate, which enables us to see how even the most undesirable aspects of social life – such as war, racism, sexism, and other forms of oppression – are bound up with otherwise "normal" functioning of societies and their institutions. Such insights are crucial, especially for those interested in bringing about social change.

See also COHESION; CONFLICT PERSPECTIVE; ECOLOGY; FUNCTIONAL IMPERATIVE; POPULATION; SOCIAL ORDER; SOCIAL STRUCTURE; THEORETICAL PERSPECTIVE.

Reading

Dahrendorf, Ralf. 1958. "Out of utopia: Toward a reorientation of sociological analysis." *American Journal of Sociology* 63: 115–27.

Durkheim, Émile. [1893] 1933. *The division of labor in society.* New York: Free Press.

——. [1895] 1938. *The rules of the sociological method.* New York: Free Press.

Gouldner, Alvin W. 1970. *The coming crisis of Western sociology.* New York: Avon.

Parsons, Talcott. 1937. *The structure of social action.* New York: McGraw-Hill.

——. 1951. *The social system.* Glencoe, IL: Free Press.

functional prerequisite *See* FUNCTIONAL IMPERATIVE.

fundamentalism Fundamentalism is a religious movement that emphasizes the absolute truth of essential – or "fundamental" – aspects of faith, especially those rooted in sacred texts such as the Christian

Bible or the Islamic Koran. Christian fundamentalists, for example, believe the Bible to be the word of God, whose accounts – such as the swallowing of Jonah by a whale or the parting of the Red Sea – are literally true rather than being metaphorical or allegorical.

Fundamentalism is sociologically important not only because of its unique place among religions, but because it easily extends itself into the political realm. In both the Middle East (in Iran, for example) and the United States. religious fundamentalism plays an important part in conservative political movements and NATIONALISM.

See also MILLENARIANISM; RELIGION.

Reading

Marsden, George M. 1980. *Fundamentalism and American culture*. New York: Oxford University Press.

Mortimer, Edward. 1982. *Faith and power: The politics of Islam*. London: Faber and Faber.

G

game theory *See* RATIONAL CHOICE THEORY.

Geisteswissenschaften **and** *Naturwissenschaften* *Geisteswissenschaften* and *Naturwissenschaften* are German words which refer, respectively, to the social, moral, or spiritual SCIENCES on the one hand and the natural or physical sciences on the other. The terms are used to distinguish two ways of knowing that involve not only different content, but, by necessity, different METHODOLOGY. They emerged as part of a debate over the question of whether and how the two modes of inquiry are separate and distinct. Max WEBER, for example, argued that it is impossible to understand human behavior without knowing something about the meaning people attach to it. No such understanding, however, is necessary to make sense of the phenomena typically studied in physics, chemistry, and other natural sciences.

See also DILTHEY; HERMENEUTICS; IDIOGRAPHIC AND NOMOTHETIC; INTERACTION.

Reading
Outhwaite, William. 1975. *Understanding social life*. London: Allen and Unwin.

gemeinschaft and gesellschaft
According to the turn-of-the-century German sociologist Ferdinand TÖNNIES, relationships in SOCIAL SYSTEMS vary along a continuum anchored by gemeinschaft relations at one end and gesellschaft relations at the other. Gemeinschaft (or "community") relations are based on a relatively homogeneous CULTURE and tend to be intimate, informal, cooperative, and imbued with a sense of moral obligation to the GROUP most often associated with KINSHIP ties. Such relationships are typical of HUNTERGATHERER, HORTICULTURAL, and other relatively small preindustrial societies.

In contrast, gesellschaft relations tend to be formal, goal-oriented, heterogeneous, and based on individual self-interest, competition, and a complex DIVISION OF LABOR. These are the kinds of relationships found most often in advanced AGRARIAN and INDUSTRIAL societies. A major theme in sociological analysis has been the dramatic impact of INDUSTRIALIZATION on such relationships, especially on the level of SOCIETIES and COMMUNITIES.

See also COHESION; PRIMARY RELATIONSHIP AND SECONDARY RELATIONSHIP.

Reading
Tönnies, Ferdinand. [1887] 1963. *Community and society*. New York: Harper.

gender and gender role *See* SEX AND GENDER.

general fertility rate *See* BIRTH RATE.

generalization   *See* STEREOTYPE.

generalized other   *See* OTHER.

generation   In its most narrow sense, a generation is a collection of people who occupy the same position in a KINSHIP system. All the grandchildren of a particular set of grandparents, for example, would belong to the same generation within that family. Demographers use this approach in defining a generation as the number of years between the birth of one set of people and the birth of their children. This is known more technically as the *mean length of generation*, calculated as the average age of mothers when they give birth to their first daughter. Numerical values for mean length of generation vary in a fairly narrow range around 29 years.

In a broader and less precise sense, a generation is a collection of people born at roughly the same time, such as those born during the Great Depression or the 1980s. The problem with this usage is the "roughly" in the preceding sentence, for the definition of where a generation begins and leaves off is completely arbitrary. We could, for example, define those born during the 1940s as a generation, but we could just as easily draw the line around the period from 1948 to 1956. One common way out of this is to define generations in terms of significant events and historical periods such as those born during the Depression or the period following World War II.

Sociologically, generation is an important concept in the study of SOCIAL CHANGE, for each new generation experiences and interprets its SOCIETY and its INSTITUTIONS in

slightly different ways. This, in turn, acts as a continuing source of change. *See also* AGE CATEGORY; COHORT.

Reading
Eisenstadt, Shmuel N. 1956. *From generation to generation.* New York: Free Press.
Mannheim, Karl. 1952. *Essays on the sociology of knowledge.* London: Routledge and Kegan Paul.
Schuman, Howard, and J. Scott. 1989. "Generations and collective memories." *American Sociological Review* 54(3): 359–81.

genocide   Genocide is the systematic attempt to kill all members of a particular SOCIAL CATEGORY, usually defined by characteristics such as race, ethnicity, religion, or nationality. The Holocaust perpetrated by Nazi Germany on the Jews of Europe, the destruction of Native American tribes in the United States, the Turkish massacre of more than a million Armenians between 1917 and 1919, and the mass killings in Cambodia in the 1970s and Rwanda and the former Yugoslavia in the 1990s are all examples of genocidal population policies designed to further the interests of social oppression, the accumulation of wealth and power, and other collective interests.
See also EXPULSION; SOCIAL OPPRESSION.

Reading
Chalk, F., and K. Jonassohn. 1990. *The history and sociology of genocide.* New Haven: Yale University Press.
Kuper, Leo. 1989. *The roots of evil: The origins of genocide and other group violence.* Cambridge, England: Cambridge University Press.

gentrification   Gentrification (or *urban recycling*) is a process of COMMUNITY change through which old, dilapidated housing is bought, refurbished, and then either inhabited by the owners or rented or sold for a profit. It is socially significant because it often displaces the original residents who tend to be lower- or working-class and replaces them with middle- and upper-middle-class residents who can afford to pay the higher price that the property now commands. It is a particularly acute problem in large U.S. cities where there is a chronic shortage of affordable housing.

See also SOCIAL CLASS.

Reading
Zukin, S. 1987. "Gentrification: Culture and capital in the urban core." *Annual Review of Sociology* 13: 129–47.

geography In relation to sociology, geography is the study of the physical features of the earth as these affect and are affected by SOCIETIES and other SOCIAL SYSTEMS. In the simplest sense, geography is about variations in social life from one place to another. Some argue for a causal relation between geography and social life, saying that factors such as terrain and weather affect the characteristics of social systems. Anthropologist Marvin Harris, for example, argues that the Hindu cultural taboo on eating cattle is based on a combination of an agricultural system that relies on cattle as a major resource and a climate of recurring droughts and famine during which eating cattle as a short-run solution to hunger would have disastrous long-term consequences. This aspect of the Hindu religion, Harris argues, results from a complex interplay of geographical, economic, and cultural elements.

The relevance of geography to social life has led to frequent pairings with various social sciences, resulting in cultural geography, political geography, and economic geography.

See also CULTURAL MATERIALISM; CULTURE.

Reading
Harris, Marvin. 1974. *Cows, pigs, wars, and witches.* New York: Random House.
———. 1977. *Cannibals and kings: the origins of cultures.* New York: Random House.
———. 1985. *Riddles of food and culture.* New York: Simon and Schuster.

gerontocracy A gerontocracy is a SOCIAL SYSTEM dominated by elderly people in positions of AUTHORITY, especially political. Most national leaders are elderly, for example, as are most of those in the highest positions of major social INSTITUTIONS such as churches, universities, and courts.

That powerful people tend to be elderly does not mean that the elderly are particularly powerful as a whole; nor does it mean that the institutions dominated by elderly leaders are run in ways that tend to favor the elderly and their interests. Indeed, most elderly people in INDUSTRIAL SOCIETIES suffer a decline in both authority and standards of living when they retire from paid employment.

See also AGING; GERONTOLOGY.

gerontology Gerontology is the study of aging as a biological, psychological, and social process, especially as it results in problems for elderly people. Social gerontology is concerned with a variety of issues, including cultural definitions of "old age," the experience of aging as it varies cross-culturally and historically, the decline in social STATUS and financial well-being experienced by the elderly in many societies, and the connection between biological aging on the one hand and how age is perceived, interpreted, and treated in SOCIAL SYSTEMS on the other. Interest in social gerontology has grown significantly in recent decades as the POPULATIONS of INDUSTRIAL SOCIETIES include increasingly large proportions of elderly people. In the United States, for example, centenarians are the most rapidly growing age category.

See also AGEISM; AGE STRUCTURE; AGING; GERONTOCRACY.

Reading
Binstock, Robert H., and Linda K. George, eds. 1990. *Handbook of aging and the social sciences*, 3rd ed. New York: Academic Press.

gesellschaft *See* GEMEINSCHAFT AND GESELLSCHAFT.

gesture A gesture is a body movement that has symbolic significance in a particular CULTURE. Hand salutes, nodding or shaking of the head, genuflections, winks, smiles, bows, curtsies, and fingers snapped to summon a waiter all have symbolic significance in many cultures. As with LANGUAGE, the same movement can have different meanings in different situations. A raised hand, for example, can signify a vote, a wave goodbye or hello, a salute, or a request for recognition and permission to speak. If the fist is clenched, the gesture can also be used to signify defiance. The sign languages used by the hearing impaired are unique combinations of gestures having the complexity of expression usually associated with spoken and written language.

See also SYMBOL.

ghetto *See* SEGREGATION AND INTEGRATION.

gift relationship A gift relationship is created through acts of giving and receiving. If someone does you a favor, for example, a relationship is created through which you will probably feel some obligation to do a favor in return.

Gift relationships are sociologically important because of their contribution to social COHESION. A sense of COMMUNITY, for example, is enhanced by people's willingness to help one another – to give and receive services or material aid in the form of food and clothing in times of hardship. In similar ways, family solidarity is based to some degree on a complex pattern of giving and receiving, first flowing primarily from adults to children and then, when children become adults themselves, from adult children to their elderly parents. In premarket societies in which cash payments play an insignificant role, a great deal of social exchange is based on variations of the gift relationship. In the colonial period of U.S. history, for example, farmers typically helped one another with seasonal tasks such as corn-husking, often turning such events into social gatherings that included food and dance. As the MARKET economy grew, however, farmers increasingly hired workers to perform such tasks in exchange for cash wages, and the social cohesion that had been grounded in the gift relationship weakened and all but disappeared.

See also EXCHANGE THEORY; POTLATCH; RECIPROCITY.

Reading
Mauss, Marcel. [1925] 1954. *The gift*. New York: Free Press.

Titmuss, Richard M. 1971. *The gift relationship*. New York: Pantheon.

Gini index *See* LORENZ CURVE.

global economy *See* WORLD SYSTEM.

globalization Globalization is a process in which social life within SOCIETIES is increasingly affected by international influences based on everything from political and trade ties to shared music, clothing styles, and mass media.

Perhaps the most powerful form of globalization is economic, in which planning and control expand from a relatively narrow focus – such as a single firm doing business on a regional or national basis – to a broad global focus in which the entire world serves as a source of labor, raw materials, and MARKETS. When business is conducted on a local level, for example, problems of dealing with workers, obtaining raw materials and other goods, transportation, and selling the final product all take place within the same social framework. In a globalized economy, however, TRANSNATIONAL CORPORATIONS operate in many different countries at once and exploit variations in local conditions for their own advantage. If workers in a more affluent INDUSTRIAL SOCIETY such as Britain or the United States, for example, go on strike in order to improve pay or working conditions, a transnational corporation can simply shift work to another country where workers are more compliant and have lower expectations. In service industries such as banking and insurance, this can be accomplished simply by transmitting work from one computer to another.

Economic globalization is important not only because it complicates economic relationships but because it further concentrates economic POWER and weakens the position of working people under industrial CAPITALISM. *See also* DEPENDENCY THEORY; WORLD SYSTEM.

Reading
Worsley, Peter. 1984. *The three worlds: Culture and world development*. London: Weidenfeld and Nicolson.

goodness-of-fit test *See* CHI-SQUARE.

government *See* STATE.

grand theory *See* ABSTRACTED EMPIRICISM; THEORY.

graphics Graphics are visual displays used by sociologists to present DATA. For example, nominal- and ordinal-scale VARIABLES such as race, religious affiliation, or educational attainment, can be presented on a *bar graph*, which uses vertical or horizontal bars to indicate the percentage or number of cases in each category, as shown in figure 2. Sometimes the area of the bar rather than its height is used to indicate the PERCENTAGE or number of CASES.

A variation on the bar graph is the *histogram*, shown in figure 3, which displays DISTRIBUTIONS for interval- and ratio-scale variables such as education, income, or age. The difference can be seen in the way the bars are separated in the bar graph (reflecting the fact that each bar represents a distinct SOCIAL CATEGORY such as race) and joined in the histogram (reflecting the continuous nature of such variables). If the midpoints at the top of each bar are joined by a line, the result is a *frequency polygon* shown in figure 3. Cumulative percentages or frequencies are displayed

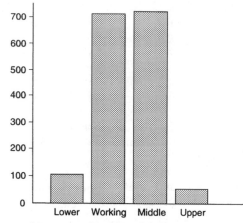

If you were asked to use one of four names for your social class, which would you say you belong in: the lower class, the working class, the middle class, or the upper class?

Figure 2 *Bar graph showing the number of survey respondents identifying with lower, working, middle or upper classes. Source*: General Social Survey (1993). Analysed from raw data.

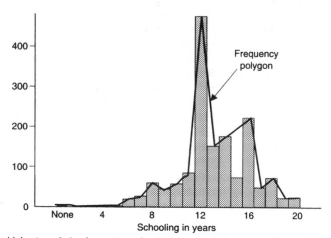
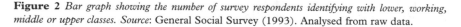

What is the highest grade in elementary school, high school, or college, that you finished and got credit for?

Figure 3 *Histogram and frequency polygon for distribution of years of schooling. Source*: General Social Survey (1993). Analysed from raw data.

by the *ogive* in figure 4, which for each score along the horizontal axis shows the percentage or number of cases that have that score or less.

One of the more ingenious graphic techniques is the *stem and leaf display*, which shows not only the distribution of scores but each individual score, as well. The first digit of each score is represented on the vertical axis, and the second digit of each score is shown on the rows extended out to

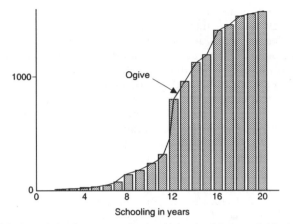

What is the highest grade in elementary school or high school that you finished and got credit for?

Figure 4 *Ogive showing cumulative distribution for years of schooling*

```
0
1    9
2    56799
3    3444555678888899999
4    011112222333444455555667777788889999
5    00001111112222223333333444444455555556789
6    01
7
8
9
```

Figure 5 *Hypothetical stem and leaf display for distribution of age at menopause for 100 women*

the right. Figure 5 shows that of 100 women, one experienced menopause at age 19 (second row), and five experienced it during their twenties (at ages 25, 26, 27, 28, and 29). The beauty of stem and leaf displays is the amount of information they display, from the quick picture conveyed by bar graphs and histograms to the frequency of each score.

All graphic displays must be constructed and interpreted with care because decisions about how they are drawn can have dramatic effects on how they are interpreted. If the vertical and horizontal scales are drawn out of proportion to each other, for example, trends over time and differences between categories can appear to be greater or less than they actually are.

Reading

Tufte, Edward R. 1982. *The visual display of quantitative information*. Cheshire, CT: Graphics Press.

gross reproduction rate *See* BIRTH RATE.

grounded theory A grounded THEORY is based on observations of the real world rather than solely on abstract reasoning. In a sense, it is impossible to construct sociological theory without some reference to the real world, which means that all theory is grounded to some degree. The concept of grounded theory arose, however, as a critical response to theory that seems to pay relatively little attention to real-world observation. In contrast, the formulation of grounded theory is more a process of discovery that begins with extensive observation from which theory emerges.

See also ABSTRACTED EMPIRICISM.

Reading

Glaser, Barney G., and Anselm L. Strauss. 1967. *The discovery of grounded theory.* Chicago: Aldine; London: Weidenfeld and Nicolson.

Glaser, Barney G., ed. 1995. *Grounded theory: 1984–1994.* Mill Valley, CA: Sociology Press.

group A group is a SOCIAL SYSTEM involving regular INTERACTION among members and a common group identity. This means that groups have a sense of "we-ness" that enables members to identify themselves as belonging to a distinct entity. A football team, for example, is a group because of the regular interactions among members – from playing together during games to socializing at other times – and a shared sense of identity that distinguishes them from other teams and from those not involved in football. Recognition that the group exists may or may not be shared by those outside the group.

Just how much interaction and we-ness there is will vary from one group to another, which means that it is not always clear whether a particular social system has enough of either quality to qualify as a group. One way around this problem is to avoid thinking of "group" as a distinct category into which every system does or does not fall, and think instead of social systems as having varying degrees of "group-ness," ranging from the intense involvement and strong identity normally associated with families, a neighborhood association, or close-knit circle of friends (all of which can be thought of as groups) to a collection of strangers riding the same city bus together, which is not a group at all. Groups also vary in how often and extensively members interact, how long the group survives, and the reasons that people join and participate.

One of the most important consequences of a group's sense of shared identity is that members tend to see one another as "insiders" and non-members as "outsiders," a phenomenon described by William Graham SUMNER as *in-group* and *out-group*. Sumner argued that such distinctions always lead to hostility across group BOUNDARIES – from tribal warfare to the kind of heated feelings that often accompany athletic contests, especially among fans. But there is abundant evidence from everyday life that while social conflict often involves opposing groups, this does not mean that feelings of loyalty that members often develop toward their own groups inevitably create hostile ATTITUDES toward outsiders.

The group is an important sociological concept because groups play such a complex and important part in social life. Group membership, for example, is an important part of an individual's SOCIAL IDENTITY. As such, the group is a key agent of SOCIAL CONTROL over individuals, for it is in groups that social pressures toward CONFORMITY can be most directly applied, especially when those who deviate risk their membership as a result.

Groups are also important because of the social consequences they produce. It is in groups that many of the most important social activities take place, from the SOCIALIZATION and care of children in families to the production of goods, religious worship, formal education, SOCIAL MOVEMENTS, scientific research, politics, and the making of war. Attention to how groups work is thus essential for a full understanding of social life.

See also AGGREGATE; COLLECTIVITY; GROUP DYNAMICS; GROUPTHINK; FORMAL ORGANIZATION; PRIMARY RELATIONSHIP AND SECONDARY RELATIONSHIP; REFERENCE GROUP; SOCIAL CATEGORY.

Reading

Bales, Robert F. 1950. *Interaction process analysis: A method for the study of small groups.* Reading, MA: Addison-Wesley.

Cartwright, Dorwin, and Alvin Zander, eds. 1968. *Group dynamics: Research and theory,* 3rd ed. New York: Harper and Row.

Olmstead, Michael, and Paul A. Hare. 1978. *The small group.* 2nd ed. New York: Random House.

Sumner, William Graham. 1906. *Folkways.* Boston: Ginn.

group dynamics Group dynamics refers to what actually happens as people interact with one another. The concept is important because it calls attention to the difference between what happens and what might be expected to happen given the group's CULTURE and STRUCTURE. A group might have a POWER STRUCTURE, for example, that grants AUTHORITY to certain members over others. In practice, however, several otherwise less powerful members might form a COALITION on a particular issue and temporarily shift power away from those who hold formal authority. Just how this is accomplished and how it affects overall group functioning are key questions in the study of group dynamics.

See also ROLE; INTERACTION.

Reading

Bales, Robert F., and Stephen P. Cohen. 1979. *SYMLOG: A system for the multiple-level observation of groups.* New York: Free Press.

Cartwright, Dorwin, and Alvin Wander, eds. 1968. *Group dynamics: Research and theory,* 3rd ed. New York: Harper and Row.

Hare, Paul A. 1976. *Handbook of small group research,* 2nd ed. New York: Free Press.

grouped data Grouped data are facts that are displayed in a format such as a TABLE in which categories of a VARIABLE are combined or collapsed to produce a smaller number of categories. The table below, for example, shows how the variable "age at marriage" might be presented with grouped categories.

Age at Marriage
Less than 15
15–18
19–20
21–24
25–29
30 or older

The advantage of grouping data is that the resulting display takes up less space and is easier to read at a glance. The risk is that by combining categories (such as lumping all those 30 and older together) important differences may be obscured (those who marry at age 60, for example, will differ in significant ways from those who marry at age 30).

group marriage *See* MARRIAGE RULES.

groupthink First developed by Irving Janis, groupthink is a process through which the desire for consensus in GROUPS can lead to poor decisions. Rather than object to poor decisions and risk losing a sense of group solidarity, members may remain silent and, thereby, lend their support.
See also GROUP DYNAMICS/PROCESS.
Reading
Janis, Irving L. 1982. *Victims of groupthink.* Boston: Houghton-Mifflin.

guild Existing prior to and during the early stages of INDUSTRIALIZATION, a guild is an association formed by craftspeople and artisans as a way to pass on KNOWLEDGE, provide mutual support, set and enforce standards, and control who is allowed to practice the craft. Guilds often held considerable POWER in COMMUNITIES and guild membership was a basis for privilege.
Reading
Thrupp, Sylvia L. 1963. "The gilds." In *The Cambridge economic history of Europe from the decline of the Roman empire,* vol. 3, 230–80. Cambridge, England: Cambridge University Press.

Guttman scale *See* ATTITUDE SCALE; SOCIAL DISTANCE.

gynocentrism *See* MATRIARCHY.

gynocracy *See* MATRIARCHY.

H

Hawthorne effect The Hawthorne effect occurs when subjects' awareness that they are participating in an EXPERIMENT affects their behavior and, hence, the results of an experiment. It is named after the Hawthorne plant of the Western Electric Company where it was first identified by sociologist Elton Mayo and his colleagues researching the effects of work conditions on productivity between 1927 and 1932. They found that no matter what they did – changing lighting, for example, or the frequency of coffee breaks – productivity increased. This led researchers to conclude that the attention paid to the workers by the experimenters had an effect of its own on subjects' behavior. Since then, such experimental effects have come to be known as Hawthorne effects.

See also ERROR.

Reading

Roethlisberger, Fritz J., and William J. Dickson. 1939. *Management and the worker*. Cambridge, MA: Harvard University Press.

Rose, M. 1988. *Industrial behavior*, 2nd ed. Harmondsworth, England: Penguin.

hegemonic masculinity *See* SEX AND GENDER.

hegemony As developed by Italian Marxist Antonio GRAMSCI, hegemony is a concept referring to a particular form of dominance in which a RULING CLASS legitimates its position and secures the acceptance if not outright support of those below it. To some degree, all dominance is based on coercion and the potential to use force; but this kind of POWER is relatively unstable. For dominance to be stable, the ruling class must create and sustain widely accepted ways of thinking about the world that define their dominance as reasonable, fair, and in the best interests of SOCIETY as a whole.

Socialist societies, for example, have until recently rested in part on the assumption that the political ELITE represents and acts in the best interests of the working class. Thus criticism of the elite was defined as an attack on society itself, and therefore was unlikely to be tolerated. In similar ways, capitalist CULTURE includes the belief that private property is sacrosanct, that what is good for corporations is good for society as a whole, and that hard work and talent are the main determinants of success. In this kind of BELIEF system, the ruling class can rely less heavily on force as a way to maintain dominance and protect their interests, although the police and other agencies of coercion can never be done away with entirely.

Hegemony, then, refers as much to the social mechanisms and bases of dominance as it does to the fact of dominance itself. As a concept, it draws attention to how dominance and subordination are defined as part of the normal structure of society and woven into the INSTITUTIONAL frameworks of major aspects of social life, from the family to education to organized religion.

See also IDEOLOGY; UPPER CLASS; LOWER CLASS.

Reading

Anderson, Perry. 1977. "The antinomies of Antonio Gramsci." *New Left Review* 100 (November 1976–January 1977): 5–80.

Gramsci, Antonio. 1971. *Selections from prison notebooks*. London: New Left Books.

hermeneutics Hermeneutics (from the Greek, meaning "to interpret or make clear") is a field of study devoted to the problem of how to give meaning to a cultural product such as a work of art or a piece of writing. The concept was originally applied to interpretations of the Bible, especially given its history of repeatedly being revised, rewritten, copied, and translated. Currently, however, the concept is applicable to any element of CULTURE.

From a hermeneutic perspective, we cannot tell what something means simply from the thing itself. We also have to look at the context in which it was produced and in which we are now trying to make sense of it. Figuring out what a document such as the Magna Carta or the U.S. Constitution means, for example, depends entirely on the subjective decision of what kind of interpretive framework to use. Do we try to imagine, for example, what those who wrote the Constitution had in mind at the time? Do we interpret the document in terms of the social conditions that applied then (including,

for example, the acceptability of slavery as an INSTITUTION and the exclusion of blacks and women from the phrase "All men are created equal")? Or do we interpret the Constitution as it applies to current social conditions? The answer to such questions cannot help but be subjective, which implies that meaning is not fixed or predictable. This makes meaning and the social life on which meaning rests difficult to identify with any certainty.

As a perspective on social life, hermeneutics challenges mainstream applications of the scientific method because it argues that there is no objective reality "out there" to be understood in a strictly scientific way. Rather, there is a more subjective, fluid reality that calls for different kinds of methods in order to grasp and understand it. Giddens, for example, uses the term *double hermeneutic* to refer to two factors that affect how sociologists interpret and explain social life and behavior. First, in order to understand people's behavior we have to know something about what they think they are doing and why, about how they make sense of their surroundings and other people. Second, when we observe social life, we also make use of concepts such as ROLE and SOCIAL SYSTEM that help explain what is going on. The people who participate in social life, however, are unlikely to use such terms to describe or interpret their own behavior. A man accused of sexually harassing a female co-worker, for example, might only be aware of personal feelings he has toward her. A sociologist, however, might also be aware of gender differences in communication and the male-dominated social system in which all of this takes place. The concept of double hermeneutic draws attention to the fact that any explanation of social life depends on both kinds of KNOWL-EDGE – the knowledge of how people make sense of their own lives and behavior and the knowledge that sociologists bring to what they observe.

See also EMPIRICAL; POSITIVISM; SCIENCE.

Reading
Bauman, Zygmunt. 1978. *Hermeneutics and social science.* London: Hutchinson.
Giddens, Anthony. 1984. *The constitution of society.* Cambridge, England: Polity Press.
Ricoeur, Paul. 1981. *Hermeneutics and the human sciences.* Cambridge, England: Cambridge University Press.

hidden curriculum Hidden curriculum is a concept used to describe the often unarticulated and unacknowledged things that students are taught in school. This is distinct from the publicized curriculum that defines what students are supposed to study and learn – subjects such as mathematics and literature. The hidden curriculum is an important issue in the sociological study of how schools generate SOCIAL INEQUALITY. Students who are female, for example, or who come from lower-class families, or who belong to subordinate racial or ethnic categories, are often treated in ways that create and reinforce inferior self-images as well as low aspirations and expectations for themselves. In addition, they are often granted little trust, independence, or autonomy and as such are prepared for working lives in which they willingly submit to AUTHORITY.

Students whose social characteristics locate them in dominant groups, on the other hand, tend to be treated in ways that enhance self-esteem,

independence, autonomy, and expectations of achievement and success. This experience also supports the development of the skills and ATTITUDES these goals require.

The concept of the hidden curriculum also draws attention to the UNANTICIPATED CONSEQUENCES of SOCIAL SYSTEMS, an important area of sociological thinking. Even teachers who are most openly committed to gender and racial equality, for example, are usually unaware of how in their own behavior they discriminate in harmful ways.

See also CULTURAL REPRODUCTION AND SOCIAL REPRODUCTION; PREJUDICE AND DISCRIMINATION; SOCIAL CLASS.

Reading
Bowles, Samuel, and Herbert Gintis. 1976. *Schooling in capitalist America: Educational reform and the contradictions of economic life.* New York: Basic Books.
Jackson, Philip. 1968. *Life in classrooms.* New York: Holt, Rinehart and Winston.
Snyder, Benson R. 1971. *The hidden curriculum.* New York: Knopf.

hierarchy A hierarchy is a distribution of POWER among different layers in a SOCIAL SYSTEM, with little ambiguity as to who has AUTHORITY over whom. The more hierarchical a system is, the greater the number of layers and, generally, the greater the distance between the top and bottom.

Hierarchy is an important concept because it describes profound historical shifts in the role of power in social life and how it is organized. As SOCIETIES have become more complex, for example, and more focused on control and domination as ends in themselves, power has increasingly taken

143

the form of the ability to control events, resources, and people and become organized in a hierarchical way. This can be seen in virtually every area of social life, from politics and economics to religion and education.

See also AUTHORITY; BUREAUCRACY; POWER.

hierarchy of needs   *See* NEED.

histogram   *See* GRAPHICS.

historical materialism   *See* MATERIALISM.

historical sociology   Historical sociology is a discipline combining the study of history and sociology. Although the two disciplines are clearly distinct, the overlap between their content and method has attracted increasing interest since the 1980s. Their differences can be readily identified however. Sociologists, for example, tend to be more interested in general THEORY about how social life works, and they rely heavily on quantitative methods such as SURVEYS. Historians tend to be more interested in events and issues that are limited in time and space, and they rely on historical records that take various forms. Nonetheless, Philip Abrams and others argue that to a great extent the basic sociological goal of understanding how SOCIAL SYSTEMS work cannot be separated from an understanding of how they change. Indeed, forerunners of modern sociology such as Karl MARX, Max WEBER, and Émile DURKHEIM devoted a great deal of their work to an understanding of the historical context in which social life is shaped. Today, historical sociology focuses in particular on the development of CAPITALISM and the NATION-STATE, RELIGION, COLLECTIVE BEHAVIOR, and SOCIAL MOVEMENTS.

See also ANNALES SCHOOL.

Reading

Abrams, Philip. 1982. *Historical sociology.* Shepton Mallet, England: Open House.

Elias, Norbert. 1978, 1982. *The civilizing process,* 2 vols. Oxford: Blackwell Publishers.

Wallerstein, Immanuel. 1976. *The modern world system.* New York: Academic Press.

——. 1980. *The modern world system II: Mercantilism and the consolidation of the European world economy, 1600–1750.* New York: Academic Press.

——. 1989. *The modern world system III: The second era of great expansion of the capitalist world economy, 1730–1840.* New York: Academic Press.

historicism   Historicism has two meanings. In its first sense, it encompasses the idea that history can be explained in terms of fixed laws or principles that explain SOCIAL CHANGE. KNOWLEDGE of such patterns enables us not only to understand the past but to predict the future.

In its second sense, historicism is a perspective that argues that any aspect of social life can be understood only in the context of the historical period in which it exists. This implies that everything from cultural ideas to the structural character of social relationships and INSTITUTIONS is historically "relative" and cannot be compared across historical periods.

See also HERMENEUTICS.

Reading

Popper, Karl R. 1957. *The poverty of historicism.* London: Routledge and Kegan Paul.

holism   *See* ATOMISM AND HOLISM.

homeostasis Homeostasis is a widely used concept whose general meaning is to keep things similar or the same. In biology, homeostasis refers to the tendency of an organism to maintain a certain degree of stability, for example, by balancing the level of various chemicals in the blood or temperature variations from one part of the body to another. In ECOLOGY, homeostasis is the tendency of ecosystems to maintain a balance among different forms of life, such as the relative number of various plant and animal species in a physical habitat. And in sociology, homeostasis has been used by functionalist theorists in particular as part of their argument that SOCIETIES are organized in ways that tend toward relatively stable forms based on, among other things, an overall consensus over VALUES and NORMS.

In both its ecological and sociological applications, the concept of homeostasis is controversial. Functionalism, for example, has long been accused by conflict theorists of assuming a level of social consensus and stability that does not exist. More recently, some ecologists have argued that physical environments do not return to predictable stable states but rather are in a continuing process of change.

See also CONFLICT PERSPECTIVE; ECOLOGY; FUNCTIONALIST PERPECTIVE.

Reading
Cannon, Walter B. [1939] 1963. *The wisdom of the body*, rev. and exp. New York: Norton.

horizontal differentiation *See* DIFFERENTIATION.

horticultural society A horticultural SOCIETY is a SOCIAL SYSTEM based on horticulture, a MODE OF PRODUCTION in which digging sticks are used to cultivate small gardens. Its development around 7000 BC in Asia Minor is sociologically significant because it was the first type of society to actually grow at least some of its own food rather than merely gathering existing food and hunting animals. As a result, horticultural societies developed settlements that had larger populations, and they stayed in one place longer before migrating in search of better conditions. Some accumulation of food and goods was now possible and, with it, a more complex DIVISION OF LABOR, more substantial dwellings, and a small amount of trade. Advanced horticultural societies sometimes included several communities with as many as 5,000 people, that supported specialists producing a variety of products such as boats, pottery, and textiles. Horticultural societies were also the first known societies to support the institution of slavery.

See also AGRARIAN SOCIETY; HUNTER-GATHERER SOCIETY; INDUSTRIAL SOCIETY AND INDUSTRIALIZATION; MODE OF PRODUCTION; POSTINDUSTRIAL SOCIETY.

Reading
Lenski, Gerhard, Jean Lenski, and Patrick Nolan. 1998. *Human societies: An introduction to macrosociology*, 8th ed. New York: McGraw-Hill.

household As a unit of sociological analysis, a household consists of one or more people who share common living circumstances, especially in sharing a dwelling and/or facilities for preparing food. As such, it differs from a FAMILY, which is organized primarily around KINSHIP ties. Most,

145

but not all, families also take the form of households; but in some societies, such as the United States, an increasing number of households are not family units. Indeed, the fastest growing type of household is a single person living alone.

As the centrality of the family declines in the social life of INDUSTRIAL SOCIETIES, the household becomes an increasingly important focus of sociological research on the shape of private life.

See also FAMILY; KINSHIP.

Reading

Santi, Lawrence L. 1987. "Change in the structure and size of American households." *Journal of Marriage and the Family* 49: 833–7.

housing class *See* CONSUMPTION CLEAVAGE.

human capital Human capital is a concept based on the belief that the role of workers in production is similar to the role of machinery and other FORCES OF PRODUCTION. For example, just as INDUSTRIAL SOCIETIES invest in factories and machinery in order to enhance productivity, they also invest in schools that enhance the training, KNOWLEDGE, and skills of their workers. In this sense, organizations, communities, and societies have a certain amount of human capital contained in the various abilities of their people. Similarly, individuals can be thought of as having varying amounts of human capital at their disposal that they can use for productive purposes, including earning a living.

The concept of human capital is used most often to explain patterns of SOCIAL INEQUALITY related to race, class, ethnicity, or gender. Human capital theory argues that women, for example, earn less money than men because they possess less human capital in the form of education, skill, and experience. Although human capital certainly accounts for some variation in WEALTH and INCOME, it does relatively little to explain persistent patterns of inequality. Roughly two-thirds of the income gap between men and women in the United States, for example, cannot be explained by differences in education, work experience and continuity, or on-the-job training.

The major problem with human capital theory is its assumption that the amount people are paid for their work is based on a rational calculation of their productive worth with no attention to factors such as race, gender, or ethnicity and the vulnerability of such groups to DISCRIMINATION and EXPLOITATION based on PREJUDICE.

Reading

Becker, Gary S. 1993. *Human capital*, 4th ed. Chicago: University of Chicago Press.

Marini, M. M. 1989. "Sex differences in earnings in the United States." *Annual Review of Sociology* 15: 343–80.

human ecology *See* ECOLOGY.

Human Relations School The Human Relations School is a THEORY explaining work and productivity under industrial CAPITALISM. It is based on the idea that workers' behavior depends strongly on their relations with one another, that groups of workers operate under informal understandings that play as important a role in the production process as the formal goals and expectations set by management. A sense of group solidarity and teamwork, for example, can enhance productivity. But that same solidarity can work to lower productivity, as when workers protect themselves from working too hard by setting and enforcing lower standards than those set by management.

The Human Relations School originated in the work of Elton Mayo and his colleagues in the famous Hawthorne Studies named for the plant in which they conducted their experiments during the 1930s. It arose in part as a response to SCIENTIFIC MANAGEMENT assumptions that workers are motivated primarily by individual self-interest in the form of higher wages. Its influence faded in the 1960s, because the theory pays little attention to the importance of CLASS CONFLICT between workers and management.

See also HAWTHORNE EFFECT.

Reading

Mayo, Elton. 1949. *The social problems of an industrial civilization.* London: Routledge and Kegan Paul.

Roethlisberger, Fritz J., and William J. Dickson. 1939. *Management and the worker.* Cambridge, MA: Harvard University Press.

Rose, M. 1988. *Industrial behavior*, 2nd ed. Harmondsworth, England: Penguin.

hunter-gatherer society The hunter-gatherer SOCIETY is a SOCIAL SYSTEM having the simplest, most technologically unsophisticated MODE OF PRODUCTION. Most hunter-gatherers depend primarily on gathering existing foodstuffs with meat serving as an occasional rather than a regular source of nutrition. They rarely generate a surplus since they have no means of storing what they cannot consume in the near future and must move from place to place, making it impractical to accumulate possessions. SOCIAL INEQUALITY is at a minimum and is based primarily on prestige conferred on those who excel at particular tasks. There is a gender-based DIVISION OF LABOR, but little if any gender inequality. The entire society is organized around KINSHIP ties, which means that the idea of individual FAMILIES existing as distinct units within society is unknown. Production is communal and cooperative and the distribution system is based on sharing.

See also AGRARIAN SOCIETY; HORTICULTURAL SOCIETY; INDUSTRIAL SOCIETY AND INDUSTRIALIZATION; POSTINDUSTRIAL SOCIETY.

Reading

Lenski, Gerhard, Jean Lenski, and Patrick Nolan. 1998. *Human societies: An introduction to macrosociology*, 8th ed. New York: McGraw-Hill.

hypothesis and hypothesis testing

A hypothesis is a prediction about the relationship between VARIABLES. It is usually, although not always, based upon theoretical expectations about how things work. In thinking about factors that promote upward SOCIAL MOBILITY, for example, we might hypothesize that the more education people have, the more upwardly mobile they will be in comparison with their parents.

In STATISTICAL INFERENCE, hypotheses generally take one of two forms: substantive and null. A *substantive hypothesis* represents an actual expectation – as in "education increases the likelihood of upward mobility." To decide whether a substantive hypothesis is supported by the evidence, however, it is necessary to test a related hypothesis called the *null hypothesis*. A null hypothesis always predicts the absence of a relationship between two variables,

147

as in "education has no effect on mobility." Note that the hypothesis "education promotes downward mobility" would be a substantive hypothesis even though it is the "opposite" of our first substantive hypothesis. Null hypotheses always predict that no relationship exists between variables.

The logic of hypothesis testing is such that we test the substantive hypothesis by assuming the null hypothesis to be true. We then compare the null hypothesis with concrete evidence and use statistical techniques to estimate the probability of getting such evidence if the null hypothesis were true. If that probability is very small – such as 0.001 or 1 in a thousand – we would conclude that the assumption that the null hypothesis is true is so incompatible with our evidence that we will reject the null hypothesis in favor of the substantive hypothesis.

In rejecting a null hypothesis, there is a probability of error (that we have rejected the null hypothesis when it is in fact true) that is equal to the probability we calculated. This probability is known as the *significance level* of the hypothesis test. In our above example, we would say that we have rejected the null hypothesis at the 0.001 level of significance. This means that, in rejecting the null in favor of the substantive, we run an estimated 0.001 probability of making a mistake.

The word "significant" can be misleading if its precise statistical meaning is forgotten. To say, for example, that two groups are "significantly different" or that education has a "significant effect" on upward mobility only means that we are confident that the two groups are not exactly the same or that the effect of education

on mobility is not exactly zero. Whether differences or effects are significant in the sense of being large or important can only be found by estimating the magnitude of the difference or the effect. By itself, hypothesis testing does not accomplish this.

See also HYPOTHETICO-DEDUCTIVE METHOD; STATISTICAL INDEPENDENCE AND STATISTICAL DEPENDENCE; STATISTICS; VARIABLE.

Reading

Bohrnstedt, George W., and David Knoke. 1994. *Statistics for social data analysis*, 3rd ed. Itasca, IL: F. E. Peacock.

Brown, Steven R., and Lawrence E. Melamed. 1990. *Experimental design and analysis*. Newbury Park, CA: Sage Publications.

hypothetico-deductive   method
The hypothetico-deductive method is an approach to research that begins with a THEORY about how things work and derives testable HYPOTHESES from it. It is a form of *deductive reasoning* in that it begins with general principles, assumptions, and ideas and works from them to more particular statements about what the world actually looks like and how it works. The hypotheses are then tested by gathering and analyzing DATA and, ideally, the theory is either supported or refuted by the results. In this approach, theory is often seen as a formal collection of assumptions and propositions that are related to one another in a logical and linear way that leads to specific hypotheses.

In practice, research rarely unfolds in such a rigid and logical fashion with formal theory as its starting point. Much of the time, the research process is a mixture of concrete observation and theoretical speculation. As often as not, we make observations of the world (by conducting surveys, for example, or examining government statistics), construct some ideas that might explain them, and formulate testable hypotheses from these which lead to the next round of data gathering, and so on. In this sense, the process blends deductive reasoning, which goes from general ideas to specific observations, with *inductive* reasoning, which begins with observations and builds more general statements from them.

See also ABSTRACTED EMPIRICISM.

Reading

Collins, H. M. 1985. *Changing order: Replication and induction in scientific practice*. Beverly Hills, CA: Sage Publications.

Zetterberg, Hans. 1965. *On theory and verification in sociology*, 3rd ed. Totowa, NJ: Bedminster Press.

I

I *See* MIND.

idealism Rooted in the philosophical work of Plato, Kant, and Hegel, idealism is a way of understanding the relationship between human beings and the world as they experience it. According to idealism, reality consists primarily of how people think about it, and this depends on human ideas and theories. People are not blank slates on which external reality writes impressions of itself; they are instead active subjects who use ideas and other elements of CULTURE to construct what they then take to be reality.

Early Marxists argued that idealists had it backward, that material conditions such as the MODE OF PRODUCTION shape thinking, not vice versa. Today, however, many Marxists take a more balanced approach reflecting the sociological importance of the active role people play in the ongoing use of ideas to construct reality.

See also BASE AND SUPERSTRUCTURE; DETERMINISM AND REDUCTIONISM; PHENOMENOLOGY; MATERIALISM.

Reading
Benton, Ted. 1977. *Philosophical foundations of the three sociologies*. London: Routledge and Kegan Paul.

ideal self *See* SELF.

ideal type Most closely associated with the German sociologist Max WEBER, the ideal type is an abstract model that, when used as a standard of comparison, enables us to see aspects of the real world in a clearer, more systematic way. SOCIALISM and free-market CAPITALISM, for example, can be described as ideal types by identifying their essential characteristics – their essence – in a pure, somewhat exaggerated form that is unlikely to actually exist anywhere other than in our minds. Socialist and capitalist SOCIETIES differ in many ways from their respective ideal types: socialist STATES usually have been authoritarian and unreflective of workers' interests, for example, just as capitalist markets are increasingly controlled by oligopolies rather than being freely competitive.

The lack of fit between ideal types and the real world is not a problem, however, for it is not the purpose of ideal types to describe or explain the world. Instead, they provide us with points of comparison from which to observe it. By comparing the ideal type of socialism with actual socialist societies, for example, we can highlight their characteristics by seeing how they match or depart from the ideal type. Sociologists use many ideal types in this way, including PRIMARY AND SECONDARY RELATIONSHIPS, bureaucracy, types of AUTHORITY (charismatic, legal-rational, and traditional), and the assumption that people act rationally.

It is important to be aware that ideal types are ideal only in the sense that they are pure and abstract, not in the more usual sense of being desirable or good. TOTALITARIANISM is no less an ideal type than DEMOCRACY, for example. Both are abstract constructs with which we can compare and contrast actual political systems in order to see their various characteristics more clearly.

Reading

Weber, Max. 1947. *Theory of social and economic organization*. New York: Free Press.

Winch, Peter. 1958. *The idea of social science*. London: Routledge and Kegan Paul.

identity, social   *See* SELF.

ideological state apparatus   Marxist theorist Louis ALTHUSSER used this term to refer to the network of INSTITUTIONS that help promote the VALUES and LEGITIMATION of the STATE, even though their supposed social function is not political. RELIGION, the MASS MEDIA, schools, TRADE UNIONS, and sport all contribute to maintaining the social order and encourage loyalty to the state and obedience to its AUTHORITY. Singing national anthems at sporting events, for example, reinforces the legitimacy of the state, as does the use of religious SYMBOLS in state ceremonies such as presidential inaugurations. Schools indoctrinate students in versions of history that encourage positive views of the state and loyalty to it.

When the ideological state apparatus proves insufficient to elicit obedience and conformity, the alternative is what ALTHUSSER called the *repressive state apparatus*. This consists of the police, courts, prison system, military, and other agencies that embody the state's monopoly over the legitimate use of force and violence.

Reading

Abercrombie, Nicholas. 1980. *Class, structure, and knowledge*. Oxford: Basil Blackwell.

ideology   An ideology is a set of cultural BELIEFS, VALUES, and ATTITUDES that underlie and thereby to some degree justify and legitimate either the status quo or movements to change it. From a Marxist perspective, most ideology reflects the interests of dominant groups as a way to perpetuate their privilege. This is especially true with oppressive systems that require elaborate justifications in order to keep going. White racism, for example, includes ideas about racial differences used to justify and defend white privilege. Similar ideologies exist in support of gender, class, ethnic, and religious oppression.

In a more general sense, the CULTURE of every SOCIAL SYSTEM includes an ideology that serves to explain and justify its own existence as a way of life, whether it be a FAMILY ideology that defines the nature and purpose of family life or a religious ideology that anchors and affirms a way of life in relation to sacred forces.

Ideology can also underlie movements for SOCIAL CHANGE. From the environmental Green movement to radical feminism, SOCIAL MOVEMENTS rely on sets of ideas that explain and justify their purpose and methods.

See also CLASS CONSCIOUSNESS AND FALSE CONSCIOUSNESS; CLASS IMAGERY; HEGEMONY; KNOWLEDGE.

Reading

Apter, David E., ed. 1964. *Ideology and discontent*. New York: Free Press.

Mannheim, Karl. 1952. *Essays on the sociology of knowledge.* London: Routledge and Kegan Paul.
Marx, Karl, and Friedrich Engels. [1846] 1976. "The German ideology." In *Collected works of Marx and Engels,* vol. 5. New York: International.

idiographic and nomothetic Idiographic and nomothetic methods represent two different approaches to understanding social life. A method is idiographic (meaning to "depict the private or singular") if it focuses on individual cases or events. Ethnographers, for example, describe entire SOCIAL SYSTEMS such as SOCIETIES or organizations by observing the minute details of everyday life and constructing from these an overall portrait. Historians also make heavy use of this approach.

A method is nomothetic (meaning to "lay down laws") if it focuses on general statements that account for larger social patterns that form the context of single events or individual behavior and experience. An analysis of how industrial CAPITALISM shapes social life, for example, typifies the nomothetic approach. Although sociological work tends more toward the nomothetic than the idiographic, it often blends the two as it tries to account for both the broad outlines of social systems and the experience of the people who participate in them. *See also* ETHNOGRAPHY AND ETHNOLOGY; ETHNOMETHODOLOGY.

immanent change *See* SOCIAL EVOLUTION.

immigration *See* MIGRATION.

imperatively coordinated association An imperatively coordinated association is a concept used by Ralf DAHRENDORF in his theory of social STRATIFICATION. Derived from the work of Max WEBER, the concept refers to organizations that are arranged as HIERARCHIES, such as corporations and government bureaucracies. It is based on Weber's definition of POWER as the ability to control other people and refers to the degree to which such control is irresistible or "imperative" within an organization or "association." Dahrendorf used the concept as part of his argument that the concentration and hierarchical arrangement of power is a key aspect of social inequality in complex industrial societies and that it is in relation to such organizations that most social conflict occurs.
See also AUTHORITY; CONFLICT PERSPECTIVE; HIERARCHY; POWER; STRATIFICATION AND INEQUALITY.
Reading
Dahrendorf, Ralf. 1959. *Class and class conflict in industrial society.* Stanford: Stanford University Press.

imperialism *See* COLONIALISM AND IMPERIALISM.

impression management *See* DRAMATURGICAL PERSPECTIVE.

incest taboo *See* TABOO.

income *See* WEALTH AND INCOME.

incorporation Incorporation is a social process through which working-class organizations such as TRADE UNIONS are integrated into larger SOCIAL SYSTEMS such as the STATE and corporate boards. Instead of identifying themselves as outsiders working against the status quo and dominant classes, members of the working class increasingly view themselves as merely citizens among other citizens, working through existing INSTITUTIONS such as political parties.

Some have argued that incorporation will eventually end class privilege by extending political POWER to the working class. Marxists, however, see incorporation as a victory for the dominant classes because it encourages working-class people to settle for the kind of superficial change that mainstream institutions will allow.
See also CLASS CONSCIOUSNESS AND FALSE CONSCIOUSNESS; CLASS IMAGERY; DOMINANT IDEOLOGY THESIS; HEGEMONY.

independent primary labor market *See* LABOR MARKET.

independent variable *See* VARIABLE.

in-depth interview *See* INTERVIEW.

index *See* ATTITUDE SCALE.

indexicality In the study of social INTERACTION and the continuing process of interpreting what people say and do, indexicality is a concept referring to the fact that the meaning of speech and action depends on the social situation in which it occurs. In other words, we can conclude that meaning is indexical. The meaning of "Fire!" for example, is quite different when shouted by someone running from a house than when commanded by the leader of an artillery unit. Similarly, the clapping of hands means one thing in a theater audience and quite another when performed by a teacher trying to get the attention of a class of noisy students. Indexicality is an especially important concept in ETHNOMETHODOLOGY.

indirect effect *See* EFFECT, STATISTICAL.

individualism Individualism is a way of thinking both about how people are related to SOCIAL SYSTEMS and about the nature of social systems themselves. In the first sense, individualism first emerged as a doctrine in early nineteenth-century France, and promoted the primacy of individual interests over those of SOCIETY. It was greeted with considerable controversy at the time and some degree of horror at the prospect of an end to obedience and SOCIAL CONTROL and the beginning of chaos. It has since become firmly entrenched in the CULTURES of Western industrial capitalist societies, the United States in particular.

In its second sense, individualism refers to the idea that social systems are comprised primarily of individuals and can be understood in terms of their choices, characteristics, and interests. As such, it challenges the core sociological premise that social systems are more than the individuals who participate in them.
See also ATOMISM AND HOLISM; CIVIL SOCIETY; METHODOLOGICAL INDIVIDUALISM; SOCIAL FACT.

Reading
Abercrombie, Nicholas, Stephen Hill, and Bryan S. Turner. 1986. *Sovereign individuals of capitalism*. London: Allen and Unwin.
Heller, Thomas C., Morton Sosna, and David E. Wellbery. 1986. *Reconstructing individualism*. Stanford: Stanford University Press.
Lukes, Steven. 1994. *Individualism*. Oxford: Blackwell Publishers.

inductive reasoning *See* HYPOTHETICO-DEDUCTIVE METHOD.

inductive statistics *See* STATISTICS.

industrial conflict Industrial conflict refers to the forms (such as sabotage, absenteeism, and strikes) and the causes of conflict that arise between employers and workers under CAPITALISM. Key questions about industrial conflict include whether it is inevitable in an ECONOMY based on INEQUALITY of AUTHORITY or private ownership of the MEANS OF PRODUCTION; and how divisions arise not only between management and workers, but among various GROUPS within those SOCIAL CATEGORIES.

See also DAHRENDORF; HUMAN RELATIONS SCHOOL; INSTITUTIONALIZATION OF CONFLICT.

Reading

Hill, Stephen. 1982. *Competition and control at work*. Cambridge, MA: MIT Press.

industrial democracy Industrial democracy is a term that refers to the degree to which workers participate in making decisions that affect their work lives, from issues concerning day-to-day working conditions to plant closings and policies that shape the GLOBAL ECONOMY. Forms of participation vary from UNIONS and COLLECTIVE BARGAINING to seats on corporate boards and, ultimately, worker ownership of business.

Reading

Poole, Michael. 1975. *Workers' participation in industry*. London: Routledge and Kegan Paul.

industrialization *See* INDUSTRIAL SOCIETY AND INDUSTRIALIZATION.

industrial relations Industrial relations is an umbrella term that refers to a fairly broad area of study involving sociology and several other disciplines. At its core, industrial relations focuses on relationships between employees and employers under CAPITALISM, but it extends from there to include relationships among worker groups and among employers. Of particular interest have been the sources and consequences of social conflict.

See also CONFLICT PERSPECTIVE.

Reading

Miller, Delbert, and William Form. 1980. *Industrial sociology in organizational life*. New York: Harper and Row.

Industrial Revolution The Industrial Revolution was a period spanning the late eighteenth to the early nineteenth centuries. It transformed much of Europe and the United States by replacing agriculturally based societies with INDUSTRIAL SOCIETIES based on the use of machines and nonanimal sources of energy to produce finished goods. It began in Britain and was based on an available labor force, highly developed institutions of trade and commerce, an excellent transportation system, wealth imported from colonies, and the wide availability of coal as a source of fuel. These factors provided ripe conditions for astonishingly rapid advances in productivity.

The Industrial Revolution went hand-in-hand with the equally rapid development of CAPITALISM as an economic system whose drive for profit and expansion of both production and MARKETS provided a vital stimulus for innovation and the exploitation of the natural environment. In response to this, SOCIALISM developed as an alternative model for organizing industrial society. Today, as socialism declines in Central Europe and elsewhere, it remains to be seen what other kinds of SOCIAL SYSTEMS will emerge as alternatives to industrial capitalism.

The Industrial Revolution is sociologically important because of its wide-ranging and profound effects on the fabric of social life, from the shape of political institutions to the rhythms of family life.

See also ENLIGHTENMENT, AGE OF; INDUSTRIAL SOCIETY AND INDUSTRIALIZATION; MODE OF PRODUCTION; POSTINDUSTRIAL SOCIETY; STATE SOCIALISM; URBANIZATION.

Reading

Mathais, P. 1983. *The first industrial revolution: An economic history of Britain 1700–1914*, 2nd ed. London and New York: Methuen.

industrial society and industrialization In the simplest sense, an industrial society is a SOCIAL SYSTEM whose MODE OF PRODUCTION focuses primarily on finished goods manufactured with the aid of machinery. This contrasts with less technological societies that focus mainly on agriculture or the extraction of raw materials such as lumber, oil, or minerals.

In a more complex sense, industrialization involves a broad range of social factors that deeply affect the character of social life. Industrial societies, for example, tend to produce enormous surpluses that support highly complex DIVISIONS OF LABOR. Production tends to shift from the home to the factory and from rural to urban settings. Industrial societies also promote the RATIONALIZATION of social life, increased literacy, and the growth of science, formal education, and mass media. INSTITUTIONS such as the STATE become stronger and more pervasive in their influence while organized religion loses much of its public power (although not necessarily its influence over people's private lives). Bureaucracy becomes a ubiquitous form of social organization. Although the level of SOCIAL INEQUALITY is typically less than that found in AGRARIAN SOCIETIES, extremes of WEALTH and POVERTY are quite common.

There are, of course, many exceptions to these generalizations. Many nonindustrial societies, for example, experience rapid URBANIZATION due more to extreme rural poverty than to urban industrialization. Although centralized factory-based production has been the norm in industrial societies, this may be due more to the goals of CAPITALISM than to something inherent in industry as a mode of production. Indeed, analytically we can separate capitalism and socialism from industrialism since there is no necessary connection between them other than a historical one.

See also AGRARIAN SOCIETY; HORTICULTURAL SOCIETY; HUNTER-GATHERER SOCIETY; INDUSTRIAL REVOLUTION; MODERNIZATION THEORY; POSTINDUSTRIAL SOCIETY.

Reading

Kerr, Clark, John T. Dunlop, Fredrick Harbison, and Charles A. Meyers. 1973. *Industrialization and industrial man*. London: Penguin.

Moore, Wilbert E. 1965. *The impact of industry*. Englewood Cliffs, NJ: Prentice-Hall.

Saunders, Christopher. 1981. *The political economy of the new and old industrial countries*. London: Butterworths.

inequality *See* STRATIFICATION AND INEQUALITY.

infant mortality rate For every 1,000 births in a given year, the infant mortality rate is the number of infants who die before their first birthday. The rate is often calculated in relation to even smaller age spans, such as the *neonatal mortality rate* which measures deaths during the first 28 days of life.

Measures of infant mortality are among the best indicators of general health conditions in a POPULATION and often are used to estimate overall morbidity and death rates in countries with incomplete vital statistics records.

Reading

Shryock, Henry S., and Jacob Siegel and Associates. 1976. *The methods and materials of demography.* New York: Academic Press.

inferential statistics *See* STATISTICS.

informal relation *See* FORMAL ORGANIZATION.

informal sanction *See* SANCTION.

information society An information society is a SOCIAL SYSTEM in which the production of goods and services depends heavily on gathering, processing, and transmitting information. In the same way that INDUSTRIALIZATION made it possible to produce huge amounts of material goods, the advent of high-speed computers and telecommunications TECHNOLOGY has made it possible to produce, process, and transmit huge amounts of information.

Sociologically, the development of the information society raises a number of issues including increased GLOBALIZATION in everything from POPULAR CULTURE to the economic WORLD SYSTEM; the changing relationship between workers, the workplace, and the home; changes in the OCCUPATIONAL STRUCTURE; the impact on political DEMOCRACY; and the increased power of TRANS-NATIONAL CORPORATIONS to control workers and operate free of restraint from national governments.

See also POSTINDUSTRIAL SOCIETY.

Reading

Beniger, James R. 1986. *The control revolution: Technological and economic origins of the information society.* Cambridge, MA: Harvard University Press.

Castells, Manuel. 1989. *The informational city.* Cambridge, MA: Blackwell Publishers.

Weinberg, Nathan. 1990. *Computers in the information society.* Boulder, CO: Westview Press.

in-group *See* GROUP.

inner city Inner city is the contemporary term for Ernest BURGESS's *zone of transition* concept, originally introduced in his concentric zone THEORY of urban development. Burgess argued that as cities grow, their core areas are increasingly devoted to businesses, hotels, banks, and other uses that tend to break down a sense of COMMUNITY among those who live there. This sets in motion a social process through which these areas become zones of transition. Lacking a basis for a strong community life, inner cities tend to become entry points for relatively poor migrants in search of work. They are crowded into substandard housing, and as poverty spreads and social conditions worsen, crime and other SOCIAL PROBLEMS proliferate and more prosperous residents and businesses flee to the suburbs. This promotes a downward spiral of falling tax revenues, poverty, declining schools, and suburban flight by all but the wealthiest and poorest, with a shrinking middle and skilled working class. Burgess's model has been criticized for paying too little attention to sources of COHESION in inner city areas, especially on the level of neighborhoods.

Concepts such as inner city and zone of transition are sociologically significant because they draw attention to how geography and the uses of space play a part in the creation and perpetuation of social patterns such as inequality.

See also CHICAGO SCHOOL; OUTER CITY; SUBURB; URBANIZATION AND URBANISM.

Reading

Dogan, Mattei, and John D. Kasarda, eds. 1987. *The metropolis era.* New York: Russell Sage Foundation.

Gottdiener, Mark. 1985. *The social production of urban space.* Austin: University of Texas Press.

Park, Robert E., Ernest Burgess, and Roderick D. McKenzie, eds. 1925. *The city.* Chicago: University of Chicago Press.

innovative deviance *See* ABER-RANT DEVIANCE; NONCONFORMIST DEVIANCE.

institution An institution is an enduring set of ideas about how to accomplish goals generally recognized as important in a SOCIETY. Most societies have some form of family, religious, economic, educational, healing, and political institutions that define the core of its way of life.

Institutions differ from one another by focusing on different social functions. The family, for example, is concerned with bringing children into the world and nurturing, protecting, and socializing them. Political institutions, by contrast, are designed to generate, organize, and apply collective POWER in order to achieve goals such as maintaining social order and stability, defending against external threats,

resolving disputes and dispensing justice, and, depending on the society, protecting dominant groups and their interests. It is important to distinguish institutions from their concrete manifestations – individual families from the family as an institution, for example, or a government from the STATE. Individual families are influenced by how their society defines the family as an institution, but day-to-day life may bear little resemblance to that model. In a similar way, the state is an institution that provides a blueprint for how governance should be conducted; but each collection of office holders that constitutes a particular government may follow those guidelines only to varying degrees. In 1814 Napoléon Bonaparte made his famous declaration to the French Senate: *"L'etat c'est moi"* ("The state is me"). Such a claim had extraordinary implications, for Napoléon was in essence identifying himself with a major component of society itself and, hence, positioned himself to transcend the limitations that would otherwise apply to his behavior and uses of power.

Like most aspects of social life, institutions are experienced as external to the individuals who participate in them; but they are also shaped and changed by that participation. For example, the family in the United States is still defined institutionally in terms of the nuclear family, but as single-parent families grow rapidly in number and lesbians and gays demand social recognition for marriages and parenthood, it is inevitable that the institution itself will change, however slowly.

See also ECONOMY; EDUCATION; FAMILY; POLITICS; POLITICAL ECONOMY; RELIGION; SCIENCE.

institutionalization of conflict
Conflict in a SOCIETY becomes institutionalized when it is absorbed and contained by mainstream SOCIAL SYSTEMS such as UNIONS and the courts. At the beginning of the labor movement toward the end of the nineteenth century, for example, unions were centers of opposition to capitalist control and EXPLOITATION and led workers on strikes that seriously threatened UPPER CLASS interests. Today, by contrast, unions are more likely to mute and soothe worker discontent and minimize conflict through COLLECTIVE BARGAINING that advances some worker interests without seriously challenging the status quo.

Reading

Hill, Stephen. 1982. *Competition and control at work*. Cambridge, MA: MIT Press.

institutionalized racism *See* SOCIAL OPPRESSION.

institutionalized sexism *See* SOCIAL OPPRESSION.

institutional oppression *See* SOCIAL OPPRESSION.

instrumental role *See* EXPRESSIVE ROLE AND TASK ROLE.

integration *See* SEGREGATION AND INTEGRATION.

intended consequences *See* FUNCTIONALIST PERSPECTIVE.

interaction An interaction is the process that takes place when people act in relation to one another in a social context. Although this may seem obvious, the concept of interaction rests on an important distinction between action and behavior.

Behavior includes everything that we do, from scratching an itch to writing a novel to playing football. *Action* (or *meaningful action*), however, is behavior shaped by how other people will interpret and respond to that behavior. In social interaction, we perceive other people and social situations and from this construct ideas of what is expected, of what VALUES, BELIEFS, NORMS, and ATTITUDES apply. On this basis, we choose to act in ways that will have the meaning we intend them to have.

When we go into a store, for example, much of what we do is based on our recognition that we are in a store situation and our knowledge of what is expected of various actors in such situations. When we point to items that we want to buy, ask their price, offer money, and so on, we base our actions on what we think they will mean to the other people in the situation. It is this thought process based on meaning that distinguishes action from behavior and which lies at the core of interaction as a social process.

The general approach to understanding what we do in terms of the meaning we attach to our own and other people's behavior is known as *action theory*. Its development is most closely associated with Max WEBER and his concept of *verstehen* (German for "understanding"). Weber argued that we cannot understand what people do without some sense of how they subjectively interpret their own behavior. This basic insight calls upon sociologists to include empathy in their approach to understanding social life along with more objective scientific methods.

See also INTERACTIONIST PERSPEC-
TIVE; METHODOLOGY.

Reading
Mead, George Herbert. 1938. *The philoso-
phy of the act.* Chicago: University of
Chicago Press.
Schutz, Alfred. 1972. *The phenomenology
of the social world.* London: Heinemann
Educational Books.
Weber, Max. 1968. *Economy and society.*
New York: Bedminster Press.

interaction effect *See* SPECIFICA-
TION.

interaction variable *See* SPECIFICA-
TION.

interactionist perspective As a
major THEORETICAL PERSPECTIVE
within sociology, the interactionist
perspective focuses on the concrete
details of what goes on among individuals in everyday life, as distinct
from the larger focus on SOCIAL SYS-
TEMS found in the CONFLICT and
FUNCTIONALIST PERSPECTIVES.

Interactionists study how we use
and interpret SYMBOLS not merely to
communicate with one another but
to create and maintain impressions of
ourselves, to forge a sense of SELF,
and to create and sustain what we
experience as the reality of a particular social situation. From this perspective, social life consists largely of a
complex fabric woven of countless
interactions through which life takes
on shape and meaning.

One of the critical issues in interactionist theory is the relationship
between individuals and social systems. Manford Kuhn, for example,
argues that social life consists primarily of networks of statuses and roles
that act as external constraints on
individuals and shape their experience and behavior as a result. Herbert

BLUMER, however, argues that social
systems exist only through interaction
among individuals without whom
there is no SOCIETY. As Georg
SIMMEL ([1902] 1950) put it, "Society
is merely the name for a number of
individuals, connected by interaction" (p. 10). As with many polar
positions, the truth is probably found
somewhere in between. We do experience social systems such as society
as external and feel constrained by
their CULTURES and structures. But it
is also true that the choices we make
as individuals cannot be predicted
merely from knowledge of our STA-
TUSES and ROLES, and that as individuals we have the creative potential to
affect the shape of social systems,
however small those effects might be.
See also DRAMATURGICAL PERSPECTIVE;
ETHNOMETHODOLOGY; INTERACTION;
MICROECOLOGY; MIND.

Reading
Blumer, Herbert. 1969. *Symbolic interac-
tionism: Perspective and method.*
Englewood Cliffs, NJ: Prentice-Hall.
Cooley, Charles Horton. [1902] 1964.
Human nature and the social order. New
York: Schocken.
Kuhn, Manford H. 1964. "Major trends
in symbolic interaction theory in the
past twenty-five years." *Sociological
Quarterly* 5 (winter): 61–84.
Mead, George Herbert. 1934. *Mind, self,
and society.* Chicago: University of
Chicago Press.
Simmel, Georg. [1902] 1950. *The sociol-
ogy of Georg Simmel.* Edited and trans-
lated by Kurt H. Wolff. New York: Free
Press.

interest group An interest (or *pressure*) group is an organization whose
purpose is to influence the distribution and use of political POWER
in a SOCIETY. This is done primarily

through influencing elected officials – a practice known as *lobbying* – by providing information promoting a particular point of view, or by offering support for reelection (or threatening to oppose a candidate's reelection). Environmental groups, for example, regularly send witnesses to testify at public hearings on issues affecting the environment, campaign for or against candidates and parties based upon their positions on environmental issues, seek meetings with officials to discuss legislation, and conduct public demonstrations designed in part to attract the attention of political office holders. In similar ways, various associations of manufacturers send lobbyists to influence legislation that affects their interests, such as laws requiring equipment to reduce pollution or to ensure worker safety.

Some interest groups, such as prochoice or antiabortion groups, exist primarily to do the lobbying of their group. For other organizations, such as labor unions, corporations, or the military, lobbying is secondary to a variety of other activities. In either case, interest groups differ sharply from political parties, whose primary goal is to place members in positions of political AUTHORITY rather than to influence those already in POWER.
See also PARTY, POLITICAL; POLITICS.

Reading
Berry, Jeffrey M. 1984. *The interest group society*. Glenview, IL: Scott, Foresman.
Held, David, 1987. *Models of democracy*. Cambridge, England: Polity Press.

intergenerational mobility *See* SOCIAL MOBILITY.

internal colonialism *See* COLONIALISM AND IMPERIALISM.

internalization Internalization is a process through which we come to identify parts of our CULTURE as parts of ourselves, especially in relation to ideas such as VALUES and NORMS that guide decisions about appearance and behavior. When children learn patriotic attitudes toward their country, for example, or to value hard work or financial success or a belief in God, they tend to acquire a sense of vested interest in such ideas and feelings as these become their own.

Internalization is a crucial process in maintaining SOCIAL SYSTEMS because it leads people to regulate their own behavior in accordance with accepted forms rather than having to be monitored and corrected by external authorities, an impossible task in all but the smallest and simplest systems. In contrast, coercion is a far less effective means of SOCIAL CONTROL.
See also POWER; SOCIAL CONTROL; SOCIALIZATION.

internal labor market *See* STATUS ATTAINMENT AND NEW STRUCTURALISM.

international division of labor The international division of labor (or *new international division of labor*) is the range of tasks that exists on several levels in the economic WORLD SYSTEM. On the corporate level, TRANSNATIONALS often divide the production process among operations in several different countries. The European version of the Ford Escort automobile, for example, is assembled from parts produced in some 15 European and North American countries.

On a national level, production is increasingly organized around country and regional specialization. Parts for electronics such as computers, for example, are typically produced in wealthier industrial countries and then assembled into finished products in THIRD WORLD countries such as Mexico and Malaysia. A similar division of labor exists for clothing and other industries.

The current international division of labor reflects the power of transnational corporations to maximize efficiency and profit by taking advantage of favorable local conditions such as cheap labor, low taxes, lax environmental and worker safety regulations, and repressive governments that control workers by discouraging TRADE UNIONS. The concept is useful because it draws attention to a DIVISION OF LABOR and class structure that operate across national boundaries with, for example, skilled workers in industrial societies privileged over workers in Third World countries. It also helps to account for economic growth in Third World countries that might not be predicted from DEPENDENCY THEORY, which sees core societies as so dominant in the world system that growth in nonindustrial societies is difficult to achieve.

See also COLONIALISM AND IMPERIALISM; DEPENDENCY THEORY; WORLD SYSTEM.

Reading

Fröbel, Folker, J. Heinrichs, and O. Kreye. 1980. *The new international division of labor.* Cambridge, England: Cambridge University Press.

interpretive sociology Interpretive sociology is a THEORETICAL PERSPECTIVE based on the idea that a sociological understanding of behavior must include the meaning that social actors give to what they and others do. When people interact, they interpret what is going on, from the meaning of SYMBOLS to the ATTRIBUTION of motives to others. As argued by SYMBOLIC INTERACTIONISM, ETHNOMETHODOLOGY, and other interpretive perspectives, this is what gives social life its patterned quality.

Interpretive sociology differs sharply from the idea that social life is governed by the objective cultural and structural characteristics of SOCIAL SYSTEMS that are external to individuals and relatively independent of them. It also conflicts with the argument that it is possible to construct rigid scientific laws that explain patterns of social behavior as fixed and determined by the social situations in which people find themselves. While some sociologists argue between the two positions, others – going as far back as Max WEBER – favor a balanced approach that incorporates both actors' subjective understandings and the consequences produced by social systems.

See also AGENCY AND STRUCTURE; EPISTEMOLOGY; HERMENEUTICS; IDIOGRAPHIC AND NOMOTHETIC; PHENOMENOLOGY AND PHENOMENOLOGICAL SOCIOLOGY; POSITIVISM; SOCIAL FACT.

Reading

Weber, Max. [1904–1917] 1949. *The methodology of the social sciences.* New York: Free Press.

intersubjectivity Intersubjectivity (meaning "between subjects") is a condition of social life that makes it possible for people to share understandings and expectations with others. How this is accomplished is of major interest to sociologists who use the INTERACTIONIST PERSPECTIVE. *See also* DEFINITION OF THE SITUATION; KNOWLEDGE; MIND; OTHER.

Reading
Berger, Peter L., and Thomas Luckmann. 1967. *The social construction of reality.* Garden City, NY: Doubleday.
Habermas, Jürgen. 1984. *The theory of communicative action,* vol. 1. Boston: Beacon Press.
Schutz, Alfred. [1932] 1967. *The phenomenology of the social world.* Evanston, IL: Northwestern University Press.

interval estimate *See* ESTIMATES.

interval-scale variable *See* SCALE OF MEASUREMENT.

intervening variable In statistical analysis, an intervening VARIABLE is one that occurs between independent and dependent variables. It is caused by the independent variable and is itself a cause of the dependent variable. For example, the more education you have (independent variable), the higher your income tends to be (dependent variable). Occupation is an intervening variable between education and income because it is causally effected by education and itself affects income: more schooling tends to mean a better job which in turn tends to bring higher income.
See also CONTROL VARIABLE; EFFECT, STATISTICAL; VARIABLE.

Reading
Rosenberg, Morris. 1968. *The logic of survey analysis.* New York: Basic Books.

interview The interview is the basic method used in SURVEY research, typically involving a trained interviewer asking questions either face-to-face or, increasingly, on the telephone, and recording the answers for later processing and analysis. Interview questions may be *structured* – printed on a form that restricts respondents to a given set of possible answers – or *open-ended*, with interviewers probing for explanations and details about a respondent's views or experience. The latter is most closely associated with the *in-depth interview* in which interviewer and respondent may spend many hours together over a period of days or weeks. This technique is most often used in the CASE STUDY method.

Sociologists have come to see the interview as a social situation in its own right that needs to be understood as such in order to better understand how it affects survey research DATA. Whites, for example, are less likely to express racist beliefs if interviewed by blacks, a form of interviewer bias that operates even when filling out anonymous questionnaires in the presence of blacks. This is related to the tendency of respondents to give what they think are socially acceptable answers in order to make a good impression on the interviewer. There is also concern that the interview situation is somewhat artificial and, as such, may elicit responses from people that do not reflect how they actually feel, think, or behave. As a result of such findings, methodological studies of interviews as social situations are an important area of sociological research.
See also ERROR; CASE STUDY; PARTICIPANT OBSERVATION; SURVEY.

Reading
Alreck, Pamela L., and Robert B. Settle. 1995. *The survey research handbook,* 2nd ed. Chicago, IL: Irwin.
Mishler, Elliot G. 1986. *Research interviewing: Context and narrative.* Cambridge: Harvard University Press.
Schuman, Howard, and Stanley Presser. 1996. Questions *and answers in attitude surveys,* 2nd ed. Thousand Oaks, CA: Sage.

interviewer bias   *See* INTERVIEW.

intragenerational   mobility *See* SOCIAL MOBILITY.

intrinsic growth rate   *See* STABLE POPULATION.

inverse relationship   *See* DIRECTION OF RELATIONSHIP.

invisible religion   Invisible religion refers to religious practice that is carried on privately, rather than through formal church attendance. It points to an alternative to the SECULARIZATION thesis, which argues that declining numbers of people attending religious services indicates that religion is losing its significance in INDUSTRIAL SOCIETIES. Instead, religious practice is seen in the broadest sense of the search for meaning in human existence, a search that can take many forms other than those measured by churchgoing.

Reading
Berger, Peter. 1967. *The sacred canopy.* New York: Doubleday.
Luckmann, Thomas. 1967. *The invisible religion.* New York: Macmillan.

iron law of oligarchy   *See* OLIGARCHY.

irregular relationship   *See* DIRECTION OF RELATIONSHIP.

isolation, racial   *See* SEGREGATION AND INTEGRATION.

J

J-curve theory *See* FRUSTRATION-AGGRESSION THEORY.

job *See* WORK.

justice In the simplest sense, justice is a concept referring to fairness and to the process of people getting what they deserve. In a legal sense, for example, justice consists of treating everyone according to the law, of guaranteeing civil rights and following prescribed procedures in a consistent and evenhanded way. Distributive or social justice, however, involves less precise notions of what is fair, especially in the distribution of resources and rewards such as WEALTH. Is a just society, for example, one that guarantees equality of opportunity or equality of outcomes? And what is the relationship between collective interests and justice for the individual?

In a highly influential work, philosopher John Rawls argued that equality should prevail unless inequality serves the best interests of everyone. Denying children rights of free speech while in school, for example, has been defended by some as a way to ensure an orderly learning environment, thereby denying equal rights and serving everyone's interests at the same time (including the learning rights of those who are silenced). Robert Nozick, on the other hand, argues that justice is done when interference with individual freedom is minimized, especially in relation to the STATE.

Reading

Moore, Barrington. 1978. *Injustice: The social causes of obedience and revolt.* London: Macmillan.

Nozick, Robert. 1974. *Anarchy, state, and utopia.* New York: Basic Books.

Rawls, John. [1971] 1973. *A theory of justice.* Oxford, England: Oxford University Press.

juvenile delinquency *See* DELINQUENCY.

K

kinship Kinship is the most universal and basic of all human relationships – that based on ties of blood, marriage, or adoption (although some societies recognize varieties of *fictive kin,* people who are treated "like FAMILY" even though technically they are not related according to established rules of kinship). In small tribal societies, kinship is the basis of all social organization. In other words, the kin GROUP and the SOCIETY are one and the same thing. As societies become more complex, kinship accounts for a shrinking portion of social life. AGRARIAN SOCIETIES, for example, include many different family units whose interests may conflict not only with one another but with those of society as a whole. The distribution of WEALTH, POWER, and PRESTIGE is strongly dependent on family ties. In INDUSTRIAL SOCIETIES, by comparison, kinship is a relatively unimportant tie except that it is through kin that much SOCIALIZATION occurs and people meet primary emotional needs. Beyond this, however, the major social INSTITUTIONS – economic, political, religious, and so on – are organized without any specific connection to kinship.

There are two basic kinds of kinship ties: (1) those based on blood ties that trace *descent* and (2) those based on marriage, adoption, or other connections (known as *affinal* ties). Descent is generally traced either through the mother's blood relatives (*matrilineal*), the father's (*patrilineal*), or both (bilateral descent). In a matrilineal system, for example, a child is related to his or her mother and the line of mothers extending back in time from her as well as their male and female siblings. But there is no kin relationship with the father and any of his relatives, including the father's mother. A woman's son is related to her, but his children are not; they will trace their descent through their mother and the line of mothers extending back from her. In a patrilineal system, these arrangements are reversed.

Kinship is socially important because of its connection to social rights and obligations, power, and the inheritance of property. This is especially true in smaller, nonindustrial societies in which kinship is a major part of social organization, but it is much less important in industrial societies. For this reason, kinship is generally of more interest to anthropologists than to sociologists.

See also FAMILY; MARRIAGE RULES.

Reading

Farber, Bernard. 1981. *Conceptions of kinship.* New York: Elsevier.

Goody, Jack. 1983. *The development of the family and marriage in Europe.* New York: Free Press.

Murdock, George Peter. 1949. *Social structure.* New York: Macmillan.

knowledge Knowledge is what we perceive to be real and true. It can be as simple and commonplace as how to tie a shoe or as rarified and complex as particle physics. Knowledge is sociologically significant because it is socially created and because we depend on it for our sense of reality.

In everyday life we carry with us knowledge of how the social world works, what sociologist Alfred SCHUTZ called *stock knowledge* (also known as *commonsense knowledge*). We know what to say when answering a ringing telephone, for example, how to tell time, how to behave in restaurants, how to dress in ways appropriate for various occasions, or how to divert attention from someone who is deeply embarrassed. Social life is based on a shared sense of what is real, and this, in turn, is based on knowledge, especially that contained in CULTURE. Without the existence of knowledge, we would not know how to participate in the countless situations that make up social life. But it is equally true that without such knowledge social life itself would not exist. There would be no such thing as "conversation," for example, without shared knowledge of what a conversation is and how people must behave in order for one to take place.

The most longstanding sociological interest in knowledge has to do with the question of where it comes from in the first place. In general, sociologists regard all forms of knowledge as socially produced and shaped by the culture and structure of SOCIAL SYSTEMS. Karl MARX argued that ruling economic classes shape knowledge in ways that promote their interests over those of subordinate classes. From a Marxist perspective, for example, the idea that WEALTH results from hard work rather than from inheritance, luck, or various forms of MARKET manipulation, serves the interests of dominant classes in capitalist societies. It does so by masking the true basis of wealth and by keeping the lower classes hard at work (which will rarely make any of them wealthy) and distracted from paying critical attention to the reality of the class system and how it works.

Following Marx, Karl MANNHEIM argued that the social basis for knowledge is much broader than the economic forces that form the core of Marx's approach. In more recent times, various approaches to knowledge have developed, including POST-MODERNISM.

See also BASE AND SUPERSTRUCTURE; BELIEF; CLASS CONSCIOUSNESS AND FALSE CONSCIOUSNESS; CULTURE; DOMINANT IDEOLOGY THESIS; ETHNOMETHODOLOGY; HEGEMONY; HERMENEUTICS; IDEOLOGY; MASS COMMUNICATION AND MASS MEDIA; PHENOMENOLOGY; POSITIVISM; WORLD-VIEW.

Reading

Mannheim, Karl. 1936. *Ideology and utopia*. London: Routledge and Kegan Paul.

Mannheim, Karl. 1952. *Essays on the sociology of knowledge*. London: Routledge and Kegan Paul.

Schutz, Alfred. [1932] 1972. *The phenomenology of the social world*. London: Heinemann Educational Books.

kurtosis *See* NORMAL CURVE DISTRIBUTION.

L

labeling theory The core idea of labeling theory is that the social response to DEVIANCE can profoundly affect how people are perceived and how they perceive themselves as well as the resources and opportunities that are then made available to them. This, in turn, affects the likelihood of future deviant behavior. To the extent that societies try to control deviance by backing people into a corner and forcing upon them a deviant STATUS and limited opportunities, societies actually promote deviance.

Drawing primarily on the INTERACTIONIST PERSPECTIVE, labeling theory starts from the idea that if appearance or behavior is perceived and interpreted by people as deviant, people will tend to label the offenders as deviant and respond with some form of punishment. Depending on what kind of NORM is violated, punishment can take many forms, from slight reprimands to social isolation to shaming to the formalities of fines and imprisonment.

For their part, offenders must cope with such consequences, and it is here that efforts at SOCIAL CONTROL can backfire to produce more rather than less deviance. If people who steal, for example, are labeled thieves, imprisoned in the company of others who have stolen, shunned upon their release, and denied opportunities to work because they are not trusted, they likely will find themselves in a position in which further stealing is a practical necessity that fits the generally accepted view of who they are.

It is important to note that labeling theory is an attempt to explain patterns of deviance that result from the social response to deviance. In making this distinction, Edwin Lemert uses the term *primary deviance* to refer to violations of norms that occur without the influence of the labeling process (such as stealing a car out of a desire to own it). *Secondary deviance* refers to subsequent deviance that is promoted by the labeling process and its consequences.

In some applications – most notably in relation to mental illness – labeling theory has been used to argue that the deviance itself is socially constructed out of the social response to a person's behavior. If we identify individuals as "crazy," for example, and refuse to treat them as "sane," labeling theory argues that over time it becomes increasingly likely that those so labeled will in fact lose their mental balance and actually behave in increasingly "crazy" ways regardless of their initial mental condition. In this sense, insanity is socially produced rather than being simply an individual's internal psychological condition. A perfectly sane but eccentric and fiercely independent artist, for example, may be treated as mentally ill – isolated, confined, whispered about, and not allowed to manage personal affairs. In response to this labeling and its effects, such individuals might become increasingly frustrated, angry, and desperate to regain control over their lives and work. This, in turn, might well be interpreted as the tragic progression of mental "disease," and prompt still more severe social responses. In this way, argue labeling theorists, societies can literally produce madness by labeling people as mad.

See also SELF; SELF-FULFILLING PROPHECY; STIGMA.

Reading

Becker, Howard S. 1973. *Outsiders: Studies in the sociology of deviance*, rev. ed. New York: Free Press.

Lemert, Edwin M. 1951. *Human deviance, social problems, and social control.* New York: McGraw-Hill.

Szaz, Thomas. 1987. *Insanity: The idea and its consequences.* New York: Wiley.

labor aristocracy *See* LABOR MARKET.

labor force The labor force is usually defined as the economically active and productive POPULATION in a SOCIETY, which includes both those who are employed and those who are actively seeking employment. In general, "employed" refers only to those who are working for money, either in the form of wages or profit.

Feminists and others object to this definition of the labor force because it leaves out huge numbers of people who engage in economically productive work. This is especially true of the domestic work that women do in all types of societies as well as the work of many men in nonindustrial societies. When people build their own houses, for example, haul their own water or care for their own

children, most societies do not count such labor as economically productive because it does not generate an exchange that includes cash. If the same people hire someone to build their house, however, or to supply them with water or to care for their children, this is considered to be economically productive. As a result, a great amount of productive labor is made invisible, not only to social scientists, but to government policy makers. This, in turn, gives a distorted picture of how much productivity is actually going on in a society and what its needs and resources truly are.

See also LABOR AND LABOR POWER; LABOR MARKET; UNEMPLOYMENT AND UNDEREMPLOYMENT.

Reading

Hauser, Philip M. 1949. "The labor force and gainful workers: Concept, measurement, and comparability." *American Journal of Sociology* 54: 338–55.

Waring, Marilyn. 1988. *If women counted: A new feminist economics.* San Francisco: Harper San Francisco.

labor and labor power As developed by Karl MARX, labor is both the process and the product of productive work. When a carpenter builds a bookcase and sells it, what is being sold is labor, the value of which is contained in the bookcase. In this sense, the concept of labor describes not simply an activity but a particular relationship between people, work, and the fruits of that work.

Under CAPITALISM, workers do not sell their labor since they have no control over the MEANS OF PRODUCTION (factories and such), the production process, or what is produced. All that they have to sell is their time – their potential to produce something – in exchange for wages.

Marx called this potential labor power.

The distinction between labor and labor power is critical in Marx's analysis of CLASS CONFLICT and capitalism, for it draws attention to the social relationships between workers, production, and the capitalist class and the consequences these produce for the nature of work and the creation of class INEQUALITY. Depriving workers of the chance to sell their labor, for example, and reducing them to selling labor power is seen as a major source of ALIENATION.

See also LABOR MARKET; VALUE, ECONOMIC.

Reading

Hodgson, G. 1982. *Capitalism, value, and exploitation.* Oxford, England: Martin Robertson.

Marx, Karl. [1867] 1975. *Capital: A critique of political economy.* New York: International Publishers.

labor market A labor market is a set of social mechanisms through which labor is bought and sold. With the rise of industrial CAPITALISM in the eighteenth and nineteenth centuries, human labor emerged not simply as a means of producing goods for use and exchange, but as a COMMODITY to be sold in return for wages. This gave increased importance to the idea of a labor market.

As capitalism has developed, the shape and nature of such markets has been important in maintaining the unequal relationship between capitalists and workers. The concept of *labor market segmentation,* for example, refers to the tendency of labor markets, and with them the WORKING CLASS, to become divided into distinct types of jobs. Jobs in the *primary labor market* tend to be highly skilled and highly paid, have clear lines of advancement and offer greater than average degrees of training and ob security to workers (who, unlike most workers, tend to be unionized). The primary market is itself divided into two smaller segments: *independent primary* and *subordinate primary.* Independent primary jobs have relatively high levels of creativity and autonomy and involve decision-making, problem solving, and initiative. Scientists, university professors, politicians, lawyers, police chiefs, and corporate executives are all in the independent primary labor market.

Although sharing many of the benefits of independent primary jobs, subordinate primary jobs tend to be more routine and emphasize discipline, dependability, and obedience to authority. Examples include police officer, computer programmer, skilled factory worker, noncommissioned officer in the military, and bank teller.

In stark contrast to the primary labor market, the *secondary labor market* includes jobs that are low in pay, PRESTIGE, and security, and offer little opportunity to acquire skills or advance. They do not encourage stable work habits and have high turnover and weak or nonexistent TRADE UNIONS. Such occupations include fast-food workers, clerks, laborers, day-care workers, bus and taxi drivers, assembly line workers, and restaurant employees.

The concept of labor market segmentation is most closely associated with the Marxist argument that segmentation serves the interests of capitalism by making it easier to control workers. This is accomplished by creating divisions within the working class so that people in various segments of the labor market will tend to disassociate themselves from workers in less privileged segments. To some degree, for example, workers in the primary labor market are relatively well rewarded and therefore feel little in common with those in the secondary market and are unlikely to join with them to work in the interests of working people as a class. Such was the case with what has been called the *labor aristocracy* of skilled trade workers in Britain at the turn of the twentieth century.

The concept of labor market segmentation is also useful for understanding how characteristics such as education, race, and gender affect occupational outcomes and, with them, SOCIAL INEQUALITY. Having a higher education, for example, "pays off" to a much greater degree in the independent primary labor market than it does in the secondary market. Since women and other minorities tend to be limited by PREJUDICE AND DISCRIMINATION to subordinate primary and secondary labor market occupations, this blunts their ability to use resources such as education to improve their standing.

See also CAPITALISM; DUAL ECONOMY; EMBOURGEOISEMENT; LABOR FORCE; STATUS ATTAINMENT AND NEW STRUCTURALISM.

Reading
Averott, Robert T. 1968. *The dual economy: The dynamics of American industry structure.* New York: Norton.
Hobsbawm, E. 1964. "The labour aristocracy." In *Labouring men.* London: Weidenfeld and Nicolson.
Reich, Michael, D. M. Gordon, and Robert C. Edwards. 1973. "A theory of labor market segmentation." *American Economic Review* 63 (May).
Kalleberg, Arne, and Aage B. Sørenson. 1979. "The sociology of labor markets." *Annual Review of Sociology* 5: 351–79.

labor market segmentation *See* LABOR MARKET.

labor power *See* LABOR AND LABOR POWER.

labor process Labor process is a Marxist term for production. It is used to draw attention to the role that human beings play in the production process, which is central to a Marxist perspective on economic life. Goods do not simply come from a faceless process, but instead are created through the application of human labor to raw materials and the MEANS OF PRODUCTION. The concept of labor process also draws attention to how production is organized as a social activity, especially the relations of production through which workers are dominated and controlled and their work is degraded as part of their EXPLOITATION under CAPITALISM.

See also LABOR POWER; PROFIT; VALUE, ECONOMIC.

Reading
Braverman, Harry. 1974. *Labor and monopoly capitalism.* New York: Monthly Review Press.

labor theory of value *See* VALUE, ECONOMIC.

laissez-faire Laissez-faire, a French phrase that roughly translates as "allow to do," has two main sociological definitions. In relation to POLITICAL ECONOMY, it is traced to a Frenchman named Legendre who, when asked what the state could do for businessmen replied, in essence, "Leave us to do it." It has also been associated with Adam Smith's description of the ideal role of the STATE in relation to CAPITALISM, which is to do nothing and leave the capitalists and the MARKETS alone to regulate themselves. Under laissez-faire capitalism, competition is supposed to ensure that the goods people want will be produced in abundance and sold at a price they are willing to pay.

The concept of laissez-faire is also used to describe LEADERSHIP styles, especially in small GROUPS. In contrast to democratic and authoritarian leaders, laissez-faire leaders do very little leading and participate minimally, offering neither guidance nor evaluation, an approach that can, depending on the situation, generate anxiety among those wanting direction.

Reading

Lippitt, R., and R. K. White. 1947. "An experimental study of leadership and group life." In *Readings in social psychology*, edited by T. M. Newcomb and E. L. Hartley. New York: Holt, Rinehart and Winston.

Viner, Jacob. [1927] 1958. "Adam Smith and laissez-faire." In *The long view and the short: Studies in economic theory and policy*, 213–45. Glencoe, IL: Free Press.

landed gentry *See* SOCIAL CLASS.

language At the core of every CULTURE is language, the collection of words and the rules of syntax and grammar that govern how words are supposed to be arranged in order to convey a particular meaning. Language is central because it is through it that we are able to create the meaning of human experience, thought, feeling, appearance, and behavior. In this sense, language enables us to create reality itself by substituting words for direct experience. When we read a newspaper, we use words to create in our minds what we then take to be KNOWLEDGE about what is happening in the world. This is no less the case with conversations in which people use words to represent who they are, or with internal conversations in which we think about and reflect upon the reality of ourselves.

Language has several uses in social life. In the most basic sense, it is a medium that enables us to store, manipulate, and communicate knowledge. *Speech communities* – the collection of all those who share a particular language – also help define the structural BOUNDARIES of larger COMMUNITIES such as tribes, ethnic groups, regions, and nations. This is also true to some extent of occupations such as law, science, and medicine (and sociology) whose specialized languages set them apart from outsiders.

In some cases, particular acts of speech, known as *performative language*, are meaningful actions in themselves. When a bride and groom utter the words "I do" at the appropriate moment in a typical Christian wedding ceremony, they actually perform a meaningful act that changes the nature of their social relationship. The same can be said of "I promise," "I swear," "You're fired," "I quit," and, to some degree, "I apologize" and "I love you" (especially when spoken for the first time). With performative language, to *say* it is to *do* it.

The sociological interest in language covers a broad terrain, from the analysis of meaning and conversation to questions about the social construction of reality to the importance of language in the process of SOCIALIZATION and identity formation to the role of language in SOCIAL INEQUALITY and OPPRESSION.

See also ETHNOMETHODOLOGY; INTER-
ACTIONIST PERSPECTIVE; MIND; PHE-
NOMENOLOGY; SEMIOTICS.
Reading
Bloomfield, Leonard. [1933] 1951. *Language*, rev. ed. New York: Holt.
Farb, Peter. 1973. *Word play: What happens when people talk*. New York: Knopf.
Spender, Dale. 1980. *Man-made language*. London: Routledge and Kegan Paul.
Whorf, Benjamin L. 1956. *Language, thought and reality*. Cambridge, MA: MIT Press.

latent consequence *See* FUNC-
TIONALIST PERSPECTIVE.

latent status *See* STATUS.

latifundia An estate system based on land grants in Latin America originally awarded by the Spanish crown during the period of European COLONIALISM AND IMPERIALISM. The system initially resembled FEUDALISM, but then adapted to CAPITALISM while retaining its essential agricultural character. Typically, absentee landlords control and profit from the labor of impoverished agricultural workers who cannot escape their authority. The latifundia system has been an ongoing target of efforts to redistribute land through either reform or revolution.

law Laws are NORMS with formal SANCTIONS – punishments or rewards that are codified and whose enforcement is generally reserved for those in positions of AUTHORITY. The punishment for burglary, for example, is specified in legal statutes as are the rules that define who may apprehend and punish burglars, under what circumstances, and with what procedures.

It is sociologically useful to distinguish between criminal law and civil law. *Criminal law* prohibits behaviors such as murder, fraud, or desecrating sacred objects or places. In contrast, *civil law* is used to regulate social relationships, such as resolving a dispute or compensating someone who has been treated unfairly or been caused injury or loss through negligence. Depending on which area of social life is involved, civil law takes many forms, from commercial, constitutional, and family law to procedural law (which regulates the functioning of courts).

DURKHEIM argues that as societies become structurally more complex and elaborate, civil law grows in importance at the expense of criminal law. In a small tribal SOCIETY, for example, most laws take the form of criminal laws because with a relatively simple structure, people's relationships can be managed informally through a common CULTURE. In industrial societies, however, the DIVISION OF LABOR is so complex and cultures are so heterogeneous that formal legal codes are needed to manage relationships that involve people who may barely know one another and have little in common except the kind of interdependency that exists between buyers and sellers of goods, between employers and employees, or between motorists who happen to collide on a highway. There is a connection, then, between the kinds of norms that predominate in a society and the nature of the cohesive bonds that hold it together.
See also COHESION; NATURAL LAW.
Reading
Durkheim, Émile. [1893] 1933. *The division of labor in society*. New York: Free Press.

Reasons, Charles E., and Robert M. Rich. 1978. *The sociology of law.* Toronto: Butterworths.

leadership Leadership is the ability to influence what goes on in a SOCIAL SYSTEM. In most cases, leadership is based on some form of legitimate AUTHORITY associated with a social STATUS such as manager or president, but this is not necessarily the case. Sociologists are particularly interested in the circumstances under which leadership emerges in GROUPS as well as how particular individuals become designated as leaders. Leaders are more likely to emerge during a crisis, and individuals who participate the most – for example, those saying the most in group discussions – are most likely to become leaders.

See also POWER; POWER STRUCTURE.

Reading

Fiedler, Fred. E. 1967. *A theory of leadership effectiveness.* New York: McGraw-Hill.

Pfeffer, J. 1981. *Power in organizations.* Marshfield, MA: Pitman.

least-squares *See* REGRESSION ANALYSIS.

legal-rational authority *See* AUTHORITY.

legitimation Legitimation is a process through which a SOCIAL SYSTEM or some aspect of it comes to be accepted as appropriate and generally supported by those who participate in it. Since it is difficult to hold a system together through coercion for long periods, the most effective way to maintain social COHESION is for people to believe in and accept the system as it is.

Legitimation is accomplished in a variety of ways, beginning with childhood SOCIALIZATION. When school children salute the flag of their country at the start of each day, for example, or study history texts that rarely criticize their political or economic system, they will tend to identify with those systems and accept them as legitimate even in the face of undesirable or even horrific consequences. As children are taught to respect AUTHORITY, beginning with their parents and teachers, they also will tend to accept as legitimate any forms of authority placed over them.

Legitimation is a crucial concept in the study of AUTHORITY and social STRATIFICATION because it plays such an important part not only in the stability of social systems of all kinds but, most importantly, in the perpetuation of SOCIAL INEQUALITY and OPPRESSION.

See also CLASS CONSCIOUSNESS AND FALSE CONSCIOUSNESS; HEGEMONY; IDEOLOGY.

Reading

Barker, Rodney. 1990. *Political legitimacy and the state.* New York and Oxford: Oxford University Press.

Mann, Michael. 1986. *The sources of social power: A history of power from the beginning to A.D. 1760.* New York and Cambridge, England: Cambridge University Press.

Weber, Max. [1921] 1968. *Economy and society.* New York: Bedminster Press.

legitimation crisis LEGITIMATION crisis refers to the inability of the STATE under modern capitalism to satisfy its various constituencies. As Marxists observe, CAPITALISM is a system that is full of CONTRADICTION and competing interests, and one of the key functions of the state is to hold society together in spite of this. It is expected for example, both to provide for the health and welfare of the people and to promote the interests of business, two goals that often work at cross-purposes. As a result, the state may be perceived as lacking legitimacy.

Reading

Habermas, Jürgen. 1975. *Legitimation crisis.* London: Heinemann.

leisure Leisure is time away from WORK that is used for recreation, healing, relaxation, and other such pursuits. From a sociological perspective, leisure is socially produced both in its content – what people do instead of work – and in people's access to it as a reward and resource. Studies of leisure include attention to the role of leisure in FAMILY life; unequal access by GENDER, RACE, SOCIAL CLASS, and age; how leisure is turned into a COMMODITY under CAPITALISM, and the domination of leisure by the demands of work.

See also CONSPICUOUS CONSUMPTION.

Reading

Parker, Stanley. 1971. *The future of work and leisure.* New York: Praeger.

Roberts, Kenneth. 1970. *Leisure.* London: Longmans.

leisure class *See* CONSPICUOUS CONSUMPTION.

leptokurtic distribution *See* NORMAL CURVE DISTRIBUTION.

level of analysis In research, the level of analysis is a measure of the size and complexity of the units being observed. In sociological work, the smallest level of analysis is the individual person (as in SURVEY INTERVIEWS), and ranges upward from there to AGGREGATES such as GROUPS,

ORGANIZATIONS, COMMUNITIES, SOCIETIES, regions, and the entire world. The distinction among various levels of analysis is important because what is actually observed varies depending on the level of analysis, and because serious mistakes can be made if we generalize from one level of analysis to another.

Observations vary from one level of analysis to another because, as Paul LAZARSFELD and Herbert Menzel show, different units have different properties. A community, for example, can have properties based on observations of the people who live in them (such as the MEAN family income or the percentage voting in an election). It can also have properties that do not rely on information about individuals, such as whether the economy is primarily industrial or service-oriented. Individuals also can have a variety of properties such as those based solely on observations of the individual (years of schooling or number of children) or properties that derive from the individual's relation to a social environment (such as whether their children attend racially integrated schools).

An awareness of levels of analysis is also important because it is often tempting to generalize from one level to another, leading to several kinds of fallacies. The most famous of these is the *ecological fallacy*, which occurs if differences observed among aggregates such as communities are used to infer that comparable differences exist among individuals. Suppose that we gather DATA showing that communities whose residents have relatively high average levels of educational attainment also tend to have relatively high rates of suicide. If we then infer from this that highly educated people are more likely to commit suicide than are less educated people, we would be committing an ecological fallacy, because differences among aggregates cannot be used to make inferences about differences among the individuals who make them up. In some cases, the pattern among individuals may turn out to be the opposite of that at the aggregate level, while in others the pattern may be the same but the differences much smaller. Also note that the ecological fallacy runs in both directions: if two VARIABLES are related at the individual level, this does not mean they will be related at the aggregate level.

See also MACROSOCIOLOGY AND MICROSOCIOLOGY.

Reading

Alker, Hayward R. 1969. "A typology of ecological fallacies." In *Quantitative ecological analysis in the social sciences*, edited by Mattei Dogan and Stein Rokkan. Cambridge, MA: MIT Press.

Lazarsfeld, Paul F., and Herbert Menzel. 1969. "On the relation between individual and collective properties." In *A sociological reader on complex organizations*, edited by Amatai Etzioni. New York: Holt, Rinehart and Winston.

Robinson, William S. 1950. "Ecological correlation and behavior of individuals." *American Sociological Review* 15: 351–57.

liberal feminism *See* FEMINISM.

liberalism *See* CONSERVATISM AND LIBERALISM.

life chances As used by Max WEBER, life chances is a term that describes social class differences. Weber defined SOCIAL CLASS in terms of people's access to goods and services, especially as these are distributed through MARKETS. These would include material goods such as food and housing; services such as medical care, police and fire protection, and public education; and cultural products such as art, music, and knowledge. Weber did not include POWER and PRESTIGE in his definition of class. These he discussed as separate dimensions of inequality (PARTY and STATUS).

The distribution of life chances is influenced primarily by the distribution of resources such as WEALTH AND INCOME (inherited, earned, and otherwise), occupational skills, and education. Depending on the SOCIETY, it also is affected by ascribed characteristics such as GENDER, RACE, and ETHNICITY.

Reading

Weber, Max. 1946. *From Max Weber: Essays in sociology*. Edited and translated by Hans H. Gerth and C. Wright Mills. New York: Oxford University Press.

life course (also called the *life cycle*). The life course is the culturally defined sequence of AGE CATEGORIES that people are normally expected to pass through as they progress from birth to death. These stages are associated with cultural BELIEFS about how aging affects people's abilities, VALUES, and so on, as well as changing distributions of social rewards and resources such as POWER and PRESTIGE.

Included in cultural conceptions of the life course is some idea of how long people are expected to live and, with it, ideas about what constitutes a "premature" or "untimely" death. Deaths among infants and children, for example, are more common in nonindustrial than in INDUSTRIAL SOCIETIES, and for this reason are less likely to be viewed as tragic.

See also AGING; COHORT.

Reading

Binstock, Robert H., and Linda K. George, eds. 1996. *Handbook of aging and the social sciences*, 4th ed. San Diego: Academic Press.

Clausen, John A. 1986. *The life course: A sociological perspective*. Englewood Cliffs, NJ: Prentice-Hall.

Eisenstadt, Shmuel N. 1956. *From generation to generation*. New York: Free Press.

life expectancy *See* DEATH RATE.

lifestyle A lifestyle is a pattern of living that includes the kinds of goods and services people make use of; taste in music, art, film, and other cultural products; and choice of leisure activities. Sociologically, lifestyle is often studied in relation to characteristics such as SOCIAL CLASS. It is also of interest to those who study DEVIANCE and alternative lifestyles; life in rural, urban, and suburban COMMUNITIES; and the effects of lifestyle patterns on emotional and physical health.
See also EMBOURGEOISEMENT.

Reading

Berkman, Lisa F., and Lester Breslow. 1983. *Health and ways of living*. New York: Oxford University Press.

Macklin, Eleanor D., and R. H. Rubin. 1983. *Contemporary families and alternative lifestyles*. Beverly Hills, CA: Sage Publications.

life table A life table is a statistical model that shows what would happen to a hypothetical group of people if they lived out their lives under a particular set of age-specific DEATH RATES. To construct a life table, we start with a hypothetical group of 1,000 newborns and, for each year of life, subtract the number who would be expected to die under current mortality conditions. As the group

ages, it will become progressively smaller until no one is left.

Life tables generate a variety of statistics of interest to demographers (and actuaries), but the most important of these is life expectancy, or the average number of years of life that people would expect to live after having attained a given age. It is a hypothetical number based on the assumption that age-specific death rates from a given year would remain unchanged throughout a person's life. It is nonetheless a very useful way of summarizing those death rates and expressing overall mortality conditions in a single number.
See also DEMOGRAPHY; STANDARDIZATION.

Reading

Shryock, Henry S., and Jacob Siegel and Associates. 1976. *The methods and materials of demography*. New York: Academic Press.

life-world *See* PHENOMENOLOGY AND PHENOMENOLOGICAL SOCIOLOGY.

Likert scale *See* ATTITUDE SCALE.

linear relationship *See* DIRECTION OF RELATIONSHIP.

lobbying *See* INTEREST GROUP.

log-linear analysis In statistics, log-linear analysis is a form of MULTIVARIATE ANALYSIS designed for nomial and ordinal-scale VARIABLES. Most multivariate techniques such as REGRESSION ANALYSIS and PATH ANALYSIS require interval- or ratio-scale variables. Prior to the development of the log-linear approach, this severely limited the kinds of CAUSAL MODELS sociologists could construct and test without ignoring crucial assumptions that might render their findings meaningless. The technique applies logarithms to CROSS-TABULA-TIONS in order to test successive models until the best explanation of the DATA is found.

Reading

Agresti, Alan. 1996. *Introduction to categorical data analysis.* New York: Wiley.

longitudinal effect *See* COHORT.

longitudinal study A longitudinal study (also known as a *panel study*) follows the same SAMPLE over time and makes repeated observations. With longitudinal SURVEYS, for example, the same group of people is interviewed at regular intervals, enabling researchers to track changes over time and to relate them to VARIABLES that might explain why the changes occur.

Longitudinal research is valuable because it enables survey researchers to get close to the kinds of CAUSAL EXPLANATIONS usually attainable only with EXPERIMENTS. Studies of occupational mobility, for example, have tracked people's occupational changes over several decades and related these to factors such as education, family, background, gender, race, and work patterns.

The major difficulty (and expense) in longitudinal research is maintaining the integrity of the original sample. People lose interest, move, or die, and this can cause a deterioration of sample size and, with it, the validity of conclusions drawn from the data. In addition, simply belonging to a panel can affect people's behavior, expectations, and perceptions of themselves and their lives in ways that make the sample no longer representative of the POPULATION.

One way of dealing with the problem of maintaining a panel is to take different samples of comparable age categories at different times. For example, researchers might INTERVIEW a sample of 20–24-year-olds, then interview a sample of 30–34-year-olds ten years later. Although the individuals may not be the same (and hence do not constitute a panel), the two samples are drawn from roughly the same population at two different times (those 20–24-year-olds will be 30–34 ten years later). It is of course not possible to use such a design to track changes in individuals, but it is possible to track changes at the AGGREGATE level, and this can be quite revealing.

See also COHORT; CROSS-SECTIONAL DATA; EXPERIMENT.

Reading

Menard, S. 1991. *Longitudinal research.* Newbury Park, CA: Sage Publications.

looking-glass self *See* SELF.

Lorenz curve In the study of social STRATIFICATION, a Lorenz curve is a graph that can be used to measure how much the distribution of something like WEALTH or INCOME deviates from a condition of equality. For a given unit of analysis (such as families), the accompanying figure shows what percentage of all income (shown along the *y*-axis) is received by what percentage of families (shown along the *x*-axis). A straight diagonal line indicates, for example, that the lowest 10 percent of the POPULATION receives 10 percent of all income; the lowest 20 percent receives 20 percent, the lowest 80 percent receives 80 percent, and so on, just as we would expect if income were distributed equally across a population.

As the line bows out into a curve extending to the lower right, however, it indicates an increasingly unequal distribution. On the upper curve, for example, the bottom 50 percent of the population receives only around 20 percent of all income and on the lower curve, the bottom 50 percent receive only around 5 percent of all wealth. These Lorenz curves show at a glance that the distribution of wealth is more unequal than the distribution of income.

In conjunction with Lorenz curves, the *Gini index* (devised by the Italian sociologist Corrado Gini) offers a numerical indicator of the degree of inequality. Notice that the diagonal line representing a condition of equality in the figure forms a triangle with the *x*-axis on the bottom and the reflection of the *y*-axis on the right. If we focus on the area contained within this triangle, we can see that as the Lorenz curve becomes more bowed to reflect greater inequality, the proportion of the area between the diagonal line and the curve increases (which is to say, there is more area between the diagonal and the wealth curve than there is between the diagonal and the income curve). The Gini index is based on the percentage of the total area of the triangle that falls between the diagonal and a Lorenz curve. The greater

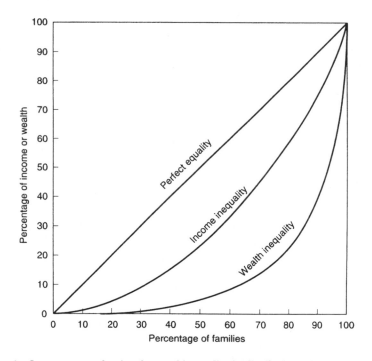

Figure 6 *Lorenz curves showing degree of inequality in distributions of income and wealth (curved lines) compared with conditions of perfect equality (straight line) in the United States. Source:* Harold R. Kerbo, *Social stratification and inequality,* 3rd ed., New York: McGraw-Hill, 1996 (first published 1991), figure 2.5, reproduced with permission of The McGraw-Hill Companies

the degree of inequality, the larger the index will be. It will vary between a value of zero (when the Lorenz curve and the diagonal coincide) to a theoretical (but practically impossible) high of 1.0.

Both the Lorenz curve and the Gini index are useful not only for describing the level of inequality in a given population, but for measuring differences between populations (such as nations) or changes over time in the degree of inequality within a population.

See also SOCIAL CLASS.

Reading

Gini, Corrado. 1921. "Measurement of inequality of incomes." *Economic Journal* 31: 124–26.

Lorenz, Max O. 1905. "Methods of measuring the concentration of wealth." *Journal of the American Statistical Association* 9: 209–19.

lower class In the study of social STRATIFICATION, the lower class is the level designated as the lowest position in virtually every dimension of inequality. Members of the lower class have no WEALTH and little INCOME. They neither own nor control any MEANS OF PRODUCTION and are at the bottom of economic and political AUTHORITY structures. They are usually without occupations, and when they do work have the most menial jobs that require little if any skill or training and offer no stability or hope of advancement. Especially in the United States, the belief is widespread that the composition of the lower class is relatively stable and passed on from one generation to the next. Although recent evidence suggests that a permanent UNDERCLASS may be forming within the black population, in general there is considerable movement between the LOWER CLASS and the working class just above it. The recurring crises of CAPITALISM, for example, produce considerable downward SOCIAL MOBILITY that swells the ranks of the homeless, detached, marginal population that Karl MARX referred to as the LUMPENPROLETARIAT.

See also SOCIAL CLASS.

Reading

George, Vic, and Roger Lawson. 1980. *Poverty and inequality in Common Market countries.* London: Routledge and Kegan Paul.

Wilson, William Julius. 1987. *The truly disadvantaged: The inner city, the underclass, and public policy.* Chicago: University of Chicago Press.

lumpenproletariat *See* SOCIAL CLASS.

M

macrosociology and microsociology
Sociologists often distinguish between macrosociology, which deals with social life on the larger scale of organizations, COMMUNITIES, and SOCIETIES, and microsociology, which focuses on the face-to-face world of social INTERACTION. There are those, however, who argue that the distinction is unclear if not false because what are identified as the macro elements of social life are constructed through what takes place on the micro level. What is known as the STATE, for example, ultimately results from complex patterns of interaction among individuals.

Reading
Hilbert, R. A. 1990. "Ethnomethodology and the micro-macro order." *American Sociological Review* 55(6): 794–808.
Lenski, Gerhard, E., Jean Lenski, and Patrick Nolan. 1998. *Human societies: An introduction to macrosociology*, 8th ed. New York: McGraw-Hill.

managerial class *See* SOCIAL CLASS.

managerial revolution The managerial revolution is a change that evolved as modern CAPITALISM shifted ownership toward publicly owned stock, and management was placed primarily in the hands of trained specialists. This was in stark contrast to the early stages of industrial capitalism, when companies were owned and managed largely by individuals and families. In the 1930s and 1940s, several authors argued that the managerial revolution would transform the face of modern capitalism and relations between CAPITAL and LABOR. Professional managers, they believed, would have codes of ethics and different interests than the old-style family capitalists, focusing less singlemindedly on profit, expansion, and the accumulation of great WEALTH and more on social responsibility and harmonious relations with workers.

Subsequent research has shown that the managerial revolution thesis was both premature and overblown. Concentrated family ownership, for example, is still the case in some large corporations; in many others managers own considerable amounts of stock in their own companies; and studies find that managers are no less concerned than owners with profit and the bottom line. In addition, the governing boards of corporations are increasingly linked through the practice of individuals serving on multiple boards ("interlocking directorates"), which reinforces a commonality and unity of purpose around the basic goals of capitalist competition and expansion. In short, the structure of capitalism has changed dramatically since the nineteenth century, but the fundamental dynamic that defines and drives capitalism as a system has not.
See also CORPORATE CLASS; POST-INDUSTRIAL SOCIETY.

Reading

Berle, Adolf A., Jr., and Gardiner C. Means. [1932] 1968. *The modern corporation and private property*, rev. ed. New York: Harcourt Brace Jovanovich.

Burch, P. H., Jr. 1972. *The managerial revolution reassessed*. Lexington, MA: D. C. Heath.

Burnham, J. 1941. *The managerial revolution*. New York: Day.

Herman, E. S. 1981. *Corporate control, corporate power*. New York: Cambridge University Press.

manifest consequence *See* FUNC-TIONALIST PERSPECTIVE.

manifest status *See* STATUS.

manor *See* FEUDALISM.

marginal *See* CROSS-TABULATION.

market A market is a social mechanism for exchanging goods and services. It can have a concrete existence in a particular time and place, such as a village market or a stock market, or it can refer to a general social pattern through which exchanges are made, such as a LABOR MARKET or even a "marriage market." Markets are based on certain principles, such as COMPETITION, a "fair deal," profit, or gaining advantage over others ("Let the buyer beware"), which distinguish it from other models of exchange, such as communal sharing and cooperation.

The historical emergence and growth of market economies are of great interest to sociologists because of their profound influence on social life, especially in relation to SOCIAL INEQUALITY. In market-dominated societies, for example, there is a tendency to measure worth in terms of monetary value. The value we assign to a particular kind of work depends to a great extent on how much income it generates, and unpaid labor (such as housework) is often viewed as not being work at all. Markets also serve as important mechanisms through which class, gender, and racial inequality and OPPRESSION are realized and perpetuated. Male privilege, for example, depends in part on the ability to limit women's access to various occupations within the labor market and to control how much women are paid in exchange for their labor.

See also LABOR MARKET; LIFE CHANCES; MARKET SITUATION; SOCIAL CLASS; WORLD SYSTEM.

Reading

Swedberg, Richard. 1987. "Economic sociology: Past and present." *Current Sociology* 35: 1–22.

Weber, Max. [1921] 1968. *Economy and society*. New York: Bedminster Press.

White, Harrison. 1981. "Where do markets come from?" *American Journal of Sociology* 87: 517–47.

market situation The market situation is a person's position in a stratified society as determined by market forces – the demand and supply of goods, services, and various skills. When certain skills become obsolete due to the introduction of computers and robots, for example, workers who depend on those skills to earn a living find their market situation deteriorating. In similar ways, when demand increases for particular kinds of workers, their market situation improves and, along with it, their access to WEALTH AND INCOME and other rewards.

See also LIFE CHANCES; MARKET; SOCIAL CLASS; UNEMPLOYMENT AND UNDEREMPLOYMENT.

Reading

Goldthorpe, John H., D. Lockwood, F. Bechhofer, and J. Platt. 1968. *The affluent worker: Industrial attitudes and behavior.* Cambridge, England: Cambridge University Press.

——. 1968. *The affluent worker: Political attitudes and behavior.* Cambridge, England: Cambridge University Press.

marriage and divorce Marriage is a socially supported union involving two or more individuals in what is regarded as a stable, enduring arrangement based at least in part on a sexual bond of some kind. Depending on the SOCIETY, marriage may require religious or civil sanction (or both), although some couples may come to be considered married simply by living together for a prescribed period (common law marriage).

In most societies marriage serves to socially identify children by clearly defining KINSHIP ties to a mother, father, and extended relatives. It also serves to regulate sexual behavior; to transfer, preserve, or consolidate property, PRESTIGE, and POWER; and, in patriarchal societies, to transfer AUTHORITY over women from fathers to husbands. Most important, it is the basis for the institution of the FAMILY.

Although in most societies marriage is defined in heterosexual terms, marriage involving partners of the same sex is not unknown and is becoming increasingly acceptable in some INDUSTRIAL SOCIETIES. Gay and lesbian marriage is legal in Denmark, for example, and in some parts of the United States homosexual couples have won some rights (such as inheritance and insurance benefits) previously reserved for heterosexual spouses.

Divorce is the socially recognized dissolution of a marriage. Like marriage, it is regulated by a variety of cultural NORMS that govern how difficult it is to accomplish and the social and personal consequences it produces. In general, divorce is more difficult to obtain in societies where marriage and divorce affect the interests of large numbers of people, as, for example, when marriages join entire families in arrangements for sharing and concentrating property and power. By comparison, divorce is relatively easy in societies where marriage is regarded as no more than a consensual union between two people, designed to produce happiness and material security for them as individuals.

See also MARRIAGE RULES; PATRIARCHY.

Reading

Cherlin, Andrew J. 1992. *Marriage, divorce, and remarriage,* 2nd ed. Cambridge, MA: Harvard University Press.

Goode, William J. 1993. *World changes in divorce patterns.* New Haven: Yale University Press.

Phillips, Roderick. 1988. *Putting asunder: A history of divorce in Western society.* New York: Cambridge University Press.

marriage rules Marriage rules are norms that regulate the choosing of spouses as well as relationships between married couples and their various kin. Under the rules of *endogamy,* for example, people are expected to marry those who have certain social characteristics in common with their own. In most societies, marriage is endogamous with regard to RACE, and, to some extent, RELIGION and ETHNICITY. Under the rules of *exogamy,* people are expected to marry those who are in some way socially dissimilar to them. This is true of GENDER, for example, in that people are generally allowed to marry those outside their own gender category. In some tribal societies, rules of exogamy are also used to encourage bonds between tribes through inter-tribal marriages.

Rules of endogamy and exogamy apply to the general problem of how much freedom is allowed in the choosing of spouses. It is typically true, for example, that the more marriage affects the distribution of power, PRESTIGE, and property among kin groups, the more control families exert over whom their children marry. Thus as the importance of the family declined with INDUSTRIALIZA-TION, individuals gained more personal control over whom to marry. In addition, children of the UPPER CLASS in industrial societies generally have less freedom of choice than do children in the classes below them. This is because control over property is a key element in the maintenance of upper-class privilege, and marriage is still a major way to ensure such control by keeping property within the family and therefore within the upper class.

Other marriage rules govern the number of spouses people may have. Although most people today live in societies that permit only one spouse per person (*monogamy*), many societies have allowed multiple spouses (*polygamy*), a practice that can take several forms. Allowing women to have several husbands (*polyandry*) has been quite rare, but allowing men to have several wives (*polygyny*) has not. Rarer still is *group marriage* in which several women are married to several men at the same time. A variation on all of these is *serial*

monogamy in which people marry one spouse at a time but due to high rates of divorce or mortality marry several times during their lives. Such marriages are monogamous in a temporal sense, but have elements of polygamy insofar as people live with the expectation of experiencing more than one spouse during their lives.

Another marriage rule governs where couples may live in relation to in-laws. Historically, in most societies couples have been expected to live near the mother's relatives (*matrilocal* marriage) or the father's (*patrilocal* marriage). In some societies, couples may choose which set of in-laws to live near (*bilocal* marriage) but they are not free to choose to live near neither, as they are in societies with a *neolocal* marriage rule.

See also FAMILY; KINSHIP; MARRIAGE AND DIVORCE.

Reading
Murdock, George P. 1949. *Social structure*. New York: Macmillan.
——. 1967. *Ethnographic atlas*. Pittsburgh: Pittsburgh University Press.

Marxist feminism   *See* FEMINISM.

Marxist sociology   Marxist sociology is a blend of Marxism and sociology. Like Marxism, it focuses on Karl MARX's concern with POLITICAL ECONOMY and the power of CAPITAL-ISM to shape social life and, in particular, various forms of SOCIAL OPPRESSION. Unlike Marxism, it has shown itself in practice to be relatively unconcerned with making class revolution.

Current Marxist sociology focuses on several areas of interest: the relation between CAPITAL and LABOR, especially the tendency of capital to devalue, degrade, and divide workers as a means of increasing control and profit; how the relations of production produce SOCIAL CLASS systems, and how these are related to other forms of oppression such as those based on GENDER, RACE, and ETHNICITY; POLITICAL ECONOMY, or the relationship between capitalism and the STATE; and the relationship between capitalism and class dynamics on the one hand and the content of CULTURE and cultural institutions such as schools and the mass media on the other.

Marxist concepts and perspectives have become increasingly influential in sociological work, especially in the United States and Europe.

See also CLASS CONFLICT AND CLASS STRUGGLE; MODE OF PRODUCTION; CULTURAL STUDIES; HIDDEN CURRICULUM; HEGEMONY.

Reading
Bottomore, Tom B. 1975. *Marxist sociology*. London: Macmillan.
Ollman, Bertell, and Edward Vernoff, eds. 1982. *The left academy. Marxist scholarship on American campuses.* New York: McGraw-Hill.
Shaw, Martin, ed. 1985. *Marxist sociology revisited. Critical assessments.* London: Macmillan.

masculinity *See* SEX AND GENDER.

masculinization *See* FEMINIZATION AND MASCULINIZATION.

mass *See* COLLECTIVE BEHAVIOR.

mass communication and mass media Mass communication is the transmission of information by trained specialists to a large, diverse audience spread out over a large territory. It is accomplished through the mass media, complex organizational and technical means that typically include television, radio, film, newspapers, books, magazines and, increasingly, the Internet.

Sociological interest in mass media research focuses on several related questions. Who controls the mass media and, with them, the information they transmit? What interests do they serve? How does mass communication affect individuals – from the products people buy to their political opinions to the tendency toward violent behavior – and how do these effects vary by characteristics such as SOCIAL CLASS, AGE, GENDER, and education? How does the cumulative effect of many mass media outlets transmitting similar messages shape POPULATIONS and their perceptions of social reality? How do mass media messages shape public definitions of SOCIAL PROBLEMS and set the agenda for public discussion and debate? How will the mass media relate to the explosion in computer TECHNOLOGY and its potential for transmitting huge amounts of information through networks such as the Internet? What is the relationship between the mass media and other major social INSTITUTIONS such as the STATE, corporations, education, and organized religion?

See also IDEOLOGY; INFORMATION SOCIETY; KNOWLEDGE.

Reading
Iyengar, Shanto, and Donald R. Kinder. 1987. *News that matters: Television and public opinion.* Chicago: University of Chicago Press.
Lasswell, Harold D. 1947. "The structure and function of communication in society." In *The communication of ideas,* edited by L. Bryson. New York: Harper.
Towler, Paul. 1988. *Investigating the media.* London: Unwin Hyman.

mass culture *See* POPULAR CULTURE.

mass media *See* MASS COMMUNICA-TION AND MASS MEDIA.

mass society According to one view, mass society is a SOCIAL SYSTEM marked by mindless uniformity and egalitarianism, the decline of religion, a sense of alienation and moral empti-ness, weak family and community ties, political apathy, and the replace-ment of high CULTURE (such as great art and literature) by low culture catering to unsophisticated and bland tastes. In the years surrounding World War II, the huge destructive potential revealed by FASCISM prompted con-cern about how the organization of social life makes it easier for popula-tions to be manipulated and con-trolled by political AUTHORITY. Many argued that industrial CAPITALISM had resulted in a mass society.

Concern over the emergence of mass society actually began in nine-teenth-century Europe when the revolutionary overthrow of monar-chies was followed by the fear of DEMOCRACY as an uncontrollable form of mob rule. Thinkers such as Alexis de TOCQUEVILLE went back and forth between optimistic and pes-simistic views of democracy's potential for good and evil. Today, the concept has little influence in sociology as research demonstrates that modern societies are far more complex than the idea of mass society would suggest.

Reading
Giner, Salvador. 1976. *Mass society*. Lon-don: Macmillan.
Le Bon, Gustave. [1895] 1960. *The crowd: A study of the popular mind*. New York: Viking.
Swinegood, A. 1977. *The myth of mass culture*. London: Macmillan.

master status A master status is a social position that tends to be among the most important positions people occupy. It lies at the core of their SOCIAL IDENTITY and influences how the ROLES associated with other posi-tions are performed. Occupation is often a master status because it forms such an important part of people's identities and affects their other roles – how they perform family roles, the friends they choose, the neighbor-hoods they live in, and so on. Depending on the SOCIETY, GENDER, AGE, and RACE are also common mas-ter statuses. They typically play an important role in SOCIAL INEQUALITY and OPPRESSION.
See also STATUS.

material culture *See* CULTURE.

materialism Materialism is a con-cept having two sociological mean-ings. The first refers to a cultural VALUE placed on the accumulation of material possessions, a process in which people base their sense of themselves, their well-being, and social standing on possessions.

In its second sense, materialism is an approach to understanding social life that rests on the idea that all aspects of human life – biological, psychological, social, historical, etc. – have a material basis flowing from human reproduction and the eco-nomic production of goods and ser-vices. Materialism views production and reproduction as fundamental social processes that greatly influence if not determine the basic character of SOCIAL SYSTEMS, the patterns of social life associated with them, and patterns of historical change and development (an approach known as *historical materialism*).

From a materialist perspec-tive, nonmaterial aspects of social life – including LANGUAGE, BELIEFS, and the structure of relationships and INSTITUTIONS such as the FAMILY, RELIGION, and the STATE – are built upon and inevitably reflect how a SOCIETY is organized around the basic tasks of production and reproduction. They do not have an autonomous, independent existence that determines material conditions of living. Rather, it is the process of producing material conditions that is most important in social life.

The materialist approach is central to the work of Karl MARX. One of the most well-known applications is his THEORY of SOCIAL CHANGE known as *dialectical materialism*. Here Marx joins materialism with the concept of a dialectic – a struggle between opposing ideas or social forces (thesis and antithesis) – that results in a new synthesis. Marx argued that social systems change through a continuing process in which socially generated internal CONTRADICTIONS create tension toward some form of resolution. The competing interests of workers and capitalists, for example, create tension in industrial capitalist societies, and this produces social change. Marx believed such change would take the form of REVOLUTION, a prediction that has thus far been shown to be false, at least in INDUSTRIAL SOCIETIES. However, his more general prediction that contradiction produces change has held up quite well. For example, the development of a variety of social programs to mollify the WORKING CLASS – from welfare, unemployment benefits, retirement and health programs to worker safety regulations and collective bargaining agreements – can all be interpreted as social responses to the inherent contradictions between the interests of different classes.

See also BASE AND SUPERSTRUCTURE; CONSPICUOUS CONSUMPTION; DETERMINISM AND REDUCTIONISM.

Reading
Marx, Karl. [1845] 1935. "Theses on Feuerbach (8th Thesis)." In Friedrich Engels, *Ludwig Feuerbach and the outcome of classical German philosophy*. New York: International Publishers.

mathematical sociology Mathematical sociology is an approach to understanding social life that attempts to describe social processes with mathematical models. The goal is to develop THEORIES that are more precise than would otherwise be possible and that reveal common underlying properties of otherwise unrelated phenomena. It may be, for example, that rumor, disease, and innovation spread through a POPULATION in ways that can be described by variations on the same mathematical model.

Mathematical sociology has been most highly developed in the study of social NETWORKS and GROUP DYNAMICS. Thus far, it has failed to attract the attention of mainstream sociologists and goes largely unnoticed and unappreciated.

Reading
Coleman, James S. 1964. *Introduction to mathematical sociology*. New York: Free Press.
Fararo, Thomas J., ed. 1984. *Mathematical ideas and sociological theory*. New York: Gordon and Breach (special issue of *Journal of Mathematical Sociology*).
Leik, Robert K., and Barbara F. Meeker. 1975. *Mathematical sociology*. Englewood Cliffs, NJ: Prentice-Hall.

matriarchy A matriarchy is a SOCIAL SYSTEM organized around the principle of mother-rule. Since mother is a family STATUS, it applies primarily to family systems. In tribal societies, however, where the family and society are one and the same, it can apply to the POWER STRUCTURE at that level as well. In societies where the family is a relatively unimportant INSTITUTION devoted primarily to the meeting of personal needs, female dominance in society at large would take the form of *gynocracy* – rule by females – rather than rule by mothers.

All of this is theoretical, however, since there is no solid evidence that a matriarchal SOCIETY or family system has ever existed. Even in societies with matrilineal descent (traced through the mother's kin only), the power structure is either egalitarian or dominated formally by the father or some other male figure such as the mother's brother. There is growing archeological evidence that for many thousands of years during the paleolithic and neolithic eras societies were *gynocentric* – organized around women's perceived reproductive power and central female symbols based upon it, especially as embodied in goddess worship. But this does not mean that the high VALUE placed on femaleness carried with it female dominance over males and society as a whole.

It should be noted that although women are the authority figures in the single-parent families that are growing so rapidly in number in some INDUSTRIAL SOCIETIES, these families are not considered matriarchal. In order for them to be matriarchal, they would need the support of a CULTURE that defined women's dominance as desirable and legitimate even if a man were to become a member of the household. Female dominance in such families is, in short, largely a matter of rule by default, not by social design, since they exist in PATRIARCHIES in which male dominance and women's OPPRESSION are the rule.

See also KINSHIP.

Reading

Bamberger, J. 1974. "The myth of matriarchy: Why men rule in primitive society." In *Women culture, and society,* edited by M. Z. Rosaldo and L. Lamphere, 263–80. Stanford, CA: Stanford University Press.

Eisler, Riane. 1987. *The chalice and the blade.* New York: Harper and Row.

Fisher, Elizabeth. 1980. *Woman's creation: Sexual evolution and the shaping of society.* New York: McGraw-Hill.

Lerner, Gerda. 1986. *The creation of patriarchy.* New York: Oxford University Press.

matrifocality Matrifocality is a concept referring to households consisting of one or more adult women and their children without the presence of fathers. Single-parent families headed by women, for example, are matrifocal since the day-to-day life of the FAMILY is organized around the mother.

See also MARRIAGE RULES; MATRIARCHY.

matrilocal marriage *See* MARRIAGE RULES.

matrilineal descent *See* KINSHIP.

me *See* MIND.

mean Like the MEDIAN and the MODE, the mean is a statistical measure of the average score in a DISTRIBUTION. It is calculated by adding up all of the scores and dividing the resulting sum by the number of scores in the distribution. Thus if three families have 1, 5, and 6 children respectively, the mean number of children is $(1+5+6)/3 = 12/3 = 4$.

The mean has the advantage of taking into account every score in a distribution. Consequently, we can, among other things, work backward from the mean to the total. If we know that the average number of children in three families is 4, we can work backward to find the total number of children in the three families combined, which is $4 \times 3 = 12$. In this sense, the mean is the most representative of all measures of the average.

If we want to use the mean to indicate the "typical" score in a distribution, however, it is less useful when the distribution has a small number of extremely high or low scores. If ten families all have numbers of children ranging from three to four, for example, the mean will fall somewhere between three and four children and will reflect the "typical" score quite well. If two families have 20 children, however, the group mean will rise to more than five, a number that does not represent the typical family in the group very well at all.

The mean can be used only with variables whose categories naturally take the form of numbers, such as income, age at marriage, and years of schooling. It cannot be used with other kinds of variables even though a researcher might assign numbers to their categories for computing purposes.

See also MEDIAN; MODE; STATISTICS; VARIABLE.

Reading

Bohrnstedt, George W., and David Knoke. 1994. *Statistics for social data analysis*, 3rd ed. Itasca, IL: F. E. Peacock.

mean independence *See* STATISTI-CAL INDEPENDENCE AND STATISTICAL DEPENDENCE.

meaningful action *See* INTER-ACTION.

mean length of generation *See* GENERATION.

means of production *See* CAPITAL; MODE OF PRODUCTION.

measurement Measurement is a key process in sociological research through which we observe the world and record the results for interpretation and analysis. In order to do this, we need a set of procedures that specifies exactly how to observe.

If our subject is RACE, for example, we might ask people "what race do you consider yourself to be?" Or, we might give interviewers a set of categories and ask them to look at each respondent and decide for themselves which is the appropriate category for each. Each of these procedures is what is known as a *measurement instrument*, and the process of devising one in order to measure a concept is called *operationalization*. The above instruments are two ways to operationalize the concept of race.

It is important to be aware that there are usually many different ways to operationalize the same concept, even with characteristics as seemingly straightforward as race. In addition to the two above, for example, we might also consult people's birth certificates as a way to measure race, or ask neighbors and friends. Or we might ask respondents to list their family trees and determine race on the basis of a formula that considers the relative numbers of ancestors with various racial characteristics. Each of these would probably yield different results (people may perceive themselves quite differently than does an interviewer, for example), which is why the operationalization process is so important. The problem is not so much one of measuring a concept "correctly" as it is of being clear about just how the concept is being defined in practice and how this will affect the interpretation of research results later on.

See also CODING; ERROR; RELIABILITY; SCALE OF MEASUREMENT; UNOBTRUSIVE MEASURE; VALIDITY; VARIABLE.

Reading
Blalock, Hubert M. 1982. *Conceptualization and measurement in the social sciences.* Newbury Park, CA: Sage Publications.
Miller, Delbert C. 1991. *Handbook of research design and social measurement.* Newbury Park, CA: Sage Publications.

measurement error   *See* ERROR.

measurement   instrument   *See* MEASUREMENT.

measurement, scale of   *See* SCALE OF MEASUREMENT.

measure of association   A measure of association is a statistical quantity used to indicate the *strength of relationship* between two VARIABLES. A large number of measures have been devised that vary in the circumstances in which they may be used as well as their interpretation. In particular, whether a measure may be used depends on the SCALE OF MEASUREMENT of the variables involved in the relationship.

By design, measures of association take on values ranging from -0.1 to $+1.0$ with the positive and negative signs indicating only the DIRECTION OF RELATIONSHIP, not the strength of the association. Whereas in normal mathematical usage a negative number is lower in value than a positive one, here the sign and number are independent of each other: values of -0.65 and $+0.65$ indicate equally strong relationships.

A value of 1.0 (regardless of sign) indicates a perfect relationship in which knowing the score on variable X (such as education) allows us to predict the score on variable Y (such as income) without making any errors. Relationships can be either conditionally perfect or mathematically perfect. If a relationship is mathematically perfect, the ability to predict scores on Y is perfect for every value of X. If the relationship is conditionally perfect, the ability to predict scores on Y is perfect for some but not all values of X. A value of 0.00 means the two variables are independent of each other.

See also CORRELATION; STATISTICAL INDEPENDENCE AND STATISTICAL DEPENDENCE; PARTIAL ASSOCIATION; RANK-ORDER CORRELATION.

Reading
Bohrnstedt, George W., and David Knoke. 1994. *Statistics for social data analysis.* 3rd ed. Itasca, IL: F. E. Peacock.
Costner, Herbert L. 1965. "Criteria for measures of association." *American Sociological Review* 30: 341–53.

mechanical   solidarity   *See* COHESION.

mechanistic   organization   *See* ORGANIZATIONAL THEORY.

median   Like the MEAN and the MODE, the median is a statistical measure of the average value in a DISTRIBUTION of scores. It is the score of the middle case in the distribution when the scores are arranged in order from highest to lowest. The middle case is the one that divides the distribution in half with an equal number of cases with scores above and below it. If three families have 1, 5, and 6 children respectively, for example, the median for the distribution is 5 children, since that is the score for the middle case. If the distribution has an even number of cases (as in 1, 5, 6, 8), the median is calculated as the arithmetic average of the middle pair of scores: $(5+6)/2 = 11/2 = 5.5$.

To identify the median, the scores must be in numerical order. Otherwise the value of the median is completely arbitrary since there are any number of ways of arranging scores in a list. If we arranged the three scores above as 1, 6, 5, for example, the middle case in the list would be 6, but it would not be the middle case in the sense of dividing the distribution in half, since there are two scores that are lower than 6 but none that are higher.

The median does not take into account all of the scores in the distribution. In fact, it makes use of only one score (if the three families had 0, 5, and 20 children, the median would still be 5). The median is generally regarded, however, as the best measure of the average score if we are interested in giving a sense of the "typical" score in a distribution, especially when there are a few extremely high or low scores. In this sense, the median is superior to the mean as a measure of the average score.

The median can only be used to summarize distributions of VARIABLES that have ordinal-scale properties, in other words, whose scores can be rank-ordered from high to low. Variables that naturally take the form of numbers (such as income, weeks unemployed, and years of schooling) have ordinal properties, as do variables that include some dimension of "more" and "less" such as SOCIAL CLASS (upper, middle, lower, etc.). The median cannot be used with variables that lack this property. For example, the categories for religious affiliation (such as Muslim, Shinto, Christian, Jewish, Buddhist) have no natural rank order.

See also PERCENTILE; STATISTICS.

Reading

Bohrnstedt, George W., and David Knoke. 1994. *Statistics for social data analysis*, 3rd ed. Itasca, IL: F. E. Peacock.

medicalization Medicalization is a social process through which a human experience or condition is culturally defined as pathological and treatable as a medical condition. In many INDUSTRIAL SOCIETIES, for example, obesity, criminal behavior, alcohol and drug abuse, childbearing, childhood hyperactivity, and sexual abuse have been defined as medical problems that are, as a result, increasingly referred to and treated by physicians.

Sociologically, this is especially significant because it vests in the medical profession AUTHORITY for defining appropriate social responses to various conditions and behaviors, and with it a degree of control over them. In rare cases a phenomenon is demedicalized, as when the American Psychiatric Association voted in the 1970s to no longer consider homosexuality a mental illness.

Reading

Turner, B. S. 1987. *Medical power and social knowledge*. Beverly Hills, CA: Sage Publications.

megalopolis A megalopolis (or megacity or *conurbation*) is a geographical area so densely settled that it forms a huge urban area flowing from one town or city to the next without a clear break between them. Examples include London, Mexico City, and the "Northeast corridor" stretching between Washington and Boston.
See also URBANIZATION AND URBANISM.

Reading
Dogan, Mattei, and John D. Kasarda, eds. 1988. *The metropolis era: A world of giant cities*, vol. 1. Newbury Park, CA: Sage Publications.

melded family *See* FAMILY.

melting pot Inspired by the title of Israel Zangwill's 1909 play about life in America, melting pot is a concept referring to the common but faulty belief that ethnic and racial groups in the United States have joined together to form a common CULTURE and national identity. This has been true to a considerable degree of European immigrants whose culture and racial background are relatively similar to the dominant Anglo POPULATION and its culture. The ghettoization and OPPRESSION of MINORITY groups, however, coupled with the rapid growth of the nonwhite, non-English-speaking population, perpetuates racial and ethnic divisions, especially in large metropolitan areas such as New York, Chicago, and Los Angeles.
See also CULTURAL CONTACT.

Reading
Zangwill, Israel. [1909] 1933. *The melting pot*. New York: Macmillan.

meritocracy A meritocracy is a SOCIAL SYSTEM in which people's success in life depends primarily on their merit – their talents, abilities, and effort. The idea of meritocracy has served as an IDEOLOGY through the argument that SOCIAL INEQUALITY results from unequal merit rather than PREJUDICE and DISCRIMINATION and OPPRESSION. It has also served as a guide for change, especially in Britain's educational system.

Keys to meritocracy include a valid way to measure merit and provide equal opportunity based upon it, a system that also forms the greatest barriers to achieving it. Critics argue, for example, that centuries of social inequality and oppression have left racial minorities and the lower classes in an inherently disadvantaged position in which they will inevitably appear to lack merit. In addition, the definition of talent and ability is biased in favor of privileged groups who set the standards to reflect themselves and their own interests and backgrounds.
See also CULTURAL CAPITAL; SPEECH CODES; HIDDEN CURRICULUM; PREJUDICE AND DISCRIMINATION; SOCIAL CLASS.

Reading
Collins, Randall. 1979. *The credential society: An historical sociology of education*. New York: Academic Press.
Krauze, R., and K. Slonczynski. 1986. "How far to meritocracy?" *Social Forces* 63: 623–42.
Young, Michael. 1958. *The rise of the meritocracy*. London: Thames and Hudson.

methodological individualism Methodological individualism is an approach to understanding social life that looks upon SOCIAL SYSTEMS as nothing more than a collection of individuals. From this perspective, the only thing we need to understand about social systems are the individual characteristics and psychological dynamics of the people who participate in them. To explain warfare, for example, we should focus on soldiers and politicians, not armies and nations.

By denying the existence of social systems as more than the people who participate in them, methodological individualism stands in direct opposition to sociological thinking (and is sometimes referred to pejoratively as *psychologism*). Indeed, Émile DURKHEIM developed the FUNCTIONALIST PERSPECTIVE in response to the widespread tendency to reduce every social phenomenon to psychological terms. The debate is less lively today because it is widely acknowledged in both psychology and sociology that individuals and social contexts are closely connected and that a full understanding of one cannot be achieved without taking the other into account. The issue now focuses more on just how individuals and social systems are related.

See also AGENCY AND STRUCTURE; ATOMISM AND HOLISM; DETERMINISM AND REDUCTIONISM; UTILITARIANISM.

Reading
Lukes, Steven. [1968] 1977. "Methodological individualism reconsidered." In *Essays in social theory*. London: Macmillan.

methodological naturalism *see* NATURALISM.

methodology In sociological research, methodology refers to the practices and techniques used to gather, process, manipulate, and interpret information that can then be used to test ideas and THEORIES

about social life. Historically, there has been some debate as to whether sociology could or should aspire to SCIENCE as a model for conducting research, especially since the only way to demonstrate cause-and-effect relationships – the EXPERIMENT – is difficult if not impossible to use with most sociological problems. Sociology cannot identify laws of social life that compare with the laws of physics, in part because social life is so complex, but also because ethical and other considerations preclude the kinds of controlled conditions and experimental manipulations so characteristic of the physical sciences. Nonetheless, sociology is quite scientific in its commitment to basic elements of the scientific method, especially those related to OBJECTIVITY, the systematic gathering of evidence, the REPLICATION of research results, and the NORMS that govern scientific work.

See also COMPARATIVE PERSPECTIVE; CONTENT ANALYSIS; EXPERIMENT; METHODOLOGICAL INDIVIDUALISM; OBJECTIVITY; PARTICIPANT OBSERVATION; SAMPLE; SCIENCE; SECONDARY ANALYSIS; STATISTICS; SURVEY.

Reading
Singleton, Royce A., Bruce C. Straits, and Margaret M. Straits. 1998. *Approaches to social research*, 3rd ed. Oxford and New York: Oxford University Press.

microecology Microecology is a field of study that focuses on individual levels of social INTERACTION. It is related to human ECOLOGY, which is usually concerned with large issues of POPULATION and the physical environment. Every interaction involves some number of people and a physical environment of some kind, both of which affect how people interpret what is going on and how they behave and appear in relation to one another.

As every college student knows, patterns of student participation differ substantially in a small seminar and in a class of 500; and a class of eight may operate quite differently in a small, somewhat cramped space and in a cavernous auditorium (hence the general principle that one way to create a sense of intimacy in a group is to choose a space that is slightly too small to hold it easily).

The physical dimensions of social interaction also come into play in how actors are positioned within a space. The elevated positions of judges, lecturers, and priests, for example, focus attention on and reinforce the AUTHORITY of those who occupy them. The chambers of Britain's parliament are arranged so that opposing speakers face one another across a relatively small space, quite unlike the U.S. Congress where members are arranged in a semicircular fashion with attention focused primarily toward the front of the room. The former lends a physical dimension to political opposition and debate, while the latter creates a more diffuse atmosphere in which individual speakers rather than parties and sides are of paramount importance. From a microecological perspective, it is not the trivial matter that it may appear to be when negotiators sometimes argue over the shape of the table at which they will sit.

One of the more interesting applications of microecological principles to social interaction lies in social considerations in architecture and interior design. Whether people in an airline terminal or a hospital lounge will tend to strike up conversations with one another, for example, depends greatly on how the space is constructed and how seats and other focuses of attention are arranged. Similar observations can be made about everything from housing projects to prisons to factory assembly lines.

See also ECOLOGY; INTERACTION; POPULATION.

Reading

Sommer, Robert. 1969. *Personal space: The behavioral analysis of design.* Englewood Cliffs, NJ: Prentice-Hall.

microsociology *See* MACROSOCIOLOGY AND MICROSOCIOLOGY.

middle class In the study of social STRATIFICATION AND INEQUALITY, middle class is a concept that has eluded precise definition. As described by Karl MARX and Friedrich ENGELS, the middle class in the eighteenth and nineteenth centuries consisted of small shopkeepers and businessmen, artisans, and professionals – the *petit bourgeoisie* – who occupied the economic territory between the large capitalists and their workers. Today this "old" middle class is distinguished from the "new" middle class that has lost much of its economic independence and is now associated primarily with the prestige attached to white-collar occupations such as clerical workers, office supervisors, government officials, professionals, and teachers.

As an analytical concept, middle class is problematic in several ways. The line separating it from the WORKING CLASS, for example, is unclear because white-collar occupations are not necessarily associated with higher levels of education, WEALTH AND

193

INCOME, and skill, or training when compared with highly skilled blue-collar jobs. This is especially true as clerical jobs are increasingly routinized, fragmented, and automated, making them more difficult to distinguish from working-class occupations.

A second problem lies in the use of the term "middle," for it is arguable that the middle class is in any sense of the word midway between the UPPER CLASS and the lower and working classes. In terms of income and wealth, for example, most of what is considered the middle class is far closer to the working class than to the upper class; most middle-class occupations involve low levels of AUTHORITY; and the middle class has no more real ownership or control over the MEANS OF PRODUCTION and the production process than does the working class. Exceptions to these generalizations are of course to be found among the upper reaches of the middle class, but this is a small portion of those who place themselves in this category. One might argue that the middle class stands midway between the working and upper classes in terms of occupational prestige; but for great segments of the upper class, occupational prestige is irrelevant since it is not through the characteristics of their occupations that members of the upper class achieve or maintain their class position.

Although the middle class is popularly perceived as the largest single class, there is evidence that its ranks are declining. In the United States, for example, there has been a steady erosion during the last half of this century in the percentage of people who identify themselves as members of the middle class, declining from 61 percent in 1964 to 45 percent in 1993.

See also BLUE-COLLAR WORKER AND WHITE-COLLAR WORKER; PROLETARIAN-IZATION; SOCIAL CLASS.

Reading

Abercrombie, Nicholas, and John Urry. 1983. *Capital, labour, and the middle classes*. London: Allen and Unwin.

Mills, C. Wright. 1951. *White collar*. New York: Oxford University Press.

Nicolaus, Martin. 1967. "Proletariat and middle class in Marx." *Studies on the Left 7*.

middle range, theories of the *See* THEORY.

migration Migration is the physical movement of people within and between SOCIAL SYSTEMS. It is important for its effects on areas that lose migrants through *emigration* and on the areas that receive them through *immigration*. Migration, for example, is a major component of POPULATION growth – particularly in low-fertility regions such as Europe and North America – and historically has been the main source of URBANIZATION. Migration also profoundly affects the social composition of populations and for this reason often plays an important role in racial, ethnic, and class relations.

Historically, the sociological study of migration patterns has focused on "push factors" and "pull factors" – conditions that cause people to leave one area and to be attracted to another. Current research on this topic has used more complex approaches that take into account larger-scale processes such as the international demand for labor and the shift of capital across national boundaries.

Reading
Fielding, A. J. 1989. "Migration and urbanization in Western Europe since 1950." *Geographical Journal* 155: 60–69.
Davis, Kingsley. 1974. "The migrations of human populations." *Scientific American* 231: 92–105.
Lee, Everett S. 1966. "A theory of migration." *Demography* 3: 47–57.
Long, Larry H. 1988. *Migration and residential mobility in the United States.* New York: Russell Sage Foundation.
Ravenstein, E. G. 1889. "The laws of migration." *Journal of the Royal Statistical Society* 52: 245–301.

military-industrial complex A term coined by outgoing U.S. president Dwight Eisenhower in 1960, the military-industrial complex is a network of intersecting and mutual interests of military and industrial organizations. Eisenhower used the term in warning: because the prime function of the military is to prepare for and conduct war, and since weapons manufacturing is highly profitable, these two powerful systems (military and economic) could be expected to work together to promote reliance on the use of military TECHNOLOGY and armed force to deal with international problems. As such, he regarded them as a threat to the development of alternative, peaceful strategies for resolving conflict and pursuing national interests, In addition, he feared that their combined influence would produce a growing drain on national resources as ever greater portions of national WEALTH are devoted to the development of war-making and defensive capabilities.
See also POLITICAL ECONOMY.

Reading
Sarkesian, Sam C., ed. 1972. *The military industrial complex.* Washington: Seven Locks Press.

millenarianism Millenarianism is a SOCIAL MOVEMENT organized around a variety of religious and quasi-religious ideas that something miraculous is going to happen that will deliver a group of people from an undesirable social condition. These movements include the fundamentalist Christian BELIEF in Christ's eventual return to rule for 1,000 years (a millennium) as prophesied by the Bible: the Melanesian "cargo cults" (in which the crash of warplanes in the jungle during World War II led to the belief that riches would come from the sky if natives built large models of airplanes); the nineteenth-century Ghost Dance CULTS of Native American tribes that predicted the demise of white rule and the return of vanishing native civilizations; and the sixteenth-century Anabaptist movement in Europe. Millenarian movements are most likely to emerge in times of social upheaval or rapid change and among those who are suffering DEPRIVATION or OPPRESSION.
See also CULT; FUNDAMENTALISM.

Reading
Cohen, N. 1957. *The pursuit of the millennium.* London: Palladin.
Lantenari, Vittorio. 1963. *The religions of the oppressed: A study of messianic cults.* New York: Knopf.
Worsley, Peter. 1970. *The trumpet shall sound: A study of "cargo cults" in Melanesia.* London: Paladin.

mind According to George Herbert MEAD, the concept of *mind* and the related concepts of *I* and *me* are key elements in the SYMBOLIC

INTERACTIONIST view of how people develop into social beings capable of interacting with others and possessing a sense of SELF.

Mead thought of the self as having two distinct aspects: I and mind. The I is preverbal and experiences everything without the reflection and thought that LANGUAGE makes possible. Hunger and thirst, fear, pain, satiation, hot, cold, the desire for human contact – all of these are elements of human life that can exist without language or language-based thought. Infants, for example, can feel hungry without thinking about and reflecting on hunger and what they would like to do about it. Since infants have no language capabilities, Mead would argue that their selves consist entirely of the I.

The transition into becoming social beings is made possible by our ability to use language in order to think about ourselves and others, to reflect upon ourselves as if we were someone else, to imagine what other people think, including what they expect of us. Mead called this ability to use language mind; the aspect of the self that uses mind to reflect upon itself he called me. The me uses mind to conduct internal conversations with ourselves, including commentary about what we experience in a more direct way (the I). This means that *empathy* – the ability to be aware of the internal lives of others – depends on the existence of language, as does any conscious awareness of ourselves as selves. Without language, we cannot think or reflect, and without thought and reflection, there would be no such thing as what we know of as self and OTHERS. All that would remain

would be the I's direct experience of stimuli and feelings.

Mead did a great deal to lay the groundwork for symbolic interactionism, the sociological perspective that focuses on the importance of language in the social construction of the self and social life.

Reading

Mead, George Herbert. 1934. *Mind, self, and society*. Chicago: University of Chicago Press.

minimax solution *See* RATIONAL CHOICE THEORY.

minority A minority is a SOCIAL CATEGORY of people singled out for unequal and inferior treatment simply because they are identified as belonging to that category. Minorities are usually defined in terms of ASCRIBED STATUS characteristics such as RACE, GENDER, and ethnic or religious background, as well as ACQUIRED STATUSES such as sexual orientation. Unlike numerical minorities, social minorities may be in the numerical majority, as blacks were in South Africa before the end of apartheid and as females still are in virtually every society in the world.

In STRATIFICATION systems, minorities are important because in contrast with CLASS inequality, upward MOBILITY is extremely difficult since the characteristics on which minority standing is based cannot be changed, although they can be concealed or misrepresented to varying degrees. In general, the more visible the characteristics that define minority standing are, the more intractable are the terms of social inequality. In the United States, for example, gender and racial inequality remain serious problems while ethnic inequality has generally disappeared.

See also PREJUDICE AND DISCRIMINATION; SOCIAL OPPRESSION.

Reading

Memmi, Albert. 1964. *Dominated man.* New York: Orion Press.

Simpson, G. E., and J. M. Yinger. 1985. *Racial and cultural minorities: An analysis of prejudice and discrimination,* 5th ed. New York: Plenum.

Wirth, Louis. 1945. "The problem of minority groups." In *The science of man in the world crisis,* edited by Ralph Linton. New York: Columbia University Press.

misogyny Misogyny is a cultural ATTITUDE of hatred for females simply because they are female. It is a central part of sexist prejudice and IDEOLOGY and, as such, is an important basis for the oppression of females in male-dominated societies. Misogyny is manifested in many different ways, from jokes to pornography to violence to the self-contempt women may be taught to feel toward their own bodies.

See also ATTITUDE; PATRIARCHY; PREJUDICE AND DISCRIMINATION.

Reading

Dijkstra, B. 1987. *Idols of perversity: Fantasies of feminine evil.* New York: Oxford University Press.

Dworkin, Andrea. 1974. *Woman hating.* New York. E. P. Dutton.

mobility *See* SOCIAL MOBILITY.

mob psychology *See* COLLECTIVE BEHAVIOR.

mode Like the MEAN and MEDIAN, the mode is a statistical measure of the average score in a DISTRIBUTION. It is simply the most common score. If ten families have 0, 1, 2, 2, 2, 2, 3, 3, 4, and 6 children, respectively, the modal number of children will be 2 since more families have 2 children

than any other number. Some distributions have no mode at all (as in 9, 1, 8, 3, 2, 6, 12, 4, 7, 5) or more than one mode (as in 0, 1, 2, 2, 2, 3, 4, 5, 5, 5). A distribution with two modes is called *bimodal* or, more generally *multimodal.*

Like the median, the mode ignores most scores in a distribution, concentrating only on the most frequently occurring. Unlike both the mean and median, however, one of its advantages is that it can be used with any type of variable, even those that simply name categories such as political party preference, type of SOCIETY (industrial, agrarian, and so on) or ETHNICITY.

See also STATISTICS; VARIABLE.

Reading

Bohrnstedt, George W., and David Knoke. 1994. *Statistics for social data analysis,* 3rd ed. Itasca, IL: F. E. Peacock.

model A model is an abstract representation, such as an analogy, that helps us think about something more clearly. When George Herbert MEAD wrote that social life was like a game, he called attention to the importance of rules and understandings that must be learned and internalized in order for people to participate. Note, however, that he did not say that social life *is* a game, for in many ways it clearly is not (since much of social life does not necessarily involve winners and losers, for example).

Sociological work involves models of various kinds. One kind of model is the THEORETICAL PERSPECTIVE whose set of basic assumptions about social life and how it works serve as basic guides to thought and research. Related to this is Max WEBER's idea of an IDEAL TYPE, a model that oversimplifies reality in order to bring out certain of its most important features. Another kind of model is used to represent statistical and theoretical relationships among VARIABLES, as in PATH ANALYSIS and other forms of MULTIVARIATE ANALYSIS. In trying to understand how social STRATIFICATION works, for example, we might create a model that connects a variable such as INCOME to a variety of variables such as educational attainment, occupation, RACE, and GENDER. As with all models, the degree to which the model fits reality is of great interest. But this is not all that matters, for models can also be useful as a form of creative play that opens up new lines of thought. In this sense, modeling is as much an ongoing process as it is a finished product.

See also CAUSAL EXPLANATION AND CAUSAL MODEL.

Reading

Blalock, Hubert M., ed. 1985. *Causal models in experimental and panel designs.* Chicago: Aldine.

Kaplan, Abraham. 1964. *The conduct of inquiry.* San Francisco: Chandler.

mode of production A central concept in Marxist analysis, the mode of production is the way a SOCIETY is organized to produce goods and services. It consists of two major aspects: the *forces of production* and the *relations of production.*

The forces of production include all of the elements that are brought together in production – from land, raw materials, and fuel to human skill and labor to machinery, tools, and factories. Along with labor, the most sociologically important part of the forces of production are the *means of production* – the tools and machinery used to transform raw materials into finished goods.

Since production is a social activity, any mode of production must also include a set of social relationships – the relations of production – through which the forces of production are used and decisions are made about what to do with the results. This includes not only relationships among people but also people's relations to the forces of production – whether they own land or means of production, for example, or whether they are paid wages to use the means of production owned by someone else.

A given mode of production consists of a particular set of forces of production combined with certain relations of production. In the pre-Civil War slave system of the U.S. south, for example, production was predominantly agricultural and the forces of production were heavily weighted toward land, human labor, and relatively unsophisticated TECHNOLOGY. In the slave economy, the relations of production centered on the ownership of slaves who used means of production owned by their masters who also had the authority to appropriate all that the slaves produced, including their children.

Under FEUDALISM, the relations of production were quite different. Here the nobility did not own the means of production but had the right to a portion of what was produced on lands over which they had AUTHORITY. The serfs were politically subjugated to the nobility but had rights to use the land and owned their own means of production.

Under industrial CAPITALISM, both the relations and forces of production are very different from slave or feudal societies. The forces include sophisticated technology through which production is primarily industrial, not agricultural, and which depends on massive inputs of energy from sources such as fossil fuels and nuclear power. The relations of production include ownership of the means of PRODUCTION by a capitalist class, control over the means of production by a managerial class, and a large WORKING CLASS that uses the means of production to produce goods in exchange for wages.

The concept of a mode of production is crucial in Marxist analysis, which argues that it underlies and shapes social INSTITUTIONS and, through them, most important aspects of social life. A high cultural VALUE placed on accumulating goods, for example, is most common in industrial capitalist societies because of the central importance of profit and expansion in that mode of production.

See also AGRARIAN SOCIETY; HORTICULTURAL SOCIETY; HUMAN CAPITAL; HUNTER-GATHERER SOCIETY; INDUSTRIAL SOCIETY AND INDUSTRIALIZATION; POSTINDUSTRIAL SOCIETY.

Reading

Lenski, Gerhard E., Joan Lenski, and Patrick Nolan. 1998. *Human societies,* 8th ed. New York: McGraw-Hill.

Marx, Karl. [1859] 1970. *A contribution to the critique of political economy.* New York: International Publishers.

——. [1867] 1975. *Capital: A critique of political economy.* New York: International Publishers.

modern community *See* COMMUNITY.

modernism *See* POSTMODERNISM AND MODERNISM.

modernization theory Modernization theory emerged in the 1950s as an explanation of how the INDUSTRIAL SOCIETIES of North America and Western Europe developed, especially through the growth of industrial CAPITALISM beginning in the eighteenth century. Modernization theory developed when it did partly because of competition between communist and capitalist ideologies following World War II and the desire of Western powers to convince Third World countries that economic development and social justice were possible under capitalism.

The theory assumes that SOCIETIES develop in fairly predictable stages through which they become increasingly complex. Development depends primarily on the importation of TECHNOLOGY and the KNOWLEDGE required to make use of it, as well as a host of political and other SOCIAL CHANGES believed to come about as a result. Modernization involves increased levels of schooling and the development of mass media, for example, both of which are seen as fostering democratic political INSTITUTIONS. Transportation and communication systems become increasingly sophisticated and accessible. POPULATIONS become more urban and mobile (both socially and geographically), and the extended family declines in importance as a result, giving way to the nuclear family model. Organizations become bureaucratic as the DIVISION OF LABOR grows more complex and RELIGION declines in public influence (although not necessarily in spiritual importance). Cash-driven MARKETS take over as the primary social mechanism through which goods and services are exchanged, replacing more informal, traditional ways in which people help one another and meet their needs.

Modernization theory has been criticized for ignoring the realities of SOCIAL INEQUALITY in the world economic system in which wealthy and powerful nations have a vested interest in keeping nonindustrial societies dependent and relatively weak economically and politically. International investment in Third World countries, for example, typically benefits most the foreign investors and their agents and managers, as well as cooperative politicians and other officials in the receiving country. At the same time, they have a variety of negative effects on the rest of their populations.

See also COLONIALISM AND IMPERIALISM; COMMUNITY; DEPENDENCY THEORY; SOCIAL EVOLUTION; SOCIAL MOBILITY; URBANIZATION AND URBANISM; WORLD SYSTEM.

Reading

Inkeles, Alex, and D. H. Smith. 1974. "The fate of personal adjustment in the process of modernization." *International Journal of Comparative Sociology* 11(1): 101–3.

Lerner, Daniel. 1958. *The passing of traditional society.* Glencoe, IL: Free Press.

Smelser, Neil J. 1973. "Toward a theory of modernization." In *Social change: Sources, patterns, and consequences,* edited by Amatai Etzioni and E. Etzioni-Halevy. New York: Basic Books.

monogamy *See* MARRIAGE RULES.

monopolistic economy *See* DUAL ECONOMY.

monopoly A monopoly is a MARKET for a particular product or service that is controlled by a single individual or organization. In the early days of capitalist expansion, it was not uncommon for kings to grant monopolies over various goods, such as the importing of tea to England. This gave traders the potential to charge whatever price the market would bear and to profit enormously as a result. Today, monopolies are granted in areas such as public utilities. Sometimes the resulting potential for abuse is balanced by creating agencies charged with regulating rates and services. In other cases, monopoly results from competition, as with the newspaper market in most U.S. cities in which there is no competition at all.

Marxists argue that the tendency for markets to move toward monopoly is built into CAPITALISM as an economic system and has been progressing since the late nineteenth century. Since COMPETITION is threatening to corporations, they tend to protect themselves and increase profits by trying to control markets by driving out or absorbing competing firms. The movement toward MONOPOLY CAPITALISM is accompanied by increased ties between economic and STATE interests. These include the purchase of military hardware; the use of foreign policy to promote competitive advantage; laws that discourage strikes; programs such as pensions and unemployment benefits that lessen the negative effects of capitalism (and thereby make workers less likely to rebel); government bailouts of failing enterprises; and the use of government policy to regulate interest rates, the flow of money, and other aspects of financial markets.

See also DUAL ECONOMY; OLIGOPOLY.

Reading

Baran, Paul A., and Paul M. Sweezy. 1966. *Monopoly capital.* New York: Modern Reader Paperbacks.

Braverman, Harry. 1974. *Labor and monopoly capital.* New York: Monthly Review Press.

monopoly capitalism *See* CAPITALISM.

monopoly economy *See* DUAL ECONOMY.

monotheism *See* THEISTIC RELIGION.

morality *See* MORES.

moral panic A moral panic is an extreme social response to the perception that the moral condition of SOCIETY is deteriorating at a calamitous pace. Most often such panics are promoted by MASS MEDIA reports reinforced by officials in various INSTITUTIONS such as the STATE. Numerous sociologists, especially in Britain, have interpreted moral panic as a device used to distract public attention from underlying SOCIAL PROBLEMS and justify increased SOCIAL CONTROL over the working class and other potentially rebellious segments of society. From this perspective, for example, the moral panic over street muggings in Britain during the 1970s can be viewed as part of a political effort to weaken the welfare state at the expense of lower- and working-class people who were the object of increased police control. In this way, resistance among MINORITIES and the poor was perceived not as political or CLASS CONFLICT but as individual lawlessness requiring repressive measures.

The concept of moral panic has also been applied to trends in youth CULTURE, reactions to AIDS and illegal drug use, and hooliganism in Britain.

See also DEVIANCE AMPLIFICATION.
Reading
Cohen, Stanley. 1972. *Folk devils and moral panics.* Oxford: Blackwell Publishers.
Hall, S., C. Critcher, T. Jefferson, J. Clarke, and B. Roberts. 1978. *Policing the crisis: Mugging, the state, and law and order.* London: Macmillan.
Pearson, Geoffrey. 1983. *Hooliganism: A history of respectable fears.* London: Macmillan.

moral statistics A term used primarily in France and Britain in the nineteenth century, moral statistics are DATA gathered to document SOCIAL PROBLEMS such as POVERTY and CRIME. The use of the word "moral" reflects sociology's long-standing concern with progressive movements for SOCIAL CHANGE.

morbidity In the study of POPULATION, EPIDEMIOLOGY and DEMOGRAPHY distinguish between mortality (death) and morbidity (conditions of ill health). Morbidity is sociologically important because in addition to its effects on mortality, it also affects social life by limiting people's abilities and producing strain on everything from families to health-care systems.
See also DEATH RATE.
Reading
Shryock, Henry S., and Jacob Siegel and Associates. 1976. *The methods and materials of demography.* New York: Academic Press.

mores A SOCIAL SYSTEM's mores (pronounced *MOR-ayz*) are a set of NORMS that define the most fundamental ideas about what is considered right and wrong, laudable and repugnant, good and bad, virtuous and sinful in human behavior. Mores are important not simply because they regulate behavior but because the moral vision on which they are based is a major source of social COHESION and continuity in human communities. Norms that prohibit incest, murder, treason and other forms of betrayal, abandonment of family obligations, and desecration of religious and civil symbols are all part of the mores of most societies. Because of their importance, mores typically take the form of LAWS with strong SANCTIONS such as imprisonment, banishment, ostracism, or death.

From a sociological perspective, moral behavior has four basic characteristics: (1) it never has the actor's self-interest as its major goal; (2) it has a quality of command through which each person feels an obligation to do what is right; (3) it is experienced as being desirable, and some satisfaction and pleasure is derived from it; and (4) it is regarded as sacred in the sense that its authority is experienced as beyond human control. Murder, for example, cannot be legalized without either tearing the moral fabric of SOCIETY or managing to cast it as something other than murder. In short, unlike other forms of norms, mores are regarded as immutable and inherent in social life, not as a social creation subject to change.
See also COHESION; CONSCIENCE COLLECTIVE; FOLKWAYS.

Reading
Sumner, William Graham. 1906. *Folkways.* Boston: Ginn.

mortality See DEATH RATE.

multiculturalism Multiculturalism is a movement occurring primarily in the United States, whose goal is to elevate and celebrate diverse ethnic backgrounds. It is reflected in educational programs that include the historical contributions by people of color; in the use of multiple languages in public life (as on voting ballots and public announcements); and in corporate programs designed to train managers to work more effectively with workers from diverse backgrounds. Multiculturalism has been promoted as part of a solution to a long history of ethnic and racial oppression. It has been criticized by conservatives as a devaluation of what they regard as an essential core of standards and wisdom traced to Western white civilization. Others argue that it is in fact merely a distraction from the underlying SOCIAL INEQUALITY of WEALTH and POWER that multiculturalism can mask but do little to remedy.
See also CULTURAL CONTACT; MINORITY; PREJUDICE AND DISCRIMINATION.

multilinear change See SOCIAL EVOLUTION.

multimodal distribution See MODE.

multinational corporation See TRANSNATIONAL AND MULTINATIONAL CORPORATION.

multiple correlation See CORRELATION.

multiple deprivation See DEPRIVATION.

multiple-nuclei theory See URBANIZATION AND URBANISM.

multiple regression See REGRESSION ANALYSIS.

multistage sample See COMPLEX SAMPLE.

multivariate analysis In statistics, multivariate analysis is a technique involving two or more independent VARIABLES in relation to a dependent variable. In trying to determine the causes of variation in income, for example, researchers typically include a variety of independent variables such as educational attainment, occupation, RACE, GENDER, and FAMILY background (such as parents' education and occupation).

Multivariate analysis can be used to answer a number of different questions, among them: How accurately can we predict values on a dependent variable such as personal income using information about several independent variables? Which independent variable has the greatest effect on the dependent variable? How are the independent variables related to one another, and how does this affect each independent variable's effect on the dependent variable? How do the direct effects of independent variables on the dependent variable compare with their indirect effects?

Multivariate techniques have grown rapidly in sociological usage, especially in the United States and especially with the advent of computers capable of analyzing large datasets such as national SURVEYS.

See also ANALYSIS OF VARIANCE; EFFECT, STATISTICAL; LOG-LINEAR ANALYSIS; MODEL; REGRESSION ANALYSIS; PATH ANALYSIS.

Reading

Bohrnstedt, George W., and David Knoke. 1994. *Statistics for social data analysis*, 3rd ed. Itasca, IL: F. E. Peacock.

myth A myth is a story about human experience involving the SACRED. In religious BELIEF systems, myth is often used to explain the origins of religious tradition, as in narratives about the birth, life, and death of Jesus, or the difficult spiritual journey of Buddha. Myth is also used to illustrate the many ways that core religious VALUES and beliefs apply to the experiences of everyday life. In short, myth often serves as a ritualistic way to affirm a shared sense of "where we came from and how we got here." In a related and broader sense, myth can be used to legitimate entire societies. Heroic myths about key figures in the formation of NATION-STATES (such as revolutionary heroes), for example, play an important part in glorifying and perpetuating current social arrangements.

Anthropologist Claude LÉVI-STRAUSS argued that the primary function of myth has little to do with explaining or justifying social reality. Instead, it embodies basic linguistic categories that are central to any cultural understanding of reality. Dualities such as love/hate, female/male, good/evil, or up/down are at the core of the cultural order that we use to make sense of reality. Myth, according to Lévi-Strauss, applies these categories in ways that reaffirm them as a legitimate way to think about the world.

Reading

Durkheim, Émile. [1912] 1965. *The elementary forms of religious life*. New York: Free Press.

Lévi-Strauss, Claude. [1964] 1970–81. *Introduction to a science of mythology*, 4 vols. London: Cape.

N

national, nation-state, and nationalism A nation is a SOCIETY that occupies a particular territory and includes a sense of common identity, history, and destiny.

A nation-state is a nation governed by a STATE whose AUTHORITY coincides with the boundaries of the nation. Until the nineteenth century, the world was not organized in terms of nation-states, but consisted instead of a diverse collection of ethnic groupings with relatively fluid political boundaries. This contrasts with the relatively rigid geographical boundaries and administrative control associated with the modern state. This was primarily because there were few if any states powerful enough to administer and control nations. In contrast, the world today is largely organized as nation-states.

Nationalism is a social process through which nation-states are formed by bringing national identities and political control into alignment. For example, the former Yugoslavia did not form a coherent ethnic whole, but appeared to because of the unifying power of the communist state which ruled from the end of World War II until the early 1990s. When the government fell, however, the old ethnic identities reasserted themselves and prompted nationalist movements aimed at creating political states whose authority would coincide with ethnic identities. Each ethnic group, in short, would form a state with authority over a clearly defined territory and people. Variations on this process have produced a proliferation of nations since World War II destabilized colonial empires in Africa and Asia.

Nationalism has become an increasingly powerful force in the world, serving as a basis not only for collective social identity but for political mobilization and action, especially through the use of warfare.

Reading

Giddens, Anthony. 1985. *The nation-state and violence*. Cambridge, England: Polity Press.

Kamenka, Eugene, ed. 1973. *Nationalism, the nature and evolution of an idea*. London: Edward Arnold.

Smith, Anthony D., ed. 1976. *Nationalist movements*. London: Macmillan.

natural area In URBAN ECOLOGY, a natural area is a neighborhood or COMMUNITY whose residents share common social characteristics such as occupation, ETHNICITY, or SOCIAL CLASS. The main sociological focus is to understand how such areas are formed and how they change.

Reading

Hawley, Amos. 1981. *Urban society: An ecological approach*, 2nd ed. New York: Wiley.

natural economy *See* SUBSISTENCE ECONOMY.

natural law and natural rights
The concepts of natural law and natural rights refer to the BELIEF that there are universal rights and principles of justice that flow from a natural moral order rather than from the AUTHORITY of the STATE to determine what is just. The right to freedom from SOCIAL OPPRESSION, for example, is regarded as inherent in the status of being human, and a law is just only to the extent that it supports it.

Reading
Reasons, Charles E., and Richard M. Rich. 1978. *The sociology of law.* London: Butterworths.

nature/nurture debate   The nature/nurture debate is a longstanding controversy about the effects of biology and SOCIAL SYSTEMS on individuals and their behavior. The "nature" side of the debate argues that people are shaped primarily by genetics and biology, an approach perhaps best exemplified by SOCIOBIOLOGY. The "nurture" side argues that our participation in social systems is the most important determinant of who we are and how we behave, that CULTURE and SOCIAL STRUCTURE are powerful enough to overcome any biological predisposition. There is disagreement, for example, over whether women and men differ because of genetic and biological factors such as hormones or whether such differences are due primarily to SOCIALIZATION and other social forces. Similar disagreements arise in trying to explain phenomena such as criminal behavior and intelligence.

Although each side has its adherents, many sociologists criticize both positions as based on the naive assumption that nature and nurture operate independently of each other.

As a result, they no longer consider the debate to be real or significant, and argue instead that biological and social factors interact with one another to shape human behavior and experience.

Reading
Bleier, Ruth. 1997. *Science and gender: A critique of biology and its theories on women.* New York: Teachers College Press.
McDougall, William. [1908] 1950. *An introduction to social psychology*, 30th ed. London: Methuen.
Watson, John Broadus. 1928. *Psychological care of infant and child.* New York: W. W. Norton.

naturalism   Naturalism (also known as *methodological naturalism*) is the name given to the belief that sociology can and should use the METHODOLOGY of the natural sciences in trying to understand social life. Naturalism is based on the idea that human beings are part of nature and, as such, can be understood with the same research methods used by biologists and other natural scientists. In practice, naturalism takes a variety of forms. SOCIOBIOLOGISTS, for example, regard sociological questions as mere extensions of biology. Other naturalists acknowledge that human beings are part of nature but argue that the profound influence of CULTURE sets human beings apart from other species and requires a different approach with its own methods. It is not possible, for example, to understand human behavior without taking into account the subjective meaning that people give to their ACTIONS.
See also GEISTESWISSENSCHAFTEN AND NATURWISSENSCHAFTEN.

need   The concept of need is used in relation to both individuals and SOCIAL SYSTEMS. In both cases, it refers to what is regarded as necessary for a person or system to survive or function or maintain a state of well-being. Abraham Maslow, for example, believed that people's needs are arranged in a hierarchy (*a hierarchy of needs*). The most essential needs such as food and shelter are at the bottom, and less essential ones such as the need to be loved or to fulfill one's spiritual potential are toward the top. He argued that we cannot satisfy needs higher up in the hierarchy without first satisfying the needs below (it's hard to concentrate on philosophy when you're starving).

Sociologists are particularly interested in understanding where needs come from and how social systems distribute resources and opportunities for people to satisfy them. Are some needs, for example, true and universal needs that all people have, while others are false and socially manufactured through SOCIALIZATION and other social forces (such as the need to own a car or to wear the latest fashions)? And if some needs are true, while others are false, how can we tell the difference?

Perhaps the most important use of the concept of need in sociological thinking is found in the FUNCTIONALIST PERSPECTIVE of Talcott PARSONS who argued that SOCIAL SYSTEMS have needs (or FUNCTIONAL IMPERATIVES) that must be met if systems are to function properly.

Reading

Maslow, Abraham. [1954] 1987. *Motivation and personality.* New York: Harper & Row.

negative relationship *See* DIRECTION OF RELATIONSHIP.

negotiated order The concept of a negotiated order refers to the idea

that SOCIAL SYSTEMS and their cultural and structural characteristics emerge from INTERACTION among the people who participate in and thereby make them happen. As such, the characteristics of GROUPS, organizations, and other systems are fluid and uncertain, rather than fixed and certain. From this perspective, for example, the POWER STRUCTURE in an organization is not a fixed feature of organizational life to which people conform in a predictable and mechanical way. Instead, it is the result of an ongoing process of negotiation, bargaining, and compromise out of which the actual distribution of POWER emerges, takes shape, and changes over time.

Reading

Blumer, Herbert. 1969. *Symbolic interactionism: Perspective and method.* Englewood Cliffs, NJ: Prentice-Hall.

Simmel, Georg. [1902] 1950. *The sociology of Georg Simmel,* edited and translated by Kurt H. Wolff. New York: Free Press.

Strauss, Anselm. 1978. *Negotiations, varieties, contexts, processes, and social order.* San Francisco: Jossey-Bass.

neocolonialism *See* COLONIALISM AND IMPERIALISM.

neo-Darwinism *See* NEO-EVOLUTIONISM.

neo-evolutionism Neo-evolutionism (or *neo-Darwinism*) is the name given to the recent renewed interest in theories of SOCIAL EVOLUTION. It is most often associated with the FUNCTIONALIST PERSPECTIVE and the work of Talcott PARSONS.

The use of biological evolution as a model for understanding the development of societies began in the nineteenth century, especially in the form of SOCIAL DARWINISM. Long discredited in SOCIOLOGY, it returned when Parsons argued that SOCIETIES evolve by adapting to their physical environment and other SOCIAL SYSTEMS and to internal changes in their own cultural and structural characteristics. Societies develop TECHNOLOGY to exploit energy more efficiently, for example, or SUBSYSTEMS that specialize in particular tasks (a process known as *structural differentiation*). As a result, societies move through various stages of development (although sometimes skipping stages by borrowing adaptations from other societies), culminating in advanced industrialization. Although Parsons was able to fix some of the problems with evolutionary theory (such as the assumption that change is always linear), he could not give an adequate account of SOCIAL OPPRESSION and other manifestations of CONFLICT in social life. For this reason, he has few followers among contemporary sociologists.

Reading

Parsons, Talcott. 1966. *Societies: Evolutionary and comparative perspectives.* Englewood Cliffs, NJ: Prentice-Hall.
——. 1971. *The system of modern societies.* Englewood Cliffs, NJ: Prentice-Hall.

neo-imperialism *See* COLONIALISM AND IMPERIALISM.

neolocal marriage *See* MARRIAGE RULES.

neonatal mortality *See* INFANT MORTALITY RATE.

net reproduction rate *See* BIRTH RATE.

network, social Although the term social networks has been around for a long time in both sociological and popular usage, it is only since the 1970s that sociologists have developed the concept as the centerpiece of a perspective on social life. A network is simply a collection of relationships that connect people, SOCIAL STATUSES, or other units of analysis such as GROUPS and FORMAL ORGANIZATIONS. By focusing on networks, sociologists can ask a variety of questions ranging from how people acquire power to why organizations function as they do.

In general, the network approach assumes that individual experience, behavior, and outcomes depend more on where people are located in various networks than it does on who they are as unique individuals. This rests on the idea that networks both impose constraints that limit options and provide resources that enable individuals to act in various ways. Thus differences among people can be understood as a result of being in different networks or of being located differently within the same network. Women, for example, often do not advance in corporations because they are excluded from informal male-dominated networks through which important information is shared. And within networks, the more centrally located people are in the flow of communication, the more POWER they tend to have as a result.

See also COMMUNICATION STRUCTURE; EXCHANGE THEORY; ROLE STRUCTURE; SOCIAL STRUCTURE.

Reading

Marsden, Peter V., and Nan Lin, eds. 1982. *Social structure and network analysis.* Beverly Hills, CA: Sage Publications.
Wellman, Barry. 1983. "Network analysis: Some basic principles." *Sociological Theory* 1: 155–99.

Wellman, Barry, and S. D. Berkowitz, eds. 1997. *Social structures*. Norwood, NJ: Abex.

neutralization When people commit acts of DEVIANCE, they may use neutralization as a coping technique to justify, deny, or rationalize their behavior. When a man commits sexual violence against a woman, for example, and justifies it by saying, "She asked for it," he is using neutralization.

Reading
Sykes, Gresham, and David Matza. 1957. "Techniques of neutralization: A theory of delinquency." *American Sociological Review* 22: 664–70.

new international division of labor *See* INTERNATIONAL DIVISION OF LABOR.

new structuralism *See* STATUS ATTAINMENT AND NEW STRUCTURALISM.

niche *See* ECOLOGY.

nominal-scale variable *See* SCALE OF MEASUREMENT.

nomothetic *See* IDIOGRAPHIC AND NOMOTHETIC.

nonconformist deviance As described by Robert K. MERTON in his THEORY of DEVIANCE, nonconformist deviance is an act that is committed openly and for social interests rather than secretly for individual gain. Civil disobedience, for example, is a deliberate law violation intended to provoke arrest and punishment. Its purpose is to focus public attention on the need for change in some aspect of social life, whether it be to end a war or protest against a perceived injustice.

Nonconformist deviance can take the form of *innovative deviance*, a situation in which NORMS are challenged rather than the cultural VALUES those norms support and enforce. People can support the value of minimizing crime, for example, but defy repressive police measures designed to control crime. Nonconformist deviance can also take the form of *rebellion* in which both cultural values and norms are rejected. In many societies, for example, accumulating material WEALTH is highly valued, but the legitimate means for accomplishing this are unequally distributed. As a result, many people are frustrated in their attempt to satisfy material needs and desires. One response to this is *rebellion*, through which people both reject the values involved and renounce the culturally defined legitimate means for achieving them. As a result, they may adopt new values, such as living simply with a minimum of material wealth and striving. Or they may try new means for achieving them, such as living in communes where sharing and COOPERATION are valued more highly than COMPETITION and in which the ownership of private property is not allowed.

See also ABERRANT DEVIANCE; OPPORTUNITY STRUCTURE; DEVIANCE.

Reading
Merton, Robert K. 1938. "Social structure and anomie." *American Sociological Review* 3: 672–82.

nonlinear relationship *See* DIRECTION OF RELATIONSHIP.

nonmaterial culture *See* CULTURE.

nonparametric statistics Statistical techniques for using a SAMPLE to describe a POPULATION often require rigorous and limiting mathematical assumptions. In some cases, for example, the DISTRIBUTION of the VARIABLE in question must have a particular shape (often that of a NORMAL CURVE) in the population, a requirement that can be overcome only if the sample is quite large. Researchers must often rely on small samples, however, and often lack justification for assuming what the population distribution looks like.

Nonparametric statistics are a group of statistics that require no underlying assumptions at all about population distributions (and, for this reason are often referred to as *distribution-free statistics*). Nonparametrics are used most commonly with ORDINAL-SCALE variables that take the form of ranks. The most widely known of these techniques are the Wald-Wolfowitz, Mann-Whitney (or Wilcoxon), and Kolmogorov-Smirnov tests.

See also NORMAL CURVE DISTRIBUTION; STATISTICS.

Reading

Neave, H. R., and P. L. Worthington. 1988. *Distribution-free tests*. London: Unwin Hyman.

Siegel, Sidney, and N. John Castellan, Jr. 1988. *Nonparametric statistics for the behavioral sciences*, 2nd ed. New York: McGraw-Hill.

nonresponse rate *See* RESPONSE RATE.

norm In everyday usage, a norm is a standard that is considered by most people to be usual practice in a statistical sense. For example, eating three meals a day is considered the norm in most Western societies.

In sociology, however, a norm is a cultural rule that associates people's behavior or appearance with rewards or punishments (SANCTIONS). As such, norms create social consequences that have the effect of regulating appearance and behavior. The consequences are artificial in that they do not naturally result from the action itself. Someone, for example, who commits slander by falsely asserting in public that someone is a thief and a liar is in fact merely speaking and, as such, creating noise and certain impressions in people's minds. There is nothing inherent in such an act that would result in someone being sued in a court of law and forced to pay damages to an injured party – an option made possible only because of legal norms that allow people to sue when they believe a particular act of speaking is slanderous. As rules, norms make a connection between an act (speaking slanderously) on the one hand and social sanctions (being sued and assessed damages) on the other. Neither the behavior nor the sanction is the norm; rather the norm is the entire rule that connects the two.

Norms have a variety of social purposes. They regulate behavior and appearance and thereby help to create the recognizable patterns that distinguish one SOCIAL SYSTEM or situation from another. In doing so, they help define and maintain BOUNDARIES that separate insiders from outsiders, since visible conformity to norms is a sign of membership in a social system and the violation of norms can result in being excluded or expelled. Norms also support cultural VALUES by attaching sanctions to the alternatives from which people choose how to behave. In this way, norms transform what would otherwise be regarded as merely a desirable form of behavior into an actual expectation with real social consequences attached.

Norms defined in the sociological sense may prohibit appearance or behavior that is, in spite of norms, quite common. A large percentage of adolescents and young adults in many INDUSTRIAL SOCIETIES, for example, have used illegal drugs such as marijuana, and an even larger percentage of those below the legal drinking age have used alcohol. Highway speed limits are regularly violated by substantial majorities of drivers, and adultery is fairly common even where LAWS prohibit it. One of the most striking findings of the Kinsey studies of sexual behavior in the United States was that large percentages of adults engaged in sexual practices such as masturbation and oral sex even though these were widely perceived as violating cultural norms regulating sexual expression, including numerous state sodomy laws. Examples such as these underscore the importance of distinguishing between norms as abstract cultural rules and actual patterns of appearance and behavior that occur in everyday life.

See also CONFORMITY; DEVIANCE; FOLKWAYS; MORES; ROLE.

Reading

Blake, Judith, and Kingsley Davis. 1964. "Norms, values, and sanctions." In *Handbook of modern sociology*, edited by Robert E. L. Faris. Chicago: Rand-McNally.

Durkheim, Émile. [1893] 1933. *The division of labor in society*. New York: Free Press.

——. [1924] 1974. *Sociology and philosophy*. New York: Free Press.

Gibbs, Jack P. 1965. "Norms: The problem of definition and classification." *American Journal of Sociology* 70: 586–94.

normal curve distribution In statistics, a normal curve distribution is one of a family of distributions that conform to a particular formula that produces a symmetrical, bell-shaped curve (see figure 7). Normal curve distributions differ from one another in how spread out or sharply peaked they are, depending on the amount of variation they contain.

Normal distributions are very useful in research because if we can assume that a distribution of scores is normally shaped, we then know what percentage of cases in the distribution lie at any given distance from the center (the average) of the distribution. For example, in a normal distribution, 68 percent of all the cases will have scores that lie within one standard deviation of the MEAN for the distribution; 95.5 percent will lie within two standard deviations; and 99.7 percent will lie within three. The ability to make these kinds of

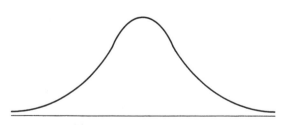

Figure 7 *Normal curve distribution*

statements is particularly important in statistical inference because it allows researchers to estimate the probability of ERROR associated with using a SAMPLE result to make inferences about the POPULATION from which it was drawn.

Although the shape of normal curve distributions changes with larger or smaller amounts of variation, not all bell-shaped symmetrical curves are normal curves. Economists in particular identify varying degrees of *kurtosis* in curves. Curves may deviate from normality, for example, by being too sharply peaked (*leptokurtic*) or too flat (*platykurtic*). One specialized platykurtic distribution that sociologists use is *student's t-distribution*

which is used to estimate population means when the sample size is small. *See also* SAMPLING DISTRIBUTION; STATISTICS; SYMMETRY; VARIANCE; Z-SCORE.

Reading

Bohrnstedt, George W., and David Knoke, 1994. *Statistics for social data analysis*, 3rd ed. Itasca, IL: F. E. Peacock.

norm of reciprocity *See* RECIPROCITY.

nuclear family *See* FAMILY.

null hypothesis *See* HYPOTHESIS AND HYPOTHESIS TESTING.

O

objectivity Objectivity can be defined in two ways. In the first, it is an absence of bias in making or interpreting observations. For example, it means designing SURVEY questions that do not encourage respondents to tell us what we want to hear; considering all reliable information that bears on our research and not merely that which supports our favorite position; and weighing and interpreting evidence according to clear criteria that would lead others to reach similar conclusions. This kind of objectivity has long been held up as an ideal in sociology, although not without some controversy. Many early American sociologists, for example, were members of the clergy dedicated to using sociological insight to change the world for the better through a clear and biased application of their VALUES. This continues to be a strong tradition in many parts of the world and especially within the realm of MARXIST SOCIOLOGY.

In its second sense, objectivity is a situation in which our representations of the world – the DATA we gather, the words we write and speak, the pictures we paint – actually correspond to a true condition of the world. To achieve this kind of objectivity, we have to describe the world free from interference from the ways in which we think about and conceptualize it, in a direct and "pure" fashion. It is doubtful that this kind of objectivity is possible in the social sciences because so much of what we study – from SOCIAL SYSTEMS to ROLES – is socially constructed and therefore unobservable without the use of ideas that are themselves socially constructed. In many ways, the same might be said even of the physical sciences. The effects of bias are easier to deal with, although always within limits. The mere process of selecting a research problem, for example, is in part an inescapable value judgment about what is most important or interesting.

See also EMPIRICAL; IDEALISM; PHENOMENOLOGY AND PHENOMENOLOGICAL SOCIOLOGY; POSITIVISM; POSTMODERNISM; SCIENCE; STRUCTURALISM AND POSTSTRUCTURALISM; VALUE RELEVANCE, VALUE FREEDOM, AND VALUE NEUTRALITY.

occupation *See* WORK.

occupational structure In a SOCIETY, the occupational structure is the mix of different types of occupations found there. Occupational structure also describes the distribution of people among those occupations, which gives some sense of which types of work predominate. INDUSTRIAL SOCIETIES, for example, include huge numbers of occupations, some of which (such as clerical and sales work) are heavily populated while others (such as brain surgeons and high church officials) are performed by a relative few.

Occupational types may be categorized in a number of ways, including distinctions among various sectors of the economy. In comparison with AGRARIAN SOCIETIES, for example, industrial societies have occupational structures that are both more complex and more heavily weighted toward manufacturing (the secondary sector) and service occupations (the tertiary sector). They are less concentrated in agriculture, mining, and other work primarily involved with raw materials (the primary sector). In the last decades of the twentieth century, the United States has lost large numbers of manufacturing jobs as its occupational structure has shifted towards service jobs.

Sociologically, occupational structure is also of great importance in its effects on SOCIAL CLASS and other forms of social inequality.

See also BLUE-COLLAR WORKER AND WHITE-COLLAR WORKER; DIVISION OF LABOR; LABOR MARKET; PRESTIGE; SOCIAL CLASS; SOCIAL MOBILITY; STRUCTURAL LAG; UNEMPLOYMENT AND UNDEREMPLOYMENT.

Reading
Blau, Peter M., and Otis Dudley Duncan. 1978. *The American occupational structure*. New York: Free Press.

ogive *See* GRAPHICS.

oligarchy An oligarchy is a SOCIAL SYSTEM under the political control of a small elite. According to Robert MICHELS's *iron law of oligarchy*, oligarchy is inevitable in large, complex societies. Such systems become oligarchic because (1) people generally prefer to let others make decisions for them; (2) the system's complexity makes it impossible for people to know enough to participate intelligently in decision-making, and, as a result, makes leaders increasingly indispensable; and (3) those who achieve AUTHORITY are unwilling to give up the resulting privileges and PRESTIGE, and thus try to consolidate and extend their POWER in order to keep them. As a result the leader's goals tend to replace the people's goals and power is increasingly concentrated.

Although Michels's THEORY was based on the study of TRADE UNIONS, it has had a profound effect on thinking about larger systems, especially the modern state.

See also AUTHORITARIANISM; AUTOCRACY; FASCISM; STATE.

Reading
Michels, Robert. [1911] 1967. *Political parties*. New York: Free Press.

oligopoly An oligopoly is a MARKET for a product or service that is controlled by a relatively small number of individuals or organizations. Within most INDUSTRIAL SOCIETIES, for example, a handful of corporations controls the supply of products and services as diverse as oil, natural gas, cigarettes, beer, breakfast cereals, aluminum, coffee, air travel, soft drinks, films, and candy.

Oligopoly is an important concept in the analysis of economic INSTITUTIONS because it draws attention to the tendency of CAPITALISM to drive out competition as economic POWER is consolidated. In the automobile industry, for example, an oligopolistic market has virtually done away with price competition among auto makers. Marxists argue that the tendency toward oligopoly and away from free markets is inherent in CAPITALISM and one of its major

213

CONTRADICTIONS as an economic system. The most extreme form of concentrated market control is the MONOPOLY.

ontology Ontology is a subfield of philosophy that focuses on the question of what actually exists and what does not. It is relevant to sociological thinking because so much of what we believe underlies social life is abstract and cannot be observed directly. For example, whether SOCIETIES can be said to exist independently of the people who participate in them is an ontological question. How we answer such questions determines how we approach the problem of understanding social life and thereby forms the basis on which all sociological work rests.

See also EPISTEMOLOGY; INTERPRETIVE SOCIOLOGY; KNOWLEDGE; SOCIAL FACT.

Reading
Keat, R., and John Urry. 1975. *Social theory as science*. London: Routledge and Kegan Paul.
Ryan, A. 1970. *The philosophy of the social sciences*. London: Macmillan.

operationalization *See* MEASUREMENT.

opportunity structure, deviance and The opportunity structure in a SOCIETY is the distribution of people's access to occupations and other ways for supporting their lives and achieving goals. The concept plays a central part in Robert K. MERTON'S THEORY of DEVIANCE. Merton argues that most societies include some degree of consensus over major VALUES, such as those that define what it means to live a "good life." In INDUSTRIAL SOCIETIES, for example, material WEALTH is highly valued, as are POWER, PRESTIGE, leisure, and so on. NORMS define the socially legitimate means for achieving such values – endorsing hard work at a legitimate occupation, for example, as well as inheritance while disallowing theft, extortion, fraud, and the like.

At the core of Merton's theory is the argument that if a CULTURE promotes shared values that define people's goals, but the STRUCTURE does not provide equal access to legitimate means for achieving those goals, higher levels of deviance will result. People will be more likely to create innovative and illegal ways of achieving the same goals everyone else aspires to. Or they may rebel against the system in various ways to protest the unequal opportunity structure or the values themselves (for example, by openly disavowing material wealth).

Opportunity structures also promote deviance when they provide equal access to legitimate means of achieving goals but those means are inadequate. If everyone can get a full-time job, for example, but many of those jobs pay much too little to live on, then deviance once again is a likely result. In similar ways, opportunity structures can also make illegitimate means for achieving goals more or less available and, in so doing, make deviance more or less likely to occur. Hiring students to xerox and collate exams, giving take-home exams, or giving exams with no monitoring in the absence of an effective honor code are all aspects of university practice that can promote cheating by making illegitimate opportunities more available.

Merton's theory has particular sociological significance because it shows how the normal functioning of a SOCIAL SYSTEM can produce undesirable consequences that are usually associated with individual failings.

See also ABERRANT DEVIANCE; NONCONFORMIST DEVIANCE.

Reading

Cloward, Richard A., Lloyd E. Ohlin. 1960. *Delinquency and opportunity: A theory of delinquent gangs.* New York: Free Press.

Merton, Robert K. 1938. "Social structure and anomie." *American Sociological Review* 3: 672–82.

oppression *See* SOCIAL OPPRESSION.

order *See* SOCIAL ORDER.

order of relationship In the statistical analysis of relationships among VARIABLES, order of relationship is the number of CONTROL VARIABLES included in the analysis. Suppose we begin with the relationship between two variables: the size of community populations and the rate of violent crime. This is the simplest kind of relationship we can have because there are no control variables; hence it is called a zero-order relationship. If we control for an additional variable, such as the number of police officers per capita, the result is a first-order relationship because we have introduced one control variable to the original two-variable relationship. If we then add a second control variable, such as the percentage of the population that lives in poverty, we have a second-order relationship.

See also CONTROL VARIABLE; VARIABLE.

Reading

Rosenberg, Morris. 1968. *The logic of survey analysis.* New York: Basic Books.

ordinal-scale variable *See* SCALE OF MEASUREMENT.

organic analogy Beginning with the work of Herbert SPENCER and Émile DURKHEIM, sociologists have often been drawn to an organic (or *biological*) analogy for societies that likens them to living organisms. This has been especially true of the FUNCTIONALIST PERSPECTIVE and its view of SOCIAL SYSTEMS as collections of interdependent parts that function together in order to make the whole survive in an effective and harmonious way, much as a body's organs relate to one another to maintain functioning and well-being. As appealing as the organic analogy can be, it has serious shortcomings that preclude its use by most sociologists. The basic problem is that it does not fit reality very well. Unlike organisms, for example, societies often include a diversity of interests that may conflict with one another or form internal systems of SOCIAL OPPRESSION.

See also SOCIAL DARWINISM.

organic organization *See* ORGANIZATIONAL THEORY.

organic solidarity *See* COHESION.

organization *See* FORMAL ORGANIZATION; SOCIAL ORDER.

organizational theory Organizational theory is the general term for THEORY intended to explain how complex organizations work as SOCIAL SYSTEMS, and how people behave as they participate in and make them happen. It distinguishes among various types of CULTURE and structure, based on characteristics such as organizational complexity, the degree to which units specialize in particular tasks, the formality of rules and procedures, how workers are controlled, who benefits most from organizational efficiency and success, the degree to which organizations stress decentralization and flexibility (the *organic* model) or are rigid and bureaucratic (the *mechanistic* model), and where an organization's structure lies along a continuum ranging from unitary and monolithic at one end to a loosely linked set of semi-autonomous divisions at the other.

The focus on individuals' behavior in organizational settings stresses primarily how organizational culture encourages people to obey NORMS and how the formation of SUBGROUPS AND SUBCULTURES can undermine those norms and the VALUES they enforce. For this reason, one of the main criticisms of organizational theory is that its primary use is to assist managers in controlling workers.

See also HUMAN RELATIONS SCHOOL; NEGOTIATED ORDER; SCIENTIFIC MANAGEMENT; FORMAL ORGANIZATION.

Reading

Blau, Peter. 1973. *The dynamics of bureaucracy*, 2nd rev. ed. Chicago: University of Chicago Press.

Burns, Tom, and George Macpherson Stalker. 1961. *The management of innovation*. London: Tavistock.

organized crime Organized (or *syndicated*) crime is a SOCIAL SYSTEM distinguished by a complex STRUCTURE resembling a FORMAL ORGANIZATION rather than a loose-knit collection of criminals. Crime organizations have a hierarchical POWER STRUCTURE, a complex DIVISION OF LABOR that includes a management system, a formal system for keeping records, and clearly articulated rules that everyone is expected to follow – all of which are characteristic of formal organizations. As criminal organizations become more complex, so do the varieties of crime they engage in, such as the drug trade, with its intricate ways of procuring, processing, transporting, and selling drugs, or the infiltration of legitimate businesses through a wide network of resources. Some crime syndicates are even organized as franchises, much like fast-food restaurants and other business chains.

Reading

Ianni, Francis A. J., Elizabeth Reus-Ianni. 1973. *A family business: Kinship and social control in organized crime.* New York: Mentor.

Posner, G. L. 1988. *Warlords of crime; Chinese secret societies.* New York: McGraw-Hill.

organized skepticism, norm of *See* SCIENCE, NORMS OF.

other In classical sociology, other is a concept in the study of social life through which we define relationships. We encounter two distinct types of others in relation to ourselves, which from a sociological standpoint differ primarily in the kind of knowledge we have of them.

The first is what psychiatrist Harry Stack Sullivan called a *significant other*, someone about whom we have some degree of specific knowledge. Because we know something about them as individuals, we pay attention to what we perceive to be their personal thoughts, feelings, or expectations. We might, for example, know that the corner grocer especially likes children, or does not like it when people ask to use the telephone, or tends to put her finger on the scale when she should not. As an "other," this grocer is significant in that we pay attention not only to what grocers are generally like but to what we know about this particular grocer.

Note that "significant" does not mean that the person is important; in fact, "specific" or "particular" are perhaps more accurate terms, especially when contrasted with George Herbert MEAD's concept of the *generalized other*. We experience the generalized other primarily as an abstract social STATUS and the ROLE that goes with it. When we enter a grocery store without any particular knowledge of the grocer, our expectations are based only on knowledge of grocers and customers in general and what usually is supposed to take place when they interact. Thus when we interact with this grocer, our only basis for knowledge is the generalized other.

Many social relationships are based on both kinds of knowledge. We may know some things about our particular grocer (just as the grocer may know some particular things about us), but most of the knowledge we rely on when we interact is based on our understanding of this social situation, the statuses it involves, and the roles that go with them.

The concepts of significant and generalized other are especially important in the study of SOCIALIZATION through which we learn to orient ourselves first to significant others and their particular expectations (especially in the form of what parents and peers expect), and then to the more generalized expectations embodied in SOCIAL SYSTEMS. It is only through our ability to understand generalized others, for example, that we are truly able to perform roles.

POSTMODERNISM and FEMINISM take different perspectives on the concept of the other. Postmodernism, for example, challenges the distinction between SELF and other as arbitrary. From this perspective, the self does not exist as an autonomous unit that can be meaningfully separated from others in the way usually envisioned by sociologists. In another vein, Simone de Beauvoir's existentialist feminism uses the word "other" to name the marginalized social position assigned to women under PATRIARCHY, by which women's lives and experience have meaning only in relation to men.

See also MIND.

Reading

Beauvoir, Simone de. [1949] 1994. *The second sex*. New York: Alfred A. Knopf.

Mead, George Herbert. 1934. *Mind, self, and society*. Chicago: University of Chicago Press.

Sullivan, Harry Stack. 1953. *The interpersonal theory of psychiatry*. New York: Norton.

outer city First identified in the United States in the late 1980s, the outer city is a SUBURB that has left behind its historical pattern of serving primarily as a bedroom community for workers who commute to a city. Instead, the outer city has developed its own business and manufacturing base – often in the form of corporate headquarters – that compete with and often hasten the decline of the INNER CITY, from which many businesses have moved. Outer cities are complete with industrial and office parks, shopping malls, hotels and restaurants.

Reading

Hartshorn, T. A., and P. O. Muller. 1987. *Suburban business centers: Employment implications*. U.S. Department of Commerce. Washington: Government Printing Office.

out-group *See* GROUP.

overdetermination The concept of overdetermination points to an important difficulty in trying to determine what causes what in social life.

Instead of one thing being caused in a simple and direct way by another, much of what happens in social life is caused by many different factors (overdetermined) which are, in turn, affected by what they "cause." Freud used the concept of overdetermination in reference to dreams, arguing that the content of a dream is based on a complex set of experiences which makes it hard to interpret in a simple way. Louis ALTHUSSER used the concept in relation to Marxism to argue against the idea that economic arrangements determine social life in a direct or linear way. Instead, he argued that nothing happens as the simple result of something else, and that what we observe as the various CONTRADICTIONS of CAPITALISM cause one another in reciprocal and complex ways.

Reading
Althusser, Louis. 1966. *For Marx.* London: Allen Lane Press.

overpopulation   On the face of it, overpopulation is a relatively simple concept that refers to a condition in which the number of people in a SOCIAL SYSTEM is larger than can be adequately sustained by the resources available to that system. There isn't enough food, housing, clothing and other things deemed essential in that CULTURE. The concept was first developed by the eighteenth-century British clergyman, Thomas Malthus, who observed that food supplies tend to grow more slowly than POPULATIONS, producing an inevitable crisis and often drastic corrective measures.

What makes the concept problematic is whether in defining and using it we emphasize the surplus of population or the deficit of resources. If we focus on the former,

the solution to the problem is to slow rates of population growth or even to shrink population size. If we emphasize the latter, however, solutions become more complex, because resources include not only raw materials but the TECHNOLOGY to make the best use of them. Perhaps most important, resources include a social system that distributes what is produced in a way that minimizes social inequality and the DEPRIVATION that results from it. Capitalist countries, for example, tend to define THIRD WORLD population problems in terms of population size. As a result, they promote birth control as a solution. Marxists, on the other hand, emphasize social inequality and exploitative relations both between and within nations as a major source of the lack of fit between population size and resources. From this perspective, there could be enough to go around if systems of production and distribution were organized differently.

See also DEPENDENCY THEORY; WORLD SYSTEM.

Reading
Johnson, D. G., and R. D. Lee. 1986. *Population growth and economic development.* Washington: National Academy of Sciences.
Malthus, Thomas. [1798] 1960. *Essay on the principle of population.* New York: Modern Library.
Mamdani, M. 1981. "The ideology of population control." In *And the poor get children*, edited by K. L. Michaelson. New York: Monthly Review Press.
Whitaker, J. S. 1989. *How can Africa survive?* New York: Harper and Row.

oversampling   Oversampling is a research practice in which members of a POPULATION subgroup are selected in greater numbers than their relative size in the population would otherwise call for. This is done most often when researchers are interested in subgroups that comprise a small portion of the total population.

In engineering schools, for example, women are a small percentage of all students. If we drew a sample of 1,000 students, the resulting number of women would be statistically too small to justify drawing conclusions about them as a group. To compensate for this, we might oversample women engineers by taking a much larger SAMPLE of them as part of the overall sample.

If we then use this sample to make statements about all engineering students, however, women will be overrepresented. We can correct for this bias through the use of SAMPLING WEIGHTS.

Reading

Kalton, Graham. 1984. *Introduction to survey sampling*. Beverly Hills, CA: Sage Publications.

Kish, Leslie. 1985. *Survey sampling*. New York: Wiley.

P

panel   *See* LONGITUDINAL RESEARCH.

pantheism   *See* THEISTIC RELIGION.

paradigm   *See* THEORETICAL PERS-PECTIVE.

partial association (also called a *partial correlation* or a *partial relationship*). In the statistical analysis of relationships among VARIABLES, a partial association is a relationship that occurs between two variables after one or more CONTROL VARIABLES have been introduced. Suppose, for example, we begin with a relationship between gender and income that shows that men have higher incomes than women. In order to help explain this relationship, we might control for occupation based on the idea that men receive more money than women because they have better jobs. In controlling for the variable occupation, we still look at the relationship between gender and income but now we restrict ourselves to people who have similar jobs. In this case, the relationship between gender and income would be called a partial relationship and any statistical measure of the strength of relationship would be called a partial association (or partial correlation) – and, in both cases, a "partial," for short.
See also CONTROL VARIABLE; ORDER OF RELATIONSHIP; VARIABLE; WEALTH AND INCOME; SEX AND GENDER.

Reading
Bohrnstedt, George W., and David Knoke. 1994. *Statistics for social data analysis*, 3rd ed. Itasca, IL: F. E. Peacock.

participant observation   Participant observation is a research method in which the researcher actually takes part in the social phenomenon being studied. In a classic study of mental hospitals, for example, researchers had themselves admitted as patients under false pretenses so that they could observe how patients, including themselves, were treated by hospital staff. The researchers found that once they had been labeled as mentally ill, hospital staff interpreted their behavior in those terms. For example, their taking of extensive notes, which was an integral part of their research effort, was interpreted in hospital records as "note-taking behavior" believed to be reflective of their pathological mental condition.

Although participant observation is most closely associated with anthropological research in tribal societies, it is used by sociologists in a variety of settings, from GROUP DYNAMICS to ORGANIZATIONS to the study of INTER-ACTION between men and women. The main advantage of this approach is that it enables researchers to study social behavior as it actually occurs. The main disadvantage is that as researchers become involved with what they are studying, they may develop interests, loyalties, and points of view that influence their observations and interpretations without their knowing it. Thus, as with many research strategies, the major strengths of participant observation are also among its weaknesses. *See also* METHODOLOGY.

Reading

Jorgensen, D. L. 1989. *Participant observation: A methodology for human studies.* Newbury Park, CA: Sage Publications.

Rosenhan, D. L. 1973. "On being sane in insane places." *Science* 179: 250–58.

particularism *See* PATTERN VARIABLES.

party, political A political party is an organization that seeks POWER over public policy by placing members in positions of AUTHORITY within the STATE, typically through elections and appointments. As an INTEREST GROUP, it also uses its resources to influence those already in office as well as the electorate. Sociological interest in parties focuses on several issues, including how they are organized and controlled: how they function as a link between CITIZENS and the STATE, shaping the interests of each; how the number of parties is established in a SOCIETY and how power is distributed among them; how characteristics such as SOCIAL CLASS and RACE affect party affiliations; to what extent office holders are subject to party discipline; and how parties mobilize people and resources for political action.

Reading

Beyme, Klaus von. 1985. *Political parties in western democracies.* Aldershot, England: Gower.

Lawson, Kay, ed. 1980. *Political parties and linkage.* New Haven: Yale University Press.

Sartori, Giovanni. 1976. *Parties and party systems: A framework for analysis.*

Cambridge, England: Cambridge University Press.

party, Weber *See* SOCIAL CLASS.

pastoral society A pastoral, or herding, SOCIETY is a SOCIAL SYSTEM in which the breeding and herding of domestic animals is a major form of production for food and other purposes. Dating back to roughly 6000 B.C., nomadic pastoral societies have been linked with several important social developments, including BELIEF in gods that watch over and take an active interest in human affairs and the introduction of PATRIARCHAL forms of social organization, especially among those that used horses for transportation and warfare.

See also AGRARIAN SOCIETY; HUNTER-GATHERER SOCIETY; HORTICULTURAL SOCIETY; INDUSTRIAL SOCIETY AND INDUSTRIALIZATION; POSTINDUSTRIAL SOCIETY.

Reading

Lenski, Gerhard E., Jean Lenski, and Patrick Nolan. 1998. *Human societies: An introduction to macrosociology*, 8th ed. New York: McGraw-Hill.

Spooner, Brian. 1973. *The cultural ecology of pastoral nomads.* Reading, MA: Addison-Wesley.

paternalism Paternalism refers to an AUTHORITARIAN relationship, especially between workers and employers. Typically, the one in power makes others dependent and powerless, tries to control all aspects of their lives, and justifies domination as in the best interests of those being controlled, based on the assumption that they are incapable of taking care of themselves. The concept has been used to describe a variety of SOCIAL SYSTEMS, including the factory system in the early stages of industrial CAPITALISM, Japanese management styles, and COLONIALISM.

path analysis Path analysis is a form of MULTIVARIATE ANALYSIS used to evaluate CAUSAL MODELS by examining the relationships between a dependent VARIABLE and two or more independent variables. The effects of each independent variable on the dependent variable are shown both directly and indirectly through other independent variables.

Path analysis has two main requirements. First, all causal relationships between variables must go in one direction only, which is to say that you cannot have a pair of variables that cause each other. Second, the variables must have a clear time-ordering since one variable cannot be said to cause another unless it precedes it in time.

A typical path diagram is shown in the accompanying figure 8. The dependent variable (income) is shown at the far right. According to the model, variations in income for employed U.S. women are due to six factors – directly by occupational prestige and education (as shown by the arrows) and indirectly by number of siblings, father's education, mother's education, and father's occupational prestige (note that the woman's own education has both direct effects on income and indirect effects through her occupational prestige). Mother's education affects income indirectly, for example, by affecting education and the number of siblings. Father's education and occupation and mother's education are shown without any variables behind them acting as their cause, which makes them *exogenous* variables in this model. The curved arrows on the left indicate that although the variables they join are correlated with each other, no argument is being made about any causal relation between them.

The arrows coming from outside the model (pointing to education, income, prestige, and siblings) indicate the relationship between these variables and all variables not included in the model. The numbers attached to these arrows (0.83, 0.89, 0.79, and 0.93 respectively) are multiple

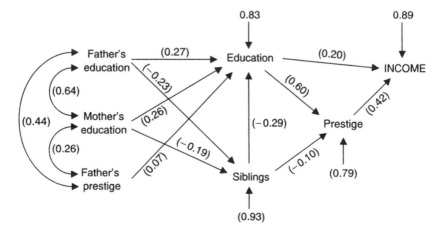

Figure 8 *Path diagram for income by occupational prestige, education, number of siblings, father's and mother's education, and father's occupational prestige, US employed women, 25–64 years old, 1972–1976. Source:* Computed from pooled 1972–1976 GENSOC Survey data.

CORRELATION coefficients indicating how strongly these variables are correlated with variables outside the model. If these numbers are squared, they indicate the percentage of variation explained by factors outside the model. In this example, $(0.89)2 = 0.79$ or 79 percent of VARIANCE in income is explained by outside variables, which means that only 21 percent is explained by variables in the model.

The numbers on the straight arrows indicate how much impact one variable has on another measured in standard deviation units. For example, the arrow joining education and income shows that for every increase of one standard deviation of education, there is an increase of 0.20 standard deviations of income. These numbers are known as *beta weights* or *path coefficients* and they allow us to compare the relative importance of different independent variables. Occupational prestige, for example, has twice the impact on income as does education (0.42 versus 0.20).

The indirect effect of one variable on another is found by multiplying path coefficients together. The direct effect of education on income, for example, is 0.20; but the indirect effect through occupational prestige is $(0.60)(0.42) = 0.25$, for a total effect of $0.20 + 0.25 = 0.45$.

In contrast with techniques such as multiple REGRESSION ANALYSIS, path analysis is theoretically useful because it forces us to specify relationships among all of the independent variables. This results in a model showing causal mechanisms through which independent variables produce both direct and indirect effects on a dependent variable.

See also EFFECT, STATISTICAL; MODEL; STANDARDIZATION; VARIABLE.

Reading
Blalock, Hubert M., ed. 1971. *Causal models in the social sciences.* Chicago: Aldine.
Duncan, Otis Dudley. 1966. "Path analysis: Sociological examples." *American Journal of Sociology* 72: 1–16.

patriarchy Strictly speaking, a patriarchy is a SOCIAL SYSTEM in which FAMILY systems or entire SOCIETIES are organized around the idea of father-rule. Since father is a family status, patriarchy is strongest in societies where the family is the primary social INSTITUTION through which WEALTH, PRESTIGE, and POWER are passed from one generation to the next. Some authors argue that patriarchy is a relatively new arrangement, whose origins date back some 7,000 years.

In industrial class societies the family is relatively unimportant as a source of wealth, power, and prestige. As a result, the position of father is no longer a basis for substantial power. This has not meant an end to male dominance and the oppression of women, only a shift from the position of father to positions outside the family – in politics, economics, and other institutions that have eclipsed the central importance of the family in most areas of social life. The new order of gender politics is *androcratic* (based on the principle of male dominance) and *androcentric* (giving primary attention and importance to men and what they do).

See also MATRIARCHY; SOCIAL OPPRESSION.

Reading
Eisler, Riane. 1987. *The chalice and the blade.* San Francisco: HarperSanFrancisco.
Fisher, Elizabeth. 1980. *Woman's creation: Sexual evolution and the shaping of society.* New York: McGraw-Hill.

Lerner, Gerda. 1986. *The creation of patriarchy*. New York: Oxford.

patrilineal descent   *See* KINSHIP.

patrilocal marriage   *See* KINSHIP.

patrimonialism
Patrimonialism is a SOCIAL SYSTEM in which a royal elite rules through personal and arbitrary control over a bureaucracy and over slaves, mercenaries, and conscripts who have no power themselves and serve only to enforce the monarch's rule. It has been found most often in Asia – China in particular – and contrasts with European monarchies, which typically depended on an alliance with landed aristocrats who provided the regime with legitimacy and ruling power. As a consequence, patrimonial systems have been far less stable and more prone to sudden palace revolutions. As Max WEBER argued, they have also been unlikely to lead to sustained economic or social development, including the emergence of CAPITALISM.

Reading
Weber, Max. [1922] 1968. *Economy and society*. New York: Bedminster Press.

patron–client relations
In the most general sense, patron–client relations are those in which a client depends upon a special relationship with a patron who is in a position of influence or POWER. Typically, the patron provides protection or the means to earn a living (such as loans or access to land for cultivation) in exchange for loyalty, support, obedience, and services from the client. It is a relationship that can exist between individuals, GROUPS, or SOCIETIES.

Although patron–client relations are often based on tradition, RELIGION, or contracts of one kind or another, the INEQUALITY inherent in the relationship makes it ripe for EXPLOITATION and abuse. This was the case, for example, in the relationship between nobles and PEASANTS under FEUDALISM in Europe, and in the SHARECROPPING system found throughout the American South, especially after the Civil War ended slavery.

Reading
Abercrombie, Nicholas, and Stephen Hill. 1976. "Paternalism and patronage." *British Journal of Sociology* 27: 413–29.

pattern variables
Talcott PARSONS used the concept of pattern variables to describe different orientations that people or entire systems can have toward "social objects," including people. Parsons saw them as important because they set us up to treat one another in particular ways and, in that, they shape patterns of social relations and experience.

For example, family members in most Western societies are treated as individuals. One child may have special needs that require a set of standards that differ from those applied to the other children. Or a child may be the parents' favorite and, for that reason, receive special attention or consideration. In school, however, children are judged according to universal standards – such as tests, grades, and rules – that apply to everyone equally and without regard to the personality or particular needs of each child or the child's personal relationship to teachers.

This example describes a pattern variable – in this case what Parsons called *particularism/universalism* to distinguish between an individual (or "particular") orientation to children at home and a group (or "universal") orientation in school.

In all, he identified four pattern variables: particularism/universalism, *affective involvement/affective neutrality*, *ascription/achievement*, and *diffuseness/specificity*. In school, for example, emotions are not supposed to affect student evaluation (affective neutrality), while family relationships depend on an active emotional tie (affective involvement). In the family, people are valued for their own sake and for who they are (ascription), while in school, children are treated more according to their performance and how well they measure up to standards of achievement. Finally, family relationships are diffuse, in that they touch on almost all aspects of their members' lives, while school relationships are more specific to the tasks of learning contained in the school curriculum.

It is no surprise that children often go through quite a shock when they first attend school. The reason for this is that they are shifting from a family system based on affective, diffuse, particularistic relations, in which they are valued simply for who they are, to a school system based on affective neutrality, specificity, and universal standards in which children are seen and valued for what they do rather than for who they are as individuals.

Reading
Parsons, Talcott. 1937. *The structure of social action.* New York: McGraw-Hill Book Company.
——. 1951. *The social system.* Glencoe, IL: Free Press.

peasants Peasants (or *serfs*) are farmers in largely AGRARIAN SOCIETIES who produce primarily within FAMILY units for their own consumption. They are typically under some degree of control by and obligation to an external power such as a landlord.

Peasants range from the relatively prosperous to the landless. Sociological interest in peasants focuses on several issues, including their role in REVOLUTIONARY movements and other aspects of SOCIAL CHANGE and the effects of CAPITALISM and emerging MARKET economies on peasant life. Under capitalism, for example, peasants often find themselves deprived of rights to use land and losing their economic self-sufficiency. This makes them increasingly dependent on the vagaries of international markets in food exports.

Reading
Moore, Barrington. 1967. *Social origins of dictatorship and democracy: Lord and peasant in the making of the modern world.* London: Penguin Press.
Shanin, T., ed. 1988. *Peasants and peasant societies.* Harmondsworth, England: Penguin.
Weller, R. P., and S. E. Guggenheim, eds. 1982. *Power and protest in the countryside: Studies of rural unrest in Asia, Europe, and Latin America.* Durham, NC: Duke University Press.

peer group *See* REFERENCE GROUP.

penology Derived from the Greek word for "punishment," penology is the study of the treatment and punishment of criminals, especially in jails and prisons. It began as a nineteenth-century reform movement dedicated to changing the social orientation to criminals from one of retribution and punishment to one of correction, reform, and rehabilitation. Today, penology is devoted more to the study of what works and what doesn't in efforts to deter and control criminal DEVIANCE.

Reading
Foucault, Michel. 1975. *Discipline and punish: The birth of the prison.* London: Tavistock.

Friedman, Lawrence M. 1993. *Crime and punishment in American history*. New York: Basic Books.

percentage   *See* CROSS-TABULATION.

percentile   A percentile is a score that cuts off a given percentage of cases in a DISTRIBUTION of scores. On a university exam, for example, if the ninety-eighth percentile is a score of 88, this means that 98 percent of the remaining scores fell below 88. The MEDIAN is equivalent to the fiftieth percentile.

Although a percentile can be used to locate a score in a distribution in terms of its relative ranking, it tells us nothing about how much better one score is than another. If there is little difference between the highest and lowest scores in a distribution, for example, a score falling in the ninety-eighth percentile might be quite close in actual value to a score falling in the fortieth.

See also MEDIAN.

Reading
Bohrnstedt, George W., and David Knoke. 1994. *Statistics for social data analysis*, 3rd ed. Itasca, IL: F. E. Peacock.

perception, social   Social perception is a general term that refers to the fact that how we perceive and interpret the world is influenced and shaped by our participation in SOCIAL SYSTEMS. This affects how we perceive, evaluate, and interpret both ourselves and other people, especially in relation to STEREOTYPES based on the social STATUSES that people occupy.

See also ATTRIBUTION, SOCIAL; EXPECTATION STATES THEORY; SELF; STATUS GENERALIZATION.

performance   expectation   *See* EXPECTATION STATES THEORY.

performative language   *See* LANGUAGE.

period data   *See* CROSS-SECTIONAL DATA.

periodicity   *See* SYSTEMATIC SAMPLE.

peripheral   economy   *See* DUAL ECONOMY.

peripheral   society   *See* WORLD SYSTEM.

personal power   *See* POWER.

petit   bourgeoisie   *See* MIDDLE CLASS.

phenomenology and phenomenological sociology   Phenomenology is the study of conscious human experience in everyday life. As first developed by Alfred SCHUTZ, phenomenological sociology is the study of the connection between human consciousness and social life, between the shape of social life on the one hand and how people perceive, think, and talk about it on the other.

Phenomenological   sociology   is based on the idea of a *social construction of reality* through INTERACTION among people who use SYMBOLS to interpret one another and assign meaning to perceptions and experience. When a woman says to a man, for example, "I love you; will you marry me?" her words play a critical part in constructing what they will experience as reality. Whether he replies, "Yes I will; I love you, too"; "No, I love someone else"; or "No, thank you," makes a world of difference in the social reality that results. In the first case, the conversation may become part of a long-term social construction of an ongoing marital relationship complete with complex expectations, understandings, and feelings (which may, of course, shift to another reality if she says one day, "I don't love you anymore").

Phenomenological sociology takes as its foremost task the study of what Shutz called the *life-world* – the taken-for-granted stream of everyday routines, interaction, and events that are seen as the source of not only individual experience but the shape of GROUPS and SOCIETIES.

See also DECONSTRUCTION; DISCOURSE AND DISCOURSE FORMATION; ETHNO-METHODOLOGY; INTERACTION; KNOWL-EDGE; OBJECTIVITY.

Reading
Berger, Peter L., and Thomas Luckmann. 1967. *The social construction of reality.* Garden City, NY: Doubleday.
Schutz, Alfred. 1967. *The phenomenology of the social world.* Evanston, IL: Northwestern University Press.
Schutz, Alfred, and Thomas Luckman. 1974. *The structures of the life-world.* London: Heinemann Educational Books.

pilot study A pilot study is a research project that is conducted on a limited scale that allows researchers to get a clearer idea of what they want to know and how they can best find it out without the expense and effort of a full-fledged study. Pilot studies are used, for example, to try out SURVEY questions and other MEASUREMENT INSTRUMENTS and to refine research HYPOTHESES.
See also METHODOLOGY.

platykurtic distribution *See* NORMAL CURVE DISTRIBUTION.

pluralism *See* POWER STRUCTURE.

pluralism, cultural *See* CULTURAL CONTACT.

pluralistic power structure *See* POWER STRUCTURE.

POET *See* ECOLOGY.

point estimate *See* ESTIMATES.

political culture Political CULTURE is the accumulated store of the SYMBOLS, BELIEFS, VALUES, ATTITUDES, NORMS, and other cultural products that shape and govern political life in a SOCIETY. This would include symbols such as mottoes and national anthems; material culture such as flags, monuments, and statues of heroic figures; beliefs about national history and destiny; attitudes of patriotism or deference (or cynicism or contempt) toward politicians and other leaders; values that shape policy choices; and norms that govern expectations ranging from the guarantee of civil rights to mechanisms for changing governments or stifling dissent. Topics of sociological interest include how various aspects of political culture affect political behavior and outcomes; the relationship between political culture and various types of political systems such as DEMOCRACY and AUTHORITARIANISM; and the SOCIALIZATION process through which political culture is passed from one generation to the next.
See also HEGEMONY.

Reading
Almond, Gabriel A., and Sidney Verba. 1963. *The civic culture: Political attitudes and democracy in five nations.* Princeton: Princeton University Press.

Pye, Lucian W., and Sidney Verba, eds. 1965. *Political culture and political development.* Princeton: Princeton University Press.

political economy

Political economy is a concept referring to the interdependent workings and interests of political and economic systems, especially in complex INDUSTRIAL SOCIETIES. So strong is this connection, that it is virtually impossible to understand the workings of one without taking into account its relation to the other.

Most closely associated with Karl MARX, the concept of political economy draws attention to how the STATE actively supports the economic system. In the process, it both protects and promotes the interests of those who dominate and benefit most from it. In return, the state depends on the economic system for its resources. The fact that leaders move freely between corporate and political realms is but one reflection of the fundamental relationship between these two critical spheres of POWER.

See also POLITICS.

Reading

Froman, C. 1984. *The two American political systems: Society, economics, and politics.* Englewood Cliffs, NJ: Prentice-Hall.

Marx, Karl. [1859] 1970. *A contribution to the critique of political economy.* New York: International Publishers.

——. [1867] 1975. *Capital: A critique of political economy.* New York: International Publishers.

political process theory

In the study of SOCIAL MOVEMENTS, political process THEORY is a concept based on the argument that the success of social movements depends not only on the movement's resources but on those of major SOCIAL SYSTEMS such as the STATE and how these are brought to bear in support or opposition.

From this perspective, it is important to understand the complex INTERACTION between the movement and the larger social environment. Political REVOLUTION, for example, is most likely to succeed if the state is vulnerable, unstable, or lacking in social legitimacy; if the revolutionary movement is better organized than the state; and if new ways of thinking undermine the state's legitimacy and promote the BELIEF that change is possible.

Political process theory was introduced into the sociological study of social movements in part as a reaction to RESOURCE MOBILIZATION THEORY.

See also POLITICS.

Reading

McAdam, Doug. 1982. *Political process and the development of black insurgency 1930–1970.* Chicago: University of Chicago Press.

Skocpol, Theda. 1979. *States and social revolutions.* New York: Cambridge University Press.

political rights

See CITIZEN AND CITIZENSHIP.

politics

Politics is the social process through which collective POWER is generated, organized, distributed, and used in SOCIAL SYSTEMS. In most SOCIETIES, politics is organized primarily around the institution of the STATE, although this is a relatively recent development. In FEUDAL societies, for example, the state was quite weak and undeveloped and political power rested primarily in nobles, vassals, and clergy whose sphere of influence was sharply limited by the extent of their lands.

Although the concept of politics is most often associated with governing INSTITUTIONS at international, NATIONAL, regional, and COMMUNITY levels, sociologically it can be applied to virtually any social system in which power plays a significant role. We can, therefore, ask questions about the politics of FAMILY life and sexuality, about "office" politics, university politics, or even the politics of art and music. This latter point is particularly important because it draws attention to the fact that every social system has a POWER STRUCTURE, not just those whose social functions are formally defined in terms of power.

See also PARTY, POLITICAL; POLITICAL ECONOMY; POWER; STATE.

Reading
Bottomore, Thomas B. 1993. *Political sociology.* Minneapolis: University of Minnesota Press.

polyandry   *See* MARRIAGE RULES.

polygamy   *See* MARRIAGE RULES.

polygyny   *See* MARRIAGE RULES.

polytheism   *See* THEISTIC RELIGION.

popular culture   Popular culture is the accumulated store of cultural products such as music, literature, art, fashion, dance, film, television, and radio that are consumed primarily by non-ELITE groups such as the WORKING and LOWER CLASSES (as well as substantial segments of the MIDDLE CLASS). It has attracted the attention of sociologists – first in Britain and more recently in the United States – for two reasons. The first is the idea that popular CULTURE is used by ELITES (who tend to control the mass media and other popular culture outlets) to control those below them. Members of the Frankfurt School, for example, argued that popular culture is trivial, homogenized, and commercialized and dulls people's minds, making them passive and easier to control. A related argument is that because popular culture is controlled primarily by elites (especially through ownership of the mass media) it tends to reflect their interests. The trivialization and sexual objectification of women in film, for example, has been criticized by many feminists as serving the interests of male viewers and male dominance.

Others, in particular British sociologists engaged in CULTURAL STUDIES, argue just the opposite, that popular culture is often a vehicle for rebellion against the culture of dominant groups. From this perspective, popular culture is not a steady, bland diet handed down from above in order to dull and pacify subordinate groups and reflect and promote elite interests. Instead, it is an arena full of diversity, conflict, and struggle over the content of culture and, thereby, the shape of social life. Lower classes, teenagers, people of color, women, and other subordinate groups do not passively absorb popular culture. Instead, they play a part in producing and reproducing a vision of what their lives are about, including some consciousness of their disadvantaged position. This struggle is reflected in a variety of cultural products, from rap and feminist music to stand-up comedy routines to rock music whose lyrics delight many young people but offend their parents.

See also CRITICAL THEORY; HEGEMONY; MASS SOCIETY; MASS COMMUNICATION AND MASS MEDIA.

Reading

Brake, M. 1980. *The sociology of youth culture and youth subcultures.* London: Routledge and Kegan Paul.

Curran, James, Michael Gurevitch, and Janet Woolacott. 1979. *Mass communication and society.* New York: Russell Sage Foundation.

Tuchman, Gaye. 1989. *Edging women out.* New Haven: Yale University Press.

population Population is a concept having two general usages. In research, a population is any well-defined collection of objects of study. For example, a research population might consist of antiwar groups, French teenagers who had babies during 1999, corporations that went bankrupt during the late 1990s, or Third World nations. Beyond sociology, of course, the populations of interest would be quite different, from computer chips produced by a particular company to wheat in a farmer's field to the artifacts left behind by an ancient CIVILIZATION. In any case, the population defines a set of objects to be studied.

In DEMOGRAPHY, a population is defined somewhat more narrowly as a collection of people who share a particular geographical territory. This contrasts with the more general notion of population offered above, which has no such restrictions.

See also CENSUS; DEMOGRAPHY; STATISTICS.

Reading

Shryock, Henry S., and Jacob Siegel and Associates. 1976. *The methods and materials of demography.* New York: Academic Press.

Singleton, Royce A., Bruce C. Straits, and Margaret M. Straits. 1998. *Approaches to social research*, 3rd ed. Oxford and New York: Oxford University Press.

population studies *See* DEMOGRAPHY.

populism Populism (from the Latin word meaning "people") is an IDEOLOGY or SOCIAL MOVEMENT having a faith in the wisdom of ordinary people and a corresponding suspicion of ELITES such as politicians, intellectuals, and big business leaders. As a political movement, populism has often promoted direct government by the people and opposed elite-driven patterns of SOCIAL CHANGE such as industrial CAPITALISM, URBANIZATION, and other forms of "progress."

Reading

Canovan, M. 1981. *Populism.* New York: Harcourt Brace.

Laclau, E. 1977. *Politics and ideology in Marxist theory: Capitalism, fascism, and populism.* London: New Left Books.

positional goods The concept of positional goods has two meanings. It can be used to refer to goods that people buy in order to indicate their status – to wear certain clothes, for example, or drive a make of car that signals to others a special or superior position (hence "positional" goods) in SOCIETY.

In the second meaning, positional goods are any product or service that is in scarce supply relative to the number of people in a society, such that not everyone can have access to it. Some goods are positional because of their high cost. Others are inherently positional because by their nature the supply is limited. Not everyone can study to be a doctor or lawyer, for example, because there are only so many places in medical and law schools. In similar ways, not everyone can go to the French Riviera for vacation or live on the seashore because, even if they could afford it, there simply isn't enough room. Access to wilderness areas is also inherently positional, in that if everyone went there, those areas would no longer *be* wilderness. Because access is limited, positional goods acquire a sense of exclusivity that sets apart those who have access from those who don't. Something like bread, by comparison, is not a positional good, and whether I have toast this morning doesn't affect other people's ability to have bread for themselves.

In his book, *The Social Limits of Growth*, Fred Hirsch argues that as societies grow wealthier, an increasing number of goods and services are positional, and this creates social CONFLICT around their DISTRIBUTION. By definition, the problem cannot be solved by economic growth and increased production, a fact that calls for other remedies.

Reading

Hirsch, Fred. 1977. *Social limits of growth*. London: Routledge and Kegan Paul.

positive relationship *See* DIRECTION OF RELATIONSHIP.

positivism As developed by Auguste COMTE, positivism is a way of thinking based on the assumption that it is possible to observe social life and establish reliable, valid knowledge about how it works. Such knowledge can then be used to affect the course of SOCIAL CHANGE and improve the human condition.

Comte believed that social life is governed by underlying laws and principles that can be discovered through the use of methods most often associated with the physical sciences. As it has developed since Comte, positivism also argues that sociology should concern itself only with what can be observed with the senses and that THEORIES of social life should be built in a rigid, linear, and methodical way on a base of verifiable fact.

Positivism has had relatively little influence in contemporary sociology for several reasons. Current views argue that positivism encourages a misleading emphasis on superficial facts without any attention to underlying mechanisms that cannot be observed. For example, we cannot observe human motives or the meaning that people give to behavior and other aspects of social life, but this does not mean that meaning and motive are nonexistent or irrelevant. Some argue that the nature of social life is such that the methods used in the physical sciences are simply inapplicable and must be replaced with a less rigid approach.

See also ABSTRACTED EMPIRICISM; EMPIRICAL; HERMENEUTICS; INTERACTION; REALISM.

Reading

Giddens, Anthony. 1974. *Positivism and sociology*. London: Heinemann Educational Books.

Turner, Stephen Park, and Jonathan H. Turner. 1990. *The impossible science: An institutional analysis of American sociology*. Newbury Park, CA: Sage Publications.

postenumeration survey A postenumeration SURVEY is a research technique that is used as a follow-up to a CENSUS. Although a census is regarded as the most complete method for counting and observing an entire POPULATION, the huge size of many populations often can result in considerable error, especially in making counts of difficult-to-observe groups such as the poor and marginalized ethnic groups. The postenumeration survey usually involves a relatively small SAMPLE but it can have as many as 50,000 respondents. Such surveys

231

allow researchers to pay more careful attention to the data-gathering, and for this reason they can serve as a check on a much larger census that precedes them. The results of post-enumeration surveys are then used to construct statistical factors that help to correct for the undercounting of various regional and SOCIAL CATE-GORIES of people.

Reading

Anderson, M. J. 1988. *The American census: A social history.* New Haven: Yale University Press.

postindustrial society A postindustrial society is a SOCIAL SYSTEM in which most economic activity is concerned with providing services based on KNOWLEDGE (such as banking, legal work, and travel) more than with producing goods such as steel, radios, and automobiles. As originally argued by Daniel BELL and others, under postindustrialism people's primary involvement is with other people rather than with raw materials or machinery. As a consequence, this leads to a change in economic relations, with more resources devoted to working out human problems such as disputes between workers and management over the conditions, rewards, and organization of work.

In some industrial capitalist countries, there has been a shift away from manufacturing and toward service industries, some of which involve specialized knowledge and skills (such as computer programming). However, there is little evidence of the accompanying SOCIAL CHANGE Bell and others envisioned. Most new service occupations, for example, are in the secondary, competitive LABOR MARKET that offers low pay, minimal training, and little opportunity for advancement.

Nor is there evidence of any widespread movement away from strict managerial control over workers in the interests of maximizing corporate profits.

See also DUAL ECONOMY; END-OF-IDEOLOGY THEORY; INDUSTRIAL SOCIETY AND INDUSTRIALIZATION; INFORMATION SOCIETY; TECHNOLOGY.

Reading

Bell, Daniel. 1973. *The coming of postindustrial society.* New York: Basic Books.

Kumar, Krishnan. 1978. *Prophecy and progress: The sociology of industrial and postindustrial society.* London: Allen Lane.

postmodernism and modernism Modernism is a particular view of the possibilities and direction of human social life. It is rooted in the ENLIGHT-ENMENT and grounded in faith in rational thought. From a modernist perspective, truth, beauty, and morality exist as objective realities that can be discovered, known, and understood through rational and scientific means. Not only does this view make progress inevitable but it provides a basis for increased control over the human condition and increased freedom for the individual.

Postmodernism argues that truth, beauty, and morality do not have an objective existence beyond how we think, write, and talk about them. From a postmodernist perspective, social life is not an objective reality waiting for us to discover how it works. Rather, what we experience as social life consists primarily of how we think about it, and there are diverse and changing ways of doing that. There are no societies, no communities, no families that exist as fixed entities. There is only an ongoing stream of conversations, abstract models, stories, and other representations flowing across every level of social life, from intimate exchanges between lovers to the products of the mass media. Although some elements in the stream are privileged or given greater weight and social legitimacy than others, ultimately one version of reality or beauty or morality is no better or worse or more true than another.

From this perspective, the Enlightenment goal of intentionally creating a better world out of some knowable truth is based on an illusion. Indeed, sociology itself along with the other social and physical sciences no longer has reason to exist. Some sociologists, however, take a less extreme view of postmodernism's implications for sociology. It shakes us, for example, from the comfortable assumption that there is a clear and fixed relationship between how we think about social life and social life as a concrete and knowable reality. It can make us more aware of the degree to which the human capacity to think symbolically gives us the ability to create in our minds what we experience as social life and human existence. And this inevitably raises important questions about our notions of truth.

The debate between the modernist and postmodernist perspectives is quite controversial because it strikes at the heart of basic assumptions that underlie attempts to understand and cope with the world and our experience of it. *See also* DECONSTRUCTION; KNOWLEDGE; STRUCTURALISM AND POSTSTRUCTURALISM.

Reading
Baudrillard, Jean. 1983. *In the shadow of the silent majorities*. New York: Semiotext(e).
Bauman, Zygmunt. 1988. "Is there a postmodern sociology?" In *Postmodernism*, a special issue of *Theory, Culture, and Society* 52(2–3): 217–38.

Lyotard, Jean-François. 1984. *The postmodern condition*. Minneapolis: University of Minnesota Press.

poststructuralism *See* STRUCTURALISM AND POSTSTRUCTURALISM.

potlatch In some Native American tribes of the Pacific Northwest of the United States and Canada, potlatch is a RITUAL practice in which men use gifts as a way to indicate their STATUS in relation to other men. It is a form of boasting intended to show how wealthy and generous a man is at the expense of those who receive the gifts. Recipients, in turn, feel compelled to act as hosts of their own at some future time so that they might gain the upper hand.
See also CONSPICUOUS CONSUMPTION; PRESTIGE.
Reading
Benedict, Ruth. 1934. *Patterns of culture*. New York: American Library.

poverty In a general sense, poverty is a condition in which people lack what they need to live; but the limits of "need to live" are a matter of definition. If poverty is defined in absolute terms – what people need to physically survive – it is relatively simple to define the point at which people become poor. But the experience of poverty also depends on how much people have relative to other people in their SOCIETY and the cultural VALUES that define the "good life." In many parts of the world, for example, indoor plumbing is regarded as a sign of affluence; but in INDUSTRIAL SOCIETIES it is taken for granted and its absence in a household is taken as a sign of poverty. How we define poverty matters a great deal, especially in industrial societies where relative poverty is more common than absolute poverty.

Understanding poverty is a major area in the study of social STRATIFI- CATION AND INEQUALITY. This includes poverty within societies and among them. Most THEORIES of poverty focus on the characteristics of the poor, rather than the relationship between poverty and the great accumulations of WEALTH found in most capitalist societies.

See also CULTURE OF POVERTY; DEPRI- VATION; SOCIAL CLASS; THIRD WORLD; WELFARE STATE; WORLD SYSTEM.

Reading

Ellwood, D. T. 1988. *Poor support: Poverty in the American family.* New York: Basic Books.

Field, F. 1982. *Poverty and politics.* London: Heinemann Educational Books.

Goldsmith, W. W., and E. J. Blakely. 1992. *Separate societies: Poverty and inequality in U.S. cities.* Philadelphia: Temple University Press.

Osberg, L., ed. 1991. *Economic inequality and poverty: International perspectives.* Armonk, NY: M. E. Sharpe.

power Power is a key sociological concept with several meanings around which there is considerable disagree- ment. The most common definition is Max WEBER's: power is the ability to control others, events, or resources – to make happen what one wants to happen in spite of obstacles, resis- tance, or opposition. This is some- times referred to, especially by feminists, as power-over. In addition to its use to control people or events, power can also be used in more sub- tle and indirect ways. These include the ability to not act (as when a par- ent withholds love from a child or a government withholds financial support from the poor) as well as the

ability to shape people's BELIEFS and VALUES, as through control over mass media or educational INSTITUTIONS.

Power defined as power-over reflects SOCIAL SYSTEMS organized in a HIER- ARCHY and is a substance or resource that individuals or social systems can possess. Power is a thing that can be held, coveted, seized, taken away, lost, or stolen; and it is used in what are essentially adversarial relationships involving conflict between those with power and those without. This kind of power takes several different forms. AUTHORITY is power associated with the occupancy of a particular social STATUS, such as the power exercised by parents over children, officers over troops, or teachers over students. Authority is a form of power that is socially defined as legitimate, which means it tends to be supported by those who are subject to it. In con- trast, *coercive power* lacks social legiti- macy and is based instead on fear and the use of force. It is the power exercised by conquering nations over those they conquer, or by schoolyard bullies over weaker classmates. Unlike authority, coercive power is particu- larly unstable, which is why even the most AUTHORITARIAN government cannot last for long without some degree of legitimacy in the eyes of those they govern.

Unlike Weber, Karl MARX used the concept of power in relation to SOCIAL CLASSES and social systems rather than individuals. Marx argued that power rests in a social class's position in the RELATIONS OF PRODUCTION, as in capitalist class ownership and control of the means of production. From this perspective, the sociologi- cal importance of power lies not in relations among individuals but in domination and subordination of social classes based on the relations of production.

Individual power that is not associated with the occupancy of a social status is *personal power*. This is the ability to influence or control others based on individual characteristics such as physical strength or the ability to argue persuasively. Of the various forms of power, personal power is sociologically less significant because it has less to do with social systems and their characteristics.

FUNCTIONALISTS such as Talcott PARSONS argue that power is not a matter of social coercion and domination but instead flows from a social system's potential to coordinate human activity and resources in order to accomplish goals. From this perspective, for example, the power of the STATE rests on a consensus of values and interests in the name of which the state acts toward the greater benefit of all.

Key sociological questions about power focus on how it is distributed within social systems, from democratic small GROUPS based on consensus to bureaucratic FORMAL ORGANIZATIONS to SOCIETIES organized around political AUTHORITARIANISM. From this perspective, power is an important component of social STRATIFICATION, both a resource and reward that plays an important part in social inequality and conflict.

A second way of thinking about power flows most recently from FEMINISM. The concept of power-to views power as something based not on hierarchy or dominance and subordination but on the capacity to do things, to achieve goals, especially in collaboration with others. Whereas the power-over view tends to focus attention on COMPETITION for power

and dominance, the power-to view stresses the potential of COOPERATION, consensus, and equality. When farmers gather to build a barn for a neighbor, for example, their collaboration generates a great deal of power (as evidenced by the result) without anyone dominating anyone else. Unlike power-over, an increase in power-to does not require that anyone lose power. Theoretically, power-to is infinitely expandable, while power-over is not.

The concept of power is controversial not only because it can take different forms but because how we look at it profoundly affects how we think about social systems and how they work. For example, the predominance of power-over in most contemporary thinking about power makes it difficult to work toward the development of alternatives.

See also CLASS CONFLICT AND CLASS STRUGGLE; CONFLICT PERSPECTIVE; FUNCTIONALIST PERSPECTIVE; HEGEMONY; MARXIST SOCIOLOGY; POWER STRUCTURE; SOCIAL CLASS.

Reading

French, Marilyn. 1985. *Beyond power.* New York: Summit Books.

Lukes, Steven. 1986. *Power.* New York: New York University Press.

Weber, Max. [1925] 1947. *The theory of social and economic organization.* New York: Oxford University Press.

Wrong, Dennis H. 1980. *Power: Its forms, bases, and uses.* New York: Harper and Row.

power elite   *See* POWER STRUCTURE.

power structure   In SOCIAL SYSTEMS, a power structure is the DISTRIBUTION of POWER among individuals or, on larger levels of analysis, among SOCIAL CATEGORIES or entire social systems such as GROUPS, organizations, COMMUNITIES, or SOCIETIES.

For sociologists, the most important dimension along which power structures vary is the degree of inequality in the distribution. In a DEMOCRACY, for example, power is distributed evenly. The more AUTHORITARIAN the system is, the more concentrated power is in the hands of a relative few.

Within nominally democratic societies such as most industrialized nations, there has been some debate over what the power structure actually looks like. One view is that key INSTITUTIONS are dominated by a *power elite*, a close network of highly placed people whose family, educational, class, occupational, and cultural backgrounds provide the basis for easy movement from one sphere of power to another and for a general consensus on issues of collective self-interest. A contrary view is that INDUSTRIAL SOCIETIES are too complex for a unified ELITE to dominate. Instead, the power structure is *pluralistic*, distributed among a variety of competing INTEREST GROUPS such as industrialists, unions, and civic, environmental, and civil rights organizations. A combined view – *elite pluralism* – argues that competition takes place primarily among elite groups that nonetheless tend to take a common position on issues of fundamental social policy that affect their elite standing.

See also AUTHORITARIANISM; AUTOCRACY; DEMOCRACY; ELITE; POWER.

Reading
Kornhauser, William. 1966. " 'Power elite' or 'veto groups'?" In *Class, status, and power*, edited by Reinhard Bendix and Seymour Martin Lipset. New York: Free Press.
Mills, C. Wright. 1956. *The power elite.* New York: Oxford University Press.
Riesman, David. 1961. *The lonely crowd.* New Haven: Yale University Press.

PPS sampling Probabilities-proportional-to-size (PPS) sampling is a COMPLEX SAMPLE design in which at each level of sampling the probability of a unit being selected is directly proportional to its size. In a cluster sample of a city, for example, the larger a block is, the larger is the number of clusters – and, therefore, respondents – who will be selected from that block. People living on a large block, then, are more likely to have their block selected than are people living on a small block. Once the block is selected, however, the probability of each household or person being selected in the final SAMPLE is also proportional to the size of the block, but inversely so. At this final stage of sampling, people on larger blocks have less overall chance of being selected than do people living on smaller blocks. As a result, inequalities in PROBABILITY of selection cancel out and are the same for all members of the POPULATION, which is a major requirement for scientific sampling.
See also COMPLEX SAMPLE.

Reading
Kish, Leslie. 1965. *Survey sampling.* New York: Wiley.

praxis In its simplest sense, praxis is ACTION, standing in distinct contrast to THEORY. It is about what we do rather than what we think. We might, for example, have ideas about what causes inequality and POVERTY (theory); but whether or how we implement those theories in an effort to eliminate poverty is a matter of praxis. Karl MARX used the term to refer to all purposeful action, the creative process through which people work, produce goods, and act upon one another and the world. It is praxis, Marx argued, that lies at the core of human existence, and thinking is important only insofar as it shapes and gives purpose to action.

See also ABSTRACTED EMPIRICISM; THEORY.

Reading

Marx, Karl. [1927–1935] 1964. *The economic and philosophical manuscripts of 1884.* New York: International Publishers.

Lefebvre, H. 1968. *The sociology of Marx.* London: Allen Lane and the Penguin Press.

prediction and projection From a methodological perspective, a prediction or a projection is a statement about the future. Concern over the question of what the future will look like (known generally as *social forecasting*) has a long history in sociology.

For some social scientists, the ability to predict what will happen under varying conditions is the true test of a THEORY; but most social science is far from being able to accomplish this. Some important social phenomena are fairly easy to predict. If we know how many babies are born each year in a SOCIETY, for example, we also know with considerable accuracy how the AGE STRUCTURE will change in the future since tomorrow's adults have already been born.

Even with POPULATION, however, accurate predictions are hard to come by. For this reason DEMOGRAPHY tends to focus on projection, a statement of what will happen if current trends continue. For example, if the use of cigarettes, alcohol, and drugs is declining, we might simply extend the trend forward in time to see what things will look like if the rate of decline continues. The problem with projections is that rates of change rarely remain constant, so that it becomes necessary to make sets of projections representing various assumptions about trends. Unfortunately, all of this caution on the part of social scientists is often thrown to the winds through the common tendency to confuse projections with predictions, especially in the mass media.

See also MASS COMMUNICATIONS AND MASS MEDIA.

Reading

Ascher, William. 1978. *Forecasting: An appraisal for policymakers and planners.* Baltimore: Johns Hopkins University Press.

Singleton, Royce A., Bruce C. Straits, and Margaret M. Straits. 1998. *Approaches to social research*, 3rd ed. Oxford and New York: Oxford University Press.

prejudice and discrimination In general, prejudice is the THEORY of racial and other forms of inequality, and discrimination is the practice. Prejudice is a positive or negative cultural ATTITUDE directed toward members of a GROUP or SOCIAL CATEGORY. As an attitude, it combines BELIEFS and VALUE judgments with positive or negative emotional predispositions. For example, racial prejudice that whites direct at blacks and other people of color includes stereotyped beliefs about racial differences in such areas as intelligence, motivation, moral character, and ability. These differences are then judged according to cultural values to the detriment of people of color and the enhanced standing of whites. Finally, emotional elements such as hostility, contempt, and fear complete the attitude to create a predisposition among whites to treat blacks in oppressive ways and to perceive their own racial category as socially superior. Since people of color in Europe and the United States live in the same CULTURE as whites, racial prejudice will also to some degree affect how they perceive, evaluate, and feel about themselves.

If we judge the importance of a prejudice by its social consequences, then prejudice focusing on RACE or gender, or on ethnic and other MINORITIES is most interesting sociologically. Technically, for example, any prejudice directed against men is sexist, just as prejudice directed by blacks against whites is racist. One objection to this view is that the consequences of prejudice aimed at minorities are very different from prejudice aimed at dominant groups by minorities, usually in self-defense. The former supports and perpetuates SOCIAL OPPRESSION. The latter, however, has relatively trivial consequences for members of dominant categories since they are unlikely to even be aware of them. Even if they are aware, they have the security of their standing as members of the dominant category to fall back on for support. For this reason, some sociologists argue that while minorities can be just as prejudiced as those who dominate them, terms such as racist and sexist should be reserved for prejudice whose ideological function is to justify social oppression.

Prejudice is sociologically important because it underlies discrimination, the unequal treatment of people who happen to belong to a particular group or category. When unequal treatment takes the form of systematic abuse, EXPLOITATION, and injustice, then it becomes SOCIAL OPPRESSION. Not all discrimination is based on prejudice, however. In the United States, for example, *affirmative action* is a government policy according to which social categories such as blacks and women that are burdened by long histories of prejudice and discrimination are actively sought out as applicants for jobs, government contracts, and university admissions. Although this kind of positive discrimination has been quite controversial, it generally has had little effect on the overall distribution of men, women, blacks, and whites among occupations. In addition, several states have recently tried to ban its use.

See also RACISM; SEXISM; STEREOTYPE.

Reading

Allport, Gordon W. 1954. *The nature of prejudice.* Garden City, NY: Doubleday Anchor Books.
Memmi, Albert. 1964. *Dominated man.* New York: Orion Press.

pressure group *See* INTEREST GROUP.

prestige According to Max WEBER, prestige is honor or deference attached to a social STATUS and distributed unequally as a dimension of social STRATIFICATION. He distinguished prestige from SOCIAL CLASS – access to material rewards and resources – and POWER, although they often go together.

If prestige is defined merely as respect, then there is nothing inherently unequal in its DISTRIBUTION. Theoretically, everyone can enjoy the same level of respect. But if prestige refers to honor that calls for some degree of deference and presumption of superiority, then, as Talcott PARSONS argues, it is inherently unequal, for these cannot be symmetrical. It is this view, in part, that led Parsons to regard prestige as the most important – and inevitable – factor in stratification systems. Prestige, he argued, is distributed according to three factors: (1) possessions, (2) qualities (such as talent and ASCRIBED STATUSES such as RACE and gender), and (3) performance (including ACHIEVED STATUSES such as educational attainment and marital status).

This view of the importance of prestige is reflected in the large body of research on SOCIAL MOBILITY in INDUSTRIAL SOCIETIES. Most research focuses on occupational prestige measured by asking SURVEY respondents to rate occupations from "excellent" to "poor" on the basis of "general standing." These ratings turn out to be quite stable over time and consistent across SOCIETIES, although with some interesting variations. The prestige gap between white- and blue-collar jobs was generally smaller in socialist societies such as the former Soviet Union, for example, than in the United States and Britain.

See also CONSPICUOUS CONSUMPTION; OCCUPATIONAL STRUCTURE; PARTY, POLITICAL; SOCIAL CLASS.

Reading

Parsons, Talcott. 1964. "A revised approach to the theory of social stratification." In Talcott Parsons, *Essays in sociological theory*, 386–439. New York: Free Press.

Treiman, Donald J. 1977. *Occupational prestige in comparative perspective.* New York: Academic Press.

primary deviance *See* LABELING THEORY.

primary labor market *See* LABOR MARKET.

primary relationship and secondary relationship Primary and secondary relationships (or GROUPS) are a classification continuum used by sociologists to describe the INTERACTIONS and ties that bind people to one another. The continuum is anchored at either end by these two general types of relationship.

Primary relationships are based on ties of affection and personal loyalty, involve many different aspects of people's lives, and endure over long periods of time. They involve a great deal of face-to-face interaction that focuses on people's feelings and welfare more than accomplishing specific tasks or goals. A primary group is one organized around this kind of relationship. Given the requirement for frequent face-to-face interaction, primary groups also tend to be what sociologists refer to as *small groups*, typically ranging in size from two to 20 with fewer than ten being most common in small group research.

As a group, the FAMILY embodies all the basic characteristics of primary relationships. The tie between spouses, for example, is generally based on deep emotional bonds and involves a great deal of interaction. There are few if any areas of a spouse's life that cannot be considered a legitimate concern for the other spouse. And the relationship is expected to last as long as the emotional tie lasts if not longer. There are no specific goals which, when accomplished, signal the end of the relationship.

In contrast, a secondary relationship is organized around fairly narrow ranges of practical interests or goals without which it would not exist. The waiter–customer relationship in a restaurant, for example, is secondary in that it involves a narrow range of activities – exchanging food and service for money – through which participants meet particular needs or desires. What makes the relationship secondary is the relatively narrow, utilitarian, task-oriented, time-limited focus of its activities. A secondary group is organized around secondary relationships. The employees in a restaurant, for example, may constitute a secondary group insofar as their relationships are narrowly focused on the work of running a restaurant.

As is often the case with concepts used to describe types of social phenomena, many relationships and groups are not purely primary or secondary, but rather are a mix of the two. For example, in societies such as India where many marriages are arranged, the relationship between spouses may be quite task oriented and involve relatively little affection, at least initially. Or, the people who work in a restaurant may over time develop feelings of affection and loyalty for one another and the establishment. These are primary aspects of their relationship that coexist with what would otherwise be a purely secondary economic arrangement.

It is important to identify the primary and secondary characteristics of relationships and groups because these have great effects on what happens in them. Military combat units, for example, are in many respects secondary groups tightly organized around the accomplishment of specific tasks. But as sociologists have found, the degree to which primary ties develop among soldiers has a lot to do with how well they fight, for soldiers tend to care more about one another than about the abstract reasons for which nations presumably go to war.

In general, secondary relationships occupy unimportant places in people's lives because their focus is so narrow and they tend to involve little emotional attachment. They can, of course, be quite important as in the case of work. Indeed, one of the dilemmas of life in INDUSTRIAL SOCIETIES is that so much of people's lives is taken up with secondary relationships.

See also GROUP; IDEAL TYPE.

Reading
Cooley, Charles Horton. [1909] 1962. *Social organization*. New York: Schocken Books.

primitive society The term "primitive society" is typically used to refer to SOCIETIES that are small, tribal, traditional, lacking TECHNOLOGY, and organized around a simple DIVISION OF LABOR. Although the term may be seen as purely descriptive, in practice it invariably implies the pejorative – and highly debatable – judgment that primitive societies are inferior to modern urban and industrial societies. For this reason, the term is avoided by most social scientists.
See also COMMUNITY.

private sphere and public sphere The private and public spheres are the two gendered spheres that it has become common practice to think of the social world as divided into. The private sphere is the stereotypically feminine world of HOUSEHOLD, FAMILY, and unpaid DOMESTIC LABOR; the public sphere is the stereotypically masculine world of politics and paid employment. The emergence of the two spheres is traced to the capitalist INDUSTRIAL REVOLUTION, which took production out of the home and into the factory, taking men with it and leaving wives and mothers behind to tend children and keep house.

This view has been criticized by feminist scholars who argue that the public/private split is an illusion that serves to reinforce women's subordination under PATRIARCHY. Because most married women work both inside and outside the home and because work life has such profound effects on all family members, it is misleading to treat work and family as inhabiting distinct and separate worlds. In addition, even women who do not work for pay outside the home are still engaged in important productive work, providing key services that reproduce the next generation of workers and sustain the working ability of the current generation. The public/private split also ignores the fact that women of color and working- and LOWER-CLASS women have never had the luxury of not working for pay outside the home while also taking care of most domestic labor.

Others argue that while the perceived split between public and private spheres may not accurately reflect the true nature of women's lives, it nonetheless is a powerful cultural image that is often used to limit women's lives and make their economic productivity invisible. In this sense, the private/public split plays an important ideological role in the perpetuation of gender inequality.

Reading
Thorne, Barrie, ed. 1992. *Rethinking the family.* Boston: Northeastern University Press.
Waring, Marilyn. 1988. *If women counted: A new feminist economics.* San Francisco: HarperCollins.
Zaretsky, Eli. 1976. *Capitalism, the family, and personal life.* New York: Harper.

privatism Privatism is the name given to the phenomenon of people increasingly turning away from public involvement and focusing instead on the more private spheres of household and FAMILY. It has been observed in RELIGION, for example, in the tendency to avoid public services and RITUAL in favor of prayer and other observances in private spaces that maintain a relationship with God that is more personal than collective. It has

also been observed in COMMUNITY life and politics as people avoid political involvement in election campaigns and social issues, spend less time in community places such as markets, and have less contact with neighbors.

The term is sometimes confused with PRIVATIZATION.

Reading
Goldthorpe, John H., David Lockwood, Frank Bechhofer, and J. Platt. 1969. *The affluent worker in the class structure.* Cambridge, England: Cambridge University Press.
Sennett, Richard. [1977] 1996. *The fall of public man.* New York: W. W. Norton.

privatization Privatization occurs when governments turn over publicly owned industries, utilities, or services to private organizations such as corporations. It has most often occurred with public utilities such as gas, electricity, and telecommunications. In the United States, however, other government functions, such as Social Security and the running of jails, prisons, and public schools, have also been discussed as candidates for privatization.

Reading
Savas, Emanuel S. 1982. *Privatizing the public sector.* Chatham, NJ: Chatham House Publishers.

probability Probability is a concept that plays an important part in QUANTITATIVE RESEARCH METHODS that use STATISTICS. It refers to the relative likelihood that something will occur. In general, the probability that something will happen is the number of ways it could happen divided by the total number of possible outcomes. Suppose, for example, there are 100 people in a room – 60 women and 40 men – and we select one of them at random and want to know the probability of it being a woman. There are 60 women in the room, which means there are 60 ways of selecting a woman. There are 100 people overall, which means there are a total of 100 possible selections. The probability of selecting a woman, then, is 60/100 = 0.60. If we call the outcome we are interested in (selecting a woman in this example) a "success," then the probability of selecting a woman can also be thought of as the proportion of the total possible outcomes that consist of successes.

Another way to think of probabilities is to take a long-run perspective. Suppose we flip a coin over and over again. If the coin is "fair," then a head is just as likely as a tail. If we flip the coin twice, we might nonetheless get two heads or two tails in a row, even though the coin is not biased one way or the other. If we flip it 1,000 times, however, we would expect the proportion of heads and the proportion of tails to be quite close to 0.50, since each outcome is equally likely to occur. Thus, the probability of flipping a coin and getting heads on a single flip is represented by the proportion of heads we would expect to find in the long run over many flips.

Since a probability is a proportion, it must always have a value that ranges from a low of 0 to a high of 1.0. It cannot be negative or greater than 1.0.

Probability is a crucial concept in quantitative research, because DATA are typically gathered through SAMPLES. Samples necessarily involve a certain amount of ERROR that must be accounted for in trying to make inferences from the sample to the POPULATION from which it came. *See also* HYPOTHESIS AND HYPOTHESIS TESTING; STATISTICS.

product–moment correlation coefficient *See* CORRELATION.

profane *See* RELIGION.

profession and professionalization
As defined by sociologists, a profession is an occupation that is based on theoretical and practical KNOWLEDGE and training in a particular field such as medicine, law, or science. Professions tend to be credentialed and regulated in relation to certain standards of performance and ethics. This makes them more autonomous and independent than other occupations. Whether a physician's performance is adequate or ethical, for example, depends primarily on judgments made by other physicians in relation to codes formulated by professional organizations.

The combination of specialized knowledge and collective self-regulation produces a relatively high social standing for professionals, including higher levels of income, WEALTH, POWER, and PRESTIGE. As a result, those in a number of non-professional occupations, such as business, often try to professionalize themselves by forming occupational organizations and fostering a public image of ethical standards and specialized knowledge and training. These have been successful in a few cases such as teaching and allied health occupations, but there are still few occupations that constitute professions as completely as medicine or law.

As professional practice in industrial capitalist societies becomes increasingly subject to economic pressures, the autonomy and independence usually associated with professional standing shows signs of eroding. In the United States, for example, an increasing number of physicians work as employees of large health maintenance organizations (HMOs) whose bureaucratic control over medical costs (and profits) often plays a significant part in professional decisions about medical care. Similarly, many large law firms employ lawyers as salaried employees whose main economic task is to generate revenues that enrich the firm's partners, with no hope of ever becoming partners themselves. In science, the dependence of scientists on large organizations such as corporations and government that will provide the huge amounts of money necessary for modern research also raises questions about professional autonomy and independence.

See also WORK; WEALTH AND INCOME.

Reading

Freidson, Eliot. 1986. *Professional powers: A study in the institutionalization of formal knowledge.* Chicago: University of Chicago Press.

Hodson, Randy, and Teresa A. Sullivan. 1994. *The social organization of work.* Belmont, CA: Wadsworth.

Ritzer, George, and David Walczak. 1986. *Working: Conflict and change.* Englewood Cliffs, NJ: Prentice-Hall.

professional authority *See* AUTHORITY.

profit In general, profit is the excess that results from an economic exchange when the price of what is sold is greater than what it costs the seller to provide or produce it.

The social importance of profit has been most highly developed under CAPITALISM. In its early stages, capitalist profit making took the form of trading goods for more than their cost. Goods such as spices, for example, were purchased at their source and then transported to regions where they were unavailable and could, therefore, fetch a higher price than that paid by the trader. Or storable goods such as grain might be held from the market until a shortage emerged (through drought or other conditions) and then brought to market where scarcity made it possible to demand a higher price.

As capitalism developed, capitalists went beyond buying and selling what others produced and acquired ownership and control over the MEANS OF PRODUCTION such as tools and factories. According to Karl MARX, this gave the capitalist leverage to extract a new form of profit. Since workers neither own nor control means of production, they depend on employers who are willing to buy workers' time in exchange for wages. Employers exploit this dependency by paying workers only a portion of the VALUE of what they produce and keeping the rest – the *surplus value* – for themselves as profit. This forms the basis for accumulations of great wealth both for individuals and families and for institutions such as corporations, foundations, universities, and the like.

Unlike other forms of profit, surplus value arises from the structure of capitalist relations among workers, capitalists, and the means of production, all of which define advanced capitalism as an economic system. It is therefore a uniquely capitalist form of profit.

See also LABOR AND LABOR POWER; VALUE, ECONOMIC.

Reading

Braverman, Harry. 1974. *Labor and monopoly capital.* New York: Monthly Review Press.

Marx, Karl. [1867] 1975. *Capital: a critique of political economy.* New York: International Publishers.

projection *See* PREDICTION AND PROJECTION.

proletarianization Proletarianization is a social process through which some MIDDLE-CLASS occupations increasingly resemble working-class jobs, resulting in downward SOCIAL MOBILITY for some segments of the middle class. There is evidence of this in the routinization of white-collar jobs (especially through office automation), the erosion of worker control, autonomy, and independence (especially through electronic and computer monitoring of worker performance), and, with these, increased boredom and ALIENATION. Thus, although white-collar jobs may retain their relatively high levels of occupational PRESTIGE, in other important respects they and the middle-class positions they anchor are losing some of their distinctive character that distinguishes them from the classes below.

Although there is considerable evidence of proletarianization in INDUSTRIAL SOCIETIES, its social consequences are less clear. Whether it will result in changes in political views and activity or increased union activity among white-collar workers, for example, remains to be seen.

See also CLASS CONSCIOUSNESS AND FALSE CONSCIOUSNESS; EMBOURGEOISEMENT; SOCIAL CLASS; BLUE-COLLAR WORKER AND WHITE-COLLAR WORKER.

Reading

Abercrombie, Nicholas, and John Urry. 1983. *Capital, labour, and the middle classes.* London: Allen and Unwin.

Braverman, Harry. 1974. *Labor and monopoly capital.* New York: Monthly Review Press.

proletariat *See* SOCIAL CLASS.

property Property is something that is owned within a system of ownership defined by people's rights and responsibilities in relation to others and SOCIAL SYSTEMS. Property rights typically include those of use, access, and disposal (to sell, destroy, or give away) as the owners see fit. This, however, varies greatly both historically and cross-culturally. Among numerous Native American tribes, for example, land was held in a form of trusteeship by those who lived on it, but the right to sell or otherwise dispose of it was unheard of. Under European FEUDALISM, PEASANTS did not own land, but they had traditional rights to its use; and the property rights of the local nobility extended only to the right to residence and to appropriate a portion of what the peasants produced. Full ownership lay with the sovereign who ruled over them all.

Property may be held individually or collectively and may be either material or nonmaterial (as in the case of ideas, writings, music, and computer software protected by copyright or patent). Human beings may be regarded as property to varying degrees, from the extreme case of slavery to more subtle ways in which people may assert proprietary interests and rights in relation to other people. A central insight of FEMINISM, for example, is that under PATRIARCHY men tend to view women as sexual property, a relationship that grants men rights of exclusive sexual access and use.

Property has been an important concept in the analysis of all forms of social inequality, but especially in relation to SOCIAL CLASS under CAPITALISM. For example, Karl MARX defined class and capitalism as a system centering on the ownership and control of CAPITAL. Alternatives to capitalism typically involve changing both the distribution of property and the primacy of the idea itself as a part of CULTURE.

Reading

Collins, Randall. 1982. "Love and property." In Randall Collins, *Sociological insight: An introduction to non-obvious sociology*, 119–54. New York and Oxford: Oxford University Press.

Hollowell, P., ed. 1982. *Property and social relations*. London: Heinemann Educational Books.

Protestant ethic The Protestant ethic is a religious ethic stressing carefully controlled behavior, methodical planning and hard work, self-denial, and vocational dedication and success. In trying to explain the cultural context in which CAPITALISM developed, Max WEBER argued that the Protestant Reformation in Europe produced an ethic that facilitated and supported capitalism's core tendencies, especially those related to investment and the accumulation of WEALTH. In rejecting the Church and its RITUALS as a sure means of salvation, Protestantism relied instead on individual autonomy and responsibility which, in turn, created considerable anxiety and need for reassurance that personal salvation was assured. The Protestant response to this anxiety was to promote an ethical consistency and way of life that helped provide a cultural environment that legitimated and promoted the very kinds of practices and values that would enable capitalism to flourish.

There has been considerable criticism of Weber's thesis on various technical grounds (such as whether Catholicism also provided some cultural support for capitalist practice).

Perhaps his most enduring contribution, however, lies simply in the argument that aspects of CULTURE profoundly affect the structure of SOCIAL SYSTEMS. This stands in marked contrast to the Marxist view that it is primarily the MODE OF PRODUCTION that shapes culture, not the other way around.

See also BASE AND SUPERSTRUCTURE.

Reading

Marshall, G. 1982. *In search of the spirit of capitalism*. London: Hutchinson.

Weber, Max. [1904] 1958. *The Protestant ethic and the spirit of capitalism*. New York: Scribner's.

psephology The study of elections and voting behavior. The term, used primarily in political sociology, is derived from the Greek word *psephos*, which means "pebbles" or "stones" and refers to the ancient practice of using stones or bits of clay pottery to cast ballots.

psychologism *See* METHODOLOGICAL INDIVIDUALISM.

public opinion Public opinion consists of the aggregated views of members of a POPULATION on various issues. It might, for example, be expressed as the percentage of adults who approve of a political leader's job performance, or the percentage who favor legalizing drugs such as cocaine or marijuana. It is of concern primarily to elected officials, both as a guide to how the electorate defines its interests and as a way to avoid offending voters. It is also, however, of interest to those looking for a standard against which to gauge their own views.

Although public opinion often reflects cultural ideas such as VALUES and ATTITUDES, it is distinct from

CULTURE. Public opinion is measured as the simple aggregation of individuals' views at a given time, while culture is part of the social environment in which individuals' views take shape. Public opinion is rooted in individuals and their changeable personal perceptions and judgments. Culture, on the other hand, is a major part of SOCIAL SYSTEMS which, sociologically, cannot be reduced to the characteristics of the people who participate in them.

See also ATOMISM AND HOLISM; SOCIAL FACT.

Reading

Ginsberg, Benjamin. 1986. *The captive public: How mass opinion promotes state power.* New York: Basic Books.

Neuman, W. Russell. 1986. *The paradox of mass politics.* Cambridge, MA: Harvard University Press.

public sphere *See* PRIVATE SPHERE AND PUBLIC SPHERE.

Q

qualitative and quantitative research methods Qualitative research methods are tools for gathering information that does not take a numerical form that can be counted and otherwise manipulated mathematically. If I live with a group of women and men and observe that males tend to dominate conversations, for example, my results consist of an interpretation based on a set of observations that I summarize in an overall impression. As such, it is a qualitative assessment of what is going on. By contrast, if I systematically count how often men and women interact and then compare the totals, my method is quantitative, because it produces numerical results.

Qualitative methods are most closely associated with PARTICIPANT OBSERVATION, HISTORICAL SOCIOLOGY, ETHNOMETHODOLOGY, ETHNOGRAPHY AND ETHNOLOGY. Quantitative methods are most closely associated with SURVEYS, EXPERIMENTS, and other forms of numerical DATA gathering. Although quantitative methods are often considered superior to so-called "soft" qualitative methods, most sociologists appreciate that each provides unique and valuable insights into the workings of social life that are beyond the reach of the other.

See also METHODOLOGY; QUALITATIVE VARIABLE AND QUANTITATIVE VARIABLE.

qualitative variable and quantitative variable A VARIABLE is qualitative if the observations cannot be described meaningfully in terms of numbers. Gender, for example, is a qualitative variable because there is no way in which numbers can be assigned to "female" and "male" in a meaningful way. This is also true of ORDINAL variables such as SOCIAL CLASS; categories such as LOWER, WORKING, MIDDLE, and UPPER CLASS have no meaningful numerical equivalents and are therefore qualitative.

A variable is quantitative if observations can be characterized in numerical terms. Income, WEALTH, AGE, fertility, gross national product, religious services attended each year, and GROUP size are all examples of quantitative variables.

The distinction between qualitative and quantitative variables is important because the two types of information often call for different research METHODOLOGIES. Quantitative information, for example, is more easily gathered through large SAMPLE SURVEYS on representative populations. Qualitative information, such as how people negotiate the complexities of everyday life, requires more intense scrutiny of smaller and typically less scientifically representative samples.

See also DISCRETE VARIABLE AND CONTINUOUS VARIABLE; SCALE OF MEASUREMENT; VARIABLE.

questionnaire *See* SURVEY.

quota sample A quota sample is a SURVEY design in which interviewers recruit respondents according to a set of guidelines that will result in an overall SAMPLE with certain proportions of people with various social characteristics. For example, the requirement might be to produce a collection of interviews that is evenly divided between women and men, has certain percentages of people from different RACES and AGE CATEGORIES, and so on. So long as the final sample has the correct proportions of people with these various characteristics, it does not matter which individuals the interviewers select.

Although quota samples can produce results with considerable accuracy, there is no scientific reason to expect this outcome since they are not based on known probabilities of selection. None of the mathematics on which STATISTICAL INFERENCE is based, for example, can be used with quota samples because they satisfy none of the theoretical assumptions associated with those techniques. As such, quota samples have little legitimacy in serious research and are used primarily in market research as a cost-cutting measure.

See also SAMPLING; STATISTICS.

Reading

Singleton, Royce A., Bruce C. Straits, and Margaret M. Straits. 1998. *Approaches to social research*, 3rd ed. Oxford and New York: Oxford University Press.

R

race   Race has often been defined as a grouping or classification based on genetic variations in physical appearance, most notably in skin color. Most sociologists (and biologists) dispute the idea that biological race is a meaningful concept, especially given the enormous amount of interbreeding that historically has characterized the human POPULATION. Instead, the consensus is that race exists as a socially constructed set of categories used primarily as a basis for social inequality and SOCIAL OPPRESSION. Distinctions such as "black" and "white" have little basis in scientifically identifiable genetic differences but have great significance in people's perceptions, evaluations, and behavior toward other people.

Race has often been used interchangeably with ETHNICITY, which refers to a common cultural background. Thus phrases such as "the British race" or "the Jewish race" are still in use. Since a great deal of research demonstrates the social consequences of skin color itself regardless of cultural background, in sociology the two terms continue to refer to separate and distinct phenomena.

See also PREJUDICE AND DISCRIMINATION.

Reading

Banton, Michael P. 1987. *Racial theories.* Cambridge, England: Cambridge University Press.

Lieberson, Stanley. 1975. "The debate over race: A study in the sociology of knowledge." In *Race and IQ*, edited by Ashley Montagu. New York: Oxford University Press.

van den Berghe, Pierre L. 1981. *The ethnic phenomenon.* New York: Praeger.

racism   Racism is most often associated with PREJUDICE based on race. From this perspective, ACTION based on racial prejudice and people who hold prejudiced BELIEFS, values, and ATTITUDES are described as "racist."

Sociologically, a more useful definition is offered by David Wellman, who argues that racism encompasses not only prejudice, but any action or characteristic of SOCIAL SYSTEMS that supports race privilege, regardless of whether people intend that to be the result. The key test of whether something is racist, then, lies in its consequences: if it supports race privilege, then it is by definition racist. For example, a linchpin of race privilege in the United States is SEGREGATION in housing and schools, because a vast range of social resources vary by neighborhood and community. In other words, white control over resources such as jobs, education, and political POWER depends on excluding people of color from white COMMUNITIES and neighborhoods. Many whites defend the right of people to sell their homes to whomever they like. They also argue for neighborhood schools, based on the idea that it is better for children to attend school near where they live. They argue that both these positions are based on principles that have nothing to do with race and are not, therefore, racist. The consequence of their position, however, is the continuation of race privilege and SOCIAL OPPRESSION based on the exclusion of people of color from resources needed to achieve equality. This, Wellman argues, makes those positions – however worthy the arguments used to defend them – racist in effect, even if they are not racist in intent.

This broader way of defining racism helps to explain why race privilege and oppression persist in spite of dramatic changes in how whites describe their own racial attitudes and beliefs. As Wellman argues, systems as complex as race privilege are held in place by institutional arrangements – such as neighborhood schools and property rights – that can transcend the intentions and feelings of individuals.

Reading

Wellman, David T. 1993. *Portraits of white racism*, 2nd ed. New York: Cambridge University Press.

radical feminism *See* FEMINISM.

random error *See* ERROR.

random sample *See* SIMPLE RANDOM SAMPLE.

range In a DISTRIBUTION of scores the range is a measure of variation that takes the difference between the highest and lowest scores. If the oldest person in a group is 110 and the youngest is 18, then the range for the VARIABLE age is $(110 - 18) = 92$. The range is a relatively crude measure of variation because it uses only two scores in the distribution. It can however, provide useful information. The range of income associated with an occupation, for example, provides a meaningful idea of the degree of inequality among those who work at it as well as the potential for advancement.

See also VARIANCE.

Reading

Bohrnstedt, George W., and David Knoke. 1994. *Statistics for social data analysis*, 3rd ed. Itasca, IL: F. E. Peacock.

rank-order correlation A rank-order CORRELATION is a MEASURE OF ASSOCIATION for relationships between ordinal-scale variables that take the form of ranks, especially when there are relatively few ties (few cases with identical scores). For example, if we rank NATIONS by their degree of economic development and then rank them by how democratic their political INSTITUTIONS are, we can then use any of several rank-order correlation coefficients to statistically measure how closely the two ranks are associated. Like all measures of association, the numerical value of rank-order correlations varies between $+1.0$ and -1.0. A value of $+1.0$ indicates a perfect relationship in which the two sets of ranks are identical, with the most highly developed SOCIETY being most democratic to the least developed society being least democratic. A value of -1.0 indicates a relationship in which the two sets of ranks are in perfect disagreement with each other, with the most developed society as least democratic and the least developed society as most democratic. A value of zero indicates no relationship between the two sets of ranks, which means that highly developed societies are no more likely to be democratic than are less developed societies.

The most widely used rank-order correlations are Spearman's r_s and Kendall's tau (τ).

See also CORRELATION; MEASURE OF ASSOCIATION; STATISTICAL INDEPENDENCE AND STATISTICAL DEPENDENCE; SCALE OF MEASUREMENT.

Reading
Bohrnstedt, George W., and David Knoke. 1994. *Statistics for social data analysis*, 3rd ed. Itasca, IL: F. E. Peacock.

rate A rate is the number of times a particular phenomenon occurs in a given period of time (typically one year) divided by a base figure such as the size of a POPULATION. Dividing by the population size is necessary in order to compare rates for populations of different sizes. Since the resulting number tends to be very small and thus awkward to read and interpret at a glance, it is usually multiplied by 1,000, 10,000, or even 100,000 to produce a more manageable figure, such as the number of suicides or homicides per 100,000 population. Among 15–24-year-old males, for example, the homicide rate in Japan is 0.5 per 100,000 people compared with 1.2 in England and Wales, 2.5 in Australia, 2.9 in Canada, 3.3 in Norway, 5.0 in Scotland, and 21.9 in the United States.

In popular usage, the term "rate" is often used to refer to what are actually percentages, such as the literacy rate which is the percentage of a population that is literate. Strictly speaking, however, rates involve events that take place over a given period of time.

See also RATIO.

rate of natural increase The rate of natural increase is the net effect of births and deaths on POPULATION growth. It is measured by subtracting the CRUDE DEATH RATE from the CRUDE BIRTH RATE, with the result usually expressed in the form of additional people per thousand population or as a percentage. If the birth rate is 20 per 1,000 population and the death rate is 8 per 1,000, for example, then the rate of natural increase is $(20-8)=12$ per 1,000, or 1.2 percent.

Although rates of natural increase take the form of relatively small numbers in an absolute sense, they, like compound interest rates on savings, can have dramatic implications for future growth. For example, the population of Africa currently grows at a rate of roughly 2.9 percent per year, which means it will double in around 24 years, quadruple in 48 years, and be eight times as large in just 72 years. By comparison, the population of Europe, which currently grows at a rate of just 0.3 percent, will require 233 years to double and 466 years to quadruple.

See also BIRTH RATE; DEATH RATE; DEMOGRAPHIC TRANSITION.

Reading
Shryock, Henry S., and Jacob Siegel and Associates. 1976. *The methods and materials of demography*. New York: Academic Press.

ratio A ratio is one number divided by another. In some cases – with percentages and RATES, for example – there is a clear numerical relationship between the numerator and the denominator. With a percentage, the numerator is a subset of the denominator. If we calculate the percent unemployed, those who are

unemployed are included in both the numerator and the denominator. In other ratios, such as the ratio of hospital beds to POPULATION, the two numbers can have quite different origins.
See also DEPENDENCY RATIO; SEX RATIO.

rational choice theory According to rational choice THEORY, SOCIAL SYSTEMS are organized in ways that structure the alternatives and consequences facing individuals so that they behave rationally. This allows them to best serve their self-interest within the constraints and resources that go with social systems and their STATUS in them. As such, this approach explains patterns of social behavior not in terms of individual psychology but rather in terms of the underlying context of "rules" and contingencies in which rational choices are made.

Decision theory is a form of rational choice theory that is applied to both COLLECTIVE BEHAVIOR and to decision-making in organizations. It argues that choices usually take the form of rational, systematic problem solving that occurs in several stages: gathering information about past, present, and likely future events and conditions; listing options and ranking them by the relative desirability of their most likely consequences; and making a final decision intended to produce the best possible outcome.

A second form of rational choice theory is *game theory*, which focuses on how people choose between COOPERATION, COMPETITION, and EXPLOITATION in various social situations. It assumes that people use rational choice to minimize costs and maximize rewards to achieve what is known as a "minimax solution."

A crucial factor in such situations is people's access to information about other people's perceptions and motivations.

The classic experiment in game theory is the *prisoner's dilemma,* in which two people play the role of accused criminals who are being interrogated separately. They are presented with the following dilemma: (1) if neither confesses, both will receive a minor punishment; (2) if both confess, the punishment will be greater, but not the maximum; but (3) if one confesses and the other does not, the one who confesses will go free and the other will receive the maximum sentence. Researchers have found that players often choose to confess, gambling that the other will not confess. In other words, players will choose not to cooperate, as in alternative (1), but to exploit. In other situations, however, especially where players have the opportunity to communicate with one another, cooperative choices are much more likely to occur.

Although rational choice theory is most highly developed in economics, it has a number of followers in sociology, especially among those who study GROUP DYNAMICS, social NETWORKS, and collective behavior.
See also UTILITARIANISM; ZERO-SUM GAME.

Reading

Luce, R. Duncan, and Howard Raiffa. 1957. *Games and decisions.* New York: Wiley.

Raiffa, Howard. 1970. *Decision analysis.* Reading, MA: Addison-Wesley.

Von Neumann, John, and Oskar Morgenstern. 1964. *Theory of games and economic behavior,* 3rd ed. New York: Wiley.

Zagare, F. C. 1984. *Game theory: Concepts and applications.* Beverly Hills, CA: Sage Publications.

rationalism Rationalism was a seventeeth- and eighteenth-century philosophical tradition that promoted reason and logic as the only valid basis for knowing about reality and as the best foundation for social progress and the solution of SOCIAL PROBLEMS. It stood in opposition to religious BELIEF, spiritual revelation, and a reliance on God's will as sources of explanation for social conditions. Instead, it placed its faith in the ability of the human mind to reason inductively and deductively in order to know the truth.

See also MODERNISM; ENLIGHTENMENT, AGE OF; SCOTTISH ENLIGHTENMENT.

rationalization Rationalization has two meanings in sociology. In its first sense, it is the practice of justifying something after the fact, as when a country attacks another in order to seize territory or resources and then creates a more noble and socially acceptable explanation later on. This meaning is directly related to Vilfredo PARETO'S RESIDUES AND DERIVATIONS.

The second definition of rationalization can be traced back to the work of Max WEBER, who was concerned that as industrial CAPITALISM developed in increasingly complex SOCIETIES, social life would become organized around impersonal principles of rational calculation, technical efficiency, and control. Feeling, spirituality, and moral VALUES would shrink in importance as societies constructed an increasingly restrictive "iron cage" of bureaucracy in every area of social life, from religion to education to work to the law. All of this would lend itself to STATE and corporate control over people's everyday lives.

Reading
Weber, Max. [1922] 1954. *Max Weber on law in economy and society*. Cambridge, MA: Harvard University Press.

ratio-scale variable *See* SCALE OF MEASUREMENT.

raw score *See* Z-SCORE.

realigning action *See* ALIGNING AND REALIGNING ACTION.

realism Realism is a philosophical approach to understanding reality that emphasizes the importance of taking into account not only what can be observed with the senses but what cannot. For example, if we confine ourselves only to what can be observed directly, we tend to focus on the most superficial aspects of social life. We cannot observe human motives, BELIEFS, and VALUES, or various structural aspects of societies such as SOCIAL CLASS systems. Indeed, the concept of a SOCIETY is itself in many ways an abstract representation of something that we cannot observe directly. Realists argue, therefore, that sociology must develop ways to identify underlying social mechanisms and to integrate these into our understandings and explanations of social life.

See also ABSTRACTED EMPIRICISM; EMPIRICAL; HERMENEUTICS; POSITIVISM.

Reading
Keat, R., and John Urry. 1982. *Social theory as science*. London: Routledge and Kegan Paul.

rebellion, as deviance *See* NONCONFORMIST DEVIANCE.

rebellion, political In political sociology, rebellion is an organized revolt against a government intended to force a change in policy without changing the nature of the government itself. In France, for example, there have been a number of student rebellions over the years spurred by unpopular government policies affecting higher education. Their goals, however, did not include changing the basic form of either the STATE or the universities as INSTITUTIONS, which distinguishes rebellion from REVOLUTION. Nor were they attempting to replace one set of government leaders with another, as in a COUP D'ÉTAT.

Reading

Barry, T. 1987. *Roots of rebellion: Land and hunger in Central America*. Boston: South End Press.

Tilly, Charles, Louise Tilly, and Richard Tilly. 1975. *The rebellious century*. Cambridge, MA: Harvard University Press.

reciprocity Reciprocity is a condition of mutual give-and-take in social INTERACTION, without which people tend to lose interest and withdraw. In a conversation, for example, while one person talks, the listener usually gives something in return in the form of attention – looking at the speaker, nodding, murmuring agreement, asking questions and otherwise showing interest. Without this, the speaker will tend to feel a sense of something missing and may even find it difficult to talk at all. So important is this exchange that there is in many situations a *norm of reciprocity*. By this we are expected to "complete the circle," whether in conversation, gift giving, or statements of commitment such as "I love you." It is for this reason problematic to give a gift to or perform a service for someone who is not in a position to respond in kind,

because it essentially places that person in the position of having to violate the norm of reciprocity and feel badly as a result.

See also EXCHANGE THEORY; GIFT RELATIONSHIP; NORM; POTLATCH.

Reading

Gouldner, Alvin W. 1960. "A norm of reciprocity: A preliminary statement." *American Sociological Review* 25: 16–78.

recursive relationship In constructing causal MODELS, a recursive relationship between two VARIABLES is one in which causal effects run in one direction only. For example, the relationship between educational attainment and occupation is typically defined as recursive: education affects occupation, but occupation does not affect education. A nonrecursive model includes relationships between variables that may run in both directions. People's BELIEFS and VALUES, for example, have a causal effect on their behavior, which in turn tends to reinforce their beliefs and values.

Nonrecursive models are so complex to work with that most multivariate techniques require recursive relationships.

See also MULTIVARIATE ANALYSIS.

Reading

Bohrnstedt, George W., and David Knoke. 1994. *Statistics for social data analysis*, 3rd ed. Itasca, IL: F. E. Peacock.

reductionism *See* DETERMINISM AND REDUCTIONISM.

reference group As first described by Herbert H. Hyman, a reference group is a collection of people that we use as a standard of comparison for ourselves regardless of whether we are part of that group. Reference groups to which we actually belong are known as *peer groups*. We use reference groups to evaluate the relative worth or desirability of our appearance, thoughts, feelings, and behavior; as a source of models that we imitate, often, in anticipation of becoming members; and as a source of expectations that we can use to judge the appropriateness of our appearance and behavior.

To a doctor, for example, other physicians constitute the most important reference group. How high should fees be set? Is it acceptable to wear jeans when interacting with patients? Is it acceptable to have sexual contact with patients? How much ongoing training should doctors receive after leaving medical school? If a doctor is incompetent, should another doctor who knows of it tell the authorities? Am I a competent doctor? These are the kinds of questions that a doctor would most likely answer in relation to physicians as a reference group.

It is not uncommon to orient ourselves to more than one reference group at a time, especially when this involves reference groups to which we do not belong. Medical students, for example, use other students as one reference group in addition to the reference group of practicing physicians whose ranks students hope to join eventually.

The concept of a reference group is important for understanding SOCIALIZATION, CONFORMITY, and how people perceive and evaluate themselves, especially in relation to the SELF. When students who stand at the top of their class go on to a top-rated university, for example, they may see themselves as less capable and confident than before, not because they had misperceived their actual abilities, but because they have a new reference group whose members are just as capable as they are, if not more so.

See also ANTICIPATORY SOCIALIZATION.

Reading

Hyman, Herbert H., and Eleanor Singer, eds. 1968. *Readings in reference group theory and research.* New York: Free Press.

Merton, Robert K., and Alice S. Rossi. 1968. "Contributions to the theory of reference group behavior." In *Social theory and social structure*, rev. and exp., edited by Robert K. Merton. New York: Free Press.

Singer, Eleanor. 1981. "Reference groups and social evaluations." In *Social psychology: Sociological perspectives*, edited by Morris Rosenberg and Ralph H. Turner, 66–93. New York: Basic Books.

reflexivity Reflexivity is the process of referring back to oneself, and it is applied both to THEORY and to people. A reflexive theory is one that refers to itself. For example, a basic idea in the sociology of KNOWLEDGE is that all knowledge is socially constructed rather than existing as an objective, external truth. This kind of statement, of course, also refers to itself, for it, too – like all of sociology – is socially constructed and can be explained as such.

As applied to people, reflexivity refers to the human ability to think of and refer to ourselves as if we were someone else. The statement, "I like myself," for example, is reflexive because I am both the subject of the verb and its object and thereby refer to myself just as I might to someone else, as in "I like Nora." Reflexivity is a crucial human ability that, according to SYMBOLIC INTERACTIONISM, makes possible the development of the SELF and the ability to participate in social life in relation to others. *See also* MIND; OTHER.

reform movement *See* SOCIAL MOVEMENT.

regression analysis Regression analysis is a statistical technique for describing and analyzing relationships between a dependent VARIABLE and one or, with *multiple regression*, two or more independent variables. To use regression analysis, the variables must be interval- or ratio-scale, which means they must naturally take the form of numbers (such as income or age). An exception to this is any variable that takes the form of a DICHOTOMY, such as gender, or a multicategory variable, such as education, that is collapsed to two categories such as "less than

university" and "some university or more."

Regression analysis is best illustrated in the accompanying figure, where a scatterplot shows the relationship between two variables: the percentage of a POPULATION that is literate (X) and the population's life expectancy (Y). Each dot in this graph represents a country, and the location (or coordinates) of each dot is determined by its level of life expectancy (on the vertical axis) and the percentage of the population that is literate (on the horizontal axis). As you can see, there is a tendency for countries low on X to also be low on Y and for countries high on X to also be high on Y (there are no dots in the upper left and lower right corners). There is, then, a positive relationship between literacy and life expectancy: the higher the literacy level is, the longer people tend to live on the average.

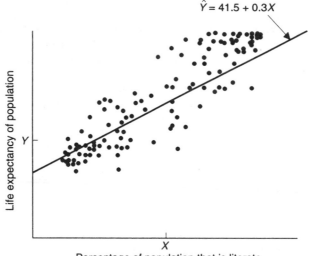

Figure 9 *Scatterplot with regression line for the relationship between life expectancy (Y) and the percentage of literate people (X) in various countries, early 1980s. Source*: US Census Bureau, 1989.

Regression analysis uses a mathematical equation to describe this kind of relationship. In linear regression the equation describes the straight line which, on the average, provides the closest "fit" to all the points at once. There is only one such line and it is known as the *least-squares* regression line. It gets its name from the fact that if we measure the vertical distance (called a *residual*) between the line and each point on the graph, square each distance, and add them up, the total will be smaller for this line than for any other. Hence, it is the line that best "fits" the data.

The general form of the equation is $\hat{Y} = a + bX$, where $\hat{Y}$ is the predicted value of the dependent variable and X is the value of the independent variable. The caret (ˆ) over the Y indicates that it is a predicted rather than an actual value. The *regression constant* (also known as the *Y-intercept*), which is represented by a in the equation, tells us the value of Y when X has a value of zero. It is also the point where the line crosses the vertical (Y) axis. The *regression coefficient* (or *slope*), which is represented by b in the equation, tells us how much the value of Y changes for each change in X.

If we apply the statistical techniques of linear regression analysis to the case shown in the figure, the resulting equation is $Y = 41.5 + 0.3X$. This means that if we want to estimate life expectancy for a country, our best bet is to take 41.5 years and add to that 0.3 multiplied by the percent literate for that country. If 75 percent of the population is literate, the best estimate of life expectancy would be $Y = 41.5 + (0.3)(75) = 64$ years. If the percent literate is 10 points higher, then because the slope is 0.3, we must increase our estimate by 0.3 years for each additional percent literate or, by another $(0.3)(10) = 3$ points. The resulting estimate would then be 67 years.

Since the coordinates for most countries (the dots in the scatterplot) do not lie directly on the line, our estimate will most likely be in ERROR to some degree, but using the regression line gives us estimates that, in the long run, involve the least amount of error. Because of this, the equation is sometimes written as $Y = a + bX + e$, where e represents the error associated with each prediction. Note that the Y no longer has a caret over it since it no longer represents an estimate of Y. Since we have included error on the right side of the equation, the actual value of Y is now represented on the left side.

A more complicated form of regression analysis is multiple regression, where two or more independent variables are used simultaneously to estimate the value of a dependent variable. To estimate personal income, for example, we might use independent variables such as years of schooling (X_1), occupational prestige score (X_2), and gender (X_3). The equation would then look like this:

$$\hat{Y} = a + b_1 X_1 + b_2 X_2 + b_3 X_3$$

For a relationship that looks more like a curve than a straight line, *curvilinear regression* may be used. In general, curvilinear techniques are more complicated to use and interpret and are less widely used in sociology than linear techniques.

Although the least-squares regression line is the line that best fits a set of data, this does not mean that it fits the data very well. To measure this, it is necessary to compute a CORRELATION.

See also COVARIANCE; STANDARDIZA-TION; SCALE OF MEASUREMENT.

Reading
Bohrnstedt, George W., and David Knoke. 1994. *Statistics for social data analysis*, 3rd ed. Itasca. IL: F. E. Peacock.

regression coefficient *See* REGRESSION ANALYSIS.

regression constant *See* REGRESSION ANALYSIS.

reification Reification is the process of taking an idea or concept and treating it as though it were something concrete and real. For example, "society" is a concept that sociologists use to describe the organization of social life. A society is not something we can see or otherwise experience with our senses; nor is it capable of thinking, feeling, or acting. Nonetheless, people often reify society by speaking of it as if it were a concrete living entity with needs, wants, intentions, and behaviors, a sentient being that can be blamed for various outcomes.

As used by Georg LUKÁCS and Karl MARX, the concept of reification reveals how we become separated and alienated from ourselves and our relations with others when we begin to view them as thing-like and largely beyond our control. We forget, for example, that computers and other technology are human inventions. Instead we think of them as an independent force capable of controlling our lives. Or we think of human labor as a COMMODITY that is sold in return for wages rather than a deeply important part of our social lives.
See also ALIENATION.

Reading
Lukács, Georg. [1923] 1971. *History and class consciousness.* London: Merlin; Cambridge, MA: MIT Press.
Marx, Karl. [1867, 1894] 1970. *Capital*, vols 1 and 3. London: Lawrence and Wishart.
Schaff, Adam. 1980. *Alienation as a social phenomenon.* Oxford and New York: Pergamon.

relationship, statistical *See* STATISTICAL INDEPENDENCE AND STATISTICAL DEPENDENCE.

relations of production *See* MODE OF PRODUCTION.

relative deprivation *See* DEPRIVATION.

relativism *See* CULTURAL RELATIVISM.

reliability Reliability is the degree to which a MEASUREMENT instrument gives the same results each time it is used, assuming that the underlying thing being measured does not change. If the temperature in a room stays the same, for example, a reliable thermometer will always give the same reading. But if the readings change even when the temperature does not, then the thermometer lacks reliability.

Note that the thermometer does not have to be accurate in order to be reliable; it might always register 3 degrees too high, for example. Its degree of reliability has to do instead with the predictability of its relationship with whatever is being measured.

We can test reliability by determining whether several observers of the same situation will give similar accounts of it. We might ask people to observe a group INTERACTION, for example, and report afterward on the amount of conflict that occurred. In this case, the measurement instrument consists simply of people watching and listening and then reporting what they observe. As a result, however, we might find that people's accounts differ a great deal, depending on how they pay attention to an interaction.

To increase reliability, we might – as Bales and his colleagues did in studying GROUP DYNAMICS – devise a set of categories of behavior, including conflict, and ask observers to put each behavior they observed into a category on a piece of paper. We might further give our observers training so that they know when to consider a behavior as conflict and when to consider it something else. As a result, we would expect that our observers would be more in agreement about what they saw than before, which would mean our instrument for measuring conflict in group interactions would have greater reliability.

See also ERROR; MEASUREMENT; VALIDITY.

Reading

Bales, Robert R. 1950. *Interaction process analysis: A method for the study of small groups.* Cambridge, MA: Addison-Wesley.

Singleton, Royce A., Bruce C. Straits, and Margaret M. Straits. 1998. *Approaches to social research*, 3rd ed. Oxford and New York: Oxford University Press.

religion Like all social INSTITUTIONS, religion is defined sociologically by the functions that it performs in SOCIAL SYSTEMS. In general, religion is a social arrangement designed to provide a shared, collective way of dealing with the unknown and un-knowable aspects of human life, with the mysteries of life, death, and the difficult dilemmas that arise in the process of making moral decisions. As such, religion not only provides responses to enduring human problems and questions but also forms a basis for social COHESION and solidarity.

Central to the social reality of religion is the distinction made by Émile DURKHEIM between the *sacred* and the *profane*. The profane world consists of all that we can know through our senses. It is the natural world of everyday life that we experience as either comprehensible or at least ultimately knowable. In contrast, the sacred encompasses all that exists beyond the everyday, natural world that we experience with our senses. As such, the sacred inspires feelings of awe because it is regarded as ultimately unknowable and beyond limited human abilities to perceive and comprehend. Religion is organized primarily around the sacred elements of human life and provides a collective attempt to bridge the gap between the sacred and the profane.

See also ANIMISM; CIVIL RELIGION; ETHICALIST RELIGION; THEISTIC RELIGION; TOTEMIC RELIGION.

Reading

Durkheim, Émile. [1912] 1965. *The elementary forms of religious life.* New York: Free Press.

Wilson, Bryan. 1982. *Religion in sociological perspective.* New York: Oxford University Press.

replication Replication is the standard scientific practice of repeating a study in order to see if the initial findings were caused by an accidental or otherwise distorting set of circumstances. Studies whose findings are regarded as significant are usually repeated, or replicated, by other researchers to see if the findings can be reproduced. If they can, then the findings gain increased credibility among scientists.

A common experience is that replication produces a variety of findings that may, nonetheless, favor one pattern over another. In the area of sex differences, for example, some studies may find men more likely than women to exhibit a certain behavior or ability; others may find women more likely than men; and still others may find no difference at all. If most results lean in a particular direction, then this may be enough to accept it in spite of conflicting findings. In other cases, the diversity of findings may leave researchers with no firm ground to stand on and force them to suspend judgment until more conclusive evidence can be found.

Researchers may find it impossible to reproduce a set of findings, which usually results in the rejection of the original claim. This happened, for example, when a pair of U.S. scientists claimed to have found a way to produce a nuclear fusion reaction at room temperature.

See also SCIENCE, NORMS OF.

Reading

Singleton, Royce A., Bruce C. Straits, and Margaret M. Straits. 1998. *Approaches to social research*, 3rd ed. Oxford and New York: Oxford University Press.

repressive state apparatus *See* IDEOLOGICAL STATE APPARATUS.

research methods *See* METHODO-LOGY.

residual *See* REGRESSION ANALYSIS.

residues and derivations Residues and derivations are key concepts in a THEORY developed by Vilfredo

PARETO to explain nonlogical aspects of social life. Pareto argued that most human behavior is governed by a relatively fixed number of universal psychological motivations that he called residues. He saw political life, for example, as governed primarily by the motivation to preserve the SOCIAL SYSTEM as it is ("persistence of aggregates") and the making and breaking of connections ("instinct for combinations") in order to gain POWER and advance various special interests. Social life also includes derivations, the explanations that people offer for their behavior and the social systems in which it occurs. Derivations are important because they provide an ideological justification that serves as a basis for social action. Thus, for example, the argument that what politicians do is for the greater good of SOCIETY and all its people is a derivation that plays an important part in political systems.

See also ELITE.

Reading

Pareto, Vilfredo. [1916] 1963. *The mind and society: A treatise on general sociology*, vol. 1, *Non-logical conduct*. New York: Dover.

resistance movement *See* SOCIAL MOVEMENT.

resocialization Resocialization is part of the ongoing process of SOCIALIZATION that extends throughout the LIFE COURSE and involves the learning and, sometimes, the unlearning of various roles. Adult roles may cover a wide range – from spouses, parents, widows, single-parents, and divorced parents to prison inmates and employees in different occupations. All of these transitions involve a kind of resocialization.

Erving GOFFMAN defines resocialization as a more drastic process of tearing down and rebuilding an individual's ROLES and socially constructed sense of SELF. The forced indoctrination of political prisoners, for example, or the "deprogramming" of former converts to religious cults are examples of resocialization, as is the attempt to rehabilitate people who have organized major portions of their lives around crime or extensive drug and alcohol abuse. Because resocialization is a drastic process that requires considerable control over its subjects, it often takes place in tightly controlled SOCIAL SYSTEMS such as prisons and hospitals.

See also SELF; SOCIALIZATION; TOTAL INSTITUTION.

Reading

Gecas, Viktor. 1981. "Contexts of socialization." In *Social psychology: Sociological perspectives*, edited by Morris Rosenberg and Ralph Turner. New York: Basic Books.

Goffman, Erving. 1961. *Asylums*. New York: Anchor Books.

resource mobilization theory

In the study of SOCIAL MOVEMENTS, resource mobilization theory argues that the success of social movements depends on resources – time, money, organizational skills, and the like – and the ability to use them. When the THEORY first appeared, it was a breakthrough in the sociology of social movements because it focused on VARIABLES that are explicitly sociological rather than implicitly psychological, as was the case with the CLASSICAL SOCIAL MOVEMENT THEORIES that preceded it. No longer were social movements viewed as irrational, emotion-driven, and disorganized. For the first time, influences

from outside social movements, such as support from various organizations or the government, were taken into account.

Resource mobilization theory has been criticized for overemphasizing the importance of outside resources, especially in regard to the civil rights movement in the United States. It also seems to be most effective in explaining what happens with movements that begin with fairly substantial resources such as those related to environmental and antinuclear issues. The theory is less useful in explaining the course of movements among racial and other minorities.

See also POLITICAL PROCESS THEORY.

Reading

Jenkins, J. Craig. 1983. "Resource mobilization theory and the study of social movements." *Annual Review of Sociology* 9: 527–53.

McCarthy, John D., and Mayer N. Zald. 1973. *The trend of social movements in America: Professionalization and resource mobilization*. Morristown, NJ: General Learning Press.

response rate

In a SURVEY, the response rate is the percentage of those selected in the SAMPLE who actually provide DATA for analysis. For example, if a national sample of 1,500 people is selected and 1,100 of these are actually interviewed, the response rate is $1,100/1,500 = 0.73$ or, expressed as a percentage, 73 percent. The nonresponse rate is the remainder, or 27 percent.

The response rate is crucial in SURVEY research because the lower it is the greater the danger that the sample is biased in one way or another. People who refuse to be interviewed, for example, can be expected to differ in socially significant ways from those who do not.

Although there are no hard and fast rules, sociologists generally regard response rates under 75 percent as suspect and those below 50 percent as virtually useless for scientific research. This does not mean that such data have no value. They can be used to generate ideas and insights, among other things, or for anecdotal purposes. However, they cannot be used to make scientific inferences about the POPULATION from which the sample was drawn.

See also ERROR; STATISTICS.

Reading

Singleton, Royce A., Bruce C. Straits, and Margaret M. Straits. 1998. *Approaches to social research*, 3rd ed. Oxford and New York: Oxford University Press.

restricted speech code   *See* SPEECH CODES.

retreatism   *See* ABERRANT DEVIANCE.

revolution   Revolution is a SOCIAL CHANGE that alters basic aspects of a SOCIETY or other SOCIAL SYSTEM. In politics, for example, a revolution consists of more than a change of leadership, however sudden or violent it may be. For political change to be revolutionary, the political system itself must undergo some basic change, as from aristocracy to DEMOCRACY or from democracy to military dictatorship. Given this definition, true revolutions are quite rare and difficult to sustain because the forces of LEGITIMATION that promote the status quo tend to be quite strong even in the most oppressive systems.

Although revolution is most often associated with politics and sudden, violent change, it can occur in any area of social life and can take place without violence over long periods of time. The INDUSTRIAL REVOLUTION is an example of one of the most profound social transformations ever to occur, as was the development of CAPITALISM as an economic system. Both changes evolved over several centuries without one order being forcibly toppled by another. What is key to the idea of a revolution is the kind of change that occurs, not how it occurs.

See also COUP D'ÉTAT; REBELLION, POLITICAL.

Reading

Goldstone, Jack A., ed. 1994. *Revolutions*. Fort Worth: Harcourt Brace Jovanovich.
Kimmel, Michael. 1990. *Revolution: A sociological interpretation*. Philadelphia: Temple University Press.
Skocpol, Theda. 1994. *Social revolutions in the modern world*. New York: Cambridge University Press.

rising expectations   *See* FRUSTRATION AGGRESSION THEORY.

rite of passage   A rite of passage is a RITUAL used to mark and accomplish the transition from one social STATUS to another. The marriage ceremony is a rite of passage marking the transition from single to married, just as initiation ceremonies in clubs and other exclusive organizations mark the transition from nonmember to member.

In many tribal societies the shift from child to adult status is marked by puberty rites. In contrast, INDUSTRIAL SOCIETIES often lack such clear indications of adult status with the exception of Jewish bar mitzvah and bas mitzvah ceremonies. Some sociologists argue that as a result of the general lack of rites of passage, the late teens and early twenties are an age marked by ambiguity, anxiety, and rebelliousness. In fact, in the United States the AGE CATEGORY in which males are most prone to violence and criminal activity encompasses the late teens and early twenties, precisely those ages when adult standing with all the privileges it entails is most desired and least clearly attained.

It is important to note that a rite of passage involves a socially recognized ritual. In this sense, experiences (such as first sexual experience) that are popularly referred to as rites of passage are in fact not because there is no rite per se (there is, for example, no generally recognized change in social position associated with having sex for the first time in most industrial societies).

See also SOCIALIZATION.

Reading
Van Gennep, Arnold. [1909] 1960. *The rites of passage*. Chicago: University of Chicago Press.

ritual In general, a ritual is a pattern of speech or behavior that is used to create or sustain the sense of connection to a SOCIAL SYSTEM. At sporting events the ritualistic singing of national anthems helps to reinforce national unity. In religious ceremonies, ritual serves to affirm the social relationship among believers as well as the relationship between believers and various forms taken by supernatural forces (in those religions that include BELIEF in the existence of such forces). Religious rituals differ a great deal in their complexity and the use of SACRED objects, and in their formality, spontaneity, and allowance for displays of emotion. Depending on the religion, ritual may make use of prayer, sacrifice, magic, meditation, and other practices.

On a smaller scale of interpersonal relations, ritual serves similar functions by sustaining social relationships and their definitions of reality. When spouses kiss each other good-night, for example, this can be interpreted as a ritual that plays a part in sustaining the shared definition of a loving relationship. Social life is full of such INTERACTION ritual. Despite its seeming triviality, it plays an important part in sustaining social systems and people's participation in them.

See also ETHNOMETHODOLOGY; INTERACTION; RITE OF PASSAGE; TABOO.

Reading
Bocock, R. 1974. *Ritual in industrial society: A sociological analysis of ritualism*. London: Allen and Unwin.
Goffman, Erving. 1967. *Interaction ritual*. New York: Anchor Books.
Turner, Victor. 1995. *The ritual process*. New York: Aldine.

ritualism In Robert K. MERTON's THEORY of DEVIANCE, ritualism is a form of quasi-deviance in which people obey NORMS outwardly by "going through the motions" but lack inner commitment to their ROLES and the underlying VALUES of the SOCIAL SYSTEM. Because the lack of commitment is usually detectable to other people, widespread ritualism can undermine the morale and commitment of others to the system (and hence the social COHESION of the system as a whole), an effect that is not balanced by technical compliance with norms.

Reading
Merton, Robert K. 1938. "Social structure and anomie." *American Sociological Review* 3: 672–82.
———. 1968. *Social theory and social structure*, exp. ed. New York: Free Press.

role A role is a set of ideas associated with a social STATUS that defines its relationship with another position in a SOCIAL SYSTEM. The role of teacher, for example, is built around a set of ideas about teachers in relation to students: BELIEFS about who they are, VALUES related to goals they are supposed to pursue, NORMS about how they are supposed to appear and behave, ATTITUDES about their emotional predispositions toward their work and students. The role of student usually includes the belief that students know less than teachers; the value that learning is good as an end in itself; and expectations that students will arrive on time, work hard, and learn what is assigned to them and that they will maintain an attitude of respect toward their teachers and other students. Neither students nor teachers are expected to approach each other sexually, to engage in exchanges of money in return for higher grades, or to be vicious or sarcastic.

Because a role is a set of ideas associated with a social status, it should be distinguished from what people actually do as status-occupants, which is known as *role performance*. This distinction is particularly important in SYMBOLIC INTERACTIONISM, which stresses the importance of creativity in social behavior. Like jazz musicians, individuals may pay attention to a general "score" but do a great deal of improvising in the process.

Along with the concept of a status, the role is a basic building block of social systems, for to a considerable degree a social system can be thought of as a network of statuses and their associated roles. Role is also an important concept because it is through roles that individuals are connected to social systems.

See also ATOMISM AND HOLISM; ROLE PARTNER; ROLE STRUCTURE.

Reading
Biddle, Bruce J. 1979. *Role theory: Expectations, identities, and behaviors.* New York: Academic Press.
Heiss, J. 1981. "Social roles." In *Social psychology: Sociological perspectives*, edited by Morris Rosenberg and Ralph H. Turner. New York: Basic Books.
Linton, Ralph. 1936. *The study of man.* New York: Appleton-Century-Crofts.
Mead, George Herbert. 1934. *Mind, self, and society.* Chicago: University of Chicago Press.

role conflict Role conflict occurs when people are confronted with contrary or incompatible role expectations in the various social STATUSES they occupy in their lives. A military field commander who is ordered to send troops into a risky operation may feel torn between the obligation to obey superior officers and the obligation to protect the lives of troops. In similar ways, a parent may feel conflicting obligations to employers who demand full devotion to the job and children who need to be cared for when they are sick.

Role conflict takes several different forms. In the above cases, the expectations associated with two different ROLES – military subordinate and commanding officer, employee and parent – are contradictory and produce strain in the person called upon to resolve the contradiction. When this involves roles associated with two different statuses, such as employee and parent, the result is known as *status strain*. When the conflicting roles are both associated with the same status – military officer, for example – the result is known as *role strain*.

Conflict may also occur when people disagree about what the expectations are for a particular role.

Employers and secretaries, for example, may disagree about whether secretarial duties include personal services such as picking up laundry. In another sense, role conflict can occur when someone simply has difficulty satisfying expectations because their duties are unclear, too difficult, or disagreeable.

There is a variety of responses for resolving or minimizing the effects of role conflict. The first is to choose which role is most important and then violate the expectations associated with the other role. A second response is to leave one of the conflicting statuses (a person might quit a job if it interferes too much with parenting responsibilities). A third response is to engage in *role* (or *audience*) *segregation*, the practice of separating various role partners from one another (doctors, for example, often refuse to treat members of their own family). A fourth response involves what Erving GOFFMAN called *role distance*, a method for minimizing role strain associated with a disagreeable role. For example, managers who must dismiss large numbers of employees in order to lower costs and make firms more competitive may resort to a variety of techniques to disassociate themselves from what they have to do. One way is to use euphemistic language such as "downsizing," "outplacement," and "letting people go" that masks the reality of what is happening. Military officials use role distance in similar ways when they refer to people as "soft targets" and civilian casualties as "collateral damage."

Role distance can also take the form of performing a role while behaving in a distracted manner. The use of macabre humor by surgeons while performing particularly difficult procedures on emergency room patients can be a form of role distance that minimizes the emotional strain of their work.

Along with the concepts of status and role, role conflict plays an important part in drawing attention to the connection between individual experience and behavior and the cultural and structural characteristics of SOCIAL SYSTEMS from which the potential for conflict and strain emerges.

See also STATUS SET.

Reading

Goffman, Erving. 1961. *Encounters*. Indianapolis: Bobbs-Merrill.

Merton, Robert K. 1968. *Social theory and social structure*, exp. ed. New York: Free Press.

Van Snell, M., A. P. Brief, and R. S. Schuler. 1981. "Role conflict and role ambiguity: Integration of the literature and directions for future research." *Human Relations* 34: 43–71.

role distance   *See* ROLE CONFLICT.

role model   A role model is someone to whom we look for examples of how to behave in the performance of a ROLE. Research on role models focuses primarily on childhood SOCIALIZATION and imitation of the behavior of adults and other models, and the role of mentors in school and occupational success, especially for women and other minorities. Role models differ from REFERENCE INDIVIDUALS. The former focuses on a specific activity while the latter is generalized to many areas of social life.

Reading

Bandura, Albert, and Richard H. Walters. 1963. *Social learning and personality development*. New York: Holt, Rinehart and Winston.

Jung, John. 1986. "How useful is the concept of role model? A critical analysis."

Journal of Social Behavior and Personality 1: 525–36.

Speizer, Jeanne J. 1981. "Role models, mentors and sponsors: The elusive concepts." *Signs* 6: 692–712.

role partner A role partner is the occupant of a social STATUS in relation to whom a person's ROLE is defined. The role of mother, for example, is defined in relation to the role of child, which makes the child the mother's role partner and, by the same token, the mother the child's role partner.

It is often the case that when we occupy a social status we find ourselves in relationships with several different role partners. A lawyer, for example, has relationships with judges, clients, opposing lawyers and their clients, police officers, colleagues, witnesses, and various court clerks and functionaries. Although each of these relationships is associated with occupying the status of lawyer, a lawyer's role or behavior in relation to a judge is going to vary considerably from the role assumed with a client or an opposing counsel.

If all of the various roles associated with occupying a particular status are combined, the result is a *role set*. This means that each status carries with it a role set consisting of a collection of roles performed in relation to different role partners.

Reading

Merton, Robert K. 1968. *Social theory and social structure*, rev. and exp. ed. New York: Free Press.

role performance *See* ROLE.

role segregation *See* ROLE CONFLICT.

role set *See* ROLE PARTNER.

role strain *See* ROLE CONFLICT.

role structure A role structure is the set of ROLES that are included in every SOCIAL SYSTEM. A family, for example, has a role structure that includes relationships between spouses, between parents and children, and between siblings, as well as more extended relationships with more removed kin such as cousins and grandparents.

Role structures differ in both their content and their complexity. College classrooms differ from government bureaucracies in that they involve different roles, with teacher and student being qualitatively different from manager and cabinet minister. Such role structures also differ in complexity, however, because a college classroom involves only two roles whose connections are relatively simple, whereas a bureaucracy involves many different roles that connect to one another in different ways.

Role structure influences what actually goes on in social systems more than any other structural characteristic because it most directly concerns the patterns of behavior of those who participate in them.

See also DIVISION OF LABOR; SOCIAL STRUCTURE.

ruling class *See* UPPER CLASS.

rural community *See* COMMUNITY.

rural/urban continuum *See* COMMUNITY.

S

sacred *See* RELIGION.

sample A sample is any subset of a POPULATION selected to represent and draw inferences about that population. As a research technique, sampling first came into use in agricultural studies as a way to estimate crop yields without having to measure the entire crop. Today sampling techniques are used widely in the social sciences to gather information on large, complex populations without the expense of conducting a CENSUS.

Although sampling is a process that inevitably produces ERROR (as does every other method of observation), when scientific procedures are followed the results are usually quite accurate and involve levels of error that are more than justified by the savings in time and money. Indeed, many studies of sociological interest would be impossible without the use of samples.

See also COMPLEX SAMPLE; FRAME, SAMPLING; OVERSAMPLING; PPS SAMPLING; QUOTA SAMPLE; SAMPLING ERROR; SIMPLE RANDOM SAMPLE.

Reading

Kish, Leslie. 1965. *Survey sampling.* New York: Wiley.

Singleton, Royce A., Bruce C. Straits, and Margaret M. Straits. 1998. *Approaches to social research*, 3rd ed. Oxford and New York: Oxford University Press.

sampling distribution In STATISTICS, a sampling distribution is a theoretical mathematical DISTRIBUTION of all the possible SAMPLE outcomes that can be obtained by selecting samples from a POPULATION. Suppose we determine the MEAN income of a sample of British households and use those figures to estimate the mean income in the entire population of British households. The sample we selected, as well as its mean income, is only one of an almost infinite number of possible samples and sample means that we could have selected. The sampling distribution contains all of those possible sample means.

In using sampling distributions we must be able to estimate the distribution's main characteristics: its MEAN, its shape, and its VARIANCE (the degree to which samples in the distribution differ from one another). Since sampling involves random ERROR, half of the sample means will be greater than the population mean and half will be smaller. Since these errors tend to cancel one another out, if we were to add up all the possible sample means and take an average, it would equal the population mean we are trying to estimate.

The shape of the distribution is determined from a mathematical theorem known as the *central limit theorem*. According to this theorem, a sampling distribution for a particular sample characteristic such as mean income will have the shape of a symmetrical, bell-shaped NORMAL CURVE DISTRIBUTION if the population is itself normally shaped for that variable. Since this is rarely the case, the theorem provides a fall-back position: the larger the sample is, the more closely the sampling distribution will resemble a normal curve. This will be true regardless of the shape of the population.

The amount of variation in a sampling distribution is measured by a statistic known as the STANDARD ERROR.

Sampling distributions are invaluable in research because they act as a statistical bridge between what we know (the DATA gathered in samples) and what we want to know (the characteristics of populations from which samples are drawn). This is accomplished through a process known as STATISTICAL INFERENCE.

See also DISTRIBUTION; ERROR; NORMAL CURVE DISTRIBUTION; SAMPLING ERROR; STANDARD ERROR; STATISTICS.

Reading

Bohrnstedt, George W., and David Knoke. 1994. *Statistics for social data analysis*, 3rd ed. Itasca, IL: F. E. Peacock.

sampling error Sampling error is an ERROR that occurs when using SAMPLES to make inferences about the populations from which they are drawn. There are two kinds of sampling error: random error and bias. Since researchers rarely can know if a particular sample is in error, the idea of sampling error applies more to the long-run probability that sample outcomes, such as the percentage of people dwho have married more than once, will differ from the corresponding POPULATION values by no more than a given margin of error.

Even the best sample design will generate a certain amount of random error, a pattern of errors that tend to cancel one another out so that the overall result still accurately reflects the true value. In general, random error decreases with larger sample size and varies directly with the amount of variation in the population from which the sample is drawn. Expressed another way, large samples tend to be more accurate than small ones. In addition, if there is a great deal of variation on some characteristic in the population (people have widely differing ages, for example), samples used to estimate population characteristics (such as average age) will be more subject to random error than will similar samples drawn from a population in which people tend to be more alike.

Since random error occurs by chance, it can be minimized through the use of various sampling techniques, such as drawing a large sample or using a STRATIFIED SAMPLE design. We cannot eliminate it entirely, however. Statistical inference, the process of using sample results to estimate characteristics of populations, is for this reason largely a matter of trying to estimate the amount of random error that is most likely to be produced by a particular sample design.

Sampling bias is more serious than random error because the pattern of errors is loaded in one direction or another, which is to say the errors tend not to balance one another and therefore produce a true distortion. A sample design that uses telephone directories to make selections, for example, will tend to produce samples that are biased toward the higher end of SOCIOECONOMIC STATUS, since those without telephones will tend to be the poor. Bias is also more serious than random error because there is little if any way to estimate its presence in a set of data, which is why researchers go to such great lengths to design samples that minimize the probability of its occurrence.

See also ERROR; SAMPLE; STATISTICS; STRATIFIED SAMPLE.

Reading

Kalton, Graham. 1984. *Introduction to survey sampling.* Beverly Hills, CA: Sage Publications.

Kish, Leslie. 1965. *Survey sampling.* New York: Wiley.

sampling weights A sampling weight is a statistical correction factor that compensates for a SAMPLE design that tends to over- or underrepresent various segments within a POPULATION. In some samples, small subsets of the population, such as religious, ethnic, or racial MINORITIES, may be selected in larger numbers than their percentage of the population would otherwise require so as to have enough cases to analyze. When these subsamples are combined with the larger sample, their disproportionately large numbers must be diluted by a sampling weight. In the case of COMPLEX SAMPLES, probabilities of selection may turn out to be unequal due to unforeseeable field conditions, a result that requires correction in the form of sampling weights.

To illustrate, let's assume that we are drawing a sample of 1,000 people from a population that is 10 percent Catholic and 90 percent Protestant. Since a representative sample would include only 100 Catholics (10 percent of 1,000), we might oversample Catholics by selecting 300. This would enable us to make statistically valid inferences about the Catholic population, but when we use the combined sample, Catholics would comprise $300/1000 = 30$ percent of the sample, which is far more than their actual percentage of the population. We can correct for this in estimating a characteristic such as average income, by applying to each Catholic's income a weight of $10/30 = 0.33$. Thus, by counting each individual Catholic in the sample at only 0.33 instead of 1.0 we effectively reduce the number of Catholics in the sample from 300 to 100. Similarly, since Protestants constitute 90 percent of the population but only $700/1000 = 70$ percent of the sample, we inflate each Protestant's income score by multiplying it by a sampling weight of $90/70 = 1.286$, which effectively increases the relative number of Protestants in the calculation from 700 to 900.

The usefulness of sampling weights underscores the importance of selecting samples in such a way that probabilities of selection are always known even if they are unequal. As long as they are known, it is possible to make corrections after the sample has been selected.

See also COMPLEX SAMPLE; OVERSAMPLING.

Reading

Kalton, Graham. 1984. *Introduction to survey sampling.* Beverly Hills, CA: Sage Publications.

Kish, Leslie. 1965. *Survey sampling.* New York: Wiley.

sanction A sanction is a reward or punishment that a NORM associates with a behavior or appearance. People who work hard at their jobs, for example, can expect to be rewarded with wages, while those who rarely show up for work and work badly when they do may expect to be punished with dismissal.

Sanctions vary in their degree of formality. *Informal sanctions* are not codified anywhere in an official and definitive form, and they have few limitations as to who may impose them and under what conditions. Verbally scolding a child who lies to a friend, glaring at a stranger who stares, or refusing to speak to someone who has committed a personal insult are all informal sanctions. *Formal sanctions*, by contrast, are generally codified and administered only by specific people authorized to do so under particular conditions. These include such sanctions as imprisonment, capital punishment, fines, loss of a job, expulsion from school, and suspension of a driving license. Norms that have formal sanctions are known as LAWS.

Reading

Garland, David. 1990. *Punishment in modern society: A study in social theory.* Chicago: University of Chicago Press.

scale of measurement The purpose of empirical research is to make comparisons – to see how BELIEFS differ from one RELIGION to another, for example, or to compare the fertility of people in different SOCIAL CLASSES. To make such comparisons, we must observe people and SOCIAL SYSTEMS and note various behaviors, characteristics, consequences, and so on. These take the form of VARIABLES, from class, RACE, and GENDER among individuals to the complexity of organizations or the POWER of NATIONS.

Variables differ in the kinds of comparisons we can make with them, and these differences take the form of four different scales of measurement: (1) nominal, (2) ordinal, (3) interval, and (4) ratio. The *nominal-scale* property allows us to classify variables simply in terms of their names, to determine whether they are the same or different. Religion, for example, is a variable consisting of categories such as Moslem, Christian, Jew, Buddhist, and Hindu. The only way that people can be compared with each other on this variable is to see whether they are alike – have the same religion – or unalike. They cannot, for example, be ranked from "high religious preference" to "low religious preference." All variables have this nominal-scale (or *categorical*) property.

If a variable has an *ordinal-scale* property, we can rank observations in terms of higher and lower, more or less, better or worse. If we ask people to rank their degree of religious commitment in terms of "high," "medium," "low," and "none," the resulting four-category variable would have an ordinal property in that we could rank people from high to low commitment. Note, however, that we cannot say anything about how great the differences are among the categories. We do not know how great the difference is between "high" and "medium," for example, or how that difference compares with the difference between "low" and "none." Note also that any variable that has ordinal-scale properties also has nominal-scale properties that enable us to categorize people on the basis of having the same or different religious commitment.

If a variable has an *interval-scale* property, the actual distances, or intervals, between categories can be compared. If we use the centigrade scale to measure temperature, for example, we can say that the difference between 100 and 150 degrees $(150 - 100 = 50)$ is half the difference between 200 and 300 degrees (300 − 200 = 100). Similarly, we can say that the difference between ages 20 and 25 is the same as the difference between ages 50 and 55, or that the difference between ages 18 and 24 is half the difference between ages 30 and 42.

There is an important difference between these two examples of variables with interval-scale properties, however. Both allow us to compare categories, but with age we can actually take the ratio of one category to another: we can say that age 30 is twice age 15. With the centigrade scale, however, we cannot do this: a day that is 30 degrees centigrade is not twice as hot as a 15 degree day. The reason for this is that zero degrees centigrade is not a true zero point; it does not represent the absence of heat (unlike the Kelvin scale). An age of zero, however, does represent a true zero, which is what enables us to take the ratio of one age to another. A variable that allows us to do this has a *ratio-scale* property.

There are four important points to be made about measurement scales: (1) scales of measurement are ranked from high to low, with nominal-scale properties considered "low" and ratio-scale properties "high"; (2) a variable is known by the highest scale properties it has; thus religion is a nominal-scale variable, degrees centigrade is an interval-scale variable, and age is a ratio-scale variable even though all have nominal-scale properties in common; (3) a variable that has one scale property will also have all the scale properties below it; thus an interval-scale variable has interval-, ordinal-, and nominal-scale properties; and (4) the appropriateness of statistical techniques used to analyze

DATA depends upon the scale of measurement of the variables involved, which is why it is so important to be able to tell one from another.
See also DICHOTOMY.

scapegoat A scapegoat is an individual, GROUP, or SOCIAL CATEGORY of people used as an object of blame in a SOCIAL SYSTEM. Scapegoating provides a mechanism for venting rage, frustration, resentment, fear and other emotions that might otherwise be expressed in ways that damage social COHESION, challenge the status quo, or attack dominant groups and their interests. Immigrants and MINORITIES, for example, are often used as scapegoats during times of economic hardship and blamed as the cause of unemployment and other SOCIAL PROBLEMS. As a result, aspects of social systems that bring about economic crises, such as capitalist competition and EXPLOITATION, are hidden from public scrutiny and possible criticism.
See also ATTRIBUTION, SOCIAL; CLASS CONSCIOUSNESS AND FALSE CONSCIOUSNESS.
Reading
Ryan, William. 1971. *Blaming the victim.* New York: Pantheon.

science From a sociological standpoint, science is a body of KNOWLEDGE about the natural world and a method for discovering such knowledge, and a social INSTITUTION organized around both. As a method, science rests on the idea that reliable knowledge of the world must be based on a systematic, objective observation of facts that will lead everyone who considers them to the same conclusion. Although much sociological work is guided by scientific principles, there is controversy over whether scientific methods are applicable to social life or, for that matter, even to the natural world.

Sociologists are interested in science not merely as a method for their own research, but as a social phenomenon in its own right. As a social institution, for example, the practice of science has become increasingly complex, expensive, and dependent on government and corporations for funding. This has in turn transformed the process of scientific work, beginning with the VALUES that influence the choice of subjects for research.

See also DECONSTRUCTION; ENLIGHTENMENT, AGE OF; EPISTEMOLOGY; FALSIFICATIONISM; HYPOTHETICO-DEDUCTIVE METHOD; METHODOLOGY; POSTMODERNISM; OBJECTIVITY; STRUCTURALISM AND POSTSTRUCTURALISM; TECHNOLOGY; VALUE RELEVANCE, VALUE FREEDOM, AND VALUE NEUTRALITY.

Reading

Barnes, Barry. 1985. *About science.* New York: Blackwell Publishers.

Merton, Robert K. 1973. *The sociology of science: Theoretical and empirical investigations.* Chicago: University of Chicago Press.

Zuckerman, Harriet. 1988. "The sociology of science: A selective review." In *Handbook of sociology,* edited by Neil J. Smelser. Beverly Hills, CA: Sage Publications.

science, norms of The norms of science, like the norms in any other SOCIAL SYSTEM, are the set of rules that govern how scientists do their work. According to the norm of *disinterestedness,* for example, scientists are expected to act in the best interests of science however this might affect them as individuals.

Scientists who falsify research results in order to make a name for themselves clearly violate this norm and threaten the credibility of scientists in general.

The norm of *communism* (which has nothing to do with economic or political systems) requires scientists to share results freely with one another in order to further scientific discovery. The norm of *universalism* requires scientists to evaluate findings solely on their objective scientific merits rather than on such subjective criteria as the personal or social characteristics of the scientists who report them. During the 1930s, for example, the Nazis regularly violated this norm by dismissing as invalid the findings of "Jewish science."

Finally, the norm of *organized skepticism* requires scientists to always question their results, to resist the temptation to conclude that any idea about how things work is once and for all proven to be true. More than anything else, this sets science apart from RELIGION as a way of arriving at ideas about truth, for most religions are taken by their believers to be bodies of truth that are not subject to ongoing critical questioning. It is for this reason that many scientists argue that "Creation science," which rejects the theory of evolution in favor of divine origins, is not science at all since it regards the truth as already established beyond doubt.

Although the norms of science generally influence scientific work in fairly predictable ways, the structure of scientific work and the great expense of scientific research often creates pressures toward DEVIANCE. For example, scientists who depend on government and corporate sponsors with conflicting interests may be required to keep their results secret from the larger scientific community. A government agency may want discoveries with military applications kept secret, or a corporation may want to protect discoveries that have profit potential. Scientists thus find themselves caught in a bind between satisfying the conditions under which their work is funded and obeying the norm of communism on which the overall success of science depends.

Reading

Merton, Robert K. 1968. *Social theory and social structure*, rev. and exp. ed. New York: Free Press.

Zuckerman, Harriet. 1977. "Deviant behavior and social control in science." In *Deviance and social change*, edited by E. Sagarin, 87–138. Beverly Hills, CA: Sage Publications.

——. 1988. "The sociology of science: A selective review." In *Handbook of sociology*, edited by Neil J. Smelser. Beverly Hills, CA: Sage Publications.

scientific management Scientific management is the systematic attempt to analyze work in order to identify the most efficient way to accomplish a given task. The theory originated in 1911 in the work of F. W. Taylor (and hence is often referred to as *Taylorism*). Taylor likened the human body to a machine and conducted time and motion studies to determine the most efficient way to make use of it. Taylorism was closely related to the development of mass production, especially in factory-based assembly lines first introduced by the American automaker Henry Ford. What came to be known as *Fordism* separated workers from one another and divided the production process into a fragmented series of tasks more easily controlled by supervisors and management.

Critics of industrial CAPITALISM identify scientific management as a major tool for controlling workers, not only to increase productivity but to undermine the power of labor in relation to management by depriving workers of control over the work process.

See also ALIENATION; AUTOMATION; DE-SKILLING.

Reading

Braverman, Harry. 1974. *Labor and monopoly capital*. New York: Monthly Review Press.

Hounshell, D. A. 1984. *From the American system to mass production 1900–1932: The development of manufacturing technology in the United States*. Baltimore: Johns Hopkins University Press.

Salaman, Graeme. 1986. *Working*. London: Tavistock.

Taylor, Frederick Winslow. 1911. *The principles of scientific management*. New York: Harper and Row.

scientific revolution As defined by T. S. KUHN in his classic analysis of how scientific work is done, a scientific revolution is a process that occurs when one THEORETICAL PERSPECTIVE, or paradigm, is discarded and replaced by another. This happens when an accumulation of scientific observations and findings, called *anomalies*, conflict with the prevailing paradigm and cannot be explained by it. The Ptolemaic paradigm of the universe, for example, was based on the false assumption that the sun revolved around the earth. Many years of astronomical observations, however, produced anomalous findings that contradicted Ptolemy's basic premise. These eventually prompted a scientific revolution through which a new paradigm – Copernicus's and Galileo's model of the sun occupying the central position in the solar system – replaced the old.

Sociology has yet to experience a scientific revolution because no single paradigm has been well-enough established to be overthrown by a competitor, although some might argue that this has occurred to some degree in the struggle between proponents of the CONFLICT and FUNCTIONALIST PERSPECTIVES.

See also THEORETICAL PERSPECTIVE.

Reading
Kuhn, Thomas. 1970. *The structure of scientific revolutions*. Chicago: University of Chicago Press.

Scottish Enlightenment The period in Scottish history known as the Scottish Enlightenment took place during the eighteenth and early nineteenth centuries. It was noted for the work of David Hume, Adam SMITH, and others, whose ideas helped to shift the way people thought about social life. This accompanied energetic economic and commercial progress and vigorous development in the arts, literature, architecture, and engineering.

Enlightenment thinkers were skeptics who emphasized the importance of lived experience as a basis for KNOWLEDGE and who saw the need for new intellectual tools for making sense of SOCIETY and SOCIAL CHANGE. People, they argued, are social and relational beings by nature, and society is a natural phenomenon, rather than something imposed as a way to control an otherwise unruly human nature. They also saw society as problematic and took a critical stance regarding the consequences it produces, especially in the form of social CONFLICT and "progress" that was not necessarily for the good.

script *See* DRAMATURGICAL PERSPECTIVE.

seasonal unemployment *See* UNEMPLOYMENT AND UNDEREMPLOYMENT.

secondary analysis Secondary analysis is the practice of analyzing DATA that have already been gathered by someone else, often for a distinctly different purpose. As a research method, it saves both time and money and avoids unnecessary duplication of research effort. The method does have its drawbacks though, since the data may not exactly fit the needs of the researchers analyzing them.

The sources of data for secondary analysis are increasingly varied and extensive, especially as SURVEY researchers, government agencies, corporations, and other organizations continue to gather far more information than they can possibly analyze themselves.

See also CONTENT ANALYSIS; SURVEY.

Reading
Hyman, Herbert H. 1972. *Secondary analysis of sample surveys*. New York: Wiley.

secondary deviance *See* LABELING THEORY.

secondary labor market *See* LABOR MARKET.

secondary relationship and secondary group *See* PRIMARY RELATIONSHIP AND SECONDARY RELATIONSHIP.

second world *See* THIRD WORLD.

sect A sect is a type of religious group that is distinguished by having broken away from a larger organization, usually a CHURCH. Members of sects are predominantly LOWER CLASS, and they have usually attained membership through conversion. The POWER STRUCTURE in a sect is informal and minimally HIERARCHICAL, and leaders are untrained and typically chosen by the members. There are few formal RITUALS and services tend to be emotional, although less intense than those in CULTS. In relation to other religious organizations, sects tend to be nonconformist and oppositional, although they are less so than cults.

Examples of sects include early Buddhism (a sect of Hinduism, as are the Sikhs today), early Christianity (a sect of Judaism), English Quakers, Mormons, and Baha'i. Christianity seems particularly prone to the formation of sects. According to Reinhold Niebuhr, this occurs when churches become well established and cater increasingly to the spiritual concerns of the middle and upper-middle classes. Their needs differ from the working and lower classes who want support and solace for their disadvantaged social position and material DEPRIVATION. As a result, disaffected lower- and working-class members leave and form their own sects.

See also AUTHORITY; DENOMINATION; ECCLESIA; RELIGION; SOCIAL CLASS.

Reading

Niebuhr, Reinhold. 1929. *The social sources of denominationalism*. New York: Holt.
Troeltsch, Ernst. [1912] 1956. *The social teachings of the Christian churches*. London: Allen and Unwin.
Wilson, Bryan. 1982. *Religion in sociological perspective*. New York: Oxford University Press.

sector model *See* URBANIZATION AND URBANISM.

secularization Secularization is a process of SOCIAL CHANGE through which the public influence of RELIGION and religious thinking declines as it is replaced by other ways of explaining reality and regulating social life. In INDUSTRIAL SOCIETIES, where secularization has progressed the farthest, SCIENCE has replaced religion as the primary approach to understanding the natural world, and civil law and the STATE have replaced religion as a source of SOCIAL CONTROL. Religious holidays have increasingly lost their religious significance and have become occasions for vacations from work or times for families to do things together. MATERIALISM has steadily replaced spirituality as a human goal, and social relationships have become increasingly rational and secondary. Even within religions there is evidence of secularization as RITUALS and SACRED texts are revised and rewritten to provide a better "fit" with the modern world.

There is some disagreement about the degree of secularization in industrial societies. The public POWER of religious institutions has certainly declined along with religious practice in all industrial societies except the United States. Also, religious explanations for natural phenomena such as evolution have lost their credibility. However, substantial majorities of POPULATIONS in industrial societies retain central religious beliefs such as the belief in life after death. In the United States, there is also evidence of renewed interest in religious and spiritual matters, especially in the form of religious FUNDAMENTALISM.

See also CIVIL RELIGION; RELIGION.

Reading

Fink, Roger, and Rodney Stark. 1992. *The churching of America, 1776–1990: Winners and losers in our religious economy.* New Brunswick, NJ: Rutgers University Press.

Stark, Rodney, and William Sims Bainbridge. 1985. *The future of religion: Secularization, revival, and cult formation.* Berkeley: University of California Press.

Wilson, Bryan. 1966. *Religion in secular society.* London: Watts.

segmented labor market *See* LABOR MARKET.

segregation and integration Segregation is the socially based separation of one category of people from another, usually perpetuating conditions of social inequality and SOCIAL OPPRESSION. Segregation most often refers to physical distributions, as in neighborhood or school segregation that concentrates people of different RACES, ETHNICITIES, SOCIAL CLASSES, or RELIGIONS in different territories, or segregated workplaces in which men and women work at different types of jobs.

Integration is the opposite of segregation. It exists when the relative number of people from various categories found in a neighborhood, school, or other units reflects their proportions in the POPULATION as a whole.

In some cases, segregation is *de jure*, or required by law, as was the case with racial segregation in South Africa until quite recently and in the United States until the mid-twentieth century. Most often, however, segregation is *de facto*, by which segregation in one area of social life (such as housing) gives rise to segregation in others (such as schools). In those areas where children attend neighborhood schools, for example, discrimination that results in segregated housing will also result in segregated schools even though neither is mandated by law.

When deprived groups are concentrated in areas from which it is difficult for them to escape – because they cannot afford it, or are limited by discrimination, or are forbidden to do so under law – the areas they inhabit are known as *ghettos*. The first known ghettos were Jewish neighborhoods of cities in Europe, the Middle East, and Africa, in which Jews were increasingly confined after the Middle Ages.

In the study of race relations, sociologists distinguish between segregation and *isolation*. Segregation occurs within an area that depends on common social services, such as towns and cities or school districts. Such an area is segregated if members of different races are not represented proportionally in various sectors of social life. If the population of a school district is 10 percent black, for example, then each school within it should have roughly 10 percent black students in order to be considered fully *integrated*. If some schools have no blacks, however, and one or two have a majority of blacks, then the schools are segregated.

Racial isolation occurs when members of different races are distributed unevenly across COMMUNITIES or other areas so that even though schools and neighborhoods technically are integrated within communities, there is little opportunity for inter-racial contact. If one city is all white and another is predominantly black, for example, then the schools within each are technically integrated since their racial composition matches that of each community as a whole. But blacks and whites have little contact with one another because they live in different communities, resulting in racial isolation. This is an increasingly prevalent pattern in the United States as whites continue to move out of inner cities. The process has led to suggestions that cities annex surrounding communities so as to achieve a greater degree of racial balance.

Reading

Massey, Douglas S., and Nancy A. Denton. 1993. *American apartheid: Segregation and the making of the underclass.* Cambridge, MA: Harvard University Press.

self From a classical sociological perspective, the self is a relatively stable set of perceptions of who we are in relation to ourselves, to OTHERS, and to SOCIAL SYSTEMS.

The self is organized around a *self-concept*, the ideas and feelings that we have about ourselves. These ideas are derived from several sources. What Charles Horton COOLEY called the *looking-glass self*, for example, is based on how we think other people see and evaluate us (which is not necessarily how they actually see us). On a more structural level, the self is also based on cultural ideas about the social STATUSES that we occupy. In this way, for example, a woman who is a mother will draw upon cultural ideas about mothers in constructing her idea of who she is. In similar ways, she may use cultural ideas about women, about various occupations, about age, and so on to contribute to an overall sense of who she is. This component of a self-concept, which is based on the social statuses that a person occupies, is known as a *social identity*.

An important part of the self is the *ideal self*, which consists of ideas about who we ought to be, rather than about who we actually are. Whether it be an "A" student, a business tycoon, a loving parent, or the perpetrator of the perfect crime, the ideal self is a standard against which we measure our self-concept – in other words, who we think we actually are. Our *self-esteem*, the level of positive or negative regard we have for ourselves, depends on how well the ideal self and the self-concept agree. Also contributing to self-esteem are evaluations that are part of the looking-glass self (we tend to think badly of ourselves if we think others think badly of us) and those that are associated with the social statuses we occupy (people in prestigious occupations will tend to feel better about themselves because they draw upon the higher cultural VALUE placed upon their positions).

The self is socially "constructed" in the sense that it is shaped through INTERACTION with other people and draws upon social materials in the form of cultural imagery and ideas. As with SOCIALIZATION in general, the individual is not a passive participant in this process and can have a powerful influence over how this process and its consequences develop.

POSTMODERNISM offers an alternative to the classical view of the self, especially through its application to FEMINISM. From this perspective, the distinction between the self and OTHERS is arbitrary and rests on the false notion that the self exists as an autonomous and separate entity. Instead, the self exists only through relationships. It is inherently relational and has no meaningful definition or existence apart from those social connections. The classical view of the self is seen as a manifestation of dualistic thinking that tends to divide everything along the lines of polar opposites – mind and body, true and false, self and other – a kind of thinking that postmodernism challenges.

Postmodernism also argues against the idea that the self is a stable unit that persists through time and space. Instead, the self is seen as fragmented and split (between, for example, its conscious and unconscious aspects) and continually in the process of being constructed.

See also MIND; OTHER; PHENO-MENOLOGY.

Reading

Cooley, Charles Horton. 1927. *Life and the student*. New York: Knopf.

Mead, George Herbert. 1934. *Mind, self, and society*. Chicago: University of Chicago Press.

Rosenberg, Morris. 1979. *Conceiving the self*. New York: Basic Books.

Tong, Rosemarie. 1998. *Feminist thought*, 2nd ed. Boulder, CO: Westview Press.

self-concept *See* SELF.

self-esteem *See* SELF.

self-fulfilling prophecy First described by Robert K. MERTON, a self-fulfilling prophecy is a cultural BELIEF that becomes true because people act as though it is true already. When teachers treat MIDDLE-CLASS students as if they will do better than working- and LOWER-CLASS students, the middle-class students tend to perform better and achieve more than they otherwise would. Similarly, when women or other MINORITIES are denied educational opportunities based on the belief that they lack ability and motivation, the denial itself may produce just that result. In some cases, a self-fulfilling prophecy takes the form of a genuine prediction, as when rumors of an impending banking crisis produce a run on banks and their subsequent collapse, or when rumors in stock markets set off waves of selling that produce the very collapse that has been predicted.

Although most often associated with the above kinds of cases, the concept of self-fulfilling prophecy points toward a more general and in some ways important point about the SOCIAL CONSTRUCTION OF REALITY. In the most basic sense, the function of cultural beliefs in social life is not only to represent reality but to further its creation and re-creation. The shared belief that a SOCIETY is a DEMOCRACY, for example, is an integral part of ensuring that it maintains, if not improves upon, existing democratic INSTITUTIONS. In this sense, it is a social function of all cultural beliefs to produce self-fulfilling prophecies.

See also BELIEF; CULTURE; STEREO-TYPE.

Reading

Merton, Robert K. 1968. *Social theory and social structure*, rev. and exp. ed. New York: Free Press.

semiotics (also called *semiology*) Semiotics is the study of signs and their use in social life. A sign uses a *signifier* such as a word in order to point to or represent a *signified* which is the mental image we have of an object, idea, or experience. The word banana, for example, is a signifier, a collection of letters arranged in a particular way that, when pronounced, produce a particular sound. A banana is an object (or referent) that we can experience and form mental images of in various ways, by looking at its color and shape, for example, or by eating it. Both the word and the image can exist in their own right. To a non-English-speaking person eating a banana, there is no connection between the word and the image. Once the two are associated with each other, however, the resulting pairing of signifier and signified is a sign.

Because any given signifier can be associated with any number of signifieds, signs can be quite complex and multileveled. A picture of a ship, for example, can be seen as a direct (or "iconic") signifier of the ship. In a more indirect (or "arbitrary") sense, the picture can be associated with feelings of adventurousness and exploration or, in the case of warships, of national might and resolve (as in "Britannia rule the waves"). The flag shown flying from the ship's mast, however, is potentially far more complex. As a signifier, a flag can merely point to a particular nation-state as distinguished from other nation-states (as in the array of flags flown outside the United Nations building in New York). A flag can also be associated with particular histories, cultural VALUES, and feelings ranging from patriotic love to the most intense hatred. From this perspective, something as seemingly simple as a flag can be nested in a complex web of meaning and association, all of which is included in semiotics as a field of study.

See also CULTURE; DECONSTRUCTION; HERMENEUTICS; LANGUAGE; SAUSSURE; STRUCTURALISM AND POST-STRUCTURALISM; SYMBOL.

Reading

Barthes, Roland. 1976. *The pleasure of the text*. London: Cape.

Hawkes, T. 1977. *Structuralism and semiotics*. London: Methuen.

Manning, Peter. 1987. *Semiotics and fieldwork*. Newbury Park, CA: Sage Publications.

semiperipheral society   *See* WORLD SYSTEM.

sentiment   *See* ATTITUDE.

serfs   *See* PEASANTS.

serial monogamy   *See* MARRIAGE RULES.

service class   *See* CORPORATE CLASS.

sex and gender   Although gender is a word with a long history of diverse usages, its sociological meaning refers to cultural ideas that construct images and expectations of females and males. This distinguishes gender from sex, whose scope is limited to biological differences such as reproductive function and secondary characteristics such as body hair and breast development. In some ways this is a misleading distinction because it ignores how sex is also a socially constructed set of ideas shaped by CULTURE. Western cultures, for example, typically define sex in terms of two sexes, female and male; but there are cultures that identify more than two categories. In this sense, the social importance of sex as a set of categories lies not in some objective reality that language merely names, but in what we think sex is as defined by cultural ideas.

Gender is usually defined around ideas about male and female personality traits and behavioral tendencies that take the form of opposites. Taken as sets of traits and tendencies, these make up *femininity* and

279

masculinity. Masculinity, for example, typically includes aggressiveness, logic, emotional inexpressiveness, and dominance, while femininity is associated with peacefulness, intuitiveness, emotional expressiveness, and submissiveness. Most cultures include multiple versions of femininity or masculinity, but one is typically regarded as having dominance or HEGEMONY over the rest (hence terms such as *hegemonic masculinity*). Among gay men, for example, definitions of masculinity may be quite different from those found in the predominantly heterosexual mainstream culture.

Although the evidence is clear that such ideas about the sexes are cultural, their sociological importance is less clear. Traits typically attributed to males and females, for example, do not in fact describe most people accurately. Wives may be relatively submissive in relation to their husbands, but, as mothers, not so in relation to their children. In this sense, to describe women as "submissive" confuses personality with cultural expectations associated with particular ROLES and social situations.

Others argue that the common emphasis on masculinity and femininity as key factors in explanations of gender inequality is misplaced. *Androgyny*, for example, is a concept describing a mixture of feminine and masculine personality traits, and has been proposed by some feminists as part of the solution to gender inequality. Critics, however, argue that the oppression of women is not based on personality differences, but on the social organization of PATRIARCHY and its INSTITUTIONS, from the division of labor in the FAMILY to the competitive, exploitative nature of CAPITALISM.

From this perspective, the concepts of masculinity and femininity serve mythic and SOCIAL CONTROL functions that reinforce male dominance. This is revealed in the selective way in which they are applied. When men are tender and physically affectionate with their children, for example, they are rarely criticized as unmasculine; but when they are this way with other men, masculine IDEOLOGY is invoked to bring them into line with the requirements of male dominance. Similarly, women are likely to be criticized if they assert POWER or dominance in relation to husbands and other men, but not if they behave in this way in relation to their children.

In the study of gender, the significance of femininity and masculinity lies in their relation to *gender roles* (sometimes referred to as *sex roles*). These are sets of expectations and other ideas about how females and males are supposed to think, feel, appear, and behave in relation to other people. In Western societies, for example, men who appear and behave in culturally masculine ways are seen as conforming to their gender role.

There is some disagreement about both the existence of gender roles and their importance for understanding gender inequality. "Feminine" women, for example, are expected to defer to husbands, but not to brothers or sons, even though in each case the status they occupy – wife, sister, or mother – is inherently female. This suggests that there is no distinct male role or female role (just as there are no distinct race roles or class roles) but only loosely connected sets of ideas about men and women which can be invoked for various purposes, including social control and maintaining PATRIARCHY as a male-dominated system.

More recent work, especially from a POSTMODERN perspective, has greatly expanded ideas about sex and gender. Gender, for example, can be seen as the name of a social position that locates women and men in relation to a system of gender privilege, rather than as a collection of personality traits or a particular body type defined in relation to reproduction. It can also be viewed as an ongoing process ("doing gender") rather than as something people *are* in some concrete sense. In other words, gender names something we *do* in ways that can shift from one situation or time to another – in how we dress or speak or otherwise present ourselves to others and behave – and doesn't simply name something fixed and concrete about who we are or the social position we occupy.

The concept of gender has itself been criticized for assuming that its categories – female and male – exist as a homogeneous whole. When we use the word "woman," for example, we tend to assume that we are referring to a homogeneous category of people who have enough in common to justify grouping them together under a single term (such as "women's music" or "the oppression of women," or "women's experience"). Some post-modernists argue, however, that there is so much diversity of experience among women – such as by RACE, AGE, SOCIAL CLASS, ETHNICITY, and sexual orientation – that to refer to them all as "women" distorts the reality of women's lives. Taken to its extreme, the argument can conclude that in some ways, there is no such thing as a "woman" or a "man" in

the unitary sense usually associated with those words. Other postmodern feminists take a less extreme view and argue instead for the need of an ongoing awareness of the socially constructed nature of such categories and the diversity of human experience that they include.

See also ANDROCRACY; IDEOLOGY; STRATIFICATION AND INEQUALITY.

Reading

Carrigan, Tim, Robert Connell, and John Lee. 1985. "Hard and heavy: Toward a new sociology of masculinity." *Theory and Society* 14: 551–603. Reprinted in *Beyond patriarchy: Essays by men on pleasure, power, and change*, edited by Michael Kaufman, 139–92. New York: Oxford University Press.

Epstein, Cynthia Fuchs. 1988. *Deceptive distinctions: Sex, gender, and the social order*. New Haven, CT: Yale University Press.

Hess, B., and M. Ferree, eds. 1987. *Analyzing gender: A handbook of social science research*. Newbury Park, CA: Sage Publications.

Kessler, Suzanne J., and Wendy McKenna. 1985. *Gender: An ethnomethodological approach*. Chicago: University of Chicago Press.

Mead, Margaret. [1935] 1963. *Sex and temperament in three primitive societies*. New York: William Morrow.

Tong, Rosemarie. 1998. *Feminist thought: A more comprehensive introduction*. Boulder, CO: Westview Press.

sexism Sexism is most often associated with PREJUDICE based on gender, with actions based on GENDER prejudice, and with people who hold prejudiced BELIEFS, VALUES, and ATTITUDES all described as sexist. So, a male manager who discriminates against women or sexually harasses them at work can be called "sexist," as can the cultural belief that men are superior to women.

Sociologically, a more useful definition borrows from David Wellman's definition of RACISM as something that encompasses not only prejudice, but any ACTION or characteristic of SOCIAL SYSTEMS that has the effect of supporting race privilege, regardless of the intentions or ideas people hold about race. The key test of whether something is sexist, then, lies in its consequences: if it supports male privilege, then it is by definition sexist. I specify "male privilege" because in every known SOCIETY where gender inequality exists, males are privileged over females.

See also SOCIAL OPPRESSION; SEX AND GENDER.

sex ratio   In a POPULATION, the sex ratio is the number of males for every 100 females. Sex ratios affect various areas of social life, including the availability of potential marriage partners and the composition of the labor force. Although sex ratios among newborns are typically around 105 males per 100 females, at older ages sex ratios can change considerably. In the United States, the sex ratio is 105 among those less than 5 years old but drops to 45 among those over the age of 85. Overall, a population with a high proportion of elderly will tend to have a low sex ratio because women tend to outlive men. High birth rates, by contrast, result in a younger population and, hence, a higher sex ratio. Since men are more likely than women to migrate, areas that receive migrants tend to have higher sex ratios than do areas from which people migrate.

Reading
Guttentag, Marcia, and Paul F. Secord. 1983. *Too many women? The sex ratio*

question. Beverly Hills, CA: Sage Publications.
Kanter, Rosabeth Moss. 1977. "Some effects of proportions on group life: Skewed sex ratios and responses to token women." *American Journal of Sociology* 82: 965–90.
Shryock, Henry S., and Jacob Siegel and Associates. 1976. *The methods and materials of demography*. New York: Academic Press.

sex role   *See* SEX AND GENDER.

shaman   *See* ANIMISM.

shame and guilt   Shame and guilt are both mechanisms of SOCIAL CONTROL, but they operate on different principles. Shame is a punishment imposed from without – for example, when members of a COMMUNITY ridicule, scold, or ostracize someone for misbehaving. This kind of punishment can be extended to relatives of the offender, which causes them to feel a strong investment in controlling the behavior of FAMILY members.

In contrast, guilt is primarily an internal psychological process. When we internalize social standards and VALUES as part of being socialized, we may also develop the capacity to punish ourselves for our own misdeeds by feeling badly about ourselves and otherwise making ourselves feel varying degrees of misery. The distinction between shame and guilt is sociologically significant because shame tends to operate in simpler systems in which it is possible to observe people's behavior directly, while guilt is more common in larger, more complex systems in which observation is more difficult. Shaming is rarely used in urban SOCIETIES, for example, but it is more common in small communities such as preindustrial tribes or

isolated communities such as the Amish in the United States.
See also DEVIANCE; SANCTION; SOCIAL CONTROL.

Reading
Lynd, Helen. 1958. *On shame and the search for identity*. New York: Harcourt Brace.
Scheff, Thomas J. 1987. "Shame and conformity: The deference-emotion system." *American Sociological Review* 53(3): 395–406.

sharecropping Sharecropping was an economic arrangement found primarily in the American South following the Civil War and the legal end of slavery. Landlords allowed tenants to cultivate portions of land in return for a share of the crops they raised. Although it generally brought a mediocre return to the landlord, to the sharecropper it was a highly exploitative system that in many ways continued the institution of slavery in a modified form. Black tenants almost always had to borrow from landlords in order to invest in each new crop, and the mountain of debt they accumulated made it impossible for them to own land and ensured their virtual enslavement to the sharecropping system.

Reading
Du Bois, W. E. B. [1903] 1996. *The souls of black folk*. New York: Penguin Books.
Royce, Edward. 1993. *The origins of southern sharecropping*. Philadelphia: Temple University Press.

sign *See* SEMIOTICS.

significance, statistical *See* HYPOTHESIS AND HYPOTHESIS TESTING.

significant other *See* OTHER.

signifier and signified *See* SEMIOTICS.

simple random sample A simple random sample is a SAMPLE design in which selections are drawn from a POPULATION in a way that gives every member and every combination of members an equal chance of being selected. The classic way of selecting such a sample is to assign a number to each member of the population and then to select the sample by choosing numbers from a random number table.

Virtually all of the mathematics of STATISTICAL INFERENCE assumes that DATA are gathered with a simple random sample design, but in practice this is often impractical and prohibitively expensive. As an alternative, researchers have devised a variety of sample designs that, while not strictly random, are approximations that entail acceptable levels of ERROR that are more than offset by the improvements in practicality and cost.
See also COMPLEX SAMPLE; ERROR; SAMPLING ERROR; SYSTEMATIC SAMPLE.

Reading
Kalton, Graham. 1984. *Introduction to survey sampling*. Beverly Hills, CA: Sage Publications.
Kish, Leslie. 1965. *Survey sampling*. New York: Wiley.

single-parent family *See* FAMILY.

situational status A situational STATUS is a position in a SOCIAL SYSTEM that is occupied only as long as someone is actually in a particular situation and actively performing a ROLE associated with it. In this sense, a situational status differs from other social statuses that people are associated with regardless of the situation they may be in at the moment. Statuses such as "African," "university graduate," and "married," are social positions that people may occupy wherever they go; they are attached to them as social characteristics; they are not "university graduates" during some days of the week but not others. But a situational status is just that: a person occupies it when entering a situation (such as assuming the status of "passenger" immediately upon boarding a bus) and drops it when leaving that situation. In short, in order to occupy a situational status, a person must be actively involved in a situation.

skewness   *See* SYMMETRY.

slope   *See* REGRESSION ANALYSIS.

small group   *See* PRIMARY RELATIONSHIP AND SECONDARY RELATIONSHIP.

social   The term social can be applied to anything that is related to SOCIAL SYSTEMS, their characteristics, and people's participation in them. When two friends talk, their behavior is social insofar as they draw upon CULTURE for LANGUAGE, their expectations of each other, their understanding of what constitutes a friendship, and so on. Note that what is social is not merely something that involves or affects many people. All human beings eat food, for example, but this does not make eating per se social. Cultural ideas that influence our choice of what to eat and how and when to eat it, however, make those aspects of eating social. In similar ways, starvation, hunger, and satiation are not in themselves social even though they involve billions of people. But the economic, political, and other social arrangements through which WEALTH and INCOME, and access to food are distributed give these human conditions a profoundly social aspect.

See also   INSTITUTION.

Reading

Mills, C. Wright. 1959. *The sociological imagination.* New York: Oxford University Press.

social category   A social category is a collection of people who occupy the same social STATUS, such as "woman," "manager," or "university student." Although members of the same social category may as a result share characteristics such as BELIEFS and VALUES, they do not necessarily identify the category as a meaningful entity to which they belong (if they did, they would constitute a COLLECTIVITY). Nor do they engage in regular patterns of INTERACTION (in contrast to GROUPS). In spite of the women's movement, for example, many women do not think of "woman" as being anything more than a social and biological characteristic; they do not consider it a larger entity with which they identify and feel some sense of solidarity. In contrast, many feminists regard "women" as the name of a recognizable body of people to whom they feel a sense of loyalty.

Social categories can be transformed into collectivities or groups by creating a sense of shared identity and by increasing the amount of interaction among members. SOCIAL MOVEMENTS typically begin in this way when members of oppressed MINORITIES identify their disadvantaged status as not merely a personal characteristic but as an indicator of their membership in a larger social entity.

See also AGGREGATE; SOCIAL.

social change

social change Social change is any alteration in the cultural, structural, POPULATION, or ecological characteristics of a SOCIAL SYSTEM such as a SOCIETY. Sociological interest in explaining and predicting patterns of change began in the eighteenth and nineteenth centuries with the social upheaval that accompanied the INDUSTRIAL REVOLUTION and the political revolutions that surrounded the development of DEMOCRACY. Although these early efforts focused on identifying universal laws that would account for the complexity of social change, this has since been abandoned in favor of THEORIES more narrowly focused on particular aspects of social life, such as POLITICS, RELIGION, ECONOMY, TECHNOLOGY, and the FAMILY.

In a basic sense, attention to social change is inherent in all sociological work simply because social systems are always in the process of change. In other words, to understand how social systems work or hold together, we must on some level understand how they change or fall apart.

See also CLASS CONFLICT AND CLASS STRUGGLE; COHORT; CULTURAL LAG; DIFFUSION; HISTORICAL SOCIOLOGY; MODERNIZATION THEORY; REBELLION, POLITICAL; REVOLUTION; SOCIAL EVOLUTION; SOCIAL MOVEMENT; STRUCTURAL LAG; SUCCESSION, ECOLOGICAL; WORLD SYSTEM.

Reading
Boudon, Raymond. 1986. *Theories of social change*. Cambridge: Polity Press.
Giddens, Anthony. 1986. *The constitution of society*. Berkeley: University of California Press.

Smelser, Neil J. 1958. *Social change in the Industrial Revolution*. London: Routledge and Kegan Paul.

social class Social class, one of the most important concepts in the study of STRATIFICATION, is a SOCIAL CATEGORY and division resulting from the unequal DISTRIBUTION of rewards and resources such as WEALTH, POWER, and PRESTIGE. Sociologists define social class primarily on the basis of how these divisions are identified.

Karl MARX argued that class divisions are based on differences in people's relationships to the process of production, especially their ownership or control over the MEANS OF PRODUCTION (such as machinery, land, and factories). Under CAPITALISM, the means of production are owned and controlled by one class – the *bourgeoisie* or capitalist class – whose members do not actually use the means of production to produce wealth. Instead, this work is performed by members of the *working class* or *proletariat* who produce wealth but neither own nor control any means of production. Since capitalists do not themselves actually produce wealth, their prosperity is necessarily dependent on the work of others. The capitalists thus control the means of production and, by extension, the wealth that is produced. Workers meet their needs through the wages they are paid in exchange for selling their time (or LABOR POWER). From a Marxist perspective, wages represent only a portion of the VALUE of the wealth that workers produce. Hence, class and class relations are based on tension and struggle over conflicting interests.

The proletariat and bourgeoisie were not the only classes Marx

285

identified, although they are the most important. Others included the *aristocracy* and the *landed gentry* (both of whom were regarded as unimportant because their influence would be nil in industrial societies), and the *lumpenproletariat*, or *underclass* (which includes today's homeless population), who have no relationship to the process of production at all. (For this reason, some sociologists argue that the underclass is too fragmented and transient to constitute a class.) More recent Marxist thinkers have identified new class distinctions to account for the rise of the *managerial class* (who generally do not own means of production but control them in the interests of the capitalist class) and professional workers (such as college professors and government officials). These classes work for wages but nonetheless enjoy a considerable degree of autonomy, which distinguishes them from other members of the working class.

Max WEBER identified class distinctions according to three dimensions of inequality: (1) class, (2) POWER, and (3) PRESTIGE. Weber used the term "class" to refer to LIFE CHANGES, or the ability of people to get what they want and need in the marketplace, to buy goods and services, to shield themselves from others, and so on. From this perspective, class position rests on a great many more factors than relations to the means of production – from occupational prestige, education, experience, and skill and intelligence levels, to inheritance, luck, ambition, and FAMILY background.

Weber's second dimension of inequality is the distribution of power, especially in relation to complex organizations such as corporations, governments, unions, and other SOCIAL SYSTEMS. Weber used the term *party* to indicate power differences. This refers not merely to political parties but to the general way that power is bureaucratically organized in INDUSTRIAL SOCIETIES, making individuals relatively powerless unless they have access to such organizations. A few sociologists argue that location in the distribution of power is the primary determinant of class position, rather than economic position or prestige.

Weber's third dimension is the distribution of prestige, or the degree of social honor, status, or deference that people enjoy in relation to others. This dimension has been most studied in the United States, especially in relation to occupational prestige as a dimension for measuring SOCIAL MOBILITY. Unlike the other two dimensions, prestige is a resource whose distribution must be unequal in order for it to exist, since deference must run from higher to lower positions just as honor elevates some above others.

Weber's multidimensional approach not only broadens the analysis of class but helps identify the complexities of class position and relations, especially if relationships are viewed in the context of the three dimensions of inequality and the factors that affect them. Although power, prestige, and wealth often go together, to some degree they vary independently. For example, a leader might rank high on power and prestige but relatively low on wealth, just as wealth does not automatically bring with it power or prestige.

In addition to the determinants of class location and the dynamics of relations between classes, fundamental issues in the study of class include questions about where to draw lines between different classes (or, in the view of some, whether such lines exist outside sociological models of stratification); the relative invisibility of women in class analysis since substantial (although rapidly declining) percentages of women are not employed outside the home and yet contribute considerably to the maintenance and reproduction of workers; and the question of whether the family or the individual should be the main unit of class analysis.

See also ALIENATION; BLUE-COLLAR WORKER AND WHITE-COLLAR WORKER; CASTE; CLASS CONSCIOUSNESS AND FALSE CONSCIOUSNESS; CLASS INTEREST; CORPORATE CLASS; EMBOURGEOISEMENT; LABOR AND LABOR POWER; LORENZ CURVE; LOWER CLASS; MIDDLE CLASS: PRESTIGE; PROLETARIANIZATION; SOCIAL MOBILITY; UPPER CLASS.

Reading

Bendix, Reinhard, and Seymour Martin Lipset, eds. 1966. *Class, status, and power.* New York: Free Press.

Marx, Karl. [1867] 1975. *Capital: A critique of political economy.* New York: International Publishers.

Weber, Max. 1946. *From Max Weber: Essays in sociology.* Edited and translated by Hans H. Gerth and C. Wright Mills. New York: Oxford University Press.

Wright, Erik Olin. 1985. *Classes.* New York: Schocken Books.

social closure   A concept first introduced by Max WEBER, social closure refers to the practice of preserving privilege by restricting other people's access to resources and rewards. It can take many forms, from residential SEGREGATION to exclusion from professional training and licensing, MARRIAGE RULES that forbid unions

with anyone from outside the privileged group, and keeping women out of "old boys' networks." Excluded groups often respond with various forms of what Frank Parkin called "usurpation" designed to gain the access that social closure would deny to them. Affirmative action programs in the U.S., for example, are a form of usurpation.

See also CASTE; SOCIAL CLASS; BOUNDARIES.

Reading

Murphy, Raymond. 1988. *Social closure: The theory of monopoly and exclusion.* New York: Oxford University Press.

Parkin, Frank. 1974. "Strategies of social closure in class formation." In *The social analysis of class structure,* edited by Frank Parkin, London: Tavistock.

Weber, Max. 1946. *From Max Weber: Essays in sociology,* edited by Hans H. Gerth and C. Wright Mills. New York: Oxford University Press.

social   conflict   *See*   CONFLICT PERSPECTIVE.

social construction of reality   *See* PHENOMENOLOGY AND PHENOMENOLOGICAL SOCIOLOGY.

social contract   Social contract is an idea that has been used as a metaphor to describe the relationship between CITIZENS and the STATE. The seventeenth-century philosopher Thomas Hobbes saw the state as a necessary INSTITUTION to keep people from doing harm to one another. It was a protection, however, that required people to surrender some of their freedom and autonomy to the state. This generated the idea of a contract, of protection in return for submission to AUTHORITY, with the understanding that both parties – state and citizenry – must live up to their part of the bargain without abusing the terms of the agreement. People do not, of course, actually enter into such a contract in a conscious way, and this is not how the state actually came into being; hence, the metaphoric nature of the concept.

The idea of a SOCIAL CONTRACT has played an important role in discussions of citizens' rights in relation to the state as well as the basis for the state's LEGITIMACY as an institution, especially as articulated during the ENLIGHTENMENT by Jean-Jacques Rousseau. Others, Talcott PARSONS among them, have argued that social COHESION rests on a concensus over VALUES, not on a social contract.

Reading

Hobbes, Thomas. [1651] 1962. *Leviathan*. Glasgow: Fontana.

Parsons, Talcott. 1937. *The structure of social action*. New York: McGraw-Hill.

Rousseau, Jean Jacques. [1762] 1950. *The social contract*. New York: E. P. Dutton.

social control Social control is a concept that refers to the ways in which people's thoughts, feelings, appearance, and behavior are regulated in SOCIAL SYSTEMS. To some degree, control is exerted through various forms of coercion, from the parent's ability to physically restrain a child to the AUTHORITY of criminal justice systems to imprison those convicted of crimes and the authority of physicians to administer drugs that make "difficult" patients more "manageable."

Coercion, however, is generally ineffective as the sole means of social control. Far more important is the process of SOCIALIZATION through which people come to identify with a social system and its VALUES and NORMS, and thereby acquire a stake

in maintaining these as well as their sense of belonging to the system. Fear of ridicule or exclusion, for example, is a powerful inducement to conform, as is the risk of being shamed. Also important is the inducement of guilt, achieved through the internalization of moral standards during socialization. Underlying all of these is the fundamental BELIEF that social systems and their norms are legitimate and therefore binding on us as participants.

See also CONFORMITY; DEVIANCE; NORMS; POWER; SELF; SHAME AND GUILT; SOCIALIZATION; SOCIAL ORDER.

Reading

Cohen, S. 1985. *Visions of social control*. Cambridge, England: Polity Press.

Lemert, Edwin M. 1951. *Human deviance, social problems, and social control*. New York: McGraw-Hill.

Parsons, Talcott. 1951. *The social system*. Glencoe, IL: Free Press.

social Darwinism Social Darwinism, a nineteenth-century adaptation of Charles Darwin's theory of evolution, is a theoretical explanation of human social life in general and social inequality in particular. As argued by Herbert SPENCER in Britain and, to a greater extent, by William Graham SUMNER in the United States, the development of SOCIETIES resembles natural evolution, with competition among various groups (racial, ethnic, class, and so on) supplying the necessary dynamic for society to progress through the victory of superior groups over the inferior and less "fit." Regarding social inequality, social Darwinism attributed the gap between the wealthy and the poor primarily to the greater "fitness" of the wealthy to survive and thrive. Society was likened to the natural world, ruled by competition and the principle of "survival of the fittest," a phrase coined by Spencer, not Darwin.

As an argument, social Darwinism is deeply flawed and has little if any credibility among contemporary social scientists. In one sense, social Darwinism is based on a tautology because it measures fitness in terms of what fitness is supposed to explain: the wealthy are wealthy because they are more fit, and the evidence of their greater fitness is their WEALTH. This argument is true by definition as long as we accept the idea that possessing great wealth is a valid measure of fitness (rather than an accident of being born into a wealthy family, for example). As such, it could always be used to justify the status quo, beginning with racial and other forms of SOCIAL OPPRESSION and IMPERIALISM.

See also SOCIAL EVOLUTION; SOCIO-BIOLOGY.

Reading

Hofstadter, Richard. 1955. *Social Darwinism in American thought*. Boston: Beacon.
Sumner, William Graham. 1883. *What social classes owe to each other*. New York: Harper.

social determinism See DETERMINISM AND REDUCTIONISM.

social distance Social distance is the degree to which people are willing to accept and associate with those having different social characteristics. An unwillingness to live next door to a FAMILY of a different RACE, for example, would indicate a high degree of social distance, while a willingness to marry someone of a different race would indicate an extremely low level of social distance.

One way to measure social distance is through use of the *Bogardus social distance scale* (named for Emery

S. Bogardus, the American sociologist). The scale is based on a series of questions asking respondents whether they would be willing to tolerate various levels of social distance – from living in the same neighborhood, to inviting to dinner, to marrying. The assumption is that respondents willing to tolerate a given level of distance will also tolerate greater levels. In other words, if they are willing to marry someone of a different race, the scale assumes they would also be willing to have them over to dinner. A scale with this characteristic is known as a *Guttman scale*.

See also ATTITUDE SCALE; SEGREGATION AND INTEGRATION.

social evolution According to some early social theorists such as Herbert SPENCER, social evolution is a process through which SOCIETIES develop in predictable ways that generally reflect progress toward "higher" or more nearly perfect forms of social life. Initially, evolutionary theorists coming on the heels of Charles Darwin and his theories of biological evolution argued that social evolution consisted of *unilinear change* that followed a prescribed path – for example, from simpler to more complex forms of social organization. *Cyclical change* is a variation on unilinear theory developed by Oswald Spengler and Arnold J. Toynbee. They argued that societies change according to cycles of rise, decline, and fall just as individual people are born, mature, grow old, and die. The theory of cyclical change was prompted to some degree by the events of the 1914–18 world war, which turned what had appeared to be a new age of enlightenment and prosperity into a nightmare of unprecedented slaughter and destruction. Related to cyclical change theory is Pitirim SOROKIN'S idea of *immanent change*. Sorokin argued that particular elements such as cultural VALUES play an important part in the direction of change in societies. For example, the value placed upon accumulation of material WEALTH in many societies has led to an emphasis on INDUSTRIALIZATION, trade, and other means of achieving it. Sorokin believed that in the long run certain elements become overdeveloped and lead to extreme conditions in which they lose their usefulness and precipitate SOCIAL CHANGE, such as reacting against materialism with a resurgence of interest in spiritual values.

A contrast to these ideas is found in *multilinear theory*, which is a more complex and, in the eyes of most sociologists, more realistic approach. It does identify some social trends as nearly universal: the progression from smaller to larger, simpler to more complex, rural to urban, and low-technology to higher-technology. But multilinear theory recognizes that these can come about in various ways (perhaps with "stages" experienced by some societies but being skipped altogether by others) and with distinct consequences, only some of which may be characterized as progress. For example, many THIRD WORLD (nonindustrialized) countries have become highly urbanized and have greatly lowered their DEATH RATES (and increased POPULATION growth rates as a result) without becoming industrialized. Countries such as China and Iraq, however, are nonindustrialized but nonetheless have access to high TECHNOLOGY such as computers and sophisticated weapons of mass destruction.

Multilinear theory is related to what is known as the *episodic approach*, which stresses the importance of accidents and unique historical, social, and environmental circumstances that help to explain a particular course of social change. Although episodic THEORY was originally developed in opposition to evolutionary theory, many argue that especially in multilinear theory there is room to consider episodic factors.

See also SOCIAL CHANGE; SOCIAL DARWINISM.

Reading

Lenski, Gerhard E., Jean Lenski, and Patrick Nolan. 1998. *Human societies*, 8th ed. New York: McGraw-Hill.

Giddens, Anthony. 1981. *A contemporary critique of historical materialism*. London: Macmillan.

Sorokin, Pitirim A. 1937–1941. *Social and cultural dynamics*, vol. 4. New York: American Book Company.

Spencer, Herbert. 1891. *The study of sociology*. New York: Appleton.

——. 1896. *The principles of sociology*. New York: Appleton.

Spengler, Oswald. 1926. *The decline of the West*. New York: Knopf.

social fact According to Émile DURKHEIM, a social fact is a cultural or structural characteristic of a SOCIAL SYSTEM, which we experience as external to us and having an influence and authority that amount to more than the sum of the intentions and motivations of the people who happen to be participating in those systems at a particular time. A "corporation," for example, has an existence as a system that involves the people who work in it but is in many ways independent of them. A corporation may go bankrupt and go out of existence altogether, but this does not mean the same fate must befall the people who work there. The corporation, then, with its CULTURE and structure that define it as a system, is a set of social facts that constrain and shape the lives of the people who participate in it. In part, sociology originated as a response to an individualistic, psychological perspective on human life (UTILITARIANISM) that dominated thinking in nineteenth-century Europe. Durkheim argued in particular that the collective nature of social life could not reduce the individuals' experience or representations of it, that experience of the law as an individual, for example, could not account for the law as a social phenomenon.

Durkheim argued that social facts must be regarded as something to be examined and understood much as if they were things, that they could be explained only in relation to other social facts. This was a major contribution to what was to become modern sociology.

See also AGENCY AND STRUCTURE; ATOMISM AND HOLISM; INTERPRETIVE SOCIOLOGY; METHODOLOGICAL INDIVIDUALISM.

Reading
Durkheim, Émile. [1895] 1938. *The rules of the sociological method.* New York: Free Press.
——. [1924] 1974. *Sociology and philosophy.* New York: Free Press.

social forecasting *See* PREDICTION AND PROJECTION.

social identity *See* SELF.

social inequality *See* STRATIFICATION AND INEQUALITY.

social institution *See* INSTITUTION.

social interaction *See* INTERACTION.

social mobility Social mobility is upward or downward movement in a stratified society. Mobility can be *intergenerational* (comparing people with their parents) or *intragenerational* (comparing positions across individual lifetimes), although the former has been of far more interest to sociologists than the latter.

The measurement and analysis of mobility patterns depend a great deal on how SOCIAL CLASS position is measured. In Europe and the United States, mobility studies usually define class in terms of occupational PRESTIGE, especially as measured by the distinction between BLUE-COLLAR AND WHITE-COLLAR jobs. There is little attention to changes in WEALTH AND INCOME, POWER, or ownership and control over the MEANS OF PRODUCTION (nor, until very recently, has research included mobility among women). This is problematic because occupational prestige is only one dimension of inequality and, in the eyes of many sociologists, a relatively minor one. It is also problematic because it ignores the top end of the STRATIFICATION system, the UPPER CLASS, whose position neither depends upon nor is defined by occupational prestige.

In general, patterns of upward or downward mobility have two causes rooted in the structure of SOCIAL SYSTEMS. *Structural mobility* is caused by a shift in the DISTRIBUTION of occupations. In Europe and the United States, there has been a general upward trend in occupational prestige simply because low prestige blue-collar jobs are disappearing and being replaced by low-level white-collar occupations. With fewer blue-collar jobs available for the children of blue-collar parents, the only alternative to unemployment is some degree of upward mobility.

Circulation mobility includes all upward and downward movement due to factors other than changes in the occupational structure. This form of mobility is also known as *exchange mobility* because those who move upward are often replaced by those who move downward.

Mobility patterns are often displayed in mobility tables that take two different forms. Inflow tables look at a group of workers and identify their origins, such as the percentage of upper-nonmanual male workers whose fathers have lower-prestige occupations. An outflow table might look at a generation of mothers and identify the class positions of their daughters, such as the percentage of mothers with lower-nonmanual occupations, whose daughters have upper-nonmanual jobs. Such tables give an idea of the balance between upward and downward mobility, the class origins from which there is the least and greatest amount of upward and downward mobility, and the patterns of recruitment from which the various classes draw their current members.

Societies differ in how open or closed their stratification systems are. CASTE systems, for example, allow no mobility at all, while class systems allow limited mobility below the level of the upper class. In general, mobility research in INDUSTRIAL capitalist societies finds that although there is considerable structural and circulation mobility, it usually involves relatively small moves and has little if any effect on the overall class structure.

See also BLUE-COLLAR WORKER AND WHITE-COLLAR WORKER; CASTE; SPONSORED MOBILITY AND CONTEST MOBILITY; STRATIFICATION AND INEQUALITY.

Reading

Blau, Peter M., and Otis Dudley Duncan. 1978. *The American occupational structure*. New York: Wiley.

Kurz, K., and W. Muller. 1987. "Class mobility in the industrial world." *Annual Review of Sociology* 13: 417–42.

Mach, B., and W. Wesolowski. 1986. *Social mobility and social structure*. London and New York: Routledge and Kegan Paul.

social movement A social movement is a sustained, organized collective effort that focuses on some aspect of SOCIAL CHANGE. *A reform movement* tries to improve conditions within an existing SOCIAL SYSTEM without changing the fundamental character of the system itself. An example would be the attempt to equalize the tax burden in a SOCIETY. A reform movement contrasts sharply with a REVOLUTIONARY movement, whose purpose it is to alter the basic structural or cultural characteristics of a system – for example, by trying to change from STATE SOCIALISM to CAPITALISM. A *resistance movement* is organized not to promote social change but rather to oppose it. In the United States, for example, a resistance movement opposes changes in laws that guarantee women the right to abortion.

Social movements have always been of great sociological interest because they are a major source of social change and social conflict.

See also CLASSICAL SOCIAL MOVEMENT THEORY; POLITICAL PROCESS THEORY; RESOURCE MOBILIZATION THEORY; REVOLUTION.

Reading

Turner, Ralph H., and Lewis M. Killian. 1987. *Collective behavior*, 3rd ed. Englewood Cliffs, NJ: Prentice-Hall.

Zurcher, Louis A., and David A. Snow. 1981. "Collective behavior: Social movements." In *Social psychology: Sociological perspectives*, edited by Morris Rosenberg and Ralph H. Turner. New York: Basic Books.

social oppression Social oppression is a concept that describes a relationship of dominance and subordination between categories of people in which one benefits from the systematic abuse, EXPLOITATION, and injustice directed toward the other. The relationship between whites and blacks in the United States and South Africa, between SOCIAL CLASSES in many INDUSTRIAL SOCIETIES, between men and women in most societies, between Protestants and Catholics in Northern Ireland – all have elements of social oppression in that the organization of social life enables those who dominate to oppress others.

Because social oppression describes relationships between social categories, it should not be confused with the oppressive behavior of individuals. A white man may not himself actively participate in oppressive behavior directed at blacks or women, for example, but he nonetheless benefits from the general oppression of blacks and women simply because he is a white man. In this sense, all members of dominant and subordinate categories participate in social oppression regardless of their individual ATTITUDES or behavior.

Social oppression becomes *institutionalized* when its enforcement is so embedded in the everyday workings of social life that it is not easily identified as oppression and does not require conscious PREJUDICE or overt acts of discrimination. In the United States, for example, the bail bond system operates as *institutionalized racism* by discriminating against black defendants, who generally are less able than whites to afford bail. Since defendants incarcerated during trial are more likely to be convicted, the bail bond system has the effect of biasing the legal system against those who cannot afford it and thereby perpetuating inequality.

Institutionalized sexism operates in similar ways. For example, minimum physical requirements for various occupations tend to screen women out and advantage men, even though the requirements may bear little relation to what is actually needed to do the job. Height requirements for firefighters in the United States screen out far more women than men. However, since Americans and Europeans tend to be taller than the Japanese, those same requirements would render ineligible many Japanese firefighters who presumably do a fine job of putting out fires in Japan.

See also EXPLOITATION; INSTITUTION; MINORITY; PREJUDICE AND DISCRIMINATION; SOCIAL CLASS.

Reading

Fanon, Franz. 1967. *The wretched of the earth.* Harmondsworth, England: Penguin.

Frye, Marilyn. 1983. *The politics of reality: Essays in feminist theory.* Trumansburg, NY: Crossing Press.

Memmi, Albert. 1964. *Dominated man.* New York: Orion Press.

social order Social order has several different although related meanings. In its first sense, it is the social COHESION through which systems are held together, one of the central concerns of the FUNCTIONALIST PERSPECTIVE. In its second sense, it is sometimes synonymous with SOCIAL CONTROL, the institutional means and other methods used to ensure that people obey NORMS and support VALUES. In its third sense, it refers to the relatively predictable patterns of behavior and experience that characterize life in the systems themselves (also referred to as *social organization*). If we were to combine all these meanings, we might say that every social system is a social order that has some degree of social order that is maintained through social order.

social organization *See* SOCIAL ORDER.

social problem A social problem can best be defined by looking at the term in its two parts: the problem and what makes it SOCIAL. For a problem (or anything else) to be social, it must involve SOCIAL SYSTEMS and/or people's participation in them in some way. This would include problems that are caused by underlying social conditions or that produce consequences that affect social systems. For example, we can describe drug abuse as a social problem because it is rooted in particular social conditions that make it possible and promote it. This includes the availability of drugs as part of material CULTURE and the widespread cultural promotion of general drug use, from aspirin to alcohol, as a legitimate and effective response to personal problems; a profit-oriented ECONOMY in which drugs serve as a COMMODITY and source of WEALTH for those who buy and sell them; and social conditions such as POVERTY and ALIENATION that make drug use an attractive way for many people to deal with the stresses of everyday life. As a problem, drug abuse is also social in the consequences it produces, from patterns of violent behavior to the strain on health services and the loss of economic productivity.

In general, something will be identified as a social problem only if it violates or interferes with cultural VALUES that define what is good, important, and desirable in a SYSTEM. This alone, however, is not enough, for the identification of social problems is itself a social process. And, as with everything else, some groups have more control than others over this process and the identification of social problems is often tied to the interests of dominant groups. The medical consequences of certain occupational hazards, for example, have often been known long before they were socially recognized as problems. In the textile industry, the effects of chronic exposure to cotton dust were known to medicine long before "brown lung" was recognized as an occupationally related condition that required corrective action by employers. The use of drugs such as cocaine and heroin generally was not considered a serious social problem until it began to spread to children of the MIDDLE and UPPER CLASSES in the 1960s. As long as drug use was limited to minority and poor populations, there was little public alarm or action.

Reading
Becker, Howard S. 1966. *Social problems.* New York: Wiley.
Merton, Robert K. 1972. *The sociology of social problems*, 4th ed. New York: Harcourt Brace Jovanovich.
Spector, Malcom, and John I. Kitsuse. 1977. *Constructing social problems.* Menlo Park, CA: Cummings.

social reproduction *See* CULTURAL REPRODUCTION AND SOCIAL REPRODUCTION.

social script *See* DRAMATURGICAL PERSPECTIVE.

social status *See* STATUS.

social structure Along with the concept of CULTURE, social structure is a crucial defining concept for sociology as a way of thinking about social life. Every SOCIAL SYSTEM has a structure, and it is this that accounts for much of the differences between systems and the patterns of human experience and behavior that constitute what we know as social life.

The structure of a social system can be analyzed in terms of two characteristics, relationships and DISTRIBUTIONS. The relationships in a system connect its various parts to one another and, hence, to the system as a whole. The "parts" can range from the STATUSES people occupy to entire systems such as GROUPS, organizations, COMMUNITIES, and SOCIETIES. The relationships that connect the parts have structural characteristics. For example, a military unit is a social system that has BOUNDARIES regulating the flow of people into and out of social statuses; a ROLE STRUCTURE that includes all the different tasks people are expected to perform in the DIVISION OF LABOR; a COMMUNICATION STRUCTURE that describes the frequency and duration of interaction between different members of the unit; and a SOCIOMETRIC STRUCTURE whose patterns of affection and dislike connect people to one another.

The second structural characteristic of a social system includes various kinds of distributions. Power may be distributed equally, as in a DEMOCRACY, or unequally as in a traditional patriarchal family. In similar ways we can describe the structural distribution of various other products and resources of social life, from WEALTH AND INCOME and PROPERTY to PRESTIGE and access to education and health care. We can also look at the distribution of people among the various positions in a social system – how many students there are per teacher, the number of wives or husbands in a marriage, or the relative numbers of people in various occupations.

See also STRUCTURALISM AND POST-STRUCTURALISM; TIME STRUCTURE.

Reading

Bates, F. L., and W. G. Peacock. 1989. "Conceptualizing social structure: The misuse of classification in structural modeling." *American Sociological Review* 54(4): 565–77.

Blau, Peter M., ed. 1975. *Approaches to the study of social structure*. New York: Free Press.

Coser, Lewis A., ed. 1975. *The idea of social structure: Papers in honor of Robert K. Merton*. New York: Harcourt Brace Jovanovich.

Merton, Robert K. 1968. *Social theory and social structure*, rev. and exp. ed. New York: Free Press.

social system A social system is any interdependent set of cultural and structural elements that can be thought of as a unit. The "parts" that make up a social system can be of almost any size or complexity. They can be as small and simple as a SYMBOL (such as the word "symbol") or a position in a social relationship (such as "friend"); and they can be as large and complex as entire SOCIETIES or groups of societies. Marriages, basketball teams, department stores, friendships, doctors' offices, armies, corporations, governments, the United

Nations, the world economy – no matter how small and informal or how vast and intricate, all can be thought of as social systems.

In general, any system can be defined as a set of interdependent elements or parts that can be thought of as a whole. In this sense, we can think of a motor or the human body as a system. As a general approach to understanding a variety of phenomena, *systems theory* is the study of how systems are organized, how they adapt to changing circumstances, how the interests of SUBSYSTEMS fit or conflict with those of the whole, and so on. It is a widely used perspective, applied to everything from assessing the risks of nuclear power plant accidents to diagnosing operational problems in large corporations or government bureaucracies.

The concept of a social system embodies perhaps the most important of all sociological principles: that the whole is more than the sum of its parts. If we take two sticks of wood, one half as long as the other, and join them together to resemble the Christian "cross," no amount of understanding of the sticks themselves can ever fully account for our perception of the cross as a particular arrangement of sticks in relation to each other. It is the arrangement of the parts that makes the whole what it is, not merely the characteristics of the parts themselves. The focus on such arrangements is what distinguishes sociology from other perspectives on human life.

The concept of a social system is arguably the most important in the entire sociological vocabulary because for many sociologists it defines what it is that distinguishes sociology from other disciplines. Although most often associated with the FUNCTIONALIST PERSPECTIVE, the concept has much broader applications. Almost everything that sociologists investigate – from INTERACTION between wives and husbands to the uses of modern warfare as instruments of political policy to Marxist critiques of CAPITALISM – flows from a basic assumption that social systems exist in a fundamental coherence among the various aspects and elements of social life. This, in the most general sense, is what the concept of a social system is all about.

See also AGENCY AND STRUCTURE; ATOMISM AND HOLISM; SOCIAL FACT; STATUS; CULTURE; SOCIAL STRUCTURE; POPULATION; ECOLOGY.

Reading
Boguslaw, Robert. [1965] 1981. *The new utopians: A study of systems design and social change.* Englewood Cliffs, NJ: Prentice-Hall.
Giddens, Anthony. 1984. *The constitution of society.* Cambridge, England: Polity Press.
Parsons, Talcott. 1951. *The social system.* Glencoe, IL: Free Press.

socialism *See* STATE SOCIALISM.

socialist feminism *See* FEMINISM.

socialization Socialization is the process through which people are prepared to participate in SOCIAL SYSTEMS. Included in this concept is some understanding of SYMBOL and idea systems, LANGUAGE, and the relationships that make up social systems. We are generally not socialized to understand systems as systems, to analyze how they actually work and produce consequences. Instead, we come to understand systems as a taken-for-granted reality that is simply as it seems to be. What is generally not included, in other words, is any kind of sociological awareness of what it is we are participating in and how we are participating in it.

Although most commonly associated with child development, socialization is a lifelong process that occurs as people acquire new ROLES and adjust to the loss of old ones. When people first marry, for example, they go through a considerable period of socialization, as they do again when they have a child. Socialization continues as their children grow older and become more independent, an inevitable development that calls upon parents to reshape their roles in relation to their children. In old age, roles may actually reverse if parents become disabled and dependent upon the care of their children.

From the perspective of individuals, socialization is a process through which we create a social SELF and a sense of attachment to social systems through our participation in them and our INTERACTION with others. From the perspective of social systems, socialization is necessary if the system is to continue and function effectively, since every social system depends upon people who are motivated and prepared to perform the various roles that it encompasses.

There has been some controversy within sociology about the power of socialization to shape people's feelings, thoughts, appearance, and behavior. Although everyone must be socialized to some degree if they are to participate in social life, there is enormous variation in how that actually happens and the results it produces. In complex societies this is due in part to the variety of experiences people encounter in families, schools, occupations, and communities. But

in all societies it is also due to the fact that individuals are not passive, and they play an important part in their own socialization as they respond in various ways to social pressures and influences.

See also ANTICIPATORY SOCIALIZATION; INTERNALIZATION; RESOCIALIZATION; RITE OF PASSAGE; REFERENCE GROUP; SELF; SOCIAL CONTROL.

Reading

Brim, Orville G., Jr. 1966. "Socialization after childhood." In *Socialization after childhood: Two essays,* edited by Orville G. Brim Jr. and Stanton Wheeler. New York: Wiley.

Bush, Diane M., and Roberta G. Simmons. 1981. "Socialization processes over the life course." In *Social psychology: Sociological perspectives,* edited by Morris Rosenberg and Ralph H. Turner, 133–64. New York: Basic Books.

Goslin, David A. 1969. *Handbook of socialization theory and research.* Chicago: Rand McNally.

Wrong, Dennis H. 1961. "The oversocialized conception of man in modern sociology." *American Sociological Review* 26: 183–93.

society A society is a particular kind of SOCIAL SYSTEM. Like all social systems, it is distinguished by its cultural, structural, and population/ecological characteristics. Specifically, a society is a system that is defined by a geographical territory (which may or may not coincide with the boundaries of NATION-STATES) within which a POPULATION shares a common CULTURE and way of life under conditions of relative autonomy, independence, and self-sufficiency. It is necessary to specify "relative" because these are matters of degree in today's world of interdependent societies. It is safe to say, however, that societies are among the most autonomous and independent of all social systems.

An additional distinguishing characteristic of societies is that they tend to be the largest system of which people identify themselves as members. People who are Japanese, American, or British, for example, are unlikely to think of themselves as belonging to some recognizable social entity larger than, respectively, Japan, the United States, or Britain. Even this may be a matter of degree, however, as confederations of nations become more common. As Europe unites, it is conceivable that people will begin to think of Europe in the way once reserved for NATION-STATES. As such, Europe may begin to take on the characteristics of a society.

The society is a central concept in sociology because it is on the level of societies that the most important elements of social life are created and organized. Virtually every social system in which we participate – from the FAMILY to RELIGION to occupations to sports – is in some way a SUBSYSTEM of a society that defines its basic character. Even subversive or revolutionary groups operate and define themselves primarily in relation to societies and their INSTITUTIONS.

As important as societies are, it is important not to impute to them characteristics they do not have. This is especially evident in the common practice of speaking of societies as if they were people capable of thinking, feeling, wanting, needing, and acting. As a social system, a society is to a great extent abstract even though it may be experienced as having a concrete reality.

See also GROUP; INSTITUTION; REIFICATION.

sociobiology Sociobiology is a branch of biology that tries to identify biological and genetic roots of behavior and the organization of life among various species. This perspective is based on the idea that behavior and organization are based on the drive to successfully reproduce genes (hence Edward O. Wilson's assertion that "the chicken is just the egg's way of making another egg").

Most work in sociobiology has been done on nonhuman species, although there have been a few notable and extensively criticized attempts to extend such arguments to human SOCIAL SYSTEMS. Among them was Wilson's initial claim that there was an "altruistic" gene determining the altruistic impulse among humans, but he has since backed away from that position and recognized the overwhelming importance of social factors in human life. Although sociology cannot deny the fact that all human capabilities ultimately have a biological basis, the creative potential of human beings to shape and give meaning to their social environment is so great that the biological factors have relatively little importance in sociological analysis. Nonetheless, there is continuing discussion within sociology about how to most effectively integrate biological factors into sociological thinking.

See also DETERMINISM AND REDUCTIONISM; ETHOLOGY.

Reading

Fausto-Sterling, Ann. 1992. *Myths of gender: Biological theories about women and men*, rev. ed. New York: Basic Books.

Sahlins, Marshall D. 1976. *The use and abuse of biology: An anthropological critique of sociobiology*. Ann Arbor: University of Michigan Press.

Wilson, Edward O. 1975. *Sociobiology*. Cambridge, MA: Belknap.
——. 1977. "Biology and the social sciences." *Daedalus* 106 (fall): 127–40.

socioeconomic rights *See* CITIZEN AND CITIZENSHIP.

socioeconomic status Socioeconomic status (SES) is a concept referring primarily to people's positions in STRATIFICATION systems as indicated by their occupational PRESTIGE and, secondarily, their educational attainment, WEALTH, and INCOME. Sociologists have devised several scales for measuring SES empirically, the most notable of which are Duncan's Socioeconomic Index and Hollingshead's Two Factor Index of Social Position. These have been faulted for paying too little attention to POWER, especially in relation to the MEANS OF PRODUCTION.

See also SOCIAL CLASS; STATUS INCONSISTENCY AND CRYSTALIZATION; STRATIFICATION AND INEQUALITY.

Reading
Powers, M. G., ed. 1982. *Measures of socioeconomic status*. Boulder, CO: Westview Press.

sociogram *See* SOCIOMETRY.

sociolinguistics Sociolinguistics is the study of LANGUAGE as a resource in social life. It includes questions about how language is used to produce various outcomes in social INTERACTION; how it is distributed as a resource among various GROUPS; and the role it plays in people's acquistion of cultural competence, on which their ability to participate effectively in social life is based. In multicultural societies, the uneven distribution of competence in the dominant language often reinforces

racial and ethnic inequality by limiting the ability of MINORITIES to gain acceptance.
See also SEMIOTICS; SPEECH CODES.

Reading
Bernstein, Basil. 1975. *Class, codes, and control*. London: Routledge and Kegan Paul.
Gumperz, John J., and Dell Hymes. [1966] 1990. *New directions in sociolinguistics*. Oxford: Blackwell Publishers.
Labov, William. 1972. *Sociolinguistic patterns*. Philadelphia: University of Pensylvania Press.

sociology Sociology is the study of social life and behavior, especially in relation to SOCIAL SYSTEMS, how they work, how they change, the consequences they produce, and their complex relation to people's lives. The term was first used by Auguste COMTE.

From its beginnings, sociology has suffered from somewhat of an identity crisis reflected in its many definitions. It is often referred to as the "study of SOCIETY," but this excludes the vast majority of social life that takes place in systems that are much smaller than societies. Studies of GROUPS, corporations, school classrooms, and dysfunctional FAMILIES are all connected with society in an ultimate sense. But we can ask many sociological questions about them without ever referring to that largest of social systems in which they find themselves. At the other end of the spectrum is the objection that there are increasingly interesting problems that take place at levels larger than societies, such as global economic and political systems.

Going in another direction, sociology is often defined as the "study of groups," but this fails to take into account that the concept of a GROUP is quite precise and narrow in sociology. Many important social systems – from complex organizations and COMMUNITIES to societies and the world ECONOMY – are not groups. In addition, the concept of a group does not include SOCIAL CATEGORIES such as those defined by RACE, GENDER, ETHNICITY, RELIGION, and AGE, which play an important part in social inequality, SOCIAL OPPRESSION and conflict.

Sociology might also be defined as the study of social behavior. However, since there is but a small range of human behavior that cannot be construed as social to some degree, this definition confuses sociology with psychology, which is far more concerned with the individual's internal workings than with their social context and their connection to it. Although human behavior is central to sociological thinking, it is not what makes that thinking distinctly sociological.

Central to any definition of the sociological point of view is the idea that the whole is greater than the sum of its parts, for the whole also includes the relations that bind the parts together, which generally cannot be derived from knowledge of the parts alone. Also central is the distinction between social systems and the people who participate in them and make them happen. It is of course true that social systems would not amount to much if there were no individual people, but it does not follow from this that social systems are therefore just a collection of individuals. Social systems are sets of arrangements in which individuals participate, much like a game that people play. This does not mean that the game is a particular group of people playing it.

To borrow from chemistry, a molecule cannot be understood solely by studying the characteristic of each element that "participates" in it. Indeed, we know next to nothing about molecules unless we understand the bonds that connect them to one another, and these are not characteristics of any of the constituent parts. In the same way, psychological profiles of workers in a corporation will not be of much use in understanding what a corporation is and how it works. It is therefore a combined focus on social systems and their connection to individual people's lives that distinguishes sociology from other disciplines and provides a unique and powerful vantage point from which to pose questions about human life.

See also ATOMISM AND HOLISM; CULTURE; SOCIAL STRUCTURE; ECOLOGY.

sociometry Sociometry is a technique developed by Jacob Moreno to identify the structure of ties in a GROUP based on affection rather than ROLE expectations. In an office, for example, the most important and extensive role obligations of secretaries are in relation to their bosses, not to one another. But within that formal ROLE STRUCTURE there often is a pattern of affective ties that can profoundly affect how the roles are performed. Secretaries may like one another far more than they like their bosses, and as a consequence feel a sense of personal loyalty to one another that may compete with their actual occupational roles and loyalty to their bosses.

To measure the existence of such patterns, Moreno developed a method of asking people in a group to report their positive and negative feelings about other members. The result is a *sociogram,* a chart in which each person is shown in relation to others: two-headed arrows show mutual liking, one-headed arrows show asymmetrical liking, no arrow shows neutrality, and so on. Although the technique has not enjoyed much use among sociologists, it can be a useful way to detect the presence of SUBGROUPS that would not be predicted on the basis of a system's other structural characteristics. Subgroups are important in part because they often develop interests of their own that may conflict with those of the larger system of which they are a part. Thus although the role and POWER STRUCTURES of an office might predict loyalty of secretaries to their bosses, the sociometric structure might predict the contrary.

See also PRIMARY RELATIONSHIP AND SECONDARY RELATIONSHIP; SOCIAL STRUCTURE.

Reading
Moreno, Jacob L. 1943. "Sociometry and the cultural order." *Sociometry* 6: 299–344.

solidarity *See* COHESION.

specification In the statistical analysis of relationships among VARIABLES, specification is the practice of seeing if a particular relationship remains the same in different segments of a POPULATION. These are also known as *conditional relationships.* For example, the relationship between college education and income in the United States is stronger among African-Americans than among whites. The reason for

this is that among whites there are more "exceptions" to the general "rule" that in order to earn a higher income one must have a higher education. Among African-Americans, however, it is much more difficult to earn a high income without a correspondingly high education. Thus education is a more accurate predictor of income among blacks and the relationship between the two variables is therefore stronger.

In this case, the act of controlling for RACE in order to see what happens to the relationship between education and income is referred to as "specifying for race." The finding that the relationship varies in strength from one category of people to another is called an *interaction effect.* In some cases, interaction effects can also take the form of actual differences in the DIRECTION OF THE RELATIONSHIP (positive in one group and negative in another) or the existence of a relationship (positive or negative) in one group and nonexistent in another.

See also CONTROL VARIABLE; DIRECTION OF RELATIONSHIP; VARIABLE.

Reading
Bohrnstedt, George W., and David Knoke. 1994. *Statistics for social data analysis,* 3rd ed. Itasca, IL: F. E. Peacock.
Rosenberg, Morris. 1968. *The logic of survey analysis.* New York: Basic Books.

specificity *See* PATTERN VARIABLES.

speech codes In his studies of SOCIOLINGUISTICS, Basil Bernstein developed the concepts of elaborated and restricted speech codes to explore the relationship between SOCIALIZATION, LANGUAGE, and SOCIAL CLASS. Bernstein argued that people use language in two basic ways. The first is elaborated code, a more formal, public language (universalistic) that can be used to communicate in ways that everyone will understand. For example, if we are trying to explain an event to someone who was not there when it occurred, we must put ourselves in the listener's place and provide enough detail to adequately describe the context for the event, especially through the use of adjectives, adverbs, and subordinate clauses. The result is a story that can stand on its own with a good chance our listener will get the point of it even while being unfamiliar with the context that produced the story in the first place.

The second way that people use language is through restricted code, which is language used in informal ways that tend to be understood only by those who share a common understanding of a particular context. When family members sit around the dinner table and recount a story from the family's past, for example, they leave out a great deal of detail because their familiarity with the circumstances makes it unnecessary to include it in order to get the meaning. A guest, however, is likely to miss the point of the story because so much detail is missing.

Bernstein argued that MIDDLE-CLASS children have more opportunity to master both elaborated and restricted speech codes while LOWER-CLASS children tend to have experience only with restricted code. Since elaborated code is the language of public life, including school, children lacking exposure to it will suffer class differences in their school performance, especially in tasks requiring abstract, universalistic kinds of

thinking. There is considerable disagreement over whether Bernstein is correct (it is possible to use restricted code and still discuss abstract concepts, for example), but his ideas remain influential in the study of social class and language.

Reading

Bernstein, Basil. 1971, 1977. *Class, codes, and control*, vols 1 and 3, 2nd ed. London: Routledge and Kegan Paul.

speech community   *See* LANGUAGE.

sponsored mobility and contest mobility   Sponsored and contest mobility are two different ways that education relates to SOCIAL MOBILITY. In a system based on sponsored mobility, students are selected on the basis of promise, CLASS background, and other criteria, and they are allowed to continue in school with financial and other support. In a system of contest mobility, all students are allowed to continue and compete with one another throughout the educational process.

In INDUSTRIAL SOCIETIES, education is one of the most important factors in social mobility. This means that unequal access to education plays a critical role in producing social inequality and class systems.

Contest mobility is most common in the United States, where educational resources are more plentiful and there is less need to select out students at lower educational levels. Sponsored mobility is more common in Europe and Japan, although less so in Britain since the decline of selection into state schools. Beneath this apparent difference, however, is the fact that within school systems there is often considerable class, RACE, and

GENDER inequality in the distribution of educational support, attention, and resources. This in turn contributes to unequal rates of social mobility and achievement.

See also HIDDEN CURRICULUM.

Reading
Turner, Ralph H. 1960. "Sponsored and contest mobility and the school system." *American Sociological Review* 25: 855–67.

spiriousness In the analysis of relationships among VARIABLES, spuriousness occurs when two variables that are statistically related to each other are found to have no causal relation. Let's assume that we have determined that when the level of ice cream consumption increases in a seaside community, so do the number of drownings. Before we conclude that the statistical relationship indicates cause and effect – that ice cream causes drownings – we might control for a third variable such as how much swimming people do. We would then find that increased ice cream consumption reflects the onset of summer and with it, an increased amount of swimming. It is this, and not ice cream consumption, that causes an increased number of drownings. We would thus conclude that the relationship between ice cream consumption and drownings is spurious; it is statistical only and not in any way causal. The third variable for which we controlled – the amount of swimming people do – is called an *extraneous variable*.

Spuriousness is a particularly important and often overlooked interpretation in statistical analysis, for it often means the difference between what is and what is not causal. Educators, for example, often point out that a university education is associated with liberal thinking and interest in public affairs. It is unclear, however, whether this is an effect of education per se or a spurious relationship. It is quite possible that those young people most likely to go on to higher education come from families that support the very characteristics that are most often associated with university graduates.

An alert and conscientious analyst will always consider the possibility of spuriousness and make every effort to identify possible extraneous variables.

See also CONTROL VARIABLE.

Reading
Rosenberg, Morris. 1968. *The logic of survey analysis.* New York: Basic Books.

stable population In DEMOGRAPHY, a stable population is a hypothetical POPULATION that would result from a prolonged period during which the age-specific BIRTH and DEATH RATES remained constant, typically around 70 years. A stable population has a constant rate of growth (called the *intrinsic growth rate*) and an unvarying age-sex composition. If its crude birth rate and crude death rate are equal, its intrinsic growth rate is zero and the population is known as a *stationary population*. The stable population model is useful for assessing the long-term effects of birth and death rate patterns independent of a population's age-sex composition.

Reading
Shryock, Henry S., and Jacob Siegel and Associates. 1976. *The methods and materials of demography.* New York: Academic Press.

standard deviation *See* VARIANCE.

standard error A standard error is a statistical measure of the amount of variation in a SAMPLING DISTRIBUTION. In general, it is calculated as the square root of the result obtained from dividing the population VARIANCE by the SAMPLE size (making it essentially a kind of standard deviation). Since sample size is in the denominator the standard error grows smaller as sample size is increased.

Because the sampling distribution contains all the possible results that might be obtained from selecting a sample from a particular POPULATION, the standard error is a crucial quantity in making inferences from samples to populations. If the standard error is large, the various samples will differ a great deal from the average, which is the population value being estimated. This means that any given sample is likely to be in considerable error. The smaller the standard error, however, the less variation there is among potential samples and, therefore, the smaller the probability that any given sample that is selected will be in error by an unacceptable margin.

Since samples are used to estimate a variety of population characteristics – from population MEANS and percentages to CORRELATIONS between VARIABLES – there is an equally large number of formulas for estimating the corresponding standard errors.

See also ERROR; STATISTICAL INFERENCE.

standard score *See* STANDARDIZATION; Z-SCORE.

standardization Standardization is a statistical technique that gives different units of measurement a common base for purposes of comparison. For example, percentages are used instead of raw frequencies in order to compare groups of different sizes. In the United States there are many more poor whites than there are poor blacks, but this is primarily because there are many more whites overall. Because the two categories of people are of different sizes, the only way to compare them is to compare the percentage of each group that is poor by dividing the number of poor by the size of the appropriate population. By standardizing in this way, we find that blacks are about twice as likely as whites to be poor.

In multiple REGRESSION and PATH ANALYSIS, standardization is used to make regression coefficients comparable to one another by dividing each by the standard deviation of its VARIABLE. The effect is to standardize the units of measurement so that the effects of different independent variables on the dependent variable can be compared. This would otherwise be impossible since the units – dollars, euros, years of education, number of previous jobs held, and so on – would not be the same and hence could not be compared with one another. These standardized coefficients are called standardized regression coefficients in regression analysis; in PATH ANALYSIS they are called *beta weights*.

DEMOGRAPHY uses a lot of standardization, especially in comparing BIRTH and DEATH RATES for POPULATIONS that differ in size or, especially, in age composition. For example, the use of RATES standardizes for population size by dividing the number of events in a given year – such as deaths – by the population size. Even if populations are of the same size, however, comparisons of rates might be misleading if other factors related to deaths – such as age composition – are not accounted for. This is illustrated by death rates in the United Kingdom and the United States, which are higher than they are in Mexico. This difference is due not to poorer health conditions or lower longevity but, rather, to differences in AGE STRUC-TURE. Mexico's population has a far higher proportion of children and a far lower proportion of the elderly. Since the elderly are especially likely to die, any SOCIETY whose age structure is older will tend to produce a larger number of deaths each year even if death rates are lower in that society for every age of life.

To standardize death rates, we take the age-specific rates for each population and apply them to the same age structure. The resulting rates, called age-standardized rates, will then reflect only differences in mortality, not age structure. Although this generally makes comparisons possible, it is not a foolproof method. The choice of an age structure on which to standardize, for example, is somewhat arbitrary and can make a large difference in the relative magnitude of the resulting standardized rates. In addition, the numbers themselves have no intrinsic meaning since they depend so heavily on which age structure is chosen for the standardization. This kind of standardization is a tricky business requiring considerable care and expertise.

See also Z-SCORE.

state As defined by Max WEBER, the state is the social INSTITUTION that holds a monopoly over the use of force. In this sense, the state is defined by its AUTHORITY to generate and apply collective POWER. As with all social INSTITUTIONS, the state is organized around a set of social functions, including maintaining law, order, and stability, resolving various kinds of disputes through the legal system, providing common defense, and looking out for the welfare of the population in ways that are beyond the means of the individual, such as implementing public health measures, providing mass education, and underwriting expensive medical research. From a CONFLICT PERSPEC-TIVE, however, the state also operates in the interest of various dominant groups, such as privileged SOCIAL CLASSES and RACES.

The state is not the same as *government*, although the terms are often used interchangeably outside of sociology and political science. The state is a social institution, which means that it consists of a form or social blueprint for how various functions ought to be accomplished. The parliamentary system, for example, is one way of accomplishing various tasks of governance, such as enacting legislation. A government, however, is a particular collection of people who at any given time occupy the positions of authority within a state. In this sense, governments regularly come and go, but, barring REVOLU-TION, the state endures and is slow and difficult to change.

Reading

Marx, Karl. 1964. *Selected writings in sociology and social philosophy*. New York: McGraw-Hill.

Parsons, Talcott. 1969. *Politics and social structure*. New York: Free Press.

Weber, Max. 1946. "Politics as a vocation." In *From Max Weber: Essays in sociology*, edited and translated by Hans H. Gerth and C. Wright Mills. New York: Oxford University Press.

state autonomy State autonomy is a condition representing the degree to which the STATE is independent of capitalist interests, especially as these are organized through corporations. Max WEBER argued that the state is an independent INSTITUTION that operates according to its own bureaucratic CULTURE. Karl MARX, however, saw the state as little more than an extension of the ELITE, controlled primarily by its own members in order to protect and promote CAPITALISM and ruling-class interests. Other more recent views argue that the state plays a more complicated role, although still one that ultimately promotes the status quo and rarely challenges capitalism as a system. It must maintain a certain degree of autonomy, for example, in order to maintain its legitimacy in the eyes of the working class.

Reading

O'Connor, James. 1973. *The fiscal crisis of the state.* New York: St. Martin's Press.

Parkin, Frank. 1978. *Marxism and class theory: A bourgeois critique.* London: Tavistock.

state capitalism State capitalism (also known as *democratic socialism*) is a POLITICAL ECONOMY in which the STATE is heavily involved in the ownership, control, or active support of capitalist enterprise. In some cases this includes owning and operating key industries such as public utilities, television stations, oil and natural gas, and mass transportation. More generally, however, the state uses its resources and AUTHORITY to stabilize capitalist markets (by prohibiting monopolies, for example, or by controlling interest rates, tariffs on imports, and price-fixing) and to otherwise protect and advance the interests of the capitalist class. For example, the recurring practice of the U.S. government using tax funds to

"bail out" large manufacturers and banks that threaten to go bankrupt (often because of mismanagement or fraud) illustrates state capitalist intervention. This deviates sharply from the capitalist ideal of a "free MARKET" in which competitive fitness is the main determinant of which firms succeed and which fail.

See also CAPITALISM; STATE SOCIALISM.

Reading

Edwards, Richard C., Michael Reich, and Thomas E. Weisskopf. 1986. "The capitalist economy: Structure and change." In *The capitalist system,* 3rd ed., edited by Edwards, Reich, and Weisskopf, 4–15. Englewood Cliffs, NJ: Prentice-Hall.

Jessop, Bob. 1982. *The capitalist state.* New York: Oxford University Press.

state socialism As envisioned by Karl MARX, state socialism is a MODE OF PRODUCTION that will replace industrial CAPITALISM, most likely as the result of a workers' revolution but also through more gradual evolutionary change. Under capitalism, the MEANS OF PRODUCTION are owned and controlled by capitalists who employ workers to produce WEALTH in exchange for wages. This is all done with the active support of the STATE, which itself depends on capitalism for its resources. Under state socialism, however, the means of production are owned and controlled by a democratic state or by collective organizations of workers (a "workers' state"), both of which act directly on behalf of the workers. The goals of socialism include destroying the CLASS system and thereby ending the EXPLOITATION, oppression, and ALIENATION of workers; replacing greed and the profit motive with concern for collective well-being; and using this concern rather than the

MARKET as a basis for making decisions about production and the use of resources. As a result, social life would be regulated democratically in ways that put human needs first and make more efficient and effective use of human and other resources.

In practice, socialism has worked quite differently. AUTHORITARIANISM rather than DEMOCRACY has been the predominant form of political POWER; inefficient central planning has generally failed to meet the needs of the people; a privileged class of bureaucrats has perpetuated the class system, although with far lower levels of inequality than previously; and chronic (until recently) conflict and competition with wealthier and more powerful capitalist nations has drained both attention and resources. To some degree this has resulted from the fact that no socialist society has met Marx's main precondition for successful socialism at the time of its REVOLUTION: a well-developed industrial capitalist society that has solved the problem of production. Rather, virtually all socialist countries either were barely beyond agrarian FEUDALISM (as in Russia and China) or were recently devastated by war (as in East Germany), or both.

Since no advanced capitalist society has yet undergone a socialist revolution, it remains to be seen if the state socialist alternative is feasible.

See also COMMUNISM; MARKET; SOCIAL CLASS.

Reading
Cole, George D. H. 1959. *A history of socialist thought*, 5 vols. London: Macmillan
Kornai, János. 1986. *Contradictions and dilemmas: Studies on the socialist economy and society*. Cambridge, MA: MIT Press.

Lenin, Vladimir I. [1917] 1949. *The state and revolution*. Moscow: Progress Publishers.
Marx, Karl. [1875] 1891. "Critique of the Gotha programme." First published by Friedrich Engels in *Die Neue Zeit*, IX, 1.

stationary population See STABLE POPULATION.

statistical independence and statistical dependence In sociological work, statistical dependence and independence are ideas that are applied to relationships between events and VARIABLES. Two events are independent of each other if the occurrence of one has no effect on the probability that the other will occur. For example, if we flip a coin fairly, the PROBABILITY is 1/2 that the result will be heads. If we get heads on the first flip (event number one), the probability of getting heads on the second flip is still 1/2 (event number two). In other words, as events the first and second flips are statistically independent of each other.

If two variables are independent of each other, then knowing the value of one variable tells us nothing about the value of the other variable. If the variables income and education are independent of each other, for example, then knowing someone's education will tell us nothing about their most likely income. The probability that college graduates have a particular income – say $50,000 a year – is the same probability that exists for everyone else. Education, in short, makes no difference in income and the two variables are statistically independent of each other.

As we all know, education does make a difference, which is to say, the probability of having various incomes changes considerably depending on how much schooling a person has. In this case we say that the two variables are statistically *dependent* on each other and therefore have a *relationship* (or "are related"). The word "statistically" is used as a qualifier because the fact that two variables are related in a statistical sense does not mean that one variable causes the other.

Statistical independence can take two different forms: *stochastic independence* and *mean independence*. With stochastic independence, each category of one variable is independent of each and every category of the other. For example, for people with a college education, the probabilities associated with each possible income level will be the same for them as for everyone else regardless of their education.

If education and income are mean independent, however, only the average income will be the same for each educational category. The difference is that the averages could be the same without the probabilities associated with particular income levels being the same. With mean independence, for example, two educational categories might have the same mean income, say, $20,000. But in the first group everyone might have the same income of $20,000 (resulting in a mean of $20,000) while in the second group half might have incomes of $40,000 and half might have no income at all (also resulting in a mean income of $20,000 overall). In this case, the two variables are mean independent since each category of the variable has the same average income; but the variables are not stochastically independent. In general, if

two variables are mean independent, they are not necessarily stochastically independent; but if they are stochastically independent, then they must also be mean independent.

The distinction between mean and stochastic independence is particularly important in REGRESSION ANALYSIS because one of the shortcomings of this technique is its inability to distinguish the two.

See also DIRECTION OF RELATIONSHIP; MEAN; MEASURE OF ASSOCIATION.

statistical inference *See* STATISTICS.

statistics Statistics is a set of mathematical techniques used to organize, analyze, and interpret information that takes the form of numbers. If we want to see how the sexual behavior of teenagers is affected by making contraceptives available to them, we might gather information on sexual behavior from teenagers who differ in how much access they have to contraception. We could calculate various indicators of sexual activity such as the percentage who are sexually active or the average number of sexual encounters per month and use these to make comparisons based on differing access to contraception. Statistics refers not only to the calculation of quantities such as percentages and averages but also to the results – the percentages and averages themselves, each of which can be referred to as "a statistic."

Statisticians identify two main types of statistics: descriptive and inferential. *Descriptive statistics* describe and explain phenomena that lend themselves to being counted and sorted, such as the frequency of sexual intercourse or the amount of income people receive each year in a given POPULATION. We might, for example, look at how sexual practices vary from one SOCIAL CLASS to another to get some clue as to why BIRTH RATES also vary across classes.

Inferential (or *inductive*) statistics perform the same functions as descriptive statistics with the additional task of reaching conclusions about entire populations by using DATA gathered from a SAMPLE rather than a CENSUS. If we want to see how the number of friends people have varies depending on whether they live in country, town, or city, we might gather information on a sample of people in each type of COMMUNITY. Whatever our sample information looks like, we will still have the problem of using it to make statements about what we are really interested in, which is the larger population the sample information comes from – country, town, and city communities in general. All of this requires an additional set of mathematical techniques known as inferential statistics.

In general, statistical inference is used to estimate population characteristics (such as MEANS, percentages, or CORRELATIONS) or to test HYPO-THESES about population characteristics. In either case, the key to the process is estimating the amount of ERROR associated with any given conclusion.

See also ESTIMATES; HYPOTHESIS AND HYPOTHESIS TESTING.

Reading

Bohrnstedt, George W., and David Knoke. 1994. *Statistics for social data analysis*, 3rd ed. Itasca, IL: F. E. Peacock.

status Status has two meanings in sociology. Max WEBER equated the term with PRESTIGE, as in "a high status occupation" or someone who is "status conscious." Most sociologists, however, define status as a position occupied by an individual in a SOCIAL SYSTEM. "Wife" and "husband" for example, are statuses in marital systems just as "lawyer," "juror," and "judge" are statuses in court systems and "goalie," "centerforward," and "fullback" are statuses on soccer teams. Note that status is a purely relational term, which means that each status exists only through its relation to one or more other statuses. "Husband," for example, makes no sense at all except in relation to "wife," just as there can be no judges without corresponding positions that comprise the rest of a judicial system.

Since statuses are positions in social systems, they exist independently of the particular individuals who occupy them. Indeed, a status can exist even though no one is occupying it at the time, such as the status of "prime minister" when the current minister has died and a new one has yet to be elected, or the status of "candidate" when there is no election forthcoming. People are associated with statuses only through their participation in the social systems that include them. In this relatively simple principle lies the core sociological insight that social systems cannot be reduced to the people who participate in them.

If we take the sum of all of the statuses that we occupy, the result is known as a *status set*. The status set locates us as individuals in relation to the multidimensional network of social systems that make up the world we live in. None of this, of course, would hold our sociological interest for very long were it not for the profound influence that occupying these positions has on human thought, feeling, experience, and behavior, an influence that is exerted through the ROLES that are attached to those positions.

Although every status set includes a large number of different statuses, we do not pay attention to all of them, or even several of them, at once. In the typical social situation, only one or a few statuses are actually relevant and identify our current position. These are known as *manifest statuses*. At a family dinner table, for example, it is most likely that only kin statuses such as parent, child, sibling, grandparent, and so on actually matter in that situation and are therefore manifest.

The other statuses we include in our status sets are "dormant" in that situation and generally do not have recognized effect. The responsibilities associated with employment would thus not be defined as relevant at a family dinner gathering. When a status is in the background in this way, it is called *latent*. Notice, however, that a latent status can become manifest at any moment, as when an employer telephones and interrupts dinner, asking for help with an emergency. Notice also that it is often the case that latent statuses affect how people perceive manifest statuses. The GENDER statuses of "female" and "male" often operate in this way, as do age, RACE, and occupation. Professionals are generally more likely to be taken seriously if they are male, for example, as are members of community groups if they happen to occupy other statuses that are highly regarded. In some cases, otherwise latent statuses are considered to be so

important that a *compound status* is created by combining them with a manifest status, as in "policewoman." *See also* ACHIEVED STATUS; ASCRIBED STATUS; STATUS GENERALIZATION.

Reading

Linton, Ralph. 1936. *The study of man.* New York: Appleton-Century-Crofts.
Merton, Robert K. 1968. *Social theory and social structure,* rev. and exp. ed. New York: Free Press.

status attainment and new structuralism Status attainment and new structuralism are the two main sociological approaches to understanding social inequality as it occurs through occupations and earned income. Status attainment is based on the idea that inequality results primarily from differences in characteristics such as education, parents' occupation and education, academic achievement, mental ability, VALUES, and motivation. From this perspective, RACE, GENDER, ethnic, and class inequality result primarily from differences in an individual's ability to compete successfully for higher status or income.

In sharp contrast to the individualist status attainment model, the new structuralism focuses on how characteristics of economic systems and organizations shape the DISTRIBUTION of opportunity for various SOCIAL CATEGORIES of people, limiting achievement for some while promoting it for others. This approach includes characteristics of LABOR MARKETS, especially the DUAL ECONOMY and the segmented labor market; changes in the structure of occupations as some jobs become obsolete or are moved to different locations; and *internal labor markets* that structure opportunities for job placement and promotion within firms. From this perspective, a factor such as gender inequality results in part from women's location in certain segments of the labor market (service rather than manufacturing) and, within firms, in relatively low-paid jobs (secretarial and clerical) in comparison with men with comparable qualifications.

See also COMPARABLE WORTH; OPPORTUNITY STRUCTURE; SOCIAL MOBILITY; UNEMPLOYMENT AND UNDEREMPLOYMENT.

Reading

Baron, James N., and William T. Bielby. 1980. "Bringing the firms back in: Stratification, segmentation, and the organization of work." *American Sociological Review* 45: 737–65.

Blau, Peter M., and Otis Dudley Duncan. 1978. *The American occupational structure.* New York: Wiley.

Sewell, Williams, and Robert Hauser. 1975. *Education, occupation, and earnings: Achievement in the early career.* New York: Academic Press.

status characteristic *See* EXPECTATION STATES THEORY.

status crystalization *See* STATUS INCONSISTENCY AND STATUS CRYSTALIZATION.

status generalization Status generalization is a process that occurs when a STATUS that is irrelevant in a situation nonetheless has an effect. Implicit in the DEFINITION OF THE SITUATION is shared understanding of which statuses and ROLES are relevant and, by exclusion, which are not. In a courtroom, for example, statuses such as judge, lawyer, court recorder, witness, and defendant are recognized as legitimate parts of the situation – which is to say, expectations

are organized around these positions in relation to one another. The status of doctor, however, is not relevant, unless a physician is asked to take the witness stand, in which case the expectations of the physician role may conflict with those of courtroom witness.

Studies of juries have found that although jury members are presumably equal, those who are male or who have high PRESTIGE occupations tend to have more influence and are more likely to be placed in leadership positions even though their occupations may have no bearing on their ability to deliberate a particular case. In other words, attributions made to people on the basis of status characteristics such as occupation are generalized to a variety of other statuses and social situations. Status generalization is particularly likely to occur in relation to MASTER STATUSES such as occupation, RACE, GENDER, and AGE.

See also EXPECTATION STATES THEORY.

Reading

Strodbeck, James L., R. M. James, and C. Hawkins. 1957. "Social status in jury deliberations." *American Sociological Review* 22: 713–19.

status inconsistency and status crystalization Status inconsistency is a condition that occurs when individuals have some STATUS characteristics that rank relatively high and some that rank relatively low. In most complex SOCIETIES, people's positions in the STRATIFICATION system are based on several characteristics such as occupational prestige, income, educational attainment, and, in many cases, RACE, GENDER, ETHNICITY, and AGE. Because several dimensions of inequality play a part for each individual, it is important to pay attention to how consistent the various dimensions are with one another. An organized crime boss, for example, ranks high in terms of WEALTH AND INCOME, but low in terms of occupational PRESTIGE. This tends to result in tension, which can be resolved by bringing the various dimensions into alignment, a process known as status crystalization. This might be accomplished by investing in "legitimate" businesses and deriving higher occupational prestige from them.

Status inconsistency can be quite pervasive, especially in societies in which ASCRIBED STATUSES such as race and gender play an important role in stratification. In white-dominated societies, for example, black professionals have high occupational status but low racial status that creates an inconsistency along with the potential for resentment and strain. Gender has similar effects as does ethnicity in many societies.

See also SOCIAL CLASS; STRATIFICATION AND INEQUALITY.

READING

Lenski, Gerhard. 1954. "Status crystalization: A nonvertical dimension of social status." *American Sociological Review* 19: 405–14.

status set *See* STATUS.

status strain *See* ROLE CONFLICT.

stem and leaf display *See* GRAPHICS.

stereotype A stereotype is a rigid, oversimplified, often exaggerated BELIEF that is applied both to an entire SOCIAL CATEGORY of people and to each individual within it. (The word is borrowed from the printing process in which one impression is used to stamp out many exact copies.) The belief that people on public assistance are lazy, for example, is a stereotype as is the belief that men cannot take care of children.

It is important to distinguish between a stereotype and a *generalization*. A generalization is any descriptive statement that applies to a category of people as a whole. An example would be the statement "In the U.S. black men are more likely than white men to commit violent crimes." Sociologists must frequently formulate generalizations because they are primarily interested in describing and understanding SOCIAL SYSTEMS and people's positions in them (which is to say, the categories they fall into).

Although people often object to generalizations as if they were stereotypes, there is an important difference between the terms: a generalization does not apply to individuals, only to collections of individuals such as social categories. That black men are more likely than whites to commit violent crimes does not mean that all, most, or even many black men do so. Anyone who uses the generalization as a stereotype, however, will tend to assume just that about any and all black men they encounter.

Stereotypes are important because they form the basis for PREJUDICE, which in turn is used to justify discrimination and both positive and negative ATTITUDES. In this sense it is important to be aware that stereotypes can be positive as well as negative. The stereotyped view of Jews as greedy, for example, is balanced by the equally stereotyped belief that Christians are not.

Although stereotypes are often regarded as undesirable because of the prominent role they play in SOCIAL OPPRESSION based on characteristics such as RACE, GENDER, ETHNICITY, and AGE, in an importtant respect they are essential for social life. When we enter a situation in which we do not know any one, for example, we must have some basis for knowing what to expect of others and what they expect of us. To accomplish this, we rely on what is known as the GENERALIZED OTHER, our perception of those who occupy particular social STATUSES. When we go to see a physician for the first time, for example, we know nothing about the individual, only about physicians in general. On this basis, however, we make all kinds of assumptions about this particular physician, assumptions that are, in essence, stereotypical.

The critical difference between stereotypes and generalizations is that they produce very different kinds of social consequences.

See also ATTITUDE; BELIEF; KNOWLEDGE; OTHER; PREJUDICE AND DISCRIMINATION; SOCIAL STATUS.

Reading

Allport, Gordon W. 1954. *The nature of prejudice*. Garden City, NY: Doubleday Anchor Books.

stigma Stigma is a negative social label that identifies people as DEVIANT not because their behavior violates NORMS but because they have personal or social characteristics that lead people to exclude them. People who are obese or physically impaired or disfigured (especially in relation to the face) have violated no NORMS, but they are nonetheless often treated as though they had. This is also true of those who are identified as homosexual, mentally ill, or infected with the AIDS virus, or who may be related to someone such as a traitor or murderer who has violated important norms. Stigma can also be applied to MINORITY groups such as blacks, Jews, and women whose only offense is simply being included in a stigmatized SOCIAL CATEGORY.

See also LABELING THEORY; PREJUDICE AND DISCRIMINATION.

Reading

Goffman, Erving. 1963. *Stigma: Notes on the management of a spoiled identity*. Englewood Cliffs, NJ: Prentice-Hall.

Schur, Edwin M. 1984. *Labeling women deviant: gender, stigma, and social control*. New York: Random House.

stochastic independence *See* STATISTICAL INDEPENDENCE AND STATISTICAL DEPENDENCE.

stock knowledge *See* KNOWLEDGE.

strain, role and status *See* ROLE CONFLICT.

stratification and inequality Stratification is the social process through which rewards and resources such as WEALTH, POWER, and PRESTIGE are distributed systematically and unequally within or among SOCIAL SYSTEMS. Stratification differs from simple inequality in that it is systematic. It is also based on identifiable social processes through which people are sorted into SOCIAL CATEGORIES such as CLASS, RACE, and GENDER. Theoretically, a system can exhibit inequality without being stratified – for example, by affording equal opportunity to all but distributing rewards based upon performance.

In general the categories that make up stratification systems take one of three forms: (1) CASTE, (2) ESTATE, and (3) SOCIAL CLASS. Castes are rigid categories determined at birth and allowing no MOBILITY from one caste to another. Caste systems are found in India and, to some degree, systems of racial subjugation are found historically in the United States and South Africa. Estates were categories in feudal systems, especially in Europe during the Middle Ages, that were less rigid than castes and allowed some (although very limited) mobility. Three estates made up the core of such systems in Europe – the clergy (the first estate), the nobility (the second estate), and everyone else from PEASANTS to artisans (the third estate).

In contrast with caste and estate systems, SOCIAL CLASS systems place less emphasis on ascriptive characteristics such as race and family background and more emphasis on universalistic criteria such as educational attainment. As such, they allow more social mobility from one level to another, although the average magnitude of individual movement is quite limited. The relatively open nature of class systems is indeed relative, however, and still qualified by the substantial role of racial, GENDER, AGE, and FAMILY background factors. Indeed, one of the greatest challenges for those who study class systems is to see clearly the intersection of class, race, gender, ethnicity and other factors that influence the distribution of resources and rewards.

See also CASTE; CONFLICT PERSPECTIVE; FEUDALISM; FUNCTIONALIST PERSPECTIVE; LORENZ CURVE; PEASANTS; POVERTY; SOCIAL CLASS; SOCIAL MOBILITY; STATUS.

Reading
Bendix, Reinhard, and Seymour Martin Lipset, eds. 1966. *Class, status, and power,* 2nd ed. New York: Free Press.
Kerbo, Harold R. 1994. *Social stratification and inequality,* 3rd ed. New York: McGraw-Hill.
Lenski, Gerhard E. 1966. *Power and privilege.* New York: McGraw-Hill.

stratified sample A stratified sample is a sampling design in which separate SAMPLES are drawn from different segments of a POPULATION in order to ensure proportionate representation of each segment in the overall sample. If we are drawing a sample of students in a COMMUNITY, for example, we will want to ensure that each level is represented in proportion to its share of the school population. To accomplish this, we can stratify the sample by level and select separate samples within each, combining them in the final stage into a single sample. In this way, the various levels cannot be under- or over-represented in the sample because their relative numbers are determined by the sample design itself. Within each level, or stratum, individuals are of course selected randomly for inclusion in the sample.

In general, stratification is a desirable feature in a sample design because it tends to improve the sample's EFFICIENCY, which is to say the sample will represent the population with the accuracy usually associated with samples of larger size. In order to select a stratified sample, it must be possible to identify the various segments of the population and draw separate samples from them – a condition that is often not the case

Reading
Kalton, Graham. 1984. *Introduction to survey sampling.* Beverly Hills, CA: Sage Publications.

Kish, Leslie. 1965. *Survey sampling*. New York: Wiley.

strength of relationship, statistical
See MEASURE OF ASSOCIATION.

structural differentiation *See* NEO-EVOLUTIONISM.

structural-functionalist perspective
See FUNCTIONALIST PERSPECTIVE.

structuralism and poststructuralism
Structuralism is a perspective on LANGUAGE that assumes there is a direct link between words and what we believe words represent. For example, "sexuality" is a SYMBOL that points to something real and concrete in the external world. In sociological language, words such as "SOCIAL STRUCTURE" or "CULTURE" point to something real and concrete that, although we cannot observe it directly, profoundly affects social life, especially by limiting and constraining what people think, feel, and do. Sociology is a perspective that argues for the existence of unobservable underlying structures that both shape social life and can be labeled and understood through the use of language.

Poststructuralism is a perspective based on the BELIEF that words point not to some concrete external reality but merely to other words that we use to construct social reality. We make the mistake of believing that this constructed reality is more than it is, that it has a concrete reality beyond the words we use to construct ideas about what is real. Since people are the ones who invent and use words, people are actively engaged in creating the social reality in which they live rather than being merely

limited and controlled by an external, underlying reality. There is also a middle ground that argues for elements of both positions – for example, that individuals both shape their social environment and are shaped by it.

See also AGENCY AND STRUCTURE; DECONSTRUCTION; OBJECTIVITY; POSTMODERNISM; SEMIOTICS.

Reading
Giddens, Anthony. 1987. "Structuralism, poststructuralism, and the production of culture." In *Social theory today*, edited by Anthony Giddens and Jonathan Turner. Stanford, CA: Stanford University Press.

structural lag
Structural lag is a condition that occurs when two related structural characteristics of a SOCIAL SYSTEM change at different rates and therefore become out of sync with each other. This often occurs in the relationship between OCCUPATIONAL STRUCTURES and AGE STRUCTURES. In occupations that depend on a supply of workers of particular ages, changes in the age structure of a COMMUNITY or SOCIETY will create a shortage or an oversupply of workers. This will in turn generate problems in the occupational market. A decline in BIRTH RATES, for example, will eventually lead to a decline in the relative number of teenagers, the main source of low-wage service workers in fast-food restaurants and retail stores. As a result, the supply of workers will lag behind the demand for them, creating structural lag.

See also CULTURE LAG.

Reading
Riley, Matilda W., Anne Foner, and Joan Waring. 1988. "A sociology of age." In *Handbook of sociology*, edited by Neil J. Smelser and R. Burt. New York: Russell Sage.

structural mobility *See* SOCIAL MOBILITY.

structural strain theory An example of CLASSICAL SOCIAL MOVEMENT THEORY, Neil Smelser's structural strain THEORY argues that CONTRADICTION, CONFLICT, and strain in a SOCIETY generate anxiety and uncertainty that people then want to alleviate. This typically occurs when social conditions such as standards of living are not what people expect them to be. Smelser believed that under such conditions people tend to adopt irrational BELIEFS – in conspiracies, for example – to explain what is going on. When there is a precipitating incident such as racially motivated violence, people respond by mobilizing for collective action and, if they are not stopped by the forces of SOCIAL CONTROL, will engage in some form of COLLECTIVE BEHAVIOR if not a full-fledged SOCIAL MOVEMENT.

Although Smelser was one of the first to theorize that social movements and collective behavior incorporate sociological factors, he has been criticized for placing too much emphasis on psychological motivation, for assuming people to be essentially irrational in their response to difficult social conditions, and for neglecting the importance of social organization and resources, especially in explaining social movements.
See also POLITICAL PROCESS THEORY; RESOURCE MOBILIZATION THEORY.

Reading
Smelser, Neil J. 1962. *Theory of collective behavior*. New York: Free Press.
McAdam, Doug. 1982. *Political process and the development of black insurgency 1930–1970*. Chicago: University of Chicago Press.

structural unemployment *See* UNEMPLOYMENT AND UNDEREMPLOYMENT.

structuration *See* AGENCY AND STRUCTURE.

structure *See* SOCIAL STRUCTURE.

student's t-distribution *See* NORMAL CURVE DISTRIBUTION.

subculture *See* SUBGROUPS AND SUBCULTURE.

subfamily A subfamily is a FAMILY that lives with another family that may or may not be related to it. If a young married couple and their children live with in-laws, for example, they are a subfamily.

The number of subfamilies tends to increase in difficult economic times as it becomes more difficult to maintain separate HOUSEHOLDS. In the United States, for example, the number of subfamilies declined by 26 percent during the 1960s and 1970s, but more than doubled during the 1980s.

Reading
Glick, Paul C., and S. Lin. 1986. "More young adults are living with their parents: Who are they?" *Journal of Marriage and the Family* 48(1): 107–12.

subgroup and subculture A subgroup is a collection of people who identify themselves as members of a GROUP that is also part of a larger SOCIAL SYSTEM to which they belong. Such groups can be formally defined (as an office unit in a corporation or government bureau or a student club) or informally defined (as a friendship clique in a labor union or a group of adolescents in relation to a COMMUNITY).

A subculture is a culture associated with social systems (including subgroups) and SOCIAL CATEGORIES of people (such as ethnic groups) that are part of larger systems such as FORMAL ORGANIZATIONS, communities, or SOCIETIES. Urban ethnic neighborhoods – from Indians in London and Moslems in Paris to Americans in Hong Kong or Chinese in New York – often share cultural LANGUAGE, ideas, and practices that differ from those of the surrounding community, and yet at the same time feel pressure to conform to some degree to the larger CULTURE in which their subculture is embedded. This can also happen in smaller social systems such as corporations, government bureaucracies, or military units, often forming around specialized interests or the bonds fostered by daily INTERACTION and mutual interdependency.

Subgroups and subcultures are sociologically important because they can be a source of diversity in social systems. They can also form a basis for conflict when subcultural VALUES, NORMS, and BELIEFS are at odds with those of the surrounding culture. This is particularly true when subcultures are associated with MINORITIES whose differences are used as a basis for rationalizing EXPLOITATION and SOCIAL OPPRESSION. It also occurs among those who tend to be marginalized in social life, as is the case with young people in many INDUSTRIAL SOCIETIES. Their exclusion from serious adult roles prolongs childhood and fosters a *youth culture* organized around peer relations rather than family or work life. Youth culture is a subculture that focuses primarily on music, concerns of fashion and style, the use of LEISURE time, the

frustrations of marginal status, and varying degrees of nonconformity and rebellion against mainstream adult middle-class culture.

See also ADOLESCENCE; COUNTERCULTURE; CULTURAL CONTACT.

Reading

Hebdige, Dick. 1991. *Subculture: The meaning of style*. New York: Routledge.

subjectivity The concept of subjectivity refers to our self-conscious awareness or perception of something, including ourselves. It is the point of view that we adopt as individual perceivers and knowers. In this sense, how I, Allan Johnson, see something is *my* subjectivity, while how you, the reader, see the same thing, is *your* subjectivity.

Subjectivity is usually contrasted with OBJECTIVITY, which refers to the existence of a point of view that transcends the particular and diverse points of view of individuals to make possible a universal point of view on the same object of perception. Objectivity is typically believed by scientists to be superior to subjectivity as a basis for knowing and understanding, although in other areas of knowledge – such as HERMENEUTICS or INTERACTION – subjectivity is regarded as essential.

subordinate primary labor market *See* LABOR MARKET.

subsistence economy A subsistence economy (or *natural economy*) is AGRARIAN and organized around production for consumption or use value, rather than for exchange value in relation to MARKETS. People produce little or no surplus, rely on simple TECHNOLOGY, and have a low level of specialization in their DIVISION OF LABOR.

See also VALUE, ECONOMIC.

substantive hypothesis *See* HYPO-THESIS AND HYPOTHESIS TESTING.

subsystem A subsystem is a SOCIAL SYSTEM that is part of a larger system without which the subsystem would not exist. The accounting depart-ment in a corporation, for example, can be understood as a subsystem – with its own CULTURAL, structural, POPULATION, and ECOLOGICAL char-acteristics – that exists only as part of the larger whole.

suburb A suburb is a COMMUNITY on the densely settled fringes of a city. Although suburbs first came into existence in the United States in the early 1800s, they did not emerge as a major form of community life until the turn of the twentieth century.

The object of intense sociological study during the 1950s and 1960s, suburbs were widely believed to con-tain a particular kind of CULTURE that included an emphasis on FAMILY life and home ownership, active commu-nity involvement, and a high degree of CONFORMITY and concern with keeping up appearances. More recent research in a variety of SOCIETIES from North America to Europe to Africa suggests that community cul-ture depends less on its suburban character than on residents' social characteristics such as SOCIAL CLASS and AGE. LOWER-CLASS suburbs, for example, are quite distinct from MID-DLE- or UPPER-MIDDLE-CLASS suburbs. *See also* INNER CITY; OUTER CITY.

Reading
Baldassare, Mark. 1992. "Suburban com-munities." *Annual Review of Sociology* 18: 475–94.

Jackson, K. T. 1986. *The suburbanization of the United States.* New York: Oxford University Press.
Stilgoe, J. R. 1989. *Borderland: Origins of the American suburb.* New Haven: Yale University Press.

succession, ecological Ecological succession is the process through which ECOSYSTEMS change. When there is change in some aspect of a physical environment (such as tem-perature or rainfall or volcanic erup-tion), in the behavior of one or more species (such as consumption pat-terns of food and other natural resources), or in the composition of the ecosystem's POPULATION (as when the size of different species' populations changes, species die out, or new species appear on the scene), the complex relations that make up an ecosystem then change. Poten-tially, this can produce many differ-ent effects on the ecosystem as a whole as well as on the physical envi-ronment and the various forms of life found there. Sociological interest in succession extends from the borders of biology and questions about the impact of human settlement on the natural environment to cities as ecosystems that change through suc-cessive waves of immigration and physical change.

For many years ecologists believed that the normal state of ecosystems was a condition of relative stability and balance which, when disturbed, would eventually reassert itself. More recently, however, some ecologists argue that ecosystems are always in a state of succession from one form to another and that stability and balance are only temporary conditions.
See also ECOLOGY.

Reading

Hawley, Amos. 1986. *Human ecology: A theoretical essay.* Chicago: University of Chicago Press.

Park, Robert E., Ernest Burgess, and Roderick D. McKenzie, eds. 1925. *The city.* Chicago: University of Chicago Press.

suicide Suicide, the act of taking one's own life, figures prominently in the historical development of SOCIOLOGY because it was the subject of the first sociological work to make systematic use of empirical DATA to test a THEORY. Émile DURKHEIM's classic work, entitled *Suicide,* was based on the premise that patterns of suicide can not be explained simply as the result of individual pathology and psychology, but are caused by SOCIAL FACTS. Durkheim argued, for example, that rates of suicide will tend to be high in COMMUNITIES with weak social ties. This led to the prediction that Protestants will have higher rates than Catholics since the former have a greater tendency to emphasize personal autonomy, independence, and achievement. Durkheim's data (government mortality records) and method have been extensively criticized for their inadequacies; but his focus on social rather than individual causes and his use of data to test theory provided a model that has profoundly influenced sociological research and thinking.

Reading

Atkinson, J. M. 1978. *Discovering suicide.* London: Macmillan.

Douglas, Jack B. 1967. *The social meanings of suicide.* Princeton: Princeton University Press.

Durkheim, Émile. [1897] 1951. *Suicide.* New York: Free Press.

Maris, Ronald, Alan L. Berman, John T. Maltsberger, and Robert I. Yufit, eds.

1991. *Assessment and prediction of suicide.* New York: Guilford.

sum of squares *See* VARIANCE.

superstructure *See* BASE AND SUPERSTRUCTURE.

suppressor variable In the statistical analysis of relationships between VARIABLES, a suppressor variable is one that, when controlled, has the effect of strengthening the relationship between two other variables. It is called a suppressor variable because when it is left uncontrolled, the relationship between the two variables is weaker than it otherwise would be.

Suppose that we are examining the relationship between occupation (BLUE-COLLAR AND WHITE-COLLAR) and income and find a relatively weak association. One explanation might be that if we controlled for gender, the relationship might then be stronger. Why? The answer lies in the relationship between gender and the two variables. We would expect that white-collar occupations would pay more than blue-collar occupations. Women, however, are usually likely to be both white-collar and badly paid since they are concentrated in lower-level white-collar jobs such as secretaries and clerks. Thus if we look at the relationship between occupation and income separately among women and among men, we would find that occupation makes a substantially greater difference in income than it did before. Since the variable gender, when left uncontrolled, "masks" or dampens the relationship between occupation and income, it is referred to as a suppressor variable.

See also ANTECEDENT VARIABLE; COMPONENT VARIABLE; INTERVENING

319

VARIABLE; DISTORTER VARIABLE; SPU-
RIOUSNESS.

Reading
Rosenberg, Morris. 1968. *The logic of survey analysis.* New York: Basic Books.

surplus value *See* PROFIT.

survey In the most general sense, a
survey is a method used to gather
DATA from a SAMPLE of a POPULATION
or, in the case of a CENSUS, from the
entire population. It has been widely
used in SOCIOLOGY since the rapid
development of empirical research
following World War II, especially in
the United States. In studies of individuals, information is gathered
either through written questionnaires
that respondents fill out themselves
or face-to-face INTERVIEWS. Although
there is increasing use of telephone
interviews, this is more often associated with commercial and political opinion polling than with serious
sociological research. In studies of
GROUPS and organizations, it is
not unusual to make use of existing
data, such as records of corporate
activities.

Survey data have several basic
uses. First, they are used to describe
a population (for example, a majority
of people in the United States place
themselves in either the working or
LOWER CLASS). The descriptive uses
of survey data extend to virtually
every aspect of social life, from opinion polling before elections to
unemployment RATES, sexual practices, how people use their time, and
health conditions in different countries. A second use of survey data is
to study relationships between VARI-
ABLES, especially those having to do
with cause and effect. The larger the
COMMUNITY in which people live, for
example, the more likely they are to
express tolerance for cultural diversity
and various forms of DEVIANCE. This
is especially true for those who spend
childhood years in larger communities. Whether a statistical relationship between variables measured
in a single survey is causal is virtually
impossible to demonstrate conclu-
sively, although analysts have developed a variety of statistical techniques
that help to minimize this limitation.

Whether for descriptive or causal
analysis purposes, surveys are increasingly used to establish trends. In the
United States, organizations such as
the University of Chicago's National
Opinion Research Center (NORC)
and the University of Michigan's
Survey Research Center (SCR) conduct annual surveys that include many
items that are asked on a recurring
basis. The NORC General Social
Survey has the added feature of inviting sociologists to add their own
questions to those asked each year at
a cost far below what it would require
to conduct a national survey on their
own. This kind of pooling of resources
has greatly expanded the access of
individual sociologists to high-quality
national surveys.

Regular national surveys make it
possible to chart trends not only for
single items such as perceptions of
SOCIAL INEQUALITY or attitudes
toward abortion, but also relationships between variables, such as sex
differences in ATTITUDES toward
GENDER inequality. These kinds of
data are then made widely and inex-
pensively available through various
consortiums such as the Roper
Center at the University of Con-
necticut.

The main advantage of surveys
over other research methods is that

they allow the gathering of large amounts of information from representative samples or, in the case of smaller populations, censuses. The main drawback of surveys is that their broad coverage makes it difficult to gather information in depth, such as detailed histories of people's lives or explanations for their views of the world and social issues. For this kind of information, sociologists tend to rely on less representative but more intensive research methods such as PARTICIPANT OBSERVATION and the IN-DEPTH INTERVIEW.

See also EXPERIMENT; SECONDARY ANALYSIS; STATISTICS.

Reading

Alreck, P. L., and R. B. Settle. 1995. *The survey research handbook.* Chicago: Irwin.

Hyman, Herbert H. 1972. *Secondary analysis of sample surveys.* New York: Wiley.

Schuman, Howard and Stanley Presser. 1996. *Questions and answers in attitude surveys.* Thousand Oaks, CA: Sage.

symbol A symbol is anything used to represent something more than itself. Words are literally nothing more than sounds (moving air) or collections of markings (print), from which it is impossible to discern their importance in social life. When the letters *e*, *l*, *v*, and *o* are arranged in a particular order to spell the word *love,* they can have an enormous effect when spoken or written in particular situations (or when not spoken, contrary to someone else's expectations). Arranged somewhat differently – into "vole," for example – the effect changes as well, since we now have an English word for a small rat-like rodent with a short tail. Like every other aspect of social life, the effect of words depends on the social context, since they will mean nothing to those who are not part of the SPEECH COMMUNITY that includes them in its vocabulary.

Although most symbols take the form of words used in spoken and written language, they can take other forms as well. Objects such as flags and religious artifacts are used as symbols, as are some physical movements (GESTURES) such as waving good-bye, thumbing a nose, or giving the "thumbs up" sign.

Symbols are the heart of cultural systems, for with them we construct thought, ideas, and other ways of representing reality to others and to ourselves.

See also ATTITUDE; BELIEF; CULTURE; HERMENEUTICS; INTERACTIONIST PERSPECTIVE; LANGUAGE; NORMS; SEMIOTICS; VALUES, CULTURAL.

symbolic interactionism *See* INTERACTIONIST PERSPECTIVE.

symmetry In mathematics and statistics, symmetry is defined in several ways. In mathematics, symmetry describes a relationship between two quantities that holds even if the quantities reverse their order. Equality, for example, is a symmetrical relationship because if $A = B$, then it is also true that $B = A$. However, if A is greater than B, then it is not true that B is greater than A, which means that the relationship is not symmetrical.

In sociological work, symmetry is used to describe relationships between VARIABLES. If variable A is independent of variable B, then it is also true that variable B is independent of variable A. Similarly, if A is statistically dependent on B, then B is also statistically dependent on *A*. If income varies by occupation, for example, then it will also be true that occupation will vary by income.

A second sociological usage focuses on the DISTRIBUTION of scores for single variables. The distribution of a variable is symmetrical if by drawing a vertical line through its center we can produce two halves each of which is a mirror image of the other. A rectangular distribution is symmetrical, for example, as is the well-known bell curve, shown at (a) in figure 10. Calculations involving the NORMAL CURVE DISTRIBUTION are made considerably simpler because we know that the distribution is symmetrical.

Distributions that are not symmetrical can assume an infinite number of shapes, but some are of particular interest in sociology. *Skewness* refers to how much the distribution of scores on a variable is lopsided in one direction or another. Cases in a skewed distribution tend to be lumped toward one end with a minority of cases with extreme scores at the other. For example, the distribution of income in most SOCIETIES is such that most FAMILIES have incomes toward the lower end of the scale and a minority have incomes at the high end, resulting in a bulge at the low end and a skinny *tail* at the upper end, as shown in figure 10 at (b). In such a case, where the small number of extreme scores is at the high end of the distribution, the distribution is described as positively skewed, or skewed to the right. If the minority is at the lower end of the distribution and most cases lie toward the upper end, the distribution is negatively skewed, or skewed to the left, as shown in figure 10 at (c). This might describe the distribution of family income at an elite university whose student body includes a small number of scholarship students from the working and LOWER CLASSES.

The concept of symmetry also applies to MEASURES OF ASSOCIATION, statistical quantities used to measure the strength of relationship between two variables. If a measure of association is symmetrical, its value will be the same regardless of which variable is considered to be the independent or dependent variable. If the measure of association is *asymmetrical*, then the value may differ depending on which variable is

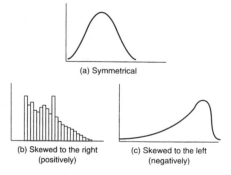

(a) Symmetrical

(b) Skewed to the right (positively) (c) Skewed to the left (negatively)

Figure 10 *Examples of symmetrical and skewed distributions*

designated as independent and which as dependent.

See also MEASURE OF ASSOCIATION; STATISTICAL INDEPENDENCE AND STATISTICAL DEPENDENCE.

Reading

Bohrnstedt, George W., and David Knoke. 1994. *Statistics for social data analysis*, 3rd ed. Itasca, IL: F. E. Peacock.

Rosenberg, Morris. 1968. *The logic of survey analysis*. New York: Basic Books.

synchronicity *See* DIACHRONIC AND SYNCHRONIC.

syndicated crime *See* ORGANIZED CRIME.

system *See* SOCIAL SYSTEM.

systematic sample A systematic sample is a design in which a list of the POPULATION is used as a sampling FRAME and CASES are selected by "skipping" through the list at regular intervals. If the population consists of 1,000 people, for example, and we want to select a SAMPLE of 250, we will take every fourth person on the list after selecting a random starting point between 1 and 4. This "skip interval" is found by dividing the population size by the sample size, in this case $1,000/250 = 4$. If we select the third case as our starting point, then we would select the following cases for our sample: 3, 7, 11, 15, 19, 23, 27, 31, 35 ... 987, 991, 995, 999. If the skip interval is not a whole number, then we follow the same process but round our selections upward or downward to the nearest whole number as the final step.

Systematic sampling assumes that the list is "well shuffled," which means there are no clear trends such as ordering DATA by AGE, income, or EDUCATION or having a characteristic recur at regular intervals (a problem known as *periodicity*). If there is an ordering, there is the danger of selecting a biased sample. If the list were ordered from youngest to oldest, for example, selecting a low random starting point would result in a sample that was biased toward young ages, while choosing a high random start point would have the opposite effect. As Blalock shows, the problem of periodicity can be seen in the example of selecting apartments from a listing of apartments in a large building. If certain kinds of apartments (such as corner units) occur at regular intervals in the list, then depending on the random start point selected, we might wind up with a sample in which corner units are under- or over-represented, anything from no corner units to nothing but corner units.

Reading

Blalock, Hubert M. Jr. 1979. *Social statistics*, 2nd ed. New York: McGraw-Hill.

Singleton, Royce A., Bruce C. Straits, and Margaret M. Straits. 1998. *Approaches to social research*, 3rd ed. Oxford and New York: Oxford University Press.

systems theory *See* SOCIAL SYSTEM.

T

table In the statistical analysis of DATA, a table is any arrangement of numerical results presented in an array of rows and columns.

See also CROSS-TABULATION; GRAPHICS.

Reading
Bohrnstedt, George W., and David Knoke. 1994. *Statistics for social data analysis*, 3rd ed. Itasca, IL: F. E. Peacock.
Zeisel, Hans. 1985. *Say it with figures*, rev. ed. New York: Harper and Row.

taboo A taboo (also spelled *tabu*) is a NORM forbidding certain behaviors as a form of RITUAL. Common taboos are the avoidance of certain foods as part of religious observance or the avoidance of a particular place that is regarded as SACRED. Sociologically, taboos are significant in several respects. The observance of taboos, for example, can serve as an indicator of GROUP membership. In a related sense, Émile DURKHEIM argued that taboos play an important part in maintaining social COHESION, as does ritual in general.

Incest taboos prohibit sexual relations between people defined as close kin. With the exception of certain CLASSES in ancient CIVILIZATIONS in Hawaii, Mexico, and Egypt, all SOCIETIES have included parents, children, and siblings in their incest taboos. Beyond this there is considerable variation. Some have argued for a biological basis to incest taboos (to prevent inbreeding) but the patterns of who is defined as close kin are often so contradictory and contrary to such concerns that this is an unlikely explanation. In some societies, for example, people commit incest if they marry a child of their mother's sister or their father's brother, but not if they marry a child of their mother's brother or their father's sister. Since the biological and genetic tie is the same in each case, the distinction clearly has more to do with CULTURE than with biology. Others have argued that incest taboos force people to marry outside of their immediate kin group, thus extending FAMILY relations and strengthening intergroup ties. There appear to be no satisfactory explanations that can account for every case.

See also MARRIAGE RULES.

Reading
Arens, W. 1986. *The original sin: Incest and its meaning.* New York: Oxford University Press.
Durkheim, Émile. [1912] 1965. *The elementary forms of religious life.* New York: Free Press.

tail of distribution *See* SYMMETRY.

task role *See* EXPRESSIVE ROLE AND TASK ROLE.

taxonomy *See* TYPOLOGY.

technocracy A technocracy is a SOCIAL SYSTEM ruled primarily by experts in SCIENCE and TECHNOLOGY. Since there has not yet been such a SOCIETY, it is a concept that describes what some social scientists fear will come to pass if INDUSTRIAL SOCIETIES continue their rapid development of and growing dependence on technology and those who both invent and control it. Signs of this include the growing importance of public issues such as nuclear power, pollution, warfare, and medicine in which most CITIZENS lack the expertise to take informed positions. By default, they feel helpless to do anything but leave such decisions to experts. A major SOCIAL PROBLEM that results is that although technical experts may be highly trained in the use of technology, their training typically does not extend to the more sociological and psychological consequences of technology.

Reading

Barnes, Barry. 1985. *About science.* New York and Oxford: Blackwell Publishers.

Habermas, Jürgen. 1971. *Toward a rational society.* London: Heinemann.

technological determinism Technological determinism is the view that social conditions and the characteristics of SOCIAL SYSTEMS are determined primarily by TECHNOLOGY and technological change. It would see the INDUSTRIAL REVOLUTION, for example, or the introduction of computer technology as primary engines driving SOCIAL CHANGE and shaping social relationships and INSTITUTIONS.

Reading

Lenski, Gerhard E., Jean Lenski, and Patrick Nolan. 1998. *Human societies,* 8th ed. New York: McGraw-Hill.

technology Technology is the accumulated store of cultural KNOWLEDGE about how to adapt to, make use of,

and act upon physical environments and their material resources in order to satisfy human wants and needs. The knowledge of how to plant and harvest crops, make steel, lay down roads, or construct computers is all part of cultural technology.

Although technology has yet to acquire a prominent place in sociological thinking, there are a number of sociologists who argue for its importance, especially in understanding the course of history and SOCIAL CHANGE. Major types of SOCIETIES – such as HUNTER-GATHERER, HORTICULTURAL, AGRARIAN, INDUSTRIAL, or POST-INDUSTRIAL – are distinguished first and foremost by differences in technology. These are associated with dramatic differences in the shape of social INSTITUTIONS such as the FAMILY, RELIGION, and POLITICS and the terms and conditions of social life. The INDUSTRIAL REVOLUTION, which produced enormous social change, was based to a great extent on technological innovations.

Technology should not be confused with SCIENCE. Technology consists of practical knowledge of how to make use of material resources, whereas science consists of abstract knowledge and THEORY about how things work. It is certainly true that technological and scientific developments often go hand-in-hand, but this is not necessarily always the case. *See also* TECHNOCRACY.

Reading

Lenski, Gerhard E., Jean Lenski, and Patrick Nolan. 1998. *Human societies: An introduction to macrosociology,* 8th ed. New York: McGraw-Hill.

teleological explanation A teleological explanation is based on the idea that things happen the way they do because they serve some ultimate purpose or contribute to some ultimate goal or end point. In this sense, it can be concluded that the cause of something is a result that it helps to bring about. Such reasoning is particularly common in explanations of animal behavior and appearance. The color of an animal's body, for example, may be explained in terms of what appears to be a consequence it produces, such as concealment from predators.

Teleological explanation is especially relevant to the FUNCTIONALIST PERSPECTIVE and its emphasis on the requirements of SOCIAL SYSTEMS. Herbert SPENCER's THEORY of SOCIAL DARWINISM argued that inequality exists because it serves the interests of SOCIAL EVOLUTION and progress. Talcott PARSONS argued that the DIVISION OF LABOR between women and men serves a higher social purpose of ensuring that key social functions will be performed efficiently and exists for that reason (rather than in support of male privilege and dominance). Outside sociology, teleological explanations are quite common, seeing gender inequality, for example, as the manifestation of a natural order or divine purpose.

The place of teleological explanation in sociology continues to be controversial. As one of the founders of sociology and the functionalist perspective, Émile DURKHEIM emphasized the importance of distinguishing between the function of some aspect of social life and the cause of it, but it is a distinction that is easily overlooked.

Reading
Durkheim, Émile. [1895] 1938. *The rules of the sociological method.* New York: Free Press.
Ryan, A. 1970. *The philosophy of the social sciences.* London: Macmillan.

Turner, Jonathan H. 1998. *The structure of sociological theory*, 6th ed. Belmont, CA: Wadsworth.

theistic religion   Theistic religion is based on a shared cultural BELIEF in the existence of gods, goddesses, or other supreme beings. *Monotheism*, as found in Christianity, Judaism, and Islam, recognizes a single deity, while *polytheism*, as found in Hinduism, includes two or more deities, often arranged in a HIERARCHY. In *pantheism*, the deity is regarded not as separate from the world but as the universe itself, with humans and the world being but manifestations of it.

Theism is sociologically significant in several ways, including the fact that religious wars, persecution, and intolerance of differences are most closely associated with monotheism. In part, this is because of its insistence that there is only one deity, a belief that places it at odds with other religions.

See also ANIMISM; ETHICALIST RELIGION; RELIGION; TOTEMIC RELIGION.

Reading
Wilson, Bryan. 1982. *Religion in sociological perspective.* New York: Oxford University Press.

theocracy   A theocracy is a SOCIETY in which the STATE is under religious authority, and religious and political leadership are one and the same.

theodicy   Theodicy refers to the idea that everything has a divine purpose and makes sense in relation to the BELIEF that God created the world and everything in it, and that God is, ultimately, just and good. From this perspective, even evil has a divine purpose – and should be endured because of it – including the evils of RACISM, SEXISM, and other forms of social injustice and SOCIAL OPPRESSION.

theoretical perspective A theoretical perspective (or *paradigm*) is a set of assumptions about reality that underlies the questions we ask and the kinds of answers we arrive at as a result. As a perspective on human life, for example, SOCIOLOGY is based on the assumption that SOCIAL SYSTEMS such as SOCIETY and the FAMILY actually exist, that CULTURE, SOCIAL STRUCTURE, STATUSES, and ROLES are real. In our work we try to understand such things and how they work, but we do not doubt their actual existence. This is true of virtually any search for truth, whether it be mathematical (whose axioms we only assume to be true), literary, spiritual, or scientific.

Theoretical perspectives are important because assumptions direct our attention and provide frameworks for interpreting what we observe. Sociologists, for example, will pay far more attention to things like the distribution of WEALTH and POWER than they will to personality differences between individuals, while psychologists will tend to do just the opposite. And in explaining patterns of human behavior, we will be drawn to explanations that rely on concepts such as social structure or culture rather than to some notion of an inherent human nature, not because we necessarily believe that human nature does not exist, but because it is not part of our theoretical perspective.

Within sociology, there are several theoretical perspectives – CONFLICT, INTERACTIONIST, FUNCTIONALIST and ecological – that bring different assumptions and points of emphasis

to the study of social life. All, however, have in common an attention to what is fundamentally SOCIAL in human life.

See also INTERPRETIVE SOCIOLOGY.

Reading
Kuhn, Thomas S. 1970. *The structure of scientific revolutions*, 2nd exp. ed. Chicago: University of Chicago Press.

theory A theory is a set of logically interrelated propositions and the implications that follow from them, which is used to explain some phenomenon. Implicit in any theory is a set of underlying assumptions and methods that are rarely questioned, a THEORETICAL PERSPECTIVE.

The simplest kind of statement about how things work is an *empirical generalization*. This is an observation about how two or more VARIABLES are related. "Women receive less in income than men," "the lower people's CLASS position is, the more likely they are to express attitudes of racial PREJUDICE," and "the more people interact in small GROUPS, the more influence they tend to have" are all examples of empirical generalizations. There is disagreement among sociologists as to whether such statements actually explain anything. Some argue that empirical generalizations merely summarize something to be explained. The generalization may hint at a related theoretical statement (as does the third example above), but this is not enough to make it fully theoretical. At the other extreme from empirical generalizations is what C. Wright MILLS called *grand theory*, which is so abstract, formalized, and general that it is often put together without any reference to empirical observation. Mills was particularly critical of Talcott PARSONS and his almost exclusive devotion to the development of grand theory.

The most common form of theory in sociology falls somewhere between the purely empirical generalization and grand theory, what Robert K. MERTON called *theories of the middle range*. Such theories are usually informed by empirical generalizations but provide a broader and more abstract context that applies to a wider range of situations. Consider, for example, Merton's theory of DEVIANCE. Here he argues that SOCIAL SYSTEMS are organized in part around a consensus in cultural VALUES that define what is regarded as important and desirable. In spite of this, however, there is often a structural inequality in access to socially legitimate means for achieving those values. As a result, the system itself encourages a variety of deviant responses among those who cannot otherwise achieve values common to all those who participate in the system.

See also ABSTRACTED EMPIRICISM; EMPIRICAL; THEORETICAL PERSPECTIVE.

Reading

Giddens, Anthony, and Jonathan Turner, eds. 1987. *Social theory today*. Cambridge, England: Polity Press.

Merton, Robert K. 1968. *Social theory and social structure*, rev. and exp. ed. New York: Free Press.

Mills, C. Wright. 1959. *The sociological imagination*. New York: Oxford University Press.

Third World Third World is a term used to refer generally to relatively poor, nonindustrial SOCIETIES often having a history of being exploited under COLONIALISM and which continue to exist in a state of relative economic and political dependence if not subordination. They are distinguished from the *first world* (industrial powers such as Britain, the United States, Japan, and Germany) and the *second world* (until recently, the former Soviet Union and its socialist satellites in Eastern Europe). *See also* DEPENDENCY THEORY; WORLD SYSTEM.

Thurstone scale *See* ATTITUDE SCALE.

time budget analysis A time budget analysis is a written account of how people spend their time. The technique can range from keeping a detailed diary to recalling the past in an interview. It is used to study a variety of sociological problems. In some INDUSTRIAL SOCIETIES, time budgets have been used to track changes in family divisions of labor in response to the women's movement and the increased participation of women in the labor force. For the most part, such studies reveal that men's participation in domestic work does not increase when their wives work outside the home. Instead, the total amount of domestic work declines as wives increase their outside commitments. As a result, the percentage of all domestic work done by men increases, but not because of greater participation by men.

Reading

Oakley, Ann. 1974. *Woman's work: The housewife, past and present*. New York: Pantheon.

Sorokin, Pitirim, A., and Clarence Q. Berger. 1939. *Time-budgets of human behavior*. Harvard Sociological Studies, vol. 2. Cambridge, MA: Harvard University Press.

Thompson, L., and A. J. Walker. 1989. "Women and men in marriage, work, and parenthood." *Journal of Marriage and the Family*, 51: 845–72.

time series analysis In STATISTICS, a time series analysis is any collection of DATA gathered from comparable POPULATIONS at regular time intervals, such as annually or, in the case of the typical national CENSUS, every five or ten years. Time series analysis has been used to describe trends in a great variety of social indicators, from PUBLIC OPINION to crime and DEATH RATES. Although usually used for descriptive purposes, time series analysis increasingly has been used to test causal models.

See also CAUSAL EXPLANATION AND CAUSAL MODEL; LONGITUDINAL RESEARCH.

Reading
Gottman, J. M. 1981. *Time series analysis*. Cambridge, England: Cambridge University Press.
Marsh, C. 1988. *Exploring data*. Cambridge, England: Polity Press.

time structure In a SOCIAL SYSTEM, a time structure is a method of organizing events in some relation to the passage of time, from annual meetings to the scheduling of school classes or when children go to bed. Time structure operates in three basic ways: (1) activities are organized to varying degrees in relation to time; (2) the length of people's participation in social systems is usually time bound: family membership is expected to be lifelong, for example, while students are expected to graduate from school in a fairly predictable way; and (3) the existence of systems themselves varies by time: ad hoc committees are designed to exist only as long as they are needed for a specific and relatively temporary purpose; INSTITUTIONS such as STATE

and church, however, are intended to endure indefinitely.

See also SOCIAL STRUCTURE.

Reading
Lauer, R. H. 1981. *Temporal man: The meaning and uses of social time*. New York: Praeger.
Sorokin, Pitirim A., and Robert K. Merton. 1937. "Social time: A methodological and functional analysis." *American Journal of Sociology* 42: 615–29.
Zerubavel, Eviatar. 1981. *Hidden rhythms: Schedules and calendars in social life*. Chicago: University of Chicago Press.
———. 1985. *The seven-day week: The history and meaning of the week*. New York: Free Press.

total fertility rate *See* BIRTH RATE.

total institution As developed by Erving GOFFMAN, a total institution is an isolated, enclosed SOCIAL SYSTEM such as a prison, mental hospital, cloister, boarding school, or military training camp whose primary purpose is to control most aspects of its participants' lives. How total institutions maintain their hold on people, the consequences they produce for individuals and social systems, and how people adapt to the limitations imposed by their circumstances are all questions of sociological interest.

See also DEGRADATION CEREMONY.

Reading
Goffman, Erving. 1961. *Asylums*. New York: Anchor Books.

totalitarianism *See* AUTHORITARIANISM.

totemic religion Totemic religion (or *totemism*) is a form of religious INSTITUTION organized around a shared cultural BELIEF in SACRED objects called totems. Émile

DURKHEIM analyzed totemic religions and argued that RELIGION is in fact a way in which people worship their own SOCIETIES by attributing supernatural power to totems associated with that society. The totems are regarded as representations of the sacred elements of society itself rather than of external deities.

Totems take many different forms but typically consist of natural objects such as plants or animals. Totems are regarded with great awe and respect since it is believed that any misbehavior in regard to a totem – such as touching it, looking upon it, or, in the case of living totems, harming or killing it – will have disastrous consequences.

See also ANIMISM; ETHICALIST RELIGION; RELIGION; THEISTIC RELIGION.

Reading

Durkheim, Émile. [1912] 1965. *The elementary forms of religious life.* New York: Free Press.

Radcliffe-Brown, Alfred R. 1952. *Structure and function in primitive society.* London: Cohen and West.

trade union A trade union is a collection of workers who organize to promote their own interests in relation to employers, especially around issues of wages, promotion, working conditions, and job security. Unions trace their history to the early stages of the Industrial Revolution in eighteenth-century England.

Sociological interest in unions focuses on several questions. First, how are union movements and working-class consciousness related to opposition to CAPITALISM? In the United States, for example, the emergence of unions had to do primarily with representing the interests of highly skilled workers, not with political organization of the broad working class (including women, various ethnic groups, and people of color). In Europe, however, trade unions had a more political agenda and posed a greater threat to capitalism as a system.

Second, what is the relationship between unions and INSTITUTIONS such as the STATE? In Britain and other European democracies, unions have a social legitimacy that often grants them a share of governing POWER. In the United States, however, unions are relatively independent and seek political influence as an outside INTEREST GROUP. In Korea and Japan, unions have little power in any arena and serve primarily as advisers to corporations in which their members are employed.

Third, as unions become larger and more complex, are they able to maintain democratic governing structures? Robert MICHELS argued that an "iron law" of OLIGARCHY prevails, making it inevitable that DEMOCRACY will give way to rule by a few. But subsequent research suggests a more complex picture, with democracy depending on a variety of conditions.

Fourth, what role do unions play in CLASS CONFLICT under capitalism? Do they, for example, ally with the establishment and serve to contain and channel worker discontent in ways that preserve capitalist interests? Are they able to organize across occupational lines so as to have the breadth needed to confront capitalism on a large scale?

See also SOCIAL CLASS; SOCIAL MOVEMENT.

Reading

Bauman, Zygmunt. 1972. *Between class and elite.* Manchester, England: Manchester University Press.

Crouch, C. 1982. *Trade unions: The logic of collective action.* Glasgow: Fontana.

Katznelson, Ira, and Aristide R. Zolberg, eds. 1986. *Working-class formation: Nineteenth-century patterns in Europe and the United States.* Princeton: Princeton University Press.

tradition Loosely put, tradition refers to a cultural practice or structural arrangement that is regarded as part of a common inheritance in a SOCIAL SYSTEM. Tradition provides a sense of unquestioned continuity with a shared perception of the past. "We do it this way because we've always done it this way, because this is who we are." Although this may be the view shared by participants in a social system, the actual cause of the phenomenon is likely to be more complex. Various aspects of RACISM and SEXISM, for example, may take on the status of tradition in a society. But they do more than preserve continuity with the past. They also preserve the privileged position of the dominant group.

Reading

Hobsbawm, Eric and Terence Ranger, eds. 1983. *The invention of tradition.* New York: Cambridge University Press.

Shils, Edward A. 1981. *Tradition.* London: Routledge and Kegan Paul.

traditional authority *See* AUTHORITY.

traditional community *See* COMMUNITY.

transitional status A transitional status is a position that exists solely for the purpose of acting as a bridge between two other statuses. "Engaged" or "betrothed," for example, are used as transitional positions linking "single" and "married," just as "on probation" is a transitional status bridging between "incarcerated criminal" and "free person." There are in fact not very many transitional statuses in most SOCIAL SYSTEMS although one might be misled into thinking otherwise by statuses that occur between other statuses in time. Thus even though different grades of schooling are typically preceded by one STATUS and followed by another, they are not transitional because their reason for existence is not merely to act as a bridge between two other statuses.

See also RITE OF PASSAGE.

Reading

Coser, Rose Laub. 1966. "Role distance, sociological ambivalence, and transitional status systems." *American Journal of Sociology* 77(2): 173–87.

transmitted deprivation *See* CULTURE OF POVERTY.

transnational and multinational corporation A transnational corporation is a business organization that operates across national borders. A multinational corporation does business in more than one country by selling goods on the international MARKET or having factories in more than one country. With transnationals, the process of production and marketing is coordinated across national boundaries, so that, for example, parts may be produced in one place and shipped to another for assembly and to yet another for final sale. This gives transnationals the potential for enormous flexibility by shifting various aspects of production to countries with lower taxes, labor costs, or standards for pollution control or worker safety. This has been greatly enhanced by recent revolutions in computers and telecommunications.

By maximizing flexibility and diversification, transnationals increase both their competitive advantage in relation to other corporations and their leverage in relation to the countries in which they operate. The size and power of transnational corporations has become so great that they rival the economic POWER of most NATIONS, especially those in the THIRD WORLD. Of the 100 largest economic units in the world, for example, half are countries and half are transnationals. The emergence and growth of transnationals is the latest stage in the GLOBALIZATION of industrial CAPITALISM.

See also CONGLOMERATE; INTERNATIONAL DIVISION OF LABOR; WORLD SYSTEM.

Reading

Chandler, Alfred D., Jr. 1990. *Scale and scope: The dynamics of industrial capitalism.* Cambridge: Belknap.

Gill, Stephen, and David Law. 1988. *The global political economy.* Baltimore: Johns Hopkins University Press.

Lall, Sanjaya, and P. Streeten. 1977. *Foreign investment, transnationals, and developing countries.* London: Macmillan.

triad *See* DYAD.

typification Typification is the process of relying on general KNOWLEDGE as a way of constructing ideas about people and the social world. As we participate in social life, most of what we know of other people does not take the form of direct personal knowledge. When we do business in a bank, for example, we usually do not know the bank teller personally, and yet we enter the situation with some kind of knowledge of tellers as a type of people and banks as a type of social situation that enables us to predict what we can expect and what will be expected of us.

See also OTHER.

Reading

Schutz, Alfred. 1962–1966. *Collected papers,* vol. 1. The Hague: Nijhoff.

typology A typology (or *taxonomy*) is a set of categories used for classification. SOCIETIES, for example, can be categorized using a typology of types of ECONOMY, which includes INDUSTRIAL, HUNTER-GATHERER, HORTICULTURAL, PASTORAL, AGARIAN, fishing, and herding. Typologies are useful for drawing attention to particular characteristics of what we observe so that we can make comparisons, such as identifying different religious BELIEFS in horticultural and industrial societies.

A typology generally has non-overlapping categories that exhaust all possibilities, which means that there is one category available for each observation and each observation fits in only one category. This is not always the case, however. Sociology identifies FOLKWAYS and MORES, for example, as two types of norms; but there are norms, such as laws governing highway speed limits, that are of neither type.

See also IDEAL TYPE.

U

unanticipated consequence *See* FUNCTIONALIST PERSPECTIVE.

unbiased estimate *See* ESTIMATES.

underclass *See* SOCIAL CLASS.

underdevelopment Underdevelopment is a concept most closely associated with DEPENDENCY THEORY and the Marxist understanding of global patterns of inequality. It describes SOCIETIES that are relatively poor and economically stagnant, with low wages and low productivity. Dependency theory argues that underdevelopment results from a WORLD SYSTEM of powerful INDUSTRIAL SOCIETIES benefiting at the expense of THIRD WORLD countries exploited through NEOCOLONIALIST trade relationships.

unemployment and underemployment Unemployment is the condition of wanting to work but being without a job. It is of sociological interest for several reasons. In the first sense, there are different types of unemployment corresponding to various causes. *Structural unemployment*, for example, occurs when the OCCUPATIONAL STRUCTURE changes (as when manufacturing jobs decline and service jobs increase), rendering some skills obsolete and throwing people out of work. Structural unemployment can occur for a variety of reasons, including technological innovation or firms deciding to close or relocate their operations to other regions or countries.

Other forms of unemployment include *frictional unemployment* (when people change jobs at their own choosing); *seasonal unemployment* (when a change in seasons lowers the demand for agricultural, recreational, or other kinds of work); *cyclical unemployment* (when companies lay off workers during a recession in order to cut costs and preserve corporate profits and protect stock holder interests). Almost all of these are tied to the way in which an ECONOMY is organized. CAPITALISM tends to generate unemployment through the profit-seeking, competitive behavior of corporations that defines capitalism as a system. STATE SOCIALISM, by contrast, tends to produce lower levels of unemployment because it is less bound by the demands of competitive efficiency and cost control.

Unemployment is also sociologically significant because of its social consequences. It tends to hurt individuals, FAMILIES, and COMMUNITIES in a variety of ways. In addition, it tends to be unevenly distributed across different SOCIAL CATEGORIES. In white-dominated societies, for example, people of color are more likely to be unemployed regardless of their educational attainment and other qualifications.

Finally, unemployment is significant in how it is measured as a social phenomenon. In the United States and Britain, official unemployment statistics define as unemployed only those who have no jobs and are actively seeking employment. This tends to underestimate the extent of unemployment by excluding those who would like to work but are so discouraged by job opportunities that they are no longer looking. It also fails to measure the extent of *underemployment*, a condition in which people must work part-time, or at jobs that do not allow them to earn enough to support themselves or their families or to utilize their skills fully. As industrial economies shift away from better-paying manufacturing jobs to lower-paying service jobs, and as corporations increase their competitiveness by turning to part-time workers, the problem of underemployment has become increasingly important.

See also LABOR FORCE; LABOR MARKET.

Reading

Ashton, D. N. 1986. *Unemployment under capitalism: The sociology of British and American labor.* Westport, CT: Greenwood Press.

Sinclair, Peter. 1997. *Unemployment: Economic theory and evidence.* Oxford: Blackwell Publishers.

Sullivan, Teresa A. 1978. *Marginal workers, marginal jobs.* Austin: University of Texas Press.

unexplained variance *See* COVARIANCE.

unilinear change *See* SOCIAL EVOLUTION.

unintended consequence *See* FUNCTIONALIST PERSPECTIVE.

union *See* TRADE UNION.

universalism *See* PATTERN VARIABLES.

universalism, norm of *See* SCIENCE, NORMS OF.

unobtrusive measure In research, an unobtrusive measure is a method of making observations without the knowledge of those being observed. One way to assess the effects of racial integration in schools, for example, is to compare the academic records of students educated in schools whose student populations vary in their degree of racial heterogeneity.

Unobtrusive measures are designed to minimize a major problem in social research: how a subject's awareness of the research project affects behavior and distorts research results. When people are interviewed, observed openly, or even fill out anonymous questionnaires, it is impossible to avoid measuring not only what researchers are trying to measure but also the subjects' reactions to the research setting and INTERACTION. The main drawback of unobtrusive measures is that there is a very limited range of information that can be gathered in this way. For this reason, they are usually used as a supplementary source of information.

See also HAWTHORNE EFFECT.

Reading

Webb, E. J. 1981. *Nonreactive research in the social sciences: Unobtrusive measures.* Boston: Houghton-Mifflin.

upper class In the study of STRATIFICATION, the upper class is identified by its dominant position in relation to the distribution of WEALTH, POWER, and PRESTIGE. In FEUDAL societies, the upper class took the form of an *aristocracy*, a collection of inherited positions of privilege based on control over land and peasant POPULATIONS, often granted in exchange for military allegiance to more powerful leaders. Under CAPITALISM, upper-class privilege is based on ownership and control of the MEANS OF PRODUCTION and the employment of workers in exchange for wages.

There are several approaches to identifying the BOUNDARIES that set the upper class apart. In one sense, the upper class is distinguished by its huge share of resources and rewards such as WEALTH AND INCOME, most of which are inherited. In Britain, for example, two out of every three chief executive officers of large corporations have upper-class backgrounds. In the United States, the richest 10 percent of the population controls 71 percent of all wealth, including 87 percent of cash assets, 94 percent of business assets, 90 percent of stocks and bonds, and 49 percent of all real estate. Whether we consider this 10 percent to constitute the upper class is somewhat arbitrary, since we could just as easily shift the definition to include the richest 12 percent or the richest 8 percent or even 1 percent.

A less arbitrary approach focuses on the fact that members of the upper class tend to have a relatively clear sense of class identity based on FAMILY ties and common experiences such as private schooling. This is reflected in practices such as compiling "Social Registers," sending children to select private schools attended by other members of the upper class, and placing tight restrictions on the choice of marriage partners. Sociologists such as William Domhoff in the United States have tried with some success to use such criteria to identify the actual boundaries of upper-class membership.

Marxists in particular argue that the upper class sometimes constitutes a *ruling class*, primarily through its control of economic and political INSTITUTIONS. This was certainly true of feudal aristocracies, but it is less clear that a true ruling class exists in modern capitalist societies. In order for capitalists to maintain control over the means of production, it is necessary to ensure that the STATE acts in their best interests at least most of the time. The upper class pursues this in several ways. They place their own members in positions of AUTHORITY such as government cabinet positions; they contribute to the political campaign expenses of candidates who support capitalism and its interests; they fund organizations such as "think tanks" that publish books and position papers and sponsor conferences that shape people's perceptions of issues related to capitalism; and they control the mass media's potential to criticize capitalism and reveal its social consequences. The degree to which the upper class actually succeeds in all of this is arguable.

See also CORPORATE CLASS; ELITE; FEUDALISM; HEGEMONY; OLIGARCHY; SOCIAL CLASS; STRATIFICATION AND INEQUALITY.

Reading

Domhoff, G. William. 1998. *Who rules America now?* Mountain View, CA: Mayfield.

Stanworth, Philip, and Anthony Giddens, eds. 1974. *Elites and power in British society.* Cambridge, England: Cambridge University Press.

Useem, Michael. 1984. *The inner circle: Large corporations and the rise of business political activity in the U.S. and U.K.* New York: Oxford University Press.

urban community   *See* COMMUNITY.

urban ecology   Urban ecology is an approach to understanding how cities develop. It originated in a group of University of Chicago sociologists known as the CHICAGO SCHOOL. The basic idea behind this perspective is to look at cities in the same way that ecologists look at various species of life in relation to natural environments. Each species makes use of the ENVIRONMENT in its own way, which often results in COMPETITION with other species or members of the same species. As a result, POPULATIONS of different species shrink, grow, or stabilize depending on climatic and other changes that affect the competitive process. In addition, if a large enough territory is examined, distinct patterns of DISTRIBUTION will also be found, with different species distributed in various ways across the land.

According to the ecological perspective, a given territory will be used in various ways by various mixes of life forms. These patterns will change over time through a complex process of adaptation and competition. Urban ecologists argue that urban growth can be described and understood in similar terms. Instead of studying different species of life, however, the focus now is on SOCIAL CATEGORIES of people who differ in characteristics such as ethnicity, SOCIAL CLASS, and RACE. As cities develop, for example, factories and other businesses tend to be built near transportation lines such as rivers and railways. This will attract housing for workers and service businesses to meet their needs. As different groups of workers adapt to these surroundings, they will form neighborhoods with distinctive class and ethnic identities whose location will depend in part on the proximity of various employment opportunities. As new populations emigrate to the city, or as businesses close, relocate, or change in character, residential patterns may change in response through a process known as ecological SUCCESSION.

The first urban ecologists regarded cultural and structural characteristics of cities as secondary in importance if not irrelevant to urban development. This rather extreme view eventually caused the ecological perspective to lose standing in sociology. More recently, however, it has been revived in a less rigidly ecological form, most notably by Amos Hawley.

See also ECOLOGY; URBANIZATION AND URBANISM.

Reading

Hawley, Amos H. 1981. *Urban society: An ecological approach,* 2nd ed. New York: Wiley.

——. 1986. *Human ecology: A theoretical essay.* Chicago: University of Chicago Press.

urbanization and urbanism   Urbanization is the process through which POPULATIONS become concentrated in large COMMUNITIES – cities – that are essentially nonagricultural in character. Instead, they are organized primarily around the production of services and finished goods.

Louis WIRTH, one of the core members of the CHICAGO SCHOOL, argued that urban ENVIRONMENTS produce a particular kind of social life. He called it urbanism. Social life in cities tends to be more anonymous and based on formal relationships and a complex DIVISION OF LABOR within a heterogeneous POPULATION. It is, for this reason, potentially more stimulating as well as more alienating.

Urbanization began its evolution around 3000 B.C., when the invention of agriculture produced great surpluses of food. This freed large segments of populations to pursue other kinds of work. From that point on, the growth of cities was relatively slow until the INDUSTRIAL REVOLUTION began in the late eighteenth century. Since then, urbanization has been an explosive phenomenon touching most parts of the world. The percentage of the world population living in urban areas rose from an estimated 3 percent in 1800 to 14 percent by 1900 and 41 percent by 1975. It is projected to reach approximately 60 percent by 2025. In addition to the sheer magnitude of its growth, urbanization also plays an important role in the functioning of the capitalist economic system, as space and urban community resources are exploited for profit.

The earliest American sociologists, especially those identified with the Chicago School, were particularly interested in the dynamics of urban growth and how it affected social life. Part of their work focused on theoretical models that described basic patterns of urban development. According to Ernest BURGESS's concentric-zone model, for example, commercial activities are concentrated in a central urban core, around which rings develop devoted to various activities. Homer Hoyt's sector model shows the effects of transportation that produce patterns of growth that, rather than looking like rings, resemble irregularly sliced pie segments that grow up around lines of transportation extending outward from the core of the city. Chauncy Harris and Edward Ullman's multiple-nuclei model describes how cities develop around several different centers, each of which focuses on a specialized activity such as manufacturing, entertainment, finance, theaters, or government.

Historically, the most rapid urbanization has been associated with INDUSTRIALIZATION in Europe and North America, but the more recent experience of nonindustrial societies is quite different. Countries such as Mexico, Egypt, and India, for example, are experiencing rapid urbanization primarily as the result of crushing rural poverty that drives migrants to cities where services and job opportunities are wholly inadequate to sustain them. The result has been what some demographers call overurbanization.

See also CHICAGO SCHOOL; COMMUNITY; MEGALOPOLIS; MIGRATION; URBAN ECOLOGY.

Reading
Castells, Manuel. 1977. *The urban question: A Marxist approach*. Translated by A. Sheridan. Cambridge, MA: MIT Press.

Harris, C. D., and E. L. Ullman. 1945. "The nature of cities." *The Annals of the American Academy of Political and Social Science* 242: 7–17.

Harvey, David. 1985. *Consciousness and the urban experience*. Oxford: Blackwell Publishers.

Hoyt, H. 1939. *The structure and growth of residential neighborhoods in American cities*. Washington, DC: Federal Housing Authority.

Wirth, Louis. 1938. "Urbanism as a way of life." *American Journal of Sociology* 44: 1–24.

urban recycling *See* GENTRIFICATION.

use value   *See* VALUES, ECONOMIC.

utilitarianism   Utilitarianism is a philosophical approach to human life that emphasizes the importance of the rational thinking individual. As developed by Jeremy Bentham and John Stuart Mill (and, more indirectly, by Thomas Hobbes, David Hume, and John Locke), utilitarianism views the core of the ideal human existence as the individual who is motivated by rational self-interest, seeking pleasure and happiness and avoiding pain and unhappiness. From this perspective, a SOCIETY is nothing more than a collection of individuals trying to make the most of what they have, using social relationships with one another toward this end. Utilitarians promoted this as an optimal way of life since they believed that when individuals act in their own rational self-interest, the result will be the greatest good for the largest number.

Although utilitarianism has influenced thinking in economics and behavioral psychology, its impact on sociology has been limited primarily to EXCHANGE THEORY and the application of mathematical models such as game theory to COLLECTIVE BEHAVIOR.

See also ATOMISM AND HOLISM; MATHEMATICAL SOCIOLOGY; METHODOLOGICAL INDIVIDUALISM. RATIONAL CHOICE THEORY.

Reading
Halévy, Élie. [1928] 1972. *The growth of philosophic radicalism*. London: Faber and Faber.
Turner, Jonathan H. 1998. *The structure of sociological theory*, 6th ed. Belmont, CA: Wadsworth.

utopia   A utopia is a vision of an idealized COMMUNITY or SOCIETY typically used to critique current social conditions and exert pressure for SOCIAL CHANGE. Most utopian visions are so far removed from social life as it has been known that they are more useful for highlighting some essential feature of society – such as inequality, AUTHORITARIANISM, or competition – than they are as practical guides for the future. Perhaps the most famous examples of utopias are found in Plato's *Republic*, Sir Thomas More's *Utopia*, and B. F. Skinner's *Walden Two*.

See also JUSTICE; MILLENARIANISM.

Reading
Mannheim, Karl. 1936. *Ideology and utopia*. London: Routledge and Kegan Paul.
Manuel, Frank E., and Fritzie P. Manuel. 1979. *Utopian thought in the western world*. Oxford and New York: Blackwell Publishers.

V

validity Validity is the degree to which a MEASUREMENT instrument such as a SURVEY question measures what we in fact think it measures. For example, when survey respondents answer "No" to the question, "Are you racist?" does this mean they are not racist or simply that they know that being racist is socially unacceptable and do not want the interviewer to think badly of them? Without a definitive answer to such questions, the validity of a particular measurement instrument is in doubt (which is why the above question is unlikely to be used by researchers).

The problem of validity is perhaps most acute in survey research because this method relies not on observations of what people do, but on people's reports of what they do and how they think about various issues. What answers mean to respondents – as distinct from what they mean to researchers – thus becomes a critical issue. As a result, studies of the effects of question wording and the characteristics of interviewers and INTERVIEW situations are important considerations in methodological research.

See also MEASUREMENT; RELIABILITY.

Reading

Singleton, Royce A., Bruce C. Straits, and Margaret M. Straits. 1998. *Approaches to social research*, 3rd ed. Oxford and New York: Oxford University Press.

value, cultural A cultural value is a shared idea about how something is ranked in terms of its relative social desirability, worth, or goodness. Values can be used to rank virtually anything, including abstractions (logic above intuition), objects (gold above lead), experience (loving and losing above never loving at all), behavior (truth telling above lying), personal characteristics (tall above short), and states of being (healthy above ill). In all cases, what makes the idea a value is its use to rank things in relation to one another rather than to compare them as merely similar or different.

We can distinguish between cultural values on the one hand and personal tastes and preferences on the other, in that the sole authority for the latter is the individual. We experience the authority for cultural values, however, as residing outside of individuals who may hold them. Honesty, for example, is valued not because you or I say it is, but because we perceive honesty as something regarded as important in our CULTURE. That we as individuals may not place much stock in it ourselves does not affect its standing as a part of culture.

Values are important parts of any culture because they influence how people choose and how SOCIAL SYSTEMS develop and change. Indeed, Talcott PARSONS argued that a social system cannot exist without a consensus around values (and, by implication, the NORMS that support them). Although some degree of consensus around at least some values is probably inherent in the very idea of a social system, it is equally true that consensus is never complete, especially in larger and more complex social systems such as SOCIETIES. Truly totalitarian social systems are exceedingly rare and short-lived precisely because they are based on coercion rather than consensus. But perhaps no less rare is a society in which the value system is not used to some degree to further the interests of some groups at the expense of others and in which some degree of coercion is not used to maintain at least the appearance of uniformity amidst underlying diversity and conflict.

See also CULTURE; VALUE, ECONOMIC.

Reading

Parsons, Talcott, and Edward A. Shils, eds. 1951. *Toward a general theory of action.* New York: Harper and Row.

Rokeach, Milton, ed. 1979. *Understanding human values: Individual and societal.* New York: Free Press.

Spates, James L. 1983. "The sociology of values." *Annual Review of Sociology* 9: 27–49.

value, economic An economic value is a cultural idea that provides a basis for determining what something is worth in a SOCIAL SYSTEM. All societies rely to some degree on *use value*: something has worth to the degree that it can be put to practical use. A highly sophisticated computer, for example, would have high use value in a university but virtually no use value in a tribe living in the Brazilian rain forest.

When there are MARKETS in a society, *exchange value* becomes important. This is determined by what one is able to get for a product or service in exchange for something else. Exchange value tends to be less stable than use value (as exemplified by the rapid changes in real estate values that often occur in INDUSTRIAL SOCIETIES). This is because it is based on several considerations, including changes in people's desires and wants, fluctuations in supply and demand, and profit motives.

It is important to be aware that use value and exchange value often vary independently of each other. Useful skills, such as the ability to craft fine furniture by hand, may become "obsolete" and lose their exchange value in the face of competition from machine-built furniture available at lower cost. Similarly, something with little use value – such as swamp land sold for residential use – can acquire great exchange value through fraudulent misrepresentation. Many luxury goods can also have exchange value that far exceeds their use value: luxury automobiles whose quality of transportation is not significantly better than many cars priced far lower, or diamond-studded watches that are not waterproof and that keep less accurate time than inexpensive digital watches.

According to Karl MARX's *labor theory of value*, the true measure of the value of something rests not on market forces but on the labor required to produce it, especially as measured by the amount of time involved. In this sense, goods "contain" human labor from which their true value is derived. If it takes twice as much labor to make a pair of shoes as it does to make a shirt, then the shoes are worth twice as much. The Marxist view of value has been much criticized and is controversial, even among Marxists.

See also COMMODITY; CONSPICUOUS CONSUMPTION; MARKET; PROFIT.

Reading

Marx, Karl. [1867] 1975. *Capital: A critique of political economy.* New York: International Publishers.

Steedman, Ian, Paul Sweezy, et al., eds. 1981. *The value controversy.* London: New Left; New York: Schocken.

value relevance, value freedom, and value neutrality First explored by Max WEBER, value relevance is an ongoing concern in sociological work. As a part of CULTURE, values are relevant as topics for research; but in the practice of sociological research they are also relevant for the part they play in the choice of what to study. Whether to study the consequences of racism, or how to improve worker productivity in the workplace, or the role of love in marriage, is a decision based not on fact or scientific method but on values. It depends, for example, on the researcher's judgment of what is most important or interesting, or what funders such as corporations or government agencies are most willing to support financially.

Although values inevitably play a part in research, the principles of value neutrality and value freedom argue for controlling their influence whenever possible. Under conditions of value freedom, researchers practice OBJECTIVITY by not choosing methods and interpreting DATA in ways that favor their values or ideological stance. To ignore evidence that contradicts a THEORY, for example, and only acknowledge evidence that supports it, violates the principle of value freedom. Value neutrality requires researchers to identify and make their own values clear rather than pretending they have no values that might influence their work, and to avoid using their AUTHORITY (especially as teachers) to advocate particular values.

Although there is general acceptance of the principles of value neutrality and freedom, it is unclear whether it is possible or desirable to adhere rigidly to them in all their particulars. The research that sociologists do, for example, has potentially profound implications for social life as people must live it, and as such many sociologists regard it as their duty to promote positive SOCIAL CHANGE.

See also OBJECTIVITY; SCIENCE, NORMS OF.

Reading

Gouldner, Alvin W. 1975. *For sociology: Renewal and critique in sociology today.* Harmondsworth, England: Penguin Books.

Weber, Max. [1904–1917] 1949. *The methodology of the social sciences.* New York: Free Press.

variable A variable is any measurable characteristic that differs from one observation to another. A *constant* is any characteristic whose value does not vary across observations. In a study of power inequality in married couples, for example, marital status would be a constant since every person observed would be married. The amount of POWER spouses have, however, would most likely be a variable since it would not be the same for everyone.

A variable differs from a concept by including some form of measurement. Age, for example, is a concept; but people's answers to the question

"How old are you?" result in a variable.

Variable is a key concept in SOCIOLOGY because the subjects of research take the form of variables. One approach to explaining racial PREJUDICE, for example, argues that ignorance breeds prejudice by encouraging people to substitute STEREOTYPES for actual experience of people whose racial characteristics differ from one's own. To test such an idea, however, we must devise a way to measure "ignorance" and "prejudice" among actual people and see whether these characteristics are related to each other. If we ask people to report the number of years of schooling they have, we create a variable that might be used as a rough gauge of the degree of ignorance which might, in turn, be related to some measure of prejudice, such as whether people regard other RACES as inferior.

In thinking about causal relationships between variables, the variable to be explained is called *dependent*, while the variable believed to produce an effect is called *independent*. If we argue that ignorance causes prejudice, then ignorance is the independent variable and prejudice is the dependent. When there is a clear time-ordering of variables, it is clear which variable must be considered dependent: if we link childhood experiences of racial differences with adult attitudes toward race, the adult attitudes clearly cannot be considered to be independent variables affecting childhood experience.

In other cases, deciding which variable to call dependent is less clearcut. A causal relationship between prejudice and ignorance, for example, might run in both directions, with ignorance causing prejudice and prejudice contributing to ignorance by closing people off to new information about people who differ from them.

See also ANTECEDENT VARIABLE; ATTITUDE SCALE; COMPONENT VARIABLE; CROSS-TABULATION; DISCRETE VARIABLE AND CONTINUOUS VARIABLE; DISTORTER VARIABLE; DUMMY VARIABLE; FREQUENCY DISTRIBUTION; GRAPHICS; INTERVENING VARIABLE; QUALITATIVE VARIABLE AND QUANTITATIVE VARIABLE; SCALE OF MEASUREMENT; SOCIAL DISTANCE; SUPPRESSOR VARIABLE.

Reading

Singleton, Royce A., Bruce C. Straits, and Margaret M. Straits. 1998. *Approaches to social research*, 3rd ed. Oxford and New York: Oxford University Press.

variance Variance is a statistical measure of the degree to which scores in a DISTRIBUTION differ from one another, especially in relation to the MEAN of the distribution. If everyone in a POPULATION has the same income, for example (which would mean that everyone's income would equal the mean income), the numerical value of the variance would be zero since the difference between each score and the mean would be zero. The more the scores differ from the mean, the larger the variance will be.

Technically, the variance is defined as the average squared deviation of all the scores about the mean. In plainer terms, the mean is subtracted from each score and each result is squared. The sum of these squared differences (known as the *sum of squares*) is then divided by the total number of scores to get an average squared difference of each score from the mean. This quantity is the variance, whose symbol is s^2 when used to describe a SAMPLE and σ^2 for a POPULATION.

The variance is a key concept in sociological research because it is a measure that reflects the key fact that there is variation in the social world, that people in different SOCIAL CATEGORIES vary in their behavior, experience, and resources, or that GROUPS, COMMUNITIES, and SOCIETIES differ from one another. In this sense the variance is one way of quantifying what it is that sociologists want to explain. The variance is also used to compare groups on the basis of their relative homogeneity: if one group has a much higher income variance than another, for example, this means that it is more heterogeneous.

The square root of the variance is the *standard deviation*, whose symbol is *s* when applied to samples and σ when applied to populations. It is used in a variety of ways to describe distributions of VARIABLES. For example, we know from Pafnuti L. Chebyshev's theorem (named for the nineteenth-century Russian mathematician) that in any distribution at least 75 percent of all the cases will have scores no more than two standard deviations above or below the mean. If the average test score is 500 and the standard deviation is 100, we know that 75 percent of all the test scores will lie somewhere between 300 and 700 (the mean of 500 plus and minus 2×100 or 200). This will be true regardless of what the distribution looks like.

See also ANALYSIS OF VARIANCE; COEFFICIENT OF ALIENATION; COVARIANCE; RANGE; STANDARD ERROR; STATISTICS.

Reading
Bohrnstedt, George W., and David Knoke. 1994. *Statistics for social data analysis*, 3rd ed. Itasca, IL: F. E. Peacock.

verification Verification refers to the principle that something may be accepted as true only if there is empirical evidence to support it.
See also FALSIFICATIONISM.

verstehen *See* INTERACTION.

vertical differentiation *See* DIFFERENTIATION.

victimless crime As first identified by Edwin Schur, victimless crime is an offense that lacks an identifiable victim who is the object of the CRIME. Rather, the offense is against SOCIETY itself through its NORMS, VALUES, ATTITUDES, and BELIEFS. Someone who smokes marijuana, for example, or uses cocaine, or engages in an illegal sexual behavior with a consenting adult, violates cultural values about appropriate behavior and the norms that support those values. There is, however, no direct victim per se, as there is when someone is robbed, beaten, or murdered, or when funds are embezzled from a bank or treason is committed against a NATION.
See also CONSCIENCE COLLECTIVE.

Reading
Schur, Edwin M. 1965. *Crimes without victims*. Englewood Cliffs, NJ: Prentice-Hall.

vital statistics Vital STATISTICS are quantitative measures that describe the RATE at which events occur that affect POPULATION processes such as BIRTH, DEATH, MIGRATION, and growth. The most important of these events are birth and death, although demographers also consider changes in marital status (marriage, annulment, separation, divorce, and remarriage) as vital events because these, in turn, affect birth rates. Countries differ a great deal in how well they register vital events, with the best registration systems typically found in the wealthiest SOCIETIES. Sweden boasts perhaps the world's oldest high-quality system. For populations with poor vital statistic registration systems, demographers have devised a number of techniques for estimating key population characteristics from other sources of information.

Reading

Shryock, Henry S., and Jacob Siegel and Associates. 1976. *The methods and materials of demography*. New York: Academic Press.

vocabulary of motives *See* ACCOUNT.

voluntarism Voluntarism refers to the idea that individual human beings originate their BEHAVIOR independent of the influence of SOCIAL SYSTEMS. As such, it opposes the basic premise of sociology that individuals are always participating in something larger than themselves – social systems – which shapes them at the same time that they make it happen.

See also AGENCY AND STRUCTURE; ATOMISM AND HOLISM; METHODOLOGICAL INDIVIDUALISM.

voluntary association A voluntary association is a GROUP or ORGANIZATION that people may join or leave freely; that is free of external control; and whose purpose, goals, and methods are up to the members to

determine. Voluntary associations take various forms ranging from informal sports clubs, church groups, and neighborhood improvement associations to national political parties. Like all groups and organizations, they vary in the formality of their structure and the purposes they serve for their members. Political parties, for example, are largely instrumental in that they exist primarily as means for achieving certain goals. Other associations, however, such as prayer groups or recreational clubs, also have important expressive purposes organized around the emotional, spiritual, or social needs of their members.

Sociologically, voluntary associations are often seen as crucial to the functioning of DEMOCRACY, especially by providing a way for individuals to become involved in public life beyond the privacy of home and FAMILY. This has been especially true in the United States.

See also INTEREST GROUP.

Reading

Gordon, C. Wayne, and Nicholas Babchuk. 1959. "A typology of voluntary associations." *American Sociological Review* 24: 22–29.

Knoke, David. 1986. "Associations and interest groups." *Annual Review of Sociology* 12: 1–21.

Smith, Constance, and Ann Freedman. 1972. *Voluntary associations: Perspectives on the literature*. Cambridge, MA: Harvard University Press.

voting behavior From a sociological perspective, the study of voting behavior focuses primarily on explaining who votes and how they vote. Early research pioneered by Paul F. LAZARSFELD and others at Columbia University concluded that voting depends primarily on people's location in SOCIAL SYSTEMS – their SOCIAL CLASS, FAMILY history of voting behavior, ETHNICITY, GENDER, RACE, RELIGION, and membership in VOLUNTARY ASSOCIATIONS such as TRADE UNIONS, political PARTIES, and civic organizations. Beginning in the late 1940s, the University of Michigan became a focal point for voter research and relied on a different model emphasizing individual characteristics such as people's sense of identification with particular political parties, their perception of which social issues are most important, and their feelings about particular candidates. From this perspective, factors such as social class are important primarily in their effects on party, issue, and candidate identification. These in turn, are what actually shape voting behavior. In recent years some researchers have used RATIONAL CHOICE THEORY to argue that voting is governed less by group loyalties and class position than by individuals' rational calculations of self-interest.

A major concern in voting studies has been the shifting dynamics that shape political parties. Until fairly late in the twentieth century, for example, lower-class voters tended to support liberal parties such as the Democrats in the United States or the Labour Party in Britain. Middle- and upper-class voters tended to support conservative parties such as the Republicans in the United States and the Conservatives in Britain. More recently, however, both countries have seen a *class dealignment* in voting behavior as working- and middle-class voters increasingly vote across liberal/conservative lines.

See also CITIZEN AND CITIZENSHIP; CONSERVATISM AND LIBERALISM; POLITICAL CULTURE; POLITICS.

Reading

Campbell, Angus, Philip E. Converse, Warren E. Miller, and Donald E. Stokes. 1976. *The American voter.* Chicago: University of Chicago Press.

Flanagan, Scott C., Kohei Shinsaku, Ichiro Miyake, Bradley M. Richardson, and Joji Watanuki. 1991. *The Japanese voter.* New Haven: Yale University Press.

Franklin, Mark, Tom Mackie, and Henry Valen, eds. 1991. *Electoral change: Responses to evolving social and attitudinal structures in seventeen democracies.* Cambridge, England: Cambridge University Press.

W

wealth and income Wealth is any valued resource that is not needed for consumption in the near future and can therefore be held in reserve and accumulated. Property, stock, bonds, savings, retirement annuities, machinery, vehicles, jewelry, art, and major household furnishings are all considered forms of wealth in capitalist INDUSTRIAL SOCIETIES.

In the study of SOCIAL INEQUALITY, wealth is distinguished from *income*, which consists primarily of money received during each year and which may be converted to wealth through investment or the purchase of things such as buildings or land. Although income inequality has important social consequences, inequality of wealth is usually more extreme and is generally regarded as more important. This is primarily because wealth is a key basis of inequality of POWER, especially when wealth takes the form of CAPITAL. In the United States, for example, the top 10 percent of all families receive roughly 40 percent of all income each year, but they hold more than two-thirds of all wealth, including roughly half of all real estate and more than 90 percent of all cash, business assets, stocks, and bonds. In the United Kingdom, the top 1 percent of the population owns 75 percent of privately held corporate stock.
See also CAPITAL.

Reading
Kerbo, Harold R. 1996. *Social stratification and inequality*, 3rd ed. New York: McGraw-Hill.

welfare state A welfare state is a SOCIAL SYSTEM in which the government assumes responsibility for the well-being of CITIZENS by making sure that people have access to basic resources such as housing, health care, education, and employment. The welfare state was first introduced in Germany in the late 1800s and subsequently in Britain and most of Western Europe and Scandinavia. It has not yet developed in Japan or the United States, the latter being the only INDUSTRIALIZED SOCIETY without a national health-care program.

Although often associated with SOCIALISM, from a Marxist perspective the welfare state has been criticized as supporting CAPITALISM by managing potential conflict between workers and capitalists. Unemployment benefits and income support programs to aid the poor, for example, are seen as mechanisms for blunting the effects of capitalist exploitation and defusing the working class's potential for CLASS CONSCIOUSNESS and revolutionary action.

Reading
O'Connor, James. 1973. *The fiscal crisis of the state*. New York: St. Martin's Press.

Offe, Claus. 1984. *Contradictions of the welfare state.* Cambridge, MA: MIT Press.

Pinker, R. 1979. *The idea of welfare.* London: Heinemann Educational Books.

weltanschauung *See* WORLDVIEW.

white-collar crime A concept first introduced by the sociologist Edwin SUTHERLAND, white-collar crime describes the concept of criminal acts that arise from opportunities created by a person's social position, especially occupation. Embezzlement, for example, can be committed only by employees such as bank officers and accountants, and it is therefore a white-collar crime. Other examples include expense account padding, corporate price-fixing, tax fraud, violation of employee safety regulations, illegal discrimination, false advertising, stealing copyrighted ideas from other companies, the use of insider information in stock market trading, and unfair labor practices.

The major significance of white-collar crime as a category in sociological analysis has been the perception that white-collar criminals tend to be middle- and upper-middle-class and that because of a class bias in the criminal justice system, their CRIMES are generally viewed as less serious and less deserving of punishment. The concept of white-collar crime has figured prominently in the study of both social STRATIFICATION and DEVIANCE.

Shapiro has argued that we should focus on the distinguishing characteristics of white-collar crime rather than the characteristics of those who perpetrate them. She argues that white-collar crime, unlike other types of criminal behavior, involves a violation of trust relationships.

Lawyers who steal from clients while managing their estates, for example, do more than steal, for they also take advantage of a trust relationship through which such theft becomes possible. The violation of a trust relationship has to do with the crime itself rather than the SOCIAL CLASS to which the criminal belongs and, as such, should be more central to the concept of white-collar crime.

Shapiro also argues that if white-collar crime is conceptualized in this way it also becomes apparent that the relatively low rate at which such crimes are detected, prosecuted, and punished is due as much to the SOCIAL SYSTEMS in which they occur as it is to class bias. The structure of the trust relationship provides criminals with a variety of ways to conceal their activities (by juggling the books, for example) and destroy evidence. As a result, they so embed their crimes in the ongoing structure of complex organizations that it is difficult to establish just what has been done and who was knowingly involved. This, argues Shapiro, will result in relatively low rates of detection and conviction for white-collar crimes and, given the difficulty of making strong cases against perpetrators, plea bargains and other arrangements that will reduce the severity of punishment.

Reading

Shapiro, S. P. 1990. "Collaring the crime, not the criminal: Reconsidering the concept of white-collar crime." *American Sociological Review* 55(3): 346–65.

Sutherland, Edwin H. 1983. *White-collar crime: The uncut version.* New Haven: Yale University Press.

white-collar worker *See* BLUE-COLLAR WORKER AND WHITE-COLLAR WORKER.

work In general, work is any activity that produces a product or service for immediate use or exchange. Sociologists have long been interested in a number of key questions about work: how work is defined and organized and how this affects the work experience; how people are distributed among occupations (such as the GENDER, RACE, or AGE composition of the LABOR FORCE); how the organization of work is connected to systems of STRATIFICATION AND INEQUALITY; and how work is related to major INSTITUTIONS such as the STATE, RELIGION, and the FAMILY.

An *occupation* is a type of work people do, such as carpentry, nursing, or child care. In MARKET societies, where people meet their needs primarily through earning money rather than producing for their own consumption or engaging in barter with other producers, work is generally considered to be an occupation only if it results in money earnings. As a result, a great deal of the work that people perform is never considered occupational. This is true not only of women's work in most societies but of both women and men in nonindustrial societies where a great deal of the work performed – from carrying water to building houses – involves neither markets nor cash.

While an occupation refers to a particular type of work, a *job* is a particular social setting in which such work is performed. Lawyer, for example, is an occupation, while partner in a particular law firm is a job performed by lawyers. Over the course of a working lifetime, people in a given occupation typically work at a number of jobs which, taken together, constitute a *career*.

It is not unusual, particularly in industrial capitalist societies, for careers to include not only a succession of jobs but occupational changes as well. As the OPPORTUNITY STRUCTURE in the LABOR MARKET changes, for example, people may find dwindling job openings in their occupations and as a result return to school to acquire new skills that qualify them for different occupations.

Occupations are sociologically important because of the role they play in the distribution of WEALTH and INCOME, POWER, and PRESTIGE and in the general process through which societies produce goods and services. *See also* ALIENATION; MARKET; OCCUPATIONAL STRUCTURE; POST-INDUSTRIAL SOCIETY; PROFESSION AND PROFESSIONALIZATION; SOCIAL MOBILITY; UNEMPLOYMENT AND UNDEREMPLOYMENT.

Reading

Cook, John, Susan Hepworth, Toby Wall, and Peter Warr. 1981. *The experience of work.* New York: Academic Press.

Kalleberg, Arne, and Ivar Berg. 1987. *Work and industry.* New York: Plenum.

Rothman, Robert A. 1998. *Working: Sociological perspectives.* Englewood Cliffs, NJ: Prentice-Hall.

working class *See* SOCIAL CLASS.

world economy *See* WORLD SYSTEM.

world system First developed by Immanuel WALLERSTEIN in the 1970s, world system is a concept referring to the complex relationships that organize countries into an international ECONOMY that governs the distribution of WEALTH, POWER, PRESTIGE, and resources for development among nations. In the process, the world system profoundly affects social life within SOCIETIES from the shape of political INSTITUTIONS to working conditions and the degree of SOCIAL INEQUALITY. Wallerstein identified three types of nations in the world system: (1) core, (2) peripheral, and (3) semiperipheral.

Core (or *center*) nations are industrial capitalist countries that control most of the world's wealth, military hardware and expertise, productive TECHNOLOGY, and financial resources. Core societies are economically diversified with a balance of manufacturing and service industries and little reliance on providing raw materials such as minerals and agricultural products. As a result, they tend to be politically stable, democratic, and relatively autonomous.

Peripheral societies include what is commonly referred to as the THIRD WORLD – relatively poor NATIONS that control few productive resources with which to compete in an international capitalist economy. As a result, they tend to depend on core nations for financial aid, for the importation of factories and technology, and for MARKETS for their main goods, which are raw materials and agricultural products such as coffee, oil, and sugar. Unlike the core, they tend to specialize in a relatively small number of products. All of this means that peripheral societies are vulnerable to fluctuations in the world demand and price paid for their products, to military intervention by core nations, or to the withholding of aid from core governments and banks. As a result, peripheral societies tend to be politically unstable and undemocratic, and to rely on large military and police establishments, often trained and equipped by core nations, to control the populace.

Wallerstein argues that the dominance of the core and the vulnerability and dependency of the periphery are a key feature in the growing inequality of income, wealth, and power on a world scale. It is a world CLASS system among nations that profoundly affects class relations among people within nations. Core societies, including their LOWER CLASSES, are able to enjoy a relatively high standard of living primarily because of the ability of the core to exploit and extract wealth from the impoverished and dependent periphery.

The *semiperipheral society*, a middle category whose membership is not always clear, is in general in the process of industrializing and providing skilled labor for core society industries. Countries such as Taiwan and South Korea are on the one hand relatively subordinate in the world system and yet engage in a great deal of sophisticated production of electronic goods, automobiles, and the like.

The world system approach to the sociological analysis of international relations is controversial. Its basic argument is that peripheral societies are poor not simply because they lack such things as technology, will, and an educated work force but because core societies exploit them by confining them to the role of providing cheap labor and raw materials, much as colonizing powers did in past centuries. One critical response to this begins with the observation that the world system approach does not explain why certain societies originally emerged as industrial powers in the first place. In addition, it is unclear that the countries of the Third World would have become industrial powers if today's core nations had not developed first. In short, there is disagreement over the history through which the current world system developed. There is less disagreement, however, over the fact that there is an increasingly unequal distribution of wealth and power in the world.

As a system of global domination, the world system was preceded by *empires* such as the Roman Empire, which ruled primarily through military dominance and sought both economic gain and political control over entire societies. The shift from empires to the current world system began in the fifteenth century as first Spain and Portugal and then England, France, and the Netherlands began to establish overseas colonies, develop market economies, and compete with one another for world dominance.

See also CAPITALISM; COLONIALISM AND IMPERIALISM; DEPENDENCY THEORY; INTERNATIONAL DIVISION OF LABOR; THIRD WORLD; TRANSNATIONAL AND MULTINATIONAL CORPORATION.

Reading

Chirot, Daniel. 1986. *Social change in the modern era*. San Diego: Harcourt Brace Jovanovich.

Wallerstein, Immanuel. 1976. *The modern world system*. New York: Academic Press.

——. 1979. *The capitalist world-economy*. Cambridge, England: Cambridge University Press.

——. 1980. *The modern world system II: Mercantilism and the consolidation of the European world economy, 1600–1750*. New York: Academic Press.

worldview Within a CULTURE, a worldview is a general way of looking upon the universe and our relation to it, a general set of assumptions about the meaning of life, about what is important, and about how things work. In comparing traditional and modern COMMUNITIES, for example, sociologists identify different points of view, with traditionalists being less receptive to change and new ideas, more reliant on religious faith, and generally suspicious of TECHNOLOGY, SCIENCE, and detached rationality as a way of approaching human life. A worldview is typically associated with a GROUP or SOCIETY, which means that, as with all aspects of culture, there is usually variation among individuals in the degree to which they share in it. Radicals and revolutionaries, for example, would by definition be at odds with the prevailing worldview of their society.

Worldview is often used interchangeably with *weltanschauung*, a German concept that is most closely associated with philosopher and historian Wilhelm DILTHEY and sociologist Karl MANNHEIM.

See also HERMENEUTICS.

Reading

Hodges, H. A. 1952. *The philosophy of Wilhelm Dilthey*. London: Routledge.

Mannheim, Karl. [1923] 1952. "On the interpretations of 'weltanschauung.'" In *Essays on the sociology of knowledge*, 33–83. New York: Oxford University Press.

X

xenocentrism Xenocentrism is a culturally based tendency to VALUE other CULTURES more highly than one's own. It is common not only in the Third World, where people tend to devalue their cultures in relation to the cultures of INDUSTRIAL SOCIETIES, but also in wealthier societies. In the United States, for example, it is often assumed that European products such as wine and cheese are superior to those produced locally.

See also CULTURAL RELATIVISM; ETHNOCENTRISM; PREJUDICE AND DISCRIMINATION; XENOPHOBIA.

xenophobia Xenophobia is a culturally based fear of outsiders. It has often been associated with the hostile reception given those who immigrate into SOCIETIES and COMMUNITIES. In some cases xenophobia is based on a genuine fear of strangers and the unknown. More often it has a more concrete basis, however, especially as it involves COMPETITION for jobs, or ethnic, racial, or religious PREJUDICE.

See also ETHNOCENTRISM; MIGRATION; SEGREGATION AND INTEGRATION; XENOCENTRISM.

Reading

Bennett, D. H. 1988. *The party of fear: From nativist movements to the new right in American history*. Chapel Hill: University of North Carolina Press.

Y

y-intercept *See* REGRESSION ANA-
LYSIS.

youth culture *See* SUBGROUP AND
SUBCULTURE.

Z

zeitgeist This German word means "spirit" (*geist*) of an "age" (*zeit*) and refers to the idea that each period in a SOCIETY's history can be characterized by a distinct set of cultural BELIEFS and practices that establish a certain tone that will be reflected in art, politics, and virtually every other aspect of social life. In the United States, for example, "the '50s" and "the '60s" point to eras commonly thought to have had a particular spirit that distinguished them from what preceded them and what came after.

zero-sum game Zero-sum game is a general term used to refer to a social situation in which one person's success must come at the expense of others. For example, when school grading is done on a curve basis so that only a certain percentage of students will get A's and a certain percentage are required to fail, grading becomes a zero-sum game. Similarly, because modern industrial ECONOMIES are so competitive and the distribution of WEALTH AND INCOME is so unequal, they are also in some respects zero-sum games.

The concept of a zero-sum game is useful for understanding how people choose among EXPLOITATION, COMPETITION AND COOPERATION as ways of interacting with others.

See also RATIONAL CHOICE THEORY.

Reading

Thurow, Lester C. 1980. *The zero-sum society: Distributions and the possibilities for economic change*. New York: Basic Books.

Von Neumann, John, and Oskar Morgenstern. 1964. *Theory of games and economic behavior*, 3rd ed. New York: Wiley.

Zagare, F. C. 1984. *Game theory: Concepts and applications*. Beverly Hills, CA: Sage Publications.

zone of transition *See* INNER CITY.

z-score In a NORMAL CURVE DISTRIBUTION, individual scores are described in one of two ways. Consider the DISTRIBUTION of IQ scores, which has the shape of a normal curve with a MEAN of 100 and a STANDARD DEVIATION of 10 points. A score, such as 120, is known as a *raw score*. We can also describe it, however, in terms of its distance from the mean of the distribution. A z-score (or *standard score*) is calculated as the difference between the score and the mean, divided by the standard deviation for the distribution. In this case, 120 corresponds to a z-score of $(120 - 100)/10 = +2.0$, indicating that a score of 120 is two standard deviations above the mean. A raw score of 80 corresponds to a z-score of $(80 - 100) = -2.0$, which indicates that the score is two standard deviations below the mean.

z-scores play a key role in calculating probabilities associated with STATISTICAL INFERENCE.

See also STANDARDIZATION.

Reading

Bohrnstedt, George W., and David Knoke. 1994. *Statistics for social data analysis*, 3rd ed. Itasca, IL: F. E. Peacock.

Biographical Sketches

Biographical Sketches

A Selected Sociological Who's Who

The entries in this section provide brief introductions to major figures who have shaped sociological concepts and thinking over the past two centuries. Readers will find here information on when and where these people lived and worked, their major interests and published works, and the concepts most closely associated with them. Most are sociologists, but there is also an occasional philosopher, economist, anthropologist or other thinker whose work is particularly relevant to sociological work. I have not included those whose work preceded the emergence of sociology as a discipline. Most selections also focus on nonliving figures, although I have also included some contemporary sociologists who have made substantial contributions to the field and whose names readers are likely to encounter.

Addams, Jane (1860–1935) One of the leading sociologists of her day, Addams is best known for helping to establish the THEORY and methods of applied sociology that would later be used by male sociologists to shape the CHICAGO SCHOOL of sociology in the United States. Addams founded Hull House, a settlement house in Chicago that attracted a fascinating and brilliant collection of sociologists, especially women who lived there and combined both intellectual work and family life.

Addams was primarily interested in combining scientific research methods with ethical and moral VALUES to work toward a more just SOCIETY. She and her colleagues applied this approach to the large and rapidly growing city of Chicago, focusing in particular on problems of POVERTY, immigration, and the plight of the working and LOWER CLASSES under industrial CAPITALISM. She became recognized as a national leader of the settlement house movement and a profoundly influential sociologist.

Addams's progressive politics included pacifist opposition to the 1914–18 world war, which resulted in censure by the U.S. government (which identified her at one point as "the most dangerous woman in America") and diminished standing among sociologists. Nonetheless, she went on to play an active role in major social reforms during the Great Depression – including social security – and received the Nobel Peace Prize in 1931.

Major works include *Hull House maps and papers* (1895); *Democracy and social ethics* (1902); *New ideals of peace* (1907); and *Twenty years at Hull House* (1910). See also *Jane Addams: A centennial reader*, edited by Emily Cooper Johnson (1960); and Mary Jo Deegan, *Jane Addams and the men of the Chicago School* (1988).

Adorno, Theodor (1903–1969) A German social philosopher with wide-ranging interests, Adorno was a member of the Frankfurt School and a proponent of CRITICAL THEORY. He was particularly interested in radical SOCIAL CHANGE and rejected EMPIRICISM, POSITIVISM, and rigid scientific methods as inadequate for discovering how to produce it. His criticism of modern SOCIETY focused extensively on the use of MASS MEDIA to produce a MASS SOCIETY of people manipulated into going along with an oppressive and dehumanizing status quo.

Major works include *The authoritarian personality* (1950); *Prisms* (1967); *Dialectic of enlightenment* (1973); and *The jargon of authenticity* (1973). See also M. Jay, *Adorno* (1984).

Allport, Gordon (1887–1967) An American social psychologist, Allport specialized in the study of cultural ATTITUDES, especially in the form of racial PREJUDICE.

Major works include "Attitudes," in *A handbook of social psychology*, edited by C. Murchison (1935); *The psychology of rumor*, with Leo Postman (1947); and *The nature of prejudice* (1954).

Althusser, Louis (1918–1990) A French Marxist social philosopher whose ideas were quite influential for a period during the late 1960s and 1970s. Althusser is best known for his criticism of traditional Marxism. On the subject of BASE AND SUPERSTRUCTURE, for example, he argued that the former does not determine the latter, but that the two exist in a complex reciprocal relationship. He also argued that IDEOLOGY amounted to more than false consciousness and played a real role in social life, especially through the cultural and social reproduction of CAPITALISM. He was criticized on numerous grounds, including being overly dogmatic in his views and ignoring contrary evidence, and has lost much of his sociological influence.

Major works include *For Marx* (1966) and *Reading Capital* (1970). See also A. Callinicos, *Althusser's Marxism* (1976).

Aron, Raymond (1905–1983) A prolific writer, Aron was a French sociologist with special interests in problems related to IDEOLOGY, INDUSTRIAL SOCIETY, POLITICS, and international relations, especially in relation to warfare. Unlike many of his French colleagues, he was critical of Marxism and argued for the social importance of pluralistic POWER STRUCTURES in political systems. In addition to his special interests, he wrote influential works on sociology as a way of thinking.

Major works include *German sociology* (1935); *The century of total war* (1951); *The opium of the intellectuals* (1955); *Peace and war* (1961); *Eighteen lectures on industrial society* (1963); *Democracy and totalitarianism* (1965); *Main currents in sociological thought* (1965); and *The industrial society* (1966).

Balch, Emily Greene (1867–1961) A colleague and friend of Jane ADDAMS, Balch was an American sociologist best known for her studies of immigration, women, GENDER inequality, and the struggle for world peace. As with many women sociologists of her time, her work was routinely ignored by male sociologists in spite of its innovations. She combined statistical studies with sociological THEORY long before it became common practice in the male-dominated sociological profession, for example. She was also one of the earliest sociologists to make frequent use of the concept of ROLE.

Like Addams, Balch was active in the pacifist movement seeking to end the 1914–18 world war and was ostracized by colleagues and hounded by the government as a result. It devastated her academic career, but she nonetheless continued working for peace. She went on to occupy important positions in the League of Nations formed after the war and the United Nations that was later to replace it. In 1946, she became the second woman (Addams being the first) to receive the Nobel Peace Prize.

Major works include *Public assistance of the poor in France* (1893); *A study of conditions of city life* (1903); *Our Slavic fellow citizens* (1910); *Beyond nationalism: The social thought of Emily Greene Balch* (1941); and, with Jane Addams, *Women at the Hague: The International Congress of Women and its results* (1915). See also Mary Jo Deegan, *Jane Addams and the men of the Chicago School* (1988).

Barthes, Roland (1915–1980) A French sociologist, Barthes was especially interested in SEMIOTICS and its application to literature and POPULAR CULTURE from a Marxist perspective. He focused on the social role of MYTH and IDEOLOGY in everyday life and was a major contributor to the CULTURAL STUDIES school of sociological thinking.

Works include *Mythologies* (1957) and *The pleasure of the text* (1975). See also J. Culler, *Barthes* (1983).

Baudrillard, Jean (1929–) A French social theorist, Baudrillard is best known for his work on POST-MODERNISM and SEMIOTICS. He argued, for example, that as the MASS MEDIA propagate images of products, the distinction between appearance and reality is blurred and it becomes increasingly unclear that anything has a fixed meaning.

Major works include *La société de consommation* (1970) and *Simulations* (1983).

Beauvoir, Simone de (1908–1986) Although trained as a philosopher, the French-born de Beauvoir produced a rich intellectual output full of sociological significance, much of which has yet to be analyzed in depth. Her interests spanned a wide range, from the MASS MEDIA, aging, and women to SOCIAL MOVEMENTS. She is best known among sociologists for her influential book *The second sex*, in which she argued that under PATRIARCHY women are regarded as "other," as marginal and mystified in a male-centered, male-identified, and male-dominated world. Her method was wide-ranging as well, blending existential philosophy with autobiography, history, biology, and fiction to produce portraits of the nature and meaning of women's existence.

In addition to *The second sex* (1949), major works include *The mandarins* (1954); *The long march* (1957); *Brigitte Bardot and the Lolita syndrome* (1959); and *The coming of age* (1970). See also *Women in sociology*, edited by Mary Jo Deegan (1991).

Becker, Howard S. (1928–) A symbolic interactionist, Becker is an American sociologist whose work has focused on a number of areas, including the SOCIALIZATION experience among physicians, DEVIANCE and LABELING THEORY, youth SUB-CULTURES, education, and the production of art.

Major works include *Boys in white: Student culture in the medical world* (1961); *The other side* (1964); *Making the grade* (1968); *Outsiders: Studies in the sociology of deviance* (1973); and *Art worlds* (1982).

Bell, Daniel (1919–) Bell is an American sociologist best known for his prediction that CLASS CONFLICT was nearing an end with the END OF IDEOLOGY and the emergence of the POSTINDUSTRIAL and INFORMATION SOCIETIES organized primarily around TECHNOLOGY and information. He later retreated somewhat from this position with the observation of a fundamental conflict among the VAL-UES of economic efficiency, individual rights and well-being, and the hedonistic lifestyle promoted by advanced capitalist societies.

Major works include *The end of ideology* (1960); *The coming of post-industrial society* (1973); and *The cultural contradictions of capitalism* (1976).

Bendix, Reinhard (1916–) A German-born immigrant to the United States, Bendix is known for his interpretation of the work of Max WEBER and for his work in comparative and HISTORICAL SOCIOLOGY, especially in relation to INDUSTRIAL SOCIETY and its ties to the WORKING CLASS.

Major works include *Work and authority in industry* (1956); *Social mobility in industrial society* (1959); *Max Weber: An intellectual portrait* (1960); and *Nation building and citizenship* (1964).

Benedict, Ruth (1887–1948) Trained first in English literature and only later in life as an anthropologist, Benedict made major contributions to the study of the relationship between personality and CULTURE. Her basic insight was that each culture promotes the development of some human potentials to the neglect of others, and that people shape themselves in ways that tend to fit their cultural context. Culture is, in Benedict's words, "personality writ large," and SOCIETIES can be seen as integrated wholes of cultural forms and human beings. An accomplished field observer, rigorous researcher, and lucid writer, Benedict combined the humanities and the scientific study of culture in often powerful ways and left a significant legacy for the study of culture and personality.

Major works include *Patterns of culture* (1934); *Zuñi mythology*, 2 vols. (1935); and *The chrysanthemum and the sword: Patterns of Japanese culture* (1946). See also Margaret Mead, *An anthropologist at work: Writings of Ruth Benedict* (1959).

Bernard, Jessie (1903–1996) Bernard was an American sociologist best known for her work on marriage, the FAMILY, the status of women,

COMMUNITIES, SOCIAL PROBLEMS, and public policy. It was she, for example, who first explored the phenomenon of "his" and "hers" marriages, recognizing that marriage has distinct advantages for men that are not shared by women. Especially during and following the 1970s, Bernard created a rich body of work detailing the nature of women's lives in contexts ranging from the family to higher education. Bernard is also known for her expertise on the history of sociology as a discipline and as a cofounder of the Society for the Study of Social Problems.

Major works include *Academic women* (1964); *Women and the public interest* (1971); *The future of marriage* (1972); *The sociology of community* (1973); *The future of motherhood* (1974); *The female world in a global perspective* (1987); and *The origins of American sociology*, with L. L. Bernard (1943). See also *Women in sociology*, edited by Mary Jo Deegan (1991).

Bernstein, Basil (1924–) Bernstein is a British sociologist specializing in education, SOCIOLINGUISTICS, and the relation between LANGUAGE, KNOWLEDGE and schooling on the one hand and SOCIAL CLASS and SOCIAL CONTROL on the other. In his THEORY of SPEECH CODES, Bernstein argues that social class affects how students learn language in FAMILY and school environments. This, in turn, affects their potential for academic achievement and SOCIAL MOBILITY. His interest in language extends to a general interest in how class systems are maintained through control over knowledge and the language needed to access and use it in complex and creative ways.

Major works include *Class, codes, and control*, 3 vols. (1971, 1973, 1975).

Blau, Peter (1918–) Blau is an American sociologist best known for his work on FORMAL ORGANIZATIONS, SOCIAL MOBILITY, the OCCUPATIONAL STRUCTURE, and EXCHANGE THEORY.

Major works include *Formal organizations: A comparative approach* (1962); *Exchange and power in social life* (1964); *The American occupational structure*, with Otis Dudley Duncan (1967, 1978); and *The dynamics of bureaucracy*, 2nd ed. (1973).

Blumer, Herbert (1900–1987) An influential American sociologist using the SYMBOLIC INTERACTIONIST perspective, Blumer was noted for the argument that SOCIAL SYSTEMS are largely abstractions that have no existence independent of what individuals actually do in relation to one another. This is a key focus in the debate over AGENCY AND STRUCTURE, a position from which interacting individuals are seen as the core of social life, providing social systems with their fundamental form and reality.

Major works include "Collective behavior," in *New outline of the principles of sociology*, edited by A. M. Lee ([1939] 1951): *Symbolic interactionism: Perspective and method* (1969); and *The Chicago School of sociology: Institutionalization, diversity, and the rise of sociological research* (1984).

Booth, Charles James (1840–1916) A British businessman by trade, Booth was also a social reformer and statistician who pioneered the use of large-scale SURVEYS to document the scope of SOCIAL PROBLEMS, most notably POVERTY in England. His studies provided a detailed description of social life under the rapid INDUSTRIALIZATION that characterized Britain at the turn of the twentieth century. His concern for the impact of poverty on the elderly also contributed to the landmark Old Age Pensions Act of 1908.

Major works include *Life and labour of the people of London*, 17 vols. (1889–1891); *Old age pensions and the aged poor* (1899); *Poor law reform* (1910); and *Industrial unrest and trade union policy* (1913). See also Thomas S. Simey and Margaret B. Simey, *Charles Booth, social scientist* (1960).

Bottomore, Tom (1920–1992) A British sociologist, Bottomore is best known for his extensive work in the analysis of CAPITALISM and SOCIALISM. A prolific author and editor, he has played an important role in helping sociologists understand the importance of Marxism and MARXIST SOCIOLOGY.

Major works include *Karl Marx: Early writings* (1963); *Karl Marx: Selected writings in sociology and social philosophy* (1965); *Classes in modern society* (1965); *Elites and society* (1966); *Marxist sociology* (1975); *A history of sociological analysis* (1978); *Political sociology* (1979); *A dictionary of Marxist thought* (1983); *Theories of modern capitalism* (1985); and *The capitalist class: An international study* (1989).

Bourdieu, Pierre (1930–) Bourdieu is a French sociologist whose main contributions are in the areas of general sociological THEORY and the link between education and CULTURE,

especially in relation to the distribution of CULTURAL CAPITAL and the maintenance of SOCIAL ORDER. He has also been concerned with developing theory that would illuminate the connection between individuals and SOCIAL SYSTEMS (see AGENCY AND STRUCTURE).

Major works include *The school as a conservative force* (1966); *Outline of a theory of practice* (1977); *Reproduction in education, society, and culture* (1977); and *Distinction* (1984).

Braudel, Fernand (1902–1985) Braudel was a French historian from the ANNALES SCHOOL who played an important role in developing history as more than a written account of political events. He focused instead on the complex interplay among cultural, demographic, economic, and political factors in order to explain the development of CAPITALISM into a WORLD SYSTEM.

Major works include *Afterthoughts on material civilization and capitalism* (1977); *The structures of everyday life: Civilization and capitalism, 15th–18th century*, vol. 1 (1981); *The wheels of commerce: Civilization and capitalism, 15th–18th century*, vol. 2 (1983); *The perspective of the world: Civilization and capitalism, 15th–18th century*, vol. 3 (1984).

Burgess, Ernest (1886–1966) A member of the CHICAGO SCHOOL, Burgess was an American sociologist largely responsible for introducing the FAMILY as a serious topic of sociological analysis. This led him to studies of the aged, especially in the context of family systems.

Major works include *Predicting success or failure in marriage* (1939); *The family* (1945); and *Engagement and marriage* (1953). See also Lewis A. Coser, *Masters of sociological thought*, 2nd ed. (1977).

Comte, Auguste (1798–1857) Comte was a French sociologist who is credited with inventing the term SOCIOLOGY, although he was not the first to think in a systematically sociological way. Reflecting the social turmoil of economic and political REVOLUTIONS, Comte was concerned with reform, progress, and the problem of SOCIAL ORDER. He was one of the first to argue for sociology as a science based in POSITIVISM and used to both understand and guide the process of social development and change. Comte believed that SOCIETIES evolve through a series of predictable stages ruled by social laws and culminating in a superior form of social life based on industry and scientific principles of morality. Most of his thinking is no longer influential in sociology, but he did leave an important legacy in his emphasis on systematic observation and the role of the COMPARATIVE PERSPECTIVE and HISTORICAL SOCIOLOGY.

Major works include *The course of positivist philosophy* (1830–1842); *Discourse on the positive spirit* (1844); *A general view of positivism* (1848); and *Religion of humanity* (1856). See also Lewis A. Coser, *Masters of sociological thought*, 2nd ed. (1977), and K. Thompson, *Auguste Comte: The foundations of sociology* (1976).

Cooley, Charles Horton (1864–1929) Cooley was an American SYMBOLIC INTERACTIONIST associated with the CHICAGO SCHOOL and George Herbert MEAD. He is best known for his work on the development of personality through the relationship between SELF and OTHERS, especially through the mechanism of the looking-glass self. He also developed the key concepts of PRIMARY and SECONDARY RELATIONSHIPS, which have been crucial to the sociological study of GROUPS, ORGANIZATIONS, and the individual.

Major works include *Human nature and the social order* (1902); *Social organization* (1909); and *Life and the student* (1927). See also Lewis A. Coser, *Masters of sociological thought*, 2nd ed. (1977).

Coolidge, Mary E. B. R. Smith (1860–1945) Mary Smith Coolidge (whose work appears under two different married names – Smith and Coolidge) was the first full-time female professor of sociology in the United States. Trained in economics and history before studying for her doctorate in sociology, she went on to do important research on POVERTY, the status of women, the aged, Chinese immigration, and Native American CULTURES. She was an early practitioner of APPLIED SOCIOLOGY, with a special emphasis on using STATISTICS to document SOCIAL PROBLEMS. Like many of her contemporaries, she believed that sociology had a crucial role to play in solving social problems and working toward progressive change. As was also the case with many early women in sociology, her work included insights that were ignored until they were included in – and often attributed to – the work of male sociologists. She developed the model of COMPETITION and ASSIMILATION in the study of immigrant adaptation, for example, well before Robert PARK and Ernest BURGESS published work based on similar insights.

Major works include *Almshouse women* (1896); *Chinese immigrants* (1909); *Why women are so* (1912); and *The rain-makers: Indians of Arizona and New Mexico* (1929). See also *Women in sociology*, edited by Mary Jo Deegan (1991).

Coser, Rose Laub (1916–) Trained in both philosophy and sociology, Coser is an American sociologist best known for her writings on WORK, FAMILY, and women. Her sociology of work focuses primarily on BUREAUCRACY in hospitals and other medical settings and its effects on the delivery of health care. She also has produced significant work on the effects of SOCIAL STRUCTURE on family life and comparisons of women across CULTURES. Throughout she has made frequent use of the concept of ROLE and contributed to clearer understandings of related concepts such as ROLE DISTANCE.

Major works include *Life in the ward* (1962); *Training in ambiguity: Learning through doing in a mental hospital* (1979); *In defense of modernity* (1990); and *The world of our mothers* (1992). See also *Women in sociology*, edited by Mary Jo Deegan (1991).

Dahrendorf, Ralf (1928–) A German-born sociologist who now works in Britain, Dahrendorf is best known for his studies of CLASS CONFLICT under industrial CAPITALISM. While traditional Marxism focuses on the division between those who own the MEANS OF PRODUCTION and those who work for wages, Dahrendorf argues that CLASS CONFLICT is based primarily on differences in AUTHORITY in ORGANIZATIONS such as corporations and government bureaus (see IMPERATIVELY COORDINATED ASSOCIATION). Dahrendorf believes that inequality of authority is inevitable, although its excesses can be contained to some degree by the political rights of CITIZENS.

Major works include *Class and class conflict in industrial society* (1959); *Society and democracy in Germany* (1967); *The new liberty* (1975); and *Life chances* (1979).

Dilthey, Wilhelm (1833–1911) A German philosopher and historian, Dilthey is best known for his ideas about the difference between natural and social phenomena. Dilthey argued that the natural world can be understood through scientific observation and objective laws. The social world, however, can be understood only in terms of the meaning given to it by the people who participate in it. Explanations of what goes on in GROUPS, for example, must include some understanding of how members see the group and themselves in it. This also means that sociologists must be aware that they are part of what they are studying and that the meaning they give to what they observe is necessarily a *part* of what they observe. In sociology, his work is most closely associated with HERMENEUTICS, the concept of *weltanschauung* or WORLDVIEW, and the work of MAX WEBER and Karl MANNHEIM.

Major works include *The life of Schleiermachers* (1870); *Introduction to the sciences of spirit* (1883); *The essence of philosophy* (1907); *The construction of the historical world in the social sciences* (1910); and *The meaning of history* (1961), edited by H. P. Rickman. See also William Kluback, *Wilhelm Dilthey's philosophy of history* (1956).

Du Bois, W. E. B. (1868–1963) William Edward Burghardt Du Bois was a sociologist who played a leading role in the struggle for black civil rights in the United States. Originally trained in history, he shifted to sociology to become a more effective agent for change by documenting the extent of racial oppression. Du Bois conducted pioneering SURVEYS that helped to map the reality of black people's lives and counter the white mythology on which RACISM depends. In his role as activist, he demanded full equality for people of color and helped organize a movement around a core of educated and talented blacks. This effort eventually merged with the National Association for the Advancement of Colored People in which Du Bois was a central figure for almost a quarter of a century. He organized the first Pan-African Congress in 1919 and urged blacks to segregate themselves from whites and form self-sufficient COMMUNITIES. Toward the end of his life he embraced SOCIALISM and became a citizen of Ghana shortly before his death.

Major works include *The Philadelphia negro* (1899); *The souls of black folk* (1903); *Darkwater: Voices from within the veil* (1920); *Black reconstruction* (1935); *Dusk of dawn: An essay toward an autobiography of a race concept* (1940); and *The world and Africa: An inquiry into the part which Africa has played in world history* (1947).

Durkheim, Émile (1858–1917) Along with Karl MARX and Max WEBER, Durkheim is considered one of the founders of SOCIOLOGY as a discipline and of the FUNCTIONALIST PERSPECTIVE in particular. Building from the POSITIVISM of SAINT-SIMON and COMTE, he played a major role in defining sociology as a systematic way of thinking distinct from the common tendency to reduce social phenomena to the experience and characteristics of individuals (see ATOMISM AND HOLISM; CONSCIENCE COLLECTIVE; SOCIAL FACT). In laying the groundwork for what would become the functionalist perspective, he pursued the problem of understanding what holds SOCIAL SYSTEMS together (see COHESION; SOCIAL ORDER), and how their organization and functioning produce various kinds of consequences for systems as a whole. In this he argued against the UTILITARIAN idea that SOCIETIES could be held together simply through individuals pursuing their own rational self-interest.

In his classic study of SUICIDE, Durkheim was the first to use systematic DATA analysis to test HYPOTHESES about the relation between SOCIAL STRUCTURE and individual behavior. He also made major contributions to the study of RELIGION in which he argued that religious practice is often used to enhance social cohesion by reaffirming fundamental cultural VALUES and images of society itself. Durkheim's legacy is immense and continues to influence sociological thinking about the fundamental nature of social life.

Works include *The division of labor in society* (1893); *The rules of the sociological method* (1895); *Suicide* (1897); *The elementary forms of religious life* (1912); and *Sociology and philosophy* (1924). See also Lewis A. Coser, *Masters of sociological thought*, 2nd ed. (1977), and Stephen Lukes, *Émile Durkheim, his life and work: A historical and critical study* (1974).

Elias, Norbert (1897–1990) Elias was a German-born sociologist best known for his work on the nature of social life. In what he called figurational analysis, he developed the idea that social life is based neither on the isolated individual actor nor on SOCIAL SYSTEMS that exist external to individuals. Rather, Elias argued that what we identify as social life consists of patterns (figures) that arise from interactions among interdependent individuals (see AGENCY AND STRUCTURE). Although largely ignored when first published, his work has attracted increasing attention in Germany, the Netherlands and Britain since the late 1970s when his writings were translated into English.

Major works include *The civilizing process* (1939); *The court society* (1969); *What is sociology?* (1972); *The loneliness of dying* (1982); and *Involvement and detachment* (1986).

Engels, Friedrich (1820–1895) A German-born British industrialist and socialist, Engels was a collaborator, friend, and financial supporter of Karl MARX and played a key role in the development of Marxist analysis of CAPITALISM and CLASS systems. He met and befriended Marx in Britain in 1845, shortly after publishing an analysis of the British WORKING CLASS under industrial CAPITALISM and the potential for bringing about socialist REVOLUTION. He went on to a lifelong association with Marx in which they coauthored several key works. After Marx's death in 1883, Engels prepared for publication the manuscript for the second and third volumes of *Capital*. He died before he could complete the fourth.

Although Engels and Marx worked closely together, Engels differed from Marx in significant ways. He believed, for example, that although equality of WEALTH and INCOME were possible under COMMUNISM, inequality of POWER and AUTHORITY would always be necessary in order to coordinate complex DIVISIONS OF LABOR. Engels is also known for his development of DIALECTICAL MATERIALISM as a mode of analysis and for being among the first to explore the connection between economic systems and the PATRIARCHAL subordination of women within families.

Works include *Conditions of the working class in England in 1844* (1845); *Dialectics of nature* (1852); *The origin of the family, private property, and the state* (1891); and, with Marx, *The German ideology* (1845); *The holy family* (1845); and *The communist manifesto* (1848). See also Lewis A. Coser, *Masters of sociological thought*, 2nd ed. (1977).

Foucault, Michel (1926–1984) Foucault was a French philosopher whose work on the connections among LANGUAGE, KNOWLEDGE, POWER, and SOCIAL CONTROL has greatly affected the thinking of many sociologists. Foucault's basic argument was that language and knowledge form a basis for power in their role in the SOCIAL CONSTRUCTION OF REALITY (see DISCOURSE AND DISCOURSE FORMATION; STRUCTURALISM AND POSTSTRUCTURALISM). Knowledge and language have been particularly powerful in their use to control the human body. From Foucault's perspective, for example, there is no such thing as an objective human sexuality apart from how we use language to think, write, and talk about it. This in turn shapes how we experience the body, which in turn serves the interests of social control.

Foucault is best known for his work on imprisonment, madness, and sexuality. Major works include *The birth of the clinic* (1963); *Madness and civilization* (1965); *The order of things* (1966); *The archeology of knowledge* (1969); *Discipline and punishment* (1975); and *The history of sexuality* (1976). See also Barry Smart, *Michel Foucault* (1985).

Freud, Sigmund (1856–1939) Most often associated with Vienna where he grew up and studied medicine, Freud developed and extended the concept of the unconscious and thereby shaped the course of modern psychology and mental therapy. Sociologically, his work has profoundly affected THEORIES of SOCIALIZATION and the relation between individuals and SOCIETY. Freud argued, for example, that there is a fundamental conflict between the individual's desire for sexual and other gratification and the forces of SOCIAL CONTROL used to maintain SOCIAL ORDER.

Freud's ideas have influenced a variety of sociological work, including the Frankfurt School's CRITICAL THEORY approach to personality development from a Marxist perspective.

Major works include *The future of an illusion* (1927); *Civilization and its discontents* (1930); and *Moses and monotheism* (1934–1938). See also Erich Fromm, *Escape from freedom* (1941) and Herbert Marcuse, *Eros and civilization* (1955).

Garfinkel, Harold (1917–) An American sociologist who founded ETHNOMETHODOLOGY as an approach within the general framework of SYMBOLIC INTERACTIONISM, Garfinkel is primarily concerned with the actual methods people use to construct and maintain an underlying sense of social reality. In emphasizing the creative abilities of individuals in social situations, he is critical of much sociological thinking organized around the influence of external SOCIAL SYSTEMS.

Major works include *Studies in ethnomethodology* (1967). See also J. Heritage, *Garfinkel and ethnomethodology* (1984).

Gellner, Ernest (1925–1995) Ernest Gellner was a British sociologist, philosopher, and social anthropologist who was born in Czechoslovakia and emigrated with his family to England to escape the German invasion in 1939. A prolific thinker and writer, his work covers a wide range of topics, including ETHNOGRAPHIES of Middle Eastern CULTURES and critical analyses of psychoanalysis, NATIONALISM, IDEOLOGY in the former Soviet Union, LANGUAGE, RESEARCH METHODS. He was particularly known for his defense of RATIONALISM and his concern with both the benefits and liabilities of nationalism.

Major works include *Language and Solitude* (1998); *Legitimation of belief* (1974); *Muslim Society* (1982); *Nationalism* (1997); *Nations and nationalism* (1983); *Plow, sword, and book* (1988); *The psychoanalytic movement* (1985); *Relativism in the social sciences* (1985); *Saints of the Atlas* (1969); *State and society in Soviet thought* (1988); *Thought and change* (1964); and *Words and things* (1959).

Giddens, Anthony (1938–) Giddens is a British sociologist who has published widely in the area of sociological THEORY. His interests include classical theory, SOCIAL CLASS and STRATIFICATION under CAPITALISM, and SOCIAL CHANGE. He is perhaps best known for his theory of structuration, which explores the connection between individuals and SOCIAL SYSTEMS (see AGENCY AND STRUCTURE).

Major works include *Capitalism and modern social theory* (1971); *Politics and sociology in the thought of Max Weber* (1972); *The class structure of the advanced societies* (1973); *New rules of the sociological method* (1976); *Studies in social and political theory* (1977); *Émile Durkheim* (1978); *Central problems in social theory* (1979); *A contemporary critique of historical materialism* (1981); *Sociology* (1982); *Profiles and critiques in social theory* (1983); *The constitution of society* (1984); and *The nation-state and violence* (1985).

Gilman, Charlotte Perkins (1860–1935) Although perhaps best known for her fictional account of a woman's nervous breakdown under the oppressive social conditions imposed by PATRIARCHY (*The yellow wallpaper*), Gilman was a prolific social scientist whose works spanned several disciplines in addition to sociology. Active in many movements for social reform, her main interest was in the status of women and the oppressive consequences of women's dependence on men and in the choice women must often make between domestic work and work outside the home. She was particularly interested in women's experiences under industrial CAPITALISM and the repression of women's intellectual and productive potential.

A contemporary of JANE ADDAMS, she cofounded the Women's Peace Party and actively promoted women's suffrage.

A visionary who believed deeply in women and the ability of individuals to act for SOCIAL CHANGE, Gilman argued against the THEORY that human development is determined by evolutionary factors. Her utopian visions of life after patriarchy leaned heavily on the idea that a world organized around women's capacities for caring, compassion, and nurturing would be superior to the masculinist model imposed by patriarchy.

Major works include *The yellow wallpaper* (1899); *Women and economics* (1898); *The home: Its work and influences* (1903); *The man-made world* (1911); *Herland* (1915); *His religion and hers* (1923); and *The living of Charlotte Perkins Gilman: An autobiography* (1935). See also *The Charlotte Perkins Gilman reader*, edited by Ann J. Lane (1980) and *Women in sociology*, edited by Mary Jo Deegan.

Glass, David V. (1911–1978) David Glass was a British sociologist and historical demographer best known for his interest in issues of SOCIAL INEQUALITY and his pioneering work on SOCIAL MOBILITY in the United Kingdom. He was a founder of the *British Journal of Sociology* and *Population Studies* and was elected a Fellow of the Royal Society.

Major works include *Numbering the people* (1973); *Population and social change* (1972); *Population in history* (1965); *Population policies and movements in Europe* (1940); *Social mobility in Britain* (1954); and *The trend and pattern of fertility in Britain* (1954).

Goffman, Erving (1922–1982) A Canadian-born sociologist, Goffman is a major figure in the SYMBOLIC INTERACTION perspective in the United States. He is best known for his DRAMATURGICAL PERSPECTIVE, which likens social life to a theater in which actors create impressions of themselves and perform before audiences, while simultaneously serving as audience to other actors. His careful and detailed observations of everyday life and the mechanisms people use to navigate through their interactions with others form a fascinating and illuminating body of work. His approach has also taken him into studies of ROLE behavior (see ROLE CONFLICT), DEVIANCE and its effects on personal identity (see STIGMA), mental hospitals (see TOTAL INSTITUTION), and the role of advertising in gender INEQUALITY.

Major works include *The presentation of self in everyday life* (1959); *Asylums* (1961); *Encounters* (1961); *Behavior in public places* (1963); *Stigma: Notes on the management of a spoiled identity* (1963); *Interaction ritual* (1967); *Gender advertisements* (1976); and *Forms of talk* (1981). See also Phillip Manning, *Erving Goffman and modern sociology* (1992).

Goldthorpe, John (1935–) A British sociologist, Goldthorpe is best known for his work on STRATIFICATION, SOCIAL MOBILITY and SOCIAL CLASS, especially through the AFFLUENT WORKER studies carried out with David LOCKWOOD and others.

Major works include *The affluent worker: Industrial attitudes and behavior* (1968); *The affluent worker: Political attitudes and behavior* (1968); *The affluent worker in the class structure* (1969); *The social grading of occupations: A new approach and scale* (1974); *Social mobility and class structure in Britain* (1980); and *Order and conflict in contemporary capitalism* (1985).

Gouldner, Alvin (1920–1980) Gouldner was an American sociologist best known for his critical analysis of the FUNCTIONALIST PERSPECTIVE and Marxism, especially as practiced in the former Soviet Union. Influenced by Max WEBER, the CRITICAL THEORY of the Frankfurt School, and the radical sociology of C. Wright MILLS, Gouldner was concerned with the reluctance of many sociologists to work for progressive SOCIAL CHANGE guided by objectively based VALUES.

Major works include *Patterns of industrial bureaucracy* (1954); *Wildcat strike* (1955); *Notes on technology and the moral order* (1962); *Enter Plato* (1965); *The coming crisis of Western sociology* (1970); *The dialectic of ideology and technology* (1976); *The future of intellectuals and the rise of the new class* (1979); *The two Marxisms: Contradictions and anomalies in the development of theory* (1980); and *Against fragmentation: The origins of Marxism and the sociology of intellectuals* (1985).

Gramsci, Antonio (1891–1937) An Italian Marxist, Gramsci first worked as a journalist and became involved in movements for worker democracy, which he saw as an alternative to the parliamentary system of government. Arrested and imprisoned as a member of the Communist Party in 1926, Gramsci spent his ten-year sentence writing his major work, the *Prison Notebooks*. In his search for an alternative to the economic DETERMINISM of orthodox Marxism, Gramsci argued that class OPPRESSION depends not merely on economic arrangements or coercion from the STATE, but on some degree of acceptance by the working class. This in turn depends on the independent role of IDEOLOGY and politics in defining oppressive CLASS relations as normal and legitimate (see HEGEMONY). As an advocate of radical SOCIAL CHANGE, Gramsci also argued for the importance of combining THEORY and practice (see PRAXIS).

Major works include *The modern prince and other writings* (1959); *Selections from the prison notebooks* (1971); and *Selections from political writings* (1977). See also C. Mouffe, *Gramsci and Marxist theory* (1979).

Habermas, Jürgen (1929–) Habermas is a German social theorist with an extraordinarily wide range of interests. Although rooted in the CRITICAL THEORY of the Frankfurt School, his work spans many disciplines – from the social sciences to linguistics to philosophy. His primary concern has been with the role of KNOWLEDGE in relation to SOCIETY in general and CAPITALISM in particular (see HERMENEUTICS).

Habermas argues that objective scientific knowledge no longer promotes liberation and enlightenment, but instead serves as an IDEOLOGY that supports the status quo. This occurs primarily because in order for knowledge to be valid, it must result from free and open dialogue, which is severely limited by political and other restraints under CAPITALISM. In other work, Habermas has analyzed the problem of legitimacy in modern capitalist societies which are, he argues, full of CONTRADICTION, crisis, and distorted knowledge.

Major works include *Theory and practice* (1963); *Knowledge and human interests* (1968); *Towards a rational society* (1970); *Legitimation crisis* (1973); *Communication and the evolution of society* (1979); and *The theory of communicative action*, 2 vols. (1984, 1988).

Halsey, A. H. (1923–) A British sociologist, Halsey has focused primarily on the relationships between education and SOCIAL CLASS, FAMILY, and SOCIAL MOBILITY. He has been particularly interested in identifying social conditions under which equality, liberty, and fraternity might be possible in any SOCIETY, as well as the social forces that leave them largely unrealized today. He was especially influential in efforts after World War II to reform the British school system to promote equality of opportunity.

Major works include *Social class and educational opportunity* (1956); *Education, economy, and society* (1961); *Trends in British society since 1900* (1972); *Power and ideology in education* (1977); *Change in British society* (1978); and *Origins destinations* (1980).

Heidegger, Martin (1889–1976) An existentialist philosopher, Heidegger is best known for his interest in PHENOMENOLOGY, conceptions of time, and the possibility of human beings understanding the nature of our own existence, especially by focusing on the details of everyday existence. Although he was tainted in the minds of many by his links to fascism, his work has been widely influential, especially in the development of POSTMODERNISM.

Major works include *Being and time* (1929) and *The question concerning technology* (1954).

Homans, George C. (1910–) An American sociologist, Homans is best known for his work on EXCHANGE THEORY and for his views on the nature of social life. From his work on small GROUPS and social INTER-ACTION, Homans made the controversial argument that social life is solely a product of individual psychology and the economic principles of exchange, rather than SOCIAL SYSTEMS and SOCIAL FACTS (see METHODOLOGICAL INDIVIDUALISM).

Major works include *The human group* (1950); *Social behavior: Its elementary forms* (1961); *Sentiments and activities* (1962); and *The nature of social science* (1967). See also Lewis A. Coser, *Masters of sociological thought*, 2nd ed. (1977).

Huber, Joan (1925–) An American sociologist and prolific writer, Huber is best known for working to include gender stratification in the overall study of social STRATIFICATION. She has done this primarily by linking women's involvement in the FAMILY and LABOR FORCE with changes in TECHNOLOGY and BIRTH RATES. Most recently, this has resulted in an overall THEORY of the FAMILY. Although her approach is essentially sociological, it also draws upon history, DEMOGRAPHY, economics, anthropology, and political science.

Huber is also prominent for her leadership in expanding sociology in the United States to include women. In addition to serving as president of the American Sociological Association, she was a cofounder of Sociologists for Women in Society.

Major works include *The social context of AIDS* (1992); *Income and ideology*, with William Form (1973); *Sex stratification*, with Glenna Spitze (1983); *Marxist theory and Indian communism*, with Charles Loomis (1970). See also *Women in sociology*, edited by Mary Jo Deegan (1991).

Hughes, Helen MacGill (1903–) Hughes is an American sociologist who has made important contributions to the progress of sociology as a profession; but these have been almost invisible in a male-dominated discipline. In addition to classic works on the news media, she served for 17 years as managing editor of the *American Journal of Sociology*, cofounded Sociologists for Women in Society, and did much to document the second-class status of women within sociology. Her sociological writings also include work on RACE relations, occupations, and human ECOLOGY, although these have gone largely unnoticed due to her gender and the overshadowing prominence of her husband, Everett C. Hughes.

Major works include *News and the human interest story* (1940); *The fantastic lodge: The autobiography of a girl drug addict* (1961); *The status of women in sociology, 1968–1972* (1973); *Where peoples meet: Racial and ethnic frontiers*, with Everett C. Hughes (1952); *Twenty thousand nurses tell their story*, with Everett C. Hughes and Irwin Deutscher (1958); and a series of edited collections on various sociological topics, intended for a high school audience and published by Allyn and Bacon. See also *Women in sociology*, edited by Mary Jo Deegan (1991).

Kollontai, Alexandra (1872–1952) Although born into the Russian aristocracy, Kollontai was an accomplished intellectual best known for

371

her work on women and the family from the perspective of revolutionary Marxism. As a feminist lecturer and author, she was politically active both before and after the Russian REVOLUTION, helping to convene the All-Russia Women's Congress and participating in postrevolutionary governing committees. Her writings included original Marxist analyses of women's right to economic independence and control over their sexuality. She produced major, innovative statements on the connection between motherhood, FEMINISM, labor, and the STATE.

Major works include *The social foundations of the woman question* (1909); *Society and maternity* (1913); *Communism and the family* (1920); *The autobiography of a sexually emancipated communist woman* (1971); *Sexual relations and class struggle* (1972); and *Alexandra Kollontai: Selected articles and speeches* (1984). See also *Women in sociology*, edited by Mary Jo Deegan (1991).

Komarovsky, Mirra (1906–1999) Mirra Komarovsky was a pioneer in the study of GENDER, WORK, FAMILY and EDUCATION in America. She offered one of the first systematic analyses of gender inequality in the post-World War II women's movement and shaped fundamental questions about the relationship between the education of women and its relation to work and to women's subordinate status in SOCIETY. She served as president of the American Sociological Association, only the second woman to be so honored.

Her major works include *The unemployed man and his family* (1940); *Women in the modern world* (1953); and *Women in college: Shaping*

new feminine identities (1985). See also *Women in sociology*, edited by Mary Jo Deegan (1991).

Kuhn, Thomas (1922–) Kuhn is an American historian of SCIENCE who has played an important role in developing sociological understandings of scientific work. Kuhn's basic argument is that science is no different from any other social phenomenon, which means it is influenced and shaped by the cultural and structural characteristics of the SOCIAL SYSTEMS in which scientific work is done. In sociology he is best known for his discussion of the process of SCIENTIFIC REVOLUTION through which one PARADIGM is replaced by another.

Major works include *The structure of scientific revolutions*, 2nd exp. ed. (1970), and *The essential tension* (1977).

Lacan, Jacques (1901–1981) A French psychoanalyst, Lacan is best known for his theory of SELF and IDENTITY development in which he combines ideas from FREUD, SEMIOTICS, and STRUCTURALISM. He argued, for example, that some of Freud's key ideas – such as penis envy – were not meant to be taken literally. Instead, they were metaphors for aspects of the development of the gendered self, which is continually under construction.

Major works include *Écrits* (1966) and *Four fundamental concepts of psychoanalysis* (1979). See also Elizabeth Grosz, *Jacques Lacan: A feminist introduction* (1990).

Lazarsfeld, Paul F. (1901–1976) Born in Austria, Lazarsfeld emigrated to the United States in 1933 and became a key figure in the development of quantitative methods in SOCIOLOGY. He founded the Bureau of Applied Research at Columbia University, the first university-based SURVEY research organization in the world. He went on to establish survey research and CROSS-TABULATION DATA analysis as major tools for testing sociological ideas. He is best known for his work on MASS COMMUNICATION, MATHEMATICAL SOCIOLOGY, and VOTING BEHAVIOR.

Major works include *The people's choice: How the voter makes up his mind in a presidential campaign* (1944); *Mathematical thinking in the social sciences* (1954); *Personal influence: The part played by people in the flow of mass communications* (1955); *Latent structure analysis* (1968); and *Qualitative analysis: Historical and critical essays* (1971).

Lévi-Strauss, Claude (1908–) A French STRUCTURALIST anthropologist, Lévi-Strauss is best known for his work on LANGUAGE, SEMIOTICS, MYTH, and KINSHIP in tribal SOCIETIES. His basic argument is that visible CULTURE reflects underlying mental constructs that are universal to and inherent in human beings as a species. Although the general idea that superficial social reality reflects underlying structures has sociological appeal, Lévi-Strauss's ideas have relatively little influence among contemporary sociologists.

Major works include *The elementary structures of kinship* (1949); *Structural anthropology* (1958); *The savage mind* (1962); *Totemism* (1962); and *Introduction to the science of mythology*, 4 vols. (1964).

Liebow, Elliot (1925–1994) Elliot Liebow is best known for *Tally's* corner, his landmark study of life among unemployed black men in Washington, DC, which prompted a major shift in sociological thinking about poverty and race in America. Formally trained in anthropology, Liebow worked for 20 years at the National Institutes for Mental Health, specializing in issues of work and mental health. His life combined scholarship with political activism in ways that drew numerous awards, including the C. Wright Mills award from the Society for the Study of Social Problems and (with Matilda White Riley) the American Sociological Association's Award for a Distinguished Career in Sociological Practice.

In addition to *Tally's corner* (1966) his other major work was *Tell them who I am: The lives of homeless women* (1993).

Lipset, Seymour Martin (1922–) An American sociologist, Lipset has been a major figure in the study of SOCIAL MOBILITY; the causes and consequences of MODERNIZATION; conditions that support and sustain the development of DEMOCRACY in STATE and unions; and SOCIAL MOVEMENTS.

Major works include *Agrarian socialism* (1950); *Union democracy* (1956); *Social mobility in industrial society* (1959); *Political man: The social bases of politics* (1960); *The first new nation: The United States in historical and comparative perspective* (1963); *Party systems and voter alignment* (1967); and *Revolution and counter-revolution* (1969).

Lockwood, David (1929–) Lockwood is a British sociologist whose work focuses primarily on

373

STRATIFICATION and SOCIAL CLASS. He collaborated with John GOLD-THORPE and others on the affluent worker studies.

Major works include *The black-coated worker* (1958); *The affluent worker: Industrial attitudes and behavior* (1968); *The affluent worker: Political attitudes and behavior* (1968); and *The affluent worker in the class structure* (1969).

Lopata, Helen Znaniecki (1925–) Daughter of the renowned Chicago sociologist Florian Znaniecki, Lopata is known for her insightful studies of women and widowhood. From her early work on suburban housewives to pathbreaking analyses of the effects of SOCIAL CHANGE on older women, Lopata has provided important resources for social policy makers and students of social life. Working primarily from the SYMBOLIC INTERACTIONIST perspective, her work also includes critiques of sex role THEORY and the debunking of numerous myths about ethnic immigrants in the United States.

Major works include *Occupation housewife* (1971); *Widowhood in an American city* (1973); *Polish Americans: Status competition in an ethnic community* (1976); *Women as widows: Support systems* (1979); and *Widows: The Middle East, Asia, and the Pacific*, vol. 1, and *North America*, vol. 2 (1987). See also *Women in sociology*, edited by Mary Jo Deegan (1991).

Lukács, Georg (1885–1971) Lukács was a Hungarian Marxist philosopher and literary theorist who was controversial both for his writings and for his political activism as a member of the Communist Party. A student of

Georg SIMMEL and Max WEBER, Lukács was primarily interested in the POWER of working-class consciousness to produce an understanding of history that was unique and had revolutionary potential. He made major contributions to the sociological study of literature as a cultural product that was shaped by and reflected the times in which it was written.

Major works include *Theory of the novel* (1920); *History and class consciousness* (1923); *The historical novel* (1937); *The destruction of reason* (1954); *The meaning of contemporary realism* (1963); *On aesthetics* (1963); *Studies in European realism* (1972); and *The ontology of social being* (1978). See also Arpad Kadarkay, *Georg Lukács: Life, thought, and politics* (1991).

Lynd, Helen Merrell (1896–1982) With broadly based training in philosophy, history, social psychology, and sociology, Lynd is best known for her classic studies (with husband Robert S. Lynd) of COMMUNITY life in America. The "Middletown Studies" set a standard for community research and in spite of being some 60 years old still have much insight to offer current researchers.

Lynd was most interested in understanding the role communities play in SOCIAL INEQUALITY and the generation of meaning in human life. These interests were related to her later work on DEMOCRACY and social identity as shaped through people's participation in social life.

Major works include *Middletown: A study in contemporary American culture*, with Robert S. Lynd (1929); *Middletown in transition: A study in cultural conflicts*, with Robert S. Lynd

(1935); *England in the eighteen eighties: Toward a social basis for freedom* (1944); *Field work in college education* (1945); *On shame and the search for social identity* (1958); *Toward discovery* (1965); and *Possibilities* (1983). See also *Women in sociology,* edited by Mary Jo Deegan (1991).

Malinowski, Bronislaw (1884–1942) A Polish anthropologist who spent a major part of his professional life in Britain, Malinowski is known both for his methods and for the findings that resulted from them. He made major contributions to the study of magic and sexual behavior, and along with Alfred RADCLIFFE-BROWNE he was a key figure in developing the FUNCTIONALIST PERSPECTIVE in anthropology. Methodologically, he did much to create the EMPIRICIST tradition in British anthropology. He specialized in ETHNOGRAPHY, offering intense, detailed observations of tribal SOCIETIES with whom he lived in the Trobriand Islands and New Guinea (see PARTICIPANT OBSERVATION).

Major works include *Argonauts of the Western Pacific* (1922); *Sex and repression in savage society* (1927); *The sexual life of savages* (1929); *Coral gardens and their magic* (1935); and *A scientific theory of culture* (1944).

Mann, Michael (1942–) Mann is a British sociologist and historian who is best known for his work on social STRATIFICATION, especially in relation to the history and nature of POWER in social life. He argues, for example, that power has several different bases – military, economic, political, and ideological – and that these account for the historically shifting nature of power in social life.

Major works include *Consciousness and action in the Western working class* (1973) and *The sources of social power* (1986).

Mannheim, Karl (1893–1947) Mannheim was a Hungarian sociologist who emigrated to England in 1933 to escape Nazi Germany. He was a powerful influence in shaping the sociology of KNOWLEDGE, especially in the form of IDEOLOGY. His basic argument was that the knowledge produced in a SOCIETY is shaped by the way the society is organized – by its CULTURE and structure. By extension, what individuals know depends on their location in the structure of their society, including but not limited to factors such as SOCIAL CLASS. As part of his work in the sociology of KNOWLEDGE, Mannheim wrestled with the problem of relativism: if what is considered true is socially located and determined, then there can be no objective basis for truth.

Prominent among his other interests was the problem of MASS SOCIETY – the lack of COHESION and meaning in modern life that Mannheim attributed primarily to the dynamics of CAPITALISM.

Major works include *Ideology and utopia* (1936); *Man and society in the age of social reconstruction* (1940); *Diagnosis of our time* (1943); *Freedom, power, and democratic planning* (1951); *Essays on the sociology of knowledge* (1952); *Essays on sociology and social psychology* (1953); and *Essays on the sociology of culture* (1956). See also Lewis A. Coser, *Masters of sociological thought,* 2nd ed. (1977).

Marcuse, Herbert (1898–1979) A German philosopher and social theorist, Marcuse was closely associated with the CRITICAL THEORY approach of the Frankfurt School, which provided a unifying theme for his varied interests. He is best known for his critical analyses of CAPITALISM, Marxism (especially as used in the former Soviet Union), REVOLUTION and human liberation, TECHNOLOGY and SOCIAL CHANGE, sexuality, and the fate of the individual in modern SOCIETY. His views appealed greatly to radicals in the United States and Europe during the 1960s.

Major works include *Reason and revolution* (1954); *Eros and civilization* (1955); *Soviet Marxism* (1961); *One-dimensional man* (1964); *Negations* (1968); and *An essay on liberation* (1969).

Marshall, Thomas H. (1873–1982) Marshall was a British historian and sociologist who focused on the problem of CITIZENSHIP and the relation between economic and political DEMOCRACY. Marshall argued that there is a basic contradiction between the political rights of citizens – such as welfare – and SOCIAL CLASS inequality as shaped by CAPITALISM. How class INEQUALITY affects political democracy, and how political democracy threatens the basis for class inequality was a major theme in his work which is widely regarded as crucial to any understanding of citizenship as a social phenomenon.

Major works include *Citizenship and class* (1950); *Sociology at the crossroads* (1963); *Social policy* (1965); and *The right to welfare and other essays* (1981).

Martineau, Harriet (1802–1876) Martineau may well qualify as the first female sociologist, ranking in the depth and breadth of her work with better-known male contemporaries such as DURKHEIM and WEBER. A prolific writer, she published dozens of books and hundreds of articles on sociological subjects ranging from occupational health and POLITICAL ECONOMY to RELIGION, SOCIAL CLASS, SUICIDE, SLAVERY, and women's rights. She was the first to translate Auguste COMTE's *Cours de philosophie positive* into English, introducing it to both her native Britain and the United States. She wrote the first systematic treatise on sociological research methods several decades before male sociologists turned their attention to such problems. She visited the United States and wrote a penetrating analysis of life in America, similar in scope and insight to that of the better-known Alexis de TOCQUEVILLE. Nonetheless, she has been largely forgotten in sociology, primarily because, like so many early women sociologists, her work was ignored by a male-dominated profession.

Major works include *Illustrations of political economy*, 6 vols. (1832–1834); *Society in America*, 3 vols. (1837); *How to observe morals and manners* (1838); *Eastern life, present and past* (1848); *Household education* (1949); *England and her soldiers* (1859); *Health, husbandry, and handicraft* (1861); and *Harriet Martineau's autobiography* (1877). See also *Women in sociology*, edited by Mary Jo Deegan (1991), and Robert K. Webb, *Harriet Martineau: A radical Victorian* (1960).

Marx, Karl (1818–1883) Along with Émile DURKHEIM and Max WEBER, Marx is generally regarded as one of the key figures in the development of sociological thinking. Trained in philosophy, law, and economics, Marx began his career as an academic but was forced to leave this post and, ultimately, his native Germany as well due to his political activism and opposition to the Prussian state. From academic life he went into journalism and political activism and then into research and writing after his move to London in 1849. There he deepened his friendship with an industrialist, Friedrich ENGELS, who became his collaborator and benefactor and helped Marx through some of his family's most difficult periods of impoverishment. For the remainder of his life, Marx devoted himself to understanding economics and its dynamic interplay with social life.

In his early work, Marx developed an interest in ALIENATION, especially as it is produced by working conditions. Later in his career, his attention shifted to the connection between economics and social life. Marx argued, for example, that the organization of economic life – whether as FEUDAL estate or industrial CAPITALISM – affects every other aspect of social life, from the FAMILY to RELIGION to POPULAR CULTURE (see BASE AND SUPERSTRUCTURE; CLASS CONSCIOUSNESS AND FALSE CONSCIOUSNESS; IDEOLOGY). One of the most profound consequences of this lies in the creation and perpetuation of SOCIAL CLASS systems in which dominant classes appropriate WEALTH produced by subordinate classes. Although class systems have existed in various forms for several thousand years, Marx was particularly interested in understanding CAPITALISM as it rapidly expanded its hold on the nineteenth-century world.

In analyzing capitalism as a dynamic system, Marx also developed a THEORY of history. He based it on the idea that systems produce their own internal CONTRADICTIONS and these, in turn, produce strain and tension that ultimately are resolved through SOCIAL CHANGE. Contradictions are particularly likely to encourage CLASS CONFLICT, which Marx regarded as the primary engine of change. Since all of this involves economic systems whose main focus is the material aspects of human life, Marx's approach to social life and history is often described as a form of MATERIALISM. Marx's heavy reliance on a materialist view of social life is perhaps the most controversial aspect of his approach, which is criticized as amounting to DETERMINISM.

Although Marx's work has been subjected to a great deal of criticism, the fact that it continues to draw so much attention testifies to its enduring relevance to understanding life under industrial capitalism. Although Marx did not explicitly identify himself as a sociologist, he played a crucial role in developing sociology as a point of view by focusing on how SOCIAL SYSTEMS shape collective outcomes as well as individual motives and behavior. To Marx, the "evils" of capitalism were not caused by evil individuals but by a system organized in ways that promoted evil consequences.

Major works include "Theses on Feuerbach," in Friedrich Engels, *Ludwig Feuerbach and the outcome of classical German philosophy* [1845] (1935); *The German ideology,* with Friedrich Engels [1845] (1965); *Manifesto of the communist party,* with Friedrich Engels [1848] (1932); *The eighteenth Brumaire of Louis Bonaparte* [1852] (1934); *A contribution to the critique of political economy* [1859]

(1970); *Capital: A critique of political economy*, 3 vols. [1867, 1885, 1894] (1975); *Economic and philosophical manuscripts of 1884*, translated by Tom Bottomore (1961); "Critiques of Hegel's philosophy of rights," in *Writings of the young Marx on philosophy and society*, translated and edited by L. D. Easton and K. Guddat [1893] (1967). See also T. B. Bottomore, *Marxist sociology* (1975); D. McLellan, *Karl Marx* (1973); and Lewis A. Coser, *Masters of sociological thought*, 2nd ed. (1977).

Mead, George Herbert (1863–1931) A sociologist, philosopher, and social psychologist at the University of Chicago (see CHICAGO SCHOOL), Mead pioneered the development of the SYMBOLIC INTERACTION perspective. He was, like his colleague Charles Horton COOLEY, interested in the relationship between individuals and SOCIETIES, especially as this affects how the SELF is formed and functions in relation to OTHERS. Along with Cooley's concept of the LOOKING-GLASS SELF, Mead developed the concepts of I, ME, and MIND to explain our ability to take on social ROLES, to view and reflect upon ourselves (see REFLEXIVITY), to internalize social expectations, and to carry on internal conversations through which we anticipate the expectations and behavior of other people.

Major works include *Mind, self, and society* (1934); *The philosophy of the act* (1938); and *The philosophy of the present* (1932). See also Lewis A. Coser, *Masters of sociological thought*, 2nd ed. (1977).

Mead, Margaret (1901–1978) An American anthropologist, Mead made important contributions to the

understanding of SOCIALIZATION, ADOLESCENCE, relations among generations, and GENDER. She is best known for her work on the importance of nature and CULTURE in the formation of human personality. Mead's studies of tribal societies led her to conclude that culture, not biology, was the primary factor in human development.

Major works include *Coming of age in Samoa* (1928); *Growing up in New Guinea* (1930); *Sex and temperament in three primitive societies* (1935); *Male and female* (1949); *New lives for old* (1956); *Culture and commitment* (1970); *Science and the concept of race* (1970); and *Twentieth century faith* (1972).

Merton, Robert K. (1910–) Merton is widely regarded as one of the leading figures in twentieth century American sociology. From his days as a student of Talcott PARSONS and subsequently as an associate of Paul LAZARSFELD at Columbia University's Bureau of Applied Research, Merton has made enduring contributions to the critical understanding of a variety of core concerns, including the concept of SOCIAL STRUCTURE, the FUNCTIONALIST PERSPECTIVE, SCIENCE, DEVIANCE (see ANOMIE, OPPORTUNITY STRUCTURE), MASS COMMUNICATION, ROLE theory, and BUREAUCRACY. His doctoral dissertation on the development of SCIENCE in the seventeenth century is generally credited with prompting a major shift in sociological approaches to science that has influenced work in the field ever since.

Throughout his career, Merton has been concerned with developing meaningful sociological THEORIES that can be tested empirically, with finding a MIDDLE RANGE between what

C. Wright MILLS criticized as the untestable abstractions of GRAND THEORY and the triviality of ABSTRACTED EMPIRICISM. Merton's overall view of social life is grounded in the idea that the choices people make as individuals are socially structured, granting them the potential for a certain degree of creativity and self-determination but also setting limits on the alternatives from which they choose.

Major works include *Science, technology, and society in seventeenth-century England* (1938); *Mass persuasion* (1946); *The focused interview: A manual of problems and procedures* (1956); *On the shoulders of giants* (1965); *Social theory and social structure*, rev. and exp. ed. (1968); *The sociology of science: Theoretical and empirical investigations* (1973); and *Sociological ambivalence and other essays* (1976). See also *The idea of social structure: Papers in honor of Robert K. Merton*, edited by Lewis A. Coser (1975).

Michels, Robert (1876–1936) A German sociologist also trained in history and economics, Michels worked on problems related to CLASS CONFLICT, REVOLUTION, DEMOCRACY, FASCISM, IMPERIALISM, NATIONALISM, MASS COMMUNICATION, and the role of intellectuals in SOCIAL CHANGE. He is perhaps most famous for his iron law of OLIGARCHY as applied to democracy in TRADE UNIONS. His influence is widely felt, however, throughout the study of political and other organizations.

Major works include *Political parties* (1911) and *First lectures in political sociology* (1927–1936).

Mills, C. Wright (1916–1962) Mills was an American sociologist noted for his often controversial critiques of both contemporary SOCIETY and sociological practice. He was critical of the tendency toward GRAND THEORY, which lacks grounding in real-world DATA and experience. But he also criticized ABSTRACTED EMPIRICISM, which focuses on the analysis of masses of data without a meaningful theoretical framework in which to interpret them. Both, he believed, distract sociologists from what he viewed as their fundamental task of helping bring about progressive change. As a practicing sociologist his major focus was on SOCIAL INEQUALITY, the power of ELITES, the declining MIDDLE CLASS, the relationship between individuals and SOCIETY, and the importance of an historical perspective as a key part of sociological thinking.

Major works include *From Max Weber: Essays in sociology* (1946), which Mills edited and translated; *White collar* (1951); *Character and social structure* (1953); *The power elite* (1956); *The sociological imagination* (1959); *The Marxists* (1962); and *Power, politics, and people: The collected essays of C. Wright Mills* (1962). See also Herbert Aptheker, *The world of C. Wright Mills* (1960) and *The new sociology: Essays in social science and social theory in honor of C. Wright Mills*, edited by Irving Louis Horowitz (1964).

Montesquieu, Charles-Louis de Secondat, Baron de (1689–1755) An eighteenth-century French aristocrat, Montesquieu is best known for laying the foundations for the sociology of law in his monumental work *The spirit of the laws*, the first sociological attempt to understand the law as a social phenomenon. His interest in government, liberty, and

379

the political dynamics of pluralism made him a figure in the ENLIGHTENMENT. His ideas influenced David Hume and others in the SCOTTISH ENLIGHTENMENT as well as the great French sociologist Émile DURKHEIM. Some regard him as one of the founders of SOCIOLOGY.

Moore, Barrington (1913–)
Moore is an American sociologist with a deep commitment to comparative and historical approaches to understanding social life. He specializes in political and economic sociology and how CLASS systems and INDUSTRIALIZATION have shaped polical systems such as DEMOCRACY, FEUDALISM, and COMMUNISM in Europe, the United States, Japan, China, and the former Soviet Union. His interests have also included the human condition, war, and privacy.

Major works include *Soviet politics* (1950); *Terror and progress USSR* (1954); *Political power and social theory* (1958); *Social origins of dictatorship and democracy* (1968); *Reflections on the causes of human misery* (1972); *Injustice* (1978); and *Privacy: Studies in social and cultural history* (1984).

Mosca, Gaetano (1858–1941)
Along with Vilfredo PARETO and Robert MICHELS, Mosca, an Italian politician and political scientist, played a major role in developing the study of ELITES. Mosca argued that domination of SOCIETY by a ruling class was inevitable, and that even in representative democracies the people do not rule.

Major works include *The ruling class* (1896). See also James H. Meisel, *The myth of the ruling class: Gaetano Mosca and the "elite"* (1958).

Myrdal, Alva (1902–1986) A Swedish-born sociologist whose work includes political science and economics, Myrdal distinguished herself through work for nuclear disarmament and world peace. In her writings she focused primarily on issues of peace and war, population planning, the family, and women's rights. She believed in the importance of sociological analysis and understanding for progressive SOCIAL CHANGE and put this into practice through years of service with the United Nations. For this work she was recognized with numerous peace prizes, including the Nobel Peace Prize in 1982.

Major works include *Nations and family: The Swedish experience in democratic family and population policy* (1941); *Women's two roles: Home and work*, with Viola Klein (1956); and *The game of disarmament: How the United States and Russia run the arms race* (1976). See also *Women in sociology*, edited by Mary Jo Deegan (1991).

Pareto, Vilfredo (1848–1923) A French-born Italian engineer, economist, and sociologist, Pareto made enduring contributions to both mathematical economics and to sociological THEORY. He is perhaps best known in sociology for his work in developing the concept of ELITES (along with Gaetano MOSCA and Robert MICHELS). Pareto saw SOCIETIES as machines governed by various elites who moved in and out of POWER in an endless cycle that leaves little room for participation by the masses of people. Pareto was also interested in theories of human action and what he regarded as the largely nonlogical aspects of human life which were, he believed, rooted in basic human psychological tendencies (see RESIDUES AND DERIVATIONS).

Major works include *The mind and society*, 4 vols. (1916). See also Lewis A. Coser, *Masters of sociological thought*, 2nd ed. (1977).

Park, Robert Ezra (1864–1944) A student of Georg SIMMEL, Park was a key member of the CHICAGO SCHOOL and played an important role in the development of SOCIOLOGY in both content and method. He was an early practitioner of the PARTICI-PANT OBSERVATION method and believed deeply in the importance of empirical research. Substantively, he is best known for his work on URBANIZATION, COMMUNITY life, RACE relations, and SOCIAL CHANGE.

Major works include *Introduction to the science of society* (1921); *The city* (1925); *Race and culture* (1939); and *Collected papers of Robert Ezra Park*, 4 vols. (1950). See also Lewis A. Coser, *Masters of sociologicol thought*, 2nd ed. (1977).

Parsons, Talcott (1902–1979) Although Parsons has relatively few followers among sociologists today, he is regarded by many as the twentieth century's most influential American sociologist. It was Parsons who first introduced the works of Émile DURKHEIM and Max WEBER to American readers, and who laid the foundation for what was to become the modern FUNCTIONALIST PERSPEC-TIVE. This evolved out of Parsons's primary interest in understanding the problem of order – what it is that holds SOCIAL SYSTEMS together. In a complex body of theoretical work, Parsons tried to lay out an overall model of social life that accounted for both the nature of social systems and the patterns of INTERACTION through which individuals participate in them. His basic approach was to see social systems as existing in their own right – as Durkheim argued before him – and as having needs of their own that must be met if systems are to function. For their part, individuals are socialized into a system and, by internalizing key VALUES and NORMS, behave in ways that support the system's needs and perpetuate its existence.

Parsons hoped that his approach would integrate the diverse strands of sociology and the social sciences. He had a powerful influence over American sociology for several decades following World War II. With the coming of the civil rights and anti-Vietnam war movements, however, a more critical consciousness led to harsh attacks on Parsons and his work. He was often accused, for example, of implicitly supporting the status quo by emphasizing the importance of values and norms in achieving social consensus over the shape of social life. This tended to ignore conflict, his critics argued, and how mainstream values and norms serve the interests of dominant groups at the expense of those below them. Parsons was also criticized for constructing GRAND THEORY with too little attention to empirical evidence; for attributing to values, norms, and SOCIALIZATION greater power than they in fact have in determining patterns of social relation; and for giving too little importance to such structural factors as CLASS and racial systems of inequality. Despite the eclipse of his once powerful status within American sociology, Parsons made enduring contributions in modeling the development of THEORY and by attempting to integrate sociology under a single model.

Major works include *The structure of social action* (1937); *The social system* (1951); *Essays in sociological theory* (1964); *Societies: Evolutionary and comparative perspectives* (1966); *Politics and social structure* (1969); *The system of modern societies* (1971); and *Family, socialization, and interaction process,* with Robert F. Bales (1953). See also F. Bourricaud, *The sociology of Talcott Parsons* (1981), and G. Rocher, *Talcott Parsons and American sociology* (1974).

Popper, Karl (1902–1994) An Austrian-born philosopher who emigrated to Britain, Poppers specialized in social philosophy and the philosophy of SCIENCE. He is best known for developing FALSIFICATIONISM as a perspective on how science is used to establish truth. He is also known for his arguments against DETERMINISM and HISTORICISM and his advocacy of METHODOLOGICAL INDIVIDUALISM.

Major works include *The logic of scientific discovery* (1934); *The open society and its enemies* (1945); *The poverty of historicism* (1957); *Conjectures and refutations: The growth of scientific knowledge* (1963); *Objective knowledge: An evolutionary approach* (1972); and *Realism and the aim of science* (1983).

Radcliffe-Brown, Alfred (1881–1955) Radcliffe-Brown was an anthropologist who, along with Bronislaw MALINOWSKI, played a major role in establishing POSITIVISM and the FUNCTIONALIST PERSPECTIVE in British anthropology. Working primarily in tribal SOCIETIES in Australia and the Andaman Islands, he pursued an interest in FAMILY and KINSHIP systems based on the idea that societies are like organisms whose INSTITUTIONS such as the family meet basic social needs that allow societies to function. He was a strong advocate of the COMPARATIVE PERSPECTIVE.

Major works include *The Andaman Islanders* (1922); *The social organization of Australian tribes* (1931); *Taboo* (1936); and *Structure and function in primitive society* (1952).

Rex, John (1925–) Rex is a South African who emigrated to England and became noted for his innovative work on RACE relations, his spirited defense of classical sociological THEORY, and his ability to join theory with empirical research.

Major works include *Key problems of sociological theory* (1961); *Race, community, and conflict* (1967); *Race, colonialism, and the city* (1970); *Discovering sociology* (1973); *Sociology and the demystification of the world* (1974); and *Social conflict* (1981).

Riesman, David (1909–) An American sociologist, Riesman is best known for his work on the relationship between SOCIAL SYSTEMS and individual character. In his influential book, *The Lonely Crowd*, Riesman argued that as CONFORMITY and the fear of losing the approval of others become increasingly important – especially in corporate settings – people grow increasingly anxious and "other-directed." This contrasts with being "inner-directed" and depending on a deeper and more stable sense of personal identity and integrity.

Major works include *The lonely crowd* (1950); *Individualism reconsidered* (1954); *Abundance for what?* (1964); and *On higher education* (1980).

Riley, Matilda White (1911–) An American sociologist, Riley has made significant contributions to understanding sociological METHODOLOGY, women in the professions, and communications. She is best known, however, for her pioneering work in defining and developing the sociology of aging, using a rich perspective that integrates sociology and anthropology, economics, medicine, and gerontology. A former president of the American Sociological Association, she has done much to lay the conceptual and empirical groundwork for research on aging and has played an important role in supporting and facilitating the research of others in the field.

Major works include *Aging and society*, vol 1: *An inventory of research findings*, with Anne Foner in association with Mary E. Moore, Beth Hess, and Barbara K. Roth (1968); *Aging and society*, vol. 2: *Aging and the professions*, with John R. Riley Jr. and Marilyn Johnson (1969); *Aging and society*, vol. 3: *A sociology of age stratification*, with Marilyn Johnson and Anne Foner (1972); *Sociological observation: A strategy for new social knowledge*, edited with Edward E. Nelson (1974); *Aging in society: Selected reviews of recent research*, edited with Beth B. Hess and Kathleen Bonds (1983); and *Social structures and human lives*, edited with Bettina J. Huber and Beth B. Hess (1988). See also *Women in sociology*, edited by Mary Jo Deegan (1991).

Rossi, Alice S. (1922–) Although her early work focused on a variety of subjects ranging from group relations and occupations to the SOVIET UNION, Rossi is best known for her innovative work in feminist sociology. Beginning with the groundbreaking "Equality between the sexes: An immodest proposal," she went on to cofound the National Organization for Women and Sociologists for Women in Society. Her work in feminist THEORY, adulthood and aging, women in occupations, parenthood, and the family has been influential, especially as she has attempted to integrate biological and psychological factors into sociological understandings of gender. See also *Women in sociology*, edited by Mary Jo Deegan (1991).

Major works include "Equality between the sexes: An immodest proposal," *Daedalus* 93 (spring, 1964); *The feminist papers: From Adams to de Beauvoir* (1973); *Feminists in politics* (1982); *Seasons of a woman's life* (1983); and *Gender and the life course* (1985).

Saint-Simon, Claude-Henri de (1760–1825) Saint-Simon was a French aristocrat whose social theorizing profoundly affected key figures in the development of sociology, among them Auguste COMTE, Karl MARX, and Émile DURKHEIM. He is best known for three basic arguments: that history is evolutionary and occurs through the relationship between new ways of thinking (such as POSITIVISM) and forms of social organization (such as FEUDALISM or INDUSTRIALIZATION); that social life is governed by laws of social organization that can be discovered through SCIENCE; and that scientists and industrialists are best equipped to solve major SOCIAL PROBLEMS and therefore should govern SOCIETY and guide SOCIAL CHANGE.

Major works include *Selected writings* (1952) and *Social organization* (1964). See also Frank E. Manuel, *The new world of Saint-Simon* (1956) and K. Taylor, *Henri Saint-Simon 1760–1825: Selected writings on science, industry, and social organization* (1975).

Saussure, Ferdinand de (1857–1913) A Swiss linguist, Saussure is best known for his work on linguistic STRUCTURALISM and SEMIOTICS. He distinguished between the language people use when they write and speak and language itself as a system of shared meaning. Words derive their meaning from both sources. The first is their position in relation to other words in a written or spoken sentence, as governed by rules of grammar and syntax. The second is their relation to other words in a language (as we discover when we look up a word in the dictionary and then follow the trail laid down by the words used to define it). As such, the system of language takes on a life of its own and develops and persists independent of the individuals who use it to communicate and independent of the objective reality we assume it represents.

His major work is *The course in linguistics* (1916), published posthumously from notes taken by his students. See also J. Culler, *Saussure* (1976).

Schutz, Alfred (1899–1959) An Austrian emigrant to the United States, Schutz was a philosopher and sociologist who was primarily interested in PHENOMENOLOGICAL SOCIOLOGY and its use in understanding social action and INTERACTION in everyday life. He focused on how we organize behavior and understandings of ourselves and others into a coherent whole that contributes to the patterns that make social life recognizable. This included the crucial role of KNOWLEDGE, meaning, and interpretation in constructing social life, which brought his work very close to ETHNOMETHODOLOGY (*see also* INDEXICALITY; REFLEXIVITY; TYPIFICATION).

Major works include *The phenomenology of the social world* (1932); *Collected papers*, 3 vols. (1962–1965); *Reflections on the problem of relevance* (1970); and *The structures of the lifeworld* (1974).

Simmel, Georg (1858–1918) Simmel was a German sociologist and philosopher who ranks second in importance only to the generally recognized giants of sociology, Max WEBER, Émile DURKHEIM, and Karl MARX. He opposed HOLISM as a view of SOCIETY and argued instead that society is a collection of people connected by their INTERACTION with one another. He was a devoted student of interaction with a special interest in the shape and role of conflict and the importance of numbers. He noted, for example, that when a third person is introduced into an interaction, the structure shifts as the possibility arises that two will combine against one and that each member will no longer control the future of the interaction. Simmel is also known for his classic analysis of the development and social significance of money.

Major works include *The sociology of Georg Simmel* (1902); *The philosophy of money* (1970); and *Conflict and the web of group affiliation* (1980). See also Lewis A. Coser, *Masters of sociological thought*, 2nd ed. (1977); David Frisby, *Sociological impressionism: A reassessment of Georg Simmel's social theory*, 2nd ed. (1992), and David Frisby, *Simmel and since* (1992).

Smith, Adam (1723–1790) A Scottish philosopher, Smith had an enormous impact on thinking about economics in general and CAPITALISM in particular. Although his work ranged over many subjects including the moral basis for social life, law, and politics, it was his account of economic life – *The wealth of nations* – that made his mark on the history of Western thought. In this work, Smith made the first serious attempt to amass enormous amounts of economic and social DATA to make sense of CAPITALISM as a system and to map out conditions for its success as a social INSTITUTION. Smith argued that the ideal ECONOMY was governed solely by individual self-interest allowed to operate in an open competitive marketplace, free from government interference and from the destructive forces of monopoly and other forms of exploitative economic control and manipulation. The result, he believed, would be a prosperous SOCIETY that met the common good through business enterprise producing goods that people want at prices they are willing to pay.

Major works include *The theory of moral sentiments* (1759); *An inquiry into the nature and causes of the wealth of nations* (1776). See also *The works of Adam Smith*, 5 vols. (1963).

Smith, Dorothy E. (1926–) A British-born sociologist who emigrated to Canada, Smith has become what many regard as the foremost feminist theorist in sociology. Her primary interest is in the sociology of KNOWLEDGE and the problem of incorporating women's perspectives into sociological views and explanations of SOCIETY. As sociology is currently practiced, what is taken to be "objective" knowledge of social life is invariably arrived at from a male-dominated, male-identified PATRIARCHAL perspective. Much of Smith's work raises critical questions for sociological theorizing, research, and practice by arguing for a sociology that views social life from a perspective informed by women's experience and positions in society. She has also made significant contributions to Marxist and feminist understandings of the relations of women and the FAMILY to CAPITALISM.

Major works include *Feminism and Marxism – A place to begin* (1977); *The everyday world as problematic* (1987); *The conceptual practices of power* (1990); and *Texts, facts, and femininity: Exploring the relations of ruling* (1990). See also Sylvia M. Hale, *Controversies in sociology* (1989) and *Women in sociology*, edited by Mary Jo Deegan (1991).

Sorokin, Pitirim A. (1889–1968) An emigrant to the United States after being expelled from the Soviet Union in 1922, Sorokin went on to become the first professor of sociology at Harvard University. His major interests included the causes and consequences of SOCIAL MOBILITY, sociological THEORY, and SOCIAL CHANGE. A prolific author, he is perhaps best known for his evolutionary theory of CYCLICAL CHANGE.

Major works include *Sociology of revolutions* (1925); *Social mobility*

(1927); *Contemporary sociological theories* (1928); *Social and cultural dynamics*, 4 vols. (1937–1941); *Sociocultural causality, space, and time* (1943); *Society, culture, and personality* (1947); *The social philosophies of an age of crisis* (1950); *Fads and foibles in modern sociology* (1956); and *sociological theories of today* (1966). See also Lewis A. Coser, *Masters of sociological thought*, 2nd ed. (1977) and Frank R. Cowell, *History, civilization, and culture: An introduction to the historical and social philosophy of Pitirim A. Sorokin* (1952).

Spencer, Herbert (1820–1903) A British social theorist, Spencer was one of the first to think of social life in terms of SOCIAL SYSTEMS. As such, he played an important role in the development of the FUNCTIONALIST PERSPECTIVE. Building on the work of the rapidly emerging field of biology, Spencer saw SOCIETIES as organisms that progressed through a process of evolution similar to that experienced by living species. From this perspective, societies adapt to their surroundings by becoming more complex and heterogeneous on the one hand and by integrating their various elements into a unified whole on the other. Individual groups within societies compete for limited resources, with the more "fit" among them emerging as dominant. This latter view is often associated with SOCIAL DARWINISM, a popular IDEOLOGY that saw social STRATIFICATION as a natural consequence of human evolution and that argued against any kind of governmental or other intervention to improve conditions for disadvantaged groups.

Spencer's attachment to biological metaphors for human societies has long since lost its appeal to sociologists because of the many differences between societies and biological organisms. His early emphasis on the importance of social systems and how they function and change, however, was an invaluable contribution to the growth of sociology as a way of thinking about social life.

Major works include *Social statics: The conditions essential to human happiness* (1850); *Education* (1854); *The principles of psychology* (1855); *First principles* (1862); *Principles of sociology* (1876–1896); *The data of ethics* (1884); and *The man versus the state* (1884). See also Jonathan H. Turner, *Herbert Spencer: A renewed appreciation* (1985).

Stouffer, Samuel A. (1900–1960) As a sociologist, Stouffer is best known as a key figure in the development of large-scale SURVEYS as a particularly American style of social research. He was the principal investigator on the massive landmark studies of American soldiers during World War II, which set a standard for research that was modest in its theorizing and rarely strayed far from hard evidence. His analysis of DATA was ingenious and his research methods had a huge impact on survey design and analysis.

Major works include *The American soldier*, 2 vols. (1949); *Measurement and prediction*, with several coauthors (1950); *Social research to test ideas* (1962); and *Communism, conformity, and civil liberties* [1955] (1992).

Sumner, William Graham (1840–1910) An American economist and sociologist, Sumner founded the department of sociology at Yale University and is best known for his evolutionary theories of SOCIAL CHANGE and development. He was a passionate advocate of SOCIAL DARWINISM but is best known sociologically for his classic work on FOLKWAYS.

Major works include *What social classes owe to each other* (1883); *Folkways* (1906); and *Essays of William Graham Sumner* (1940). See also Maurice R. Davie, *William Graham Sumner* (1963).

Sutherland, Edwin H. (1883–1950) Sutherland was an American sociologist who has received primary credit for establishing CRIMINOLOGY as a field of inquiry. He is best known for his distinctly sociological approach to criminal behavior, which focuses on the influence of CULTURE and social INSTITUTIONS in shaping individual personality and behavior. His THEORY of DIFFERENTIAL ASSOCIATION was a landmark attempt to explain broad patterns of diverse criminal behavior using a single theoretical approach. Sutherland is also known for his pioneering research on WHITE-COLLAR CRIME and crime as an occupation.

Major works include *Criminology* (1924); *The professional thief* (1937); *White-collar crime* (1949); *The Sutherland papers*, edited by Albert K. Cohen et al. (1956); and *White-collar crime: The uncut version* (1983).

Szaz, Thomas Stephen (1920–) Szaz is an American psychiatrist whose work has influenced sociologists interested in the LABELING THEORY of DEVIANCE. Szaz argues that in many ways mental illness does not exist but is a socially created category used for purposes of SOCIAL CONTROL. It gives physicians and others the AUTHORITY to label people as mentally ill and then control them by, for example, forcing them into therapy or committing them to mental hospitals.

Major works include *The myth of mental illness* (1961) and *Insanity: The idea and its consequences* (1987).

Taeuber, Irene B. (1906–1974) An American demographer and statistician, Taeuber played an important role in developing the field of DEMOGRAPHY within sociology. From 1937 to 1954 she took primary responsibility for editing the bibliographic journal, *Population Index*, which was for many years the only demographic journal available. She also served as director of the U.S. Bureau of the Census and as president of the Population Association of America.

In addition to such crucial support roles, Taeuber's interest in the populations of East and Southeast Asian societies introduced a cross-cultural perspective to American demography that was otherwise focused primarily on the United States. She also did much to develop the view of POPULATION processes – BIRTHS, DEATHS, and MIGRATION – as fundamentally social phenomena that needed to be explained from a sociological perspective.

Major works include *General censuses and vital statistics in the Americas* (1943); *The population of Tanganyika* (1949); *The population of Japan* (1958); *The changing population of the United States*, with Conrad Taeuber (1958); *China's populations – some approaches to research* (1964); *Population trends in the United States* (1965); *People of the United States in the twentieth century*, with Conrad Taeuber (1971), and *Population growth* and development in Southeast Asia (1972). See also *Women in sociology*, edited by Mary Jo Deegan (1991).

Taft, Jessie (1882–1961) Trained in philosophy and then the SYMBOLIC INTERACTIONIST tradition in sociology, Taft provides a compelling example of brilliant women whose careers and contributions have been severely curtailed and lost because of women's status in society. Unable to find teaching positions in universities, she spent most of her life as a sociologist working within a network of women who were kept outside the BOUNDARIES of academic sociology. Her major work was to extend George Herbert MEAD'S theories of SELF and SOCIETY to include women, especially young girls. Becoming better known as a social worker than a sociologist, Taft made unique contributions to feminist understandings of SOCIALIZATION and the development of the female self.

Major works include *The dynamics of therapy in a controlled relationship* (1933); *Day nursery care as a social service* (1943); *A functional approach to family case work* (1944); and *Family casework and counselling* (1948). See also *Jessie Taft: Therapist and social work educator*, edited by Virginia P. Robinson (1962); Rosalind Rosenberg, *Beyond separate spheres* (1982); and *Women in sociology*, edited by Mary Jo Deegan (1991).

Thomas, Dorothy Swain (1899–1977) A noted American statistician and demographer, Thomas is best known for her work on the relationship between INDUSTRIALIZATION and economic growth and the movement and distribution of POPULATIONS, especially through MIGRATION. She

was a dedicated researcher who promoted the use of rigorous scientific methods in sociology, and pioneered methods of observation in her studies of nursery school children. Her work also included a landmark documentation of the experience of Japanese-Americans forcibly interned during the 1939–45 world war. In addition to her research and writing, she served as president of the Population Association of America and was the first woman elected as president of the American Sociological Association.

Major works include *Social aspects of the business cycle* (1925); *The child in America: Behavior problems and programs*, with William I. Thomas (1928); *Some new techniques for studying social behavior*, with several associates (1929); *Observational studies of social behavior*, with several coauthors (1933); *Social and economic aspects of Swedish population movements* (1941); *The spoilage: Japanese American evacuation and resettlement*, vol. 1, with Richard S. Nishimoto (1946); *The salvage: Japanese American evacuation and resettlement*, vol. 2, with Charles Kikuchi and James Sakoda (1952); and *Population redistribution and economic growth, United States 1870–1950*, 3 vols, with various coauthors (1957, 1960, 1966). See also *Women in sociology*, edited by Mary Jo Deegan (1991).

Thomas, William I. (1863–1947) Thomas was a member of the CHICAGO SCHOOL of sociology. His interests included social history as seen from the viewpoint of individual biography and the complex relation between CULTURE and personality. He is perhaps best known for his famous quote on the relationship between reality and the DEFINITION OF THE SITUATION: "If men define situations as real, they are real in their consequences" (1928).

Major works include *Sex and society* (1907); *Sourcebook for social origins* (1909) (with Florian Znaniecki); *The Polish peasant in Europe and America*, 2 vols. (1918–1920); *The unadjusted girl* (1923); *The child in America* (1928); *Primitive behavior* (1937); and *Social behavior and personality* (1951). See also Lewis A. Coser, *Masters of sociological thought*, 2nd ed. (1977).

Tilly, Charles (1926–) An American sociologist with a special interest in historical studies, Tilly has made major contributions to the use of empirical DATA to test HYPOTHESES about the role of SOCIAL MOVEMENTS and COLLECTIVE BEHAVIOR in large-scale patterns of SOCIAL CHANGE. Tilly sees collective action as purposeful and strategic in bringing about change in response to large processes such as URBANIZATION, capitalist INDUSTRIALIZATION and expansion, and the growing POWER of the STATE.

Major works include *The vendée* (1964); *Strikes in France: 1830–1968*, with Edward Shorter (1974); *The rebellious century*, with Louise Tilly and Richard Tilly (1975); *From mobilization to revolution* (1978); *Historical studies of changing fertility* (1978); *As sociology meets history* (1981); *Big structures, large processes, huge comparisons* (1985); *Coercion, capital, and European states: A.D. 990–1900* (1990); and *European revolutions, 1492–1992* (1993).

Tocqueville, Alexis de (1805–1859) A French aristocrat, de Tocqueville is best known for his insightful work in comparative and historical sociology. As a young man, he traveled to the United States in the 1830s to compare its democratic system with that emerging in France and produced a two-volume work that has become a classic. He was most interested in the positive and negative consequences of various forms of democracy on various aspects of social life, from economics and law to religion and art. He argued, for example, that a purely democratic system could easily lead to what he called the "tyranny of the majority." His other major work compared France and England to explain why REVOLUTION occurred in the former but not the latter.

Major works include *On the penitentiary system in the United States* (1833); *Democracy in America*, 2 vols (1835, 1840); *The old regime and the French Revolution* (1856); and *Recollections* (1893).

Tönnies, Ferdinand (1855–1936) Tönnies was a German sociologist best known for his work on the effects of URBANIZATION, INDUSTRIALIZATION, and MODERNIZATION on social COHESION in COMMUNITIES. He developed the two key concepts of GEMEINSCHAFT AND GESELLSCHAFT to describe SOCIETIES held together primarily by traditional ties based on a shared CULTURE and way of life and those held together through differences bridged by complex DIVISIONS OF LABOR and the interdependencies that go with them. His work was influential in the development of the CHICAGO SCHOOL.

Major work includes *Community and society* (1887) and *Custom: An essay on social codes* (1909). See also Louis Wirth, "The sociology of Ferdinand Tönnies." *American Journal of Sociology* 32 (1926): 412–22.

Veblen, Thorstein (1857–1929) An American sociologist and economist, Veblen concentrated on criticism of CAPITALISM as an exploitative, predatory system; the dominant SOCIAL CLASSES – what Veblen called the leisure class – who benefit most from it (see CONSPICUOUS CONSUMPTION); and the influence of economic VALUES on social life. He was particularly critical, for example, of what he saw as the corruption of education by the singleminded pursuit of economic success.

Major works include *The theory of the leisure class* (1899); *The theory of business enterprise* (1904); *The instinct of workmanship and the state of the industrial arts* (1914); *Imperial Germany and the Industrial Revolution* (1915); *The higher learning in America: A memorandum on the conduct of universities by businessmen* (1918); *The place of science in modern civilization and other essays* (1919); and *The vested interests and the common man* (1919). See also David Riesman, *Thorstein Veblen: A critical interpretation* (1953).

Wallerstein, Immanuel (1930–) Wallerstein is an American sociologist and historian who has been the central figure in the development of WORLD SYSTEM theory and a highly influential practitioner of multidisciplinary approaches to understanding the dynamics of CAPITALISM.

Major works include *Africa: The politics of unity* (1967); *The modern world system* (1976); *The capitalist world-economy* (1979); *The modern world system II: Mercantilism and the consolidation of the European world economy, 1600–1750* (1980); *The politics of the world economic system*

(1984); *Africa and the modern world* (1986); and *The modern world-system III: The second era of great expansion of the capitalist world-economy, 1730–1840* (1989).

Webb, Beatrice (1858–1943) A prolific writer and dedicated social activist, Webb is best known as a major intellectual leader in socialist criticism and reform efforts in Britain. With her husband, Sidney Webb, she cofounded the London School of Economics and *The New Statesman*. Her studies of the working poor and consumer cooperatives were landmarks that formed the basis for her public activism, including serving on numerous government commissions and playing a prominent role in creating the British social welfare system. She was the first woman to be elected to the British Academy.

Major works include *The cooperative movement in Great Britain* (1891); *Industrial democracy*, with Sidney Webb (1897); *Problems of modern industry* (1898); *English poor law policy* (1910); *The wages of men and women* (1919); *A constitution for the socialist commonwealth of Great Britain* (1920); *The decay of capitalism* (1923); *English poor law history*, 3 vols. (1927–1929); and *Methods of social study* (1932). See also *Women in sociology*, edited by Mary Jo Deegan (1991).

Weber, Max (1864–1920) Along with Karl MARX and Émile DURKHEIM, Weber is considered to be a key founding figure in the history of sociology. Broadly trained in economics, history, law, and philosophy, Weber brought to his sociological work a complex and rich perspective on social life. He provided one of the first major discussions of research methods in the social sciences (see Harriet MARTINEAU), including issues such as OBJECTIVITY and VALUE NEUTRALITY. With his THEORY of ACTION, he combined method with content by providing a framework for linking individuals to SOCIAL SYSTEMS. Systems, he argued, are patterns of action and INTER-ACTION, and the only way to study and understand them is by examining the meaning that actors give to what they do. In this sense, a purely objective social SCIENCE is both impossible and undesirable since the very nature of social life requires us to use empathy in order to take into account subjective understandings and meaning.

Weber made major and classic contributions to the study of RELIGION, economic history, CAPITALISM, and LAW. He was an early practitioner of the CONFLICT PERSPECTIVE, especially in his pioneering work on the development of BUREAUCRACY as a pervasive form of social organization. Weber argued that RATIONALIZATION was becoming an increasingly powerful principle under industrial capitalism as cost, profit, and efficiency grew in social importance. The result, he believed, was an "iron cage" that would increasingly hold people's lives in its grip with little hope for escape or relief from its suffocating effects on the human spirit.

As with Durkheim and Marx, Weber's influence on sociology is enduring and provides a point of reference for an extraordinary range of theory and research.

Major works include *The Protestant ethic and the spirit of capitalism* (1904); *The city* (1912); *The methodology of the social sciences* (1904–1917); *The religion of China* (1915), *The religion of India* (1916); *Ancient Judaism* (1917); *The sociology of religion* (1922); *Economy and society* (1921); *General economic history* (1923); and *The theory of social and economic organization* (1925). See also *Max Weber on law in economy and society*, edited by M. Rheinstein (1922); and *From Max Weber: Essays in sociology*, edited by Hans H. Gerth and C. Wright Mills (1946). See also Lewis A. Coser, *Masters of sociological thought*, 2nd ed. (1977).

Wilson, Bryan R. (1926–) A British sociologist specializing in the study of RELIGION, Wilson has been a major proponent of the SECU-LARIZATION thesis. This argues that major SOCIAL CHANGES such as INDUSTRIALIZATION, URBANIZATION, and the spread of CAPITALISM have greatly diminished the influence of religion, especially in public life. Wilson has also done major work on religious SECTS.

Major works include *Religion in secular society* (1966); *Youth culture and the universities* (1970); *Magic and the millennium* (1973); *Contemporary transformations of religion* (1976); and *Religion in sociological perspective* (1982).

Wilson, William Julius (1935–) Among US sociologists, Wilson is a leader in the study of urban POVERTY, especially in relation to RACE. He is especially well known for developing the concept of an under-class as a key concept in the study of RACISM and INEQUALITY. Works include *The declining significance of race* (1978); *The truly disadvantaged: The inner city, the underclass, and public policy* (1987); and *The ghetto underclass* (1989).

Wirth, Louis (1897–1952) Wirth was an American sociologist who believed in the importance of using sociology to promote progressive SOCIAL CHANGE. As a member of the CHICAGO SCHOOL, he pursued interests in RACE relations, urban ECOLOGY, sociological THEORY, and the role of KNOWLEDGE and IDEOLOGY in social life. He was a founder of the American Council on Race Relations and served as a government adviser in his work to integrate sociological theory and research with public policy and action.

Major works include *The ghetto* (1928) and *Louis Wirth on cities and social life: Selected papers* (1964). See also Reinhard Bendix, "Social theory and social action in the sociology of Louis Wirth." *American Journal of Sociology* 59 (1954): 523–29.

Wittgenstein, Ludwig (1889–1951) An Austrian philosopher, Wittgenstein's most sociologically relevant work focused on the importance of LANGUAGE, social context, and how individual interpretations of reality shape patterns of social life. Sociologically, his ideas are most closely connected to ETHNOMETHODOLOGY and PHENOMENOLOGICAL SOCIOLOGY.

Major works include *Philosophical manuscripts* (1953).

Znaniecki, Florian (1882–1938) A Pole who emigrated to the United States, Znaniecki became a member of the CHICAGO SCHOOL and is perhaps best known for coauthoring *The Polish peasant in Europe and America* with William I. THOMAS. He was interested in understanding the relationship between sociology and other disciplines and argued that although the best sociological practice adhered to scientific principles and methods, its focus on social rather than natural phenomena made it a unique discipline. He was also interested in the general problem of how SOCIAL SYSTEMS are constructed through social INTERACTION among individuals.

Major works include *The Polish peasant in Europe and America*, 2 vols. (1918, 1920); *Cultural reality* (1919); *The laws of social psychology* (1925); *The method of sociology* (1934); *Social actions* (1936); *The social role of the man of knowledge* (1940); *Cultural sciences* (1952); and *Modern nationalities: A sociological study* (1952). See also Lewis A. Coser, *Masters of sociological thought*, 2nd ed. (1977).

Index